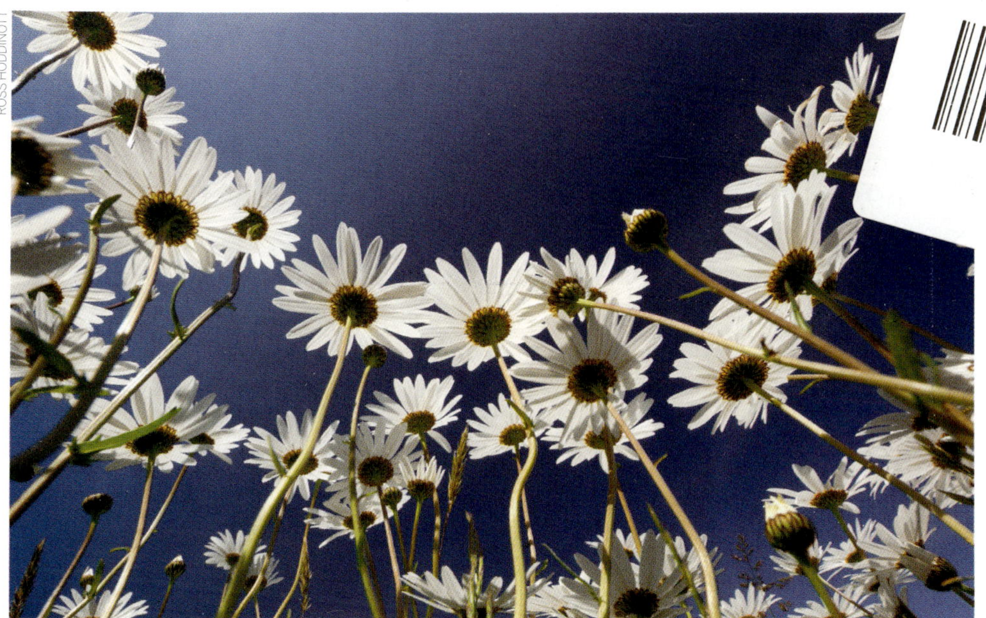

ROSS HODDINOTT

Welcome...

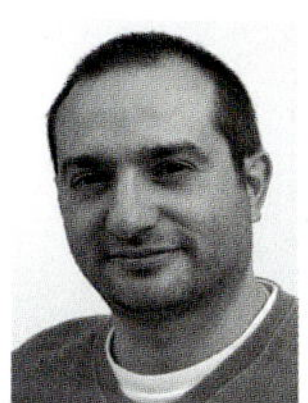

"The world is a beautiful place and few know that better than the dedicated outdoor photographer. Exploring the diversity of locations and life on our planet must rank as one of the most desirable pastimes. The UK, despite its relatively small size, is blessed with appealing photo opportunities that could keep most photographers busy for a lifetime. From stunning scenics to captivating wildlife and beautiful flowers, there's no shortage of subjects to cover. Of course, this barely scratches the surface of the wonders that await those of us who travel abroad. But regardless of where you may live, this *Essential Guide to Outdoor Photography* aims to provide advice and inspiration to passionate outdoor photographers looking to take their best ever images. Our team of experts not only provide in-depth advice to wildlife, nature and landscapes, they also provide essential techniques to shooting outdoor portraits using daylight or flash, as well as providing the core skills you need to take brilliant night photographs. This guide also features major sections dedicated to filters and other essential kit. We trust it helps you develop your photo skills and passion for photography and leads to your best ever outdoor images. All the best!"

DANIEL LEZANO, EDITOR

Meet our outdoor photography experts

All our experts are regular contributors to *Digital SLR Photography* magazine. For expert advice and inspiration to help you improve your photo skills, pick up the latest issue, available on the second Tuesday of every month. For further information, visit: www.digitalslrphoto.com

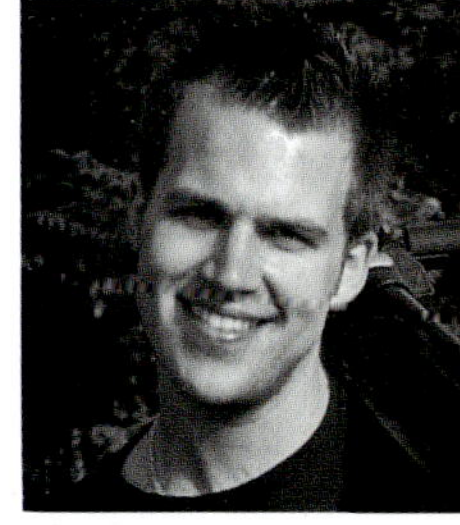

ROSS HODDINOTT
Ross is an award-winning photographer with many years of experience capturing the diverse beauty of Britain's landscapes and wildlife.
www.rosshoddinott.co.uk

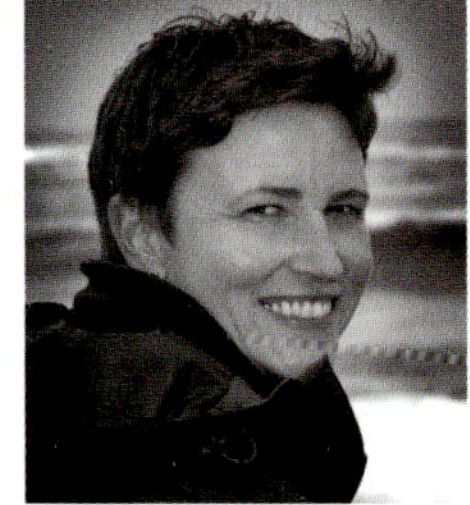

HELEN DIXON
Helen is living the dream, having given up a full-time job to become a professional landscape photographer. She is one of the UK's brightest talents.
www.helendixonphotography.co.uk

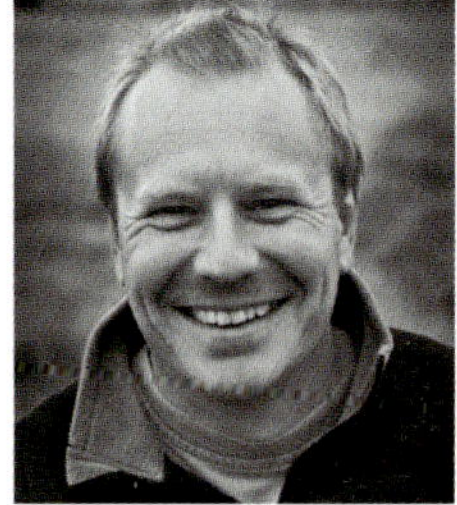

LEE FROST
A pro for two decades, Lee Frost's one of the best-known names in the UK photography business, with 20 books to his name and worldwide image sales.
www.leefrost.co.uk

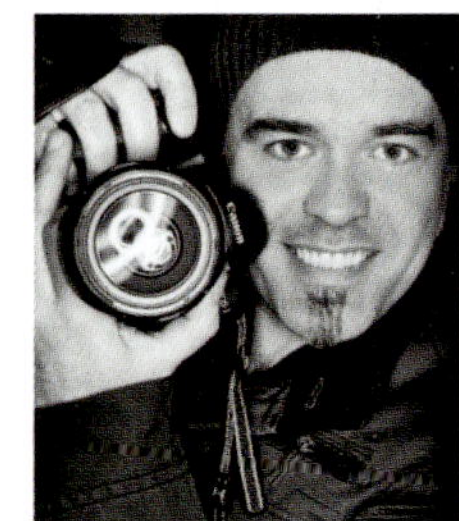

BRETT HARKNESS
Brett is one of the UK's leading portrait and social photographers and runs regular photo workshops in the UK and overseas. For further details visit:
www.bretthharkness.com

COVER IMAGE

The Essential Guide to Outdoor Photography

Produced by *Digital SLR Photography* at:
6 Swan Court, Cygnet Park,
Peterborough, Cambs PE7 8GX
Phone: 01733 567401. Fax 01733 352650
Email: enquiries@digitalslrphoto.com
Online: www.digitalslrphoto.com

Editorial

To contact editorial phone: 01733 567401
Editor **Daniel Lezano**
daniel_lezano@dennis.co.uk
Art Editor **Luke Marsh**
luke_marsh@dennis.co.uk
Features Editor **Caroline Wilkinson**
caroline_wilkinson@dennis.co.uk
Features Writer **Jordan Butters**
jordan_butters@dennis.co.uk
Designer **Luke Medler**
luke_medler@dennis.co.uk
Editorial Co-ordinator **Jo Lezano**
jo_lezano@dennis.co.uk
Editorial contributors:
Mark Bauer, Helen Dixon, Lee Frost, Brett Harkness and Ross Hoddinott

Advertising & Production

Display & Classified Sales: 020 7907 6651
Advertising Sales **Guy Scott-Wilson**
guy_scott-wilson@dennis.co.uk
Sales Executive **Joshua Rouse**
joshua_rouse@dennis.co.uk
Production Controller **Daniel Stark**
daniel_stark@dennis.co.uk
Digital Production Manager **Nicky Baker**
nicky_baker@dennis.co.uk

Management

MAGBOOK PUBLISHER **DHARMESH MISTRY**
OPERATIONS DIRECTOR **ROBIN RYAN**
MD OF ADVERTISING **JULIAN LLOYD-EVANS**
NEWSTRADE DIRECTOR **DAVID BARKER**
COMMERCIAL & RETAIL DIRECTOR **MARTIN BELSON**
PUBLISHING DIRECTOR **JOHN GAREWAL**
CHIEF OPERATING OFFICER **BRETT REYNOLDS**
GROUP FINANCE DIRECTOR **IAN LEGGETT**
CHIEF EXECUTIVE **JAMES TYE**
CHAIRMAN **FELIX DENNIS**

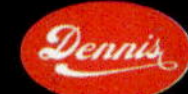

The Essential Guide to Outdoor Photography ISBN 1-78106-018-5

Licensing & Syndication: To license this product please contact Carlotta Serantoni on +44 (0) 20 7907 6550 or email carlotta_serantoni@dennis.co.uk. To syndicate content from this product please contact Anj Dosaj Halai on +44(0) 20 7907 6132 or email anj_dosaj-halai@dennis. co.uk

Printed at Benham Goodhead Print (BGP)

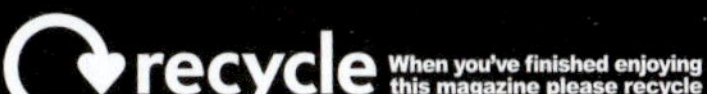

CONTENTS

THE ESSENTIAL GUIDE TO OUTDOOR PHOTOGRAPHY **2ND EDITION**

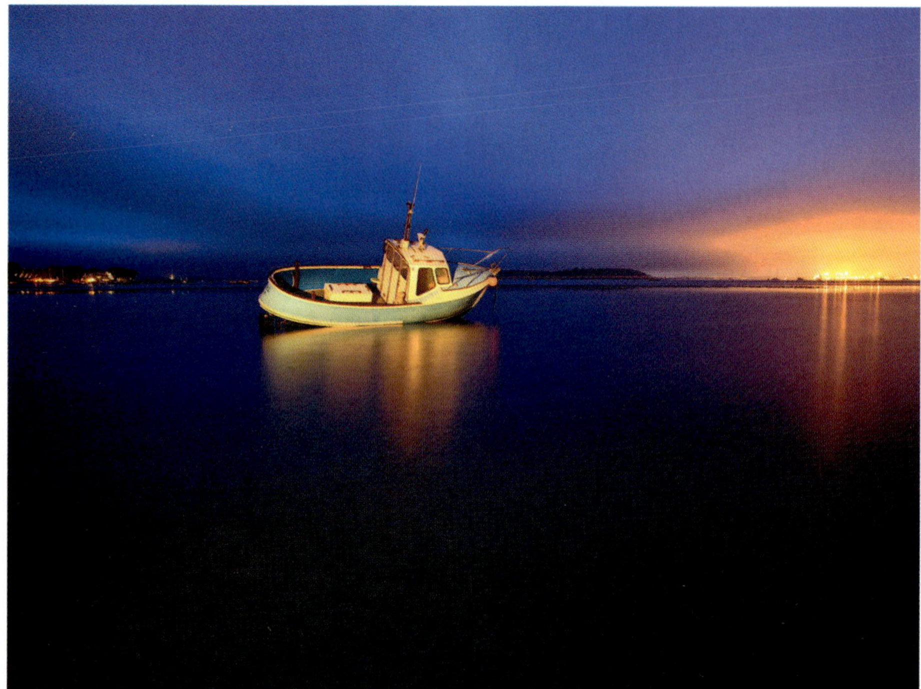

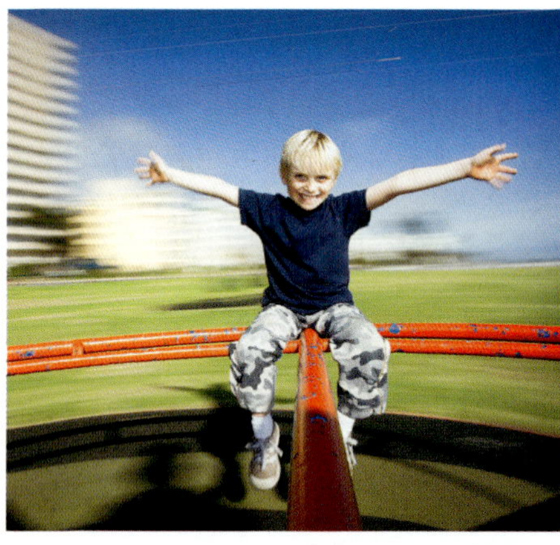

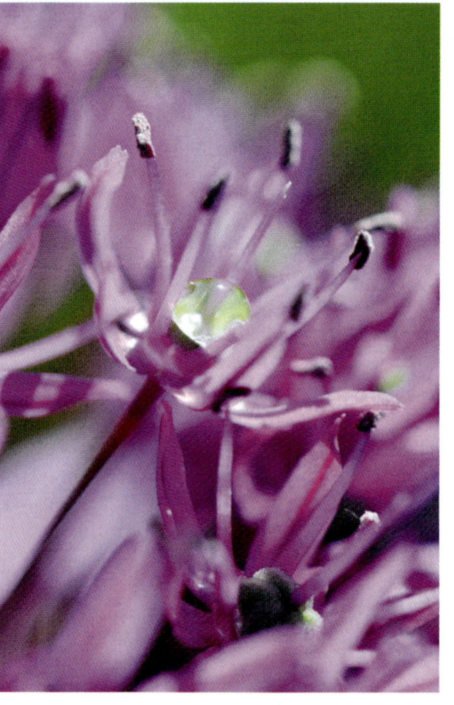

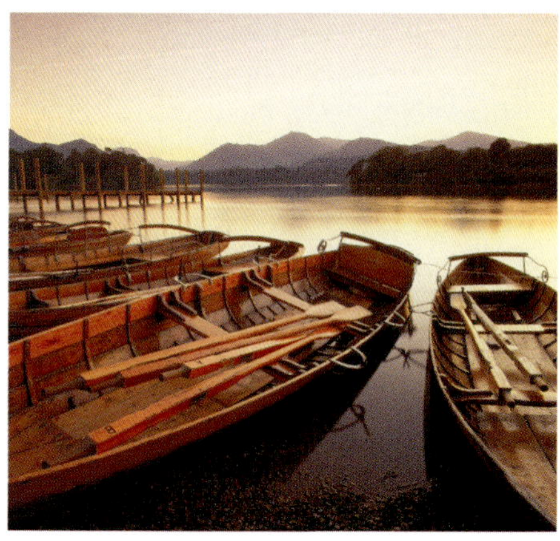

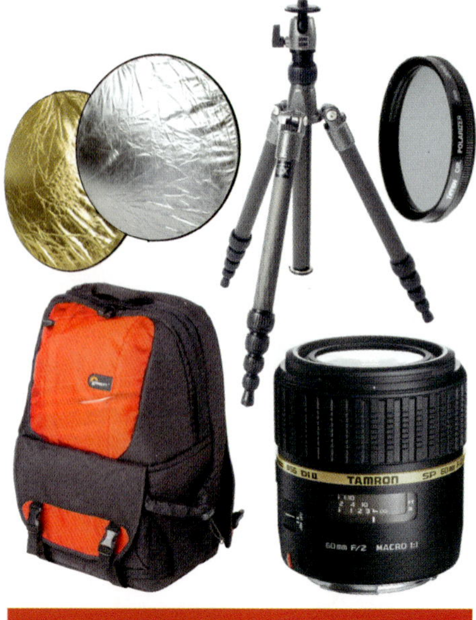

TURN TO PAGE 142 TO FIND OUT ABOUT OUR FANTASTIC SUBSCRIPTION OFFERS

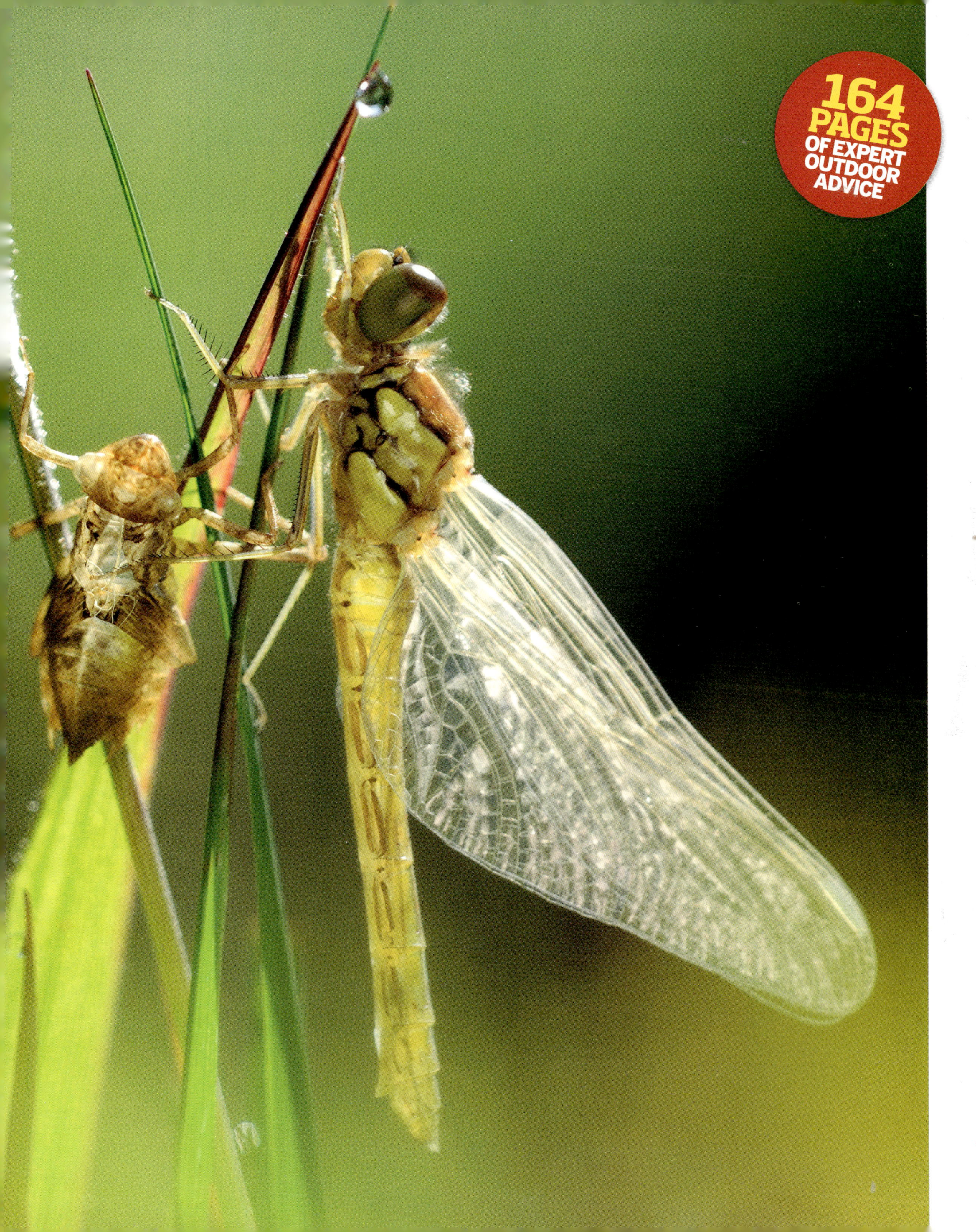
164 PAGES
OF EXPERT OUTDOOR ADVICE

Exposure: Understanding the fundamentals

Learning the basics of exposure is an essential stage in every photographer's path to success

IF YOU WANT to become a proficient photographer, then one of the first areas you want to get to grips with is how to correctly expose a scene. For many, the first stage of an exposure is the moment they press the shutter button and activate the camera's metering system. However, more experienced photographers have mentally assessed the scene well in advance of this stage and worked out whether the camera can be expected to handle the situation well, or whether some user intervention is required. While it's the camera that determines the exposure, it is the photographer who needs to ensure that the camera has been set up to give the best possible result. To do this requires a knowledge of the fundamental workings of what makes up an exposure and how a camera calculates it.

So let's look at the basics of an exposure first. The aperture controls how much light is allowed through the lens, much like the iris of an eye, while the shutter speed determines the duration the sensor is exposed to this light by lifting a barrier (the shutter curtain) in front of the sensor. For newcomers to photography who tend to use the full-auto or program mode, the ability to control exposure is limited as the camera selects all the variables to make up the exposure. Using one of these modes is ideal for those not looking to learn more about picture-taking, but for those of us who are, we would be better off switching to a semi-automatic mode (and at a later stage trying manual mode) as this will help us learn the relationship between apertures and shutter speeds.

So now we know that these two variables are intrinsic to exposure, the next question is: How does a camera look at a scene, read all the information and calculate the correct exposure? You may be surprised to discover that the principles of the system used by digital SLRs are very similar to those used by all cameras through the eras that boasted built-in exposure systems. The metering system works on the assumption that the average of tones in the area being metered – regardless of whether it's a portrait, the petals of a flower or a seascape – will work out to be a mid-tone. More accurately, it assumes that this area corresponds to 18% grey, which is a median measurement of the colour spectrum. To put it another way, if you squeezed all the tones from the scene into a blender and hit the 'on' switch, 18% grey would be the mushy result. This might all sound like techy talk, but it's worth learning about as it may help you understand what has gone wrong if you suddenly find your images suffer from incorrect exposures.

As we mentioned, today's metering systems are very efficient and are capable of exposing brilliantly in most situations – but they're not totally foolproof. If a scene is predominantly light, it can cause the metering to underexpose the image, while an overly dark scene may well be overexposed. This is as a result of the camera trying to average out the tones in the scene to 18% grey. Your camera's multi-zone metering pattern is the best choice in most conditions, but in tricky situations, other patterns may be called into use. In some circumstances, you may have to override the settings made by the camera to ensure a correct exposure. This guide will help you identify these situations and inform you of what action to take.

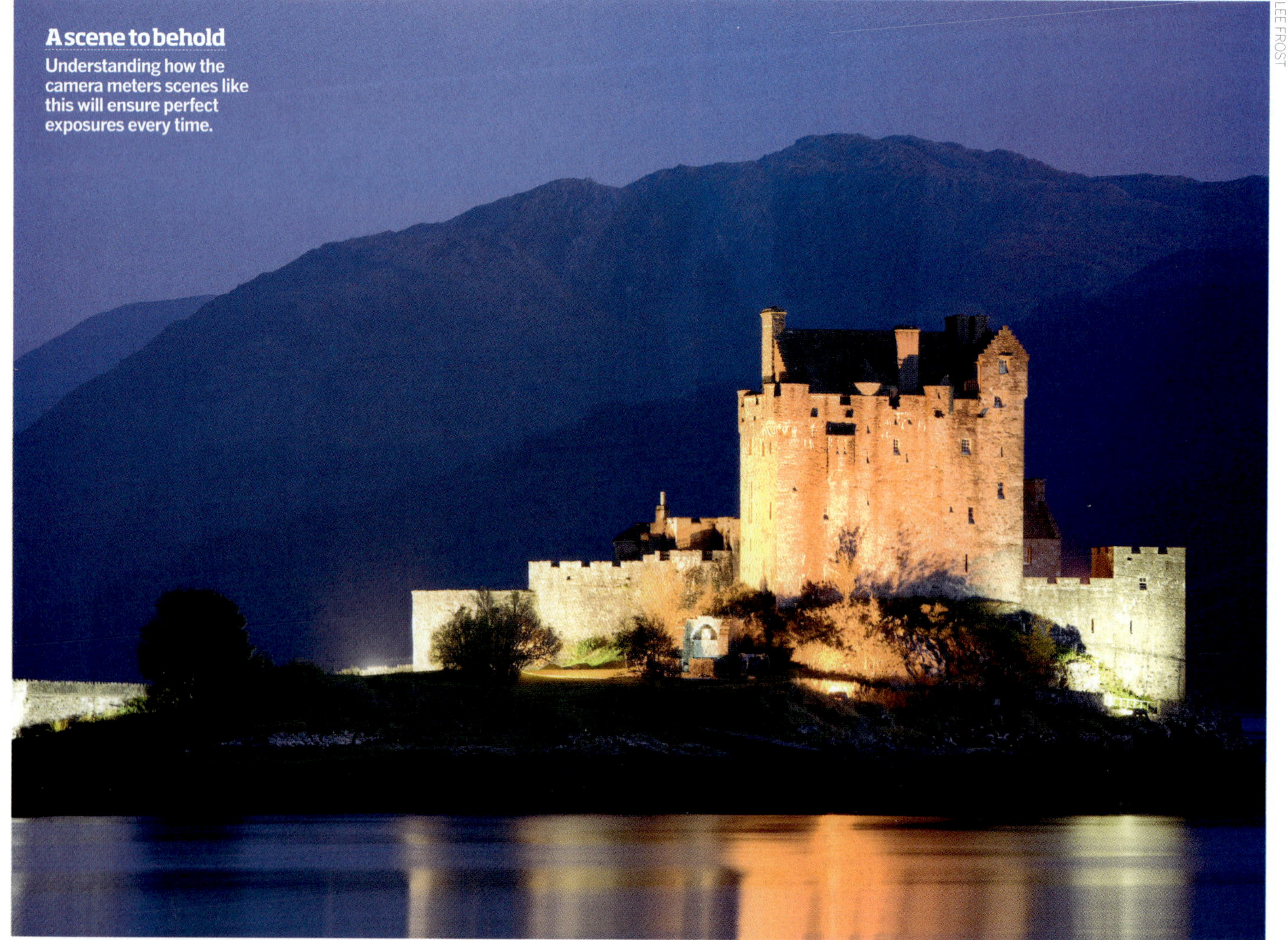

A scene to behold

Understanding how the camera meters scenes like this will ensure perfect exposures every time.

LEE FROST

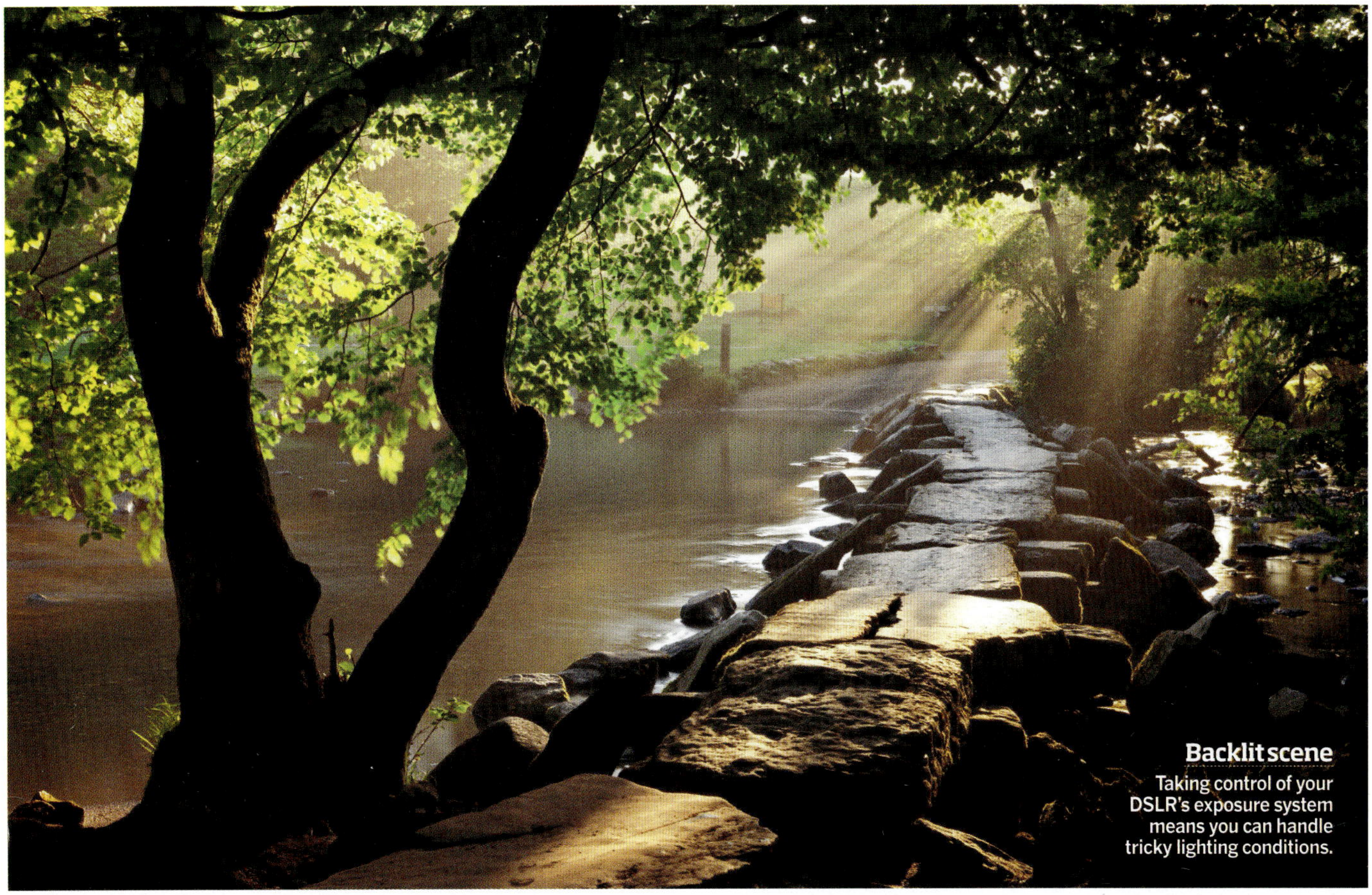

Backlit scene

Taking control of your DSLR's exposure system means you can handle tricky lighting conditions.

Aperture and shutter speeds

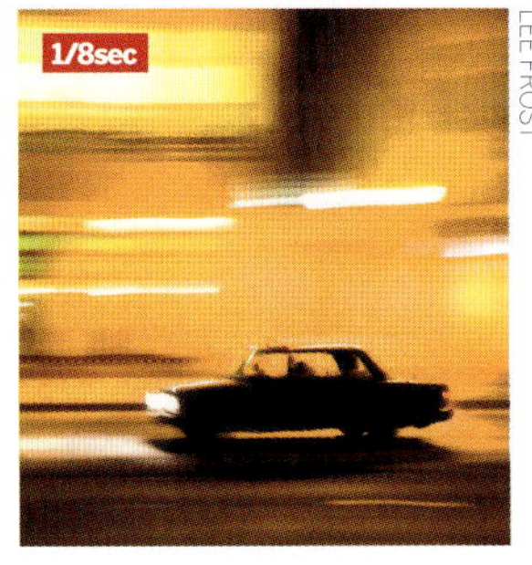

LEE FROST

Shutter speeds These are changed in increments of a fraction of a second. Each doubling or halving of an exposure is referred to as a 'stop'. For instance, changing from 1/500sec to 1/250sec doubles the exposure. Depending on your camera, you can alter shutter speeds in increments of ½ or ⅓ of a stop. Most cameras have a shutter-speed range of 30 seconds to 1/4000sec. Our diagram below shows the shutter-speed range in full stops from one second to 1/4000sec, as well as the shutter speeds that are used when changing in ½-stop increments.

Full stops	1sec	1/2sec	1/4sec	1/8sec	1/16sec	1/30sec	1/60sec	1/125sec	1/250sec	1/500sec	1/1000sec	1/2000sec	1/4000sec
1/2 stops	0.7sec	1/3sec	1/6sec	1/10sec	1/20sec	1/45sec	1/90sec	1/180sec	1/350sec	1/750sec	1/1500sec	1/3000sec	

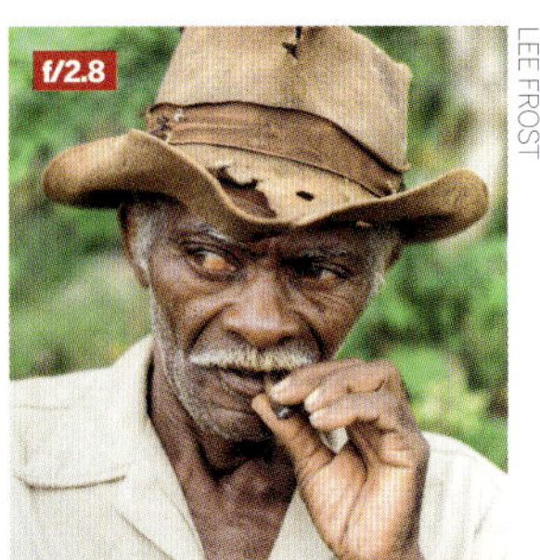

LEE FROST

Aperture Aperture settings are normally stated as 'f/numbers', such as f/4. The aperture setting affects how much light is allowed to pass through the lens. Light is controlled by a set of blades known as an iris that can be opened and closed, much like the pupil in an eye, to regulate the light passing through the lens. Each one-stop increment allows double or half of the light through. The maximum aperture refers to when the iris is wide open, while the minimum aperture refers to when the iris is at its smallest (f/22 in this case). Below are the most common aperture settings.

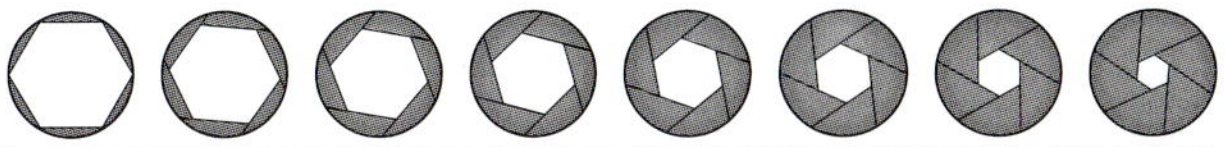

Full stops	f/2.8		f/4		f/5.6		f/8		f/11		f/16		f/22		f/32
1/2 stops		f/3.5		f/4.5		f/6.7		f/9.5		f/13		f/19		f/27	

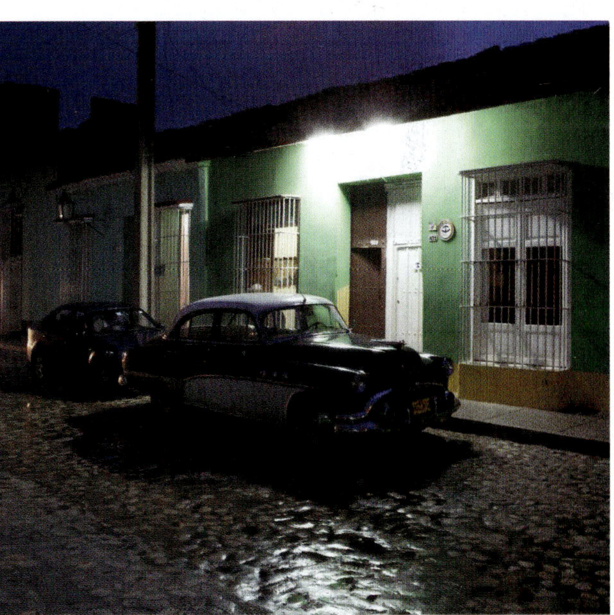

LEE FROST

ISO and exposure

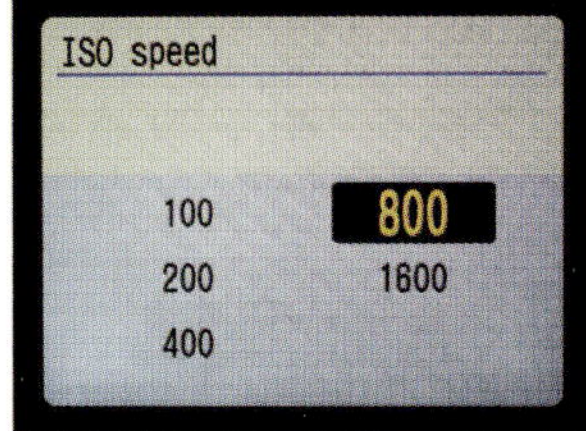

To understand how ISO can affect your exposure, we first need to understand exactly what this term is. ISO is a rating that determines how sensitive the sensor is to light. A low setting, such as ISO 100, results in less sensitivity, while ISO 800 results in higher sensitivity. The ISO rating you dial on your DSLR will affect the shutter speed and aperture settings, but remember that upping the ISO will result in increased digital noise. For most conditions, an ISO of between 100 and 400 will be sufficient.

Exposure modes: The key to taking control

Your camera offers you a choice of exposure modes, all designed to deliver a perfectly exposed image, but each is designed to do this in slightly different ways. Knowing how each exposure mode works and what shooting situation suits it best is essential if you are to improve as a creative photographer

Aperture-priority mode (Av or A)

Almost universally acclaimed as the most useful and versatile mode, aperture-priority can be left set on your camera for the majority of the time, as it is useful in most shooting situations. Labelled as Av (Aperture value), or as A, aperture-priority is the most popular and commonly used exposure mode on cameras.

Because you determine which aperture to use and the camera then decides the appropriate shutter speed, it's known as a semi-automatic mode and can be used when shooting all manner of subjects. Controlling the depth-of-field is particularly useful for photographers who seek front-to-back sharpness in their images, which is why it proves to be a very popular mode with landscape photographers.

It's a favourite amongst portrait photographers, too, who often set a wide aperture which throws the background nicely out of focus and directs attention onto their subject. Aperture-priority mode is also popular with photographers because it's incredibly easy to use, but also because controlling the depth-of-field allows you to be creative with your picture-taking, selecting points of interest that you'd like to keep in focus.

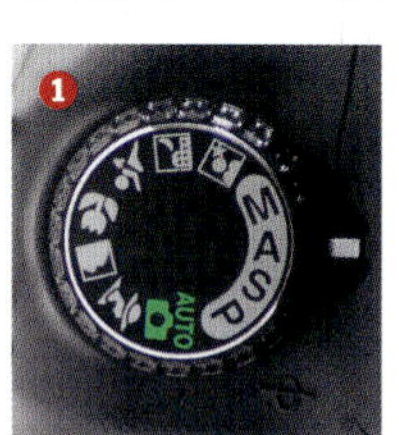

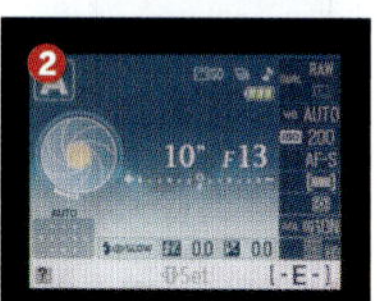

USING aperture-priority:
1. Turn the mode dial until it reads either Av or A.
2. Use the input dial to select your desired aperture, which will be displayed on the top-plate and/or rear LCD monitor.

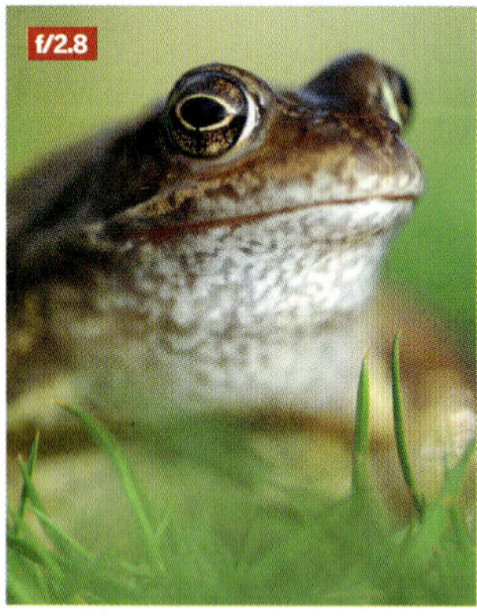
f/2.8

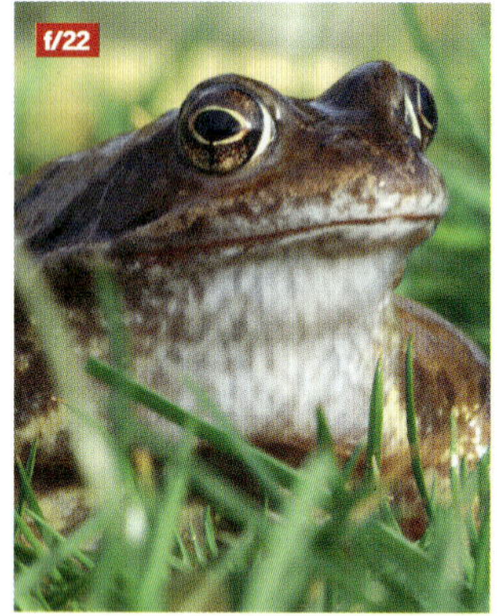
f/22

What is depth-of-field? Depth-of-field describes the amount of the scene that appears in sharp focus. The focal length and focus distance contribute to the effect, but the most important factor to controlling depth-of-field is your choice of aperture.

Aperture-priority: Perfect for...

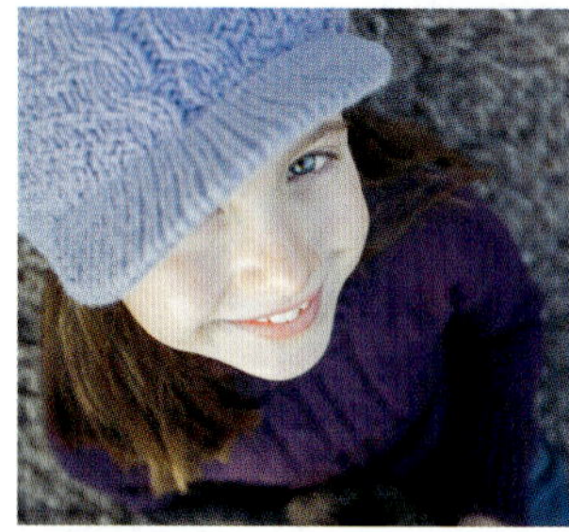
PAUL STEFAN

Portraits
A wide aperture provides shallow depth-of-field, ideal for directing attention on the subject.

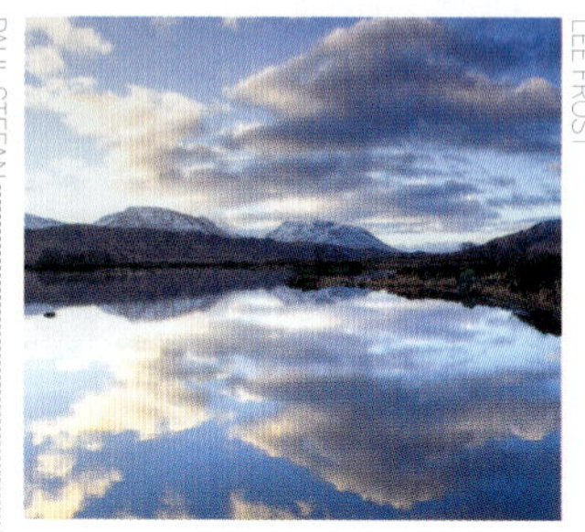
LEE FROST

Landscapes
Using a small aperture gives plenty of depth-of-field so that the entire scene appears sharp.

Shutter-priority mode (Tv or S)

Another semi-automatic function, Tv (or S) works in the opposite way to aperture-priority mode. So rather than choosing the aperture, the photographer dials in their chosen shutter speed and the camera duly works out the best aperture to use to create a correct exposure.

Most photographers prefer this mode when there is a moving object in the scene that they wish to capture pin-sharp in the image, or alternatively blur for creative effect. For example, when photographing a cyclist or car speeding by, you either have the option to set a fast shutter speed, which freezes the action, or you can select a slower one that allows you to pan the movement and therefore emphasise the movement of the subject through the frame.

A similar option presents itself when shooting landscapes with water in the frame: do you use a fast shutter speed to freeze the water's motion or select a very long shutter speed and capture a long exposure that transforms water into an ethereal mist? All of these options are possible simply by selecting the appropriate shutter speed. Try it out for yourself to get a feel for the different results.

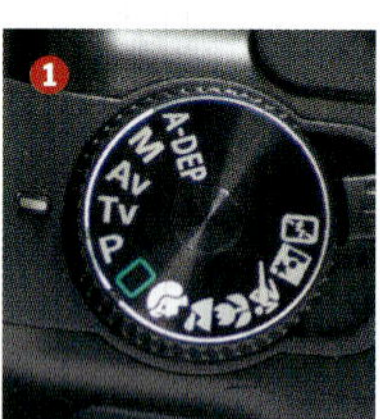

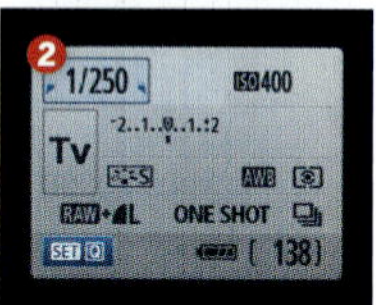

USING shutter-priority:
1. Turn the mode dial until it reads either Tv or S.
2. Now use the input dial to select your chosen shutter speed and this will be displayed on the top-plate and/or rear LCD screen.

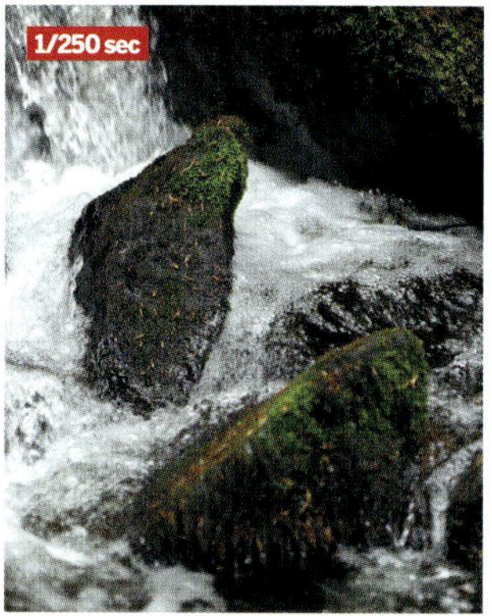
1/250 sec

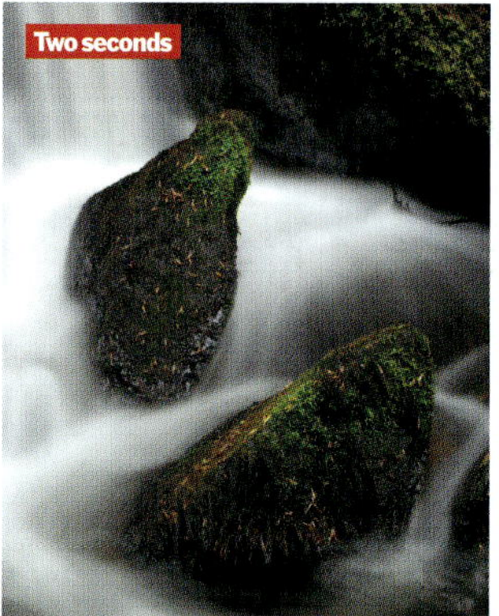
Two seconds

Slow it down! Two different shutter speeds; two very different results. A fast shutter speed will freeze moving water, but a shutter speed of a couple of seconds will create misty-looking water – a favourite with lots of professional photographers.

Shutter-priority: Perfect for...

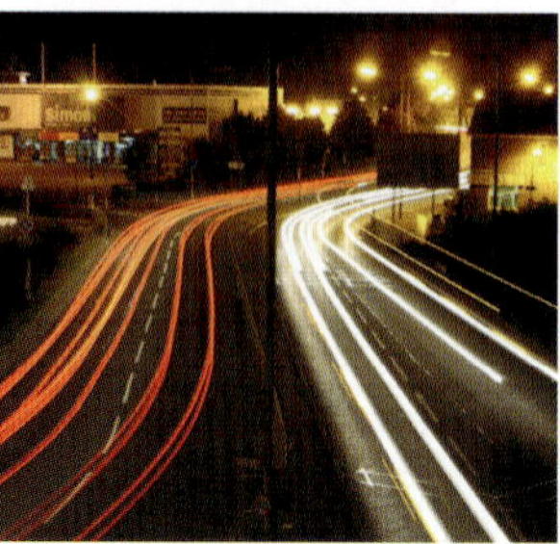

Light trails
Place your DSLR on a tripod and use a long exposure to capture creative light trails.

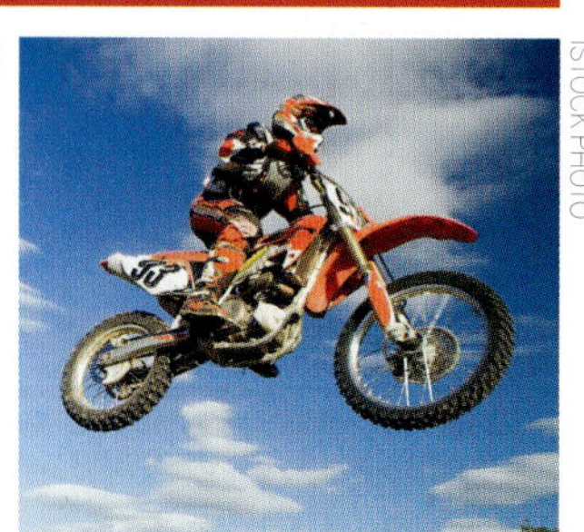
ISTOCK PHOTO

Sports & action
Selecting a fast shutter speed is essential to capture fast-moving subjects in sharp detail.

LEE FROST

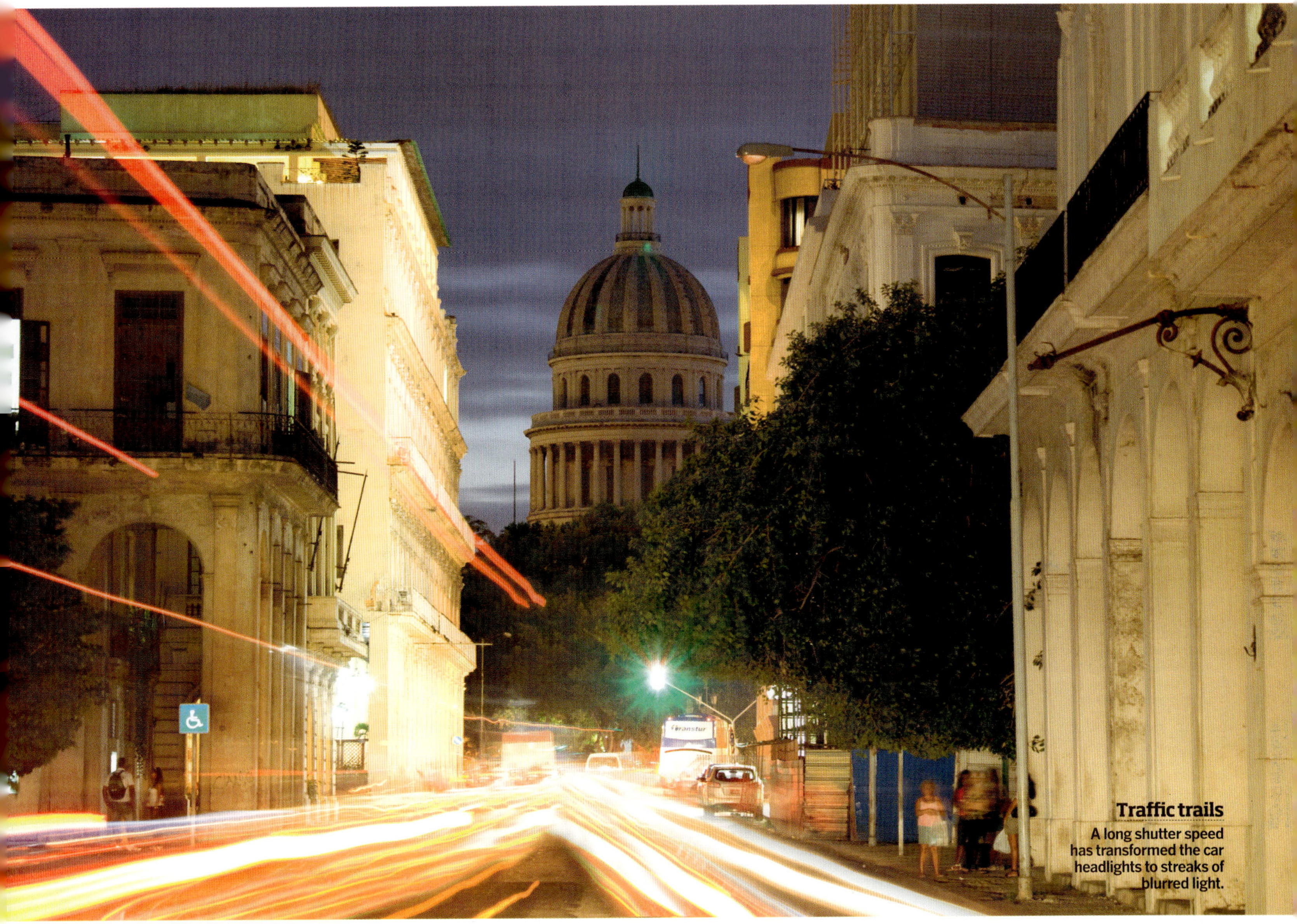

Traffic trails
A long shutter speed has transformed the car headlights to streaks of blurred light.

Other useful modes to consider

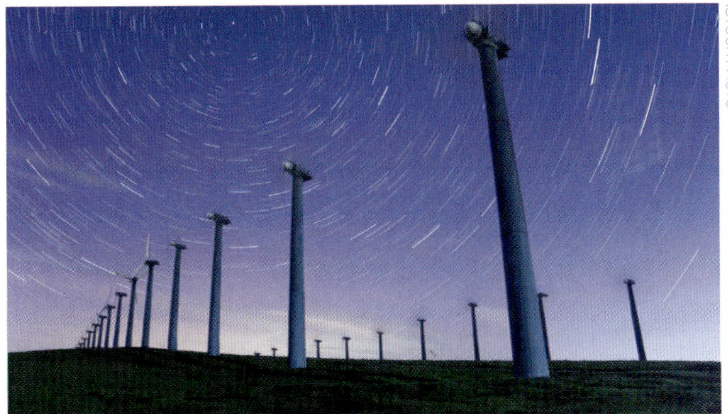

ISTOCK PHOTO

Bulb mode: For very long exposures (usually longer than 30 seconds) you'll need Bulb mode (B). Almost all DSLRs offer this mode, which allows the photographer to lock open the shutter, allowing exposures of minutes or even hours! Perfect for star trails and night photography, or for when you're shooting fireworks.

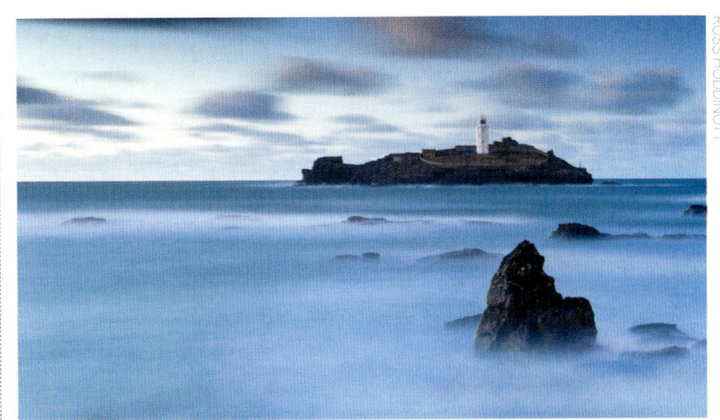

ROSS HODDINOTT

Manual mode: For complete control, manual mode is what you need. As its name suggests, the photographer selects both the key variables involved in exposure: the aperture and shutter speed. Many professionals keep their mode dial on manual as they believe in having full control over all the exposure parameters.

Master metering patterns

Your camera is equipped with different metering patterns. Learn which one to use for particular shooting situations to give you the best control over exposure

AS WE'VE ALREADY MENTIONED, the job of your camera's metering system is to assess the scene you'd like to capture and work out the aperture and shutter speed settings that will result in a correct exposure. The camera assumes the average tone within the scene is a mid-tone of 18% grey and works out the exposure based on this assumption. All metering patterns use the mid-tone principle, but how each measures the scene varies from pattern to pattern. For example, the multi-zone system divides the image frame into zones, takes individual readings from each and uses sophisticated algorithms to determine the final exposure. Partial and spot-metering patterns, however, take an exposure reading from a very small area (usually between 3-9%) at the centre of the frame.

Why have different metering patterns? Well, the option of taking a reading from the whole frame or just small elements of it gives the photographer a tremendous amount of control for precise metering.

Of course, care must be taken when selecting your metering pattern to make sure it's suitable for the subject you are attempting to capture. For example, if you are shooting a typical landscape scene with a bright blue sky, lush green grass and a dark shaded tree, you will want to use multi-zone instead of spot metering, because if you meter for the dark shaded tree, the camera will think that it is taking a reading from a mid-tone and will overexpose the scene. With multi-zone metering, however, the camera takes into account the variation from every zone – the sky, grass and dark tree etc – and uses this to calculate an accurate exposure.

We've covered each metering pattern below, along with how to identify it on your camera and a suggestion of situations where using this metering pattern may pay dividends, so that when you're next taking pictures, you'll know which mode will work best for you and avoid taking pictures that turn out to be poorly exposed.

Spot & partial metering

Ideal for situations when you wish to take a reading from a specific area of the frame, the spot and partial metering modes must be used with care by the photographer to avoid metering mishaps. These precise modes operate by metering from a small area, usually at the centre of the frame.

Most spot meters have a precise metering circle that reads off 3% of the image frame, while partial metering isn't so precise, taking readings from an area of 9% or so.

To get a correct exposure when using these patterns, the metering area must be placed over a mid-tone otherwise you run the risk of the scene being over- or underexposed. This mid-tone doesn't have to be grey; it could be any other mid-tone colour, such as green grass, brown dirt or brickwork. Most digital SLR cameras offer spot metering these days, some have partial metering, while a few have both.

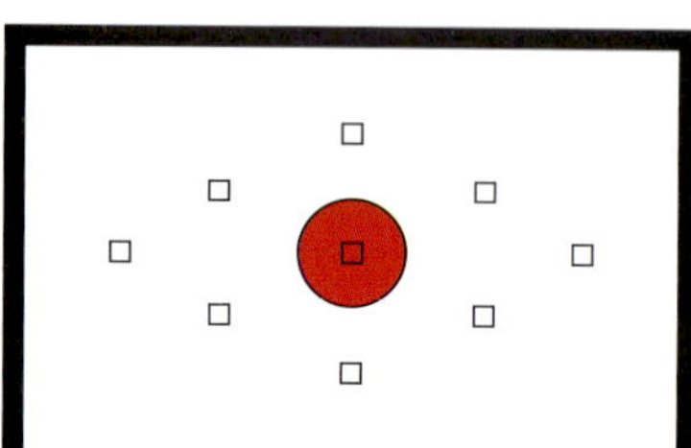

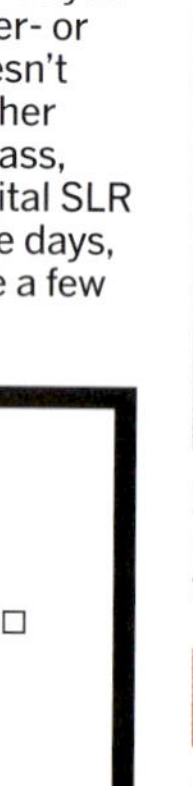

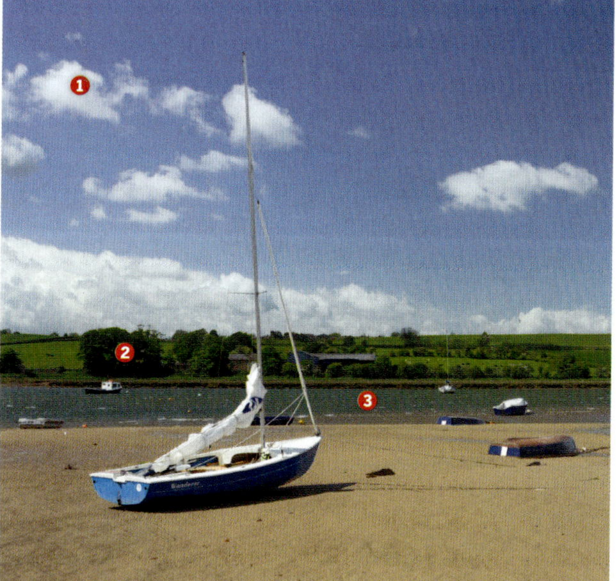

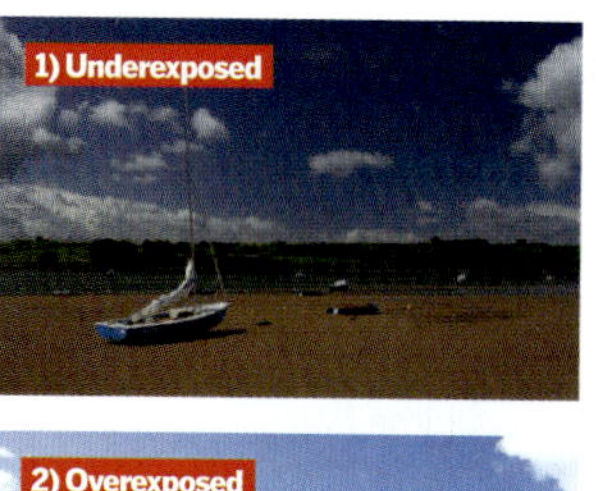

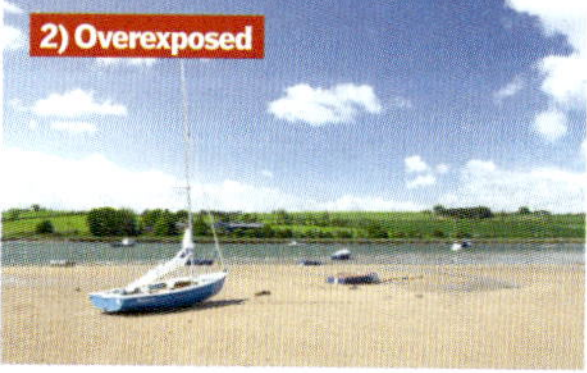

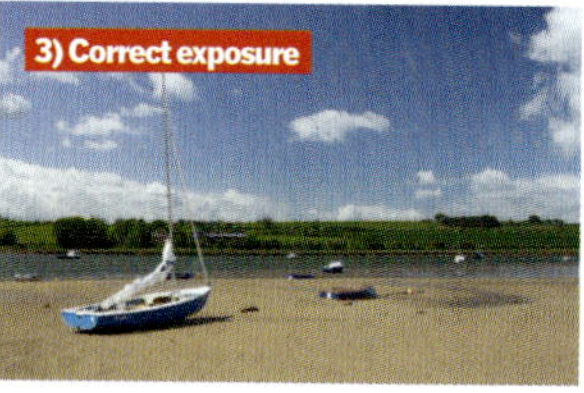

Exposing from a mid-tone: When using spot or partial metering, it's important to remember that you must place the metering area over a mid-tone to achieve the correct exposure. In this typical scene, we took spot readings from different areas of the frame to show you how the exposure varies.

Spot & partial icons

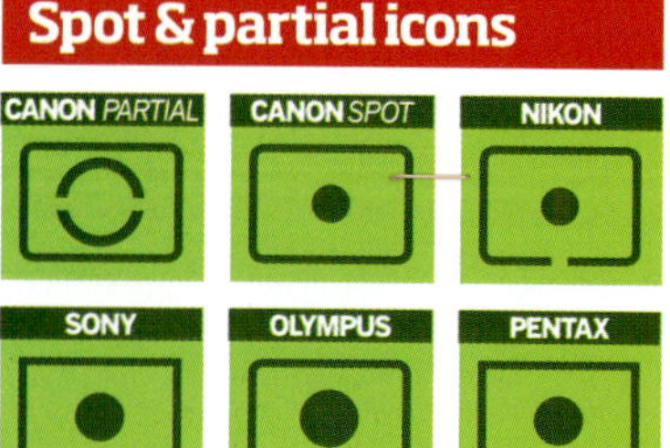

Spot & partial metering: Perfect for...

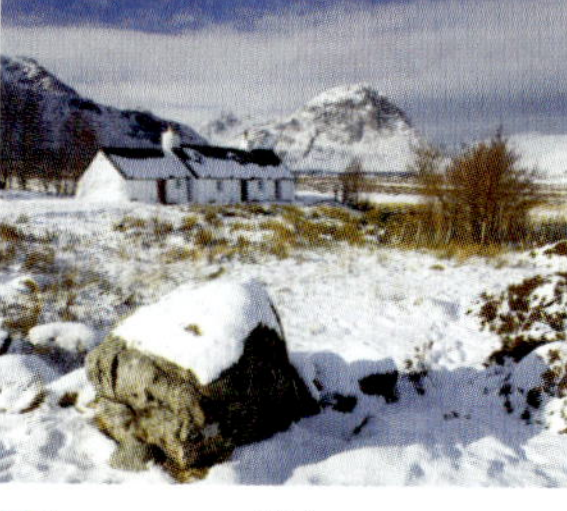

Snowy conditions
Aim the spot meter at an area with mid-tones to prevent the snow causing underexposure.

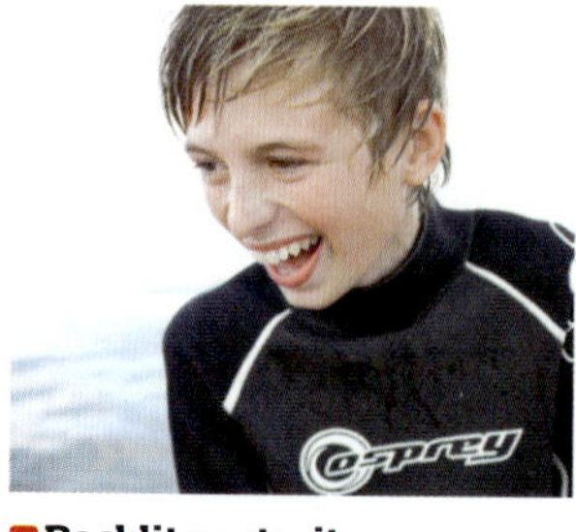

Backlit portraits
The intense backlight from the sky can fool multi-zone systems, so spot-meter from the face.

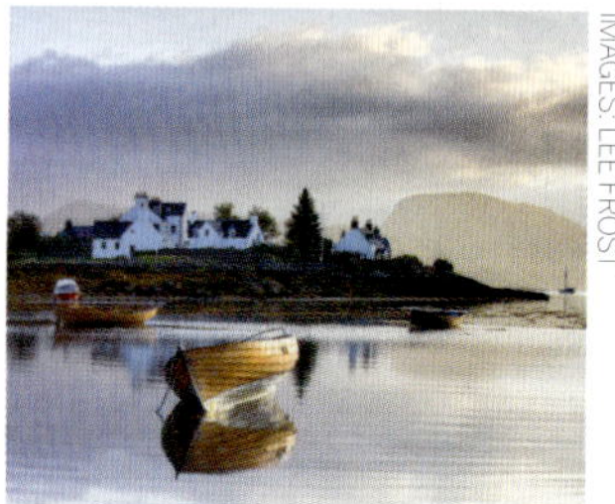

Scenes with highlights
Meter from a mid-tone when scenes are dominated by highlights like reflections.

IMAGES: LEE FROST

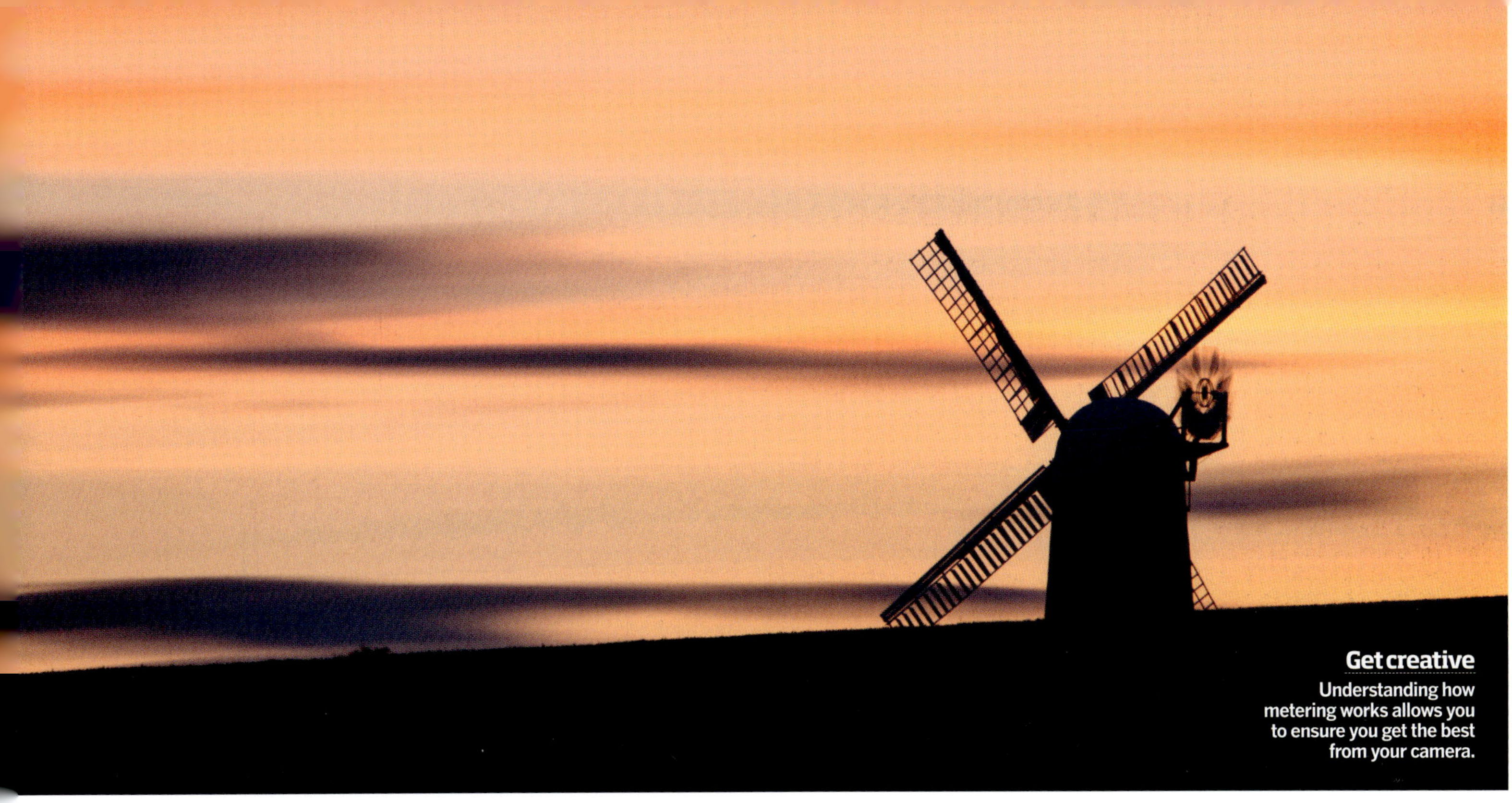

Get creative
Understanding how metering works allows you to ensure you get the best from your camera.

ROSS HODDINOTT

Multi-zone metering

Multi-zone metering systems are incredibly reliable and return a correct exposure for the vast majority of scenes. That's because the multi-zone pattern is the most sophisticated metering system available. It works by dividing the entire frame into zones, with individual meter readings taken from each zone. The data from these readings is then run through a series of algorithms, and often the data is compared to a database of images which helps to determine and calculate the final exposure.

The various brands have each given names to describe their own multi-zone mode – Nikon's mode is called Matrix, Canon calls its system Evaluative, while Pentax has multi-segment. The number of zones vary from camera to camera, and while the general rule is that the more zones a pattern has, the better its accuracy, this isn't always the case.

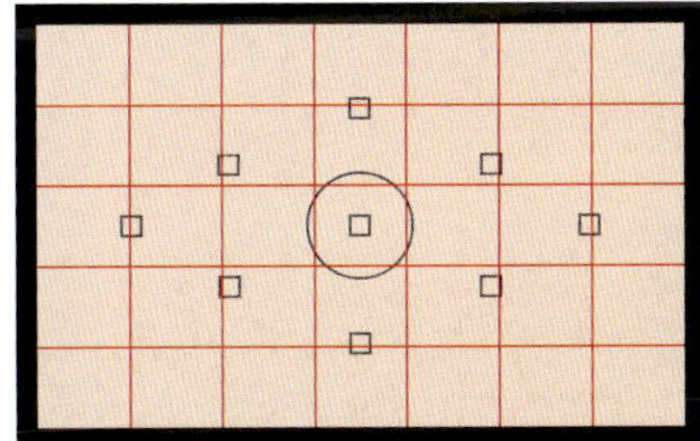

Multi-zone icons

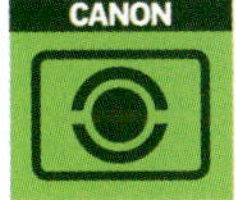

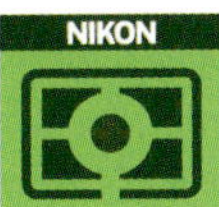

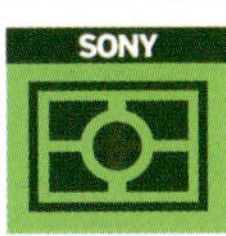

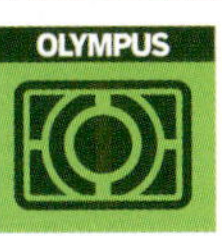

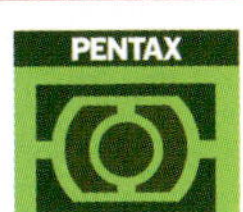

Multi-zone: Perfect for...

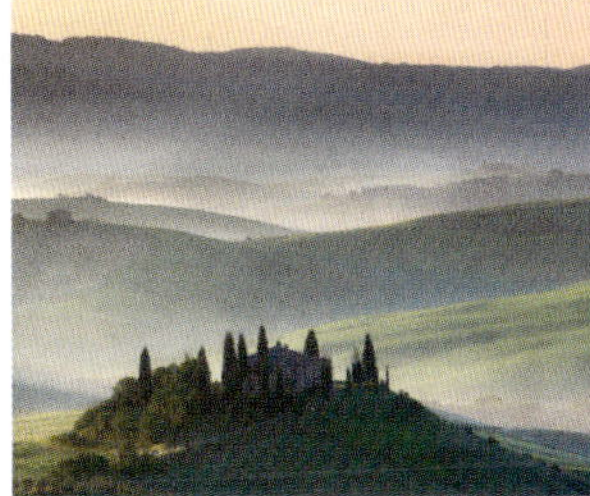

Landscapes
Scenes with sky and foreground that have a variation in exposure are easily handled.

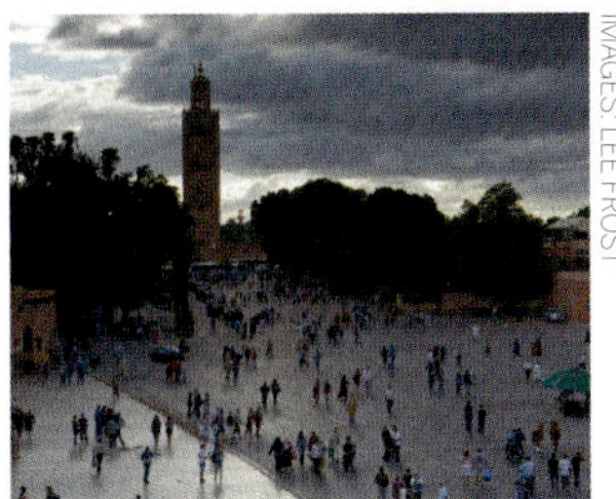

General scenes
Unless your scene has unusual lighting conditions, you'll have no problems with multi-zone.

IMAGES: LEE FROST

Centre-weighted average

Film camera enthusiasts will recognise centre-weighted average from the darkroom days. This mode has been used for years on SLR cameras, but has been superseded by multi-zone metering. Centre-weighted average works by taking an average reading from the entire frame, giving most emphasis to the central area. Those who are familiar with this pattern are more likely to use it, and it's also the recommended choice when using AE-Lock.

The bias towards the centre of the frame varies from brand to brand, but it is generally 60-80% towards the centre of the frame. The main problem with this pattern comes when you're photographing landscapes. This is because the expanse of sky in bright conditions can lead it to underexpose the scene, unless you're experienced enough to know what to do to get around these issues (see below).

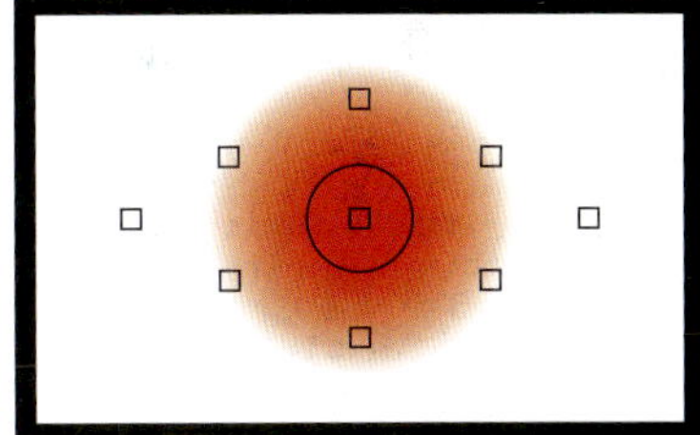

Centre-weighted average icons

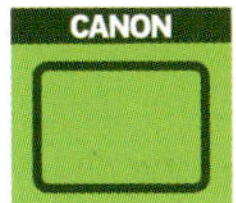

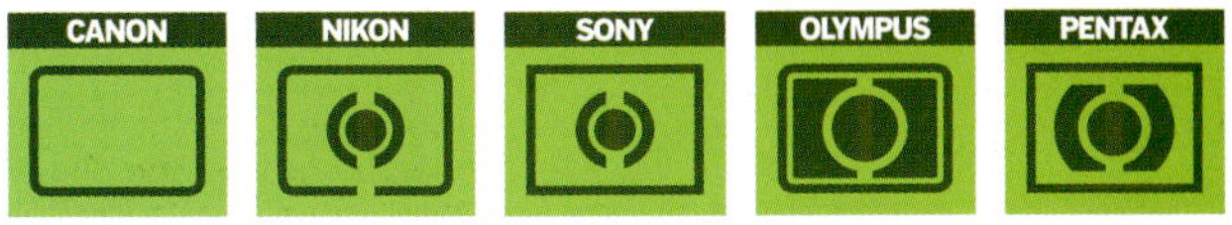

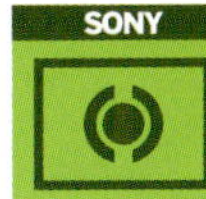

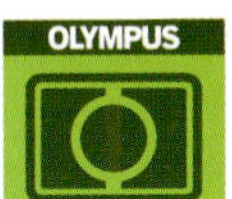

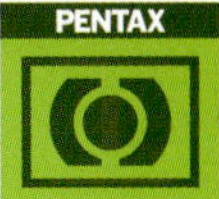

Centre-weighted average: Perfect for....

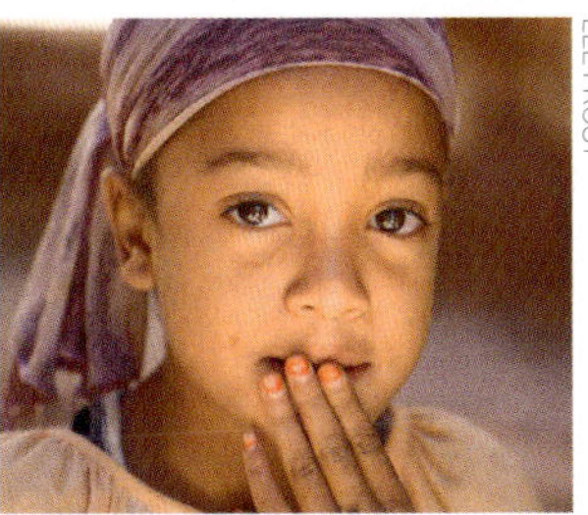

LEE FROST

General portraits
Variances between light and dark shades are well handled to ensure accurate results.

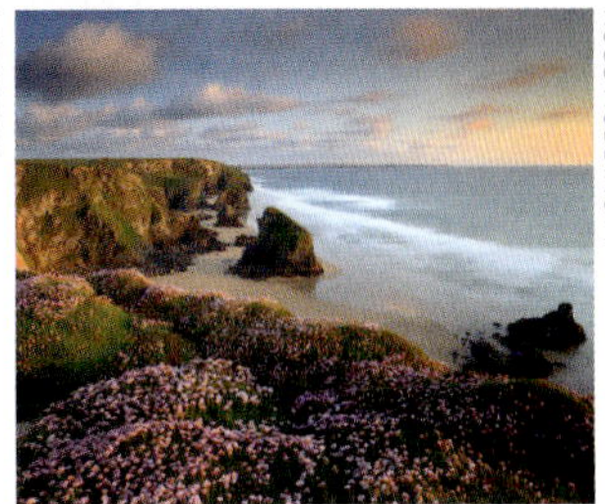

ROSS HODDINOTT

Landscapes with AE-L
In scenes with bright sky, point the camera at the ground, use AE-L then recompose and shoot.

Exposure overrides: Taking more control

Although cameras have very sophisticated metering systems, they're not infallible and will occasionally produce incorrect exposures. Lighter- or darker-than-average scenes, as well as tricky lighting situations like backlighting, are the most common situations that lead to poor results. Therefore it is important to know how to override your camera's meter reading to ensure you can take control and achieve a perfect exposure

Exposure compensation

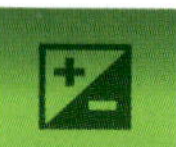

The most common and simplest override is exposure compensation – a feature that you'll find on every DSLR and one that allows the user to increase or decrease the camera's suggested exposure. Exposure compensation is incredibly easy to use as you adjust the exposure in set increments of either ⅓ or ½ stops, depending on your camera.

Applying a positive (+) value increases the amount of exposure, with the aim of lightening the image, while dialling in a negative (–) value, on the other hand, will darken it. Because the compensation is applied in incremental steps that correspond with adjusting apertures and shutter speeds, it shouldn't take too long to get used to. Before long, you'll be automatically using exposure compensation without even having to think about it.

The amount of exposure compensation is usually displayed on a scale or as a figure on the LCD, or in the viewfinder. It's often stated as an EV (Exposure Value), so adding half a stop will appear as +½EV. How the camera applies exposure compensation depends on which exposure mode you use.

In aperture-priority mode, it's the shutter speed that is changed, while in shutter-priority mode, the compensation is applied via the aperture setting. In program mode, the camera alters either variable, depending on light levels and the risk of camera shake. The general rule to remember is that if the subject or scene is dominated by a light subject, the camera may underexpose, so dial in a positive (+) value to avoid this. When photographing a very dark subject or scene, the camera is likely to overexpose it, so set a negative value (–) compensation to obtain a correct exposure.

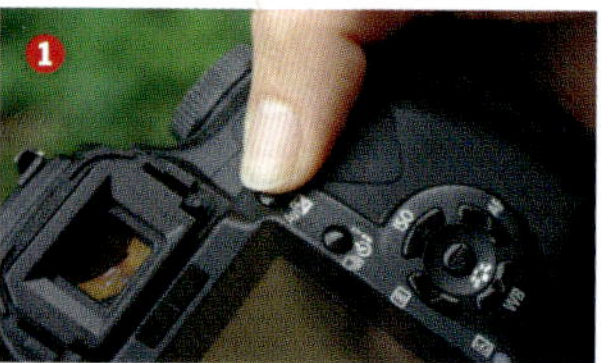

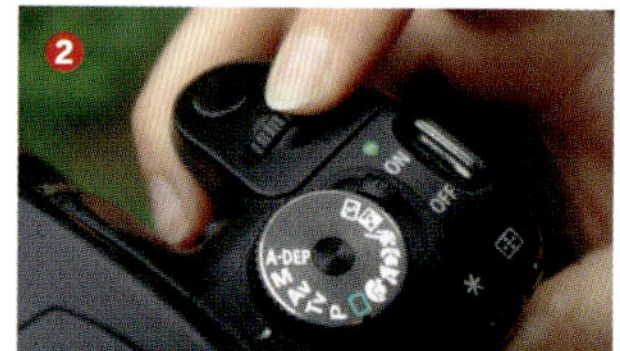

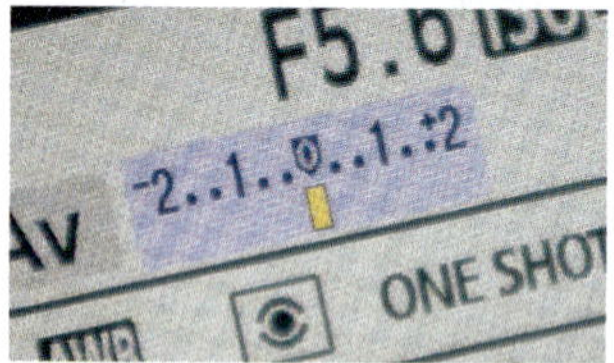

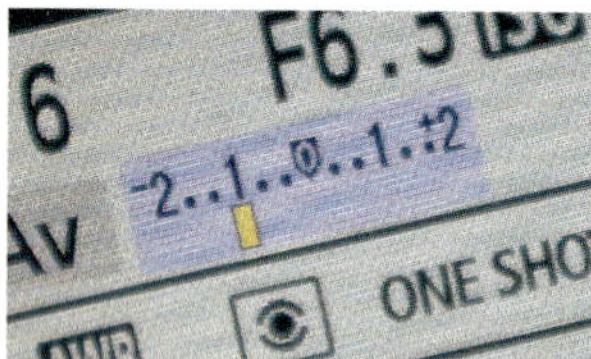

How to use exposure compensation:
1) Locate and press your DSLR's exposure compensation button (usually indicated by a +/- icon).
2) To dial in the desired amount of exposure compensation, turn the input dial in either direction. A negative input results in less exposure being applied, while a positive input increases exposure. Once you've taken a shot, check the LCD to review your results.

Exposure compensation: Perfect for...

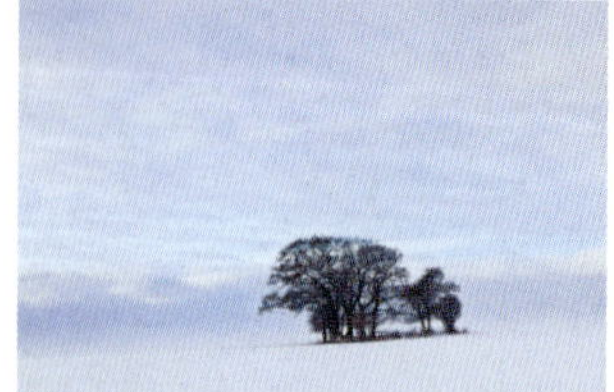

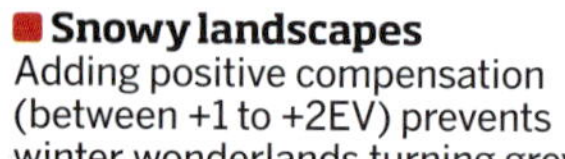

MARK BAUER

Snowy landscapes
Adding positive compensation (between +1 to +2EV) prevents winter wonderlands turning grey.

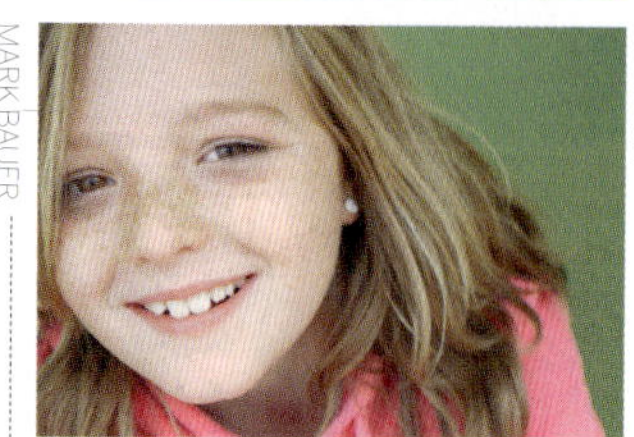

LEE FROST

Managing skin tones
Exposure compensation can help balance the skin tones of tanned or dark-skinned subjects.

Autoexposure Lock (AE-L)

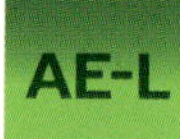

Using this exposure override doesn't actually lead to an increase or decrease in the exposure, but rather allows you to specify the area from which the camera takes a reading. It is an override function that is nowhere near as popular amongst photographers as exposure compensation, mainly because it requires users to be more experienced in picture-taking and have a broader understanding of what lighting situations and scenes demand its use.

As its name suggests, the Autoexposure Lock facility allows you to lock an exposure reading, which is retained even when you recompose the scene. Normally when you take a picture, pressing the shutter button halfway engages the autofocus and exposure systems simultaneously, which is suitable for most scenes. However, in some situations this can lead to exposure error where the subject or scene is very bright or dark, or where there is very high contrast or unusual lighting conditions. In these conditions, taking a reading from a mid-tone and locking this with the AE-L facility on your camera can ensure perfect results.

While you can use multi-zone metering with Autoexposure Lock, you'll find you are better off switching to spot or partial metering to ensure the exposure reading is taken off a mid-tone. This is relevant whether you are taking a reading off an area of grass, brickwork or a grey card. Just remember that the lighting on the area you use AE-L with should be the same as that for your main subject. So, for example, if you use AE-L to meter from an area which is bathed in bright sunshine, while your subject is sat in shade, this will only result in a very overexposed subject.

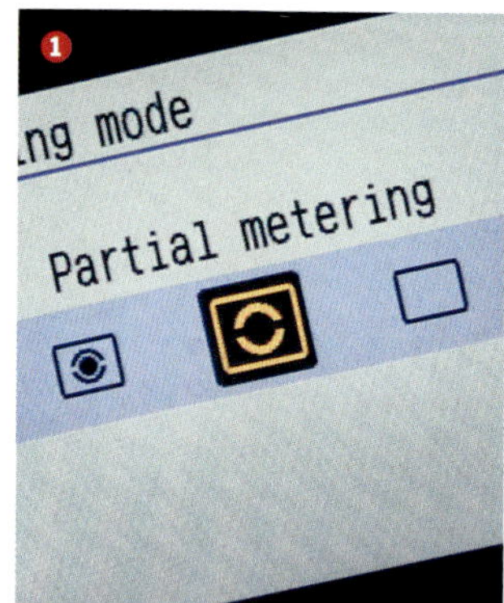

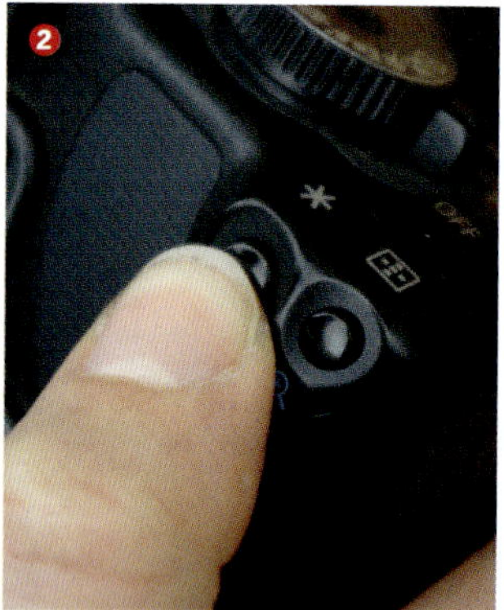

How to use Autoexposure Lock (AE-L):
1) Set your metering pattern to either spot or partial. Access the scene, find the area that you want to meter from and press the shutter halfway to activate the metering system.
2) Now press the AE-L button to lock in the exposure settings. Recompose your scene and, when happy, press the shutter button to capture your image, which should be perfectly exposed.

Autoexposure Lock: Perfect for...

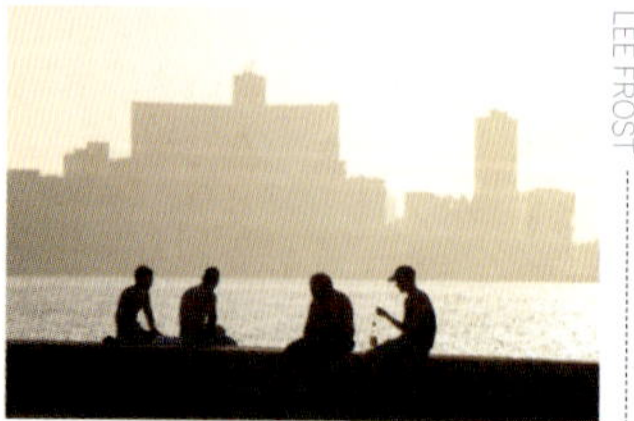

LEE FROST

Silhouettes at sunset
Meter off the sunset and hit AE-L. Other elements in the scene will become silhouetted.

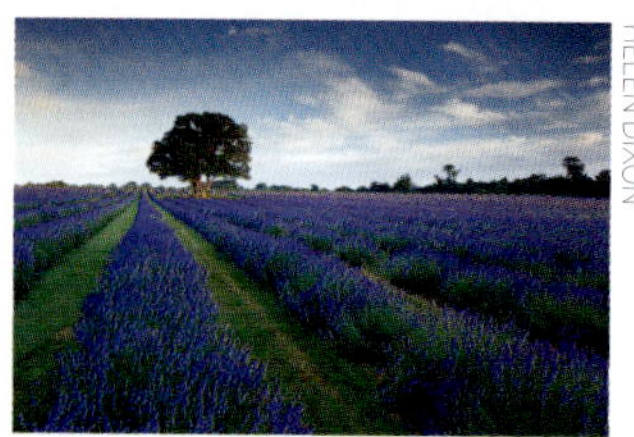

HELEN DIXON

Scenes with bright skies
Large expanses of bright sky can lead to underexposure. Use AE-L to take a reading off grass.

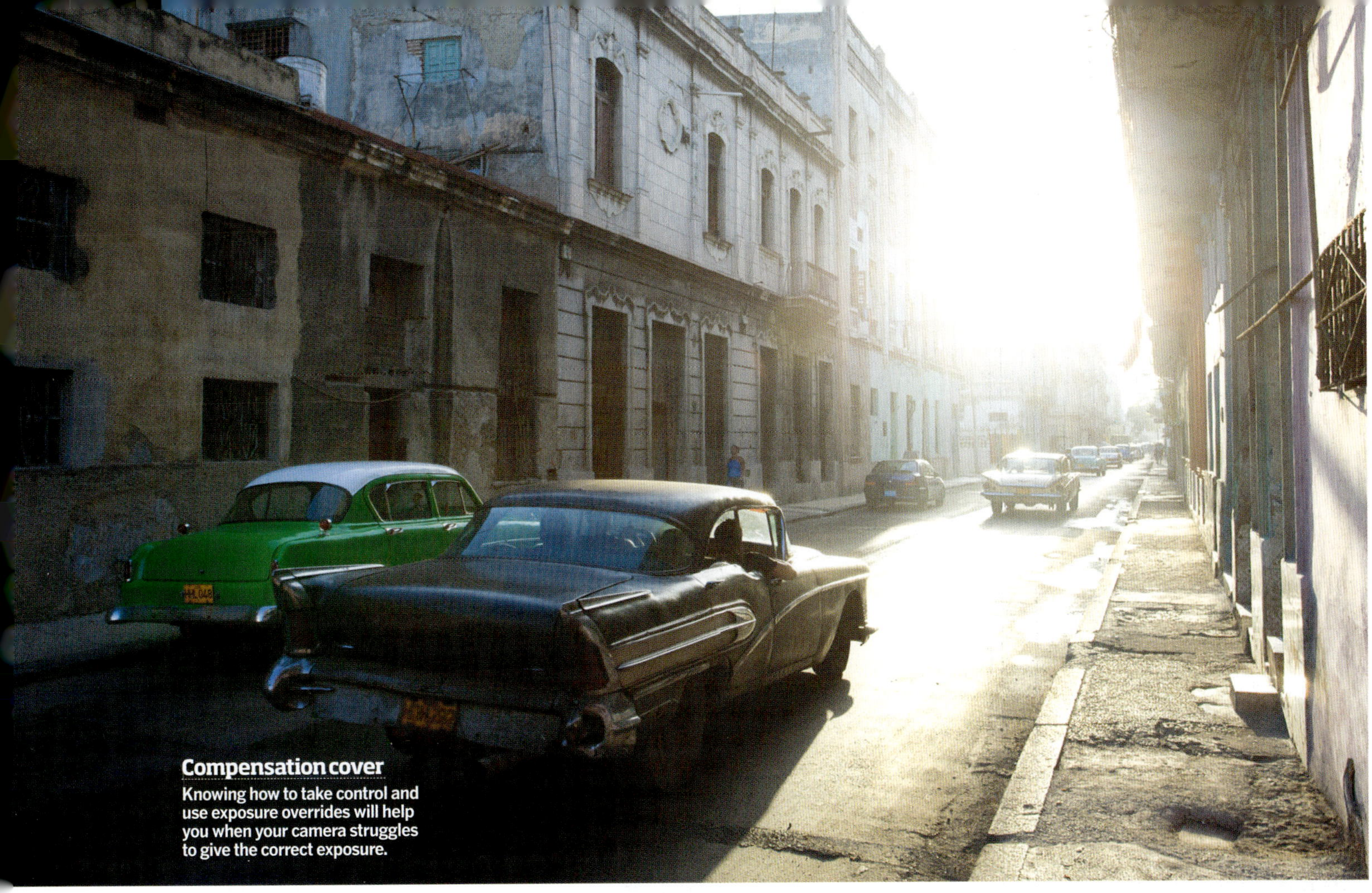

Compensation cover
Knowing how to take control and use exposure overrides will help you when your camera struggles to give the correct exposure.

LEE FROST

Autoexposure Bracketing (AEB)

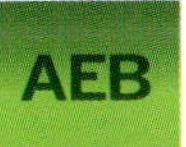

Autoexposure Bracketing (AEB) allows the photographer to capture a series of three images at different exposures without the need to adjust any settings between each frame. Most cameras allow sequential shots at +/– three stops from the base exposure, although some cameras offer up to five stops of AEB, and the function is available whether you're shooting in program, shutter-priority, aperture-priority or manual mode. The feature was originally introduced as a way to allow inexperienced photographers shooting in very difficult situations to take three exposures in combination with exposure compensation, ensuring one good result.

So how does it work? Well, it's like this: imagine you're faced with shooting a bright-white snow scene and you're not sure if you need to apply +1 or +2EV. To get around it, set +1.5EV in exposure compensation and in AEB set +/-0.5EV. When you come to shoot your sequence of images, the final result will be a set of three images at +1, +1.5 and +2EV.

Today, AEB is predominantly used to capture frames that are then used to produce High Dynamic Range (HDR) images, which are normally processed later using Photoshop or a third-party software like Photomatix. When shooting HDR, the photographer needs to be very careful not to move the camera between frames as this will render the rest of the sequence completely useless. It's also recommended that focus is achieved prior to taking the first of the AEB sequence and then make the switch to manual – the last thing you want is your lens hunting around for a focal point in between shots while someone walks into your frame and spoils the result. A remote release or the self-timer can be used in conjunction with AEB so you only have to press the shutter button once.

1

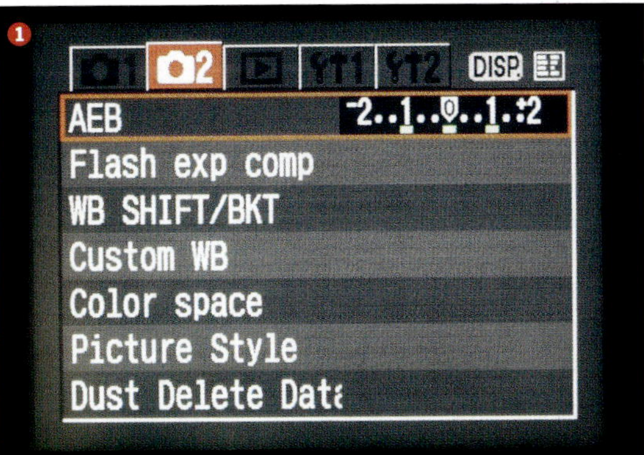

How to use AEB: 1) Access the AEB function via your menu's screen and use the input dial to select how many stops you want the bracket to cover.
2) Half-press the shutter button to exit the menu screen.
3) Set up your shot and depress the shutter button three times (or use a remote release) to capture the bracket.

AEB: Perfect for...

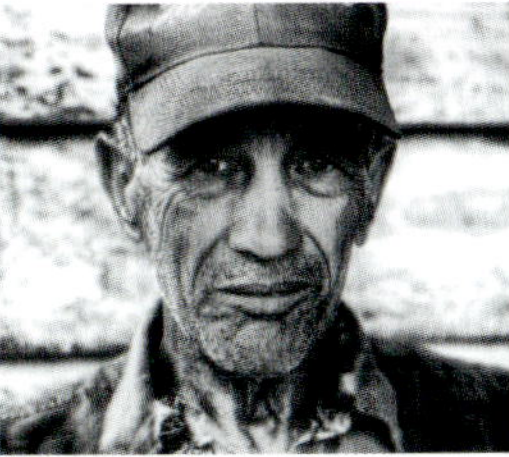

HDR images
Bring out the shadows and highlights of your scene using this popular technique.

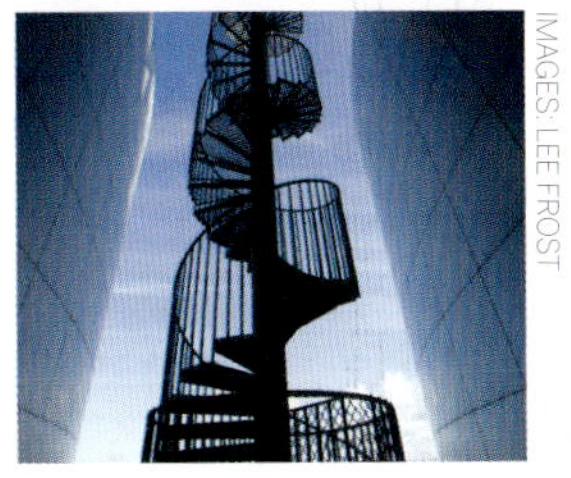

Hedging your bets
Use AEB with exposure compensation to ensure one out of three shots is perfect.

IMAGES: LEE FROST

Flash Exposure Lock (FEL)

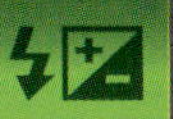

Flash Exposure Lock is an often overlooked facility available when using flash in difficult situations. It's worth noting that FEL isn't available on all DSLRs and only works with certain flashguns, so you need to check your camera and instructions to ensure you can use it. Usually, it works by pressing the partial meter button (*) or AE-L button to fire a pre-flash, which effectively takes a spot meter reading with flash. The information is stored for a short length of time (anything from six to 20 seconds, depending on your DSLR), giving the photographer time to recompose and take the shot. Flash Exposure Lock is particularly useful in scenes where there are highly reflective surfaces, such as mirrors or glass, or scenes that include light sources like neon lights. These can fool the camera's metering system by reflecting flash back, which could lead to poorly exposed flash pictures. Using FEL in these circumstances helps avoid this problem.

WILDLIFE

Whether large or small; feathered or furred; cute or creepy, wildlife is a hugely varied and popular photographic subject. From majestic deer stags to secretive stag beetles, every creature presents different challenges to photographers. To take great wildlife shots, you'll need stealth, skill, oodles of patience… and our extensive guide to shooting wildlife

WITH SO MANY OF US fascinated by the natural world, it is hardly surprising that wildlife photography is such a popular subject today. There is never a shortage of great photo possibilities when shooting mammals, birds, reptiles, amphibians, bugs and beetles. The UK is home to a wealth of great subjects – you really don't have to travel far, or go on safari, to discover and photograph impressive wildlife. Our largest land mammal is the red deer, with stags boasting imposing antlers and growing up to 120cm tall (at shoulder height). At the opposite end of the scale, ladybirds are under a centimetre in length, but are brightly coloured, appealing and equally photogenic. The UK is home to a huge diversity of habitats, each supporting a different range of wildlife and their own unique photo opportunities. Moorland and heathland is home to raptors, grouse, basking adders and lizards; while woodland offers shelter to deer, woodpeckers, squirrels, beetles and nests of ants. Our countryside is alive with bird life and home to playful rabbits and delicate butterflies; while you'll find waders, ducks, kingfishers, colourful dragonflies and raft spiders when visiting rivers and wetland habitats. Along our rugged coast and offshore islands, you may discover bobbing seals and noisy colonies of nesting sea birds; while in gardens, parks and cities, songbirds and foxes have quickly adapted to urban life.

At night, owls, hedgehogs, badgers and moths emerge, and in summer and winter the UK is invaded by a variety of migrating birds. Quite simply, the UK is an amazing island for wildlife photography. That isn't to say taking memorable nature images is easy to do, though. Although wildlife residing in parks and gardens might be more approachable, truly wild animals are shy, easily disturbed and difficult to get close to. Getting within photographic range of wild subjects requires stealth, fieldcraft, knowledge of the subject, preparation, patience… and often an element of luck. Photographing wildlife can be frustrating and time-consuming, but also extremely rewarding. Capturing truly intimate, eye-catching and original nature shots is hugely satisfying. However, before you rush outdoors, dressed head to foot in camouflage clothing, waving about your longest telephoto, be sure to first read this section on wildlife photography thoroughly.

Do your research

While some wildlife images are the upshot of pure opportunism, the best images are normally the result of careful planning. Having selected a subject to shoot, do your homework. Research subjects thoroughly online, or through reference books, to discover their preferred environments, key aspects of behaviour, diet and habits. A good knowledge and understanding of your subject is essential, helping you to first locate and then get close to the animal. Doing your homework first will save time long-term and maximise your chances of photographing it successfully.

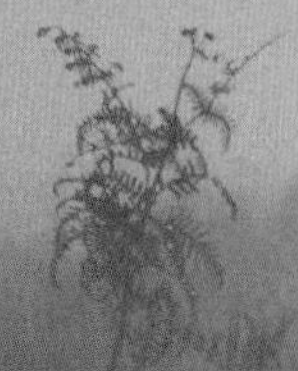

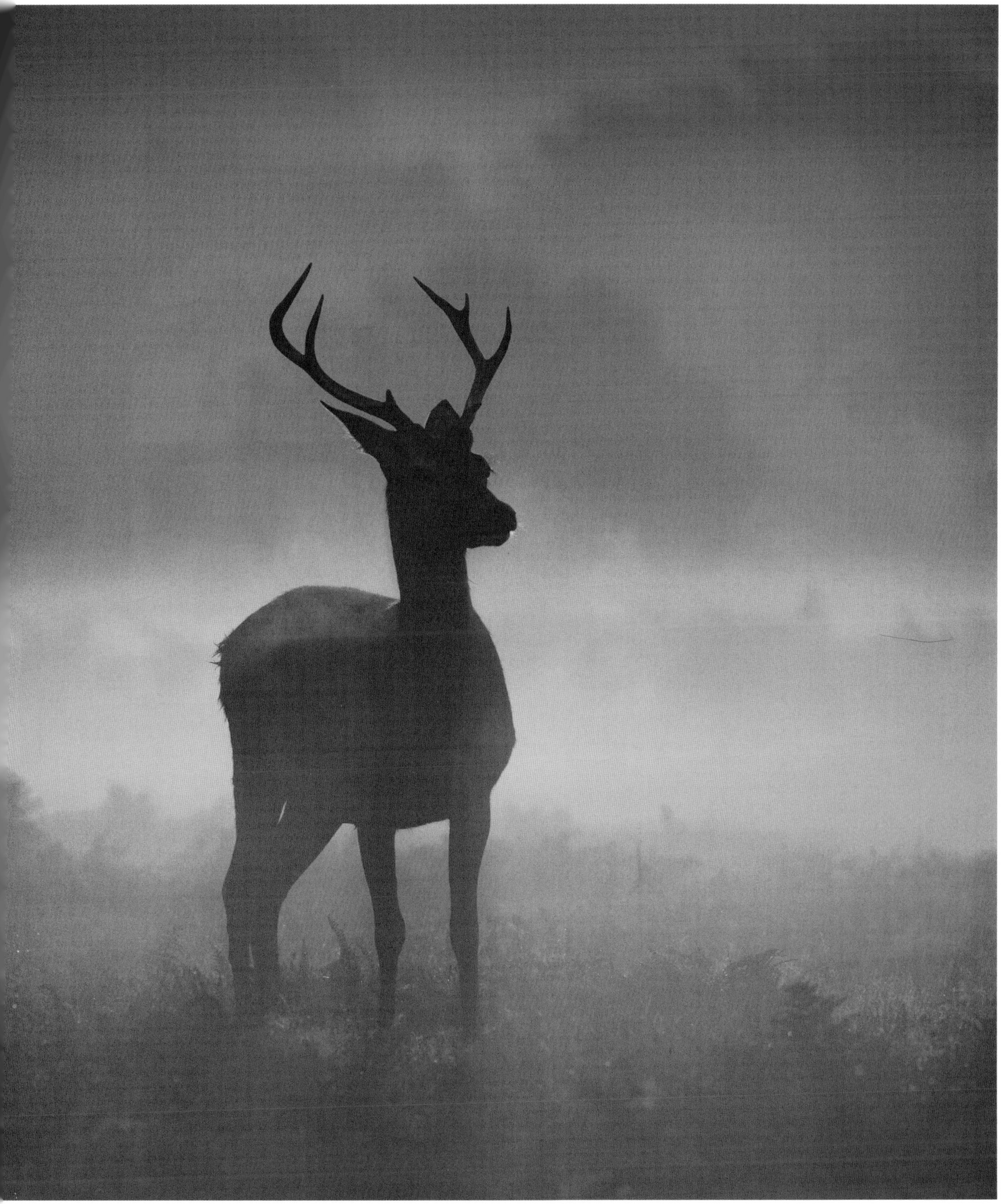

MAIN IMAGE: ISTOCK PHOTO

Get the gear and go wild!

Wildlife photography requires specialist equipment so be sure to spend wisely on the best kit for the job

THIS IS A GREAT TIME to be a wildlife photographer. The speed, reliability, focusing and high ISO performance of digital SLRs today make it possible to capture images that were simply not possible before. Despite what we're often led to believe, you don't have to have huge telephotos to capture great wildlife shots. Smaller subjects, like butterflies, frogs and lizards, can be photographed using a standard lens coupled with a close-up attachment, while the long end of a 70-300mm telezoom should prove sufficient for capturing garden birds and park wildlife. The key is to always work within the limitations of your equipment. Our gear overview will help you select the right kit for the job, from shooting close-ups of small animals and insects to larger wildlife at a distance.

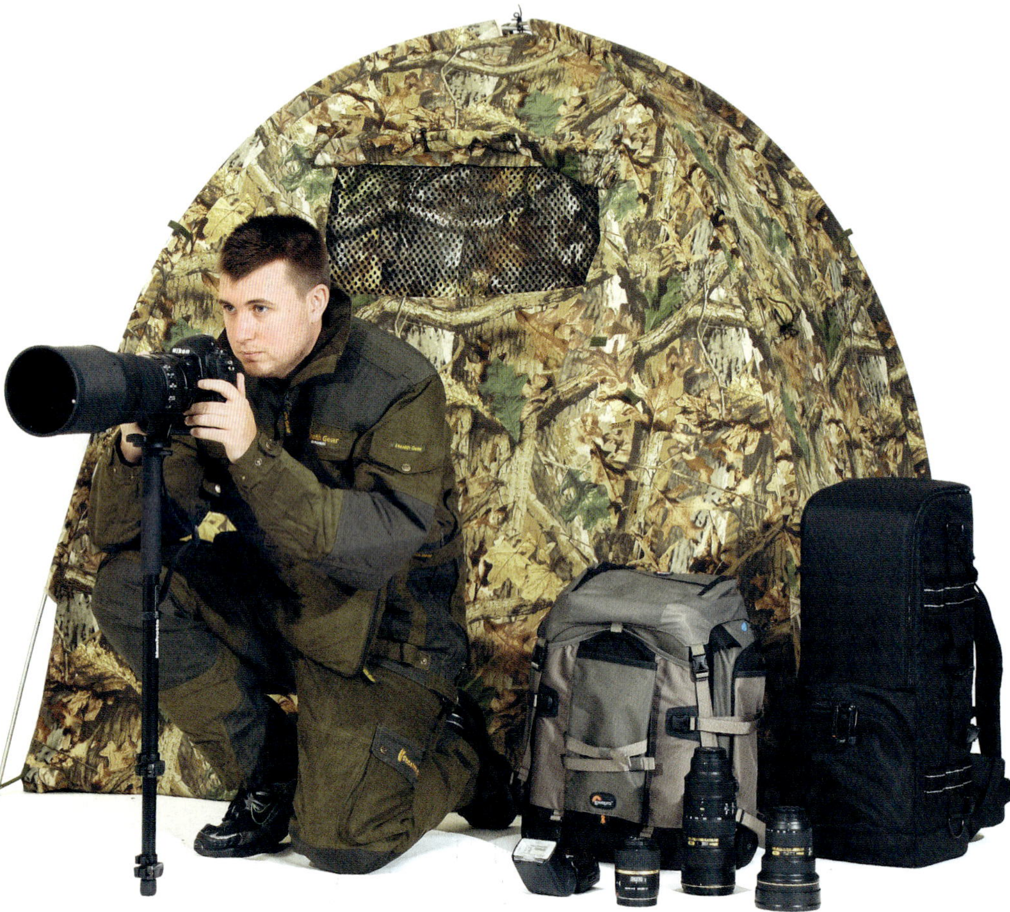

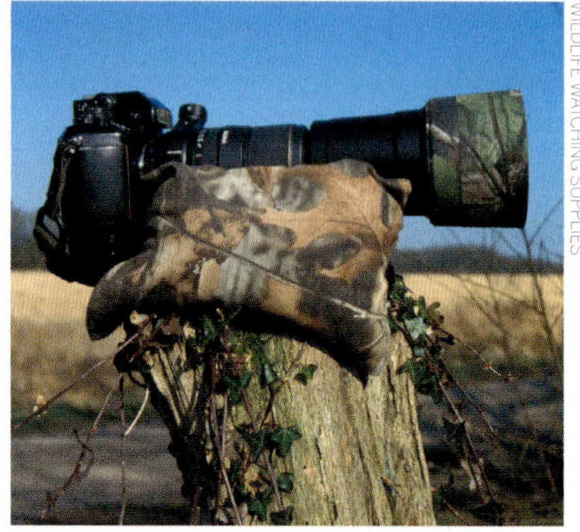

WILDLIFE WATCHING SUPPLIES

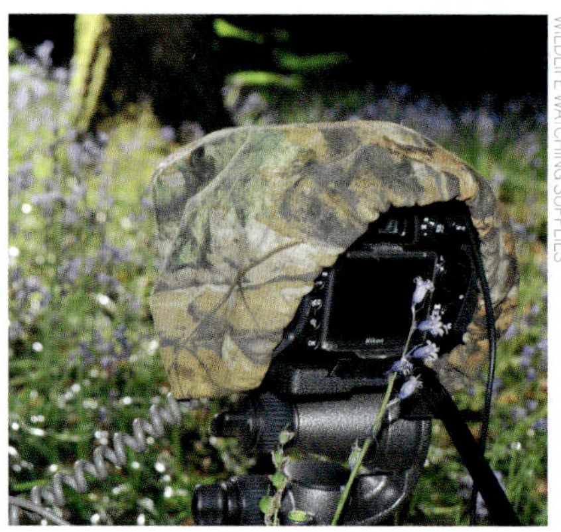

WILDLIFE WATCHING SUPPLIES

Get geared up for wildlife
As it's a specialist area of photography, it's important to choose the best kit for your needs to give you the best chance of success.

Suggested lenses for wildlife photography

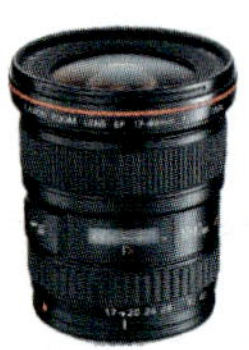

Wide-angle

Wide-angle lenses with a focal length shorter than 35mm can capture great wildlife images. Their field-of-view is suited to environmental portraits, and showing the subject in context with its habitat can convey more about the subject and its environment than a frame-filling shot might.

A key characteristic is how they seem to stretch the relationship between near and far. Also, they have an extensive depth-of-field and a fast maximum aperture, so suit low-light situations. They also have a useful short minimum focus. A wide-angle zoom, in the region of 17-35mm, will offer the most versatility, and will therefore prove a good choice.

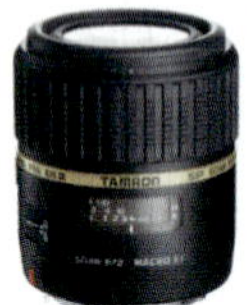

Macro lens

A dedicated macro lens is optimised for close focusing, making them the best choice for photographing smaller wildlife, like spiders and insects. You'd find a multitude of uses for it if you added one to your kit.

A true macro will offer a reproduction ratio of 1:1 life-size or larger. They are typically produced in prime lengths, ranging from 40mm up to 200mm. Shorter focal lengths – 40-90mm – tend to be compact and lightweight, making them suited to handheld work. Telephoto lengths – 100-200mm – provide a larger, more practical working distance, which makes them ideal for photographing timid subjects from a distance.

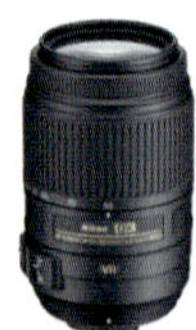

Telephoto/ telezoom

To photograph birds and mammals, a telephoto is essential. They are available in a wide range of strengths. 'Long' telephotos, with a focal length upwards of 300mm – prime or zoom – allow photographers to work further away from the subject, minimising the risk of them running or flying away. They foreshorten perspective and have a shallow depth-of-field – useful for isolating subjects from their surroundings.

Opt for one with image-stabilising technology designed to minimise 'camera shake'. OIS technology is ideal for nature photographers who often use cameras handheld.

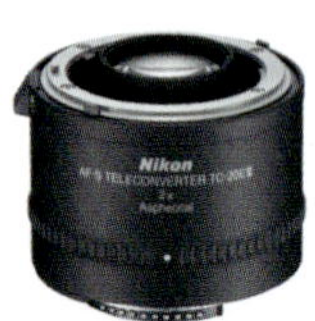

Teleconverter

Teleconverters are optical components that are placed between camera and lens. They magnify the focal length by either 1.4x or 2x. Although converters do degrade image quality to a small degree and absorb light – 1.4x extenders incur a one-stop loss, while using a 2x converter results in a two-stop light loss – they are a genuinely useful addition to a wildlife photographer's kit bag, increasing the versatility and range of their lens system.

If you can't afford to buy a decent telezoom, then this is the best budget option. Avoid three-element models and opt for those with at least seven elements for improved quality.

Tripods & tripod heads

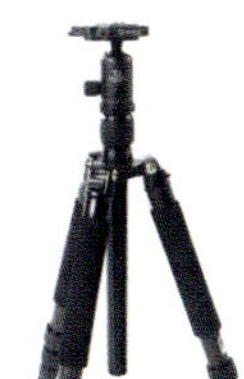

Tripods Wildlife photographers regularly find themselves using long, weighty telephotos, so a tripod is essential – particularly when working from a hide. There are a wide range of models and designs on the market, from leading brands like Benbo, Giottos, Gitzo, Vanguard and Manfrotto. Opt for solid, well-constructed legs, boasting a good maximum load capacity, capable of adequately supporting a heavy camera and lens set-up.

Look for a design that lets you work from a low shooting angle, with legs that can be splayed wide – almost to ground level – and with a centre column that can be removed or positioned horizontally. If your budget allows, carbon-fibre legs are a good option being lighter in construction, but still offering excellent stability.

Due to the wide choice of designs, weights, heights and materials, always try before you buy. We'd recommend that you look to spend at least £100 to buy a lightweight but sturdy set of tripod legs.

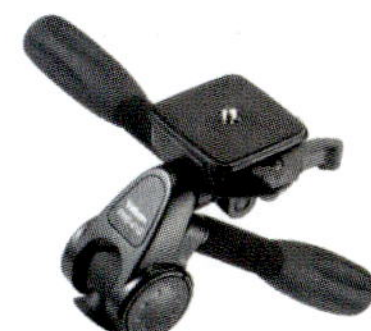

Tripod heads Although there is a wide choice of tripod heads, most are a variation on either a traditional pan-and-tilt head or a ball-and-socket design. Ball-and-socket heads allow photographers to smoothly rotate the camera around a sphere and then be locked into position.

They are rapid to adjust and position, making them popular for nature photography. A pan-and-tilt design offers three separate axes of movement – left-right tilt, forward-back tilt and horizontal panning. For long-lens work, a bracket design is a popular choice, providing better balance for panning and tilting. Gimbal heads are particularly popular for nature work.

The camera and lens is balanced at their natural centre of gravity, so they are easier to manoeuvre – perfect for tracking movement. The likes of Benro, Custom Brackets, Jobu and Really Right Stuff make gimbal heads. Again, test a variety of different designs before deciding which to go for and look to spend at least £40 for a solid choice.

Alternative supports

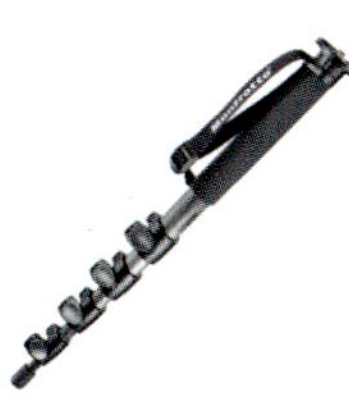

Monopod A monopod is a simple camera support with a single leg. They normally have two or three sections and, once it is adjusted to the height you require, you are ready to begin shooting. While they're unable to offer the same level of stability as a tripod, their design, simplicity and great manoeuvrability make them well suited to stalking wildlife, or when using non-image stabilised optics. It's worth noting that most monopods are supplied without a head, so to add to its versatility, either use the head from your tripod or ideally buy a compact ball-and-socket head (check out those by Giottos, Cullman, Manfrotto and Vanguard).

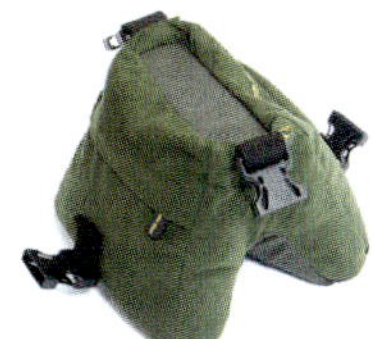

Beanbag Beanbags offer surprisingly good support for your set-up when rested on a stable surface like a car roof or placed on the ground. The bag's filling moulds around the camera and lens, absorbing the majority of movement. They are cheap, easy to use and, in the right situation, a very practical and useful support, so will be a valuable addition to your kit. There are various designs available, including the excellent £14 'Grippa Bag' (www.nature-photography.co.uk). The 'H' shape of its design allows it to grip a car door with the window wound down – perfect for photographers who use their car as a hide to shoot wildlife.

Camouflaged accessories

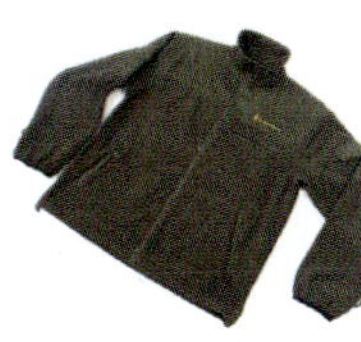

Clothing What you wear is an important consideration when photographing wildlife, particularly if you are stalking. It is important you stay warm, dry and comfortable when waiting patiently for subjects to appear, so it is hugely worthwhile investing in high-performance, tough outdoor clothing.

Stealth Gear is among the brands that produce a range of specialist clothing boasting reinforced panels, padding and extra durability. Although you don't necessarily need to be dressed head to foot in camouflage clothing, always wear dark, drab colours – like dark green and brown – and go for garments that don't rustle or make too much noise when you move to avoid disturbance of your subject.

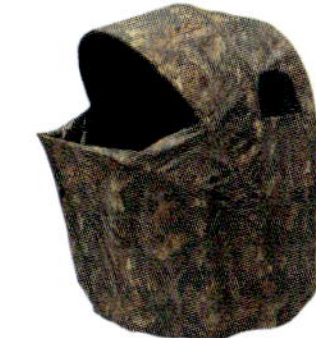

Hides Bird and mammal photographers rely on hides to disguise their whereabouts. While it is possible to construct your own hide or build one using natural materials, most photographers favour a portable, ready-made version that they can use wherever and whenever they need it.

Wildlife Watching Supplies is among the leading producers of collapsible hides and camouflaged accessories – for example, lens sleeves, clothing and scrim netting. Its popular Dome Hide is constructed from proofed and breathable material and is lightweight, compact, freestanding and quick to erect and pack away again. While hides aren't essential for casual nature photographers, they're a great choice if you regularly shoot wildlife.

Q&A Wildlife kit

I can't afford a macro lens. Are there any good budget alternatives?
Yes, there are a couple of good, inexpensive close-up attachments available. The cheapest option is a close-up filter, which screws onto the front of the lens and acts like a magnifier. They are available in a range of strengths and filter diameters and will adapt a standard or zoom into a makeshift macro lens. Filters can cost as little as £10, but they will degrade image quality to some degree. Auto extension tubes are a better option, but more costly. They are hollow tubes that fit between camera and lens in order to reduce its minimum focusing distance. They work best in combination with shortish focal lengths, like a 50mm prime.

What is the highest ISO you suggest I use when photographing wildlife?
Only a few years ago we would recommend you kept ISO below 800, but certain models today are capable of producing usable results at values up to a staggeringly high 25600, due to advancements in sensor technology. For example, Nikon's FX-series of digital SLRs – particularly the Nikon D4 – performs brilliantly at extreme ISOs. Good high ISO performance is hugely beneficial to wildlife photographers, helping them generate a fast enough shutter speed to freeze rapid subject motion, or work in low light. Therefore, if you own a relatively new camera, don't be afraid to shoot at ISOs of 3200, 6400 or above should the subject or situation require. After all, it's better to capture a slightly noisy sharp image than a noise-free image that is blurred.

Photographing wildlife can be quite memory intensive. How do I ensure I don't run out of card space?
When photographing wildlife action, you will often shoot large continuous bursts of images and can quickly fill memory cards. Therefore, have multiple high-capacity cards to hand – ideally in the region of six 8GB cards. If you are very trigger happy, carry a portable storage device, too. For example, the LaCie Rugged Mini is compact but has a large 500GB capacity and will ensure you can keep valuable images backed up at all times.

When shooting close-ups of insects, what is the best lighting accessory - a reflector or flash?
It depends on the subject and situation. Small, collapsible reflectors are handy for bouncing light onto small subjects, with the advantage that you can see and alter its effects instantly. They produce the most natural-looking results and often prove the best choice for static subjects, but they can prove fiddly without an extra hand. Flash is more reliable and instant; better suited to when you need to generate a fast shutter speed, to suspend subject movement or use a smaller aperture to capture a larger depth-of-field. Ring or twin flash units are designed specifically for close-up work. Heavily diffuse flash bursts with a softbox or handheld diffuser to soften the light.

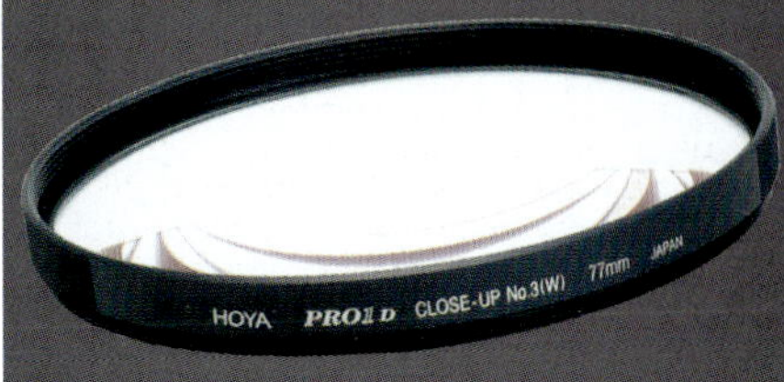

Discover life in your garden

Your back garden is teeming with interesting wildlife, so take time to explore the potential close to home

YOU DON'T HAVE TO TRAVEL to far-flung places to capture great wildlife images. The average garden, or allotment, is home to a wealth of wildlife – you might be surprised at just how many animals reside or regularly visit your backyard. For example, squirrels, hedgehogs and mice all enjoy garden environments, while blackbirds, blue tits and robins are among the most common garden birds. Look closely among your flower beds and underneath plant pots and you will probably find spiders, beetles, ladybirds and snails lurking. If you are really lucky, you might even find a slow worm or frog. Although they might all be quite widespread animals, don't let that deter you. After all, it is far better to photograph a common, everyday animal well and imaginatively than capture an average shot of a more unusual creature.

Quite simply, the garden is a great place to take wildlife images and also to hone your skills as a natural history photographer. Other than flexibility, there are many advantages to taking photos so close to home. For example, you can easily monitor subjects, their comings and goings, and behaviour from your house. Birds and mammals will already be accustomed to your activity, making them more approachable. You can also react to changing light or conditions quickly – for example, if there is snowfall, you can begin taking photos before it thaws or gets disturbed. You can create artificial backgrounds or set-ups and leave them in place without risk of theft or damage. Also, as there is no travel involved, photographers are able to maximise the amount of time that they can spend behind the camera.

IMAGES: ROSS HODDINOTT

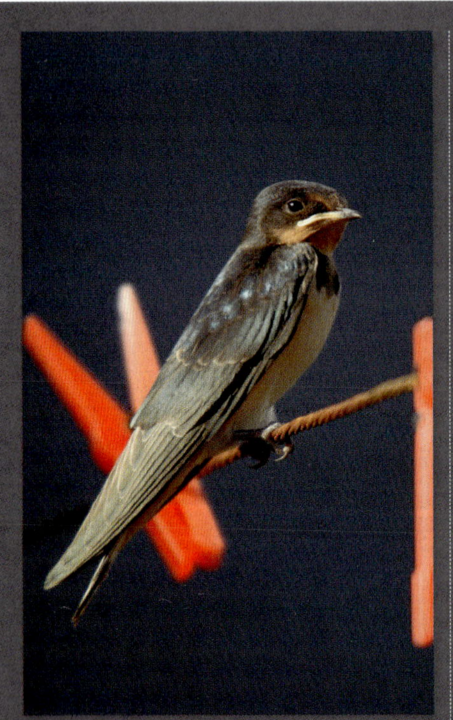

Songbirds: Gardens are great places to photograph small birds. Try enticing photogenic songbirds by 'baiting' – placing out food, like nuts, seed or mealworms. If you have a bird feeder, move it to a spot that's suited to photography. Select a position that will be well lit at the time of day you intend taking photos – mornings and evenings provide the most attractive light. Also, make sure your feeder is situated where you'll be able to place plenty of distance between the subject and an uncluttered background to ensure a clean diffused backdrop. Next, set up a hide within three metres of your feeder or place your feeder within range of a window so that you can take photos from inside your house – disguise yourself by pulling a curtain partly across the window or hang scrim netting over it. A focal length of around 300mm should allow you to fill the frame with the subject, particularly if you use a digital SLR with an APS-C sensor. Consider introducing a few props to make your shots more interesting, which the birds can rest on between feeding. You could use a blossom-covered branch, or place a spade handle nearby. Pre-focus on the prop and wait patiently until a bird perches before taking photos.

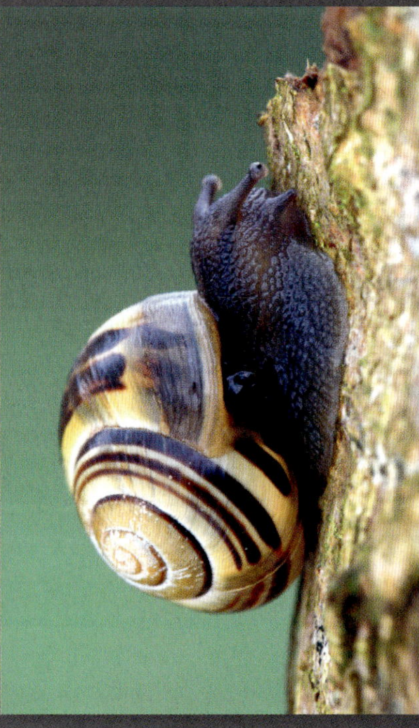

Snails: They might not be the most glamorous of animals, but snails can be highly photogenic. They are often found sheltering in shady spots in the garden, underneath rocks, pots and loose paving slabs. Try carefully moving them to a more photogenic spot; a position where there is a more interesting or colourful background maybe, or something interesting for it to climb – like a flower stem or a plant pot. At first, the snail will stay safely in its shell, but if you wait patiently for a few minutes, it will soon emerge. As snails are slow moving, photographers have longer to get the composition, lighting and exposure just right, so they're ideal subjects for wildlife photography newcomers to practise on. But that's not to say it is easy to achieve good shots of snails – it will involve shooting at a high level of magnification, using either a macro lens or close-up attachment. Depth-of-field will be shallow, so place your point of focus carefully and supplement the light if required using a reflector or flash. Be as imaginative as possible. Try shooting from a low angle or employ a wide f/stop, like f/2.8 or f/4, to create a wafer-thin depth-of-field and throw everything but your focal point intentionally out of focus.

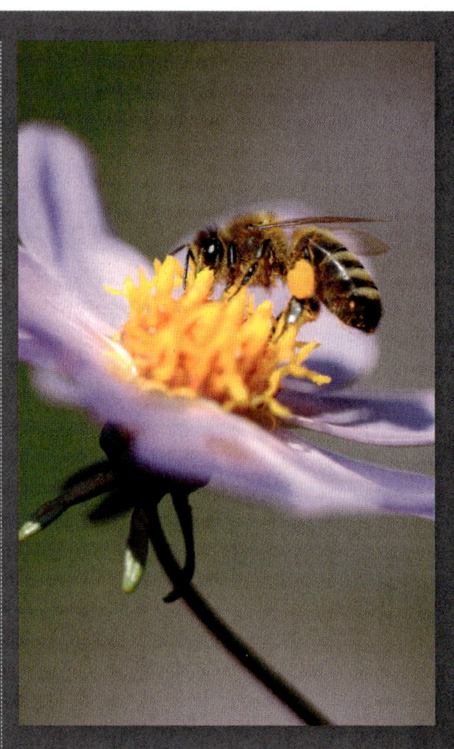

Insects: If you have nectar-rich flowers growing in your garden, you are guaranteed to attract bees, hoverflies, ladybirds and butterflies all summer long. In the mornings and evenings, insects are less active, so this is a good time to take photos. When shooting close-ups, the zone of sharpness is shallow, but by keeping the camera's sensor plane parallel to the subject, you'll ensure you don't waste any of the depth-of-field available to you. Select a position close to flowers that is regularly visited by insects, being careful not to cast your shadow over the subject or disturb other flowers nearby as this will probably scare your subject away. Waiting patiently in one position is more effective than chasing them around your garden. Insects, like bees, normally only visit flowers very briefly to feed, so you'll need to work quickly. Autofocus systems can struggle when shooting at high magnifications, searching back and forth in order to locate the subject. Therefore, we highly recommend manually focusing. It can even be worthwhile prefocusing your lens on the plant, so that you only have to move the camera slightly forward towards the subject, until it appears in focus through the viewfinder or on the LCD monitor, if working in LiveView.

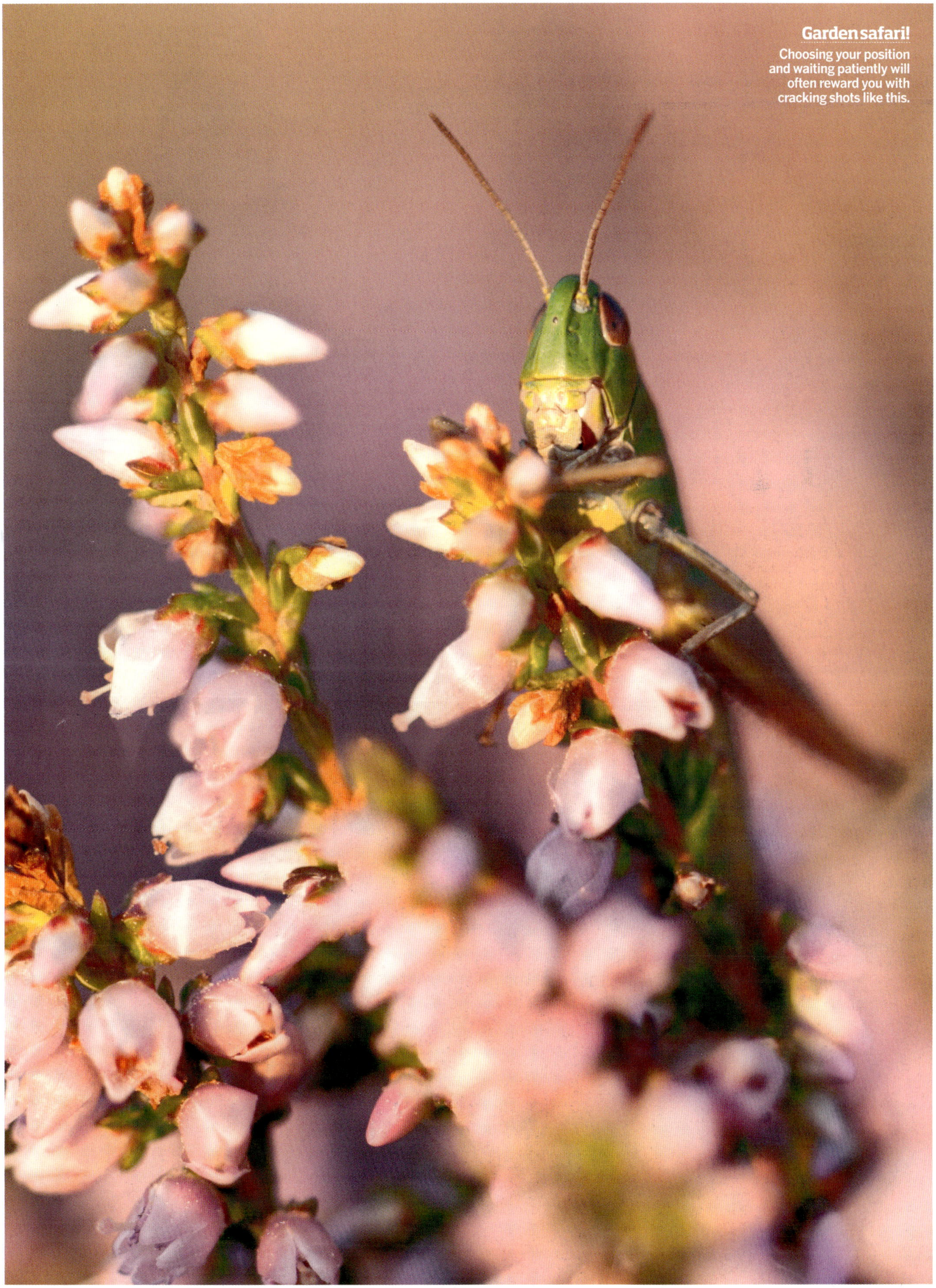

ROSS HODDINOTT

Garden safari!

Choosing your position and waiting patiently will often reward you with cracking shots like this.

Head to your local wetland

Wildlife abounds at a reserve near you. Here's what to look out for and how to photograph it…

WETLAND HABITATS support an abundance of wildlife. Lakes, rivers, estuaries, canals, ponds and marshes are home to otters, water voles, a wide variety of waders and water birds, frogs, toads, dragonflies, mayflies and a whole host of other creatures. Few habitats offer wildlife photographers such a wide variety of subjects, so hunt out suitable wetlands near you and visit regularly with your camera.

The UK is home to some excellent wetland reserves and many already have hides to aid photography of ducks, geese and waders. Discover what is in your area by joining your local Wildlife Trust or the RSPB. Winter is a particularly good time of year for photographing water birds, as large flocks of winter migrants invade these shores.

A long focal length is often required – ideally a telephoto of 400mm; or a shorter telephoto coupled with an extender is a good alternative. Flight photography isn't easy – it'll be trial and error – but with practice you can capture some great pictures.

It's a good idea to attempt flight shots of larger birds at first – like geese and swans – as they are slower and easier to track with your camera. Use your DSLR's predictive autofocus mode to help achieve pin-sharp action shots. Employ a fast shutter, upwards of 1/500sec, to suspend the subject's movement. Alternatively, opt for a slow shutter speed, in the region of 1/30sec, if you wish to creatively blur the subject movement to give your images added energy and visual interest.

Along thriving rivers, you may find kingfishers, wagtails and dippers. Kingfishers tend to be quite secretive birds, but dippers and wagtails are more approachable. They will often rest on boulders jutting out of the water and can be photographed with a long telephoto. Rivers and streams often flow through woodland, so light can be in short supply. If necessary, select a higher ISO to generate a fast enough shutter speed.

As well as birds, wetland habitats are great to capture close-up shots of frogs and toads in springtime, and exotically coloured dragonflies and damselflies, mayflies, pond skaters and other aquatic insects all through summer. A high level of magnification is required to capture frame-filling shots of small animals – if you don't own a macro lens, use a close-up filter or extension tubes.

Depth-of-field will be shallow, so focus carefully, ensuring the insect's eyes are sharp. This type of photography often requires kneeling among damp vegetation, so wear waterproof trousers to stay dry.

Top UK wetland spots

Slimbridge, Gloucestershire
Hundreds of thousands of birds visit the reserve throughout the year. With 13 hides looking out onto the reserve, this is a great place to see and photograph the wildlife of the Severn Estuary.
www.wwt.org.uk/visit-us/slimbridge

Rutland Water, Rutland
Rutland Water is one of the most important wildfowl sanctuaries within the UK. Covering a total area of 1,000 acres, it's home to upwards of 20,000 water birds and is an excellent spot to photograph dragonflies in the summer.
www.rutlandwater.org.uk

Martin Mere, Lancashire
Thousands of migrant wild ducks, geese, waders and swans overwinter at this internationally important wetland. There is a also a beaver lodge, otter enclosure, bird hides and, most importantly, potential for fantastic photography throughout the year.
www.wwt.org.uk/visit-us/martin-mere

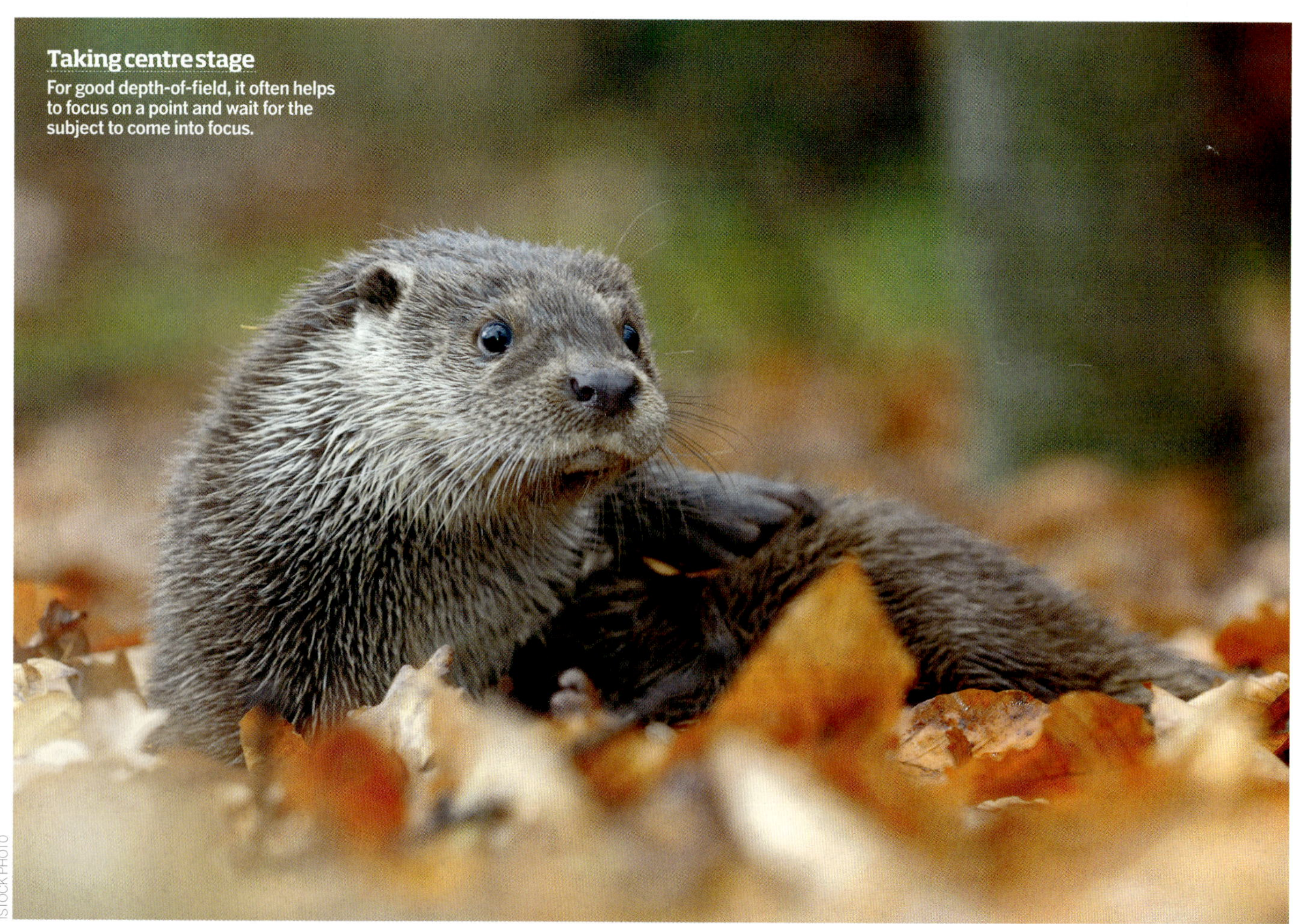

Taking centre stage
For good depth-of-field, it often helps to focus on a point and wait for the subject to come into focus.

ROSS HODDINOTT

Ready for your close-up?
Capturing great shots of insects will require a macro lens or close-up attachment for best results.

IMAGES: ROSS HODDINOTT

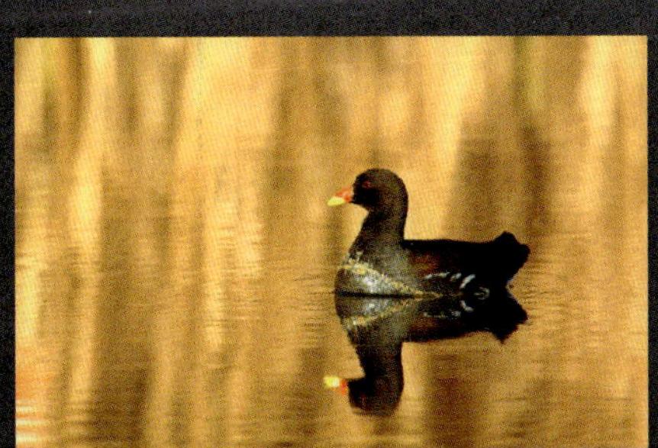

Waterfowl: To shoot captivating waterfowl photos, timing and technique are crucial. Autumn and winter are ideal times of year when wetlands support large populations of birds and plumage is immaculate. Waterfowl are most active shortly before sunrise until mid-morning and again from mid-afternoon until just after sunset. Arrive an hour before these prime times to get in position and allow wildlife to get accustomed to your presence. Pay close attention to the birds' movements to help you anticipate and capture photogenic behaviour – ie when birds are about to take off, dive, squabble or flap their wings. When possible, expose creatively. At sunrise and sunset, try silhouetting waterfowl against the warm colours reflected in the water. Try panning when shooting birds in flight, too. Select a slow shutter speed of around 1/15sec and follow the bird's movement during exposure to render it sharply against an attractively blurred background. It takes practice, but the results can look stunning.

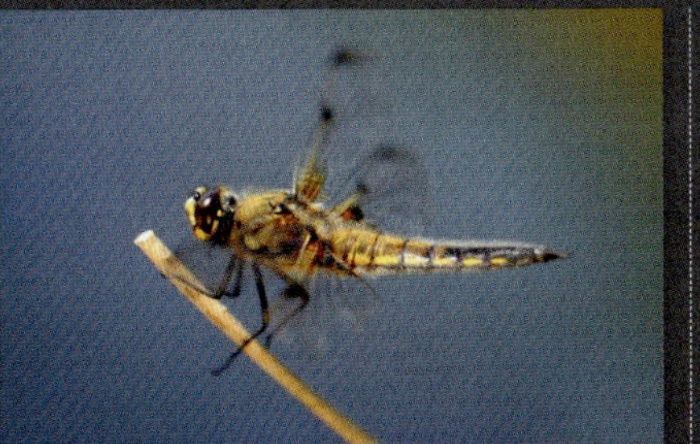

Dragonflies: In spring and summer, wetland habitats are home to a colourful variety of photogenic dragonflies. They can prove challenging subjects, resting infrequently and being prone to flying away as soon as you get near them, but you'll have more success in the morning or evening when they're less active. Use a macro lens with a focal length of at least 100mm and look for resting insects close to the water's edge where you can shoot them against an uncluttered background: their wings will get lost against a messy backdrop. Dragonflies are highly territorial, often patrolling the same stretch of water and returning again and again to the same place of rest. So spend time observing and identify a regular resting spot where you can await their return. Don't be afraid to experiment with viewpoints – dragonflies suit being shot from a number of angles: overhead highlights their wings; a side angle shows off their body shape; while a head-on view emphasises their large eyes.

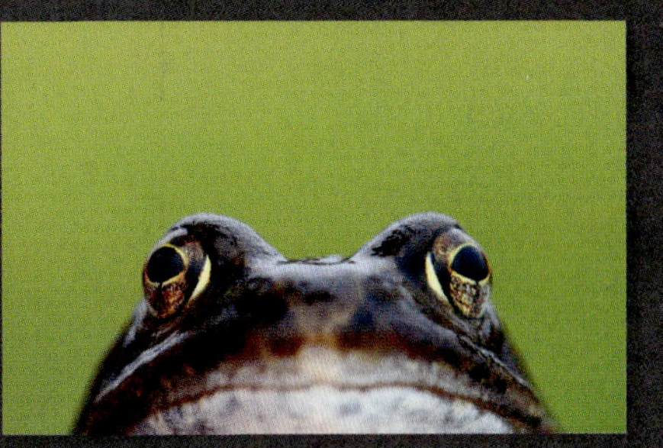

Amphibians: When shooting frogs and toads, the initial challenge is locating them; they're often well camouflaged and hide among thick foliage. They are easiest to find in spring when they are breeding: pools and ponds will be a hive of activity. Kneel by the water's edge and wait for them to poke their heads above the water to breathe. Including their reflection will add an extra dimension. Frogs and toads look equally photogenic out of the water. Having found one to photograph, ask a friend to assist you – they can carefully reposition the frog or toad, placing it just where you want while you wait, with your lens already focused on that point. Uncluttered compositions work best, so remove any distracting grasses and vegetation. If the light is dim, flash can create vivid, well-lit results or help you generate a larger depth-of-field. Flash will also add a catchlight to the subject's eye. Heavily diffuse flash bursts, though, to avoid distracting hotspots forming on the amphibian's reflective skin.

Make the most of your local park

There's more to the average park than you might think – so get out there with your camera…

PHOTOGRAPHING TRULY WILD ANIMALS can involve weeks of planning and, potentially, hundreds of hours stuck inside a hide. Unsurprisingly, the majority of photographers simply can't commit to such lengthy, time-consuming projects. If you are among those who only have limited free time due to the commitments of work and family life, then regular visits to your local park should be high on your list of priorities.

Parks, large or small, are great places for wildlife photography. Most are home to a wealth of animals, including deer, playful grey squirrels, rabbits, swans, herons, geese and ducks. Animals residing in parks quickly get accustomed to walkers, joggers and human activity, making them far easier to get closer to and photograph.

For example, squirrels will often venture within just a metre or two of your lens if you entice them with a few nuts. Parks, like Richmond Park in London and Bradgate Park in Leicestershire, are well known for their deer, being home to healthy populations of majestic fallow and red herds. Arguably, autumn is the best time of year to visit parks, when stags are rutting and the surrounding trees are ablaze with reds and golds.

Most parks are home to large ponds or lakes where swans, geese, herons, coots and moorhens often reside. They are normally very approachable and great subjects to hone your photography skills on. On still days, you can usually capture eye-catching images of birds swimming on the water and their reflections for strong symmetrical results.

In spring, birds will have young in tow, too, and these bundles of fluff are particularly photogenic, especially if shot close up for a frame-filling portrait or swimming in formation. In the winter months, water will freeze over and you can capture interesting shots of birds standing on the ice. A low shooting angle normally works best, appearing most natural. Therefore, lay flat on the ground if necessary, using either a beanbag or your elbows to support your set-up.

Parks are also home to lots of other creatures, including rabbits, robins, pigeons, starlings and beetles. Again, they tend to be very tolerant of a close approach, so don't overlook them just because they are fairly common, everyday species.

It is normally best to visit parks early in the morning or in the evening. Not only will the light be softer and more dramatic, but there will be fewer people around, minimising the risk of you or your subject being disturbed.

The UK's top parks

Richmond Park, London
Our best-known park is home to a varied landscape of hills, woodland gardens and grasslands, offering plenty of opportunity for photographers. Great shots are guaranteed as wildlife abounds – it's particularly good for deer.
www.royalparks.org.uk

St James's Park, London
The park may only cover 23 hectares and be in the centre of London, but it is home to lots of wildlife, including squirrels, geese and pelicans.
www.royalparks.org.uk

Bradgate Park, Leicestershire
Located within the Charnwood Forest in rural Leicestershire, the park is home to unspoilt countryside, where nature conservation is a priority.
www.bradgatepark.org

British Wildlife Centre, Surrey
If you want wildlife at your fingertips, look around for wildlife centres in your local area. This one in Surrey is one of our favourites and even has photo days and workshops.
www.britishwildlifecentre.co.uk

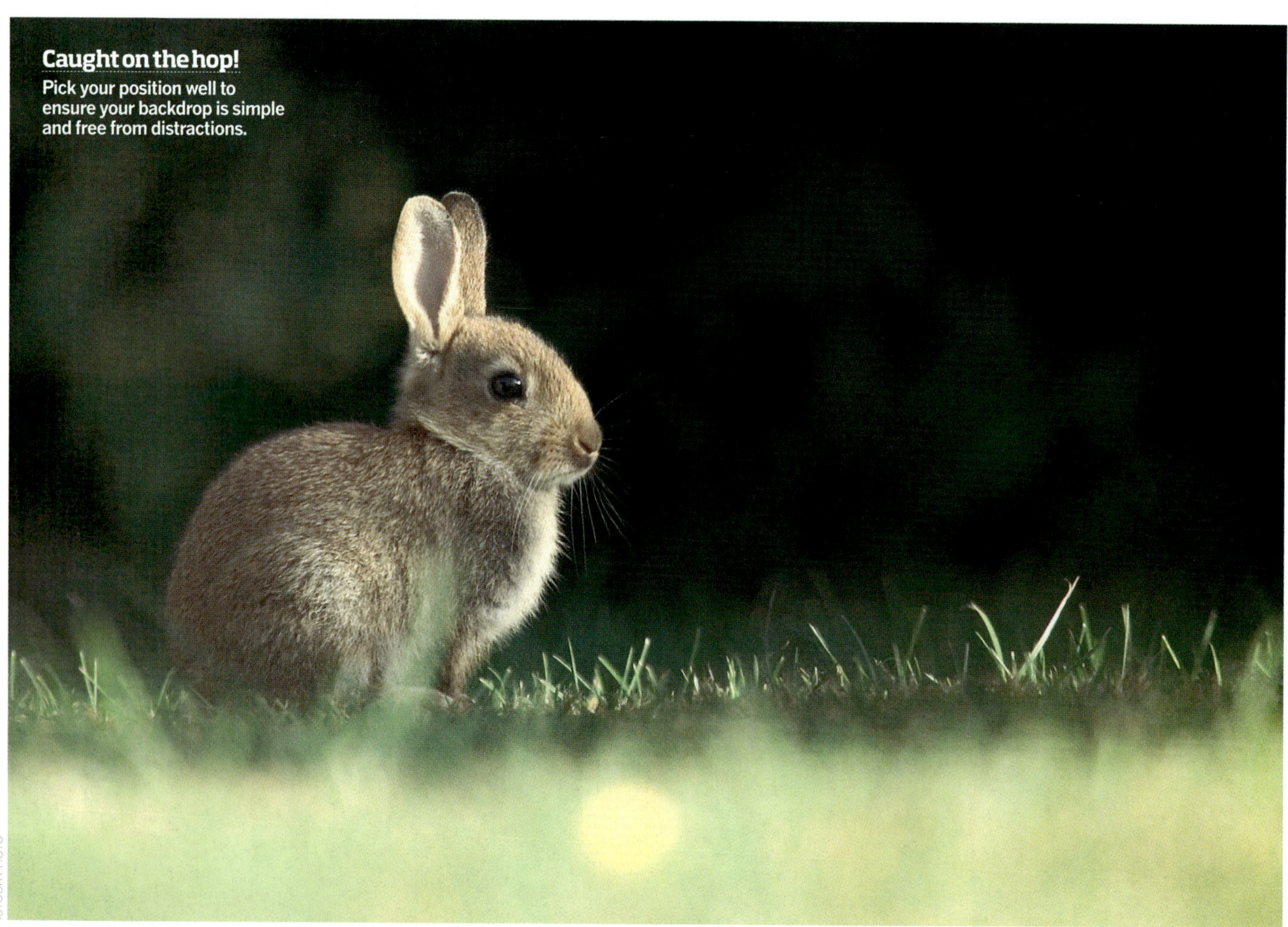

Caught on the hop!
Pick your position well to ensure your backdrop is simple and free from distractions.

ISTOCK PHOTO

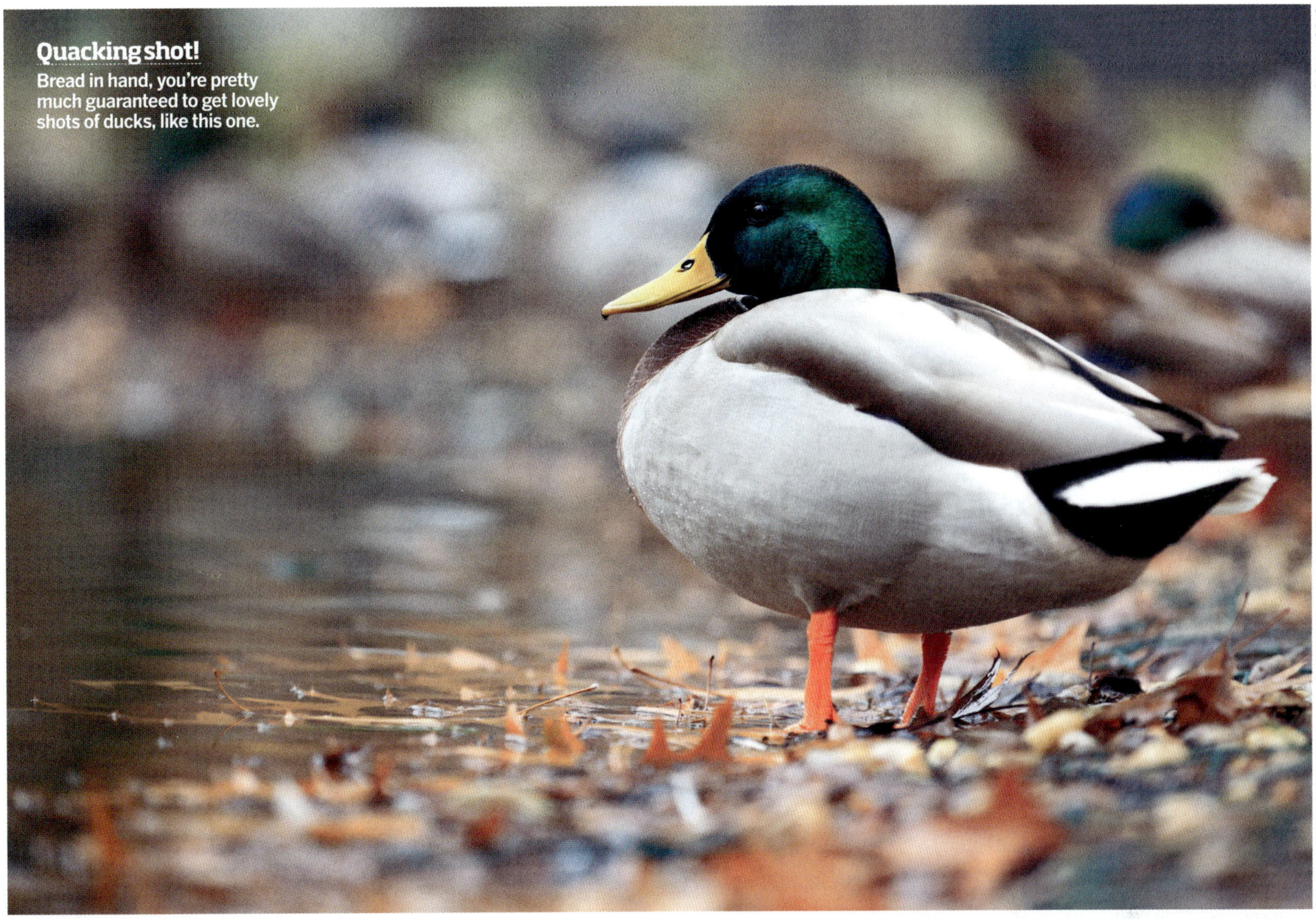

Quacking shot!
Bread in hand, you're pretty much guaranteed to get lovely shots of ducks, like this one.

ISTOCK PHOTO

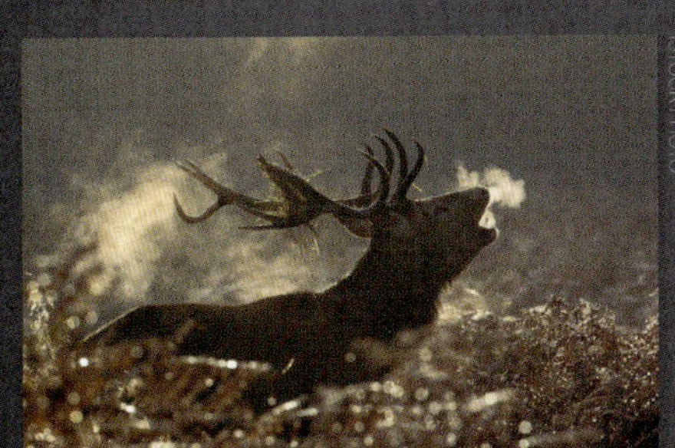

ISTOCK PHOTO

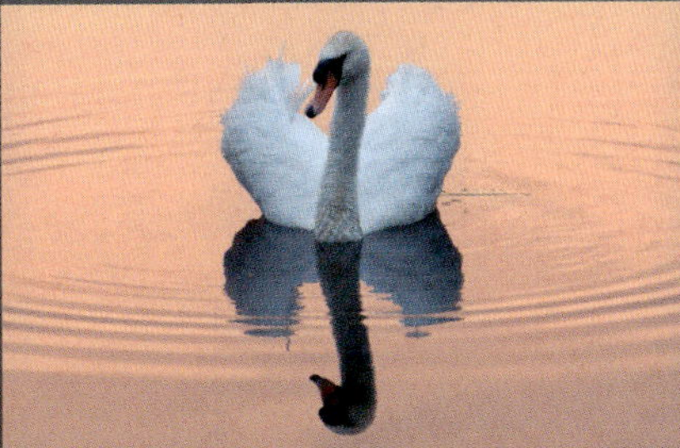

ISTOCK PHOTO

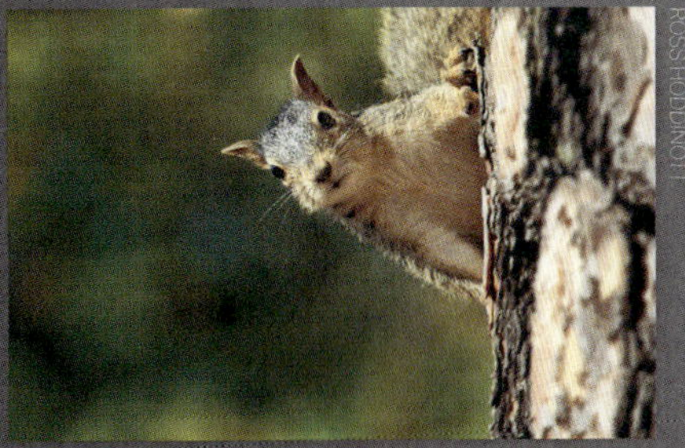

ROSS HODDINOTT

Deer: Many parks are home to large herds of deer. While most like to keep a safe distance from visitors, some are very approachable, making it possible to capture wild-looking images with ease. Visit in advance to discover which areas the animals favour and are most suited to photography, so you'll know where to head with your camera.

A 300mm lens will enable you to capture frame-filling shots. Shorter focal lengths also work, capturing the animal in context with its surroundings. In spring and autumn, low-lying mists often form after clear, cool nights. Shots of stags shrouded in mist are incredibly striking, so go at the crack of dawn when conditions look promising.

During the mating season in late autumn, stags bellow and fight. Great action shots are possible, but keep your distance. Wear neutral-coloured clothes, and approach animals slowly, in a zigzag direction, so you don't startle them. Mammals have an acute sense of smell, so keep downwind of your subject.

Swans: Few creatures are more photogenic than mute swans. They look particularly beautiful when they're reflected in calm water. Their bright white plumage can fool metering systems into thinking the scene is brighter than it is, though, resulting in underexposure, so check images using your camera's histogram. If results are too dark, apply a degree of positive exposure compensation.

Aside from the obvious shots, consider isolating details, like plumage, the 'S' shape of the swan's neck, or its eyes and bill – offering bread to get them closer. The direction and quality of light are key considerations. Avoid shooting in the harsh light of midday, as the white feathers may 'burn out'. Overcast light can be flattering, but results can lack impact. Backlighting is one of the most dramatic sources of light, so consider your position carefully. In spring and summer, swans will have cygnets which can make lovely shots. Adults will rightly be protective of their young, though, so stay well back.

Grey squirrels: They might not be very popular, but there's no denying that grey squirrels are highly photogenic. Squirrels are curious and confident, so the long end of a 70-300mm should be all you need to capture good shots. They are at their most active in autumn, collecting and storing nuts for the winter months. Collect a few handfuls of acorns and hazel nuts and place them where the light is good and the backdrop is flattering to entice squirrels within range of your lens.

Lively animals generally require you to work handheld, preferably using a lens with image stabilisation. Use continuous frame advance and fire in bursts to get the shots you want. Some animals are so tame that they'll come within 30cm of your camera. In this case, switch to a short focal length and capture wide-angle views, creating a distorted but eye-catching perspective. Also try placing your camera on a beanbag and wait nearby for a squirrel to investigate before firing the shutter remotely using a remote device.

Take a trip to the coast

We're spoilt for choice with magnificent coastlines so grab your gear and capture coastal wildlife

WITH OVER 7,000 MILES OF COASTLINE, the UK is a great place for photographing coastal wildlife. It is an exciting and diverse habitat where marine animals and birds – like seals, puffins, gannets, razorbills and terns – can be photographed against a dramatic coastal backdrop.

In the UK, you are never more than a two-hour drive from the sea and many of us are lucky enough to live much closer. In addition to our long, rugged coastline, there are over 1,000 islands offshore, of which around 300 are inhabited. Scotland is home to a large percentage of these little islands, and many are home to a wealth of wildlife, including nesting colonies of seabirds.

Islands like Skomer, the Farnes and the Orkneys are home to large populations of birds that are relatively easy to get near. It is possible to stay on some larger islands, while others can be visited for the day via organised boat trips – a brilliant way to get up close to unusual species. Wildlife photographers will find such places well worth visiting. You can capture stunning frame-filling portraits and close-ups of birds in flight – with beaks loaded with fish – as they return to their nests to feed their young.

A 300mm or 400mm lens is a must for shooting coastal wildlife, together with plenty of memory cards and fully-charged spare batteries. If you are only able to take photos during the day – when light is contrasty and less flattering – consider using fill-flash when shooting. By doing so, you will help relieve dark shadow areas and also ensure that there is a catchlight in the subject's eye. Just remember: the aim is to lighten shadows, not to remove them altogether, so begin by reducing flash output by a stop or two and reduce it further still if you feel it's required.

Seals populate much of the UK coast. They are highly photogenic mammals, but getting near to them is rarely easy as they often frequent remote, rocky beaches. Donna Nook, Blakeney, the Orkney Islands and the Moray Firth are among the best places to see and photograph seals.

Avoid getting too near to animals if they have young and always place the welfare of the subject first. A low angle will yield the best results, but sand and spray can be an issue when taking photos so close to the sea. Therefore, protect the front element of valuable optics by attaching a UV or Skylight filter.

If you fancy trying to photograph dolphins, porpoises and other marine wildlife, it's best to go on an organised wildlife boat trip, which guarantees close encounters with wildlife.

Coastal hot spots

Skomer Island, Pembrokeshire
A wonderful little island where you can get close to nesting puffins, guillemots and razorbills.
www.welshwildlife.org/skomer-skokholm/skomer

The Orkney Islands, Scotland
Home to an abundance of birds and marine wildlife. Orkney is a particularly good place for seals, with an estimated population of 50,000.
www.visitorkney.com/nature/index.asp

The Farne Islands, Northumberland
Arguably the best seabird colony in England. Home to 37,000 pairs of puffin and offering excellent photographic opportunities.
www.nationaltrust.org.uk/farne-islands

Bempton Cliffs, Yorkshire
Home to more than 200,000 seabirds (from April to August), the cliffs are a great place to see photogenic puffins.
www.rspb.org.uk/reserves/guide/b/bemptoncliffs/about.aspx

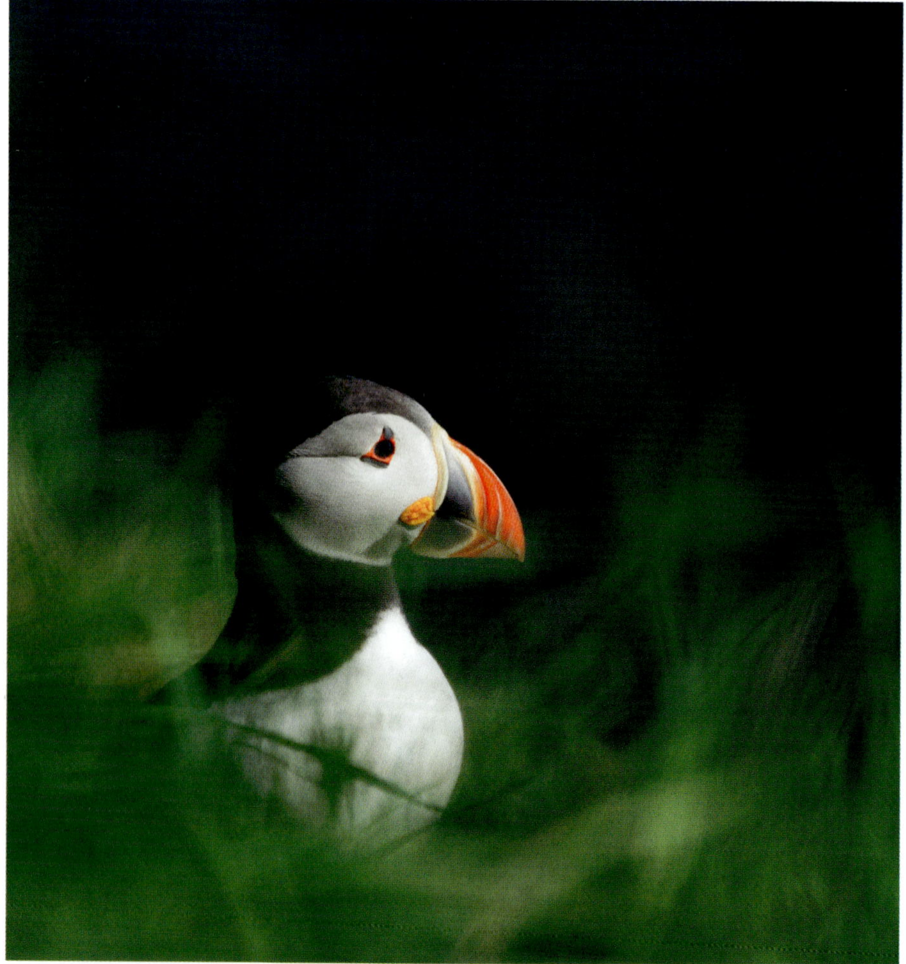
ISTOCK PHOTO

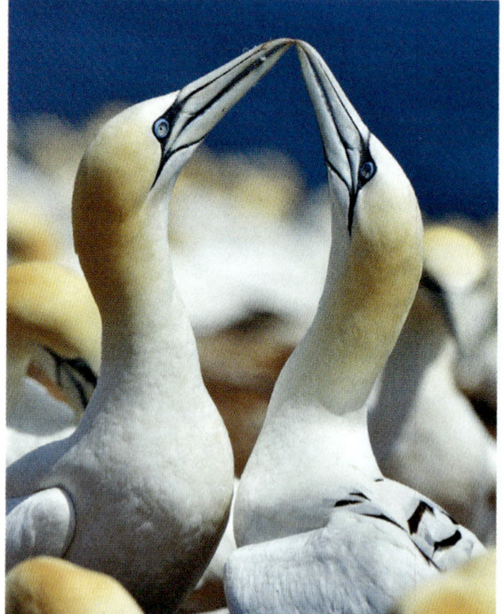
ISTOCK PHOTO

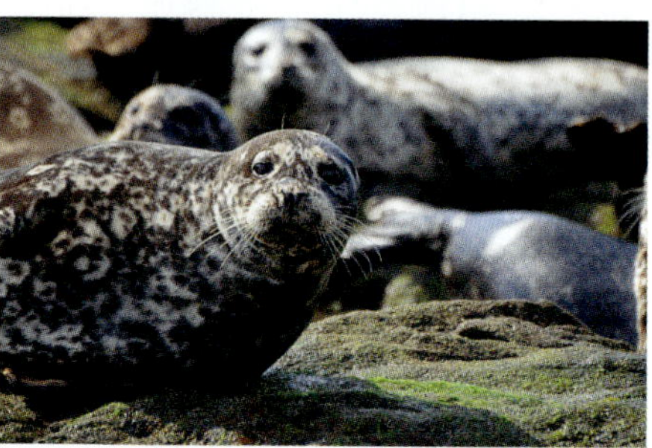
ISTOCK PHOTO

Animal magic You don't have to travel far in the UK for great wildlife shots – we're incredibly lucky to have amazing subjects like puffins, gannets and seals dotted around our coastline.

Meet your urban neighbours

Wildlife is on your doorstep, too – here's how to take great shots of inner-city animals…

YOU DON'T HAVE TO VISIT lush green countryside, woodland or the coast to photograph wildlife. Cities and towns are inhabited by foxes, hedgehogs, pigeons, starlings and peregrines, all of whom can look striking photographed against an urban backdrop. Visit harbours and quaysides, town parks, hotel gardens, train stations and near dumps for potential subjects. Foxes in particular have quickly adapted to city life, living in gardens and landfill sites, and feeding on human rubbish. They are much easier to photograph than their country cousins, being far more tolerant of people.

It can be possible to photograph them during the day, but foxes are mostly nocturnal, so be prepared to stay out late and either use flash or employ a high ISO rating to achieve a workable shutter speed. Often the key to succeeding is research. Ideally, find out where the animals live or the places or streets they regularly visit to feed. Once you have done your groundwork, it is a matter of positioning yourself accordingly and waiting. It may be possible to use a car as a hide, but try to be discreet when taking photos in towns, otherwise you might attract the attention of the police or even thieves.

When photographing urban wildlife, avoid filling the frame with your subject. If you do, you're in danger of only capturing generic-looking results. Instead, shoot with a shorter lens in order to include a sense of the animal's urban environment. As always when photographing wildlife, the background is vitally important – either helping to highlight the subject or place it in context with its environment. Look for evidence of suburbia – trains, cars, houses, shops and signs – and try to incorporate them into your shots.

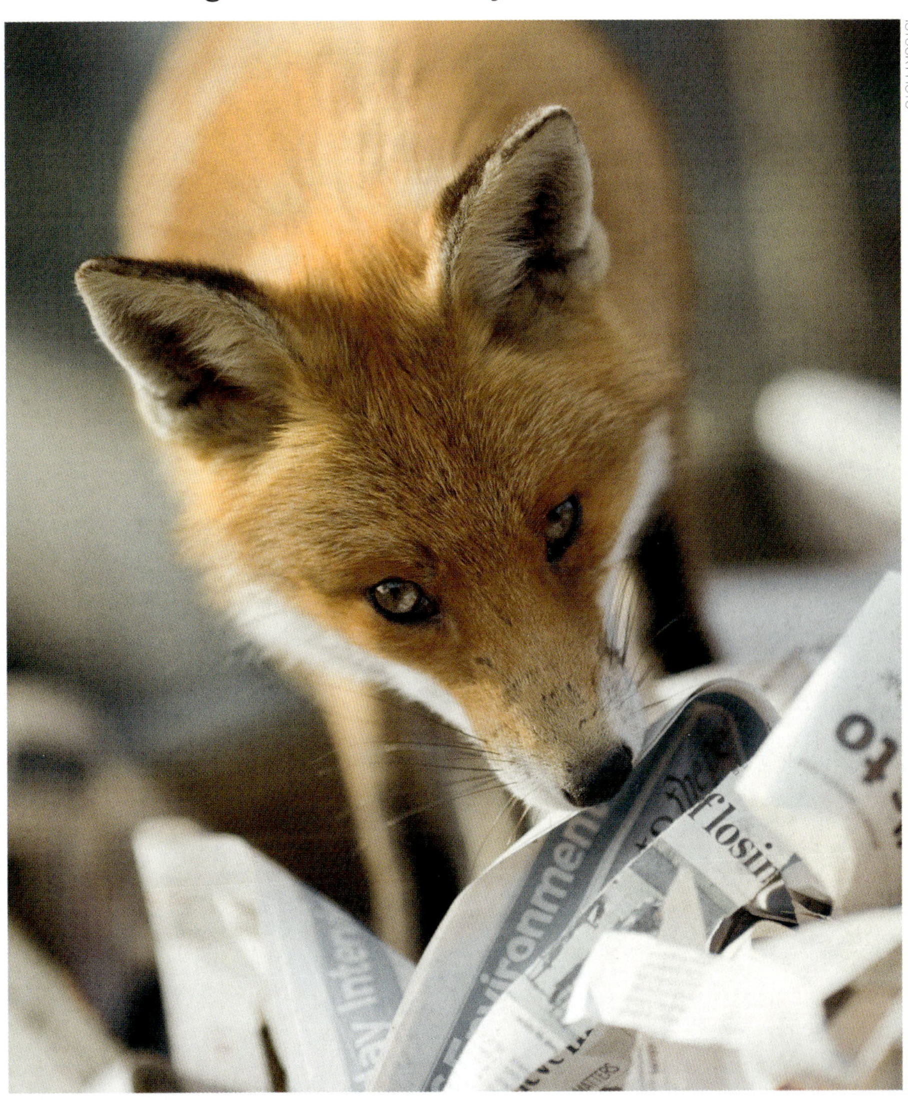

ISTOCKPHOTO

Urban legends **Foxes make really interesting subjects to photograph –the difficult part is finding them as they're nocturnal animals. Be prepared to stay out beyond nightfall!**

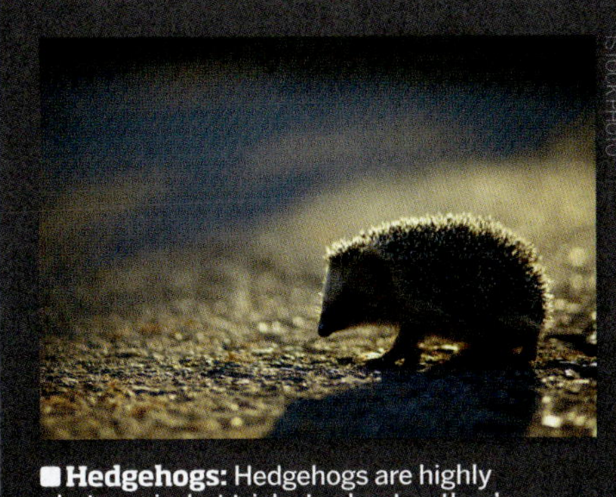

ISTOCKPHOTO

Hedgehogs: Hedgehogs are highly photogenic, but tricky to shoot as they're surprisingly fast and nocturnal. Ask friends and neighbours if they have a family living in their garden, then place out a meal of tinned dog food to entice them within range of your camera – they love it! Using a wide-angle lens will create an unusual perspective and allow you to include its urban or garden environment which will add interest.

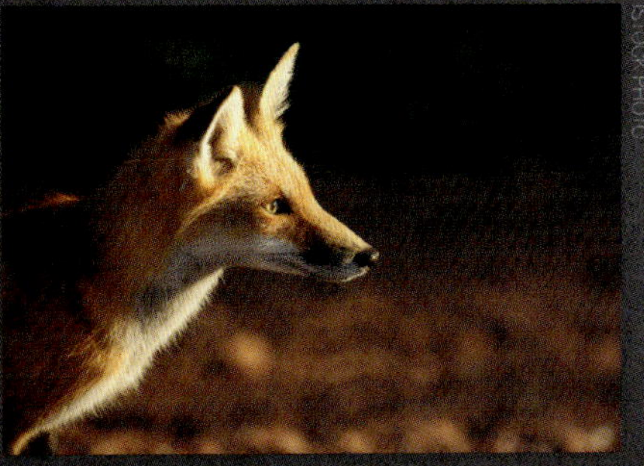

ISTOCKPHOTO

Foxes: Most towns support a large number of urban foxes – you'd be surprised at how many live near you. They can be very tolerant of people, making them easier to photograph. If you know where their earth is located, you may be able to photograph cubs playing in the late-evening or early-morning summer sun. If possible, try to photograph urban behaviour, maybe a fox pushing over a dustbin or peering into a bin .

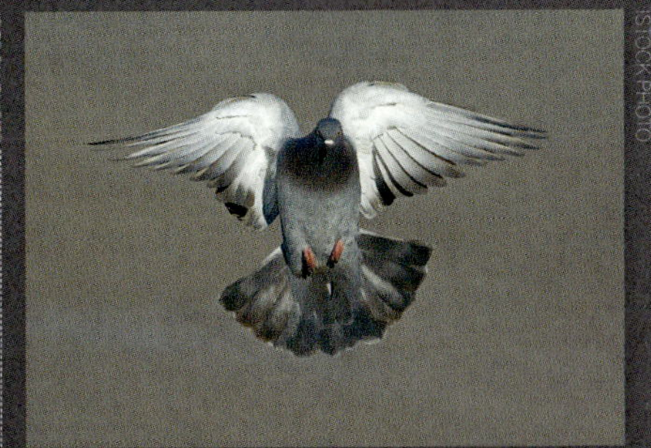

ISTOCKPHOTO

Pigeons: They might be considered pests by some people, but with a little imagination, you can capture great shots of pigeons and doves, especially as they normally allow you to get very close. Attach a wide-angle or fisheye lens to your camera for weird and wacky portraits. Also look for pigeons perched on signs or statues, as it can be possible to capture interesting or even humorous results.

Springtime garden safari

Head out into the garden to capture great macro shots of spring's smallest ambassadors – bees, butterflies and all kinds of bugs

THE WARMTH OF SPRING entices insects, like butterflies and bees, out of hibernation. Other insects – like damselflies and dragonflies – will complete their incredible metamorphosis and emerge as adult insects. There is no better time to capture great pictures of bugs.

Due to the small size of insects, you will need a close focusing lens or close-up filter if you wish to capture frame-filling images. A macro lens is the best option, offering high image quality and a 1:1 (life-size) reproduction, which is ideal for spring insects. They are quite pricey, so unless you plan to use it extensively, you may be better saving your money and buying a set of close-up filters (see panel) or extension tubes. Extension tubes fit between the camera body and lens in order to reduce the lens's minimum focusing distance. Being hollow – without any optical elements – they don't affect image quality. They can be bought in different lengths – the longer the tube, the greater the magnification. Always opt for auto extension tubes as they retain the camera's automatic functions, like metering and focusing. Like close-up filters, they are best combined with a short focal length – for example, a 50mm lens.

Insects are renowned for being challenging subjects to shoot. They can be difficult to locate and will quickly fly or scurry away if disturbed. However, the results will make all your hard work seem worthwhile. At this time of year, insects are buzzing about everywhere. Gardens, parks and woodlands – which are brimming with nectar-rich plants in spring – are all good places to look. Also, it is worth visiting local nature reserves, meadowland and wetland habitats.

Early mornings are a good time to photograph insects, as they can remain torpid until the sun's rays warm their bodies. After clear, cool nights, they may even be smothered in tiny droplets of dew, adding interest and scale to your shots. However, you need sharp eyes to spot them while they are resting. Walk slowly and search thoroughly – a careless foot can prove fatal to resting bugs. When you find a suitable subject, try to position your camera parallel to it. This maximises available depth-of-field. If an insect is resting, it might be possible to use a tripod. This is a welcome aid when shooting close-ups, as at high magnifications, the smallest movement is exaggerated and depth-of-field is shallow. When shooting hand-held is the only option, lie prone if possible and use your elbows for support.

When shooting insects, it is normally best to select the widest available aperture that will keep your subject acceptably sharp. In other words, don't aim for more depth-of-field than you actually need. Not only will this help keep the shutter speed fast enough to avoid shake, but it will also ensure surrounding vegetation is rendered nicely out of focus.

Essential accessories

Wimberley Plamp: A handy accessory for close-up photographers wishing to shoot spring foliage and insects. It is a ball-and-socket segmented arm with a clamp fixed at each end. One end can be attached to a tripod leg, while the other can hold a flower stem still, a branch in position or a reflector in place.

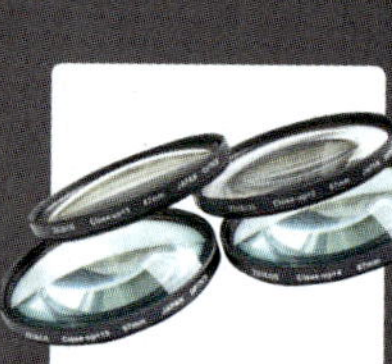

Reflector: A small (30 or 45cm) handheld reflector is a useful lighting aid – particularly when shooting in woodland. They reflect natural light onto small objects in order to relieve ugly or harsh shadows. Alter the intensity of light by moving the reflector towards or away from the subject.

Close-up filters: If you don't own a macro lens, close-up filters are a great cut-price introduction to macro photography. They are available in a variety of diameters and simply screw onto the front of your lens. They act like a magnifying glass, allowing you to focus nearer to the subject.

Fantastic creepy crawlies to shoot this spring

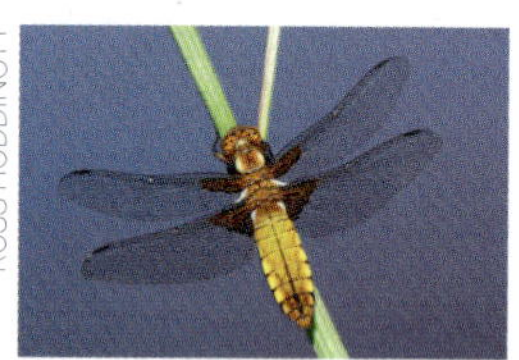
ROSS HODDINOTT

Dragonflies
A variety of dragonflies emerge during springtime. They can be found hunting close to ponds and other wetland habitats. Shoot from above, looking down on open wings.

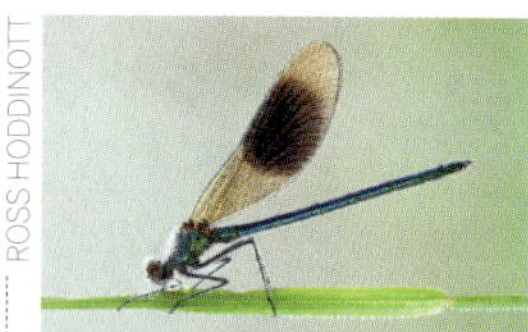
ROSS HODDINOTT

Damselflies
Colourful, attractive aquatic insects, damselflies are found emerging on grasses and reeds close to the water's edge on warm spring mornings. They are best shot from a side angle.

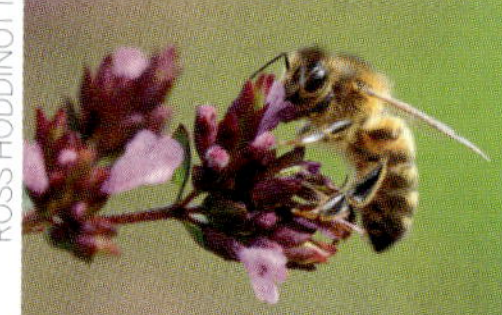
ROSS HODDINOTT

Bees
Honey and bumblebees are photogenic, but challenging subjects to shoot as they're always on the move. Opt for a fast shutter speed and shoot handheld in order to react quickly.

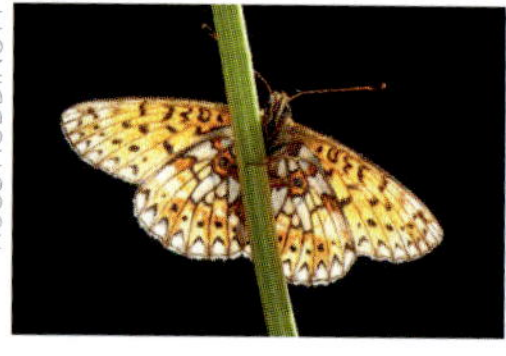
ROSS HODDINOTT

Butterflies
One of the most popular insects to capture due to their colourful, patterned wings. Great images are possible from all sorts of angles, so experiment. See page 28 for more details.

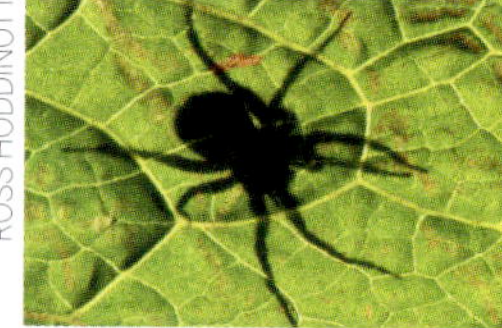
ROSS HODDINOTT

Spiders
A menace to many arachnophobes, but can make for startling close-ups. Get in close to focus on their many eyes or try for an unusual backlit silhouette.

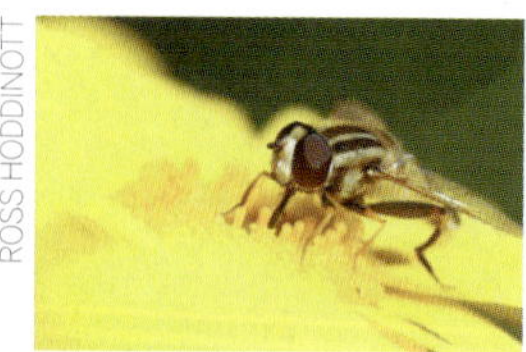
ROSS HODDINOTT

Hoverfly
Hoverflies are beautifully coloured. They often land on garden flowers, which create interesting and bright backdrops. Use an aperture smaller than f/8 to generate sufficient depth-of-field.

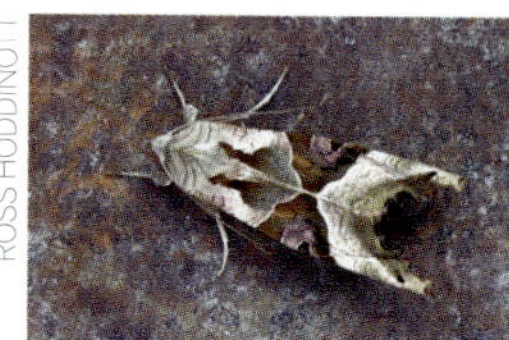
ROSS HODDINOTT

Moths
Moths are not too colourful, but some are interesting to look at, such as the Elephant Hawk Moth. Search among hedges and foliage as this is where moths often rest and shelter during daytime.

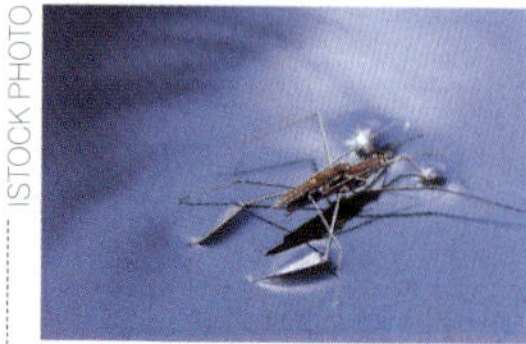
ISTOCK PHOTO

Pond skater
Pond skaters are common pond creatures. They 'skate' over the water's surface with their body supported on the tips of their legs. Photograph them as parallel as possible or from overhead using a macro lens or attachment.

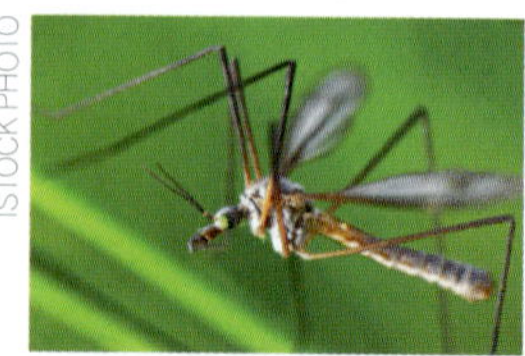
ISTOCK PHOTO

Crane fly
Don't overlook crane flies, more commonly known as Daddy Longlegs. Their gangly appearance is best captured close up and in front of a clean, uncluttered backdrop. Try to shoot them at eye-level.

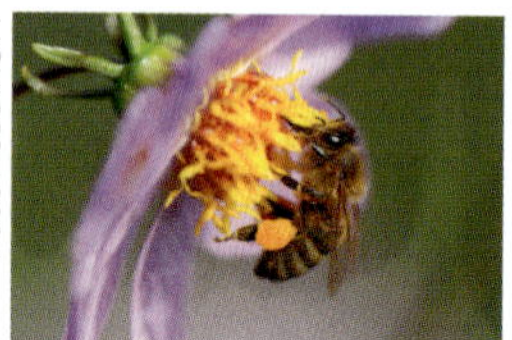
ROSS HODDINOTT

Wasps
Wasps, like bees, are regular visitors to our back gardens. They will be drawn to nectar-rich plants and are always on the move, so switch from AF to manual focus if your lens struggles to lock on.

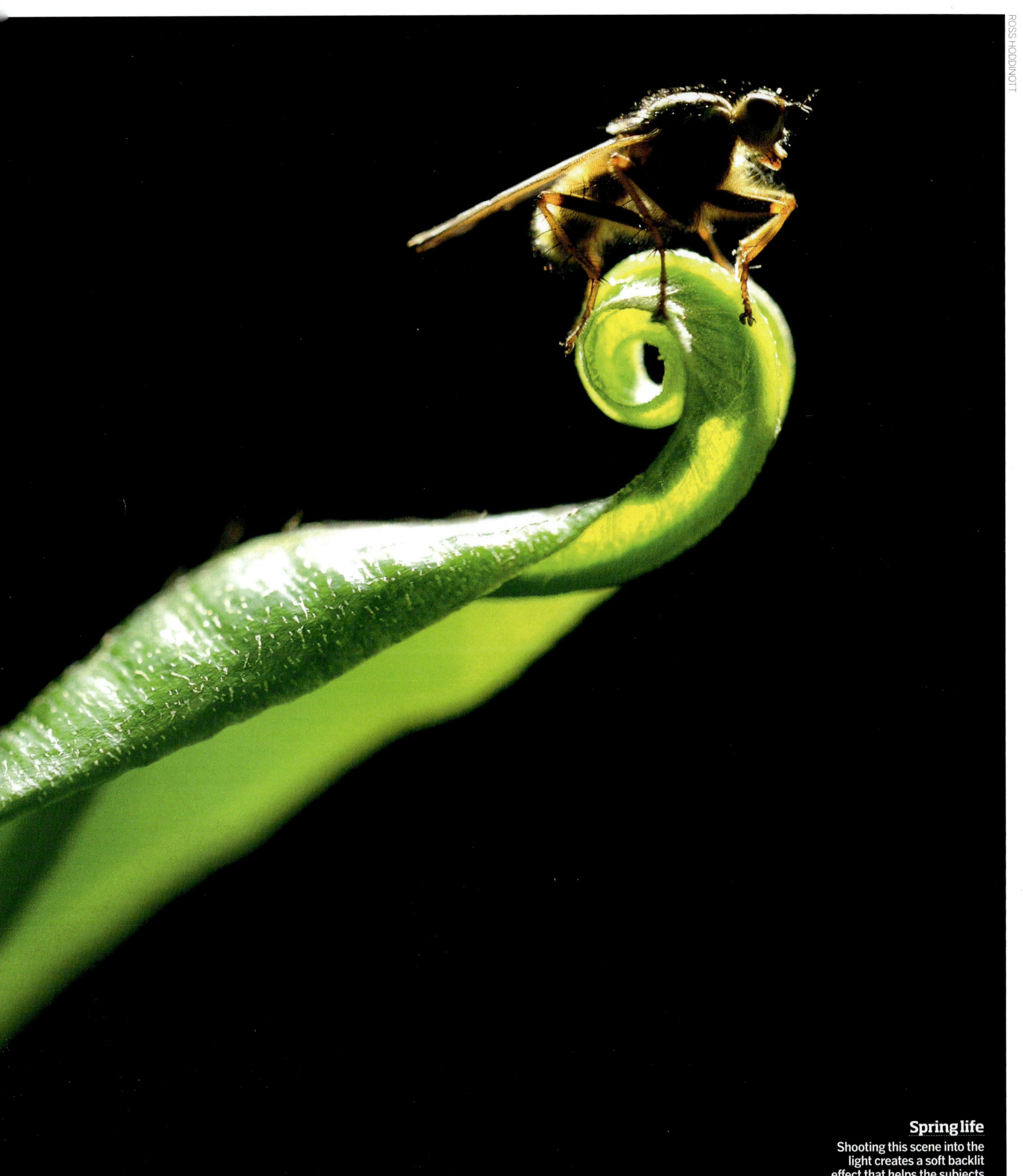
ROSS HODDINOTT

Spring life
Shooting this scene into the light creates a soft backlit effect that helps the subjects stand out from the backdrop.

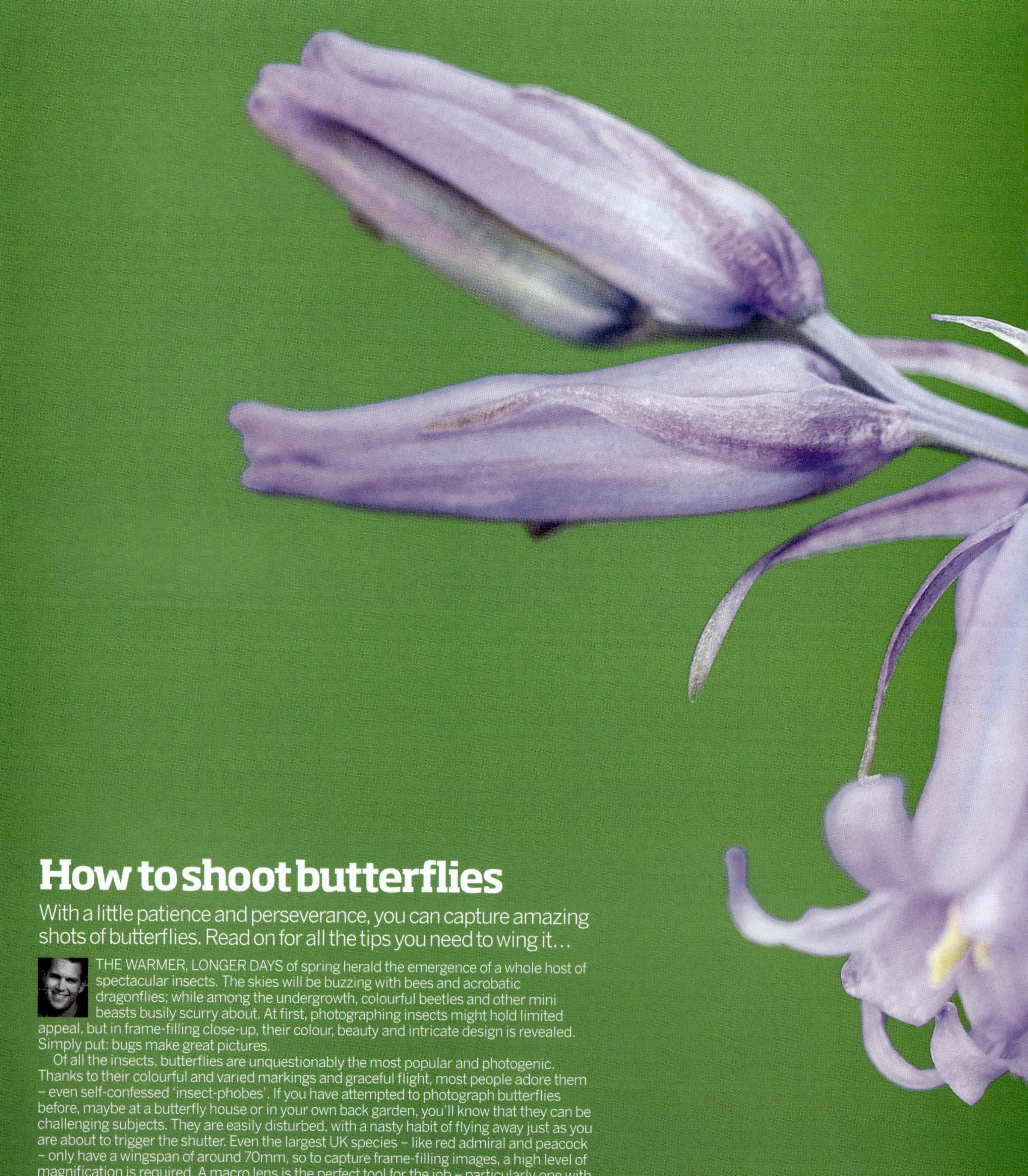

How to shoot butterflies

With a little patience and perseverance, you can capture amazing shots of butterflies. Read on for all the tips you need to wing it…

THE WARMER, LONGER DAYS of spring herald the emergence of a whole host of spectacular insects. The skies will be buzzing with bees and acrobatic dragonflies; while among the undergrowth, colourful beetles and other mini beasts busily scurry about. At first, photographing insects might hold limited appeal, but in frame-filling close-up, their colour, beauty and intricate design is revealed. Simply put: bugs make great pictures.

Of all the insects, butterflies are unquestionably the most popular and photogenic. Thanks to their colourful and varied markings and graceful flight, most people adore them – even self-confessed 'insect-phobes'. If you have attempted to photograph butterflies before, maybe at a butterfly house or in your own back garden, you'll know that they can be challenging subjects. They are easily disturbed, with a nasty habit of flying away just as you are about to trigger the shutter. Even the largest UK species – like red admiral and peacock – only have a wingspan of around 70mm, so to capture frame-filling images, a high level of magnification is required. A macro lens is the perfect tool for the job – particularly one with a focal length upwards of 90mm, as this provides a practical working distance.

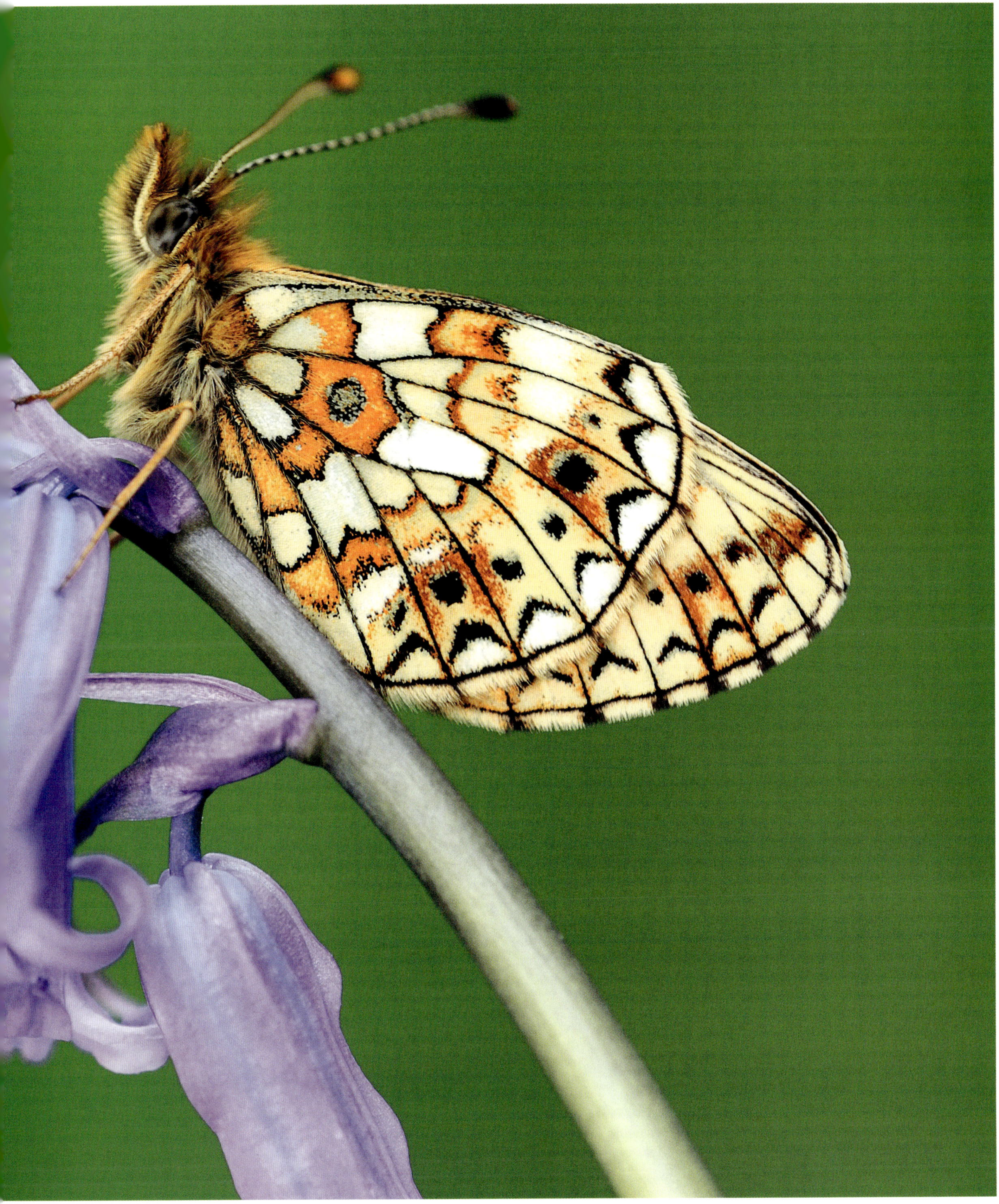

The perfect choice of optic is a macro lens – but as this is a costly item, it makes more sense to opt for an inexpensive close-up attachment instead, unless you are a dedicated close-up enthusiast. While cost-effective, the big disadvantage of using either a close-up filter or extension tube is that you have to get closer to the subject, increasing the risk of frightening the flighty insects away. They do, however, provide a great introduction to the fascinating world of close-up photography.

At the risk of stating the obvious, before you can photograph butterflies, you first need to locate them. Butterfly numbers are sadly in decline, so you may have to travel a few miles in order to find suitable environments. Different butterflies require different habitats and food plants – some enjoy grassland, while others prefer heathland, woodland or chalky downs. Research is the key. Spend time reading about butterfly types, where to find them and when. Search the internet for suitable local reserves, or better still, join your local Wildlife Trust and mix with the experts.

It is easiest to find butterflies during the day, when they are most active. However, you will probably find they rarely settle or allow you close enough to take pictures. Instead, it is better to visit habitats early in the morning, or during the evening, when butterflies are less active or roosting among vegetation or tall grasses. Search carefully – always watching where you tread. Still days are best, as even the slightest breeze will move the subject about.

Having located a butterfly, move yourself into position slowly. Avoid disturbing the surrounding vegetation or casting your shadow across the insect – doing so will frighten it away. On cool mornings, before it's warm enough for the insect to fly, it may be possible to use a tripod. This is hugely advantageous, aiding both pinpoint focusing and considered composition. If you have to shoot hand-held, switch on the image stabiliser if you have it, or employ a workable fast shutter speed, upwards of 1/200sec, to eliminate camera movement. Before releasing the shutter, search the background for anything distracting. If necessary, adjust your shooting position to exclude anything that might draw the eye away from your subject. Alternatively, select a wider aperture to help throw background detail quickly out of focus. Do bear in mind that, at high magnifications, depth-of-field is naturally shallow. Therefore, in order to keep the insect sharp throughout – and maximise the depth-of-field available at any given f/stop – keep your camera parallel to the subject.

Admittedly, photographing butterflies can prove a fiddly and frustrating business. Be prepared to crawl through the undergrowth and put up with lots of 'near misses'. However, with good preparation and perseverance, you too will soon be taking great butterfly images.

Close-up attachments

You can quickly and cheaply transform your standard lens (or a short telephoto) into one capable of capturing great insect images by using a close-up attachment.

Auto extension tubes

These are hollow rings that fit between the camera and lens to reduce the minimum focusing distance. Being constructed without optical elements, they do not degrade image quality. However, they do incur a degree of light loss. Auto extension tubes are compact, light and retain all the camera's functions. Tubes can be bought individually or in a set. The most common lengths are 12mm, 25mm and 36mm – the wider the tube, the larger the reproduction ratio.

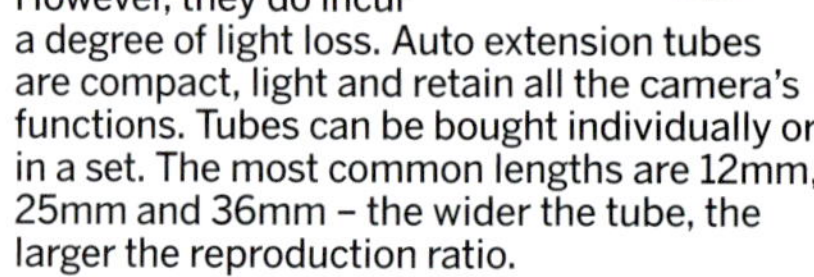

Close-up filters

These screw onto the front of the lens and act like a magnifying glass. They are inexpensive, lightweight and available in varying filter diameters. Most are a single element construction and available in a range of strengths, typically +1, +2, +3 and +4. The higher the number, the greater their magnification. They do not affect normal camera functions, like metering or autofocus, or restrict the light entering the camera. However, edge sharpness can suffer, and they are prone to 'ghosting', and spherical and chromatic aberration. Maximise image quality by selecting an aperture no smaller than f/8.

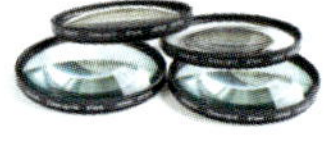

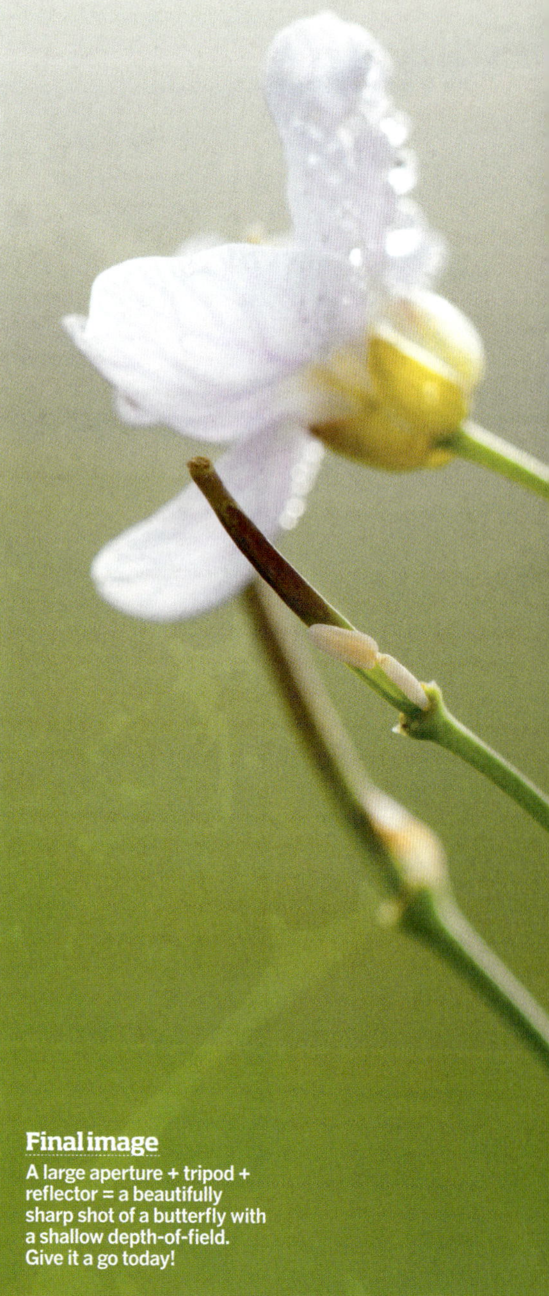

Final image

A large aperture + tripod + reflector = a beautifully sharp shot of a butterfly with a shallow depth-of-field. Give it a go today!

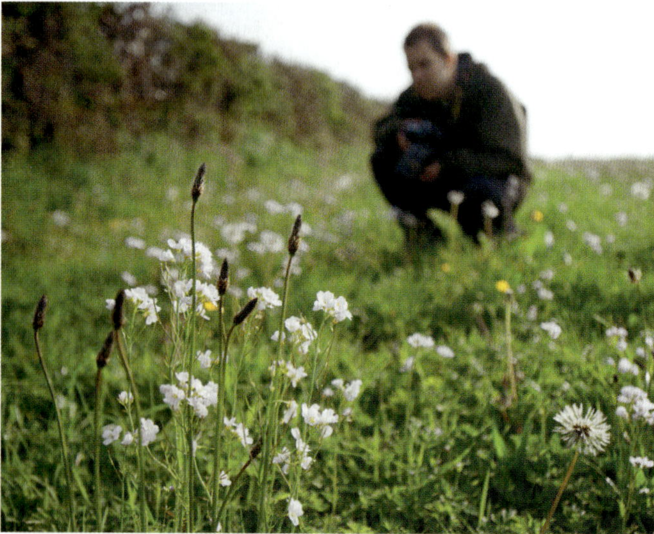

1 Locate the subject To photograph butterflies, you first need to know where, when and what to look for. For example, a local reserve close to me is home to hundreds of cuckoo flowers – a food plant of orange-tip butterflies. I set my alarm for daybreak and, after careful searching, find a butterfly clinging to one of the blooms.

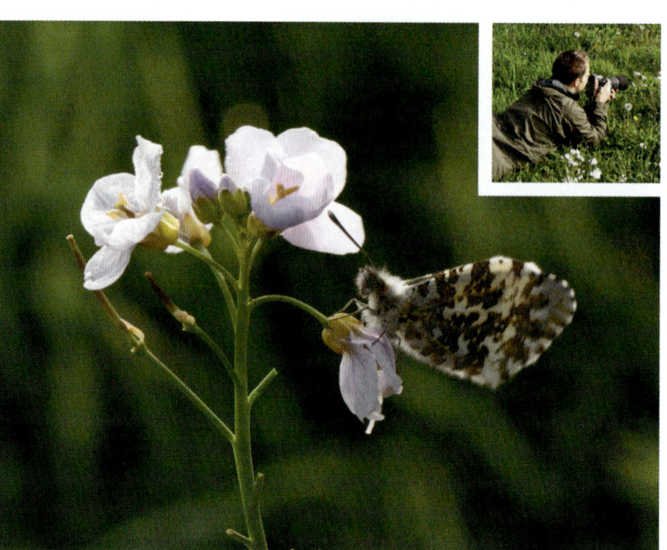

2 Getting into position I slowly move into picture-taking range, being careful not to disturb surrounding vegetation. A low viewpoint will often provide the most natural-looking results, so I lay on the ground and use my elbows as support. I select a small aperture of f/16 to help generate a wide depth-of-field, but doing so creates a distracting, messy background.

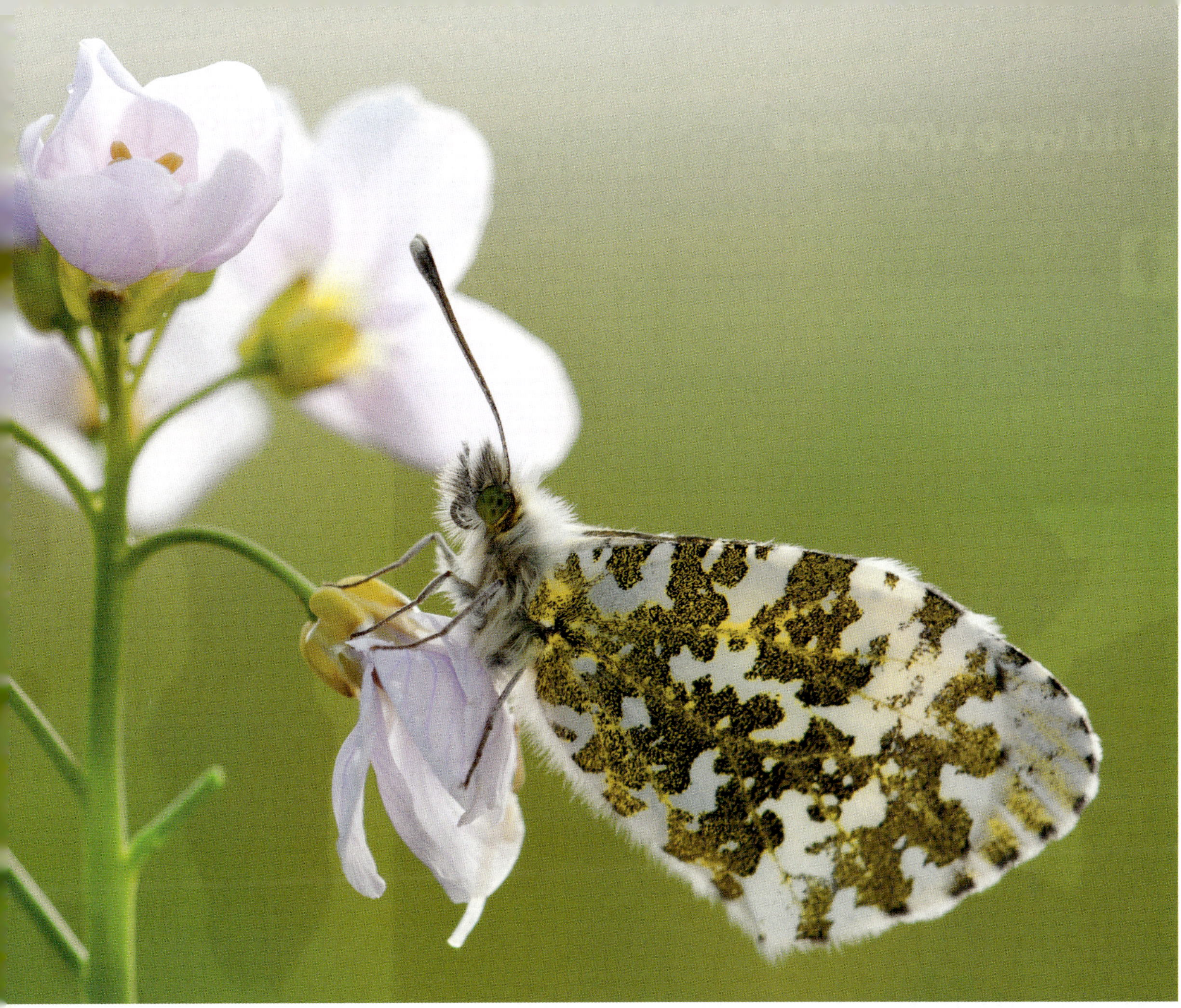

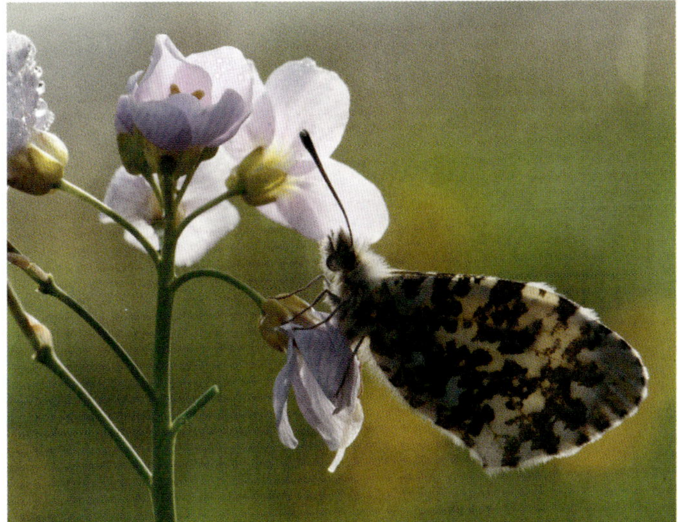

3 Blurred background To help the butterfly stand out from the rest of the scene, I set a wide aperture of f/5.6 to render the background as an attractive blur. The disadvantage of employing a larger aperture is that focusing has to be very precise, due to the limited depth-of-field. To aid focusing, I carefully set up my tripod nearby and use LiveView.

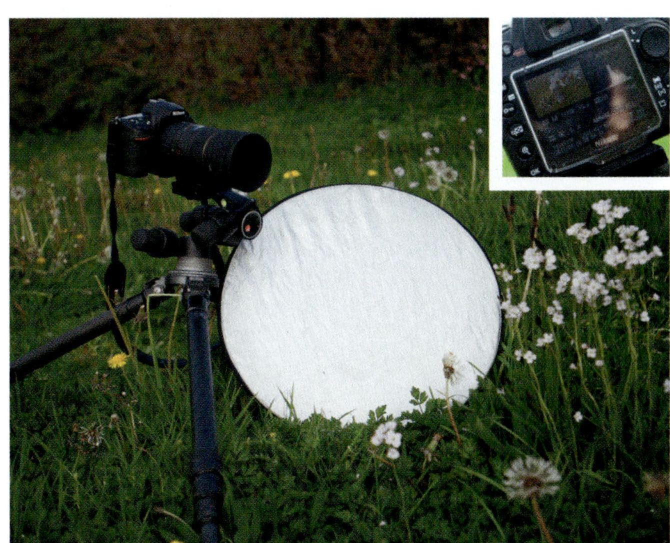

4 Lighting Although the result was better, detail in the wing was obscured by shade. To relieve the shadows, I use a small reflector to angle light onto the butterfly to reveal the beauty and detail in its under-wing. In situations like this, when the subject is static, a reflector gives more control than using flash, and the final result still looks natural.

Wild web wonders

Spiderwebs are exceptionally photogenic due to their intricate design. Ross Hoddinott shows you how to make the best out of them

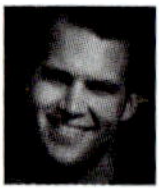

Ross Hoddinott RATHER THAN SEARCHING the web for ideas, why not get outside with your digital camera and search for a real web? Spiders spin beautiful cobwebs of sticky silk, and their constructions are intricate, often symmetrical and look stunning close up. Therefore, if you own a close-focusing zoom, close-up filter, extension tube or – better still – a dedicated macro lens, you will be able to capture stunning, frame-filling images.

Spiders live everywhere, so you shouldn't struggle to find a suitable web to photograph. They're easiest to find, and look their most photogenic, when smothered in tiny water droplets. Therefore, early in the morning after a clear, still night is the best time to look, as there should be plenty of dew around.

Alternatively, you could carefully spray a web with water using a gardener's spray bottle to create a fine mist that won't damage the web and gives a similar effect. In autumn and winter, after a cold and frosty night, you might even find a frozen web, which is particularly photogenic and can make for arty, abstract-looking images by using a shallow depth-of-field, together with careful focusing.

Essential kit

Collapsible reflector
A compact, fold-away reflector is an essential close-up accessory. They are designed to bounce natural light onto miniature subjects in order to relieve shadows. A reflector will normally create a more natural-looking illumination than flash. However, I have often employed a reflector as a makeshift background for small subjects, too. Its black cover can be held behind the subject to create a clean, simple backdrop. In some situations, you can even use a reflector's silver or white side in order to create high-key results.

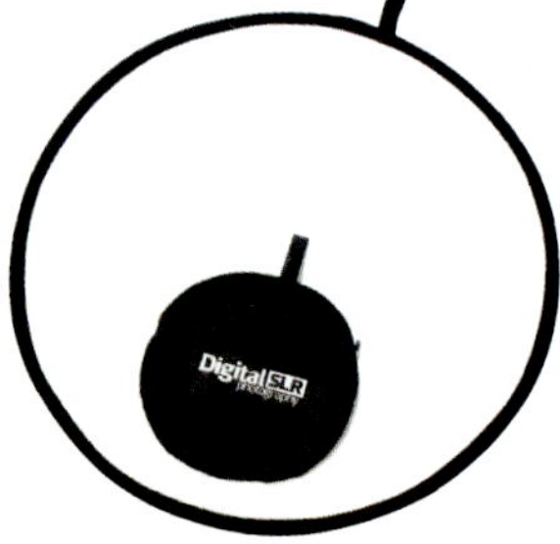

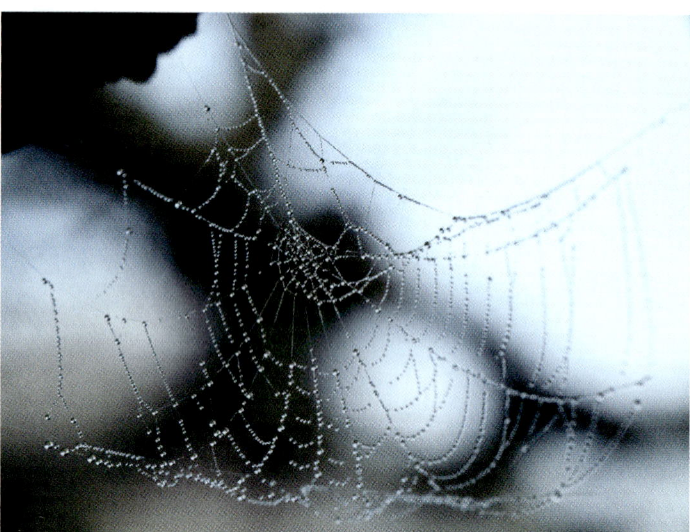

1 Test shot I don't have to search my local area long before finding a dew-laden web. I compose the image quickly, and decide to include the entire web in the frame. I opt for an aperture of f/8, hoping that this will create sufficient depth-of-field to keep the web sharp, while not recording too much background detail. However, I didn't pay enough attention to the background and the web doesn't stand out very well against the light backdrop.

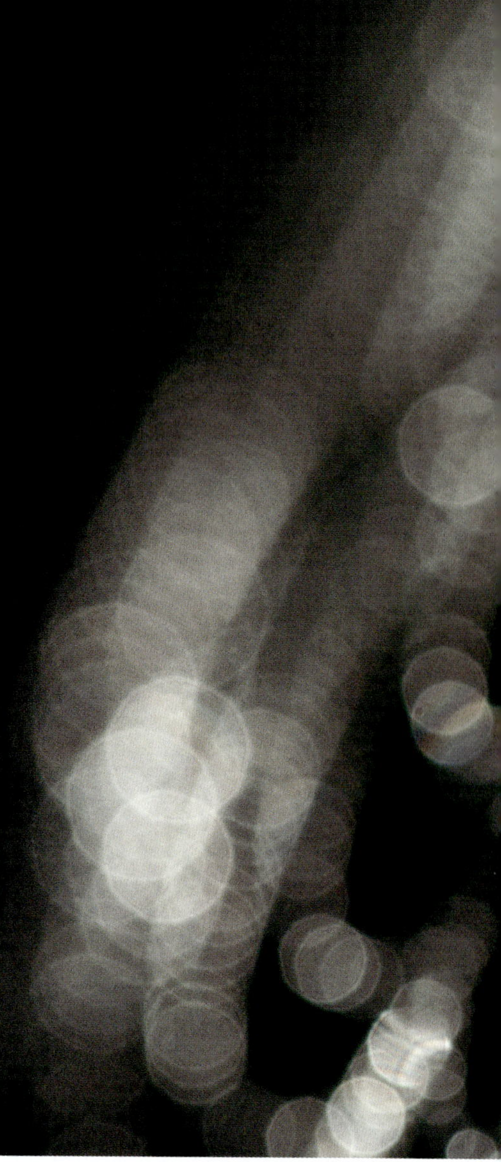

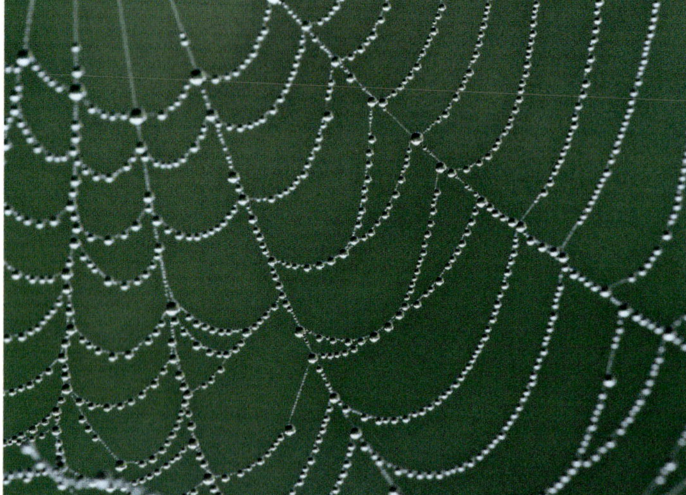

2 Get rid of distractions The subject's backdrop is often a major contributing factor to a photo's success or failure. By simply changing viewpoint, shooting angle, focal length or aperture, you can alter the background's colour and appearance. To eliminate the white sky from the image frame, I select a higher angle by extending the legs of my tripod. A grassy bank now creates a more attractive green background. I also opt for a tighter composition.

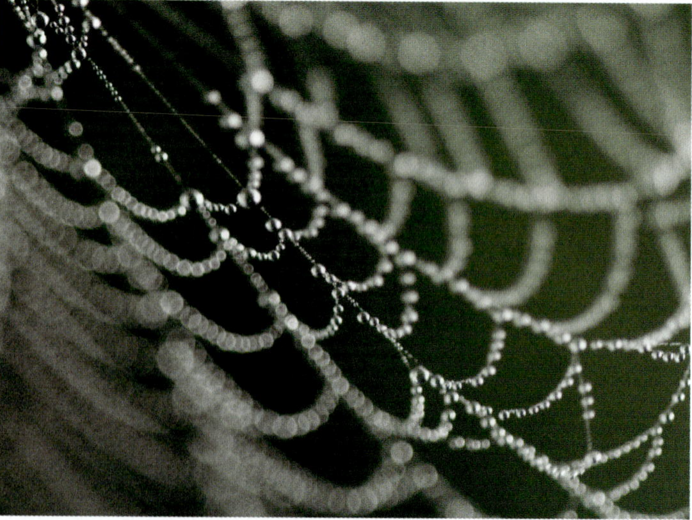

3 Experiment with depth-of-field To create a more artistic result, I select a wider aperture of f/4, and place my set-up at an angle to the web. This allows me to record just part of the web in focus. Focusing needs to be accurate when working with such a shallow depth-of-field. I check the image on the LCD monitor, zooming in to check the subject's sharpness. Unfortunately, my focusing isn't precise enough and the image is slightly too soft.

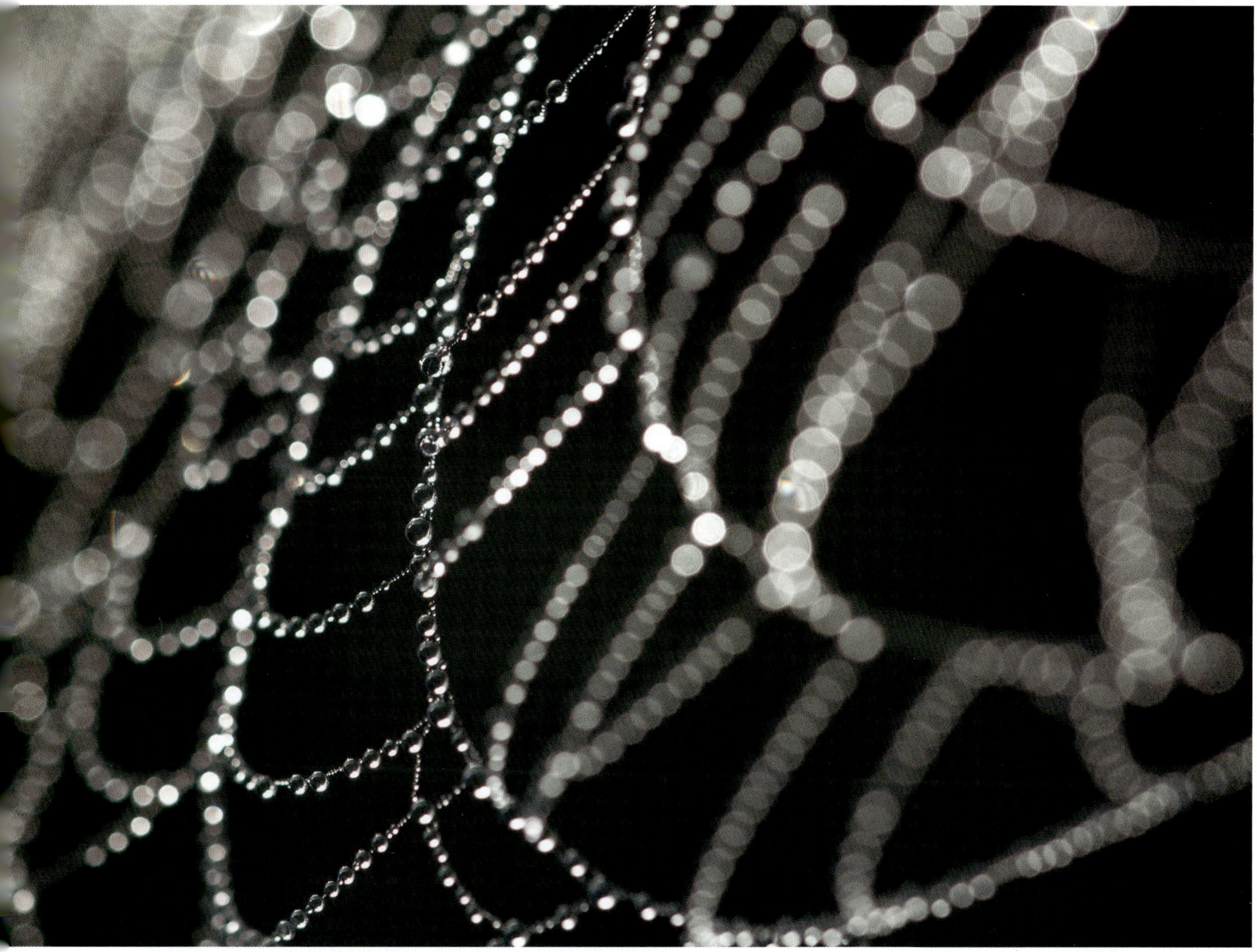

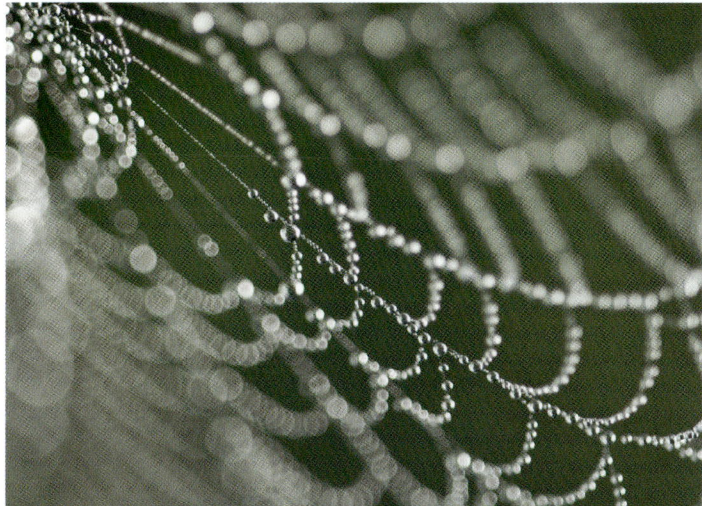

4 Refine focus Using a shallow depth-of-field at this level of magnification allows the photographer to direct the viewer's eye to a specific point of focus. If your camera has a preview button, use it to review the distribution of depth-of-field. This time I take an extra few moments to ensure my focusing is accurate and release the shutter via a remote release to prevent any camera movement spoiling the image.

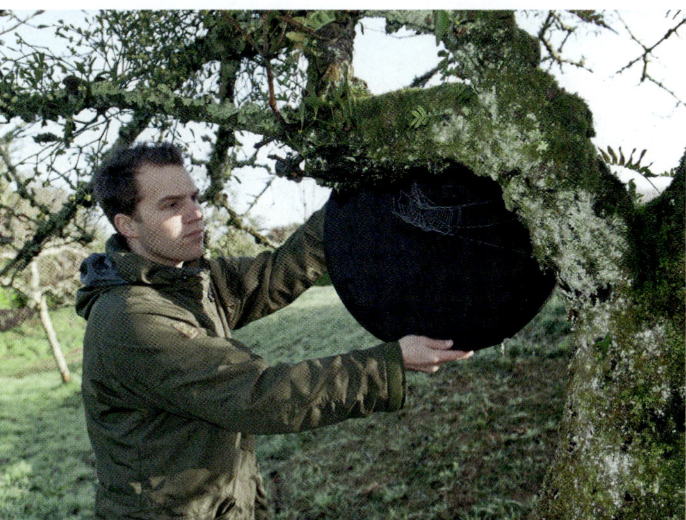

5 Try a different background Although happy with the previous shot, a black backdrop would suit the subject better; contrasting starkly with the glistening water droplets. The cover of my foldaway reflector is black, so I hold it around 40cm behind the web and use the self-timer to trigger the shutter. Finally, I have the result I wanted. If you'd prefer a more colourful look, you could try using brightly coloured card to alter the appearance of the background.

How to shoot garden birds

Ross Hoddinott reveals how you can set up your garden to help you capture great images of the small birds that visit throughout the year

REGARDLESS OF WHERE YOU LIVE in the UK – rural or urban – common and widespread songbirds are rarely far away. Due to their familiarity, it's easy to overlook just how attractive our popular garden residents are. For example, blue tits, great tits and greenfinches are all hugely photogenic. They also tend to be fairly tolerant of human activity and can be enticed near to a camera using suitable food. However, getting close enough to birds to take pictures is just the beginning. A good photograph is the result of a combination of background, surroundings, light and exposure. All these things can be controlled and influenced by the photographer; they shouldn't be left to chance. Once your set-up is complete, you then need to wait. Nature is unpredictable, so patience is required. However, photographing birds can prove addictive. You just never know what might happen next… That once-in-a-lifetime shot might be just around the corner.

1) Camouflage

Baiting garden birds with nuts and seed will only entice them close to you if your set-up is carefully concealed. Otherwise, your every movement will frighten them away and leave you without any good shots.

In this instance I simply hung scrim netting across my studio window. This allowed me to change memory cards and camera settings without risk of disturbing the birds feeding just a few metres away.

If you don't have a suitable window or shed that you can use in this way, consider buying a hide. The foldaway Dome hide, available from Wildlife Watching Supplies (WWS), is quick to erect using aluminium flexipoles.

The hide is free-standing, but in strong winds the guy ropes and pegs provided can be used. To further disguise your whereabouts, buy a camouflaged lens hood sleeve. The scrim netting from WWS is a soft, quiet lightweight material, ideally suited to wildlife photography.

For more options, visit: www.wildlifewatchingsupplies.co.uk and www.stealth-gear.com.

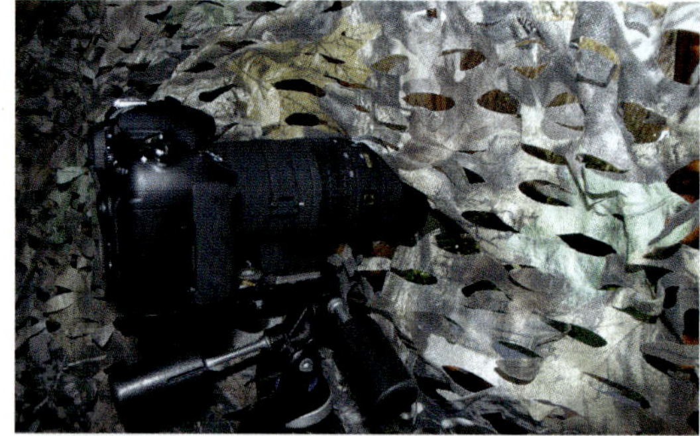

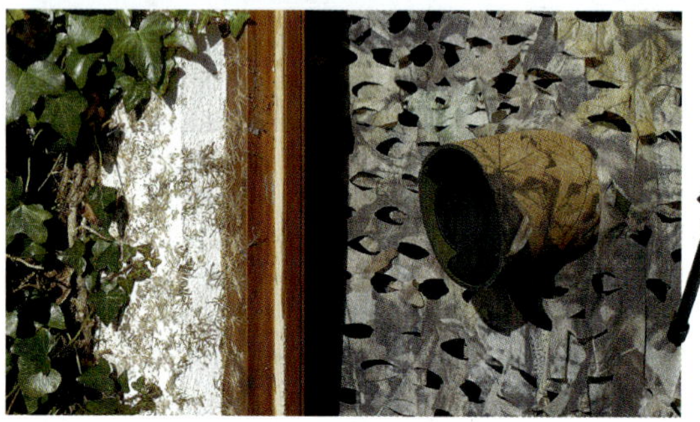

Gear up for birds!

To photograph birds of this size, you will need a minimum focal length of 300mm, otherwise they will appear too small in the frame. A 70-300mm zoom is good, or you could even combine a shorter focal length like a 55-200mm with a 1.4x or 2x teleconverter. A sturdy tripod is essential to support your set-up.

Select your digital SLR's continuous shooting mode, so when your subject is in position, you can capture a quick burst of images. As you will be shooting a large number of frames, keep spare memory cards nearby ready to replace full ones. Whether you focus using autofocus or manual focus is personal preference. Finally, don't worry if your success ratio is small at first. Digital doesn't cost and it really doesn't matter how many images you take to achieve a good one.

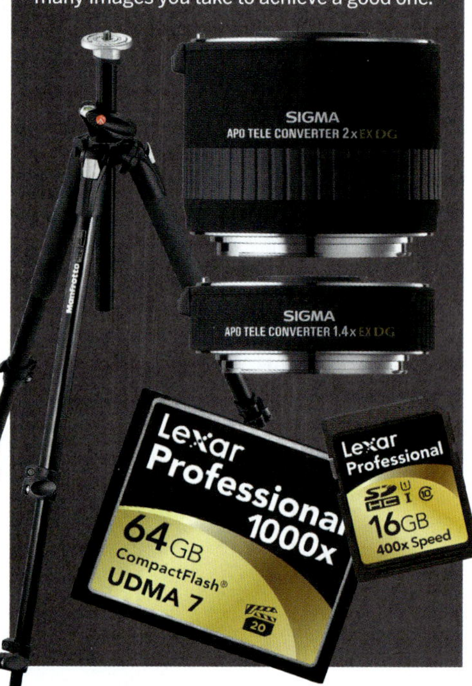

2) Bait the subject

Enticing birds within range of your camera is only possible using bait. They will soon learn to visit a feeding station to supplement their natural diet. It's important to provide suitable food which is safe for wild species to digest.

Common garden birds like tits and finches enjoy wild bird seed and peanuts – available at your local garden centre. Remember to keep food replenished regularly – while this can prove quite costly, it will be money well spent when you see the results.

Once birds are regularly visiting your feeding station, introduce a hide or move the food source within range of a window for easy set-up of your kit. I took all the images for this feature from my studio in Cornwall.

My simple set-up used two feeding poles placed 2m from my window. I hung a seed feeder from one and a nut feeder from the other in an attempt to attract a greater range of species. I placed the poles parallel to each other, with a 0.5m gap between, where I fixed a perch for birds to use when not feeding before laying in wait for my feathered visitors…

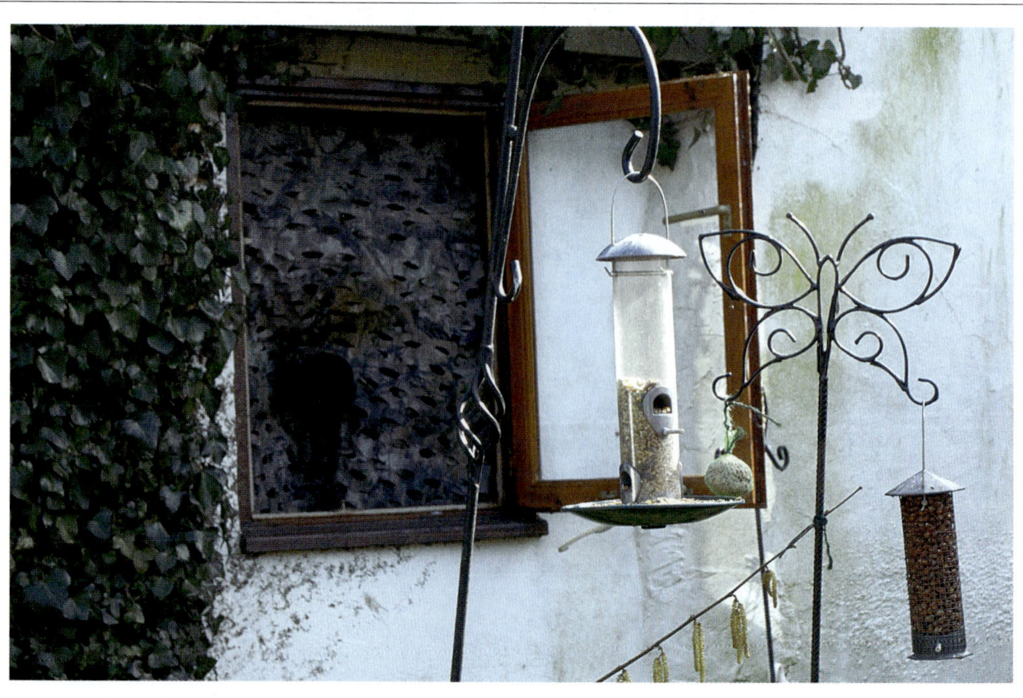

3) Create your own background

Many wildlife images fail as a result of insufficient attention being paid to the subject's background. A dull or messy backdrop will ruin an otherwise technically good image, so this is a key area to keep in mind.

When photographing small garden birds, you will normally be using a focal length upwards of 300mm. A useful characteristic of telephoto lenses is that they condense perspective, creating an attractive, diffused background at wider apertures. However, to ensure you create a clean, simple backdrop, your perch should have a minimum of 2m of empty space behind it. Any twigs or background elements nearer than this in the shot will remain defined and draw the eye away from the subject.

The background colour is also important. A vibrant backdrop will help give your image added punch. Therefore, try to align your set-up so that a colourful shrub or painted garden fence creates your background.

If this isn't possible – or you are taking pictures in winter when colours are more subdued – introduce an artificial backdrop. In this instance, I constructed a simple wooden frame (1m square), which I erected roughly 2m behind my feeding station. I then attached coloured cloth to the frame using finger tacks, being careful to keep the material taut to prevent distracting creases from forming. Alternatively, you could use a sheet of card, but this is more likely to tear if it's windy.

Positioned at this distance behind the subject, the material is rendered in soft focus, creating a clean, flattering backdrop. Any colour will do, so experiment. However, greens, blues and browns will create the most natural-looking results.

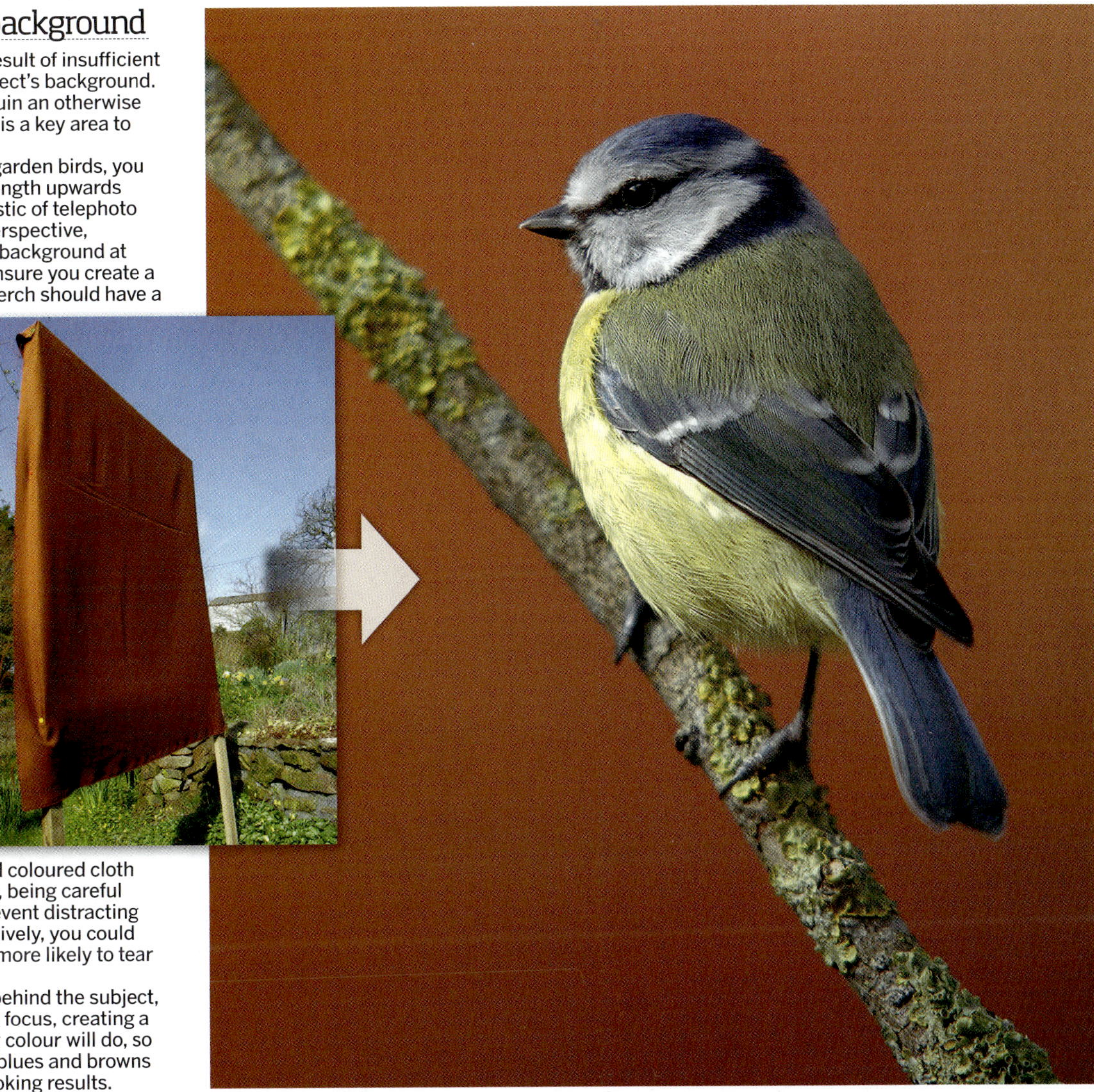

4) Choosing the shutter speed

Small garden birds are extremely flighty and active. They rarely remain still long to allow you to comfortably compose and focus on them, and even when they are resting, they are constantly looking about and altering position. Therefore, you need to prioritise a relatively fast shutter speed to freeze their rapid movement. Ideally, a speed of 1/400sec or faster is required. Otherwise you will take a high percentage of images that suffer from subject blur. If necessary, select a higher ISO sensitivity to generate a fast enough shutter speed. Even at ISO 800, levels of noise remain acceptable. However, to maximise image quality I recommend you do not exceed a sensitivity of ISO 400. Being able to increase the ISO rating at the flick of a switch is hugely beneficial to wildlife photographers who need to set a faster shutter speed to freeze movement or flight. It can make the difference between a blurred image or one that's pin-sharp.

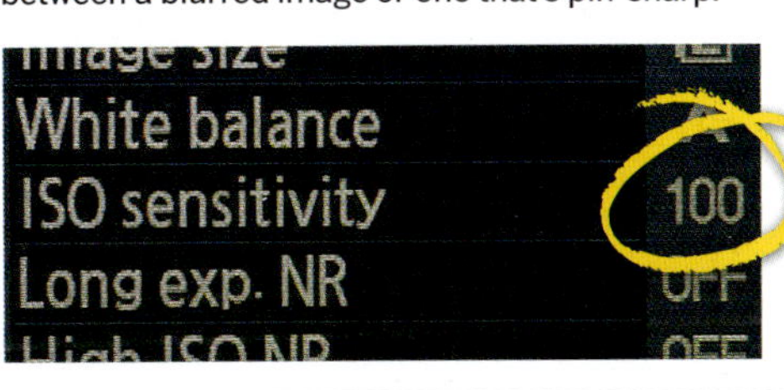

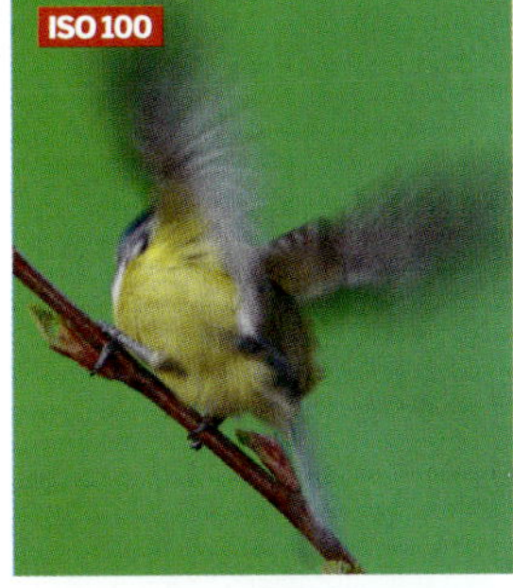

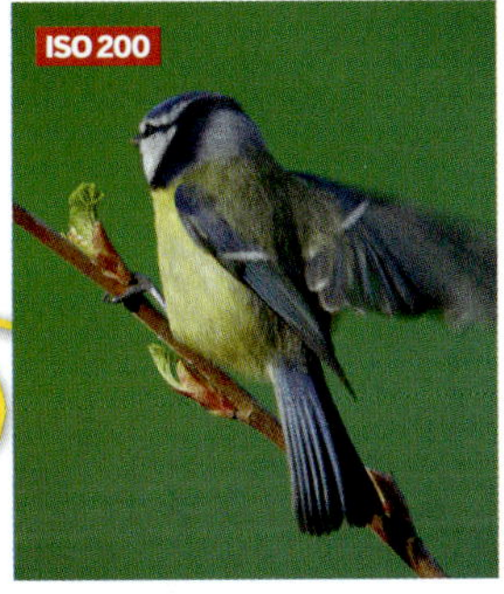

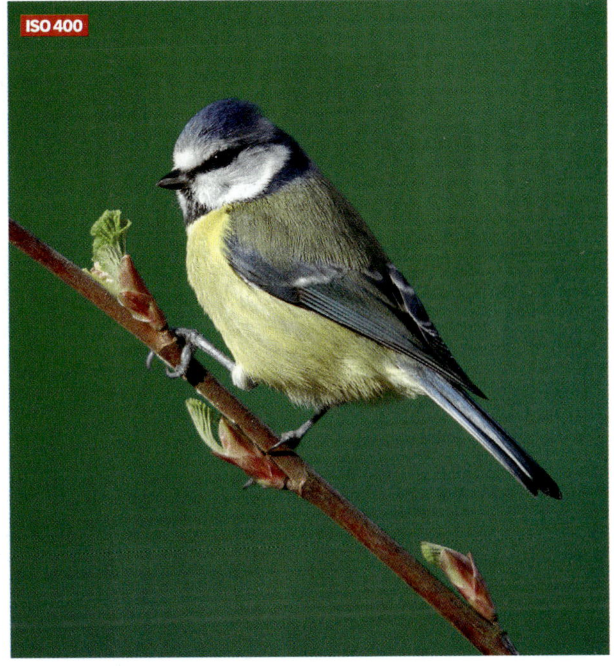

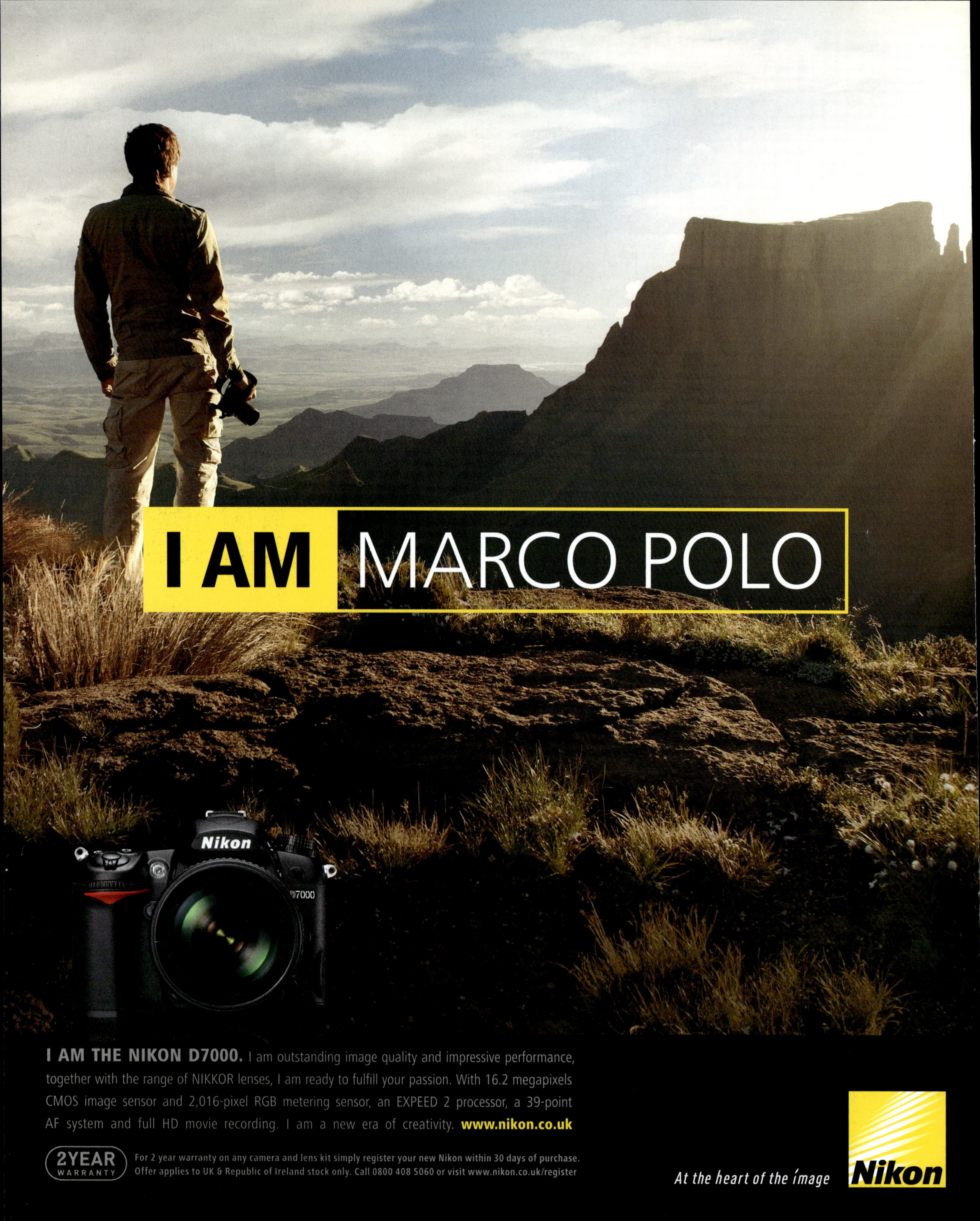

5) Consider using props

Using feeders is the perfect way to bring birds within range of your longest lenses. However, images of birds clinging to a feeder don't look very natural and you will soon get tired of taking this type of shot. To make your images look more wild and natural, introduce a prop near to your feeding station that the birds can use as a perch. This can be anything as long as it is photogenic and in keeping with the species. An attractive, colourful branch works well. You can even make your images look seasonal by utilising a sprig of spring blossom or branch of autumn berries.

If you want to be more adventurous, try using a rusty piece of barbed wire, washing line or maybe a milk bottle. Just use your imagination. The drawback of using a prop is that typically birds will only rest on the perch very briefly before hopping onto the feeder. Therefore, you will need to react quickly and remain patient. Experimentation is key. You will find that some props look and work better than others. If you're using an artificial background, you might also want to alter its colour to complement the type of perch you are using. Introducing a prop allows you more control and creativity over the look and feel of the final image. You're also able to create a more interesting overall result. Another advantage of using an attractive perch is that it will allow you to place less emphasis on the bird and, as a result, employ a shorter focal length. Shooting at a lower magnification is technically advantageous, as depth-of-field is extended.

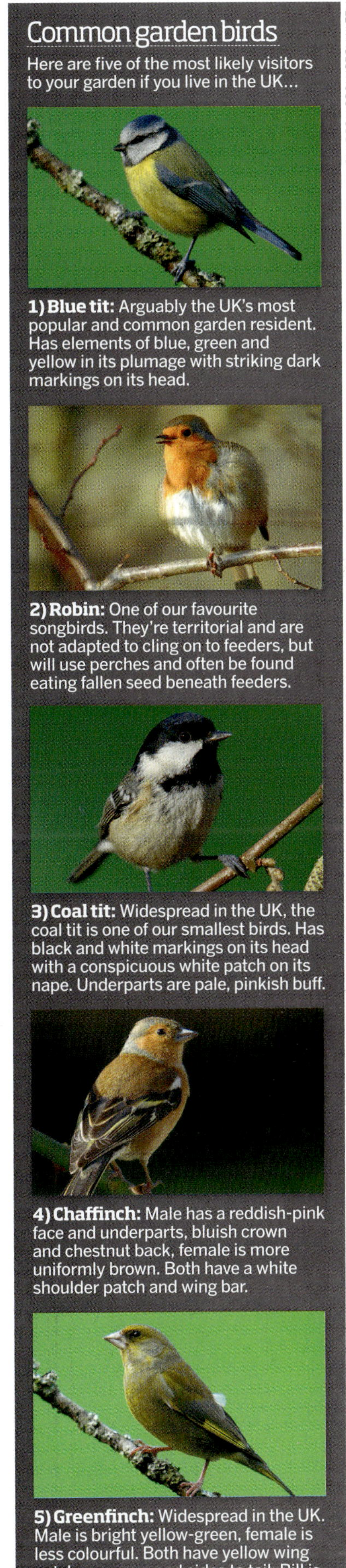

Common garden birds

Here are five of the most likely visitors to your garden if you live in the UK...

1) Blue tit: Arguably the UK's most popular and common garden resident. Has elements of blue, green and yellow in its plumage with striking dark markings on its head.

2) Robin: One of our favourite songbirds. They're territorial and are not adapted to cling on to feeders, but will use perches and often be found eating fallen seed beneath feeders.

3) Coal tit: Widespread in the UK, the coal tit is one of our smallest birds. Has black and white markings on its head with a conspicuous white patch on its nape. Underparts are pale, pinkish buff.

4) Chaffinch: Male has a reddish-pink face and underparts, bluish crown and chestnut back, female is more uniformly brown. Both have a white shoulder patch and wing bar.

5) Greenfinch: Widespread in the UK. Male is bright yellow-green, female is less colourful. Both have yellow wing patches, rumps and sides to tail. Bill is pink and conical for feeding on seed.

ALL IMAGES: ROSS HODDINOTT

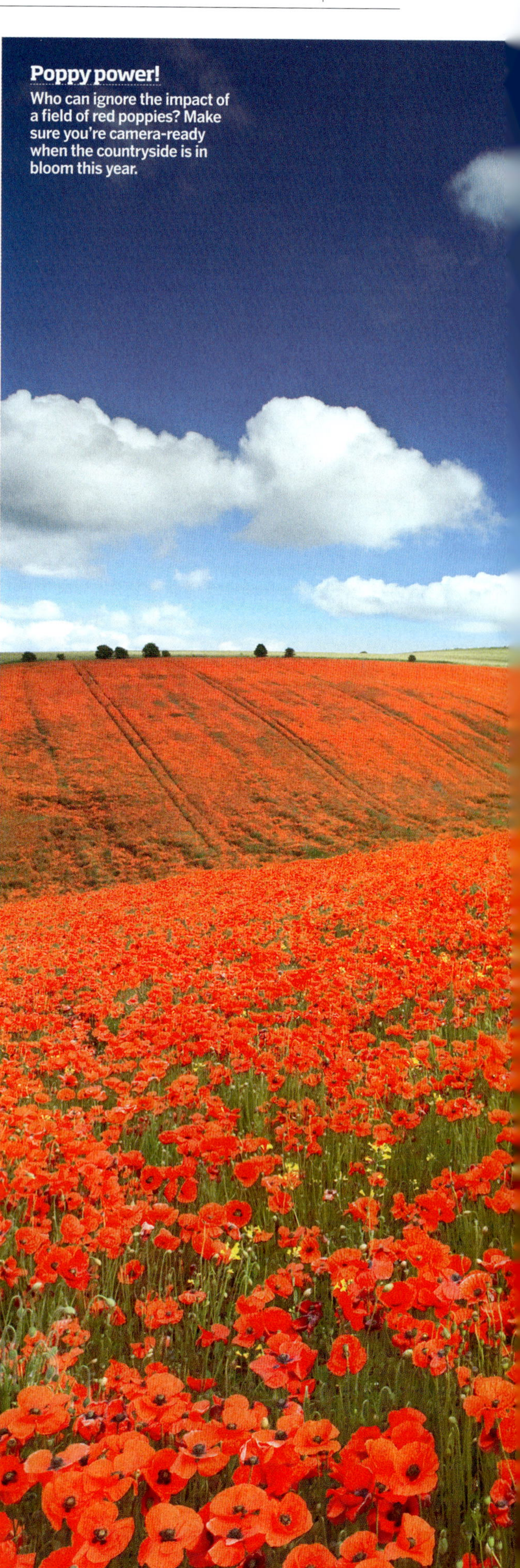

Poppy power!
Who can ignore the impact of a field of red poppies? Make sure you're camera-ready when the countryside is in bloom this year.

FLORA

It is hardly surprising that plant life is so popular among photographers. Wildflowers, plants and fungi are varied, beautiful and easily accessible subjects for everyone. Regardless of where you live, or the equipment you own, great nature scenes are well within your reach and can make for stunning images packed with colour

THE FLOW, COLOUR, DESIGN and delicacy of plants – flowering or non-flowering – make them a popular and rewarding photographic subject. In frame-filling close-up, photographers can highlight fine detail and colour; while from further away, plants can be shown in context with their surroundings. By adopting a shallow depth-of-field, or creatively using subject or camera motion, photographers are able to capture abstract or painterly results. Plants can be vibrant or dull, tall or low growing, form large carpets of colour, or be found growing singularly. Some have colourful, impressive blooms, while others, like fungi and lichen, don't flower at all. With such great variety and diversity within the natural world, there is never a risk of running out of inspiration.

As the seasons change, photographers are presented with fresh subjects and photo opportunities. During spring, new growth is everywhere. Visit woodlands, parks and gardens to discover delicately unfurling ferns, emerging leaves, swathes of bluebells and colourful blossom. During the summer months, the countryside is brimming with colour. Meadows nurture a wide array of wildflowers, while foxgloves and willowherb stand tall along hedgerows and banks. When summer gives way to autumn, foliage turns golden, the light softens and, while many plants stop flowering, the sudden emergence of weird and wonderfully shaped toadstools and fungi present new challenges for nature photographers to enjoy.

When you look at great nature images – for example, the work of German photographer Sandra Bartocha – they look stunningly effortless. However, great shots are rarely accidental. Although plants are static subjects – meaning photographers enjoy a great degree of control over the look of the final image – highlighting a plant's beauty, form and design in a single frame is still far from easy. In fact, in some respects, the level of control plant photographers have over their results just adds to the pressure to get things right – both technically and aesthetically. Simplicity is often key, while background choice and lighting are also particularly important when photographing plants. A clean, flattering backdrop, free of any distraction, will help your subject stand out boldly; while the light's quality and direction will dictate the image's mood and help highlight fine detail.

Plants, in all their many guises, provide great subject matter for photography. It is time to hone your close-up skills and begin exploring the wonderful world of plants. Read on to learn how to shoot a variety of flora...

Working in the wind

Although plants are static subjects, they can be badly affected by the wind. Tall flowers are particularly prone to movement in breezy conditions, making it difficult to focus and compose images in natural light. Plant photography is best attempted in still conditions, with a wind speed below 10mph. However, it is not always possible to be this choosy. Light, intermittent winds won't create too many problems – just wait for a brief pause in the breeze before quickly fine-tuning focus and triggering the shutter. In windier conditions, consider only photographing sheltered subjects, or use an umbrella or windbreak. You can make your own windbreak using heavy, clear polythene held in position by aluminium rods. Alternatively, the Lastolite Cubelite will help shield small subjects and also diffuse harsh directional light. Another option is to use a Wimberley Plamp – a ball-and-socket segmented arm, with a clamp fixed at either end. One can fasten to your tripod leg, while the other holds your subject still. However, be careful not to damage plants when attaching the clamp to delicate flower stems.

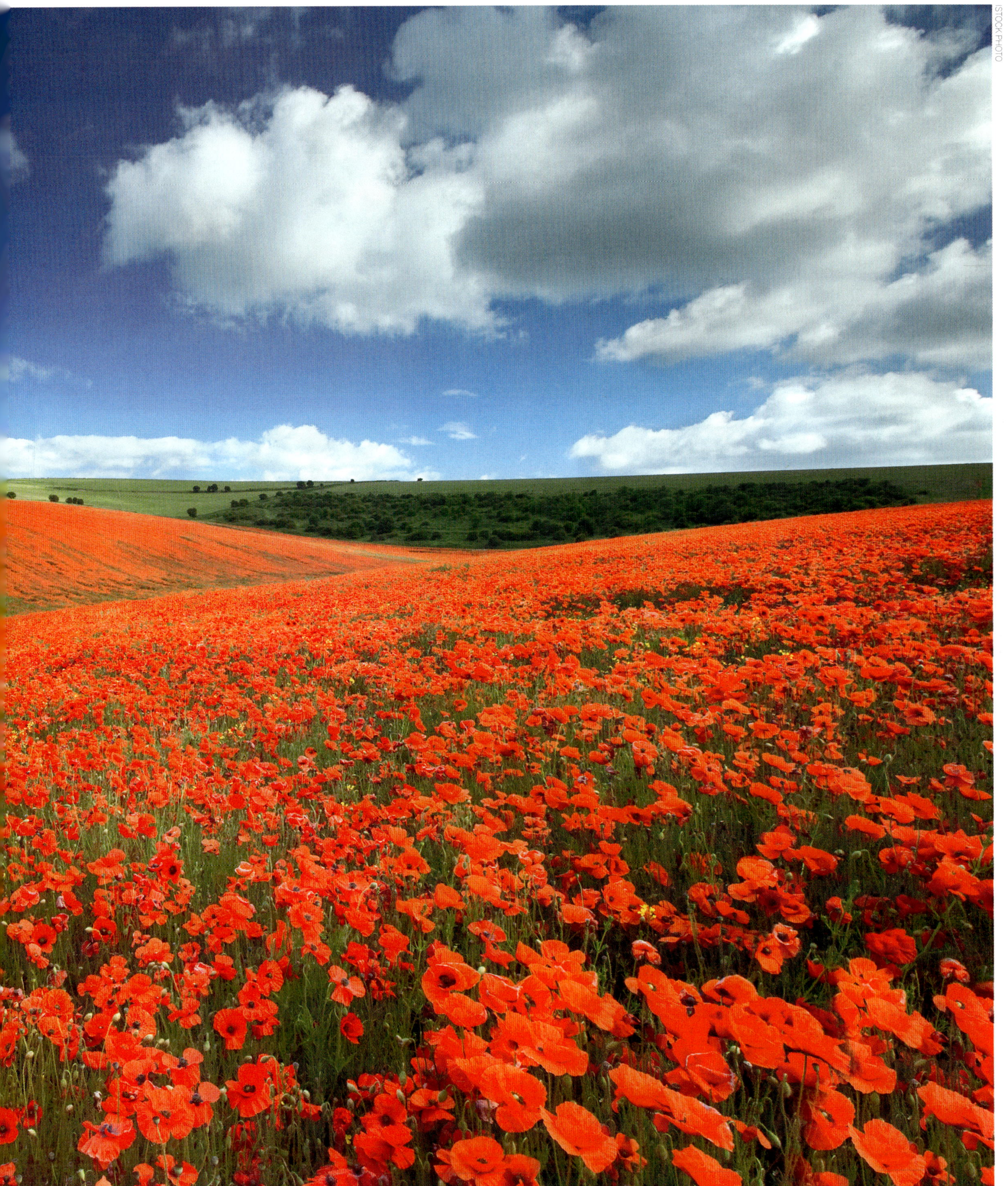

ISTOCK PHOTO

Get the gear!

Nature photography requires a modest kit investment to capture the best results. Here we summarise the type of gear you need

WHILE SOME SUBJECTS require costly, specialist kit to photograph, nature photographers can get by with a comparatively basic set-up. While a good range of focal lengths will naturally give you greater options and flexibility, it's possible to get good results using just a standard zoom. However, most plant photographers will want to capture frame-filling close-ups of their subjects from time to time, so a macro lens or close-up attachment is high up on the list of priorities. Aside from lenses, a number of useful accessories, lighting aids and supports are available that will benefit your nature images.

Get the lowdown!
Choosing the right gear for your requirements – in this case, choosing kit which will aid close-up photography and get you low to the ground – is essential for getting the results you want.

Lenses for nature

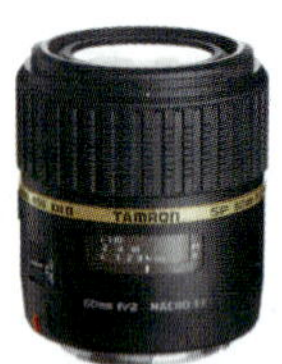

Macro: Being optimised for close focusing, a dedicated macro lens is an ideal choice for nature photography. They typically have a maximum reproduction ratio of 1:1 life-size and have a large maximum aperture – typically f/2.8 – which helps provide a bright viewfinder image to aid focusing and composition. A focal length longer than 70mm (ideally 100mm) is a good choice, as it provides a useful working distance.

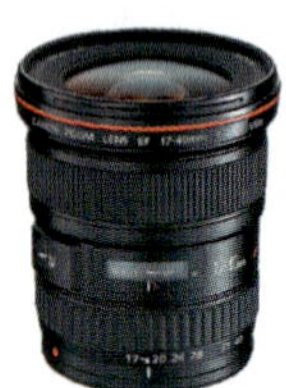

Wide-angle: A wide focal length, in the region of 18-28mm, is ideal for showing plant life in context with its surrounding environment. By getting close to subjects, you can create unusual, distorted perspectives. Wide-angles are particularly useful when shooting from low angles looking upward, or views of vast swathes of flowers. Wide-angles naturally possess a large depth-of-field, making it possible to achieve front-to-back sharpness. For more extreme results, consider using a fisheye lens.

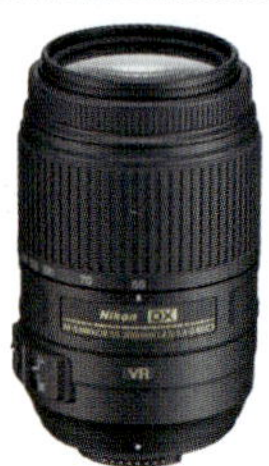

Telephoto/telezoom: Telephoto lengths – in the region of 200-300mm – are perfect for isolating single flowers. Combined with a large aperture, depth-of-field is shallow at longer lengths, so with the use of a telephoto it is possible to render one flower sharply against an attractively diffused backdrop. You don't need a fast, costly lens either – the telephoto end of a 70-300mm will suffice. Extension tubes can be useful to reduce a telephoto's minimum focusing distance, but they do restrict the light reaching the sensor.

Len accessories

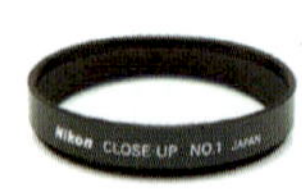

Close-up filters: You don't need a macro lens to get frame-filling shots – adapt a standard or zoom lens with a close-up filter. Available in a range of filter threads and strengths, they screw on to the front of your lens and act like a magnifying glass. A +3 or +4 dioptre is ideal for nature. Close-up filters can be bought individually, or in sets, and cost between £10-£20. They degrade image quality slightly, so for best results select a mid-range aperture in the region of f/5.6 or f/8.

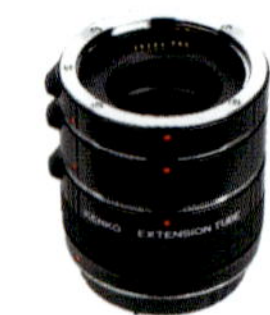

Extension tubes: Auto extension tubes cost more than close-up filters, but, unlike filters, they don't affect optical quality. They are hollow tubes that fit between the camera and lens, reducing the lens's minimum focusing distance. Auto extension tubes retain all the camera's automatic functions. They are best used with short focal lengths, ie a standard 50mm lens. They don't generate a large working distance, though, so be prepared to work close to the subject.

Lighting aids

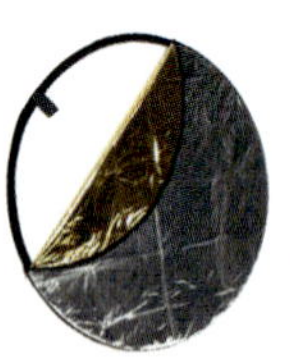

Reflector: Small, collapsible reflectors are available from the likes of Lastolite, and are useful for reducing contrast and relieving shadows on plants. The reflector is positioned at an angle that bounces light onto the subject and the light's intensity can be altered by moving the reflector closer or further away. One of the biggest advantages of using a reflector is that you are able to see its effects instantly. Use a gold reflector for a warm light, the silver side for a cooler light and the white for a soft fill-in.

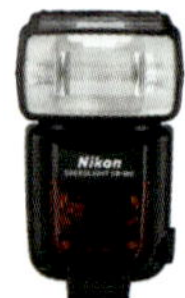

Flashgun: Light can be limited when working in close proximity to the subject and in shaded conditions. Therefore, a flashgun, or the camera's built-in unit, can be useful when shooting plant life. Flash will not only enable you to use a smaller aperture setting to improve your depth-of-field, it will also allow you to select a faster shutter speed – useful if your subject is being windswept. It is often best to shoot at a reduced output, or through a diffuser, if you want the results to look natural.

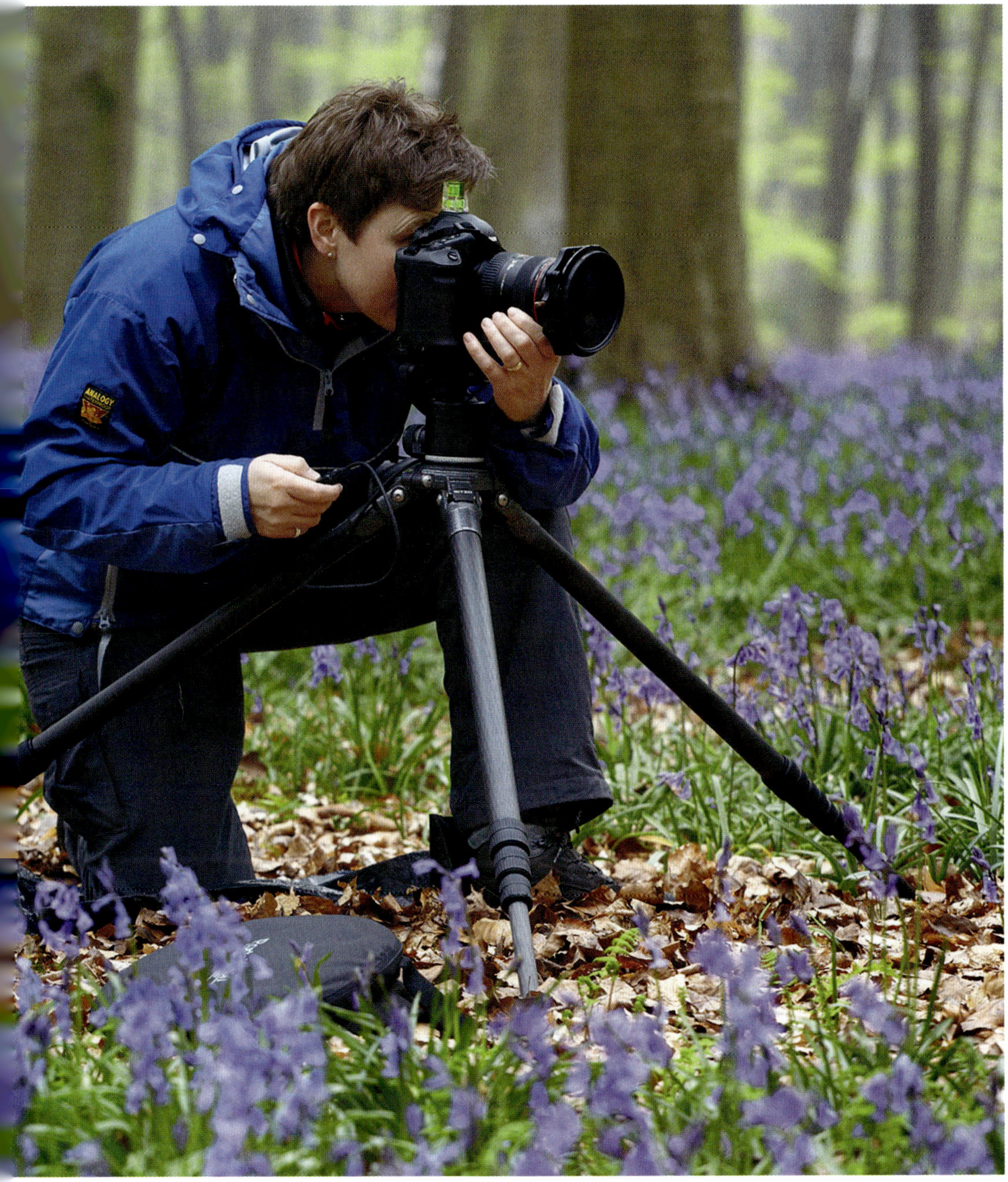

Nature kit Q&A

I struggle to look through the viewfinder when shooting plants from ground level. What can I do?
Unless you own a camera with a vari-angle LCD – like the Nikon D5100 or Canon EOS 600D – shooting from low angles can prove awkward. Rather than having to lie flat on the ground and contort your body to peer through the viewfinder, buy a right-angle finder. This L-shaped attachment fits onto the eyepiece, allowing photographers to comfortably compose images at right angles to the camera's optical axis. Most marque brands have their own range of these attachments, so visit their websites for details and models.

Do you have any tips for maximising sharpness when shooting flowers?
Firstly, always use a tripod whenever it is practical to do so. Also, avoid physically depressing the shutter button as the pressure of your finger can produce enough movement to introduce camera shake. Instead, trigger the shutter remotely – either using a remote device or your camera's self-timer facility. Finally, if your camera has a mirror lock-up facility, use it. By 'locking-up' the camera's reflex mirror prior to taking pictures, you eliminate the risk of internal vibrations or 'mirror slap' softening image quality.

I've heard polarisers are useful for plants, too. Is this true?
Yes, it is. When rotated correctly, polarisers reduce glare and reflections from foliage, petals and shiny fungi. By using the filter, you can restore natural colour saturation and capture images with added vibrancy. However, polarisers do have a filter factor of around two stops, so shutter speed is lengthened as a result of using one. In good light or still conditions, this won't be a problem, but in low light or blowy weather, it might be impractical.

How can I avoid getting damp and grubby when photographing plants?
Wear waterproof layers to protect your clothing when kneeling or lying on the ground or invest in a groundsheet. Consider the Linpix Photography Mat to help keep you clean and dry. Using garden kneeling pads is another good option. You should also think about wearing photographer's shooting gloves like those from Just Ltd (www.cameraclean.co.uk) to protect fingers and hands from thorns and nettles.

Tripods and alternative camera supports

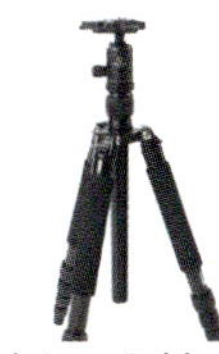

Tripod: A good, solid tripod will give you support, stability and guarantee your pictures are sharp. It will also slow down the picture-taking process, making you think about composition and viewpoint. A tripod also assists with precise focusing, so you can fine-tune your point of focus. For nature, opt for one that can be positioned low to the ground. A design that lacks a centre column or one that can be positioned horizontally is a good option. A geared tripod head, like the Manfrotto 410 Junior, is the perfect choice for close-ups.

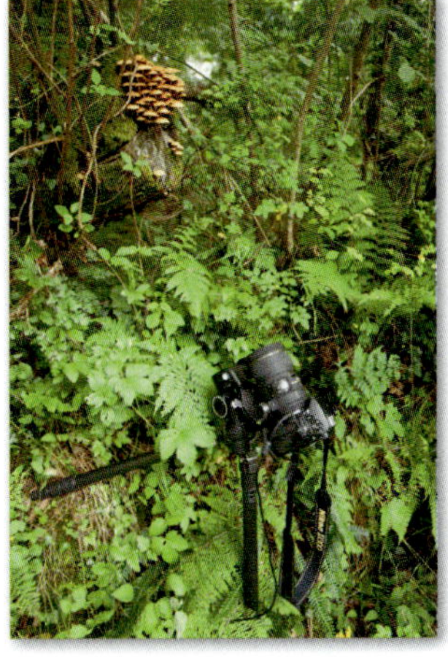

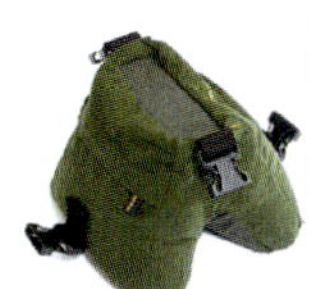

Beanbag: Beanbags offer surprisingly good support for your set-up when placed on the ground. The bag's filling naturally moulds around the camera and lens, and absorbs the majority of movement. When shooting at ground level – which nature photographers do regularly – they provide perfect camera support, being hassle-free and easy to arrange. For specialist photography beanbags, look at products provided by Wildlife Watching Supplies. A crumpled-up jumper or a fleece can also be used as a substitute beanbag.

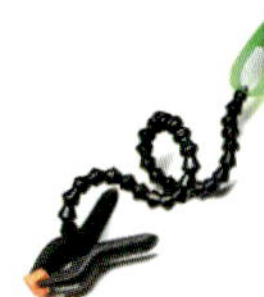

Wimberley Plamp: A Wimberley Plamp opens up many more opportunities for nature photography, allowing you to shoot things you wouldn't normally be able to. Clamp one end of the Plamp to anything from your tripod to a tree branch, and use the other to grasp your subject – it's the perfect tool for steadying delicate plants or flowers if you're shooting in windy conditions. Costing around £30, it's a great investment that you'll find a number of uses for in the studio or out on location. A must-have accessory.

Focusing on flowers

Getting the right shot takes skill – and a little knowledge of lighting, depth-of-field, viewpoint and exposure control goes a long way

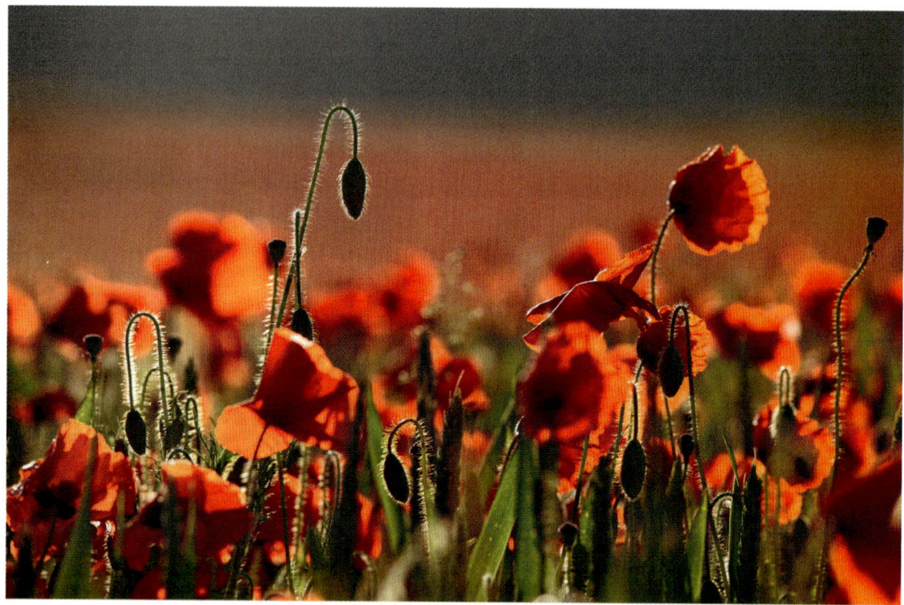

HELEN DIXON

UK's best wildflowers

ISTOCK PHOTO

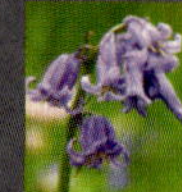

Bluebells: One of our best known and most photogenic wildflowers. They look good photographed solo or as part of a wide-angle view. They typically peak in the UK in the first week of May (see page 50 for a tutorial on how to shoot bluebells).

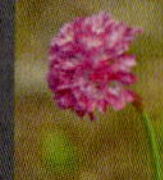

Thrift: During late April, thrift will carpet clifftops along the UK coastline. Bright and colourful, it creates ideal foreground interest for wide-angle coastal views.

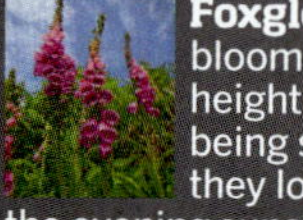

Foxgloves: These wildflowers bloom in early summer. Their height makes them well suited to being shot in vertical format and they look photogenic backlit by the evening sunshine.

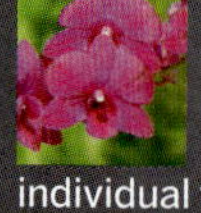

Orchids: The UK is home to around 60 species of wild orchid. They enjoy a wide variety of habitats, so research species first. Try cropping in tight to isolate individual flowers.

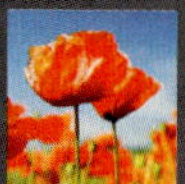

Poppies: Poppies are summer flowers, thriving on neglected ground. They can grow in large numbers, creating great swathes of colour. Try shooting from a low angle or as part of a wider view.

WILD OR CULTIVATED, plants and flowers grow in many different guises. But while they can vary greatly in size, shape, colour and appearance, most plants can be approached in much the same way photographically – for all kinds of plant life, the technique and way in which you light them is actually quite similar. Therefore, whether you visit a local park, public gardens, stately home, wild meadow, moorland, coastline or ancient woodland, our advice will ensure you return with incredible images time after time.

Depth-of-field

The aperture you select will have a large influence on how your nature images look. The size of the aperture greatly dictates the amount of depth-of-field – the zone of acceptable sharpness in front of, and behind, your point of focus. A wide aperture (small f/number) like f/4 produces a shallow depth-of-field, ideal if you wish to render background detail pleasantly out of focus. A small aperture (large f/number) like f/16 generates plenty of depth-of-field, which is best suited to images where you want the subject to be sharp throughout. It is important that you don't let your camera automatically control aperture selection, which would be the case if you were using program or shutter-priority mode. Instead, manually select apertures by using either your camera's aperture-priority or manual exposure mode.

Depth-of-field is also affected by the focal length of the lens and camera-to-subject distance, with the zone of sharpness appearing progressively shallower at longer focal lengths and at higher magnifications, as would be the case with a macro lens. Nature photographers will often have to contend with a limited depth-of-field, so focusing must be pinpoint accurate. A tripod will aid focusing, helping photographers to fine-tune and position their point of focus.

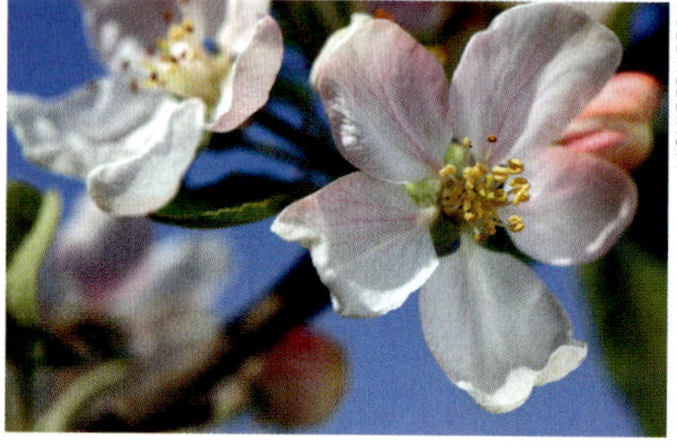

ROSS HODDINOTT

Lighting: You might think a sunny day provides the perfect conditions for nature photography, but the reverse is true. An overcast day, or shooting in the morning or evening, gives your flower shots better colour and detail as the light is softer and shouldn't cast harsh shadows.

When photographing plants – particularly in close-up – it is often better to switch to manual focusing to give you greater control. Admittedly, working with such a limited zone of sharpness can prove challenging, but you can also use it to your advantage. A shallow depth-of-field can be a useful creative and visual tool. Using a large aperture, like f/2.8 or f/4, you can isolate your subject against a diffused backdrop – perfect for picking out a single flower from all the others growing around it. Arty or even abstract-looking results are possible by intentionally using wafer-thin depth-of-field to highlight small, interesting details – like a petal or stamen. There is no secret formula as to how much or how little depth-of-field is best for nature images. The trick is to experiment. Try different focal length and aperture combinations until you achieve the level of depth-of-field that suits your particular subject. Review results regularly on the LCD monitor and zoom into your images to scrutinise sharpness and depth-of-field. If your camera has a depth-of-field preview button, use it.

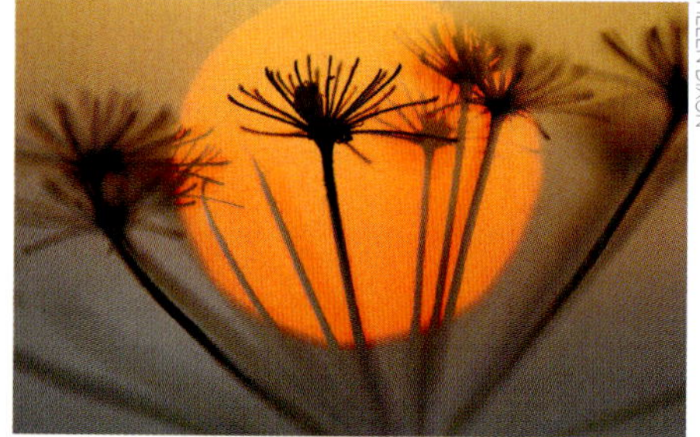

HELEN DIXON

Lighting

The light's quality and direction is a key ingredient for any nature image. Strong sunlight is often best avoided as it can be too harsh to capture the finest detail. While shadowless light might be considered dull and lifeless for some subjects, a bright but overcast day is perfect for flower or woodland photography. On days like this, the cloud cover simulates one huge softbox, producing beautiful, evenly lit results. In fact, in strong light, it can be worthwhile casting your subject in shade – using your shadow or an umbrella – to lower contrast and allow you to capture authentic colour and detail.

Generally speaking, overhead light is best avoided as it casts ugly shadows. However, you can relieve shadows by placing a reflector nearby or by using a small burst of fill-in flash. Traditionally, the best light is during early morning and evening, when it is naturally softer and warmer. The sun's low position casts longer shadows that accentuate shape and form – so it is well worth setting your alarm early and staying out late. Also, at either end of the day, the sun's low position makes it easier to shoot subjects in beautiful backlight.

Backlighting – when the principal light source is positioned behind the subject – is particularly well suited to plants and flowers. It highlights the intricacy of

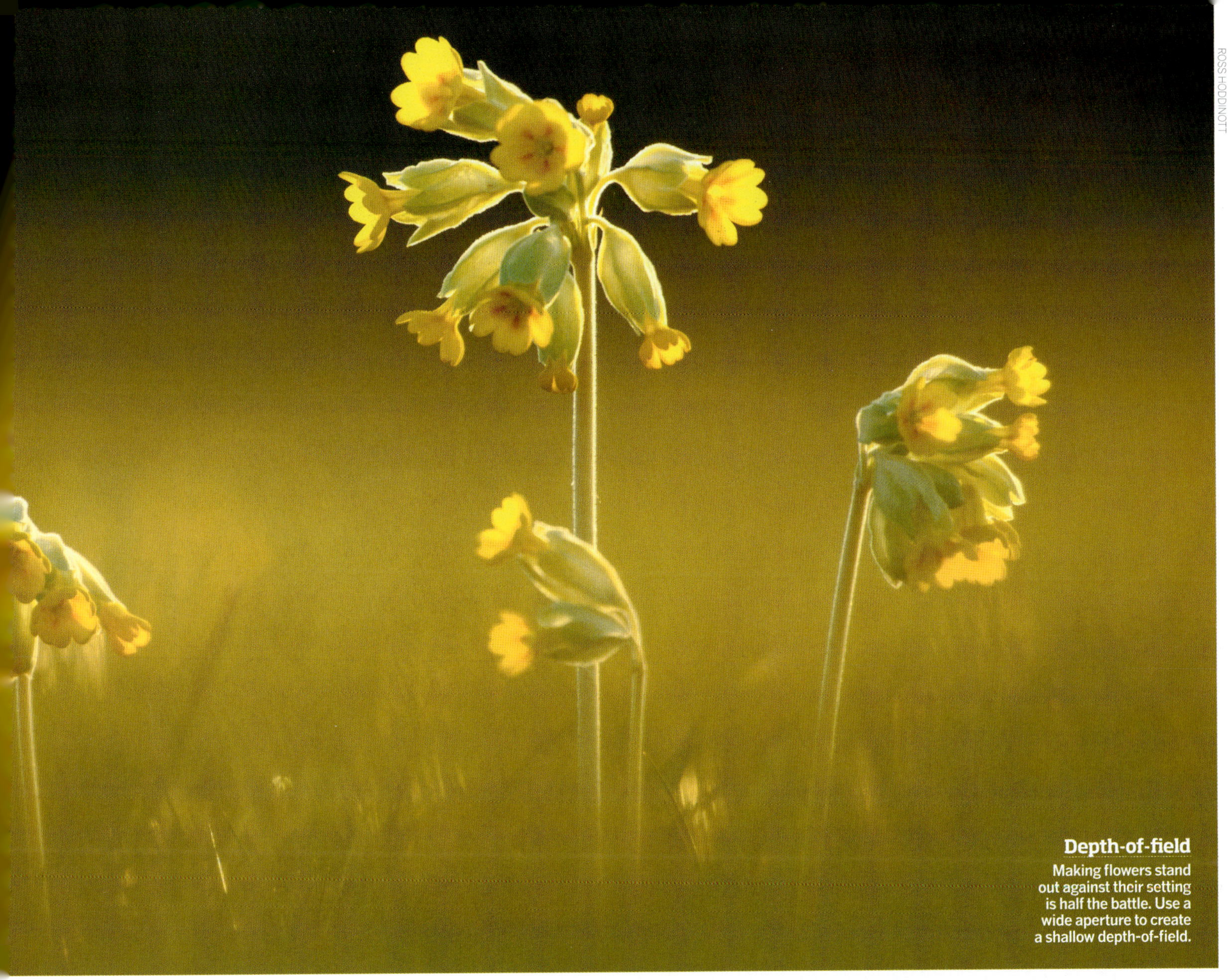

ROSS HODDINOTT

Depth-of-field

Making flowers stand out against their setting is half the battle. Use a wide aperture to create a shallow depth-of-field.

translucent subjects like leaves and petals, and places emphasis on shape, form and fine detail – like tiny hairs or prickles on flower stems. The drawback of shooting towards the light, however, is the risk of flare. Attach a lens hood or shield the front of the lens to help prevent flare and a reduction in contrast. Backlit subjects also tend to trouble metering systems, fooling the camera into underexposing results. While this is a benefit if you want to shoot silhouettes, if you don't it can spoil an image. Check your histogram regularly and increase the exposure by applying positive (+) exposure compensation.

Lastly, don't overlook flash. If you don't have a reflector to hand, flash can fill in areas of distracting shadow. Shoot at a reduced output to ensure you retain the soft qualities of natural light. Flash can create ugly hotspots on reflective foliage or petals, though, so it is worth softening flash bursts. You can use anything for this from tissue paper to a flashgun's dedicated diffuser or third-party softbox. Flash can also be useful for simplifying a subject's background, as the fall-off in light can create a pure black backdrop if surrounding vegetation is outside the range of the burst. While the effect can look slightly unnatural, it can still be a more desirable option than capturing your subject against an ugly, distracting background.

Backgrounds & 'gardening'

It is easy to underestimate just how important a subject's background is and the overall effect it has. What you exclude from the frame is often just as important as what you include. Ugly background elements like partially out-of-focus highlights and distracting bits of vegetation draw the viewer's eye away from the subject. Peer through the viewfinder and explore the subject's surroundings. Distracting elements can often be excluded easily, either by changing viewpoint or using a larger aperture to create a shallower depth-of-field. It is often possible to remove distracting vegetation by gently flattening it by hand or using scissors – nature photographers call this 'gardening'. Keep a pair of scissors in your camera bag just for this purpose. Just be careful not to damage other flowers in the process.

When a subject's background is particularly messy, small tweaks are unlikely to suffice. In situations like this, an artificial background may be best. To create your own backdrops, spray different coloured paints onto a piece of card to simulate an out-of-focus backdrop, or simply photograph foliage – with your lens defocused – before printing the results at A3 or A4 size and attaching them to stiff card to create an authentic-looking artificial background. It's times like this that you may find a Wimberley Plamp particularly helpful.

ROSS HODDINOTT

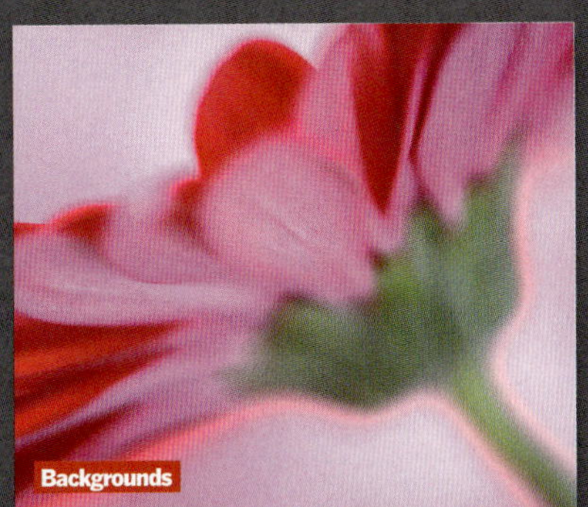

Backgrounds

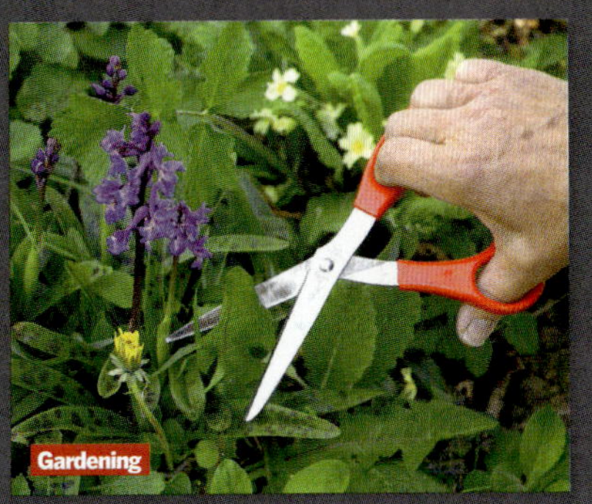

Gardening

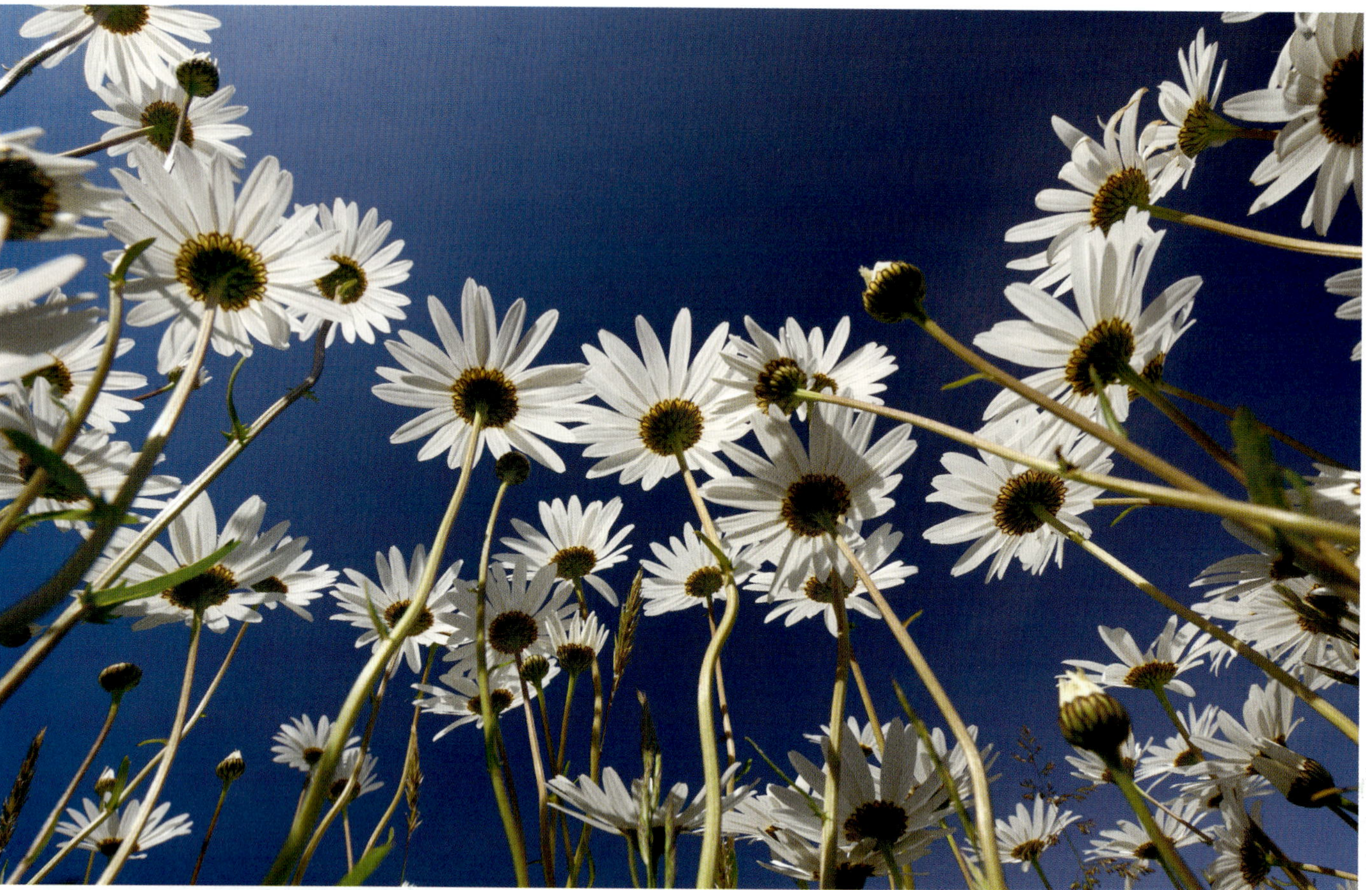
ROSS HODDINOTT

Water droplets

Tiny water droplets add scale, sparkle, depth and interest to your flora shots, so one of the best times to photograph nature is after rainfall or on dewy mornings. You can also create your own droplets using a gardener's spray or atomiser. Spray your subject from a short distance until droplets form. They will glisten attractively in the sunlight and also project a refracted image of the subject directly behind them. In fact, why not use a macro lens or close-up attachment and make the refracted image the focal point of your photo? Still conditions, a tripod and pinpoint focusing are a must. Keep depth-of-field as shallow as possible to ensure the background subject isn't too sharp. The best results will come from a careful set-up: spray a leaf or blade of grass so that droplets form, then align a colourful flower behind it – in a pot or vase – to produce the refracted image. Glycerine works better than water; its higher viscosity makes it more stable and it is less affected by evaporation. You can find it in eye drops and stain remover, or purchase food glycerine from health shops.

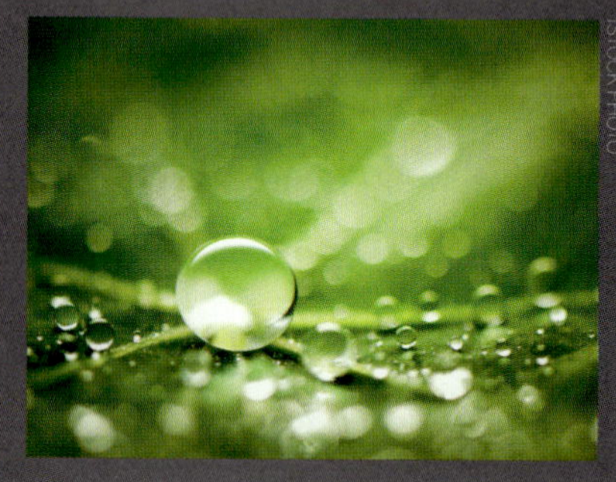
ISTOCKPHOTO

Viewpoint

A photographer's viewpoint has a significant bearing on the look of the final result, so select your shooting angle carefully. Nature photographers are often advised to shoot from a parallel angle, as this creates the most natural-looking perspective and will also help maximise the available depth-of-field. Certainly shooting at eye-level will work in many circumstances, producing engaging and intimate results. However, you should avoid getting in to the habit of always shooting at the same angle as your images will begin to look repetitive and you won't always capture the best result. Break out of your comfort zone and approach every subject with an open mind: don't be afraid to adopt a low or overhead viewpoint. An overhead shooting angle is particularly well suited to relatively flat, open flowers – like ox-eye daisies, corn marigolds, roses and gerberas. Position your camera parallel overhead to maximise depth-of-field and crop in tight to fill the frame. Placing the subject centrally can work well in this instance, creating a feeling of symmetry. An overhead angle will also prove effective when you wish to emphasise a subject's texture or detail.

The shift in perspective caused by simply lowering or raising your camera angle can have a huge impact on pictures. When photographing subjects significantly above eye-view, the subject immediately looks smaller and less imposing. In contrast, when shot from a worm's-eye view, a subject appears to loom larger. A low viewpoint can look very striking when photographing flowers or fungi. Lie on the ground and point your camera upwards, or, alternatively, hold your camera close to the ground and use a right-angle finder or an articulated LCD to compose your shots. It is best to use a wide-angle or fisheye lens for the most striking results. Plants will appear artificially tall and imposing, while flowers will stand out boldly against the sky. If the sky is clear and blue, a polarising filter can saturate its colour further and give your shots added punch.

Viewpoint: Shooting your subject from underneath gives a whole new dimension to your flower photographs, making your subjects appear taller and more imposing.

Your viewpoint has a significant impact on the strength of your composition, so always take a few moments to walk around your subject and explore the possibilities before deciding on your shooting angle.

Creative blur

Who said you have to capture images of flowers sharply or realistically? Creativity is often what leads to original, stand-out nature images. Subject or camera blur can transform an otherwise ordinary shot into a Monet-like masterpiece. If flowers or foliage are being wind-blown, emphasise that movement rather than trying to freeze it. Set your camera to shutter-priority or manual exposure mode and select a slow shutter speed in the region of ½sec to intentionally blur your subject. This works well with bright, colourful flowers like poppies or tulips. You need to achieve just the right level of motion blur: too much and the subject won't be recognisable; too little and the level of movement won't appear to be deliberate. The length of shutter you require will vary depending on the wind speed and the effect you desire. You'll need to employ trial and error – simply experiment with different shutter speeds. And, if necessary, attach a

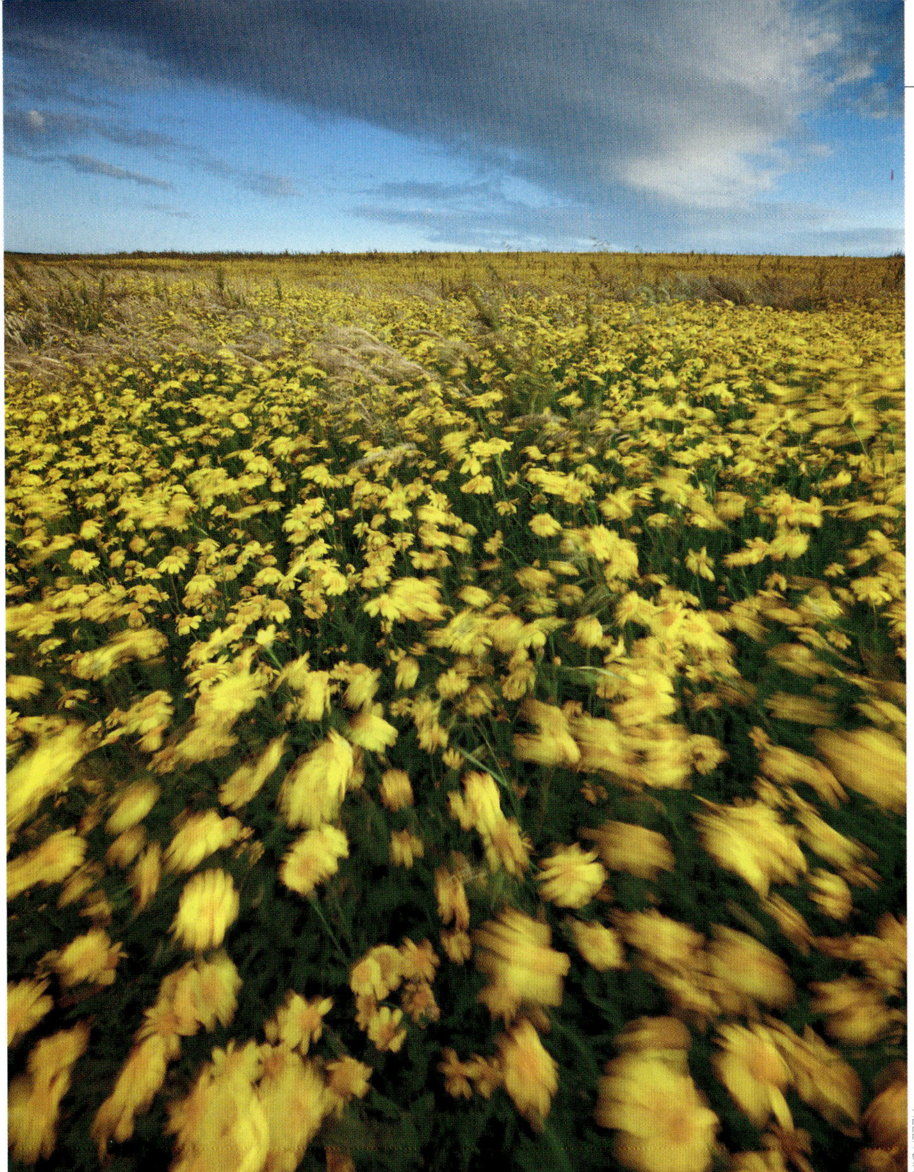
HELEN DIXON

Creative blur: This is a fantastic technique if you get the level of motion blur spot on. It's a great way to add a feeling of movement and life to your nature photography.

solid Neutral Density (ND) filter to artificially lengthen the exposure time. A polarising filter will also lengthen your shutter speed by up to two stops, as well as intensify the sky.

Another fun and effective technique is to move or 'pan' the camera during exposure. This can work in close-up or when shooting a larger expanse of flowers – bluebells, for example. Simply move the camera during exposure to create beautiful, artistic streaks of colour and texture. Try moving the camera from top to bottom, or side to side. If you are using a lens with a tripod collar, you could even try rotating the camera in a circular motion. (See our tutorial on how to create these effects on page 50).

Finally, if you are using a zoom, try a zoom burst. This is another simple technique, but results can look surreal and striking. Select a shutter speed long enough to allow you time to adjust the zoom from one extreme to the other during exposure, and zoom the lens smoothly for the best results. Again, this is a hit-and-miss technique and results won't be to everyone's taste. However, digital capture promotes this type of creative experimentation. It doesn't cost anything but time to try these things – and you might be surprised at how good the results appear.

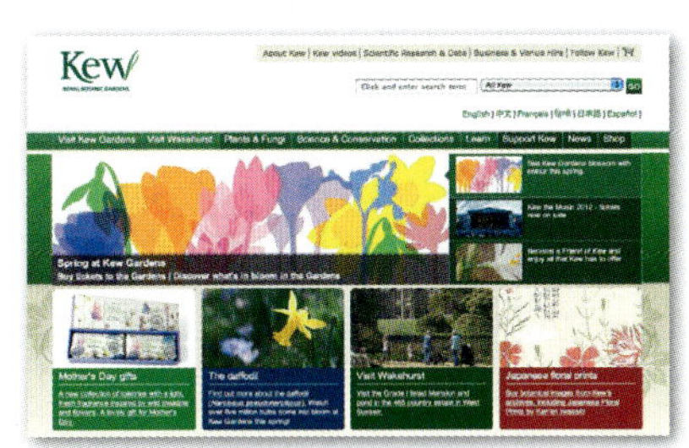

Top 5 public gardens

■ **Kew Gardens:** Kew is the UK's most famous garden. There is never a shortage of beautiful subjects to shoot. The large glasshouses ensure you can take photos whatever the weather.
www.kew.org

■ **Lost Gardens of Heligan:** Located near St Austell in Cornwall, this spectacular garden fell into decline during the First World War. Restored to its former glory in the mid-90s.
www.heligan.com

■ **Wisley:** Wisley, in Surrey, is the Royal Horticultural Society's flagship garden. With rich borders, colourful rose gardens and a state-of-the-art glasshouse home to an impressive plant collection.
www.rhs.org.uk/Gardens/Wisley

■ **Eden Project:** Eden, in Cornwall, boasts the world's largest greenhouse. Its artificial biomes are home to plants from all around the world. You will find no shortage of picture potential here.
www.edenproject.com

■ **National Botanic Garden of Wales:** The gardens, in Carmarthenshire, are home to an amazing collection of over 8,000 different plant varieties, spread across 560 acres of beautiful countryside, as well as themed gardens.
www.gardenofwales.org.uk

Double exposures

By combining one sharp image with a second out-of-focus frame, it is possible to add a beautiful, dreamlike quality to your flower images. The effect is similar to using a soft-focus filter, producing ethereal-looking results that particularly suit images of backlit flowers. The technique relies on the use of a tripod, as both images need to be identically composed so they can overlap seamlessly.

Many DSLRs allow you to create a double exposure in-camera – with the camera combining the two images to produce a single file. Select the camera's multiple exposure setting via the camera's menu (check your camera's manual for details of how to do this), select a total of two frames and then take two images: one sharply focused and the other blurry. The amount you defocus the lens will affect the strength and look of the final result. It can take several attempts to get the right effect. However, not all cameras have a multiple exposure facility and you have limited control over the look of the final result when combining images in-camera. An alternative is to blend the images during processing, combining the images in layers. Doing so allows you greater control, as you can vary the strength of each frame. It is even possible to create a soft-focus effect using just one sharply focused image: simply create a copy of the photograph and add a degree of Gaussian blur to this layer before combining it with the original, sharp frame.

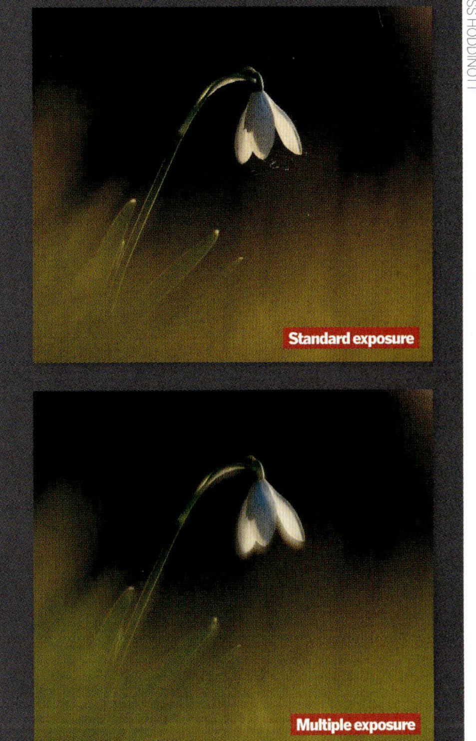
Standard exposure

Multiple exposure

ROSS HODDINOTT

Water droplets

Daniel Lezano explains how adding water droplets to a subject can give visual interest to flower images

Daniel Lezano WITH SO MUCH rain falling in the UK, it's easy to understand why producing a guide to mimicking raindrops could be deemed a little odd. Unfortunately, most of our rain falls during the colder months when garden flowers are sparse, so with fewer showers during the summer, the only way to photograph raindrops is to create them ourselves.

This can easily be done using a water spray bottle, a watering can or garden hose. If you're using one of the latter two options, be sure that the nozzle has an attachment that sprays water, rather than one that provides a heavy stream that could damage delicate plants.

There are a number of different ways that droplets can settle on garden foliage, each providing the opportunity for a different type of image. One of the most popular is capturing droplets hanging off a stem, usually in groups of two or three. This is an effective technique that has an added dimension if there are flowers nearby that can be refracted in the droplets, as seen in the adjacent image. If you want to try this technique, choose a viewpoint that takes the backdrop into account. The other favoured image is a far simpler one, but equally pleasing, and requires you to cover the surface of a leaf or petals with dozens of small droplets by spraying them with water.

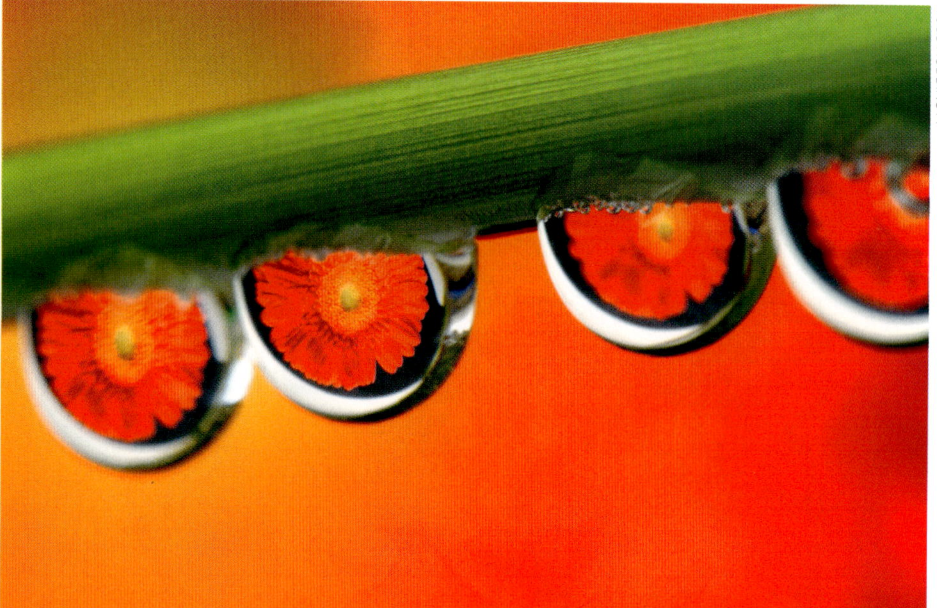
ROSS HODDINOTT

For this step-by-step, I wanted to try a technique that I'd not seen before and that was to create a single droplet that rested on a flower, rather than hanging from it. My chosen flower was a purple allium, one of my favourites to photograph due to the intricate nature of its multi-flowered bloom. As I'll be moving around trying different angles, I'm shooting hand-held and using a 100mm macro lens to help me get close. The bright sunlight means avoiding camera shake won't be a problem, but the odd breeze means I need to keep shutter speeds relatively high to avoid blur caused by the subject's movement during the exposure. I use aperture-priority mode as I want to retain close control of depth-of-field.

One final point, droplets tend to form more easily and hold their cohesion better on humid days when there is more moisture in the air. Therefore, if a summer storm is brewing, head into the garden and you'll find this technique easier to achieve than on hot, dry days.

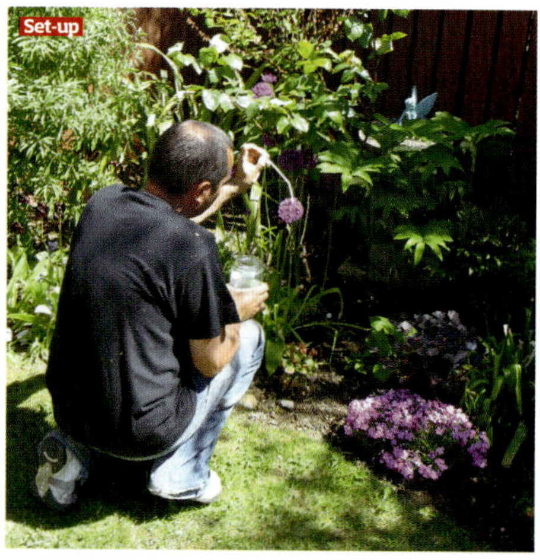
Set-up

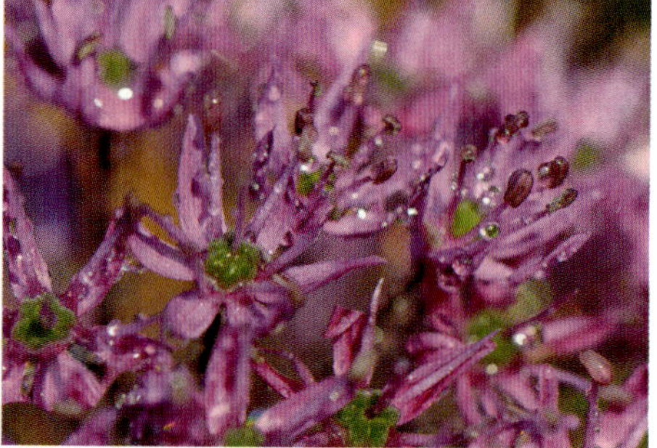
1 Apply the water Try applying a light dusting of water on the flower using a spray to see the effect it has. Unfortunately, for this technique, I find the spread of water is good, but the droplets are too small and not large enough in the frame. I need to find an alternative!

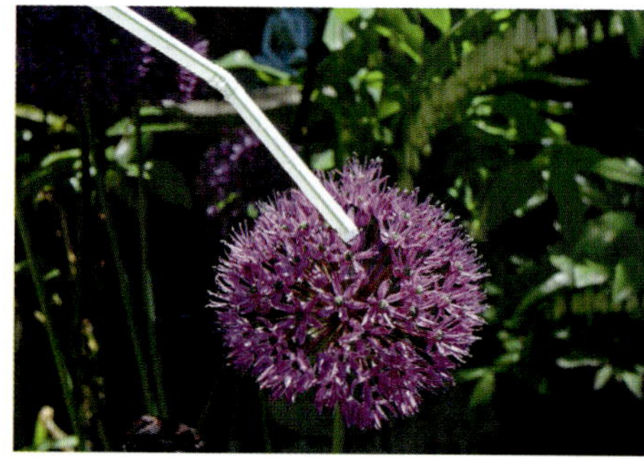
2 Experiment I try using a hose, but the result is the same. I decide I need to apply a larger drop with more control and attempt to do this using a straw dipped into a jar of water. By using my finger on the end of the straw, I do my best to control the release of water onto the allium.

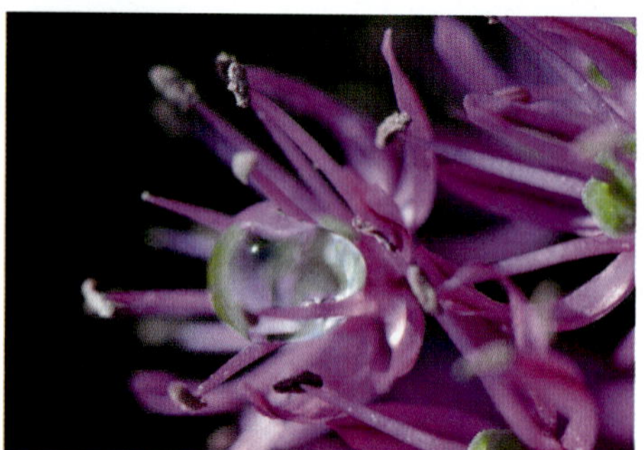
3 Keep trying It takes a few attempts, but I eventually manage to settle a large droplet of water on a flower. It's proof that with a little patience and luck, the straw method can work. This particular droplet is too large, so I shake the allium and keep trying until I manage to do better.

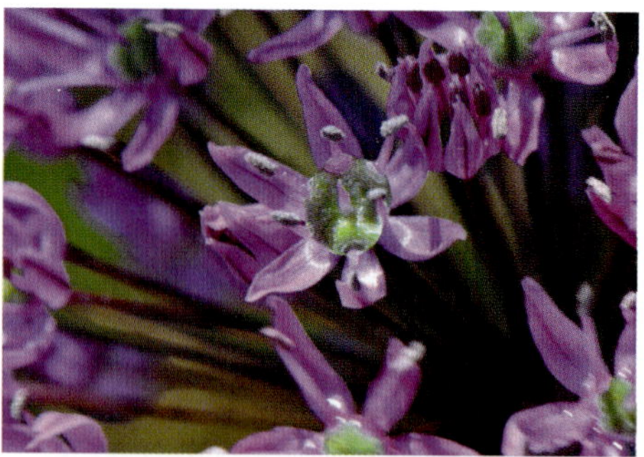
4 Find your viewpoint It takes a few more attempts, but I have a droplet that is a more suitable size. Now it's a case of trying to find a good viewpoint and the best aperture setting. I start by shooting from above, but the result is flat, so I shift my position and look for alternatives.

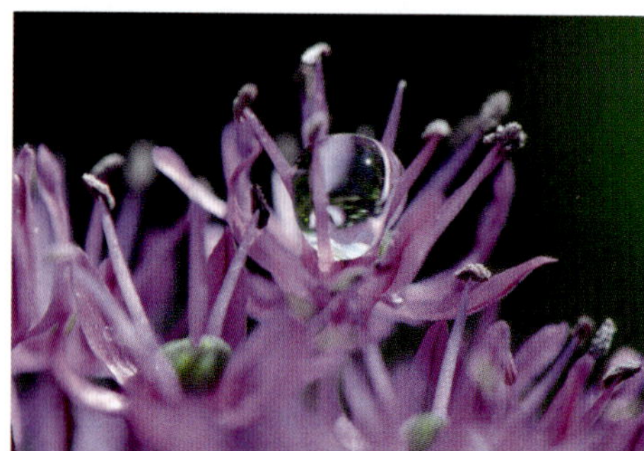
5 Get eye-level with the subject Adopting a lower viewpoint gives the image more three-dimensionality and the droplet is clearly visible due to the shallow depth-of-field. However, the out-of-focus foreground is distracting and the dark backdrop is unattractive.

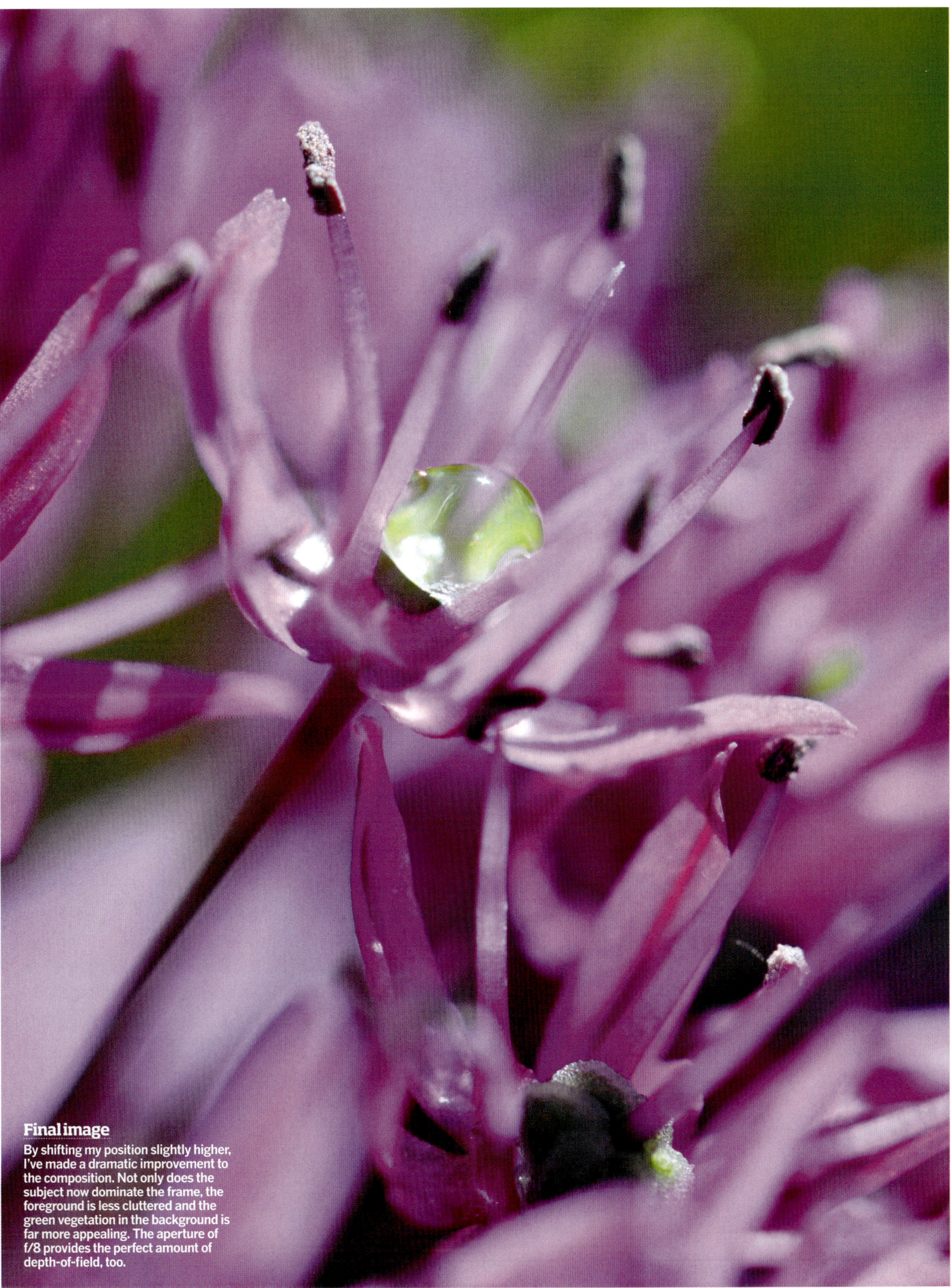

Final image

By shifting my position slightly higher, I've made a dramatic improvement to the composition. Not only does the subject now dominate the frame, the foreground is less cluttered and the green vegetation in the background is far more appealing. The aperture of f/8 provides the perfect amount of depth-of-field, too.

Fungi

Usually hidden from view in dark, moist places, come the autumn, fungi make for attractive results

FUNGI ARE NOT GENERALLY considered very attractive or glamorous subjects – particularly when compared to colourful flowers and blossom. Don't overlook the picture potential of mushrooms and toadstools, though – they are surprisingly photogenic. They've existed for millions of years, evolving into an extraordinary variety of types, which range hugely in shape, colour and form – from waxcaps, stinkhorns, puffballs, death caps to shaggy ink caps. Autumn is the best time of year to find and shoot fungi, emerging all over the UK in parks, woodlands and on garden lawns. If you haven't tried photographing fungi before, it is about time you did…

Finding fungi

There are many different types of fungi, all requiring different growing conditions and habitats. Most prefer ancient deciduous woodland and enjoy rotting tree matter. From September through to mid-November, visit woodland near where you live and look at the base of trees, amongst fallen branches, dense leaf deposits and decaying stumps. Some are relatively large, grow in big clumps and will prove easy to spot; while others will be small and well camouflaged. Look up as well as down – you will find some growing above you on overhanging branches and on tree trunks, but still within range of a telephoto. Fungi can emerge suddenly, without warning, and disappear again just as quickly. Therefore, it is worthwhile visiting the same locations regularly – what you find there will change from day to day.

Photographing fungi

Much of the practical and creative technique already discussed in this section can be applied to fungi; the equipment required is also the same. However, many species of fungi enjoy dark, damp environments, so natural light is often more restricted. Inevitably, the gills and stem receive less light then the mushroom's cap, so fill-flash or reflected light is normally required. One of the biggest advantages of using a reflector over flash is that you can see its effects instantly and you can quickly and easily change the angle or intensity of the bounced light. A sheet of white card, mirror or tin foil can also be used to reflect light onto subjects. Unlike other plant life, fungus is rarely affected by wind movement, being sturdy and often growing in the shelter of trees. Therefore, as long as you are using a tripod, the length of shutter speed doesn't really matter. Even if exposure time reaches several seconds long, don't worry. However, push the feet of your tripod firmly into the mud/ground to guarantee stability. With autumn comes dirt and damp in woodland, so use a ground sheet to keep you and your kit clean and dry. A right-angle finder, or a camera with a vari-angle LCD, will greatly assist focusing and composition when shooting fungi at ground level.

In terms of composition, simplicity often works best. Don't overcomplicate things by trying to include too much in the frame – isolating one or two mushrooms can have more impact than if you photograph a large group. You will normally want to capture the beauty and texture of the gills underneath the cap, so a low shooting angle is often the best choice. You don't even have to include the entire subject. Filling the frame will highlight detail, colour and texture.

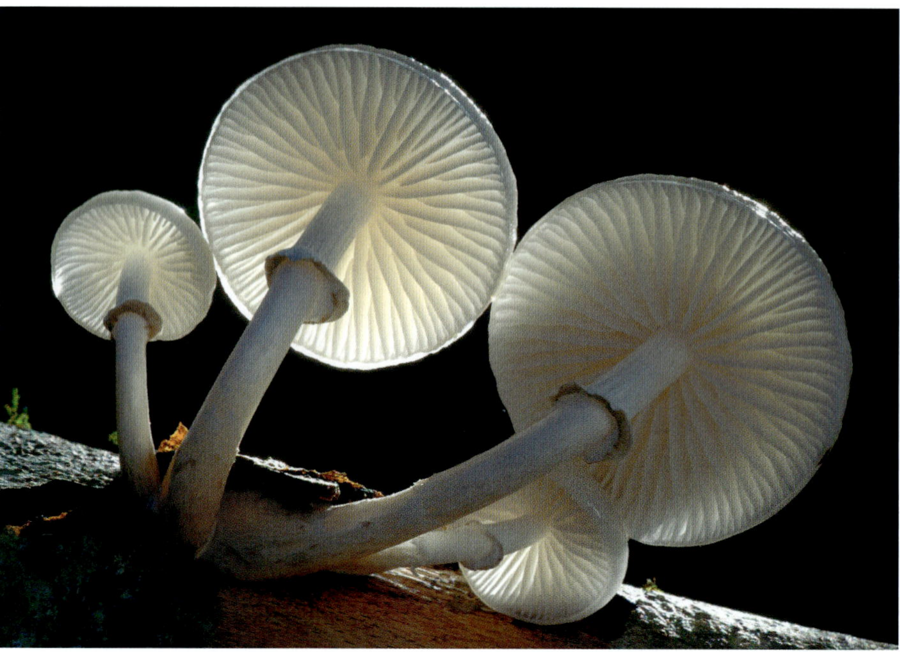

ALL IMAGES: ROSS HODDINOTT

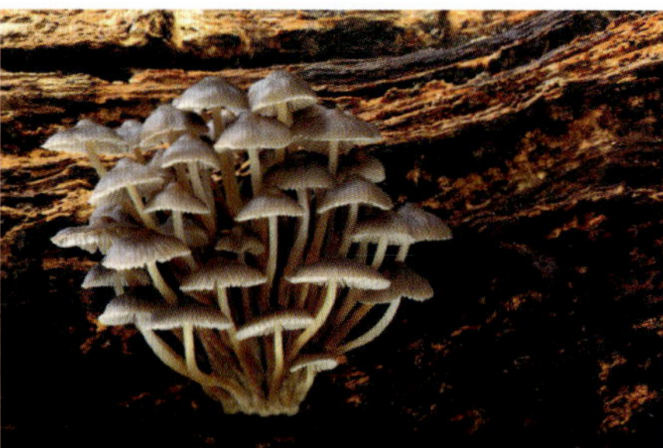

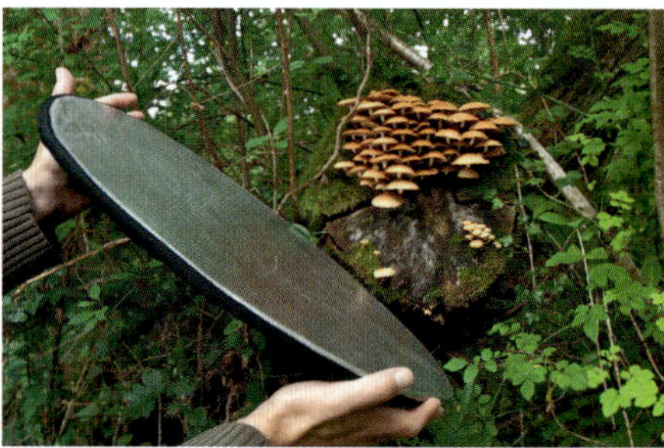

Choose your specimen: **Fungi are hugely photogenic, and if conditions are right, you'll be spoilt for choice with subjects. Find a pristine specimen for the best picture potential whether it's for a close-up or for group shots.**

Fungi hotspots

The New Forest, Hampshire, is arguably the best place for finding and photographing fungi in the UK. With around 2,700 types recorded, it is well worth a visit this autumn. Remember to never pick or damage subjects, though. Visit: www.newforestnpa.gov.uk

Shoot pristine subjects

When photographing plant life, only shoot pristine subjects. In close-up, even the slightest imperfection will be greatly exaggerated, proving distracting in the final image and requiring you to perhaps do unnecessary work in post-production. Study your subjects carefully before reaching for your camera. Fungi will quickly go past their best as they can be easily damaged by the weather or insects, such as slugs and snails, so hunt out the best specimens. Also, as fungus often grows up through decaying wood and leaf matter, subjects can be smothered in specks of dirt and vegetation: we advise using a blower brush or a soft-bristled paint brush to carefully remove any dirt. Doing so will save you a lot of time 'tidying up' the image in Photoshop, using the Clone Tool or Healing Brush.

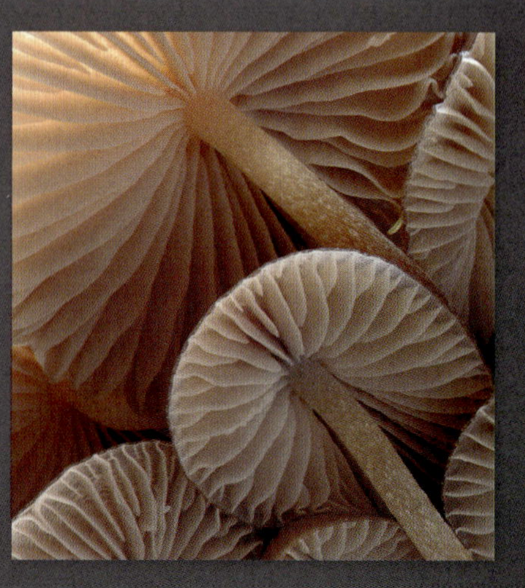

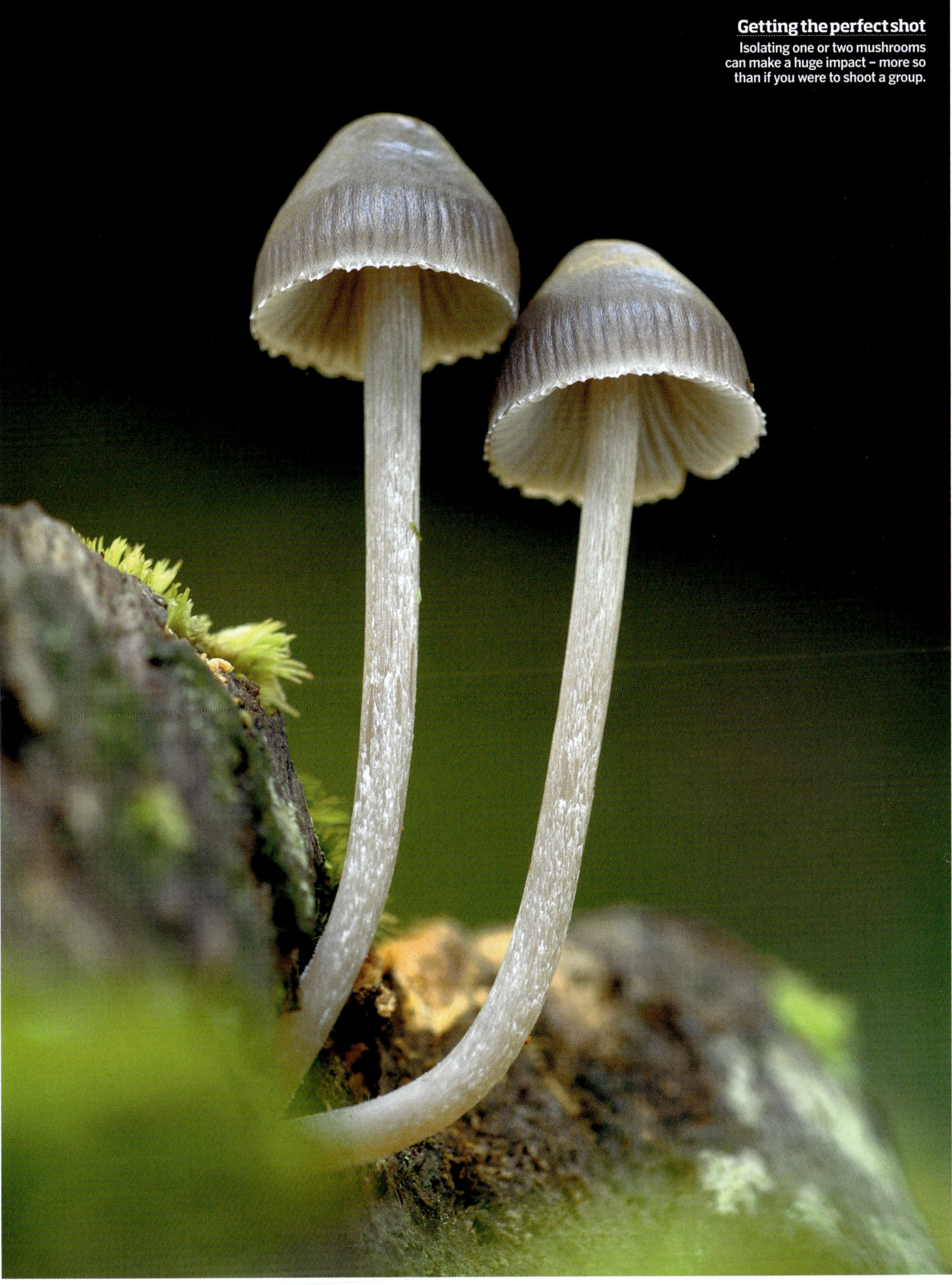

Getting the perfect shot
Isolating one or two mushrooms can make a huge impact – more so than if you were to shoot a group.

Exploit the beauty of bluebells

Plan to take a day or two off and head to a bluebell wood to try out one of several creative techniques to capture striking images

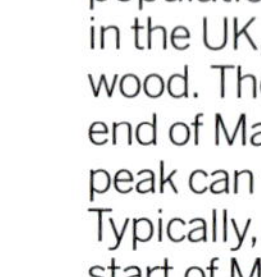

THE UK IS THE BEST PLACE in the world to photograph common bluebells – it is estimated that around 70% of their entire population is found here. So, wherever you live in the UK, you will not be far from a bluebell wood. They flower between mid-April and the end of May, but the time when they are at their peak can vary slightly from year to year. Typically, they are most photogenic at the start of May, but it is worthwhile making an early visit just to assess what stage they are at – doing so ensures you time your visit correctly and don't miss them at their best.

Weather and timing are key considerations. There is no bad weather for photographing bluebells, but a bright overcast day can often yield superb results. As the light is low in contrast, it makes it easier to achieve the correct exposure. The quality of light is soft and muted, and the colours of woodland flowers and fresh green foliage look naturally more saturated. Early morning and late evening can produce magical light for woodland photography, too. The light is warmer and the long shadows add depth to your shots. In bright overhead sunshine, the sun-dappled woodland floor can look attractive to the eye, but the level of contrast can often exceed the capabilities of your sensor's dynamic range. With so much contrast, achieving a good exposure can be difficult, if not impossible – so it is often better to avoid shooting in midday sun. It is also a good idea to visit on a still day, when bluebells remain still during exposure.

When visiting woodland with large swathes of bluebells, identifying 'the shot' can prove tricky as your choice of composition is almost limitless. To ensure you take great images, a creative eye is vital. Keep composition simple. Avoid clutter, like fallen branches, and look for interesting woodland detail that you can make a feature of, like a mossy stump or large ferns. Narrow paths winding into the distance can be used to draw the viewer's eye into shot.

Lens choice is important so take a range of focal lengths with you. Wide-angles are great for capturing vast carpets of flowers, but often a mid-telephoto – in the region of 50-100mm – is best suited to photographing bluebells. A short telephoto will foreshorten perspective, creating the impression that the carpet of flowers is denser than it is. This type of focal length is also good if you wish to focus attention on a particularly photogenic group of trees. A macro lens, or the long end of a telezoom, is ideal to isolate individual flowers.

In overcast light, achieving the right exposure is relatively straightforward. Your camera's multi-zone meter shouldn't have any problems. In early morning or late evening light, it is often preferable to shoot in the direction of the light, so that it 'bleeds' through foliage. However, when shooting towards the light, metering can be deceived and results underexposed. Keep an eye on the histogram and apply exposure compensation if required.

Shutter speeds are often slow in the shade of woodland, so a tripod is essential. For sweeping, wide-angled images of woodland interiors, opt for a small aperture, like f/13. This creates a large depth-of-field which will render everything from front-to-back in focus. However, a shallow depth-of-field will suit some scenes better. For example, isolate a single plant or attractive fern and select a wide aperture like f/4 or f/5.6 to render background flowers as an attractive out-of-focus blue haze.

UK's best bluebell woodland

Search online for woods in your area. Below are a few, just to get you started.

- **Micheldever Wood, nr Winchester**
  OS Grid Reference: SU530363
  Visit: *www.forestry.gov.uk*
- **West Woods, nr Marlborough**
  OS Grid Reference: SU163667
  Visit: *www.forestry.gov.uk*
- **Yoxall Lodge, nr Burton upon Trent**
  OS Grid Reference: SK1521
  Visit: *www.bluebellwoodsofyoxalllodge.com*

For further information on bluebell woods, visit: *www.woodlandtrust.org.uk*

Other woodland flowers

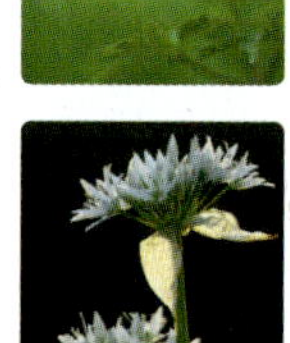

Wood anemone: Widespread and locally common woodland perennial, often growing in large clumps. Its white flowers are beautiful and delicate. Best shot individually in close-up or in context with its woodland surroundings using a wide-angle.

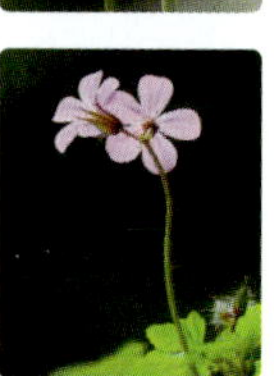

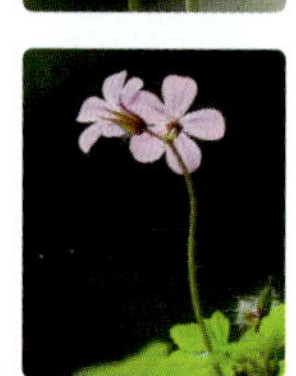

Ramsons: Often growing among or near bluebells. They smell strongly of garlic and can grow in vast numbers in damp woodland. Very attractive backlit or in frame-filling close-up. Attach a polarising filter to saturate the colour of the leaves.

Herb Robert: Common and widespread, its photogenic pink flowers appear from April onwards. Using a macro lens or close-up filter will reveal its delicate beauty. A small silver/white reflector bounces natural light and relieves harsh shadows.

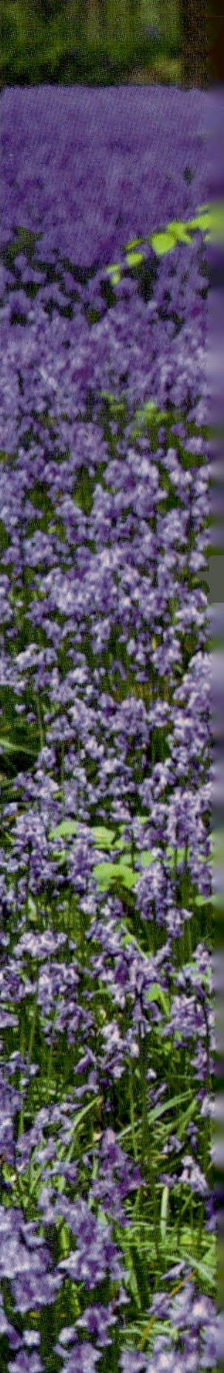

Step-by-step to bluebell magic

Bluebells are unquestionably beautiful, but that is not to say they are easy to photograph. Being such a popular, well-photographed subject makes it even harder to produce original, creative images. Ross Hoddinott provides inspiration by visiting his local woodland in order to see what variety of bluebell picture he could shoot. His expert advice will help you know what to look for, techniques to try, and what to avoid when shooting bluebells.

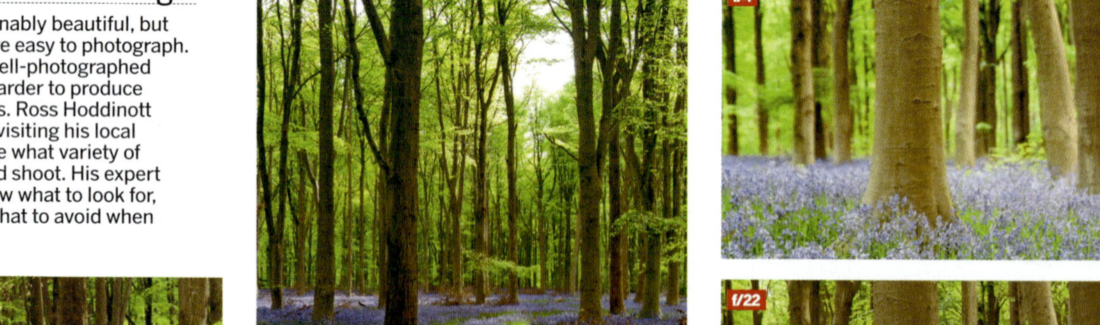

1 Avoid clutter and distraction When I took this image, I was seduced by the vibrancy and colour of the bluebells and overlooked the fallen branches and cluttered woodland floor. Keep compositions clean and simple.

2 Look for compositional aids A winding path or mossy stump can make for a strong lead-in line. This will give your images a three-dimensional feel. Without this, images may sometimes lack depth and interest.

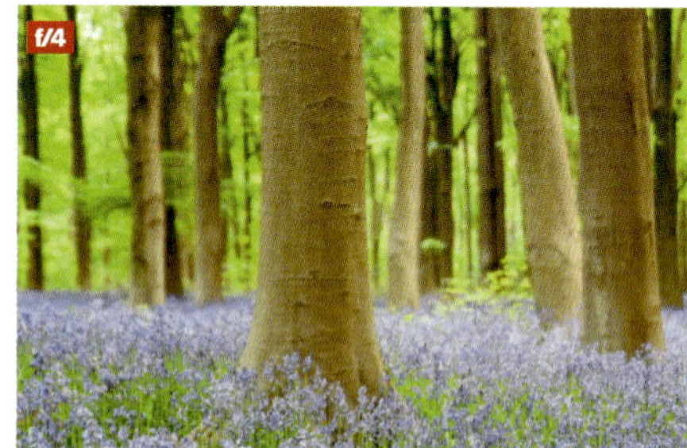

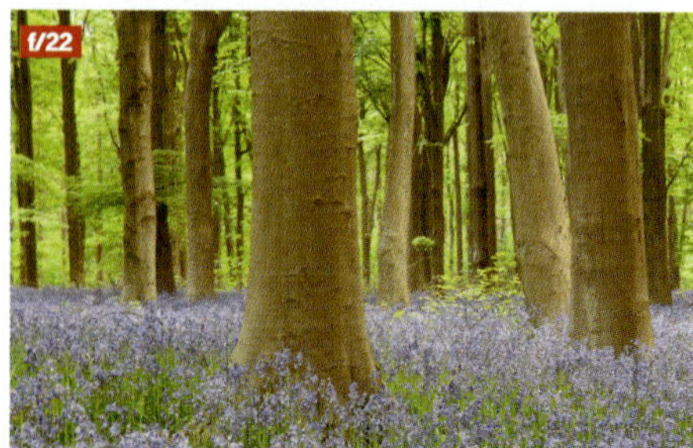

3 Experiment with depth-of-field Shallow focus can work well when photographing woodland subjects. Select a wide aperture to diffuse background detail. This will place emphasis on your point of focus.

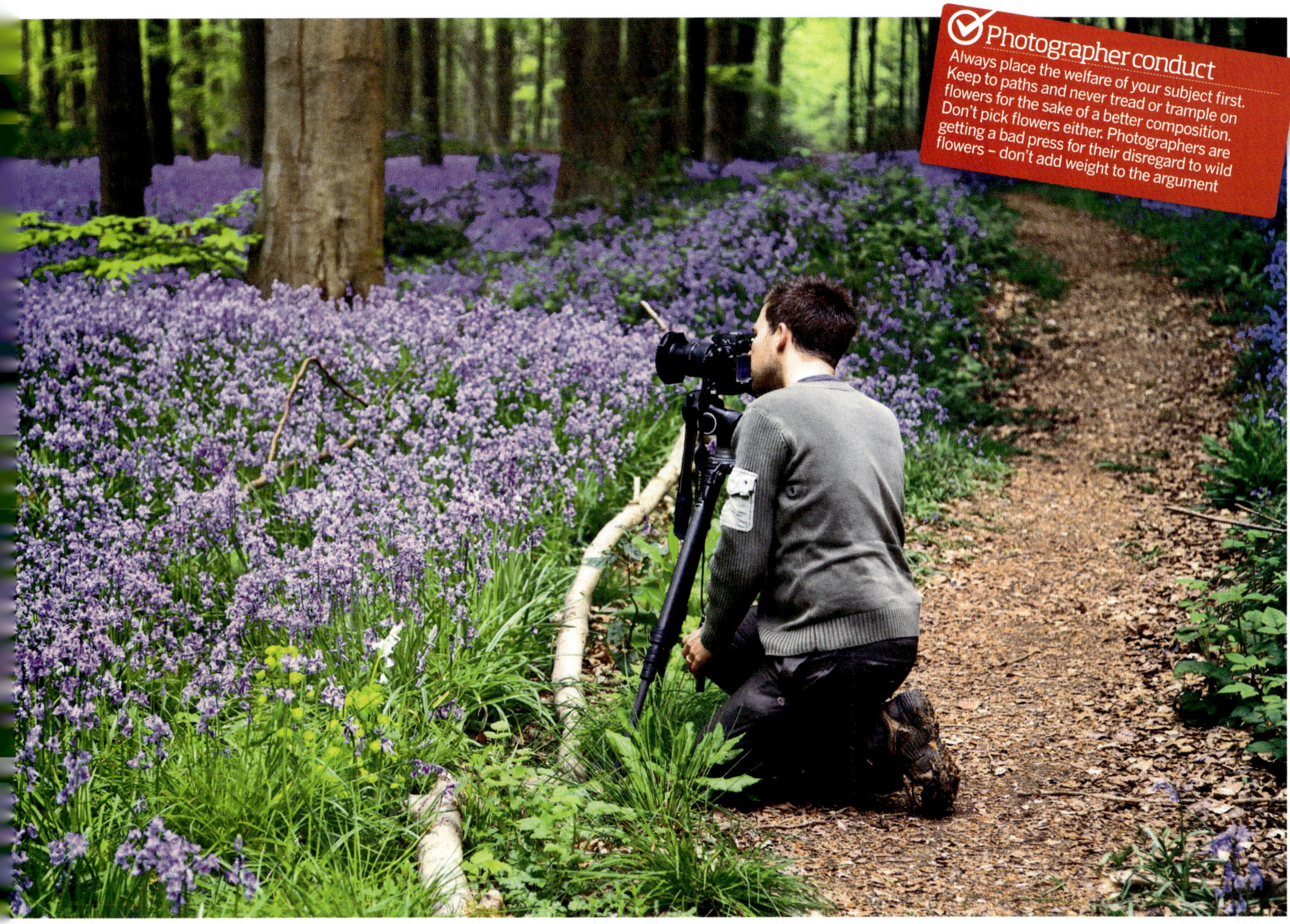

Photographer conduct

Always place the welfare of your subject first. Keep to paths and never tread or trample on flowers for the sake of a better composition. Don't pick flowers either. Photographers are getting a bad press for their disregard to wild flowers – don't add weight to the argument

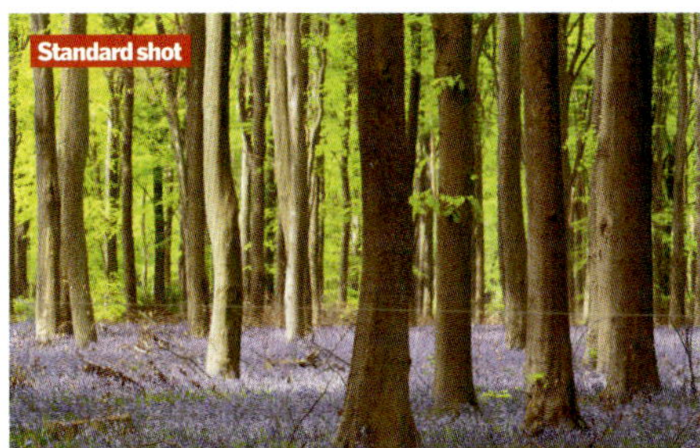

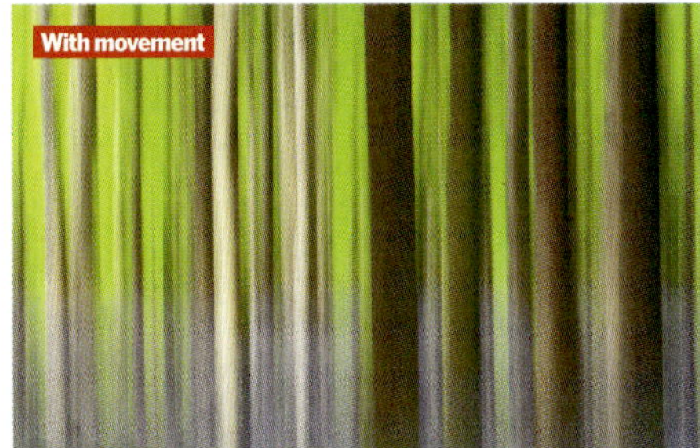

4 Be creative Set a shutter speed of one second and move the camera up and down during the exposure to artistically blur the trees. It is a hit-and-miss technique and may take many attempts to get a result that you like.

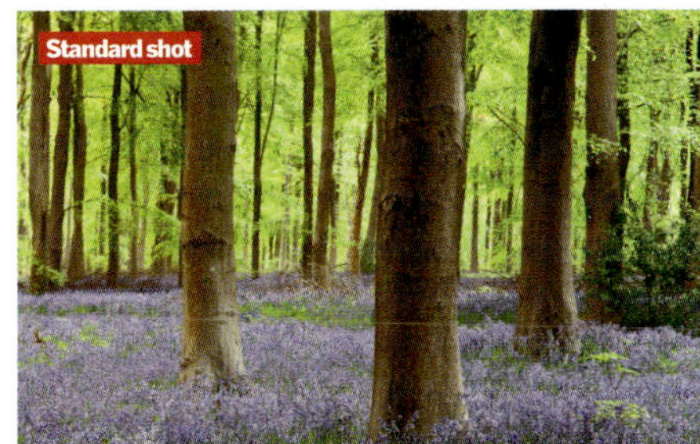

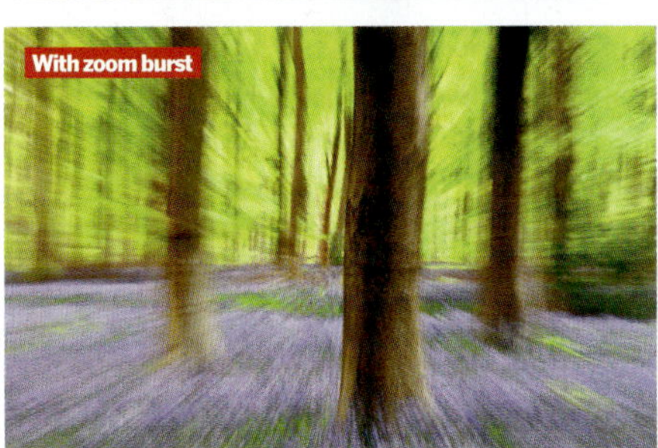

5 Try a zoom burst This is another easy, creative technique. Compose your shot using either the zoom's shortest or longest end. Then, during exposure, smoothly adjust the zoom ring to the opposite end of the lens's range.

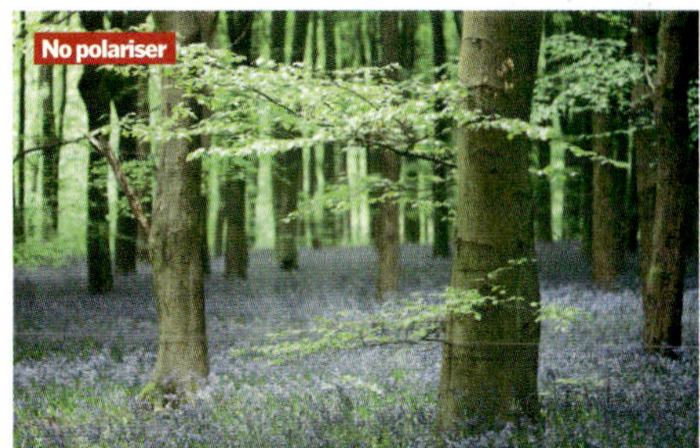

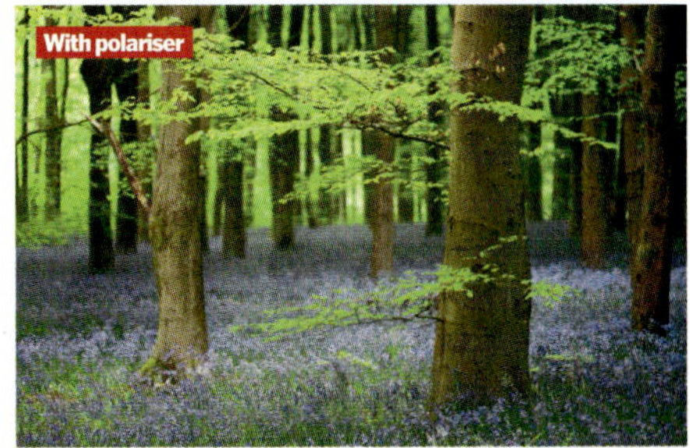

6 Use a polarising filter A polariser will reduce the glare and reflections from foliage and flowers. The filter helps restore natural colour saturation and give woodland images added impact. Note it will lengthen your exposure.

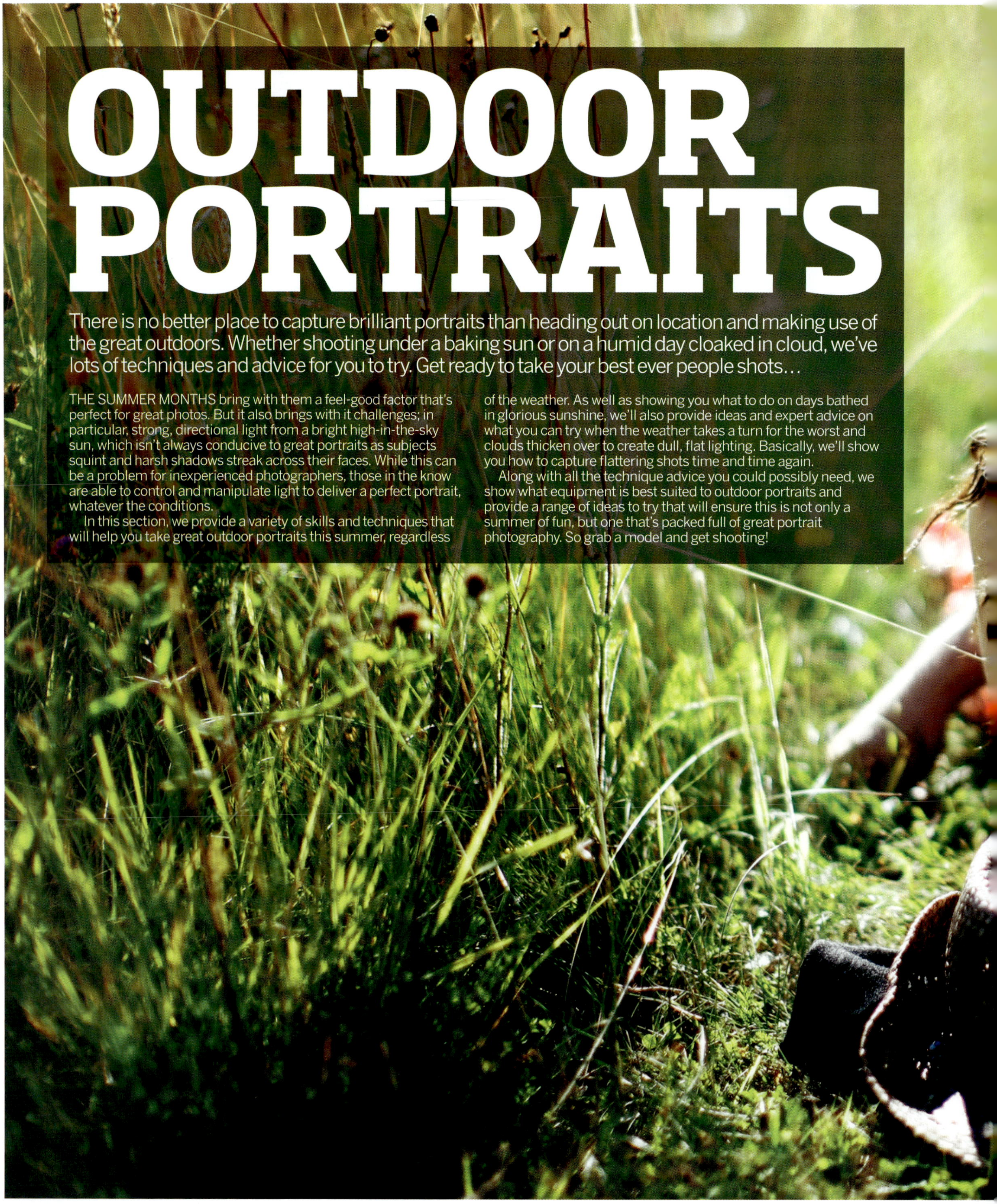

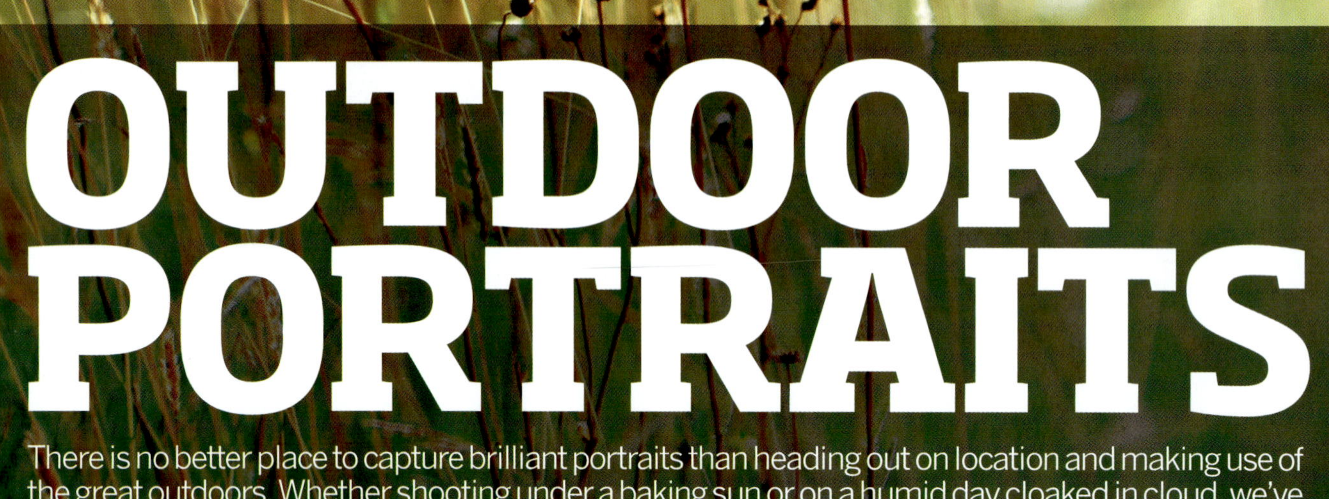

OUTDOOR PORTRAITS

There is no better place to capture brilliant portraits than heading out on location and making use of the great outdoors. Whether shooting under a baking sun or on a humid day cloaked in cloud, we've lots of techniques and advice for you to try. Get ready to take your best ever people shots…

THE SUMMER MONTHS bring with them a feel-good factor that's perfect for great photos. But it also brings with it challenges; in particular, strong, directional light from a bright high-in-the-sky sun, which isn't always conducive to great portraits as subjects squint and harsh shadows streak across their faces. While this can be a problem for inexperienced photographers, those in the know are able to control and manipulate light to deliver a perfect portrait, whatever the conditions.

In this section, we provide a variety of skills and techniques that will help you take great outdoor portraits this summer, regardless of the weather. As well as showing you what to do on days bathed in glorious sunshine, we'll also provide ideas and expert advice on what you can try when the weather takes a turn for the worst and clouds thicken over to create dull, flat lighting. Basically, we'll show you how to capture flattering shots time and time again.

Along with all the technique advice you could possibly need, we show what equipment is best suited to outdoor portraits and provide a range of ideas to try that will ensure this is not only a summer of fun, but one that's packed full of great portrait photography. So grab a model and get shooting!

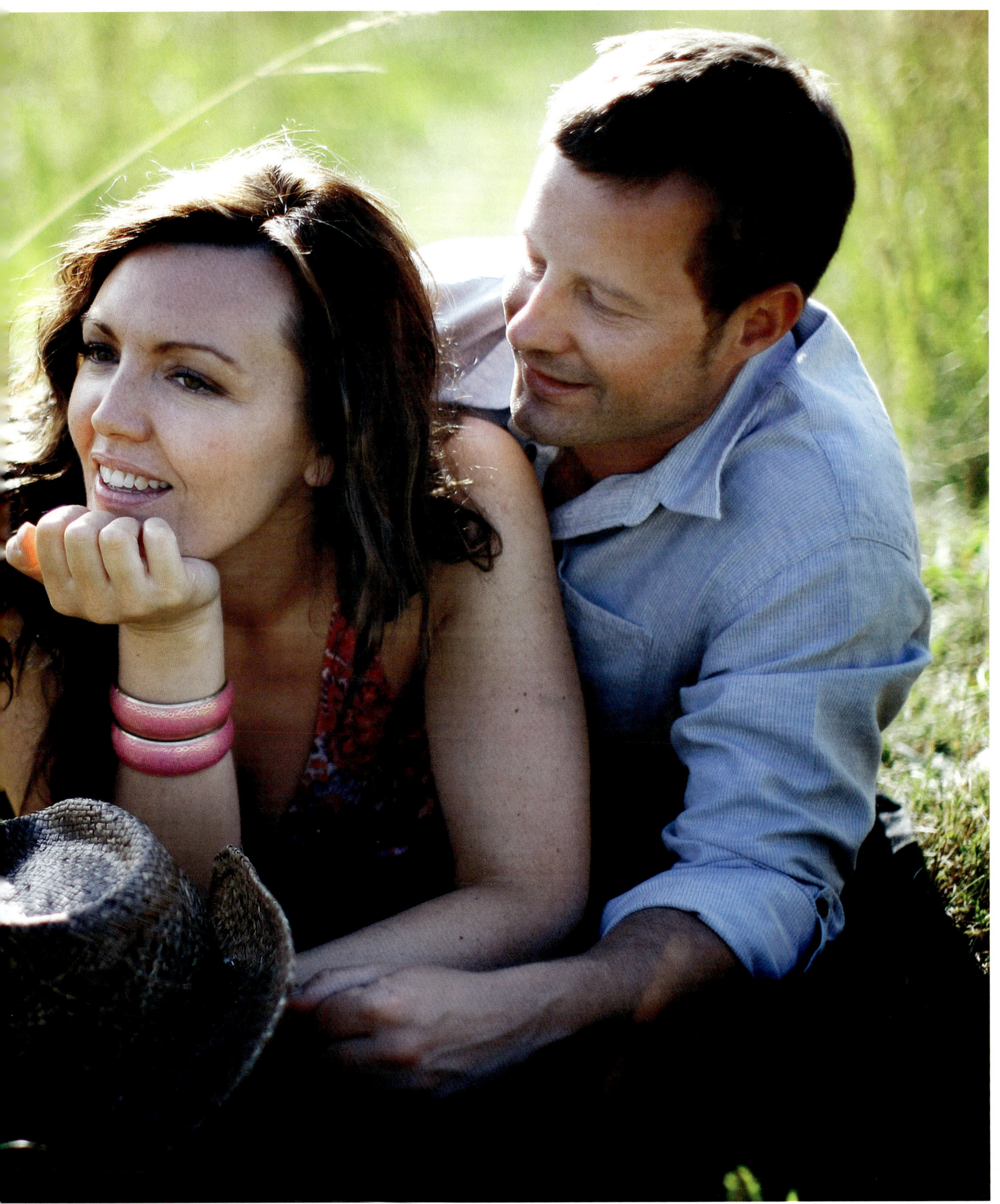

Are you ready to step outside?

Shooting on location opens up a whole world of portrait possibilities and there is no better time than summer for you to take great shots

OUTDOOR PORTRAITS, in particular those shot in summer, are all about capturing colour, feelings and memories. It's one of the best times of year for bright sunshine, romantic golden sunsets, lush landscapes and lots of outdoor fun for the whole family; a real feel-good season. Photographically, however, it's one of the hardest to work in if you don't know what you're doing. So when you get it right, it's certainly the most rewarding.

Most people thinking of summer conjure up images of blue skies and sunny days, happy faces and vivid colours. But for those of us who live in the UK, or countries with a similar climate, weather like this is cherished as its arrival is few and far between. On the plus side, though, this means we don't often have to deal with harsh and direct sunlight, which can be tricky to control, but it also means few of us know how to handle it when the sun does appear. Get it wrong and your subject could be overexposed, silhouetted or covered in harsh shadows, all of which can be controlled and corrected with a little know-how.

Success at summer portraits depends not just on how you control strong natural light through diffusers, reflectors, shade and camera settings, but how you manipulate the light creatively, evaluate a scene and compose the shots to make use of colour and your subjects' personalities. Different times of day bring a variety of challenges and shooting options. If the sun is high in the sky, usually between noon and 3pm, then look to use a diffuser or shoot in the shade, and use a reflector to bounce light onto your subject. But in the early or late hours of the day, when the sun is lower in the sky, the light is often softer and golden and far more flattering for portraits. Try to avoid placing the light directly behind your subject, instead move them so it's at an angle to create some shadows. Backlighting can cause exposure problems if you keep your camera set to multi-zone metering. Unless you want to create a silhouette against a golden sky, spot-meter from the subject's face, or take a reading from a mid-tone.

Even if you're confronted with an overcast day, the summer is generally warm and beckons photographers to shoot outdoors. Look for parks and fields with high grass or colourful flowers for beautiful foreground and backdrops. The grass will also offer protection for your subject from the low sun if you have them lie on the ground. Why not grab the whole family and take a trip to the beach? Just look to set up base near a pier so that you have access to shade if you need it. Sand dunes are great for adding depth, while forests have stunning potential for backlighting. But you needn't go far as a back garden has potential: garages and sheds are fantastic, too. Sit your subject just inside a doorway, underexpose by at least one stop, and you'll find they're beautifully lit by diffused sunlight while the shaded background is rendered black.

Colour is crucial if you want to capture that summertime feel, so look for backdrops such as a blue door, red gate or textured wall. If your environment lacks colour then it's up to you to inject some by having your subject wear colourful clothing. Coordinate clothing for family shots, have them all wear the same colour or at least block colours. Avoid patterns at all costs as it will look too busy. Finally, keep the football shirts as a treat for the last few frames and don't bring them out before then!

The biggest challenge with summer portraits is balancing shadows and working with kids, as all they want to do is run and play. It's about getting the balance between keeping the experience for your subject and getting the shots you want. Sometimes you need to kick a football or build sandcastles for a while before you can expect them to cooperate. But the key is to make sure they play in the best light so you can fire off some frames while they are having fun.

The hardest thing about photographing adults, on the other hand, is evoking joy. To get a response, you may find you need to coax them out of what's comfortable; for instance, have them roll up their trousers and paddle in water. What you give to the subject is what you get back from them: show enthusiasm, energy and push them outside their comfort zone. So what are you waiting for? Grab your camera kit and head outdoors to capture memories worth treasuring.

Top kit for outdoor portraits

Lenses: A short telephoto zoom like the 50-200mm is the ideal lens, as its versatile focal length is perfect for filling the frame. Another option is a 50mm f/1.8, a budget lens with an incredibly fast maximum aperture that is ideal for throwing the background out of focus.

Lighting aids: A reflector is a must. A silver/white is a great first choice, but also consider a sunfire or gold option. A 5-in-1 kit offers the most versatility. A diffuser is very handy when you're shooting in strong daylight. See our kit section for our favourite reflector choices.

Flashgun: Flash isn't just for low light – it's a creative tool that can be used on bright days, not only for fill-in, but to also create mood when shooting portraits during broody summer storms, as well as when used wirelessly behind a subject to create a hairlight.

Don't forget the flash!

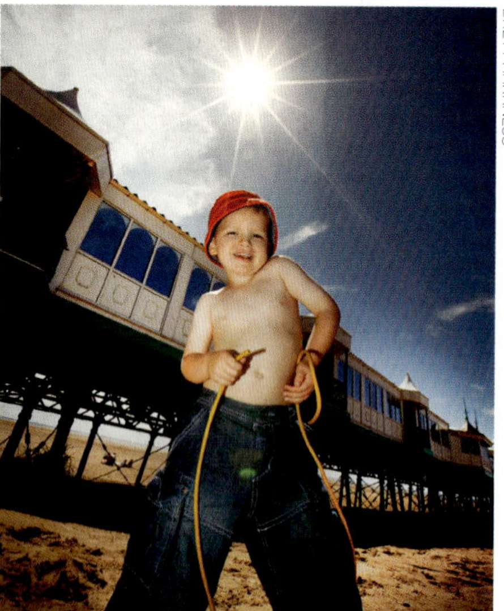

BRETT HARKNESS

Just because you are in bright sunshine, don't pack away your flashgun. Mix daylight with flash to help fill in any shadows created by strong, directional daylight and add dynamism to images. It's an advanced technique, but if you practise (try a couple of shots at the end of one of your outdoor portrait shoots), you'll find it opens up a whole range of possibilities. Using flash correctly, you can overpower the ambient light to give your subject punch against a darkened sky. Give it a go by setting your flashgun to TTL metering, then reduce your camera's exposure by dialling in -1 or -2 stops of negative exposure compensation. You'll find that the flash will expose your subject correctly, while your camera will underexpose the rest of the scene, creating a moody sky.

Setting up your camera for outdoor portraits

1) Exposure mode: Aperture-priority allows you to control depth-of-field and is our favoured choice.

2) Metering: Multi-zone metering should be suitable for most lighting, but consider switching to spot or partial and using the AE-Lock facility in tricky lighting conditions.

3) White Balance: Auto White Balance is fine, but ideally switch to the preset to match the lighting.

4) ISO rating: In bright light, use ISO 100 or 200, but raise to ISO 400 or 800 in overcast conditions.

5) Focusing: Use centre-point AF set to single-shot and focus on the eyes.

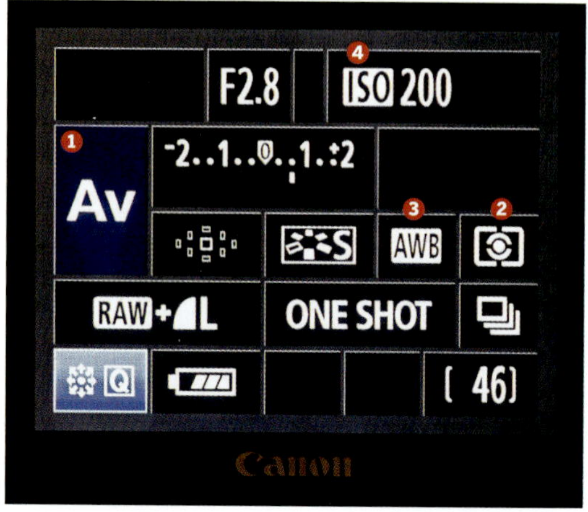

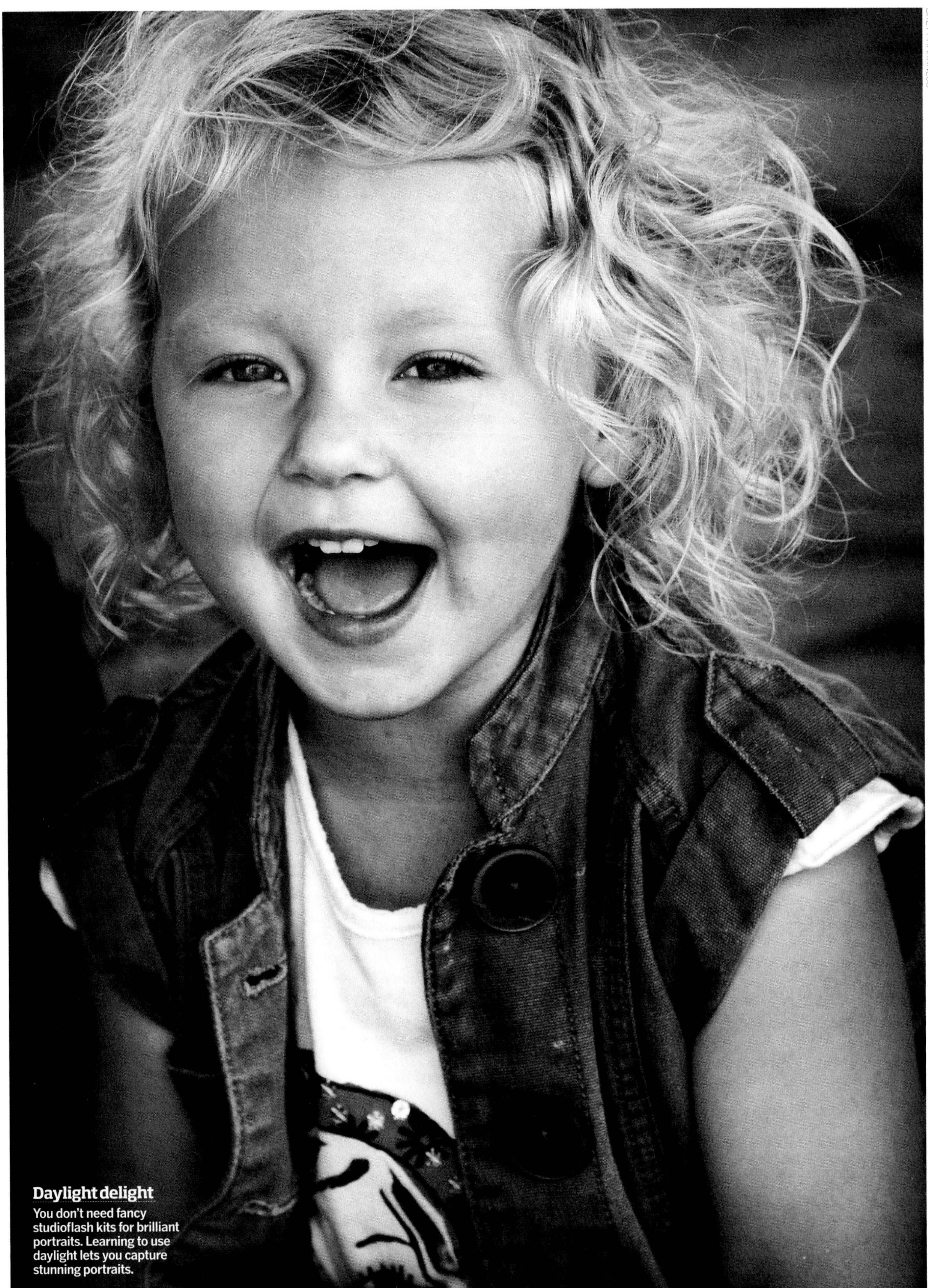

BRETT HARKNESS

Daylight delight

You don't need fancy studioflash kits for brilliant portraits. Learning to use daylight lets you capture stunning portraits.

Controlling bright sunlight

A bright summer's day may seem the ideal time to shoot outdoor portraits, but only if you know how to diffuse harsh sunlight to produce flattering results

THERE ARE MANY BENEFITS to taking photos outdoors on a day when the sky is blue and the sun is beaming. Light levels are very high, so you've a full range of apertures and shutter speeds to choose from, even with the ISO rating set to a low sensitivity for maximum image quality. Also, because the weather is warmer, subjects are happier to sit and pose for you and you've a full choice of outfits for them to wear. Plus, because the light is so bright, colours tend to be punchier and saturation higher, which all help add extra impact to images.

However, there are also drawbacks to take into account. The first is the most obvious: sunlight is very bright and direct, so if your subject is facing it, they will most likely be squinting and their face and chin will have very harsh shadows, which amounts to a very unflattering portrait. Facing them away from the sun is one solution, but you'll then need to watch out for flare, as well as cope with a subject whose face is in deep shadow. The high contrast between the bright background and the subject also means that you'll have to be careful with metering to ensure that the subject isn't underexposed.

The other solution, which we illustrate here, is to use a diffuser panel, placed between the sun and the subject, to bathe the model in a far more flattering light. In effect, you're shading the subject from the sun, but using a diffuser offers a number of differences to placing the subject within a shaded location. The nature of light passing through a diffuser is very non-directional, much like shade, but because the light has passed through a white material, it's neutral, clean and retains a relatively high level of illumination. Whereas in the shade, the light is reflected off surfaces, which, if coloured, will influence the light falling on the subject. And, because the light has bounced off one or more surfaces, it will be dimmer, meaning you have less choice with exposure settings.

The other key difference is that by diffusing direct sunlight, you're not limited in terms of location. You can shoot from the middle of a garden, beach or park, or anywhere else that suits your fancy, as you're able to use the diffuser panel to control the light falling on the subject. And as the diffused light is even, you can shoot from any direction, therefore being able to place the subject against a backdrop of your choice.

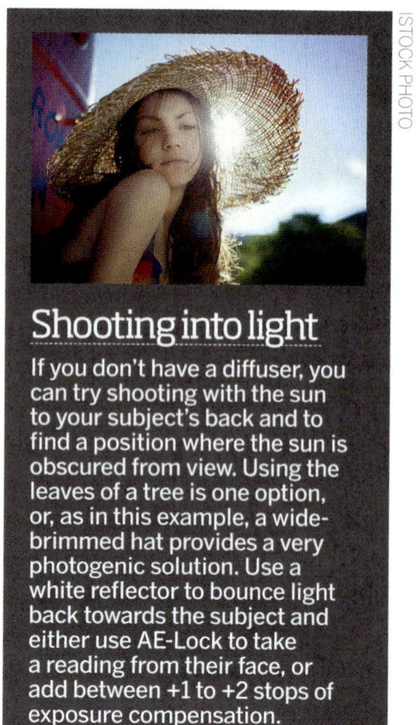

ISTOCK PHOTO

Shooting into light

If you don't have a diffuser, you can try shooting with the sun to your subject's back and to find a position where the sun is obscured from view. Using the leaves of a tree is one option, or, as in this example, a wide-brimmed hat provides a very photogenic solution. Use a white reflector to bounce light back towards the subject and either use AE-Lock to take a reading from their face, or add between +1 to +2 stops of exposure compensation.

Sunlit step-by-step

For this simple step-by-step, Daniel Lezano took some pictures in a garden using a Lastolite Skylite, which is a large diffuser panel that requires at least one person to hold it in position. Smaller panels that are easier to handhold are available, but bear in mind that the area of diffused light will therefore also be smaller. Take a look at the kit section for further details on the types of reflectors and diffusers that are available. As you'll see, reflectors also have their part to play in manipulating the light to better illuminate the subject and to help produce the effect that you want. In this shoot, the camera was set to aperture-priority mode at f/5.6 (ISO 100) and the White Balance was set to Daylight.

1 Set-up Here's the basic set-up for the pictures. We're shooting around 3pm so the sun's still very high in the sky, and the diffuser has to be held over Ruby's head. You can see the large area of diffused light it produces beneath her.

2 Test shot This is the result of this basic set-up. Because the sun is obscured by the panel, Ruby isn't squinting and as the diffuser is just above her head, her hair has an attractive highlight. However, while the light on her face is fairly even, there are still some faint shadows that need removing.

3 Add a reflector To add a little colour to the diffused light, I place a Lastolite Sunfire reflector on the grass within the diffused shade, angled up towards Ruby's face. It's a powerful reflector, but as I'm positioned under the panel its effect doesn't cause Ruby to squint.

4 Spot-on lighting The resulting image is much better than the shot captured using the diffuser alone. The light from the Sunfire's surface has added warmth to Ruby's skin and has evened out the shadows. The result is more than satisfactory, but I'm not happy with the pose so I want to try something else.

1
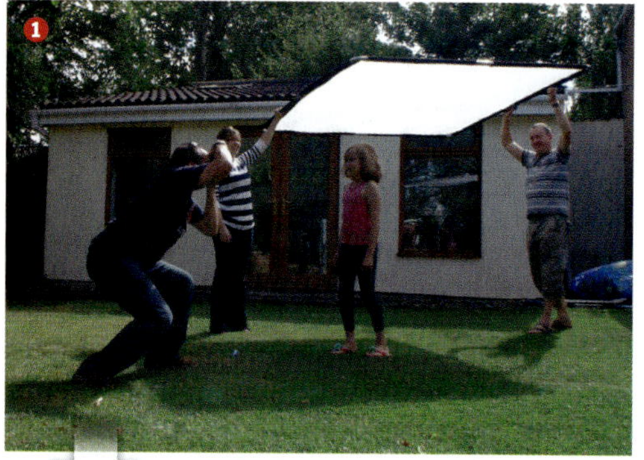

2
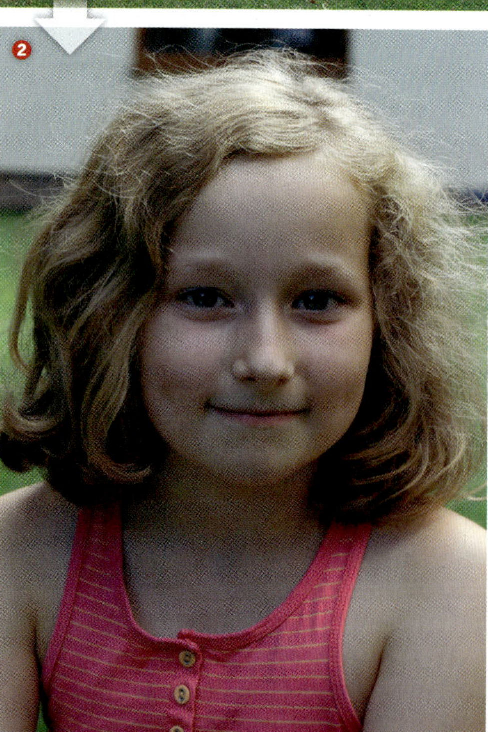

3
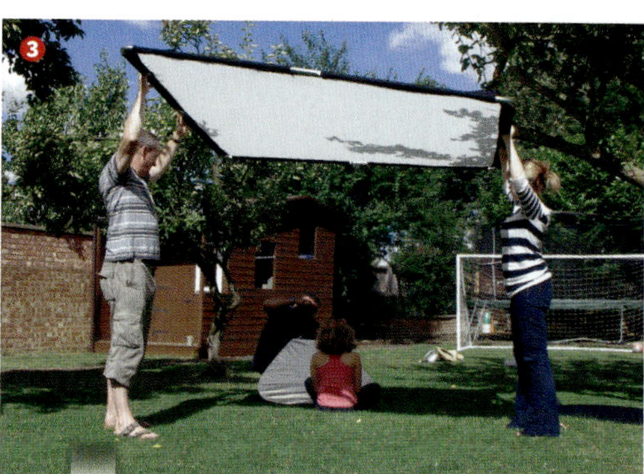

4
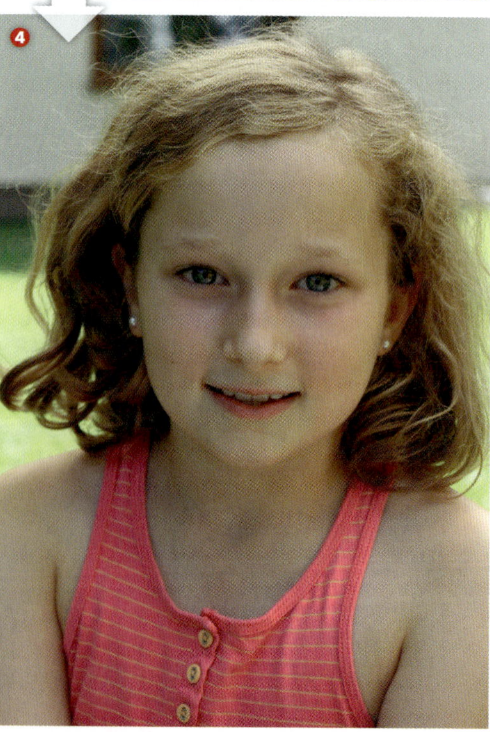

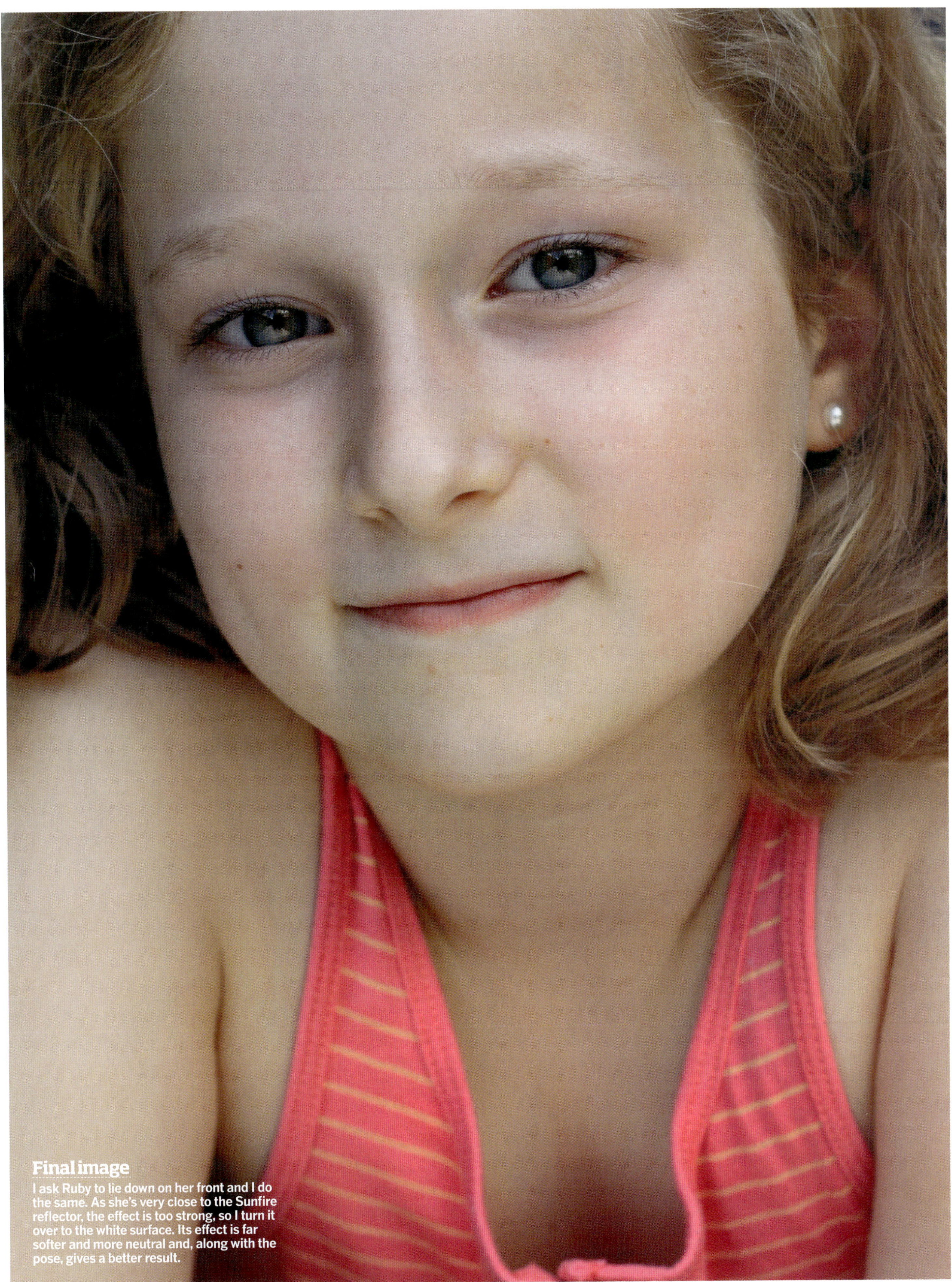

Final image
I ask Ruby to lie down on her front and I do the same. As she's very close to the Sunfire reflector, the effect is too strong, so I turn it over to the white surface. Its effect is far softer and more neutral and, along with the pose, gives a better result.

How to take portraits under cover

If you're ever struggling to work with harsh direct sunlight, one easy way to control the light is to step into some shade. We show you how to go about it...

WHEN THE SUN IS STRONG and high in the sky, there's often nowhere to escape its harsh rays and high-contrast conditions. So if you're after a wide, smooth tonal range with limited contrast and better control but you don't have a diffuser, your best chance for success is to find cover in a spot of shade, such as under a tree or beside a building.

Placing your subject in some shade instantly improves lighting and gives you more control over the strength and direction of the ambient light. Just remember that the light will be softer, cooler and more diffused, so you'll also have lower light levels to consider, as well as potential colour casts.

As shade is naturally cooler than sunlight, as well as setting your White Balance to Shade, you may want to opt for a reflector that adds warmth, such as a gold reflector or Lastolite's sunfire/silver reflector. You will also need to be aware of surrounding colours because dark surfaces absorb light while pale ones reflect it. Watch out for strong coloured surfaces too as they may reflect coloured light, so don't place your subject too close and be aware that you may need to adjust your White Balance settings appropriately, or shoot in Raw so you can correct any colour cast later.

When shooting in shade, you need to be aware of where the light is coming from, which can be tricky as it's likely to be bouncing off different surfaces like walls and floors at various angles, but with practice you'll learn how to master it. By placing your subject in the shade, an easy way to control the strength and direction of light is to vary the subject's distance from the shade and sun; the closer they are to leaving the shaded area, the stronger the light. You can further control light by moving a reflector towards or away from the subject. You can also control the contrast by where you position your subject; for instance, half in the light and half in the shadow or with their back to the light so they're backlit. If you try the latter technique, position a reflector in front of your subject to reflect light onto the face to fill in any shadows. You could also try turning your back to the sun, and have your model face you – it will cast a very flattering, soft and low-contrast light over their face.

Learning how to work with shade is useful when shooting on sunny days, especially if you're dealing with subjects who are wearing clothes that are near white or black in tone, or are dark-skinned, as bright conditions can be an exposure nightmare.

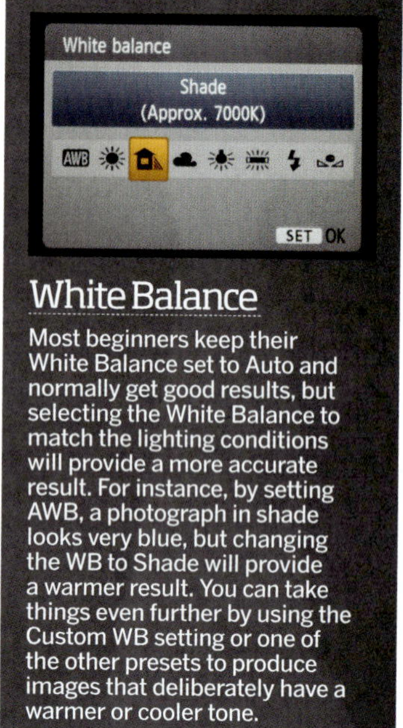

White Balance

Most beginners keep their White Balance set to Auto and normally get good results, but selecting the White Balance to match the lighting conditions will provide a more accurate result. For instance, by setting AWB, a photograph in shade looks very blue, but changing the WB to Shade will provide a warmer result. You can take things even further by using the Custom WB setting or one of the other presets to produce images that deliberately have a warmer or cooler tone.

Shooting in shade

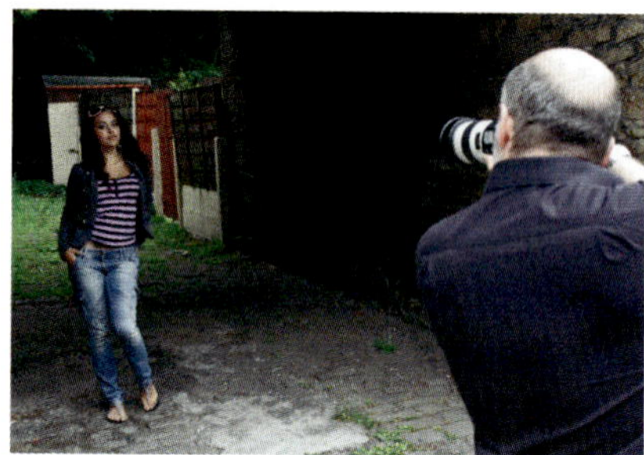

We asked pro photographer Brett Harkness to show us his process for shooting in shade. This alleyway was perfect; it offered some shade and the contained light meant it was soft and easily controllable. To get the right level of light on Emma, his model, he had her walk very slowly from inside the alley, towards him and the light until he was happy with how her face was illuminated.

1 Try different settings As light levels were low, Brett started with a wide aperture of f/4 and cranked up his ISO to 640 to generate a fast enough shutter speed to shoot handheld. The first few shots he took were good but even though the background is blurred, there's still a lot going on. Brett zoomed his lens in closer to make a tighter head-and-shoulder crop. Much better!

2 Experiment with poses For a different shot, he positioned Emma leaning against a wall – but by moving her, the light on her face was reduced, so he brought in a reflector. We opted for the silver-strong side of the Lastolite Sunfire reflector as it gave the strongest reflectance and filled in a lot of the shadows.

If you're using a wide aperture, you need to be very careful where you place your focus point. Here, Brett has focused on Emma's eyes using selective focusing, which has thrown the foreground and background out of focus. The wall also provides useful lead-in lines to Emma's face, strengthening the composition.

1

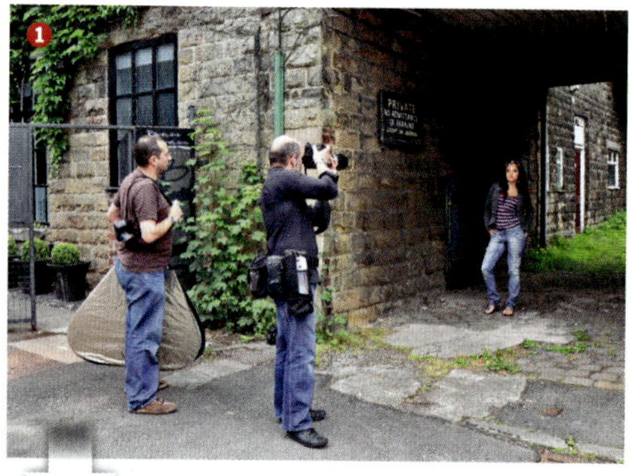

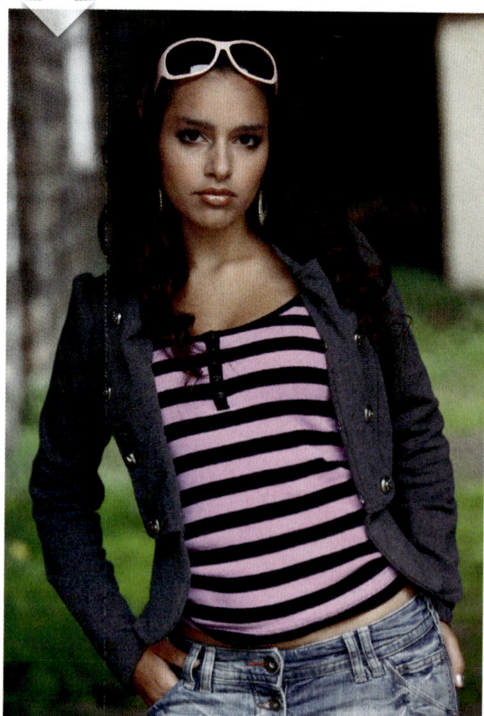

2

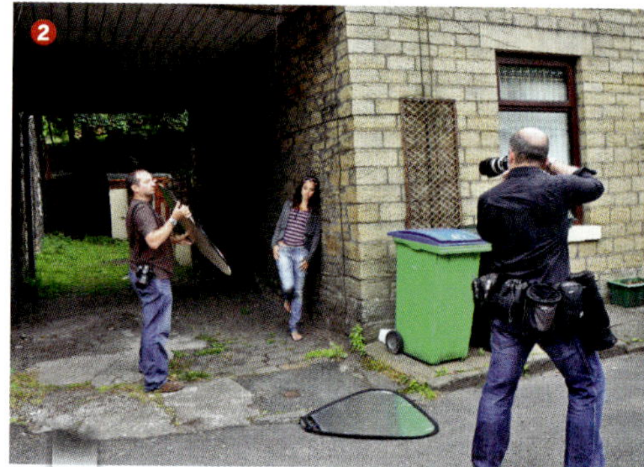

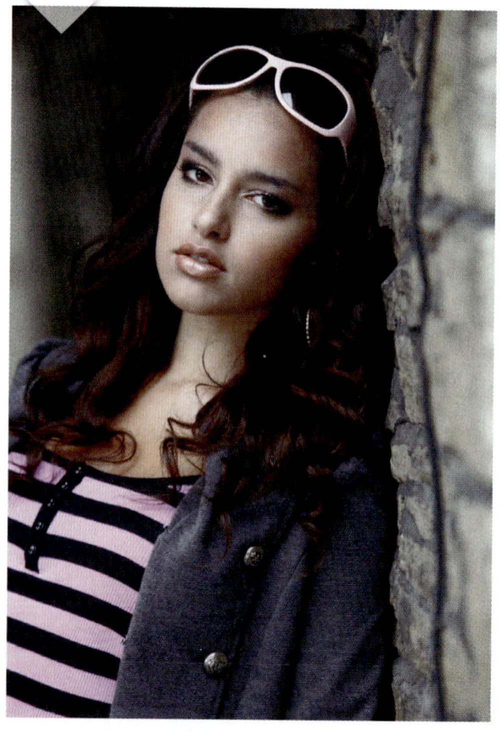

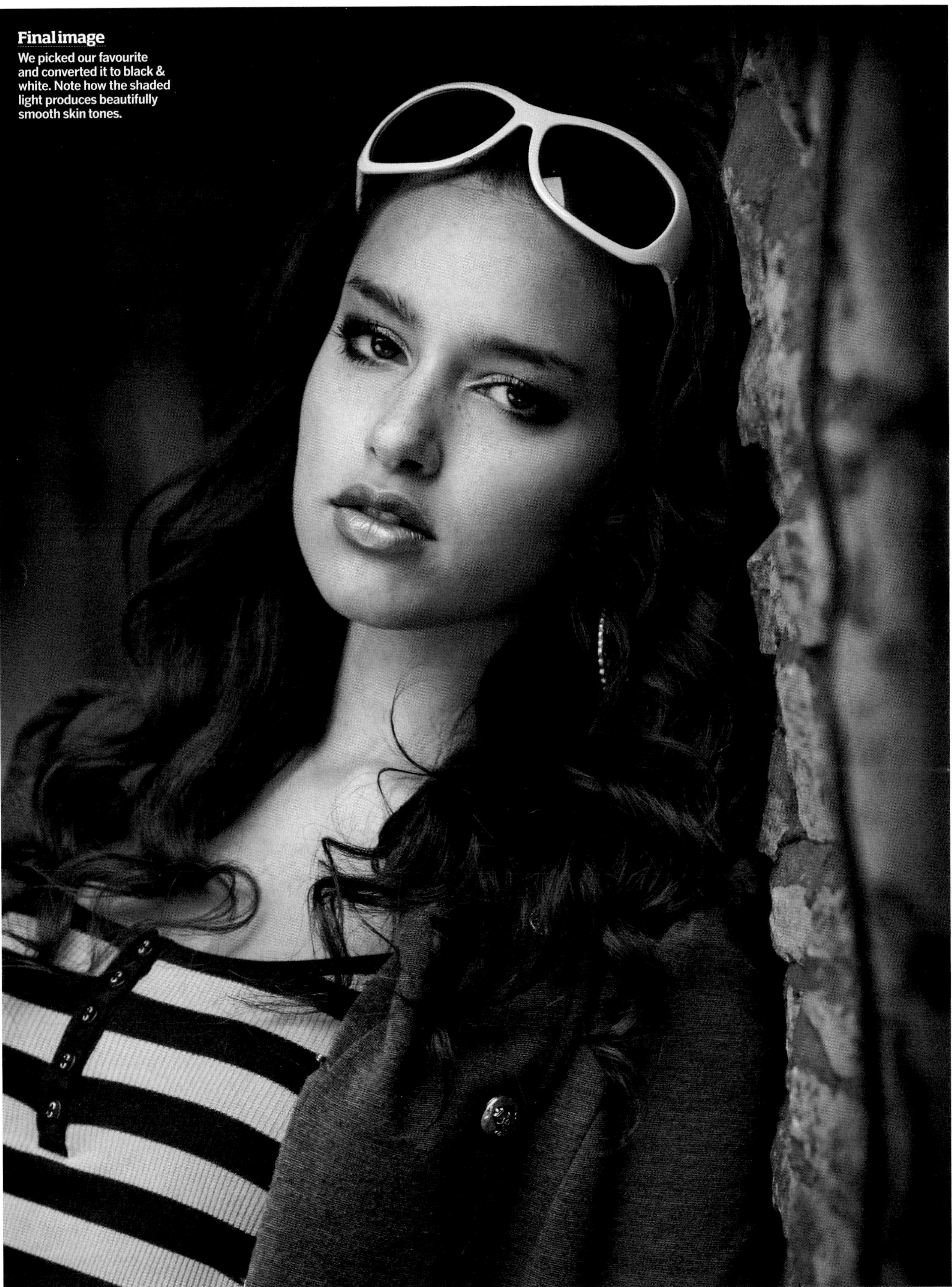

Final image

We picked our favourite and converted it to black & white. Note how the shaded light produces beautifully smooth skin tones.

Shooting in overcast conditions

Cloudy days are a blessing in disguise for portrait photographers. We show you how simple it is to manipulate Mother Nature's softbox…

ANYONE WHO LIVES IN THE UK will know we're blessed with more cloudy days than clear skies and sunshine, even in the summer months. For most, this might not sound an ideal scenario, but for a portrait photographer it's perfect; a blanket of grey cloud acts as a natural diffuser, providing even, malleable light for you to control with ease using lighting aids such as reflectors. A cloudy day offers the greatest scope for manipulating sunlight as the angle, strength and tone of the light hitting your subject simply depends on what type of reflector you choose to use and how it's positioned. As there is no direct sunlight to contend with, you're also free to place your subject anywhere you please, even at high noon, without having to worry about harsh sunlight creating unsightly shadows and stark highlights. As you're dealing with flat lighting, to add a summer feel to your shots, try to have your subject dress in brightly coloured clothing and find an environment with lots of colour impact, like a lush green field, or head to a garden filled with summer flowers.

How well your subject is lit doesn't always depend on your environment, but often your skill in using lighting aids. As the light will be descending through the clouds, it is a good idea to position the reflector below and angled upwards towards the subject to fill in any shadows. Also try varying the distance of the reflector from the subject to get the light intensity you're after. If you're dealing with young children, why not have them sit on the reflector? It will fill in any shadows by bouncing the maximum amount of light back onto the subject from the sky and it doubles up as a 'magic carpet' – ideal for keeping those little ones occupied long enough to rattle off a couple of frames. Looking around your environment for reflective surfaces, such as marble or white-coloured walls, can also be useful for bouncing light onto your subject: watch out for colour surfaces, though, as they will reflect coloured light.

There are several types of reflectors to choose from, with a 5-in-1 kit being the best option for beginners, as they include a gold, white and silver side that vary in reflectance. In some scenarios, though, you may find the silver reflector is too harsh and cool, while the gold is too warm. In cases like this, you may want to invest in a mixed reflector such as Lastolite's TriGrip sunfire/silver reflector, which Brett Harkness uses here in the following step-by-step.

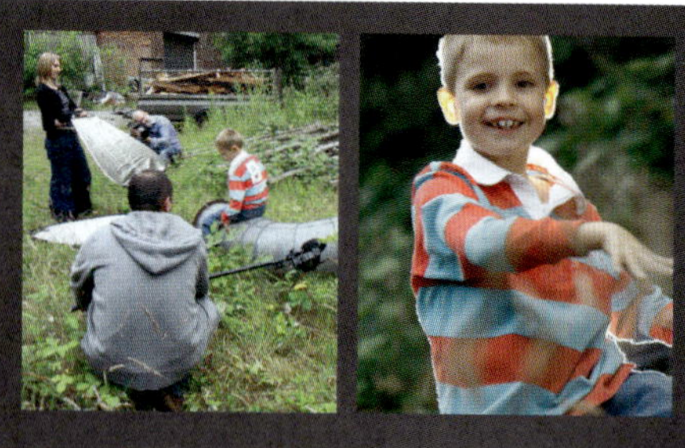

BRETT HARKNESS

Create backlighting with flash

More often than not, bright sunshine won't make an appearance when you want it to. So the next best thing is to use a flashgun. Mixing daylight with flash can, from a practical point of view, help fill in any shadows and, from a creative point of view, catapult your images to a new level of dynamism. It's a more advanced technique to tackle, but if you continue to practise it, you'll find it opens up a whole range of possibilities. One technique that you could try is placing a flashgun behind your subject to mimic a sunlit backlight. As your flash is off-camera, you'll need to be able to fire it wirelessly with a remote trigger. If you're trying this technique for the first time, set your camera to program mode and your flash to TTL. If you find that the flash effect is too low, boost its power by dialling in (positive) flash exposure compensation.

Handling overcast light

Working with kids is tough at the best of times, so shooting in overcast conditions is ideal because you can allow them to move around freely knowing you don't have to worry about harsh shadows or squinting in direct sunshine. We helped Brett Harkness on a typical lifestyle shoot as he worked his magic in very overcast lighting conditions.

Brett's model is a typical eight-year-old boy, unable to sit still for more than a few frames before running off to explore and play. The beauty of a cloudy sky means Brett can let him do this and then when the opportunity arises for a good shot, simply manoeuvre a reflector to improve the quality of light. When photographing your kids, or someone else's, remember to have fun: you're more likely to get better shots of them if you succumb to a few games than if you force them to comply with your shoot.

1 Set-up Having scouted the location for suitable backgrounds, Brett started by sitting his subject in front of a green door and set an aperture of f/5.6. As the light levels were low, we positioned a Lastolite Sunfire/Silver reflector to the side of him to create a little contrast from the flat, low light.

2 Test shot With his face in focus, Brett rattled off a few frames, encouraging the subject to give a few different expressions and to mess around with the grass. To get a more dynamic picture, Brett twists his camera to get a diagonal composition.

3 Alter position After letting the subject play for a while, Brett sat him on top of a mesh cage to stop him moving around. We held two Lastolite TriGrip reflectors below and to the side of him to bounce the light descending from the sky. We used one close to him and the other further away to create slight contrast in his face.

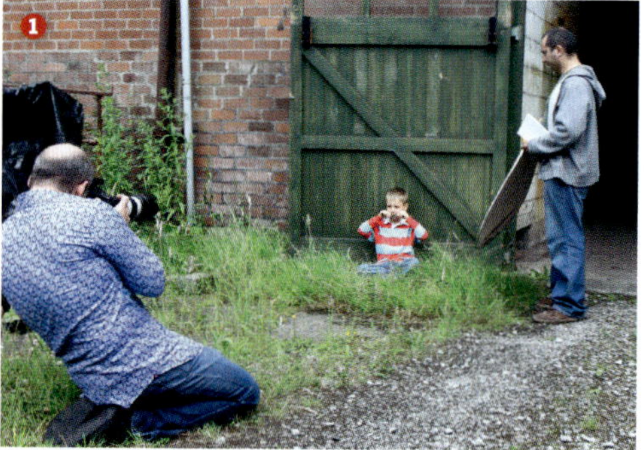

1

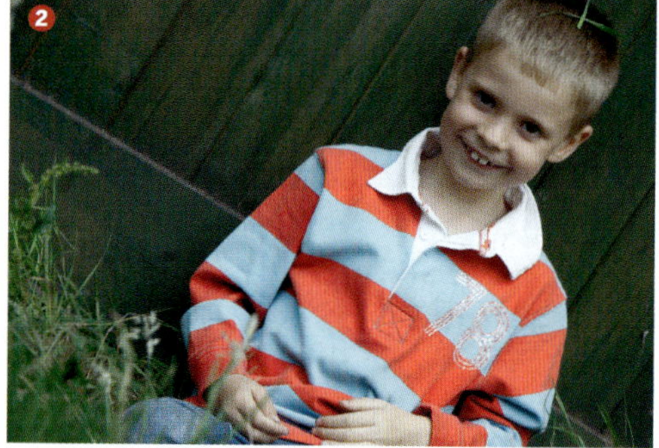

2

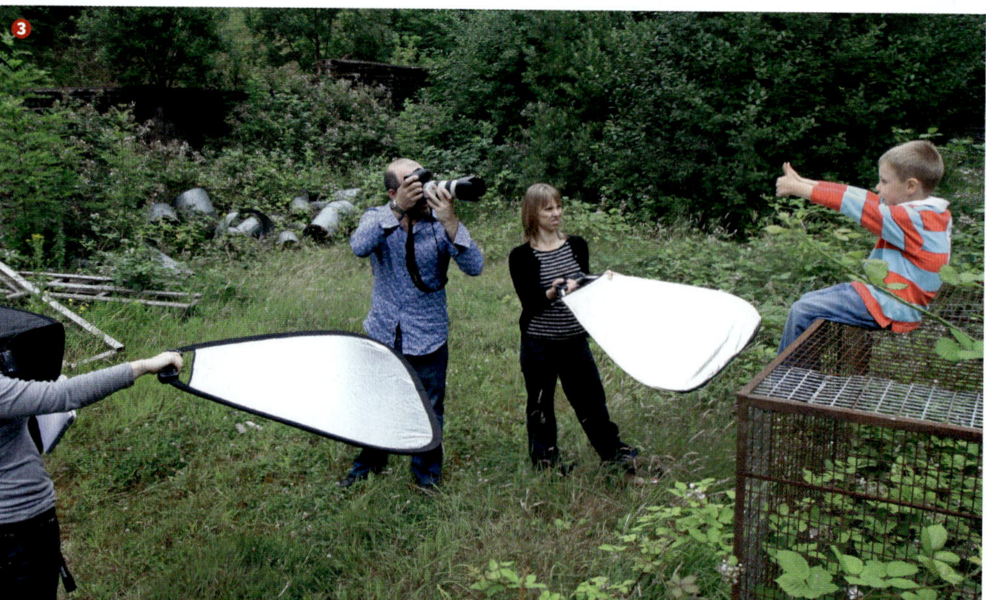

3

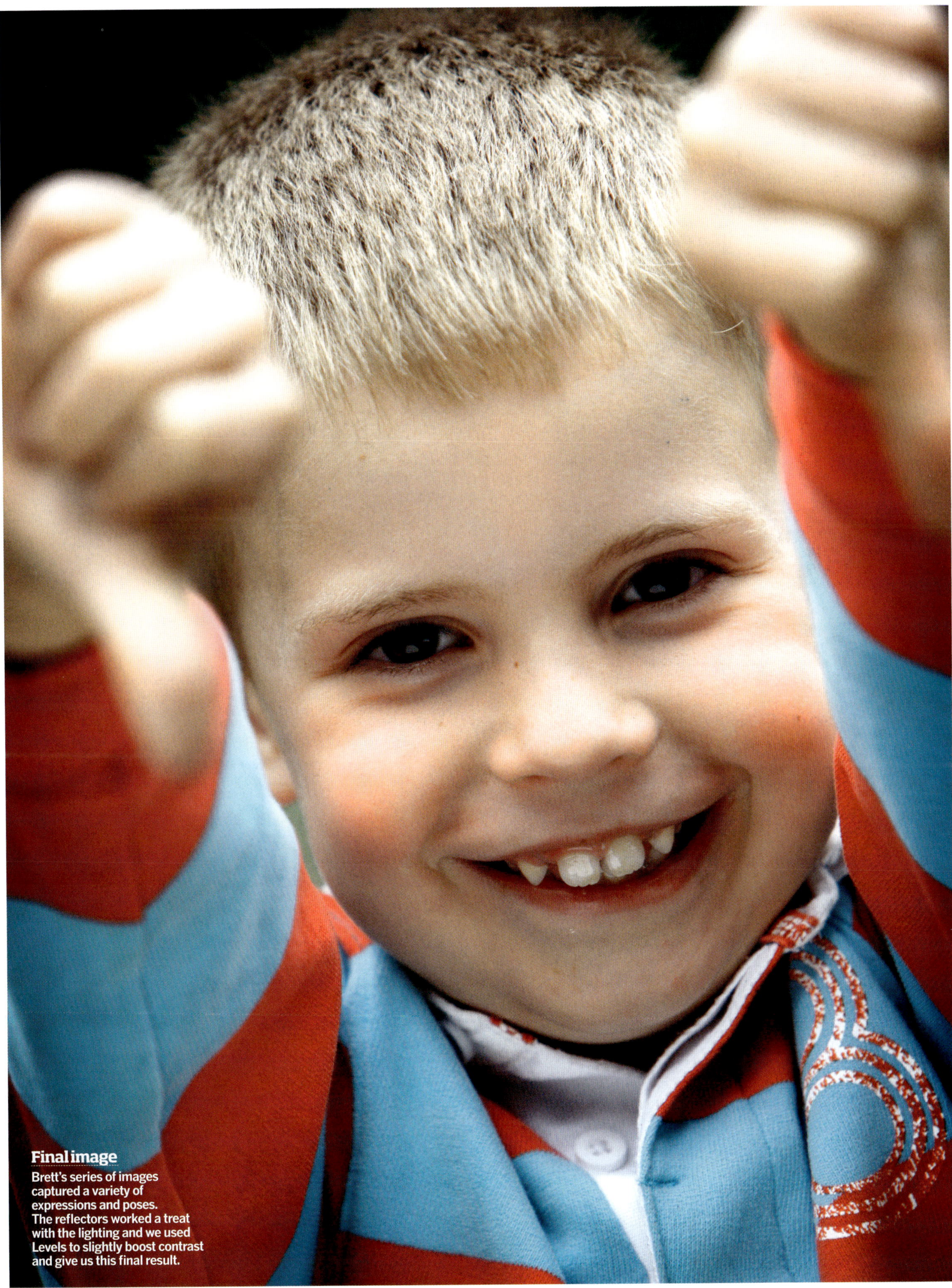

Final image

Brett's series of images captured a variety of expressions and poses. The reflectors worked a treat with the lighting and we used Levels to slightly boost contrast and give us this final result.

Shooting late in the day

Daniel Lezano reveals the challenges and rewards of shooting in the final minutes of the day's light

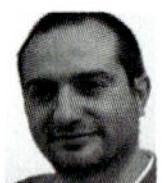

Daniel Lezano THE 'MAGIC HOUR' IS A PHRASE commonly used by landscape photographers to describe the period of time early in the morning or late in the day when the sun is so low in the sky that the light has a strong golden hue. For landscape images, this light can give scenes a three-dimensional feel as it creates shadows that reveal the depth and contours of the scenery. For portrait photography, this golden light adds warmth to a subject's skin tone and backdrop. You have to work fast, though, as you literally have minutes to take advantage of the setting sun before it disappears. You also need to be aware that you're at the mercy of the weather as, if it's cloudy, you will have little or no golden light to play with. However, if you are lucky enough to have this wonderful light appear, as well as shooting with the subject facing the light, it's also worth using the sunset as a colourful backdrop.

You're guaranteed soft light once the sun is low in the sky, as the entire scene will be in shade. This means you can work without any lighting aids, although even with low-light levels, you'll find reflectors still produce some illumination. The extra reflectance will come in useful when trying to avoid camera shake, as the very low light results in a longer shutter speed.

To provide an example, I headed to a park to capture some shots of a friend's daughter. Ruby has blonde curly hair – perfect for backlighting. Rather than go for colourful clothing, I arranged for Ruby to wear neutral tones to complement the natural colours of the scenery.

With such a short time period to work in, arrive at your location ten minutes ahead of when you plan to shoot to spot potential viewpoints and backgrounds. I decided on the bank of a pond, as it meant the horizon was unobstructed and I'd have the light for longer than if I was to shoot within the park where trees block the falling sun.

I took a white, silver and gold reflector, which Ruby's mum was happy to hold in position. The white reflector, while a favourite for most daylight shoots, might be too inefficient to bounce enough daylight when light levels fall very low. In which case, the silver or gold reflector could prove more useful, although care would need to be taken with the gold reflector when combined with the already golden light from the low sun that it doesn't create too warm a cast.

As with the majority of my portrait shoots, I used my DSLR (with 50mm f/1.8 lens) set to aperture-priority, with the initial aperture setting at f/5.6. The White Balance was set to AWB and I shot in Raw + JPEG to allow me to tweak WB if necessary in post-production.

Avoiding camera shake

Due to the relatively slow shutter speeds that occur when shooting at this time of day, avoiding camera shake should be at the forefront of your mind. The easiest way to do this is to use image stabilisation if your camera or lens has it, stick to a wide aperture of around f/4-5.6 and set the ISO rating to at least 400. You should also use a moderate telephoto lens of between 50mm and 100mm, rather than a longer telephoto, which increases the risk of shake. Using the reciprocal rule can help you determine when you run the risk of shake. To do this, ensure your shutter speed is at least equal or faster than the reciprocal of the lens in use. For instance, if you are using a focal length of 100mm, ensure the shutter speed is at least 1/100sec; at 200mm use 1/200sec or faster; and so on.

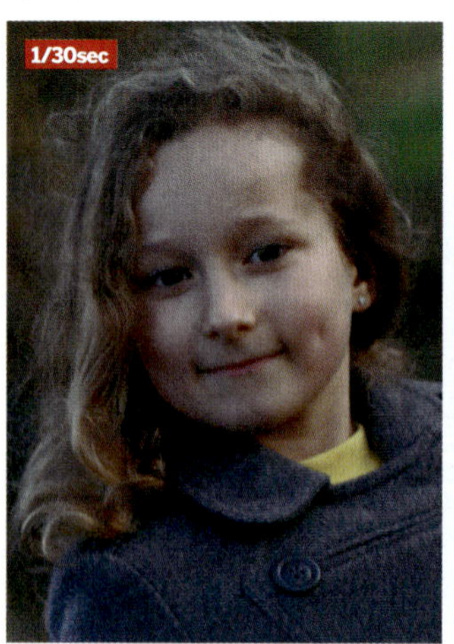

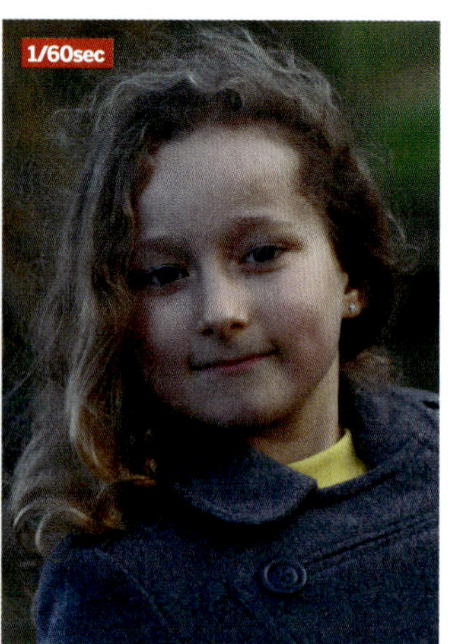

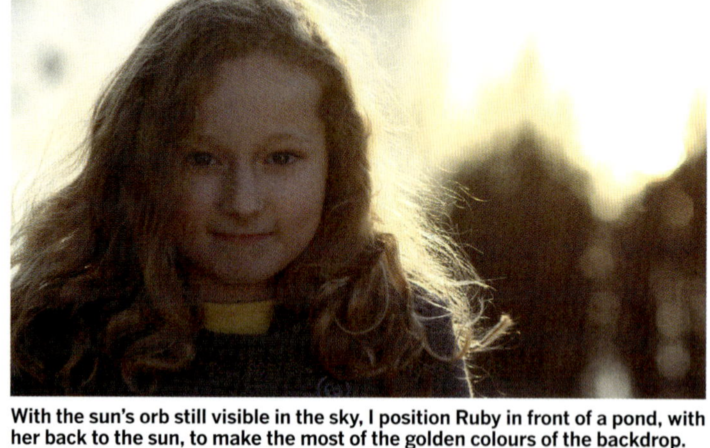

With the sun's orb still visible in the sky, I position Ruby in front of a pond, with her back to the sun, to make the most of the golden colours of the backdrop. While the low sun creates a glow in her hair, the glare effect is too strong, reducing contrast and adversely affecting the image.

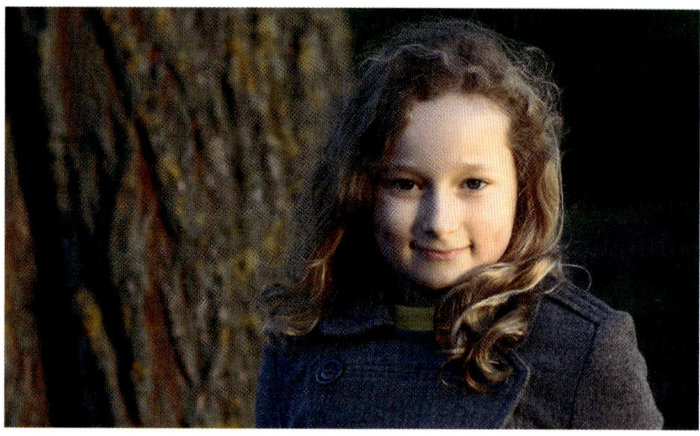

I move Ruby to stand in front of a tree and try shooting from a variety of viewpoints, remembering to alternate the format by taking portrait and landscape images. The texture of the tree adds interest and the golden light from the sun, to Ruby's left, adds a lovely warmth to her skin.

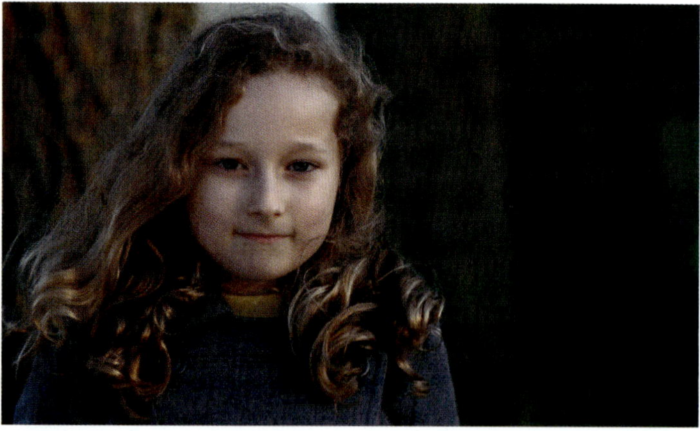

Before the sun has completely set and the scene becomes totally shaded, the light still has a very slight touch of gold to it, adding colour to her hair. Positioning a white reflector to Ruby's left side allows me to bounce a little extra light in to fill any shadows, yet retain the skin's natural tones.

Going too gold!

Take care with the gold reflector: using it with a setting sun can overdo the warm effect, especially if the reflector is positioned too close to the subject. Save the gold for when the subject is in deep shade and try a silver or white reflector instead.

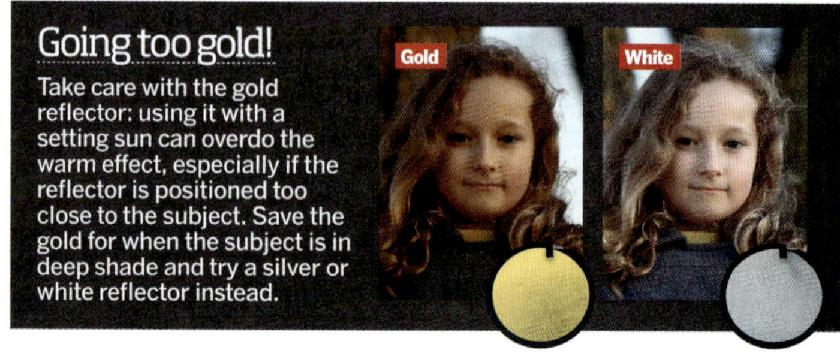

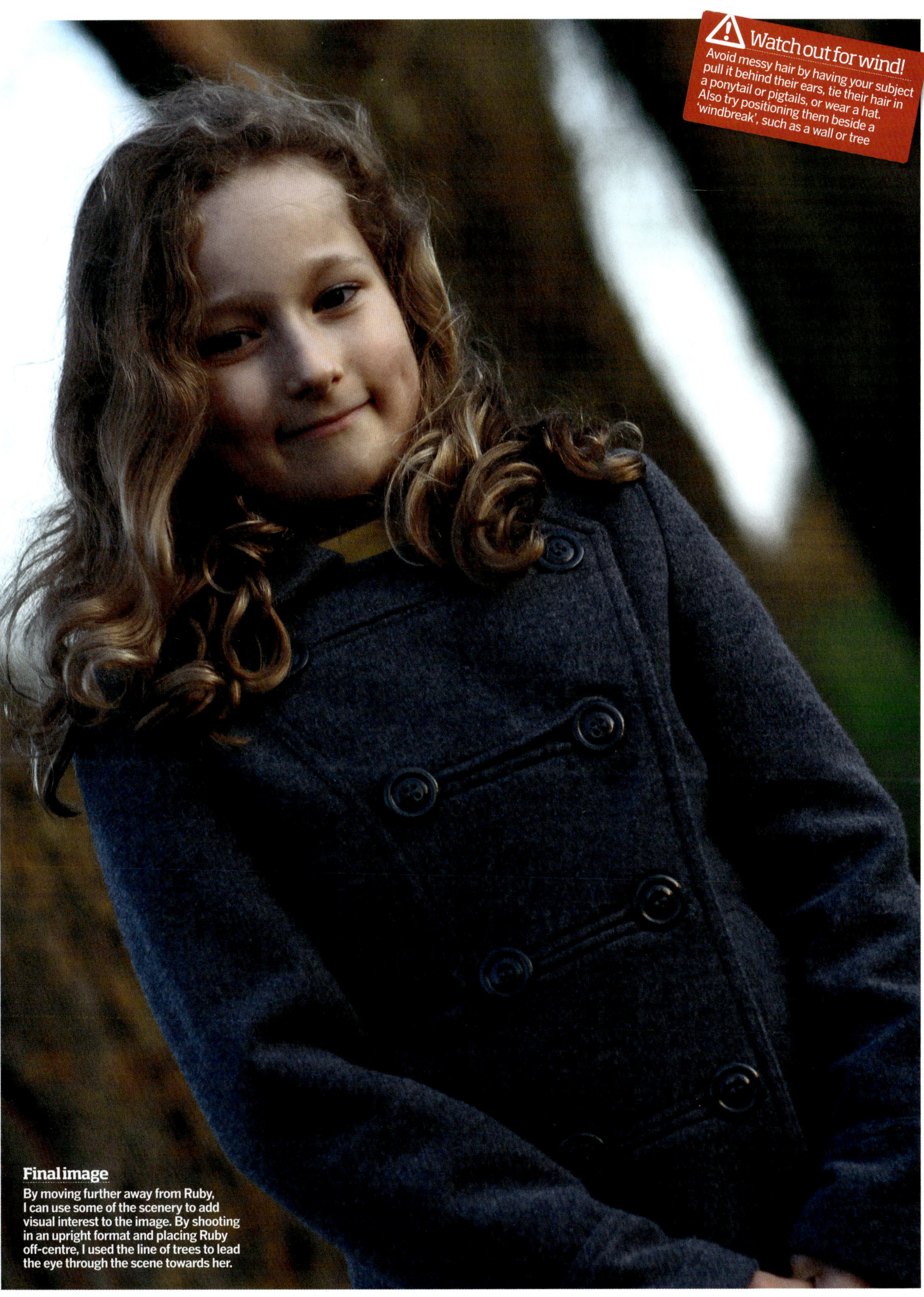

Final image

By moving further away from Ruby, I can use some of the scenery to add visual interest to the image. By shooting in an upright format and placing Ruby off-centre, I used the line of trees to lead the eye through the scene towards her.

Add flare to outdoor portraits

Pro photographer Paul Ward shows how deliberately letting the sun encroach in the frame to add a touch of flare can work with portraits

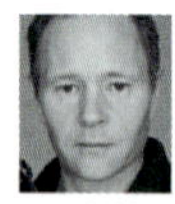

Paul Ward FEW THINGS DIVIDES opinion like lens flare. Some photographers love it, while others abhor it, going to great lengths to avoid it. Lens flare is caused by direct light travelling through a lens and bouncing off its glass elements, usually having one of two effects: bleaching colours with a white haze, reducing contrast, and creating rings of colour (known as artefacts) that dart across the frame from the sun. Using a lens hood or shooting with your back to the sun helps avoid it, but lens manufacturers have developed such effective lens multi-coatings that it's difficult to create flare with some lenses. If you struggle, try an older uncoated lens: good quality secondhand manual focus lenses can be picked up for just a few quid. Artefacts vary depending on the type of lens, too: flare from a zoom will look very different from that of a prime lens, so experiment a little.

When using aperture-priority mode, you'll find that every time you change position, your exposure changes. You can avoid this by working in manual mode, but for the sake of beginners I'll show you how to achieve it in aperture-priority mode. Start with a test shot using between f/3.5-f/5.6 to get a shallow depth-of-field. The trick is to then position the model in front of the sun. Depending on how high the sun is, you might need to kneel and shoot from a lower than normal perspective. Winter, or early morning and evening, is perfect, as the sun is never that high in the sky. Nearly every lens produces flare if it's aimed in the direction of the sun, but it takes the right kind of lens to give artefacts, which gives pro photographers that stylised finish they like.

Old lenses can create flare

Often older lenses create better flare because they lack anti-flare multi-coatings. If you're lucky enough to have only new kit that's not proving very effective, have a look on eBay for a lens adaptor so you can buy an old lens to fit to your camera. I bought an 'M42 for Canon' adaptor and a 28mm Vivitar lens for £15 each. Car boot sales and secondhand stores are also good places to pick up a bargain lens.

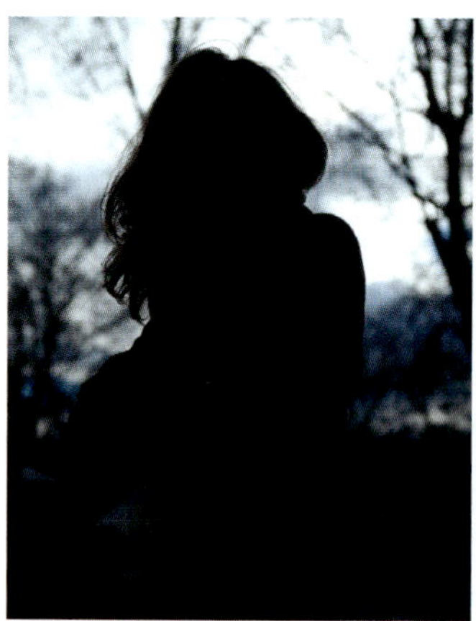

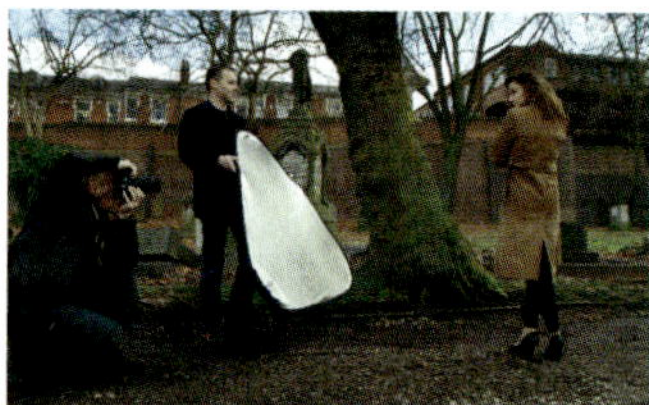

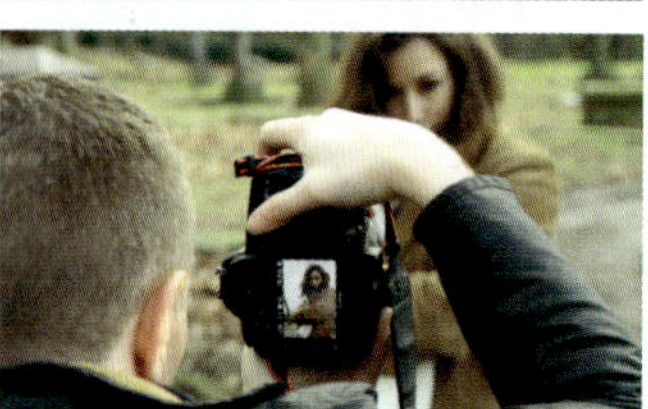

1 Use a reflector As the subject is backlit, you can expect the multi-zone metering of your camera to produce an underexposed result. You could add positive exposure compensation, but there is another option. Using a reflector is an easy and effective way to bounce the sun's rays back on to the subject's face. A gold reflector gives a warmer light than a silver or white reflector, which suits this technique. If the model squints, have them close their eyes and then open them moments before you take the shot.

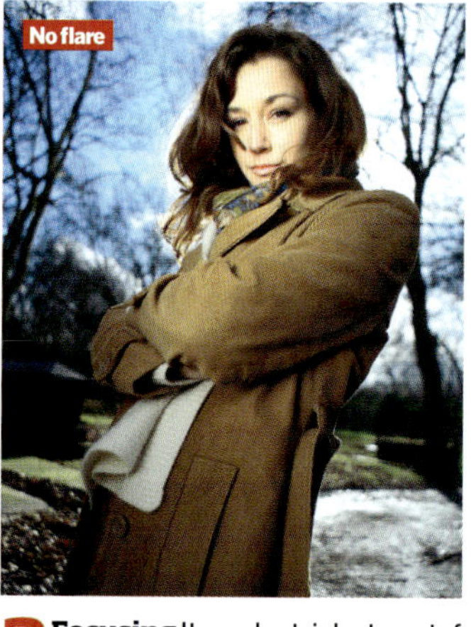

No flare

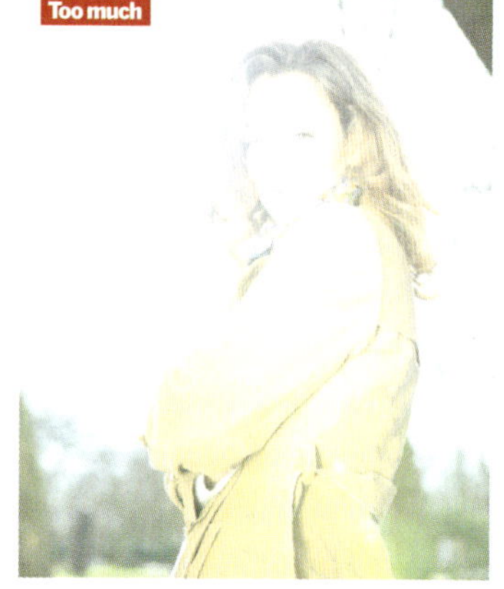

Too much

2 Focusing It can be tricky to autofocus on a subject when the sun is in the frame, as it causes a lack of contrast. To get around this, use the subject to block the sun and focus, keep the shutter button half-depressed to lock focus, and then move slightly to the side so the sun enters the frame. This can mess around with your exposure, so it takes a little trial and error. Depending on where you put the sun in the frame, it may cause too much flare, leading to blown-out highlights, so be patient and keep trying.

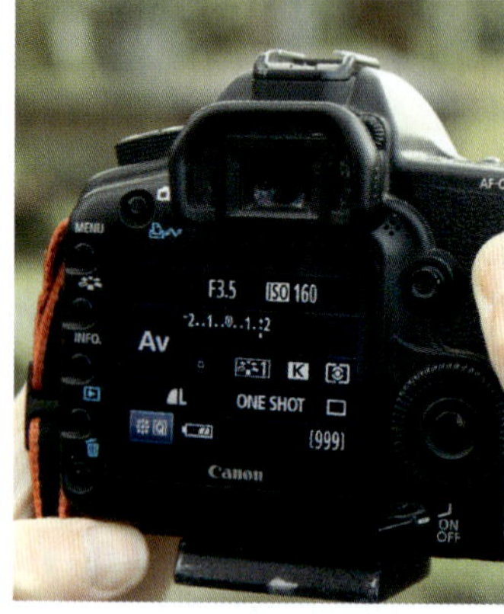

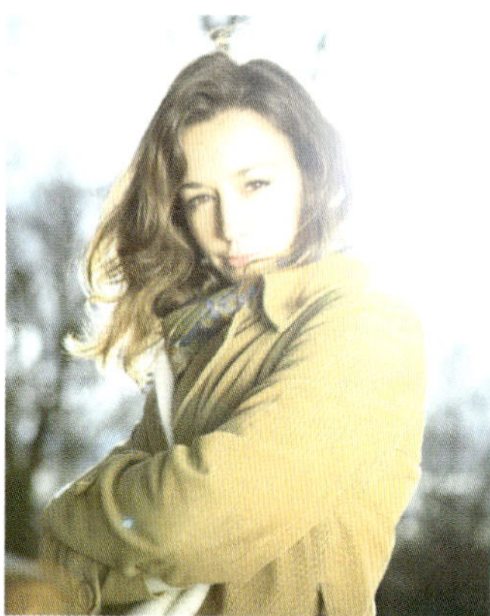

3 Exposure If the shots look too bright, dial in a couple of stops of negative exposure compensation or don't let as much sun encroach into the frame. If the shots are too dark, but the sun is as much in the frame as you want it to be, dial in a couple of stops of positive exposure compensation. For this image, as the sun is just peeping past her head, I used two stops of positive exposure compensation to overexpose, but it's slightly too much. For the next shots, I try to replicate the position of the sun and use one stop of positive exposure compensation.

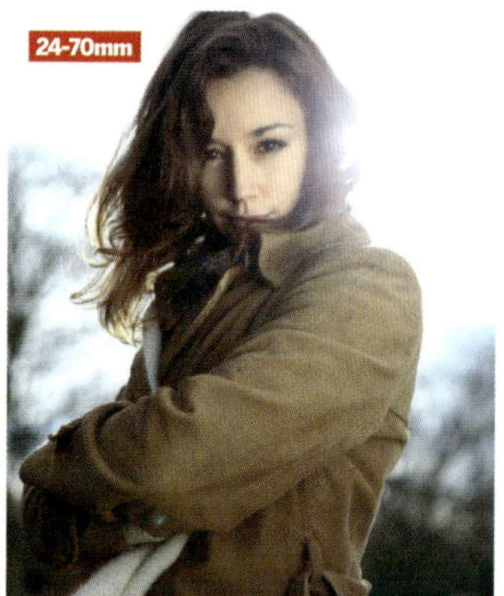

24-70mm

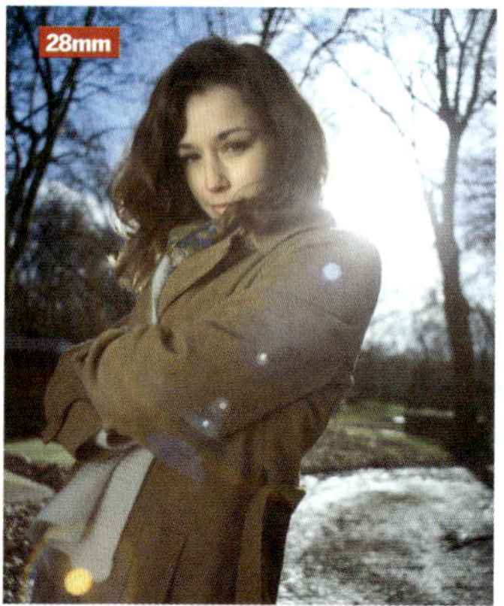

28mm

4 Different optics The Canon EF 24-70mm f/2.8L USM lens I've been using is so efficient at blocking flare that I'm struggling to get any artefacts in the picture, and am only getting the haze. The more I overexpose the shot, the more streaks of white flare expand across the subject's face, which is not the effect I want. I switch to my new, 20-year-old 28mm Vivitar lens (not anti-flare coated) to see if it does a better job. With the model in the same position, I take another shot that produces some excellent artefacts running across the picture, giving me the stylised effect I'm looking for.

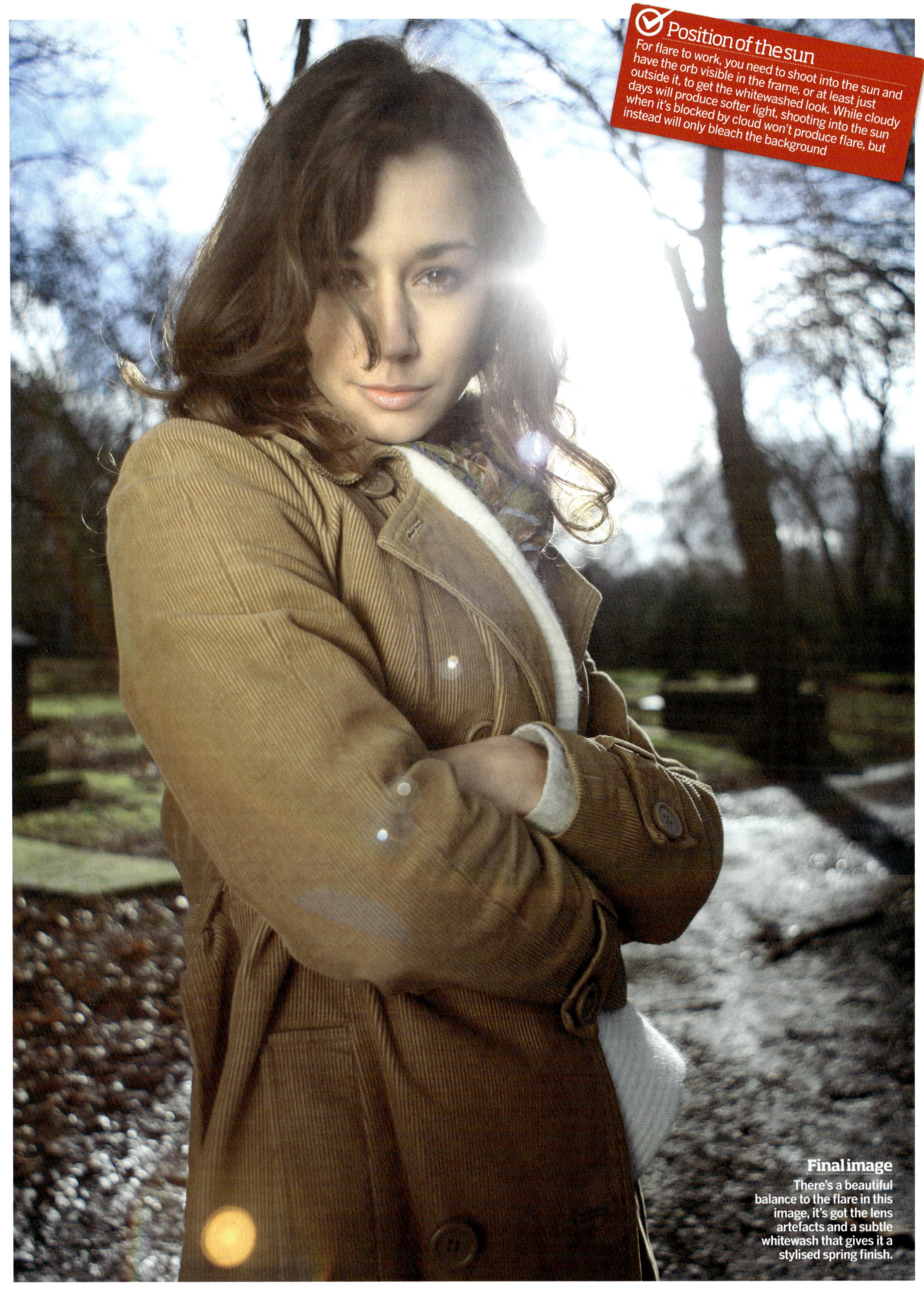

Position of the sun

For flare to work, you need to shoot into the sun and have the orb visible in the frame, or at least just outside it, to get the whitewashed look. While cloudy days will produce softer light, shooting into the sun when it's blocked by cloud won't produce flare, but instead will only bleach the background

Final image

There's a beautiful balance to the flare in this image, it's got the lens artefacts and a subtle whitewash that gives it a stylised spring finish.

Preparing for flash

Flash isn't as frightening as you might think it is. It's just a matter of knowing what to do and when to do it

WE'VE ALL BEEN DISAPPOINTED WHEN using a flashgun has produced an image that failed to capture the mood of a scene. This usually happens when we shoot in auto mode with no real thought for what we are doing or why. The secret to good flash photography lies in using the full range of your camera's exposure modes, and thinking carefully about how light from the flash – and from other sources – affects the final result.

The quality of a flash-lit picture depends on what settings you use with your camera and flash; for instance, whether you use aperture-priority or program mode, or whether you have auto or slow-sync flash set. This is all because, by changing modes, you are altering settings such as shutter speed, which in turn affects the amount of ambient light that reaches the sensor. Additionally, different flash modes command the flash to fire at the beginning or end of the exposure. Either option changes how moving objects will be rendered in the final photograph. While all this may seem complicated, it isn't. The beauty is that you can experiment and learn from your mistakes. Take inspiration, try it out and adapt it with your own ideas. Before long you'll use flash as an everyday part of your photography – rather than be afraid of it – no matter what your subject.

Common flash modes you'll find on DSLRs

The way your DSLR and flash work together is governed by the flash mode that you use. Here are the most common flash modes that you'll find on your digital SLR or dedicated hotshoe-mounted flashgun.

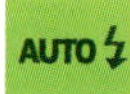

Auto In low light, your DSLR will activate the built-in flash. It calculates aperture via TTL metering, but sets a high shutter speed to avoid camera shake. Convenient, but not creative.

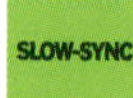

Slow-sync It uses a slower shutter speed to record ambient light properly. Good for night-time portraits where the mood needs to be recorded too, but be careful of camera shake.

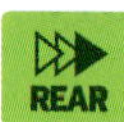

Rear/second-curtain sync Works the same as slow-sync mode, except that the flash is fired at the end of the exposure, rather than at the start. Great for leaving a trail of light behind moving subjects.

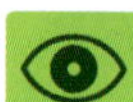

Anti red-eye Aims to prevent or reduce so-called red-eye in flash portraits by using a series of pre-flashes to make a subject's pupil narrow before the exposure is taken.

Flash-off Stops a camera from automatically engaging the built-in flash. More useful than you may think, especially when trying to shoot low-light scenes on a tripod.

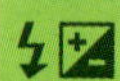

Flash exposure compensation Your DSLR automatically calculates the amount of flash needed for an exposure. Use to increase or decrease the amount of flash output to your liking.

Flash accessories

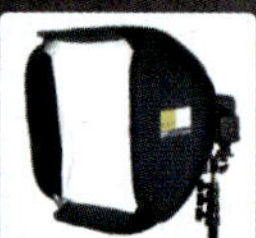

Lighting aids: There are a wealth of softboxes, diffusers, brollies, beauty dishes and other aids available to soften or direct the output from your dedicated flashgun. They vary in price from under £20 for a simple diffuser to up to £200 for a decent softbox. Check out the £17 Stofen Omni-bounce £17 (www.newprouk.com); £170 Lastolite Ezybox (38cm) www.lastolite.com; £70 Speedlight Pro (www.speedlightprokit.co.uk) and £120 Strobies kit www.interfitphotographic.com).

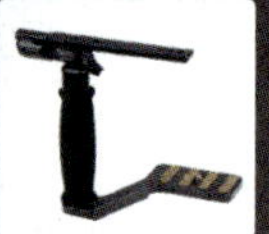

Brackets: These hold your flash to the side of your camera, rather than have it mounted on your hotshoe, which improves the lighting effect and frees your hotshoe for dedicated accessories like a remote trigger. Check out the range by Custom Brackets (www.flaghead.co.uk).

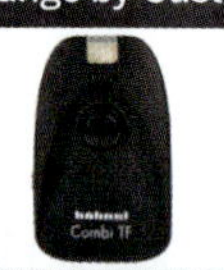

Off-camera triggers or leads: If you want to use your flashgun off-camera, you'll need these to retain dedication with your flash (unless they have a built-in wireless trigger). Manufacturers have their own, but Hama (www.hama.co.uk) Hahnel (www.hahnel.ie) and Phottix (www.intro2020.co.uk) offer affordable options.

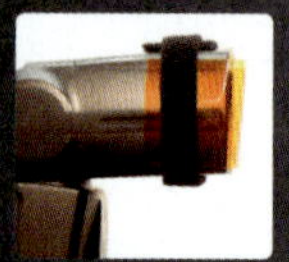

Gels: Slip a coloured gel over the flashhead and you can bathe the scene in colour. Many pros use it with an off-camera flash to illuminate a backdrop. Honl (www.flaghead.co.uk) and Hama (www.hama.co.uk) offer excellent flash gel sets.

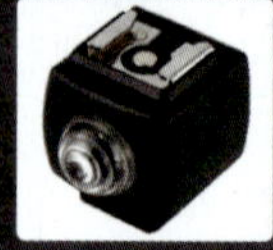

Slave cell: Pop one on the bottom of a flash and it will fire when the sensor detects a flash output. If you have non-dedicated manual flashguns, it's an inexpensive way of using multiple flash set-ups. Hama's Slave cell costs £20.

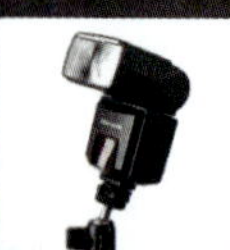

Ball & socket flash platform: If you use the flash off-camera, you'll need a 'foot' to stand it on a surface or a ball & socket head with a flash-compatible platform bracket to hold it securely. Cullmann (www.newprouk.com), Interfit (www.interfitphotographic.com) and other independent brands have several options.

Basic flash modes

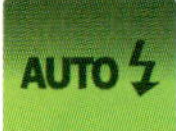

Auto: DSLRs don't have an Auto-flash mode as such, but rather have certain exposure modes that pop up the flash automatically. Some CSCs do have an Auto setting among their flash modes and this works much like it does on a compact camera, firing the flash when needed in low light and taking pictures without in brighter conditions.

When to use Auto flash

- Leaving your flash set to Auto mode makes sense when shooting general snapshots as it's most likely that shooting using ambient light only and no flash may result in camera shake ruining images.

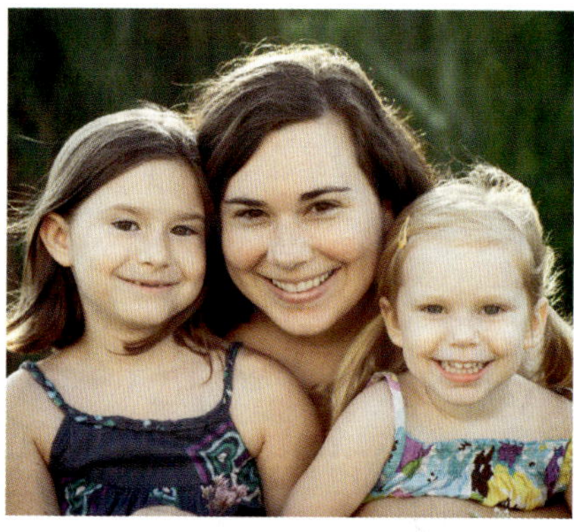
ISTOCK PHOTO

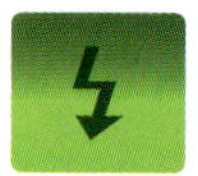

Forced-on (fill-in): You don't have to wait for the camera to suggest you need to use the flash – you can pop it up yourself by pressing the flash button. Do this to add a touch of fill-in flash to remove shadows and add catchlights to daylight portraits, or when your subject's face is in shadow. The amount of fill-in flash is determined automatically by the camera, but you can boost or reduce it using flash exposure compensation (explained over the page).

When to use fill-in flash

- The subject is standing with their back to the sun, so fill-in flash is used to reveal detail.
- Your subject is positioned under a tree with dappled shadows across the face.

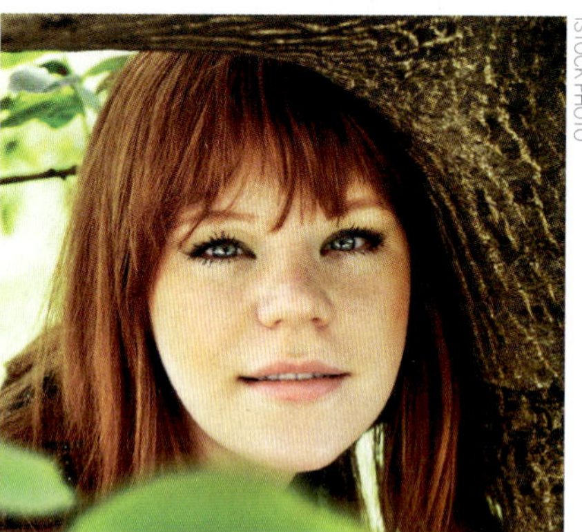
ISTOCK PHOTO

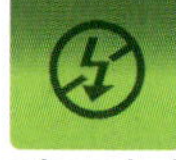

Flash-off: This mode isn't found on the majority of SLRs, as there is no auto pop-up flash facility unless the camera is set to a scene mode where it decides if the flash is needed or not. However, it does exist on some DSLRs as a mode on the mode dial and is designed to be used to prevent accidentally firing the flash in locations where flash photography is not allowed or where it would prove ineffective, such as whe the subject is out of range.

When to turn the flash off

- When shooting through glass, leave the flash off to avoid reflections.
- In locations where flash is not suitable, such as when shooting at open air concerts where the stage is outside the flash range.

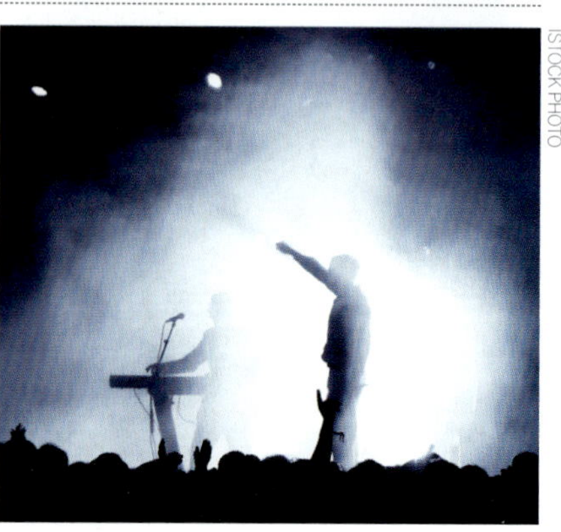
ISTOCK PHOTO

Anatomy panel: Know your flashgun...

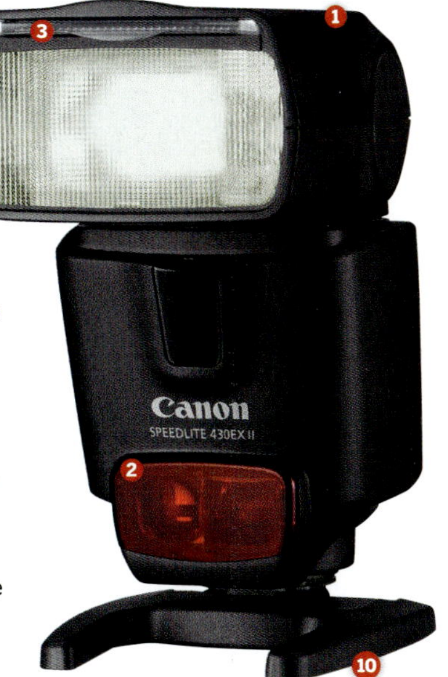

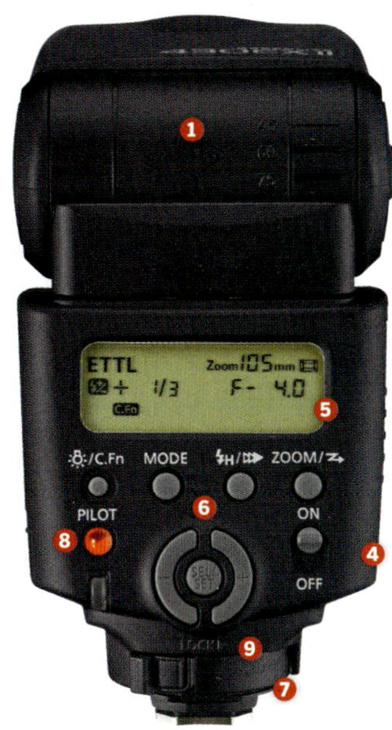

1) Flash head: Your flash head will most likely angle vertically and horizontally: an action commonly referred to as bounce and swivel actions. Most flashguns have a zoom head, where the light coverage changes to suit the lens in use to optimise the range.

2) AF assist lamp: In low light, you may see a red patterned beam emitted by the flashgun to help the camera lock focus.

3) Built-in diffuser/reflector: Slide out the diffuser and drop it in place over the flash window to soften the light, or use the reflector to redirect some of the flash output.

4) External power socket: Many mid- to top-end flashgun models accept an external power source.

5) LCD monitor: The sophistication of its features means that many flashguns have an LCD panel offering a wealth of information about what modes have been selected, as well as a flash-distance scale to give you a visual representation of the flash range at your current chosen settings.

6) Control buttons: The advanced features on flashguns mean there are a large number of buttons, with most controlling more than one function. You're advised to spend a little time getting used to the layout, as they're not always straightforward to use.

7) Hotshoe fitting: The hotshoe fitting has pins that touch contacts on the camera's hotshoe to communicate information and trigger the flash when the shutter is released. All DSLR hotshoes follow the same design, with the exception of Sony's Alpha series. Some CSCs have accessory shoes, while others lack this facility.

8) Ready/test lamp: Most models have a two-stage lamp that lights green then red to indicate partial and full charge. With many, you can press this lamp to test-fire the flash.

9) Locking mechanism: This facility prevents your flash slipping off the hotshoe by locking it in place.

10) Stand: Many flashguns that sport a wireless facility come supplied with a stand that allows the flashgun to be positioned, ready for use off-camera. An alternative is to buy a ball & socket tripod head, like the £25 Cullmann CB2 (www.newprouk.co.uk), which allows you to precisely position the flashgun while mounted on a lighting stand or tripod.

Choosing the correct exposure mode to use with flash

While the TTL flash exposure system on your camera will aim to give you perfectly exposed images every time, it's worth noting that the actual result varies depending on the exposure mode the camera is set to. How this works depends on the camera brand and model, but our easy reference table provides information on how using flash with each of the core creative modes affects how the image is captured.

Brand	Canon	Nikon	Pentax	Olympus	Sony
Program	Camera sets shutter speed and aperture, but raises shutter speed to avoid camera shake. The background may be dark.	Camera sets exposure, but raises shutter speed to avoid camera shake, unless slow-sync mode is set. Background may be dark.	Camera sets exposure, but raises shutter speed to avoid camera shake, unless slow-sync mode is set. Background may be dark.	Camera sets exposure, but raises shutter speed to avoid camera shake, unless slow-sync mode is set. Background may be dark.	Camera sets exposure, but raises shutter speed to avoid camera shake, unless slow-sync mode is set. Background may be dark.
Aperture-priority	User picks aperture; camera calculates flash exposure accordingly. Shutter speed is picked to render ambient light correctly. Be aware of camera shake.	User picks the aperture and the camera selects flash exposure accordingly. Shutter speed is limited to prevent camera shake, unless slow-sync mode is selected.	User sets aperture and camera sets shutter speed to correctly expose background, up to the maximum sync speed. Risk of camera shake in low light.	User picks aperture and camera selects flash exposure accordingly. Shutter speed limited to prevent camera shake, unless slow-sync mode is also selected.	User picks aperture and camera selects flash exposure accordingly. Shutter speed limited to prevent camera shake, unless slow-sync mode is also selected.
Shutter-priority	User picks shutter speed and camera picks corresponding aperture for ambient light, then calculates flash output according to this aperture.	User picks shutter speed and camera picks corresponding aperture to expose ambient light correctly, then calculates flash output according to this aperture.	User picks shutter speed and camera picks corresponding aperture to expose ambient light properly, then calculates flash output according to this aperture.	User picks shutter speed and camera picks corresponding aperture to expose ambient light correctly, then calculates flash output according to this aperture.	User picks shutter speed and camera picks corresponding aperture to expose ambient light correctly, then calculates flash output according to this aperture.
Manual	You set the aperture and shutter speed (at or below the flash sync) to ensure the scene receives enough ambient light. The TTL flash system ensures the subject is correctly exposed.	You set the aperture and shutter speed (at or below the flash sync) to ensure the scene receives enough ambient light. The TTL flash system ensures the subject is correctly exposed.	You set the aperture and shutter speed (at or below the flash sync) to ensure the scene receives enough ambient light. The TTL flash system ensures the subject is correctly exposed.	You set the aperture and shutter speed (at or below the flash sync) to ensure the scene receives enough ambient light. The TTL flash system ensures the subject is correctly exposed.	You set the aperture and shutter speed (at or below the flash sync) to ensure the scene receives enough ambient light. The TTL flash system ensures the subject is correctly exposed.
Exposure compensation	Affects ambient light exposure only.	Affects ambient and flash exposure.	Affects ambient and flash exposure.	Affects ambient light exposure only.	Affects ambient and flash exposure.
Flash exposure compensation	Affects flash exposure only.	Affects flash exposure only.	Affects flash exposure only.	Affects flash exposure only.	Affects flash exposure only.

* Please note that the stated information relates to most general shooting conditions. However, in certain situations, the camera and flash will operate differently.

How to use fill-in flash

What you need to know to create flattering portraits

FILL-IN FLASH DOES EXACTLY what it claims to. It fills in shadows and is most commonly used when photographing people outdoors on sunny days when the sun is casting shadows across their faces. On older, manual flashguns, it was very tricky to get right, but is much easier to achieve with current flash systems. However, some understanding of your kit and how it works will help you to get the balance right. You can work with fill-in flash by popping up your camera's integral flash (with the option to select slow-sync if you want) and shoot away in whatever exposure mode you are comfortable with. The idea is to record the scene exactly how you normally would, but then fire a blip of flash to lighten the shadows slightly. If the daylight conditions require a shutter speed that exceeds your camera's sync speed, your DSLR will automatically make adjustments, or you'll have to use a smaller aperture, depending on the exposure mode you're using. You could also engage high-speed flash (see p72). An external flashgun works in a similar way but gives you more control and extra power. Depending on the conditions, this straightforward approach may cause the effect of the flash to be too obvious, so whenever you can, it's worth using a flash off-camera, and by simply applying some negative flash exposure compensation, it will reduce the flash's effect. Setting -1EV compensation is the equivalent of halving the amount of light from the flash, taking the ratio of daylight to flash from 1:1 to 2:1. Also consider your distance from the subject; the closer you are, the less power you'll need. Below, Brett Harkness provides a step-by-step guide to how he uses fill-in.

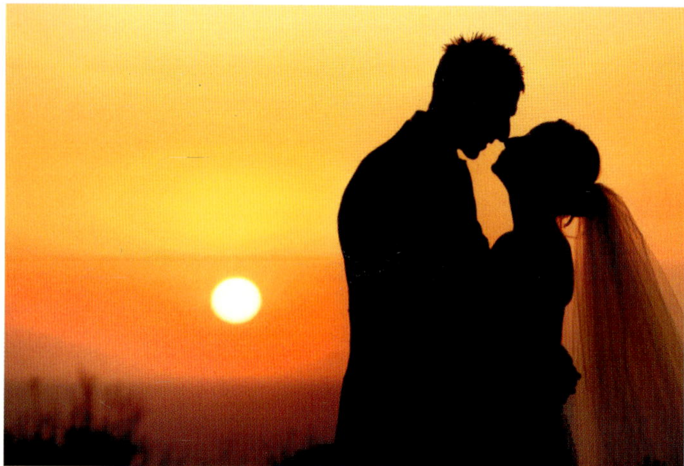

No fill-in flash Portraits taken outside on sunny days are hard to get right because of the high contrast created. Your subject may have shadows under their eyes or across their face from their nose. In extreme backlighting, your subject could be completely silhouetted, as in the shot above, but all of this can be remedied by adding a bit of flash to fill in the shadows.

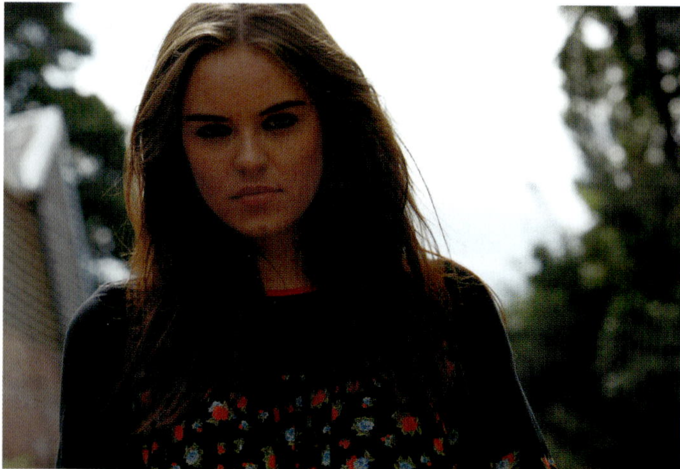

1 No flash This portrait, taken in program mode, is exactly how the camera saw it. The hard shadows across the face could benefit from some fill-in flash, which will fill in the darker areas and even out high contrast.

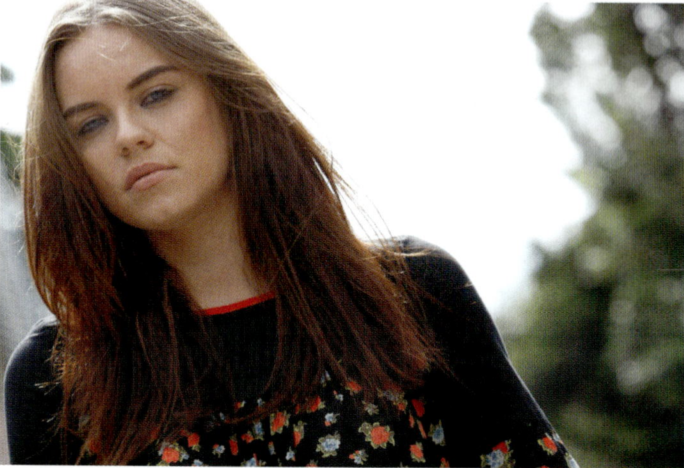

2 Dial in exposure compensation Before attaching my flash, I dial in +1EV of exposure compensation on my camera and take a shot. The result is brighter, but I'm starting to lose background detail, so fill-in flash is called for.

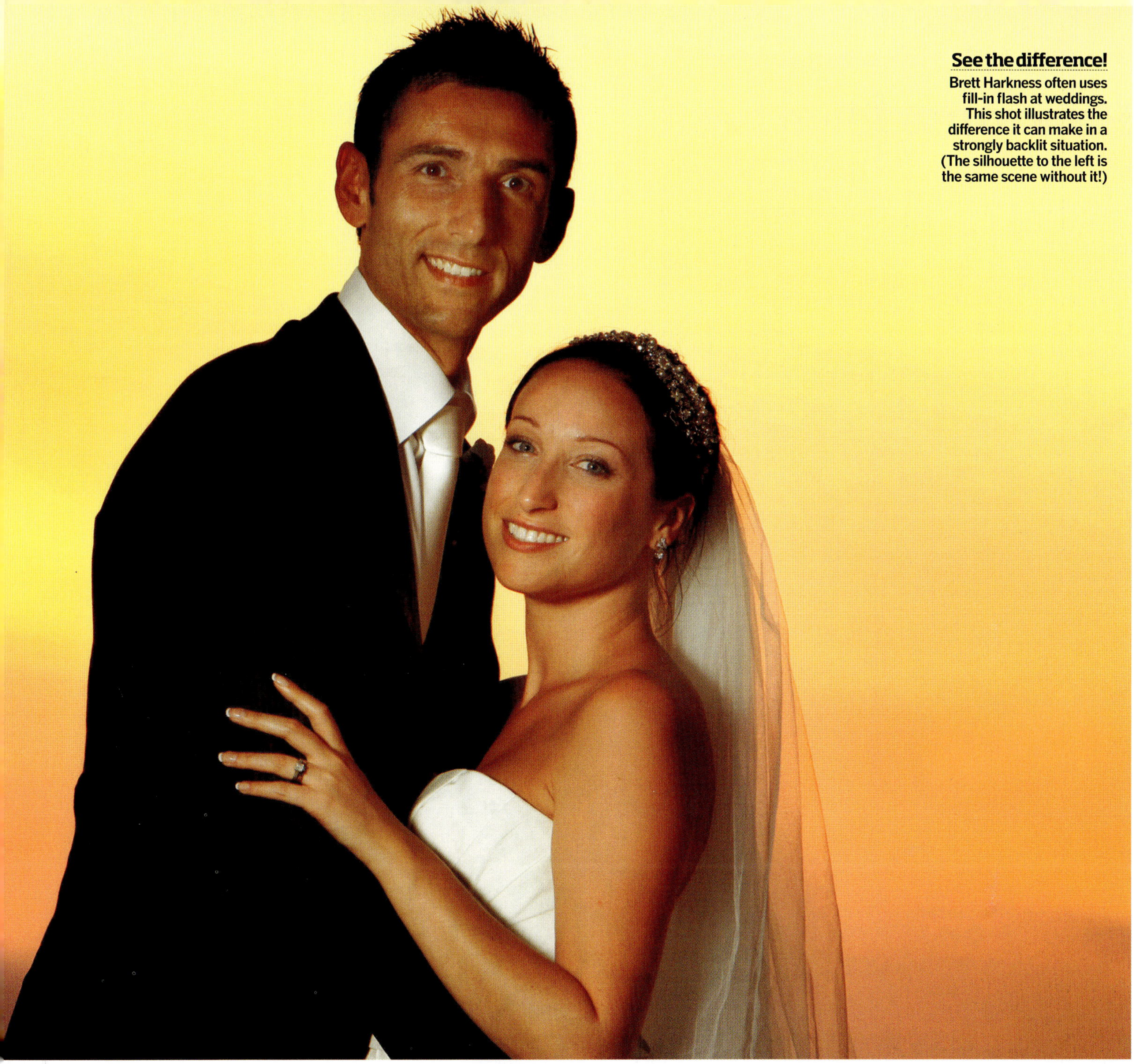

See the difference!

Brett Harkness often uses fill-in flash at weddings. This shot illustrates the difference it can make in a strongly backlit situation. (The silhouette to the left is the same scene without it!)

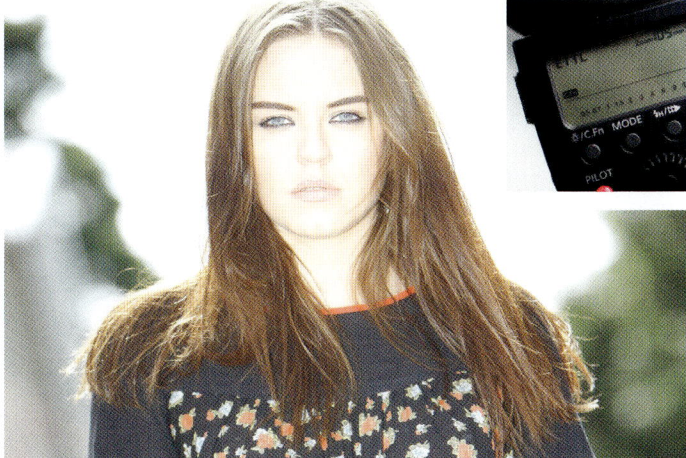

3 Use fill-in flash I switch on my Canon Speedlite 580EX II and set it to E-TTL mode. Program mode automatically selected the maximum flash sync speed of 1/250sec and chose an aperture of f/8, but the result is too bright.

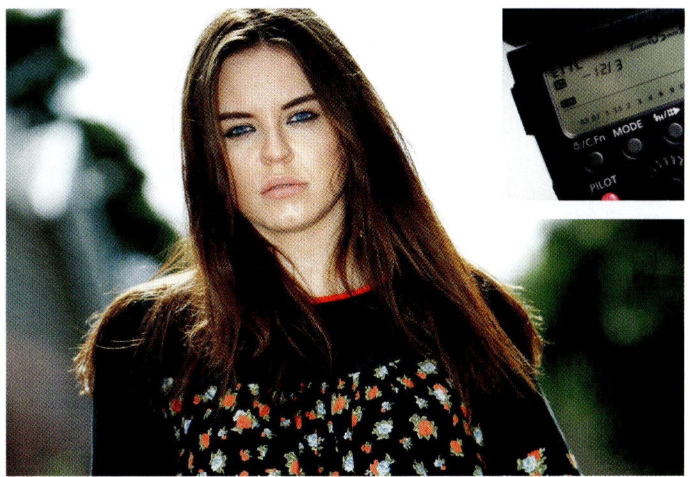

4 Adjust exposure Still shooting in program mode, with the flash in E-TTL mode, I set the flash exposure compensation to $-1\frac{2}{3}$ stops. This exposed my subject perfectly, while maintaining the background detail.

Slow-sync flash

While flash is most commonly used to freeze movement in a scene, by selecting slow-sync flash, you can get creative and add some motion to your flash

IN AUTO MODE, most digital SLRs set a relatively fast shutter speed of around 1/100sec when the flash is switched on. This can be a problem if you are trying to use a slow shutter speed for creative reasons, such as capturing ambient light in a low-light scene, as you'll end up losing all the natural light and the mood and atmosphere that comes with it. There is a solution, though – engaging slow-sync flash mode maintains the convenience of automatic TTL flash, but forces your camera to use whatever shutter speed you have set, no matter how long. Effectively, this means you can mix flash and natural light together in the same exposure.

Slow-sync flash isn't just a good feature for night-time photography, though: it's good in any situation where a longer shutter speed is required. You might be panning while shooting a moving subject and want to blur the background, or why not record the blur of objects as they move through the frame after the flash exposure has gone off? You'll end up with a 'frozen' image from the short burst of flash, followed by a trail of movement in front. This could be motion blur or light trails, for instance.

In this last scenario, you have a further option. In normal slow-sync flash modes, the flash fires at the beginning of the exposure and then the shutter stays open to record movement. However, many DSLRs and flashguns have another flash mode, called rear-curtain sync, or sometimes second-curtain sync. In this mode, the flash fires at the end of the exposure rather than the beginning, meaning that any motion recorded during a long exposure is captured before the 'frozen' image is captured by the flash. As a result, any trails appear behind the moving subject, giving a more realistic impression of speed and movement in the image.

Slow-sync with second-curtain sync

While using your flash in auto mode delivers well-exposed results, certain types of scenes, such as children at play, can be injected with energy by using slow-sync flash. As you can see from the comparison set below, the slow-sync flash is slightly more dynamic. The camera has followed the subject down the slide, resulting in streaks of movement in the background. By also setting the flashgun to second-curtain sync (also know as rear-curtain sync), a burst of flash occurs at the end of the exposure rather than at the start. Try this technique the next time you're shooting a moving subject in low light and add a little extra creativity to your flash photography.

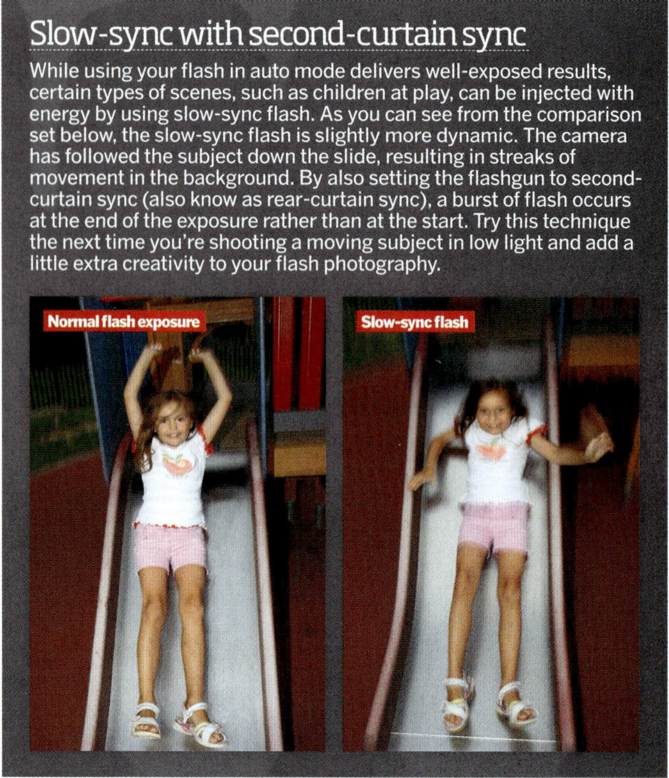

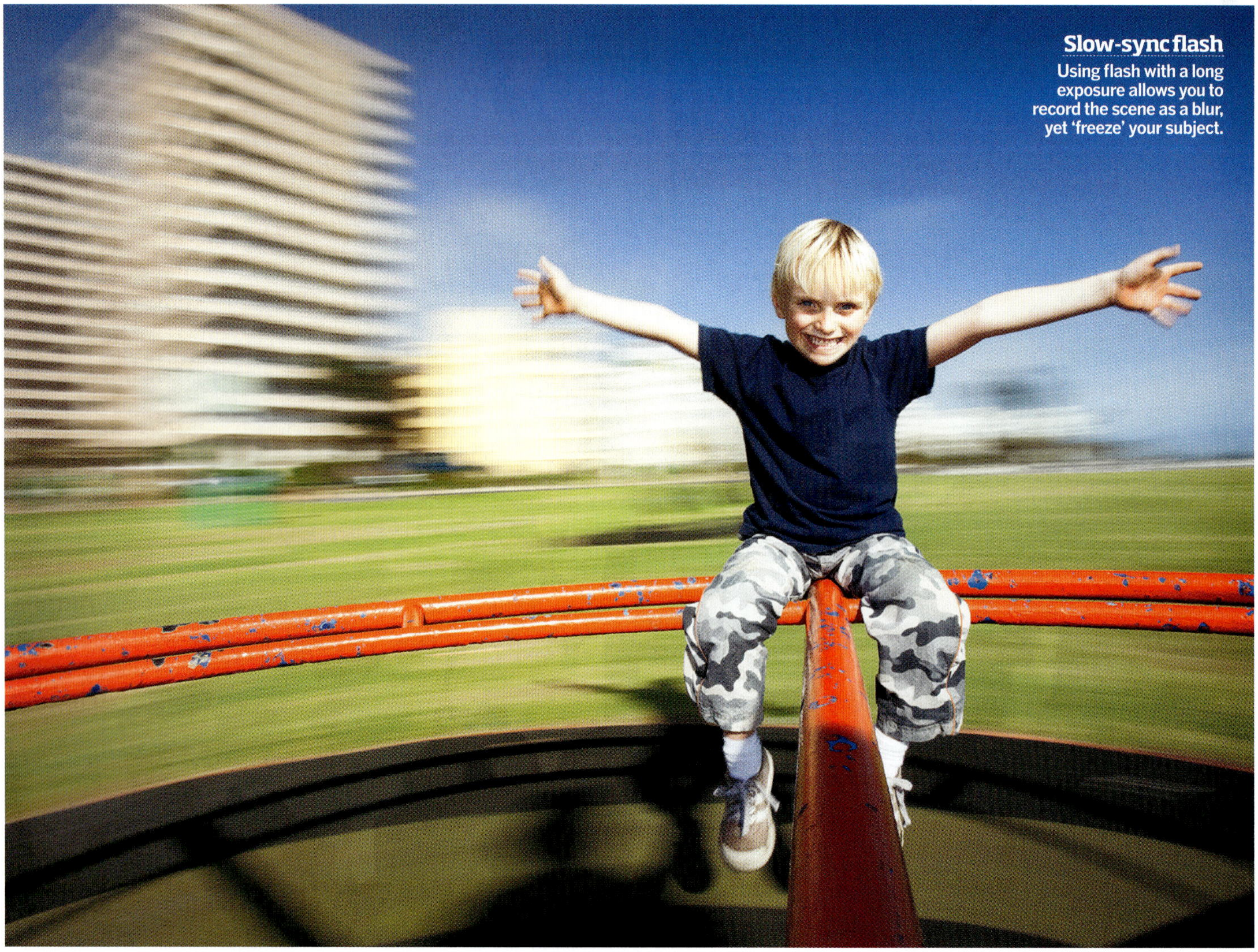

ISTOCKPHOTO

Slow-sync flash
Using flash with a long exposure allows you to record the scene as a blur, yet 'freeze' your subject.

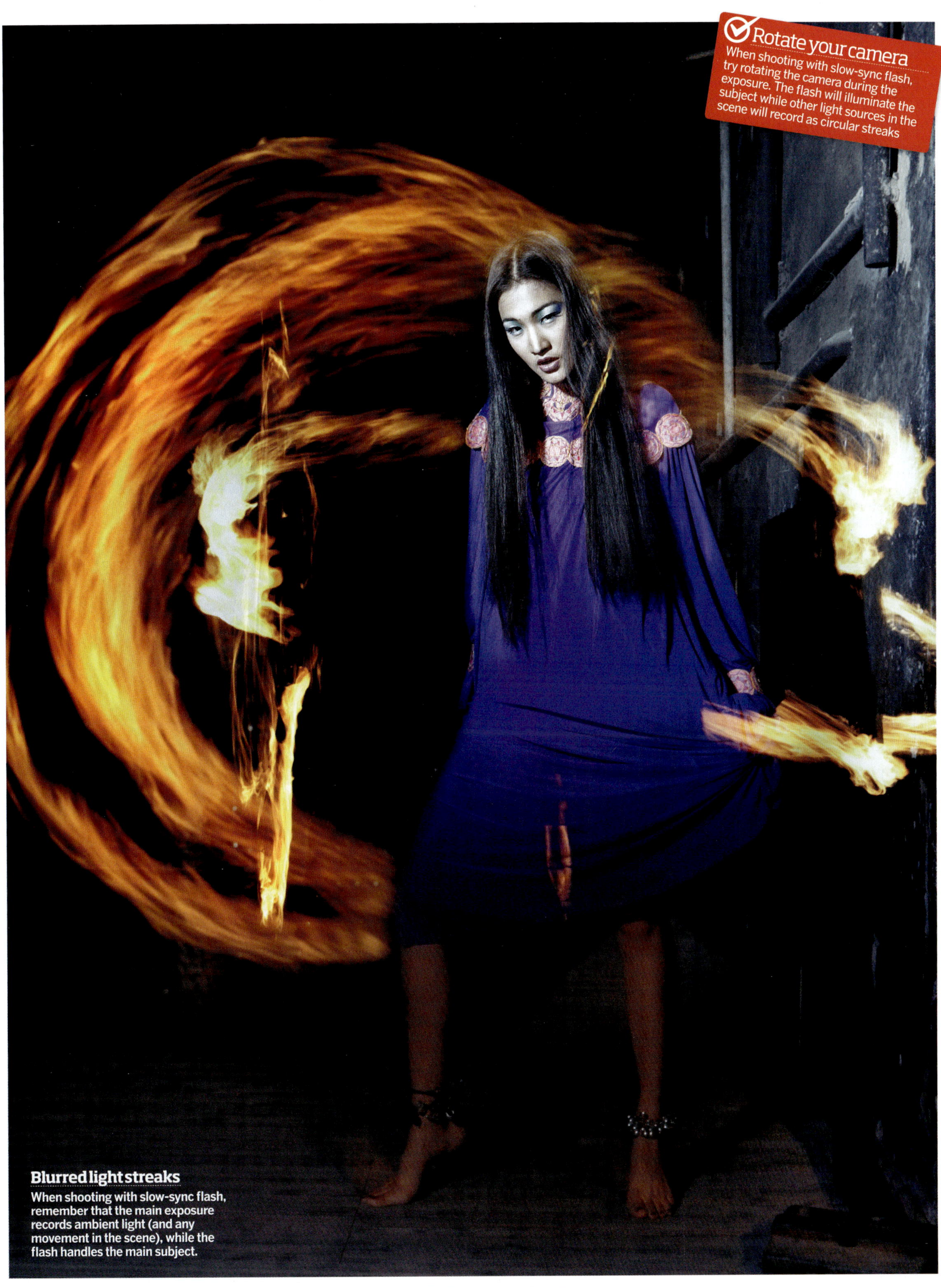

Rotate your camera

When shooting with slow-sync flash, try rotating the camera during the exposure. The flash will illuminate the subject while other light sources in the scene will record as circular streaks

Blurred light streaks

When shooting with slow-sync flash, remember that the main exposure records ambient light (and any movement in the scene), while the flash handles the main subject.

Using high-speed flash in bright daylight

Faced with bright sunlight when shooting portraits? Time for a quick blast of high-speed flash…

WHEN USING FLASH, you'll find that your DSLR has a maximum shutter speed that you cannot exceed, known as the camera's sync speed. This is usually between 1/125sec and 1/250sec and corresponds to the fastest shutter speed at which your DSLR's focal plane shutter is entirely open.

If you could open the back of your camera, you'd see that the shutter consists of two metal curtains. One of these starts the exposure by moving down vertically, which allows light through to the sensor. After a fraction of a second, the second curtain follows, shielding the sensor and ending the exposure. As the second curtain starts closing before the first one has finished opening, the sensor would not be fully exposed if you were to select a shutter speed that was faster than the camera's sync speed. Most cameras prevent you from being able to do this, but if you could, you'd see a dark band across the image – a result of the shutter obscuring the sensor during the burst of flash, preventing it from reaching the sensor.

A few years ago, Olympus found a way around this and other marques followed suit. The result is FP flash (FP stands for 'Focal Plane'), also known as High-Speed flash on Canon Speedlites. In this mode, a flashgun outputs a sequence of pulses over the course of the whole exposure, rather than blasting out all of its output in one go. The result is usable flash at shutter speeds up to 1/8000sec, although it has limitations: the power of the flash drops off as the shutter speed is shortened; FP mode drains the life from batteries more than normal flash photography; and it's only recently that FP flash has worked with automated TTL exposure systems. This means older DSLRs and flashes only work this way in manual mode.

Despite these drawbacks, FP flash can be vital when shooting portraits outdoors and mixing daylight with flash. Especially on bright, sunny days (when some fill-in flash is required), which force shutter speeds up above a sync speed, especially if you are using wide apertures to blur backgrounds.

Brett Harkness explains how to use high-speed flash for portraits

High-speed flash works best when you're shooting with a wide aperture while trying to balance flash with daylight for fill-in effects. Wide apertures mean fast shutter speeds, but with conventional flash, the options open to you are limited by the flash sync speed. Wide apertures are important in portraiture for making your subject stand off the background and this is where FP flash comes into its own. Most mid-range to high-end flashguns offer a high-speed facility, but not all DSLRs can be used with it, so consult your instruction manual (or local dealer) before you go out and buy a flashgun!

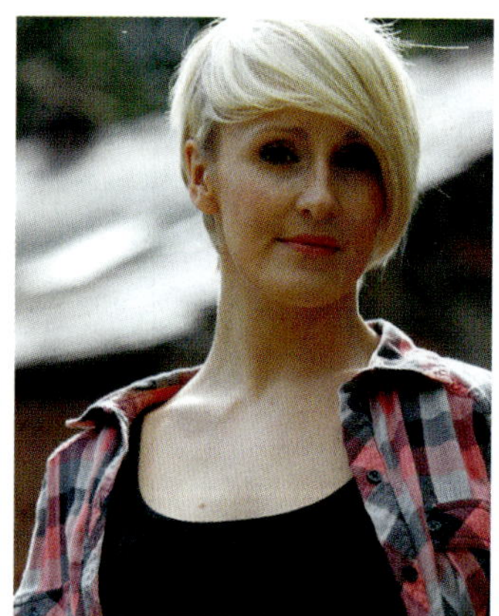

1 No flash This portrait desperately needs fill-in flash, but it was taken with an exposure of 1/640sec at f/6.3. Coming down to my camera's sync speed of 1/250sec would mean an aperture of f/11 – not the best for getting a shallow depth-of-field.

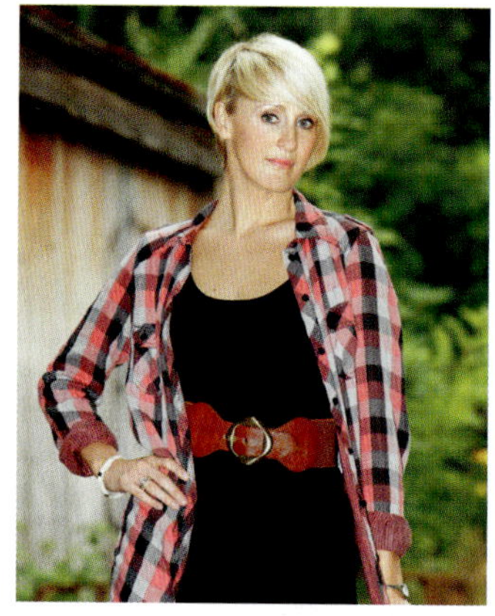

2 Set exposure Moving my model to a darker location and reducing my ISO to 50 helped me get an exposure of 1/250sec at f/7.1. Although this is a wider aperture than f/11, the background isn't very blurred. I get better results using FP flash.

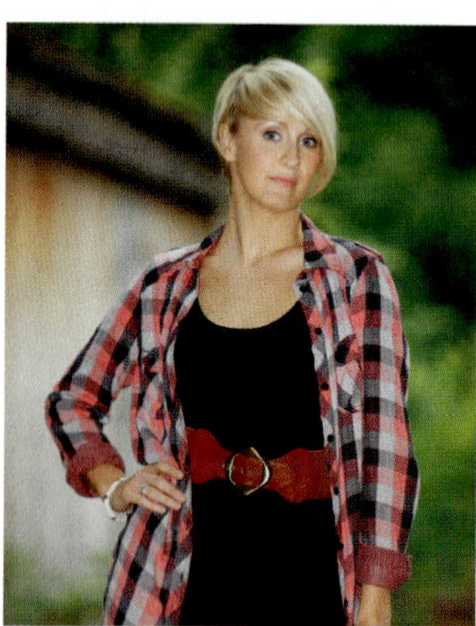

3 Use FP flash Switching on FP flash lets me shoot wide open at f/2.8 and set the required 1/1250sec shutter speed. The background is now nicely blurred thanks to the restricted depth-of-field, and my subject stands off it well.

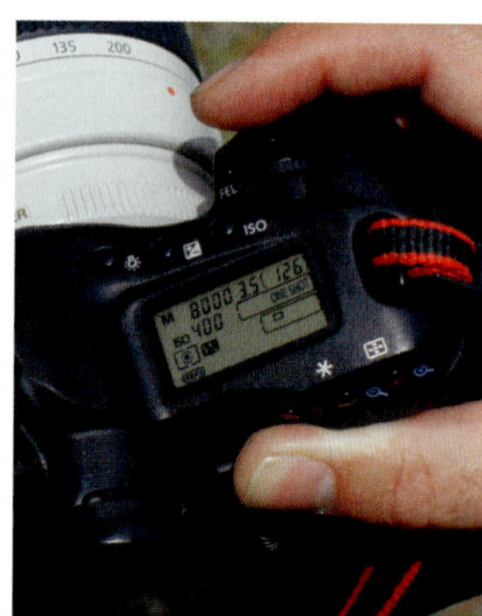

4 Increase shutter speed In bright conditions, I can take the shutter speed up to 1/8000sec – the maximum. It's no wonder wedding photographers (who rely on fill-in flash on sunny days) love the flexibility that high-speed flash gives them.

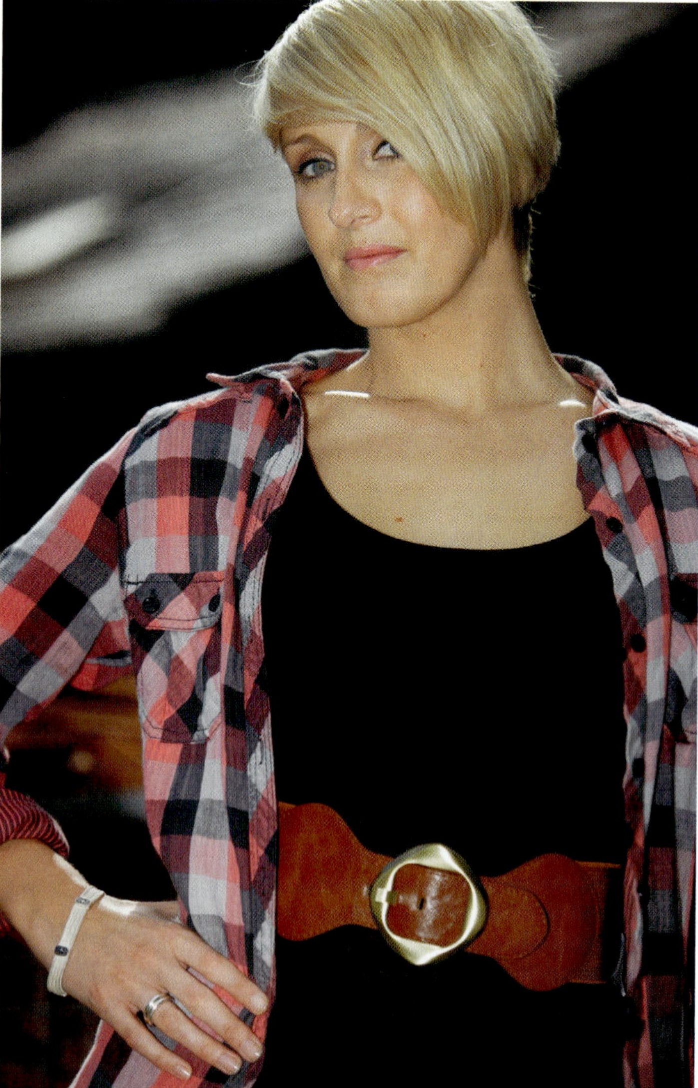

ALL IMAGES BRETT HARKNESS

5 Add fill-in flash Combining fill-in flash with an exposure of 1/8000sec at f/3.5 means my subject is properly exposed but stands out from the blurred background. It's a technique that is indispensible in my line of work.

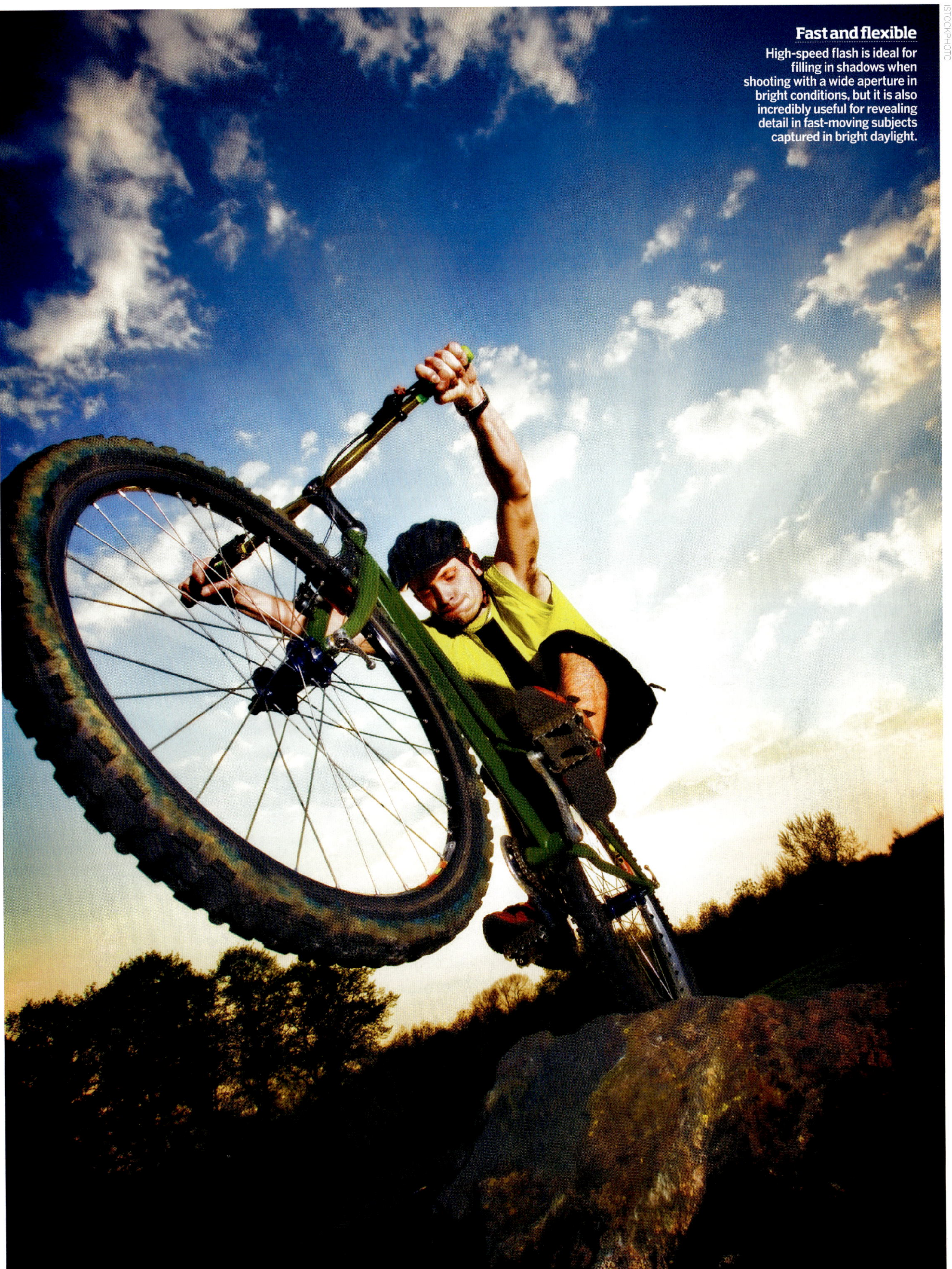

Fast and flexible

High-speed flash is ideal for filling in shadows when shooting with a wide aperture in bright conditions, but it is also incredibly useful for revealing detail in fast-moving subjects captured in bright daylight.

How to add drama to sky for outdoor portraits

Underexposing the scene and using flash to light the subject is a great way to add impact to portraits

MORE OFTEN THAN NOT, flash is used to balance flash and ambient lighting, or to fill in shadows, but now and again, it pays to use flash to overpower the ambient light and completely transform a scene.

A great technique to try is to capture a dramatic sky by underexposing the scene, leading it to appear far darker than it does in reality, while allowing the flash to correctly expose the subject. You can do it two ways: use the exposure compensation facility to dial in a negative value, or work in manual mode, both of which we'll explain in further detail.

Regardless of which you choose, for the best results, avoid using the camera's integral flash or mounting a flash on the hotshoe and instead trigger a remote flash via a slave or off-camera flash cord. Simply reposition the flash to the side of the subject to immediately change the function of the flash from a flat fill-in light to one that's directional and contrast-enhancing. For the purpose of this step-by-step, we'll explain how to do this technique using manual settings rather than relying on your camera's TTL system, as it offers greater control and a chance to learn and experiment.

Different camera and flash systems work in different ways, so if you do want to try the exposure compensation method with TTL, check your camera's instruction manual.

Remember: when working with manual flash, the shutter speed controls the amount of ambient light reaching the sensor, while aperture controls flash output. For this technique, shutter speed is paramount as you're exposing for the sky, not the subject. The faster the shutter speed, the darker the ambience will be; the slower the shutter speed, the more you encourage the influence of ambient light.

Using radio triggers

Most of the time, once a flash is off-camera and triggered by a radio release it loses its TTL capabilities, so it's important your flash has manual settings. To retain TTL, you could opt for a dedicated off-camera lead, but you will be restricted by the length of the cord. However, if you're comfortable using manual flash, the more affordable option is a slave cell or a flash remote trigger – there are many available, varying in price and functions. While PocketWizards are brilliant, and a market leader for performance, they're also expensive. Camera manufacturers also have their own remotes but we'd recommend independent versions by the likes of Calumet, Kenro, Hähnel and Seculine as they're cheaper and do the job well enough. The Hähnel Combi TF, for instance, is a bargain at around £50 and doubles up as a remote flash trigger and shutter release. Seculine's highly efficient Twin Link T2D Wireless Radio Flash Trigger Kit can be bought for around £120. Regardless of what remote you buy, remember you need a transmitter to sit on your camera's hotshoe and a receiver to attach to each of your off-camera flashguns for it to work.

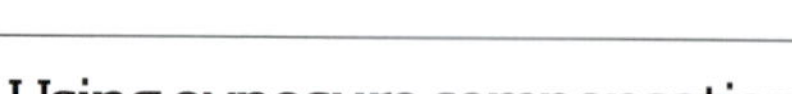

Using exposure compensation

Instead of using manual mode, set your camera to aperture-priority mode, your flash to TTL and meter for the background. Dial in the aperture you want and then set a negative value on the camera's exposure compensation to at least two stops to underexpose the scene: the flash will take care of the subject. If you're shooting with a Nikon, you may have to increase your flash exposure compensation by two stops too, as the flash and exposure compensation are linked. Have a play and experiment with results.

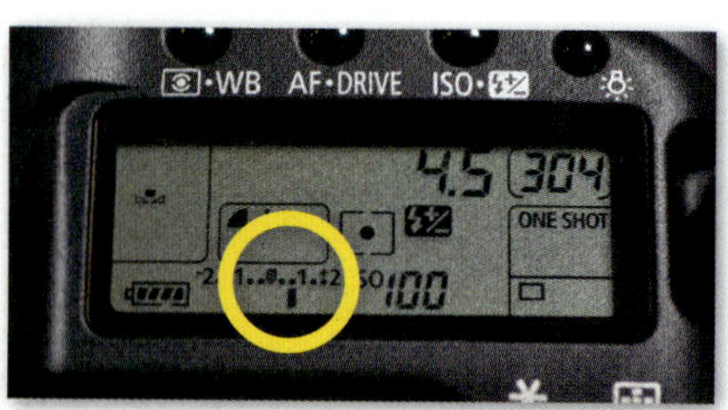

Getting a dramatic sky with an outdoor portrait

This is an advanced technique, so requires practice. Pro photographer Brett Harkness, who regularly uses it, explains how to make the most of manual flash and moody skies. On this shoot, it's overcast and there's a mass of detail in the sky to capture. As Brett likes his shots sharp front-to-back, he uses a small aperture of around f/13 and sets his flash to ¼ power to compensate. If you want shallow depth-of-field, keep the flash close to your subject, set the flash to ⅛ power and open the aperture.

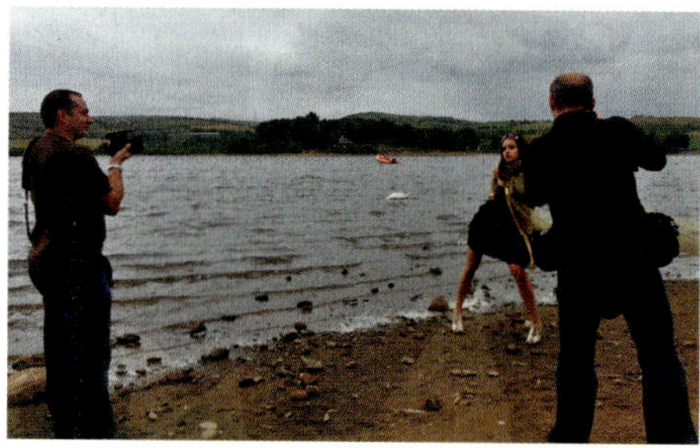

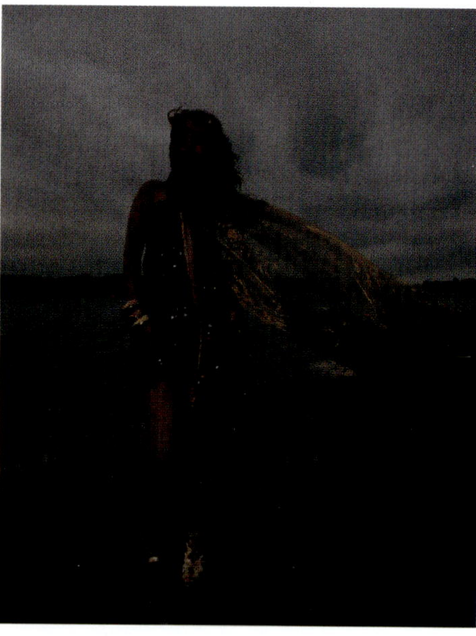

1 (Above) Prepare the flash I ask my assistant to hold the flashgun several feet away from the model, Emma. Because we're not using any diffusion accessories, I have him hold the flash vertically to get a bigger spread of light over her. Sunglasses and gold fabric add a fashion-shoot feel.

2 (Right) Underexpose the scene To capture a moody sky, I have to dramatically underexpose the scene using a fast shutter speed to retain detail in the sky. As you can see, a fast shutter speed has underexposed the scene, but without using flash it means the subject is also very dark.

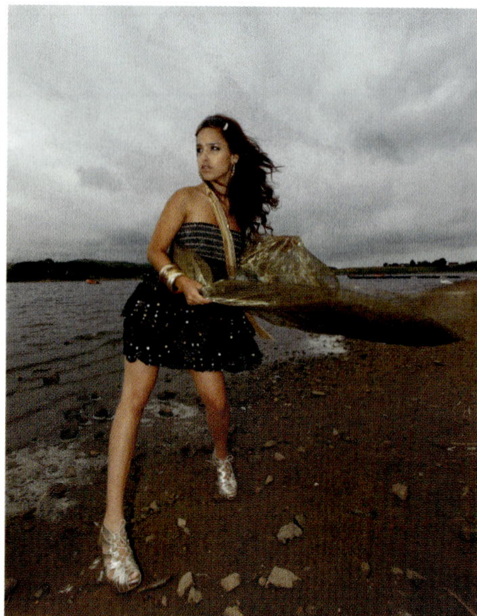

3 (Left) Set exposure Once I start using flash, my shutter speed is immediately limited to the camera's sync speed – in this case 1/250sec. With my camera set to manual, I set the aperture that gives the scene the correct exposure for the ambient light. I then set the flashgun to ¼ power, which exposes Emma well, but the scene lacks drama and mood.

4 (Below) Raise the flash To improve the effect, my assistant raises the flash and points it down on Emma. However, the key to darkening the scene behind her is to close down the aperture (in this instance by two stops) so that the background is underexposed, resulting in a far moodier result.

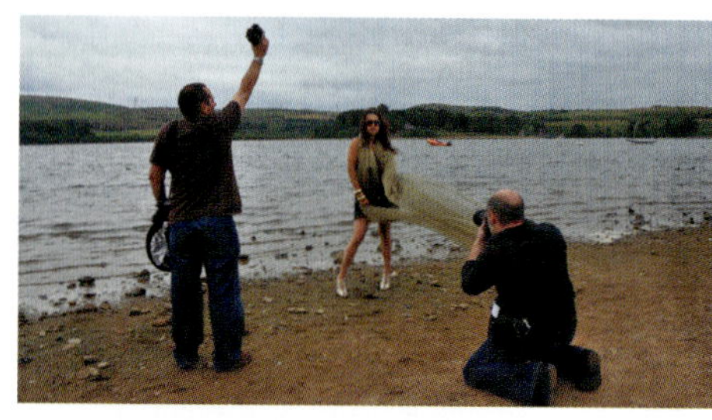

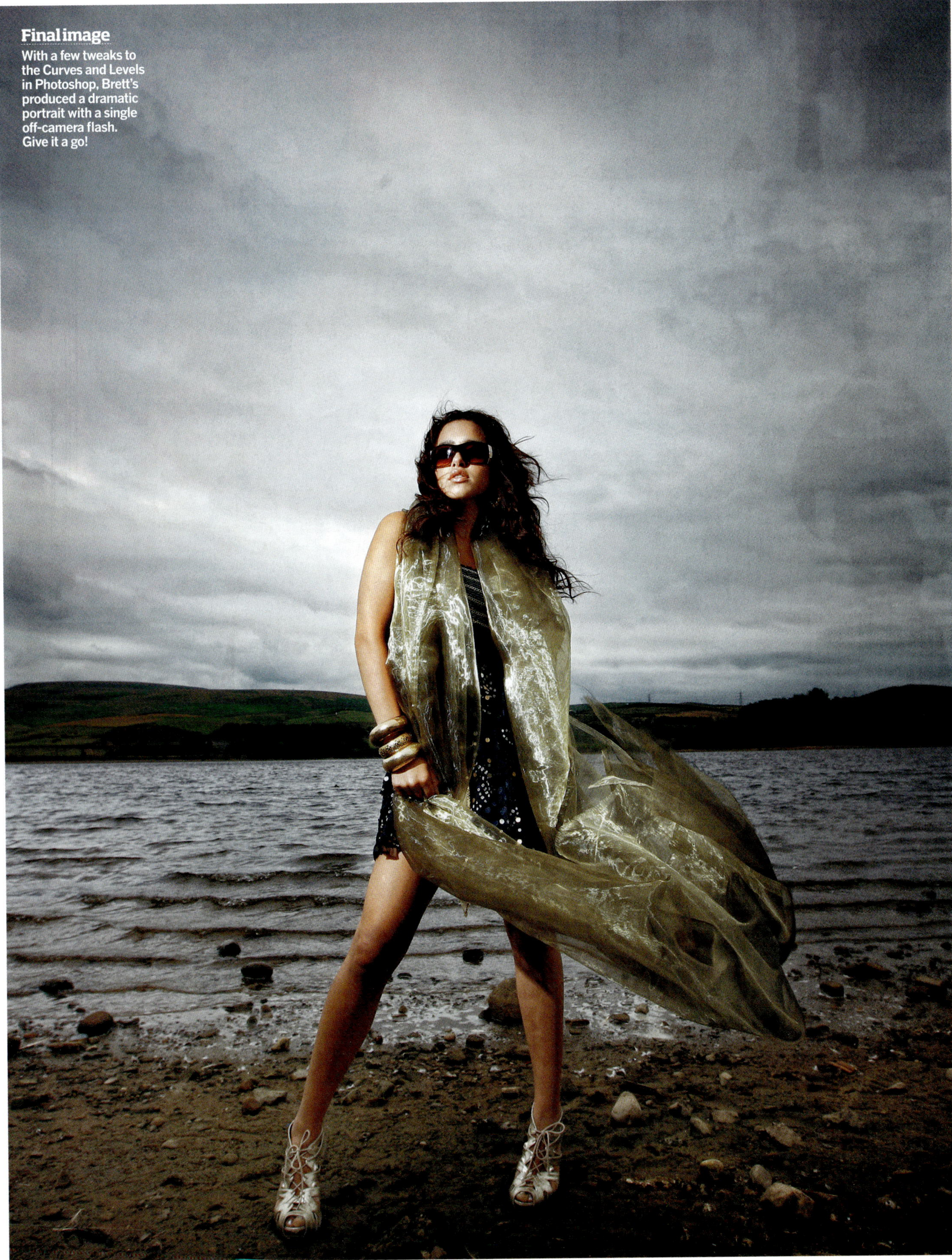

Final image
With a few tweaks to the Curves and Levels in Photoshop, Brett's produced a dramatic portrait with a single off-camera flash. Give it a go!

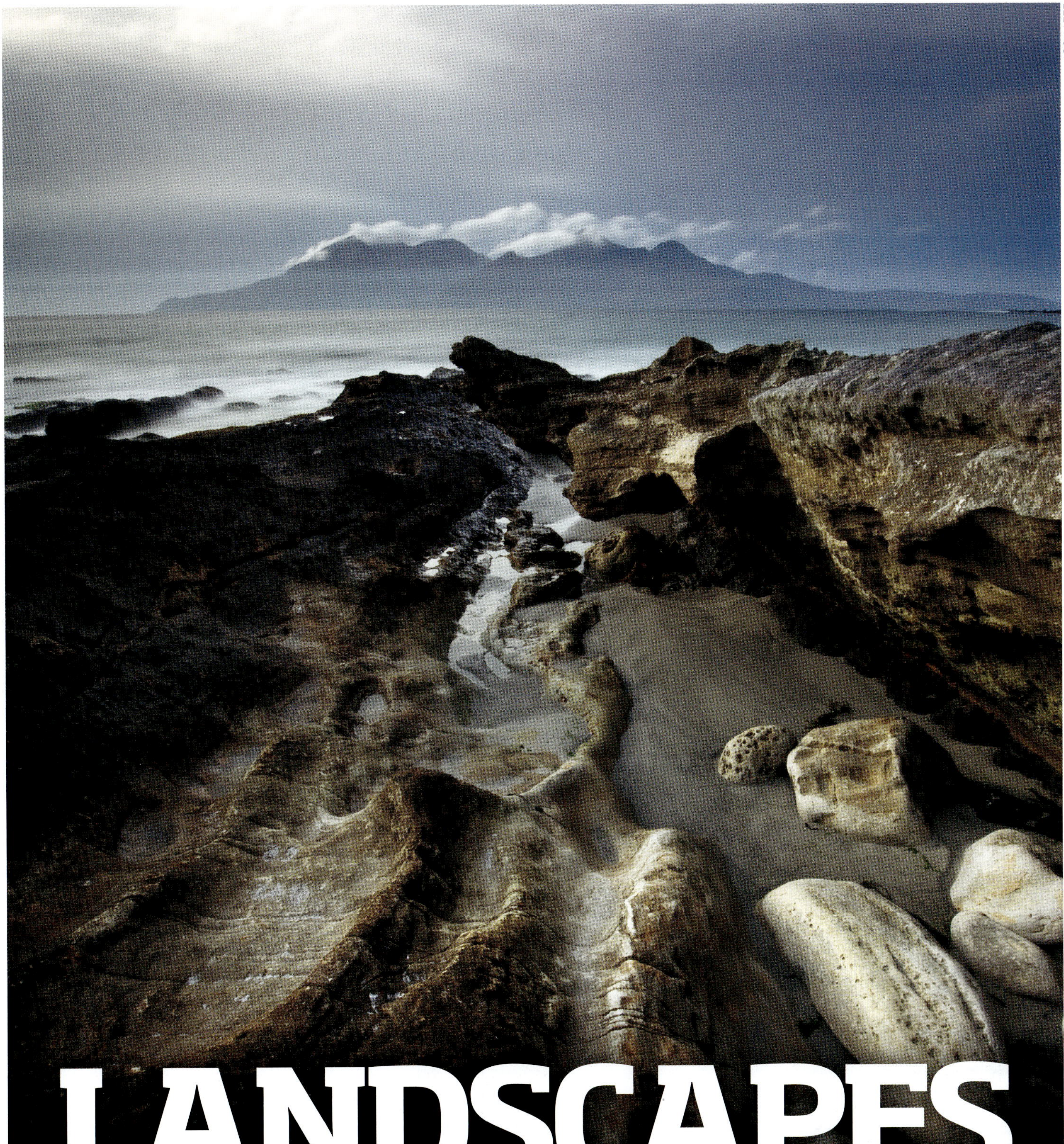

LEE FROST

LANDSCAPES

The wonders of the great outdoors offer endless potential for stunning photography. This major section provides all the essentials you need to take your best ever landscape images

CAPTURING BEAUTIFUL LANDSCAPES is a pursuit shared by millions of photographers around the world. Whether shooting in the UK or abroad, the diversity of the scenery and how it appears at different times of day, in each of the seasons and under different weather conditions, means that the great outdoors can offer an ever-changing range of scenery for you to photograph. We cover all the core principles and techniques that will help you to take your best ever landscape photographs, as well as provide a huge selection of stunning images to inspire you each time you venture out with your camera kit.

Creating balance: The rule-of-thirds

Before you shoot a single image, you need to practise this simple framing technique

THE WORD 'BALANCE' implies an equal weighting. In a picture, this would mean symmetry, but visual balance – or rather harmony – is not usually achieved this way. Placing a subject centrally in the frame usually results in a static, rather than a dynamic, composition. An off-centre subject, on the other hand, encourages the eye to move around the scene, resulting in a more engaging picture.

One way of dividing the frame up to achieve harmony is to use the rule-of-thirds. This is a simplified version of the 'Golden Section', a proportion that has been used in art and architecture for centuries. This proportion also occurs with great frequency in nature, and there is research to suggest that our brains are hardwired to respond positively to images and objects that follow this rule of proportions – for example, people whose faces are proportioned according to the Golden Section tend to be thought of as more attractive.

The practical application of this in landscape photography is to divide the frame up into thirds, horizontally and vertically, and organise the elements in the scene to fit into the grid, for example by placing the horizon line on one of the dividing lines. The points where horizontal and vertical lines intersect can be particularly powerful places for putting strong focal points in a scene.

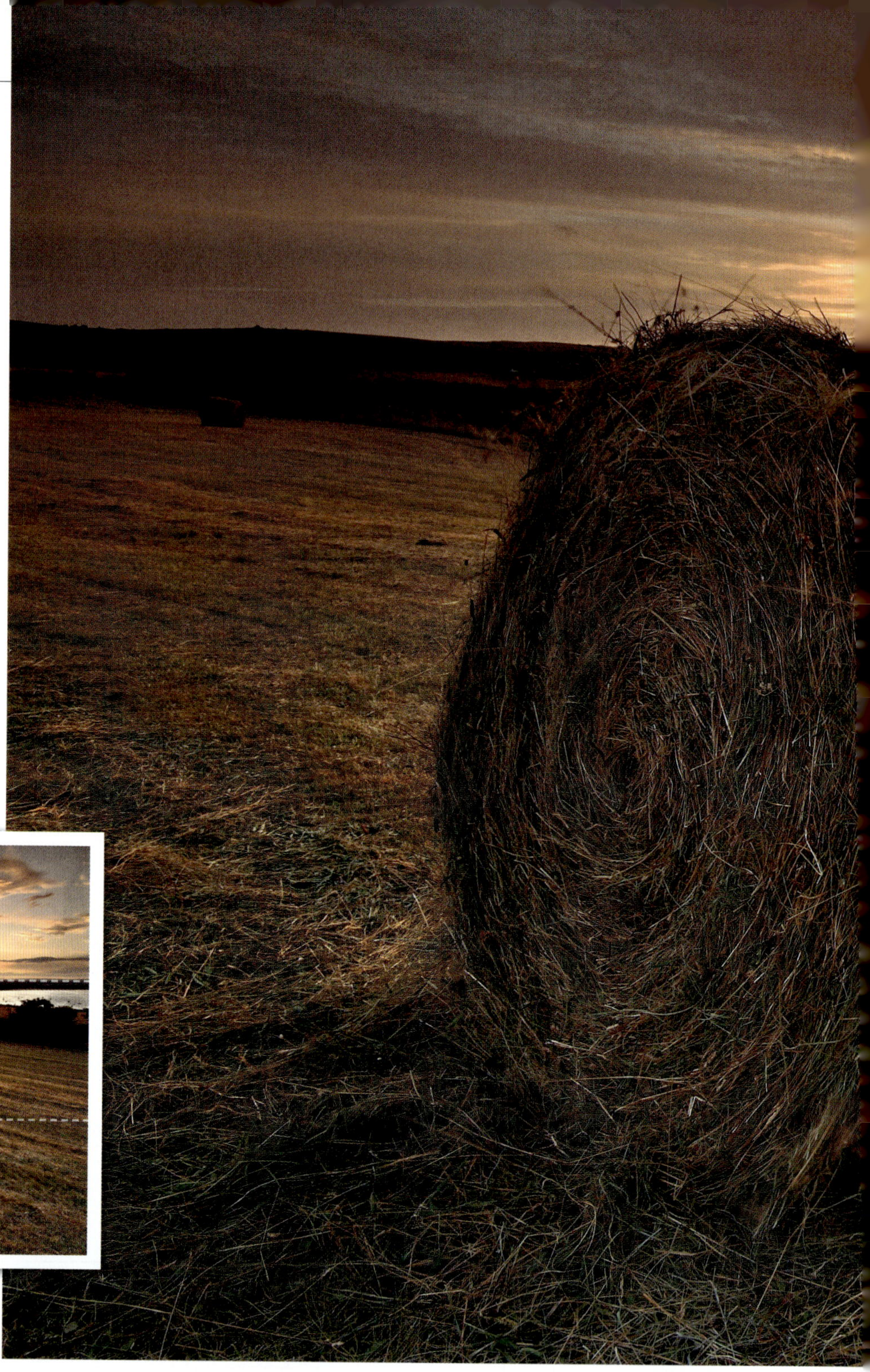

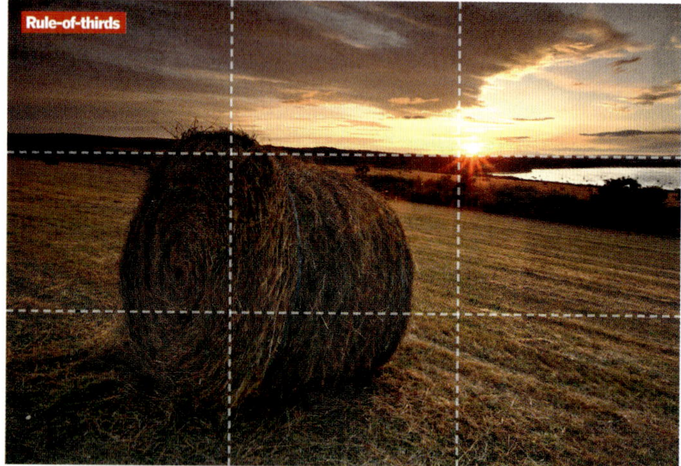

Right: This image follows the rule-of-thirds quite closely. There is approximately two-thirds land and one-third sky, the main part of the hay bale is in the left third of the frame and the sun is placed on an intersection of thirds.

Breaking the rules: Horizons

Like all rules, however, the rule-of-thirds needs to be applied with judgement rather than as a matter of course, and there will always be situations where it needs to be ignored. It's best if you think of the rule-of-thirds more as a guideline as there will be instances where applying this 'rule' doesn't strengthen an image. For example, when shooting a scene where the sky is reflected in water, you might well want to place the horizon across the middle of the frame, giving the two elements of the shot – sky and reflection – equal weighting. If there is no interest in the sky, the horizon can be placed higher in the frame or cropped out altogether, or to increase a sense of emptiness and isolation, the horizon can be placed very low in the frame for a big sky landscape. The beauty of shooting digitally is reviewing your efforts and shooting to ensure the perfect composition for the scene.

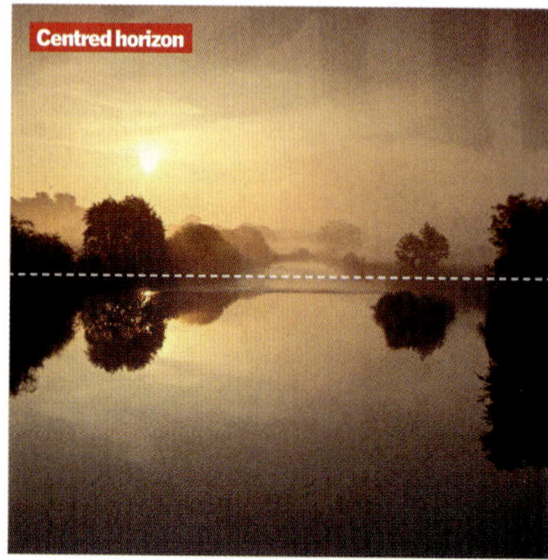

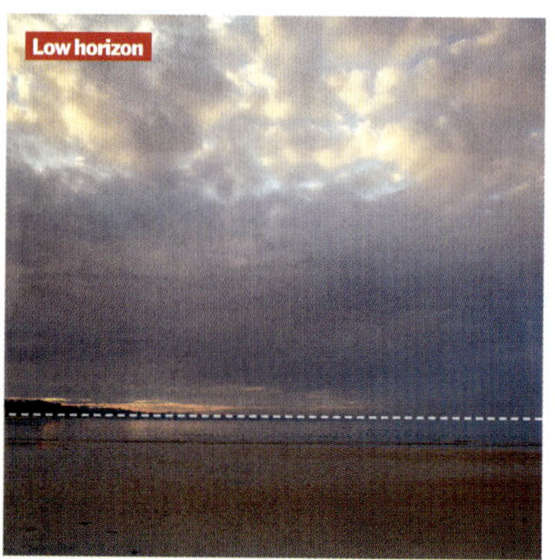

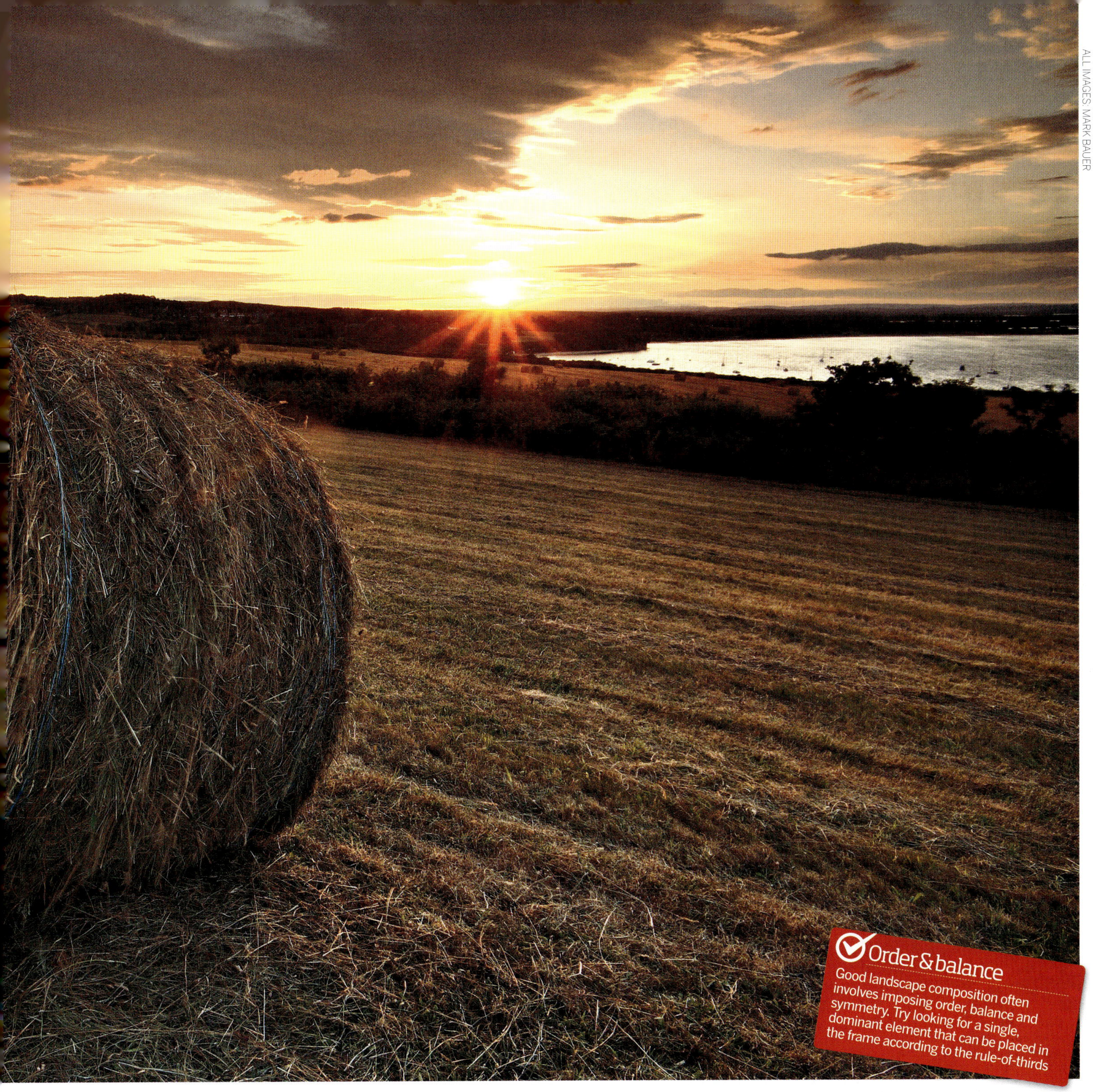

ALL IMAGES: MARK BAUER

Order & balance

Good landscape composition often involves imposing order, balance and symmetry. Try looking for a single, dominant element that can be placed in the frame according to the rule-of-thirds

Experiment with viewpoints

Finding the right viewpoint is important to achieving a successful landscape composition. Rather than shooting everything from head height, experiment with high and low viewpoints. Higher viewpoints have the effect of opening up the planes in the image and are useful with standard and telephoto lenses. Shooting up from a low vantage point, it can add immensity to your shots. When photographing well-known landmarks, it's tempting to use the established viewpoints, but spend time looking for a fresh view, as it's much more satisfying to capture an image that's original.

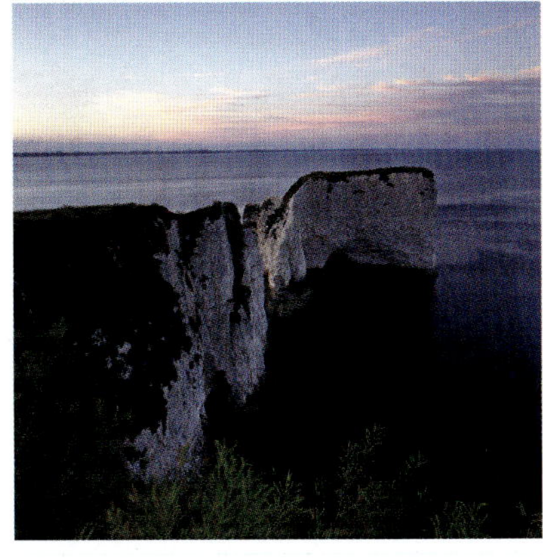

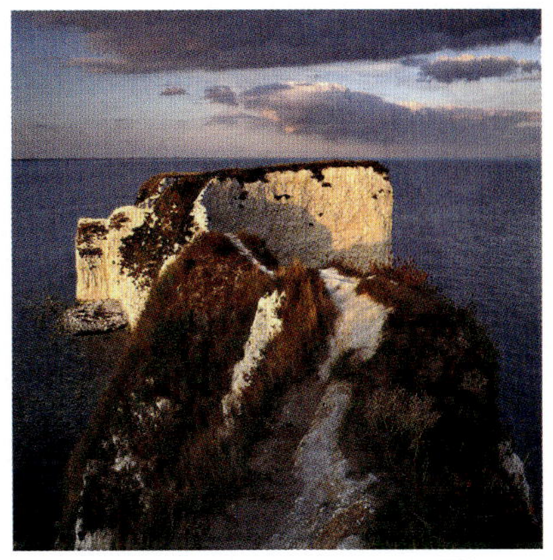

While there's nothing wrong with the first picture, it's the standard view of Old Harry Rocks in Dorset, taken by countless photographers before. Without having to move very far, however, a less photographed viewpoint was found and more dramatic image was achieved.

Lead-in lines

Master one of the most important compositional tools: lead-in lines

FEW COMPOSITIONAL DEVICES can improve the impact and add depth to your landscape pictures as well as lead-in lines.

When you think of lead-in lines, what comes to mind? Rows of crops, a seemingly never-ending road, a bendy stream? What about shadows, footprints, clouds, the coastline, windows, piers, cracks, paths or rocks – the list can go on and on. Although lead-in lines come in many guises, some natural, others man-made, all of them tend to either lead the viewer in and out of the picture or towards a focal point. The latter being the preferred choice as it allows the eye to settle within the scene, but both can work well depending on the picture.

Some of the most effective lead-in lines start from the bottom edge of the frame and go straight in to the centre of the picture, like a pier towards the horizon, but there are many variations that can have just as much impact, depending on the scene. While straight lines quickly draw the eye to the point of interest, curved lines force the viewer to take a more leisurely journey through the image. Vertical lines, shot from a low angle, like those on a building, add tension to a picture and diagonal lines work well if they travel from the bottom left to the top right of a picture, as that's where the human eye naturally gravitates. It doesn't have to be a single line either: multiple lines only strengthen the effect of one line, as long as they're clearly defined and heading in the same direction. It's very important to try to keep the elements within a scene connected, as any break in the flow of the line will leave the composition feeling disjointed and allow the viewer's gaze to wander aimlessly in and out the frame.

You can enhance your lead-in lines depending on what viewpoint and lens you choose, as both can either flatten or stretch perspective. The most dynamic distortion of lead-in lines is converging verticals. Converging diagonal lines create a powerful impression of distance and depth, especially if they converge in to the centre of the frame and run parallel to each other. By standing in the middle of them, you'll find that the further the lines are away from the camera, the closer they get to each other, creating what's known as a vanishing point when they join. A wide-angle lens can greatly enhance this effect as it stretches perspective – so the lines seem wider at the start and narrower in the distance – whereas a telephoto lens compresses perspective and hinders the feeling of depth.

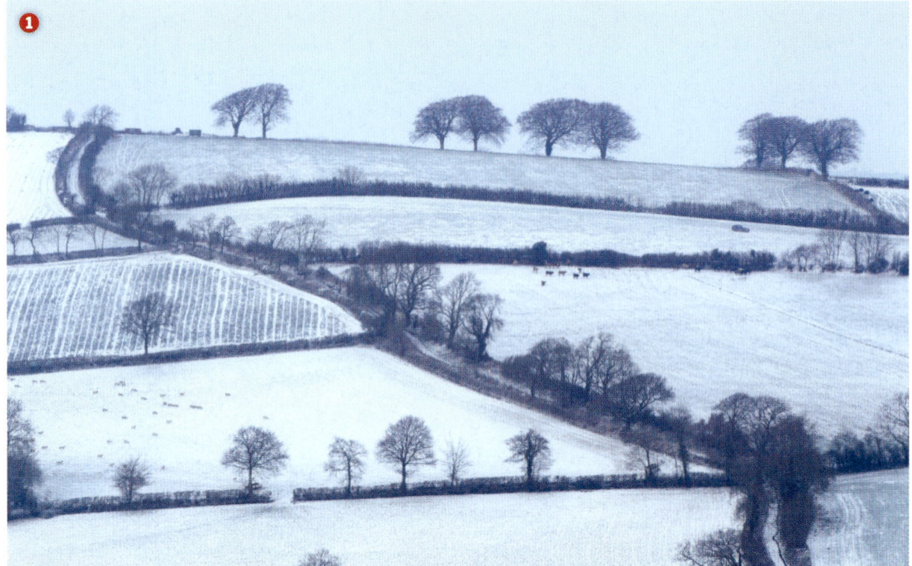
ADAM BURTON

1) Lead-in lines don't have to be straight or lead to a focal point: the line can also be the interest in the picture. Note how your eye is led through the scene by the wintry tree-lined road.

2) When using converging verticals, you need to get the entire scene in focus. Set the camera on a tripod and select a small aperture (f/11-f/22) and focus on the hyperfocal distance for maximum depth-of-field.

3) Simple compositions can sometimes be the most effective. Think about creating a graphic coastal landscape with nothing more than groynes or a pier as a lead-in line. By connecting it to the horizon, too, it means the viewer's gaze is led in to the far reaches of the scene and led out of the frame by the horizon line.

4) Diagonal lines can be used to draw the gaze from bottom left to top right, where the eye naturally gravitates, as in this coastal landscape where the lines of rocks converge towards the stunning sunset sky.

5) The fence in this picture is used as a neat device to draw the eye in towards the focal point: the elevated castle in the distance.

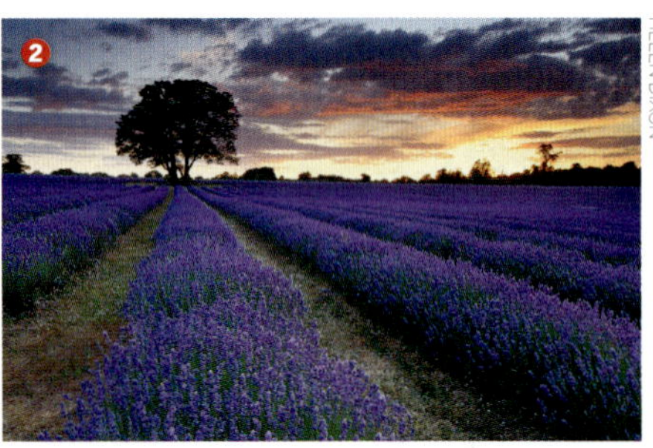
HELEN DIXON

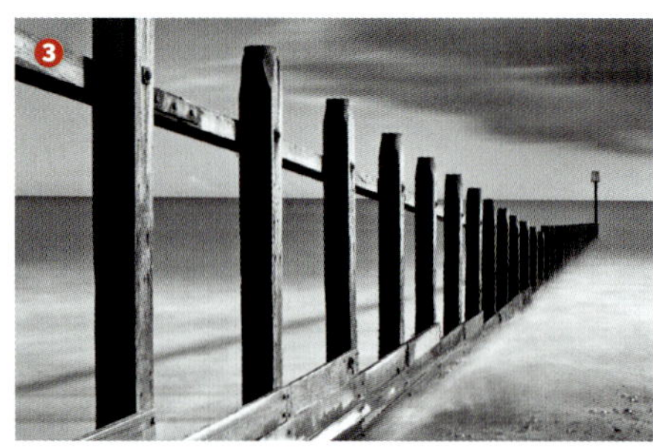
ROSS HODDINOTT

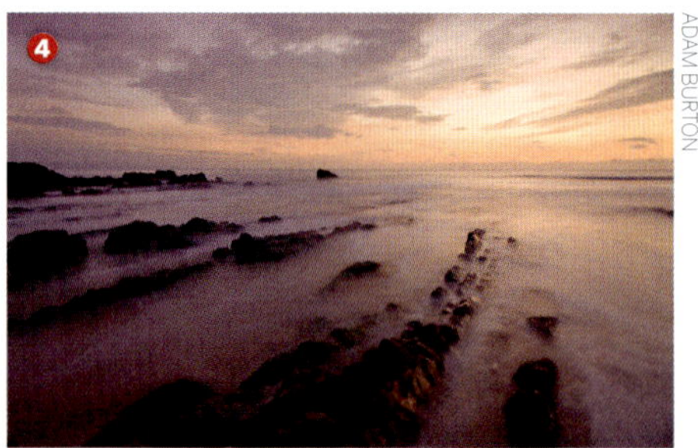
ADAM BURTON

Lead-in lines: Think differently

Try photographing lead-in lines from different angles. You may find that photographing the lines entering the frame at an angle work better than if you captured them starting within the frame. The opposite can be true, too. Try different perspectives: get low to the ground for extreme converging verticals. Tilt the camera up to see what vertical lines you can find and try to elevate your position by standing on a bridge, for instance. Above all, keep your eyes and your mind open for less obvious linear aspects and don't forget the other guidelines for composition, including foreground interest and the rule-of-thirds.

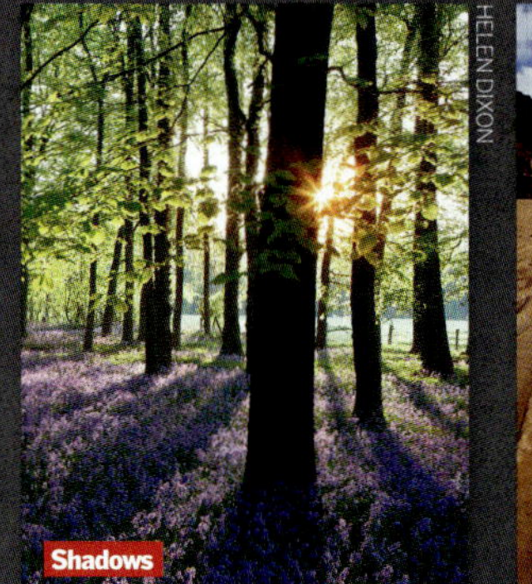
HELEN DIXON

Shadows

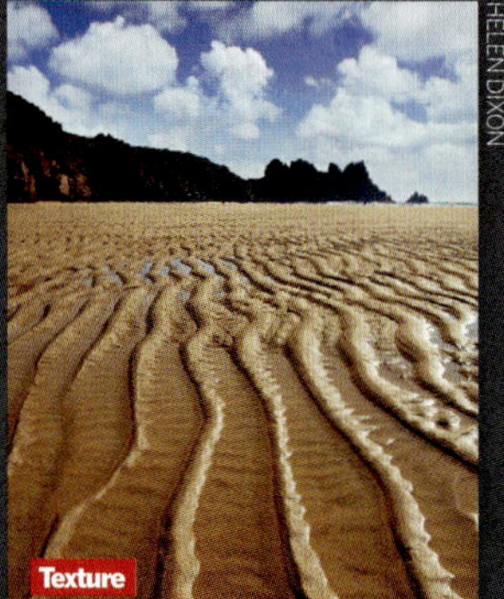
HELEN DIXON

Texture

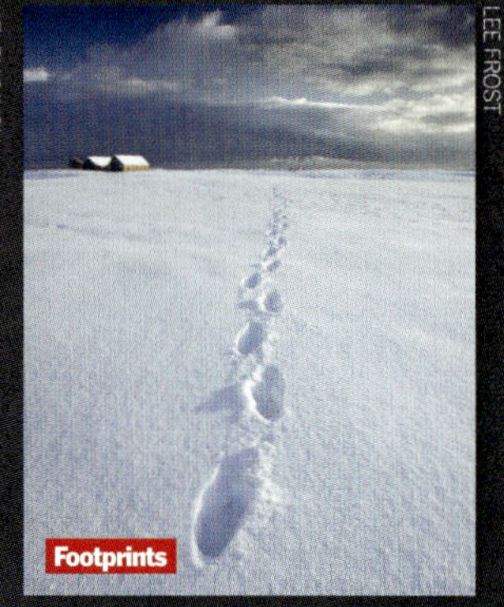
LEE FROST

Footprints

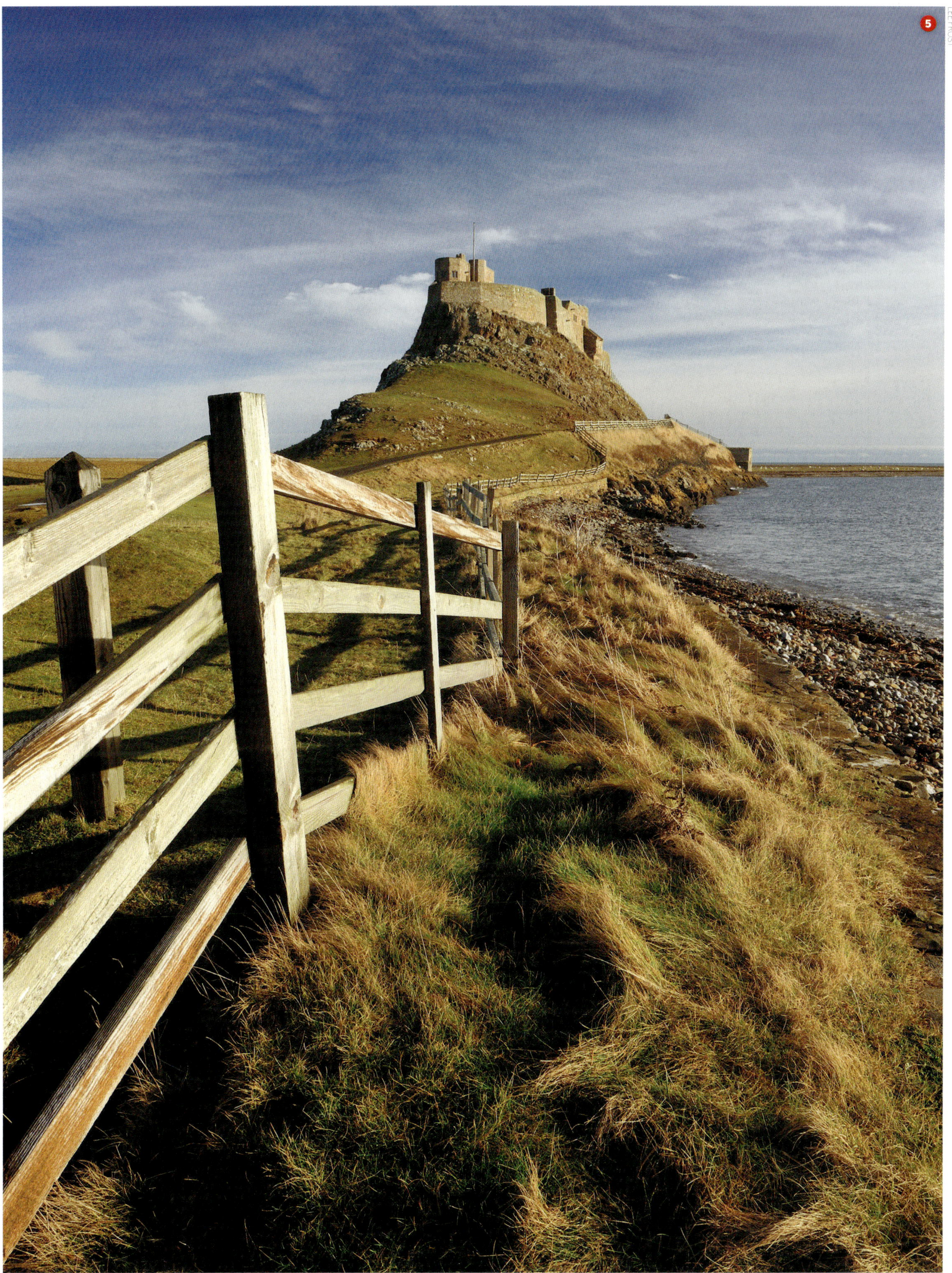

5

LEE FROST

How to use natural frames

For ideas, inspiration and information on how to improve your landscape pictures by using environmental frames, read on...

ONE OF THE MOST effective ways to produce a tight, structured composition is by framing the scene or subject you're shooting. Not only does this help to direct the viewer's eye towards the most important part of the picture, but frames can also be used to hide uninteresting areas, such as a broad expanse of empty sky. Natural frames can be used in all types of photography, but are abound in the landscape if you keep your eyes peeled.

When you think of natural frames, what comes to mind? The overhanging branches of a tree are perhaps the most obvious. The gap between trees that frames the scene beyond? How about overhanging cliffs or the entrance to a cave? On the coast, the gaps between rock outcrops or cliffs can be used to frame the beach and sea beyond.

These are all fairly obvious options, but if you start to think laterally, other ideas will present themselves. For example, the shape of a hillside or mountain can be used to frame features positioned in front of it. Clouds in the sky can act like a frame, too – containing elements on the ground and forcing the eye down towards them.

When shooting using a frame and the sun is behind you, light will fall onto the entire scene, so everything will be of a similar brightness and should record more or less as you see it. If you're shooting into the light, however, or the sun is to the side of the camera's position, the main part of the scene may be well lit, but little or no light will fall directly onto the frame and it will record dark or even as a silhouette. If the frame and the scene beyond it is evenly lit, you shouldn't experience any problems obtaining well-exposed images. If you're standing in the shadow of the frame, however, overexposure is likely. If this proves to be the case, step beyond the frame and out of the shade, take an exposure reading, set it on your camera using the AE-Lock or by shooting in manual exposure mode, and don't change anything once you recompose with the frame included. Alternatively, take a shot from your shooting position, check the preview image and histogram, then apply negative or positive exposure compensation as required and retake your exposure.

Finally, if you want the frame and the scene beyond to be rendered in focus, select a small lens aperture, such as f/13, and use hyperfocal focusing to maximise depth-of-field (see page 86 for details). Alternatively, by setting a wide aperture such as f/4 and focusing on the scene beyond the frame, depth-of-field will be reduced so that the frame itself is thrown out of focus and all attention is directed towards your main subject.

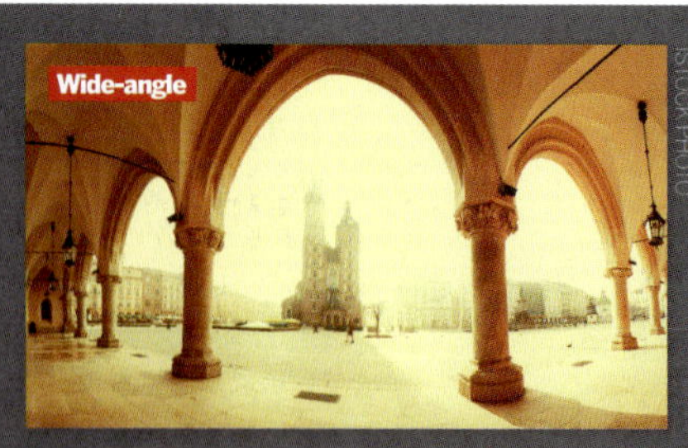

Wide-angle

ISTOCK PHOTO

Wide-angle or telephoto?

The effect the frame has on the composition is partly determined by your lens choice. Wide-angle lenses stretch perspective so the apparent distance between the elements in a scene is increased. If you move close to a natural frame, you can include it in the shot, but you'll still get a clear view of the scene beyond. Telephoto lenses have the opposite effect – they compress perspective so the elements in a scene appear closer together. This makes them less suited to shooting natural frames, though they can be handy at times if you're unable to get close to an effective frame and you're happy for the scene beyond the frame to be more selective.

1) **Using archways is something we've seen many times before, but they always lend themselves beautifully to frame a focal point. It works particularly well with this church because the detail in the frame complements the subject.**

2) **Think about symmetry when looking for natural frames; it is always pleasing to the eye. Even the most simple of arrangements can create impact, as seen here.**

3) **Using natural frames is a great way of adding foreground interest to a scene. While the castle is the focal point in this image, it's the dramatic spikes that add impact for the viewer.**

4) **Your subject doesn't have to fill the frame to be striking – here the extra space in fact helps to frame and draw emphasis to the small chapel. Try using subtle but graphic shapes in the landscape, such as clouds or hills, to improve your composition – simply centring the church would fail to create the same energy as it does here. Think outside the box and you'll begin to see frames in the most unlikely places.**

5) **The dark frame here is a striking contrast to the lighter scene beyond. Look for differences in colour to emphasise your frame and add impact.**

1

ISTOCK PHOTO

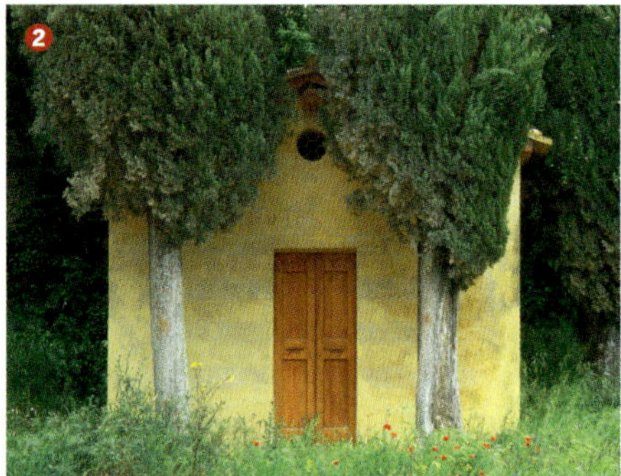

2

LEE FROST

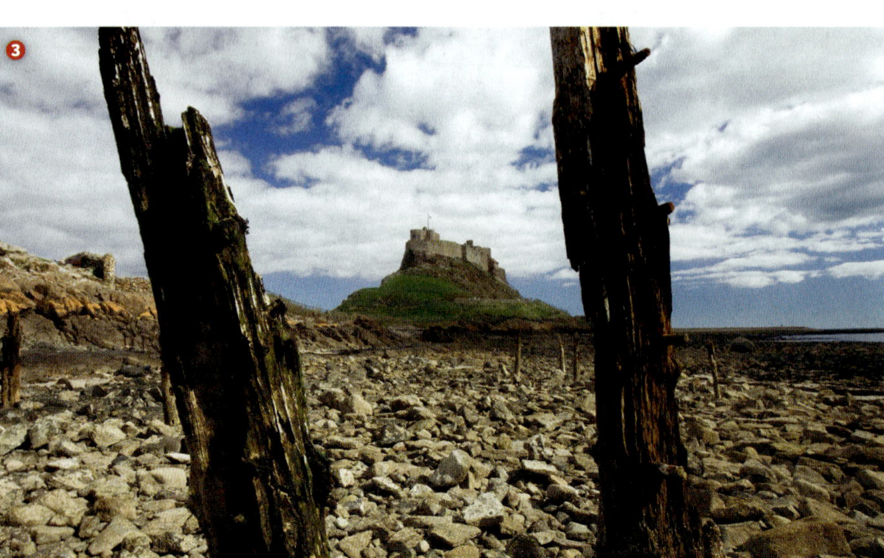

3

LEE FROST

4

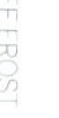

LEE FROST

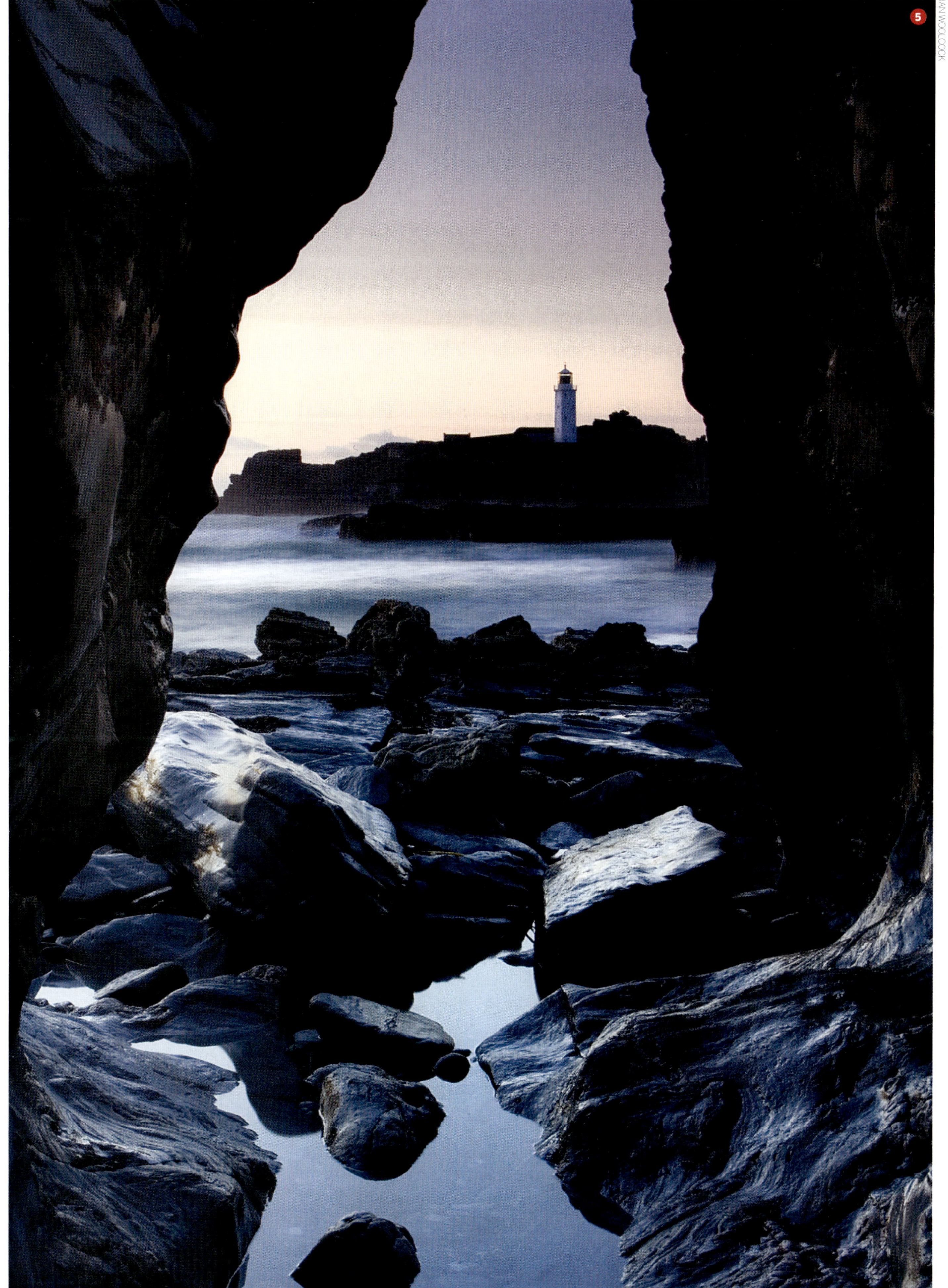

IAN WOOLCOCK

Foreground interest

Swot up on how you should use foreground interest to give your shots depth and scale and improve the impact of your images

THE LATE, GREAT war photographer Robert Capa once said, "If a picture's not good enough, you weren't close enough." He was talking about capturing the drama of human conflict, of course, and the need to be in the heart of the action – an approach that unfortunately eventually cost him his life. However, the same maxim can easily be applied to landscape photography because if you want to capture the drama of a great scene, you need to move in close and make the most of the foreground – it's one of the important elements you need to create a dynamic composition.

Foreground interest is useful for a number of reasons. First and foremost, emphasising the foreground will help to give your photographs a sense of distance and scale. This is due to perspective – features close to the camera look much bigger than those further way, so our brain immediately registers that the smaller features must be in the distance and we see the image as three-dimensional, making it more realistic.

Second, the foreground provides a convenient entry point into the composition for the viewer's eye, which then naturally travels up through the scene to the focal point or the background. A successful composition needs a 'hook' to entice the viewer and hold the attention. With landscapes, the foreground is that hook.

Third, the foreground contains more information than the rest of the scene, and being closest to the camera allows you to record the fine detail that isn't affected by haze, mist and fog, like features that are more distant.

Wide-angle lenses are the most useful for exploiting foreground interest as they allow you to include elements in a shot that are literally at your feet. The way wide-angle lenses 'stretch' perspective also makes those elements loom large in the frame while everything else seems to rush away into the distance. The lower the viewpoint you adopt, the more the foreground will dominate.

Lenses with a focal length of 16-18mm (24-28mm on full-frame sensors) are a relatively safe bet to begin with as they're wide enough to include lots of foreground interest without being so wide that you end up with all foreground and nothing else. Once your confidence grows, you can produce amazing images with ultra wide-angle lenses from 10-15mm (15-22mm full-frame), but you need to get really close to the foreground, otherwise it will seem miles away due to the excessive 'stretching' of perspective that you get with these wider lenses.

Telephoto lenses are less dynamic in this respect, as the foreground interest you include is formed by elements or features in the scene that are obviously further away, while the foreshortening of perspective 'squeezes' the elements together so that you don't get the same sense of distance and three-dimension as with a wide-angle. Nevertheless, the effect can still be strong, with a single feature dominating the foreground.

What can be used as foreground interest? Pretty much anything – rocks, rivers, walls, gates, fences, trees, moored boats, sand ripples, reflections, people. Features and elements in the scene that create natural or assumed lines work the best of all, as they lead the viewer's eye into and through the scene. Lines that travel vertically work well, lines that travel diagonally from bottom left to top right work even better, and lines that converge into the distance, such as railway tracks or straight roads, are the most powerful of all. To make the most of vertical and converging lines, turn your camera on its side and shoot in portrait format. Diagonal lines are better shot in landscape format as they have further to travel through the composition, holding attention for longer.

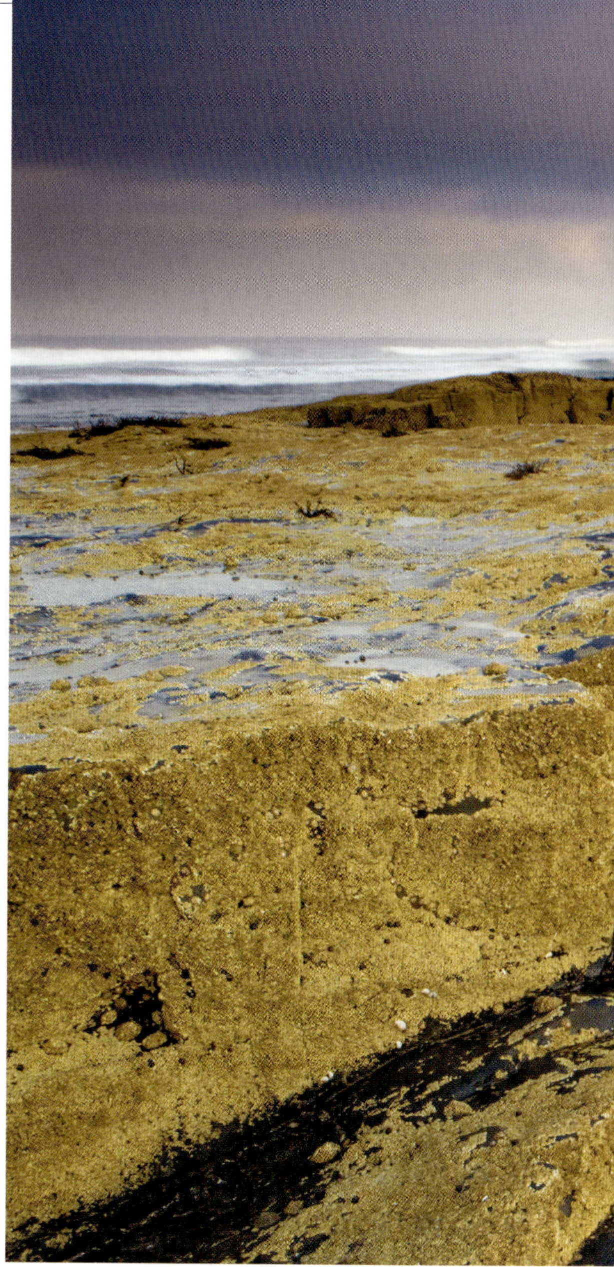

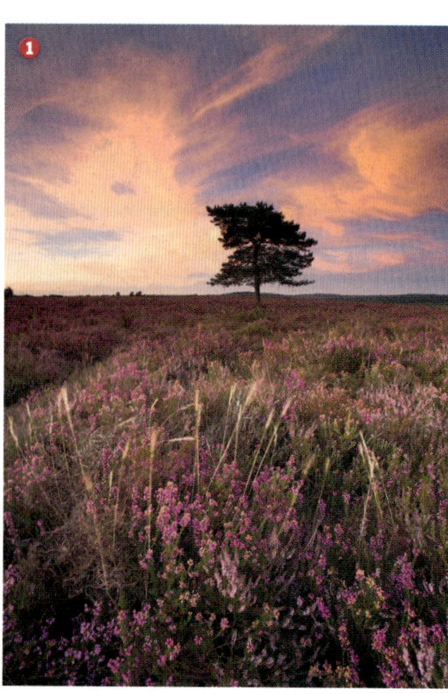

ADAM BURTON

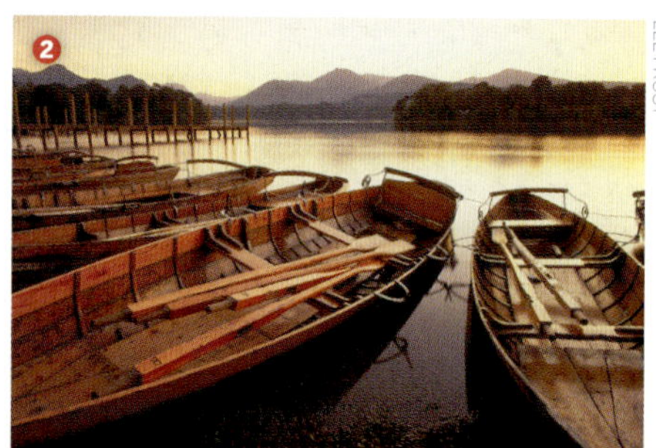

LEE FROST

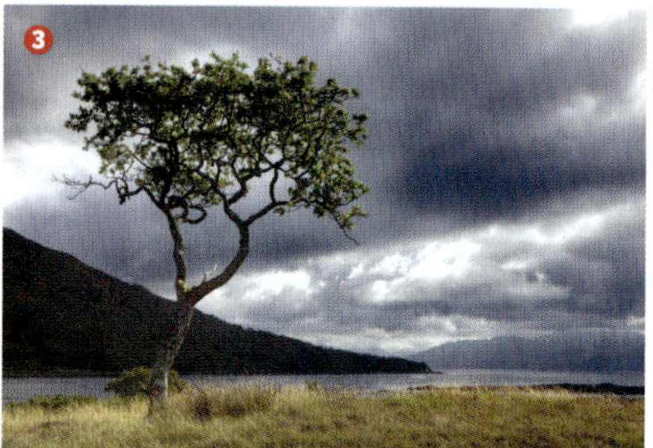

LEE FROST

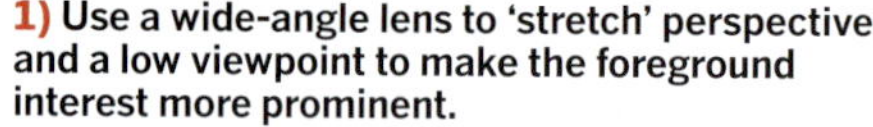

1) Use a wide-angle lens to 'stretch' perspective and a low viewpoint to make the foreground interest more prominent.

2) Try picking subjects that form diagonal lines leading from the bottom left to the top right of the frame, like these boats do, as it draws the viewer into the picture.

3) Instead of using foreground interest as a prelude to a distant focal point, try composing pictures where the dominant subject is in the foreground and keep the background simple.

4) One good reason why you shouldn't leave home without an array of ND grad filters is to ensure your foreground is correctly exposed. In low-light conditions, like a sunset, it's easy to render the foreground dark and distracting.

5) Practically anything can work as foreground interest, as long as it's composed well and fits with the rest of the scene. Look for unusual subjects or for objects that you may never have considered using before, such as driftwood, shells or wreckage remains.

6) Rocks are the most popular subjects to use in a coastal landscape and can be the most effective when used as a lead-in line, also. Jetties and piers work well, too, and have the added bonus of you being able to introduce converging verticals.

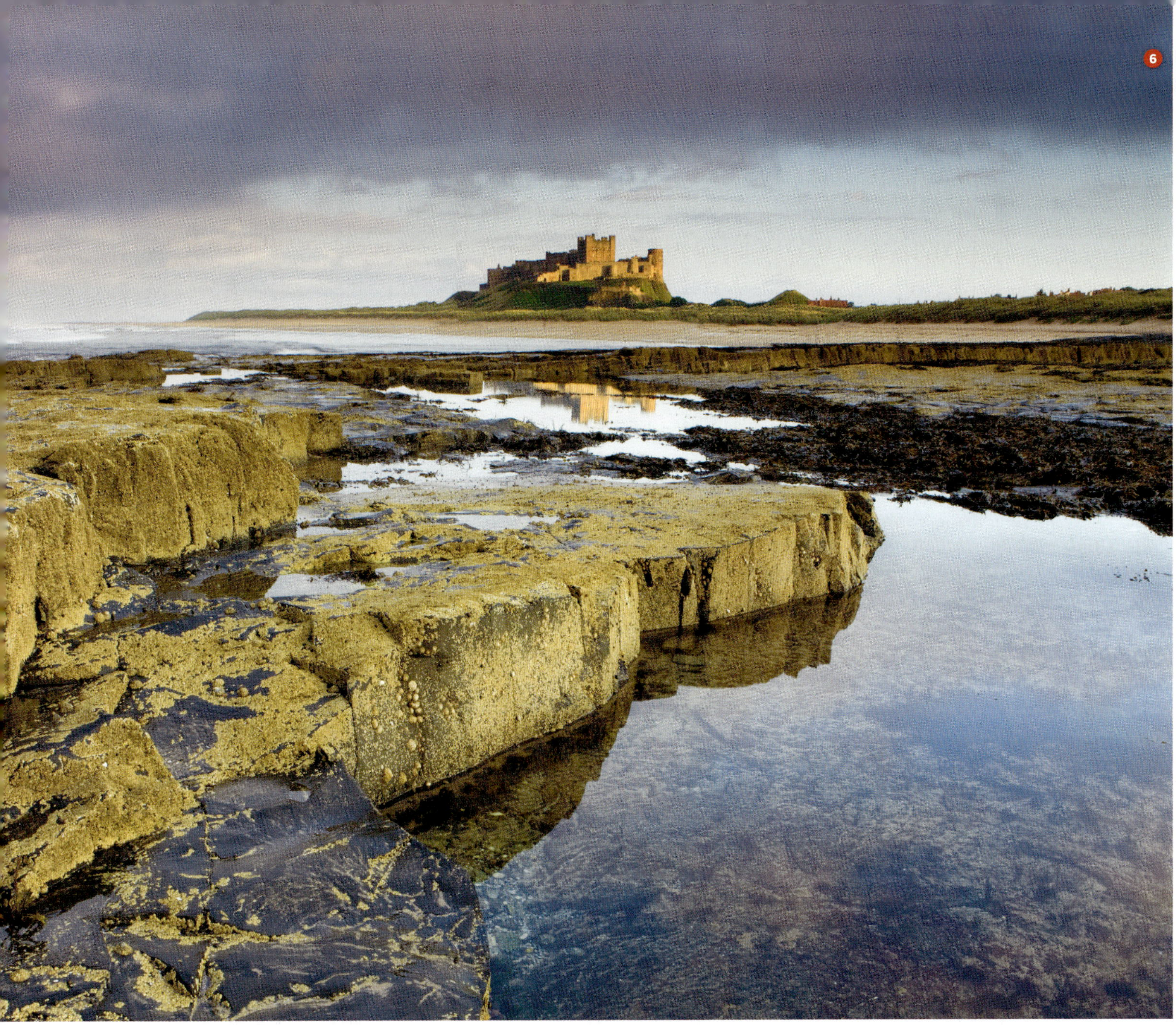

6

LEE FROST

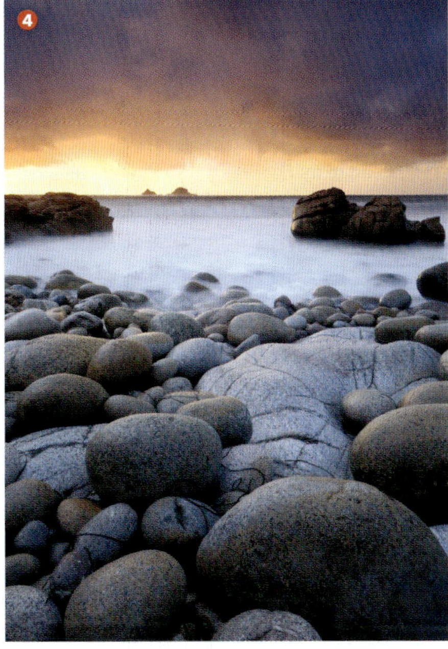

4

ROSS HODDINOTT

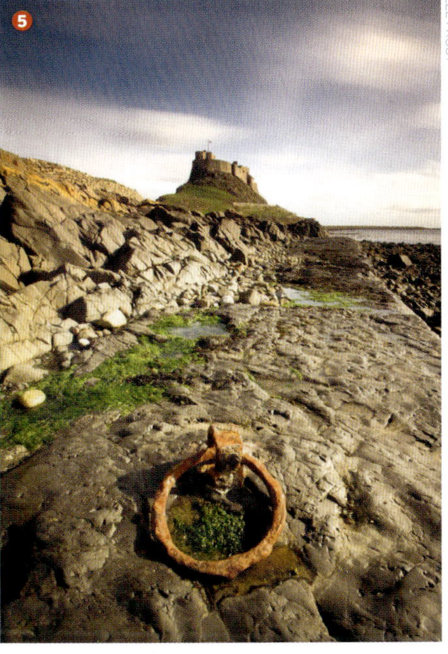

5

LEE FROST

Maximise depth-of-field

There's no point including fantastic foreground if it's out of focus; what you need is enough depth-of-field for front-to-back sharpness. As a rule of thumb, if you use a camera with an APS-C sensor with a focal length around 16-18mm, focus the lens on a point 1.5m from the camera, stop down to f/11 and everything will be sharp from around 75cm to infinity. For wider focal lengths in the 10-15mm range, focus on a point one metre away, stop down to f/11 and everything will be sharp from around 50cm to infinity. For full-frame DSLRs with a focal length in the 24-28mm range, focus on a point 1.5m away, stop down to f/16 and depth-of-field will extend from around 75cm to infinity. For wider lenses in the 16-20mm range, focus on 1m, stop down to f/16 and you'll get depth-of-field from around 50cm to infinity. Basically, to maximise depth-of-field with wide-angle lenses, you need to focus on a point relatively close to the camera; many photographers focus further into the scene, resulting in an unsharp image.

How to maximise your depth-of-field

Including foreground interest can make it difficult to achieve front-to-back sharpness, but Ross Hoddinott shows you how…

Ross Hoddinott FLICK THROUGH the pages of any photo or country magazine, and you will quickly notice that foreground interest is an important component in the majority of great landscape images. It provides an entry point into the composition and helps add context, depth and interest to views. As long as it complements the overall scene, practically anything can work as foreground interest – rocks, a stone wall, winding footpath, colourful reflections or reeds. Flowers are another good subject to include in the foreground of your shots. Not only do they help to add scale to wider views, but they will also add a welcome splash of colour. There is no better time of year than spring to look for flowers to include in your shots, particularly along the coast where pink thrift flowers. Thrift can carpet clifftops, providing colour and interest to views of sandy bays and rugged coastline.

Including foreground interest typically requires a large depth-of-field to render everything from front to back acceptably sharp. Opt for a small f/stop in the region of f/16, but avoid stopping down even further as the effects of diffraction (softening of the image) will grow more apparent. You also need to select your point of focus carefully. Depth-of-field falls roughly two-thirds beyond the point of focus and one-third in front of it. Therefore, if you focus too far into the frame, you will waste the depth-of-field available to you. A rough-and-ready method to maximise front-to-back sharpness is to simply focus a third of the way into the frame. However, a more precise method is to focus on the hyperfocal distance (see panel). It seems like a complicated calculation, but it's much easier than you may think.

To help give your images a three-dimensional appearance, opt for an ultra wide-angle lens – in the region of 17-24mm and get near to your foreground. This exaggerates the size of foreground subjects and stretches perspective, resulting in eye-catching shots.

Hyperfocal point

The hyperfocal distance is the point where you can maximise depth-of-field for any given aperture – everything from half this distance to infinity will be recorded acceptably sharp. Calculating and focusing on this point is important if you require extensive depth-of-field. Although the hyperfocal distance can seem daunting, it is not actually as complex as it first seems. If you use a prime lens with good distance and depth-of-field scales, simply align the infinity mark against the selected aperture. However, few modern lenses – particularly zooms – are designed with adequate scales, meaning photographers have to calculate it themselves. Thankfully, there are depth-of-field calculators and hyperfocal charts available to download online. Visit www.dofmaster.com – it also offers an app for your smartphone.

Below are two hyperfocal distance charts covering the most popular focal lengths and various apertures for full-frame and APS-C sensors. Photocopy or cut out the chart relevant to your camera type and keep it handy for when you come to compose and focus your shots.

APS-C size sensors

Aperture	12mm	15mm	17mm	20mm	24mm	28mm	35mm	50mm
f/8	3.2ft	5ft	6.4ft	8.9ft	12.6ft	17ft	27ft	55ft
f/11	**2.3ft**	**3.5ft**	**4.5ft**	**6.2ft**	**9ft**	**12ft**	**19ft**	**39ft**
f/16	1.7ft	2.5ft	3.3ft	4.4ft	6.4ft	8.6ft	14.5ft	27ft
f/22	**1.2ft**	**0.9ft**	**2.3ft**	**3.2ft**	**4.5ft**	**6ft**	**9.5ft**	**19.2ft**

Full-frame sensors

Aperture	16mm	20mm	24mm	28mm	35mm	50mm
f/8	3.8ft	5.6ft	8ft	11ft	17ft	35ft
f/11	**2.6ft**	**3.9ft**	**5.8ft**	**7.8ft**	**12ft**	**25ft**
f/16	1.9ft	2.9ft	4ft	5.5ft	8.5ft	17.5ft
f/22	**1.4ft**	**2ft**	**2.9ft**	**3.9ft**	**6ft**	**12.5ft**

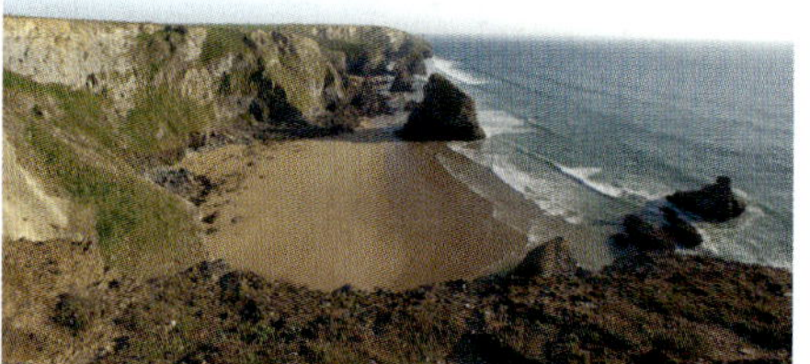

1 Find your view Images lacking foreground interest can look flat and boring. Despite finding this impressive vista, by not including anything of aesthetic value in the foreground to complement the view and direct the eye into the photo, this shot is nothing more than a snap.

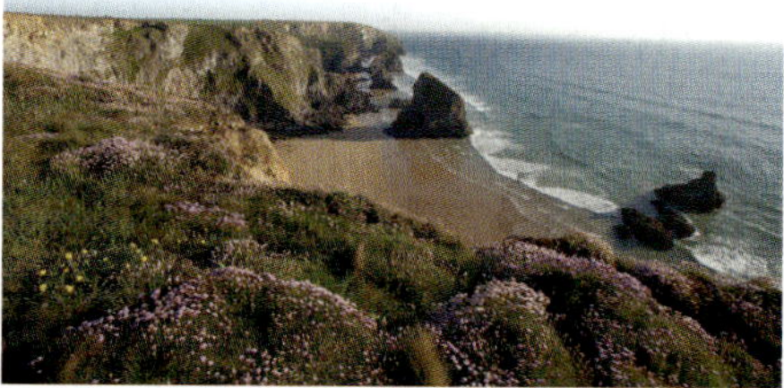

2 Alter your viewpoint By simply moving a few metres, my next image is much better. By including some flowering thrift in the foreground, the image immediately has more depth and interest. However, the sky is overexposed, so filtration or exposure blending is needed.

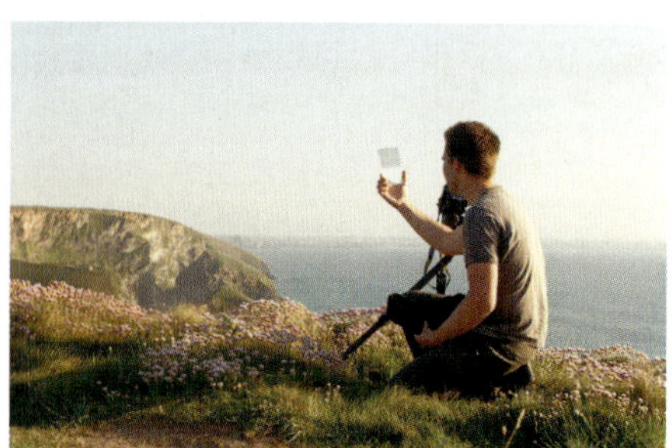

3 Set your exposure I take a meter reading from the sky and another from the foreground thrift. The difference in light is around four stops. I don't want to even out the light completely as our eyes naturally perceive the sky to be brighter than the land. Therefore, I attach a two-stop (0.6) graduated Neutral Density filter to help me record detail throughout the scene.

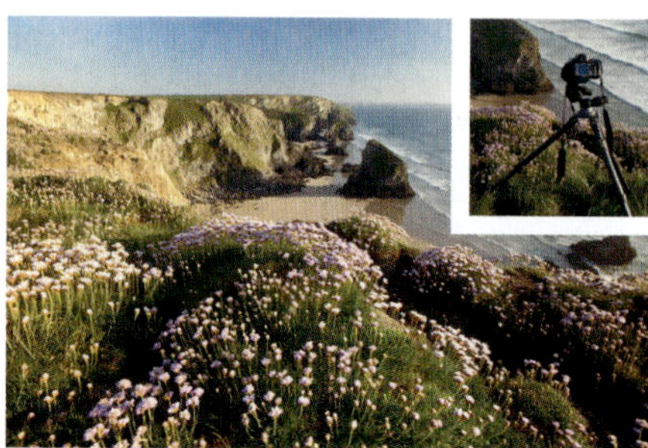

4 Perfect your composition With the correct exposure achieved, it is time to focus on composition. To place more emphasis on foreground, and to create depth, a low, close viewpoint is often best, together with a short focal length. I do this, opting for the wide end of my 17-35mm zoom. The nearest flowers aren't in sharp focus, though, due to inaccurate focusing.

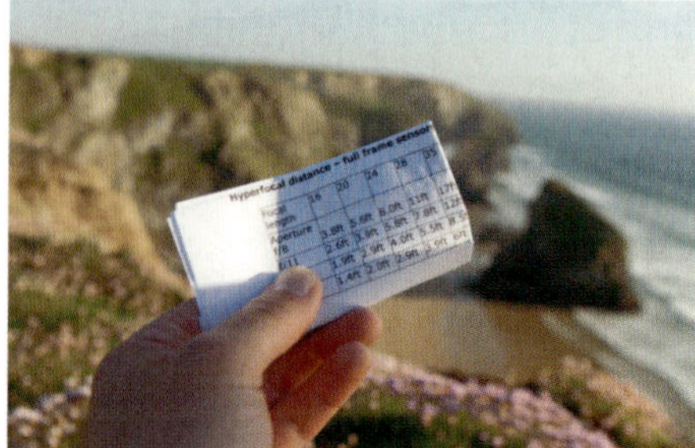

5 Calculate the hyperfocal distance To ensure everything from nearby foreground to the distant view is acceptably sharp, focus on the hyperfocal distance. The chart tells me that, with a focal length of 17mm and aperture of f/16, the hyperfocal distance is just over 2ft. I manually focus the lens to this distance and reshoot. This time, I achieve front-to-back sharpness.

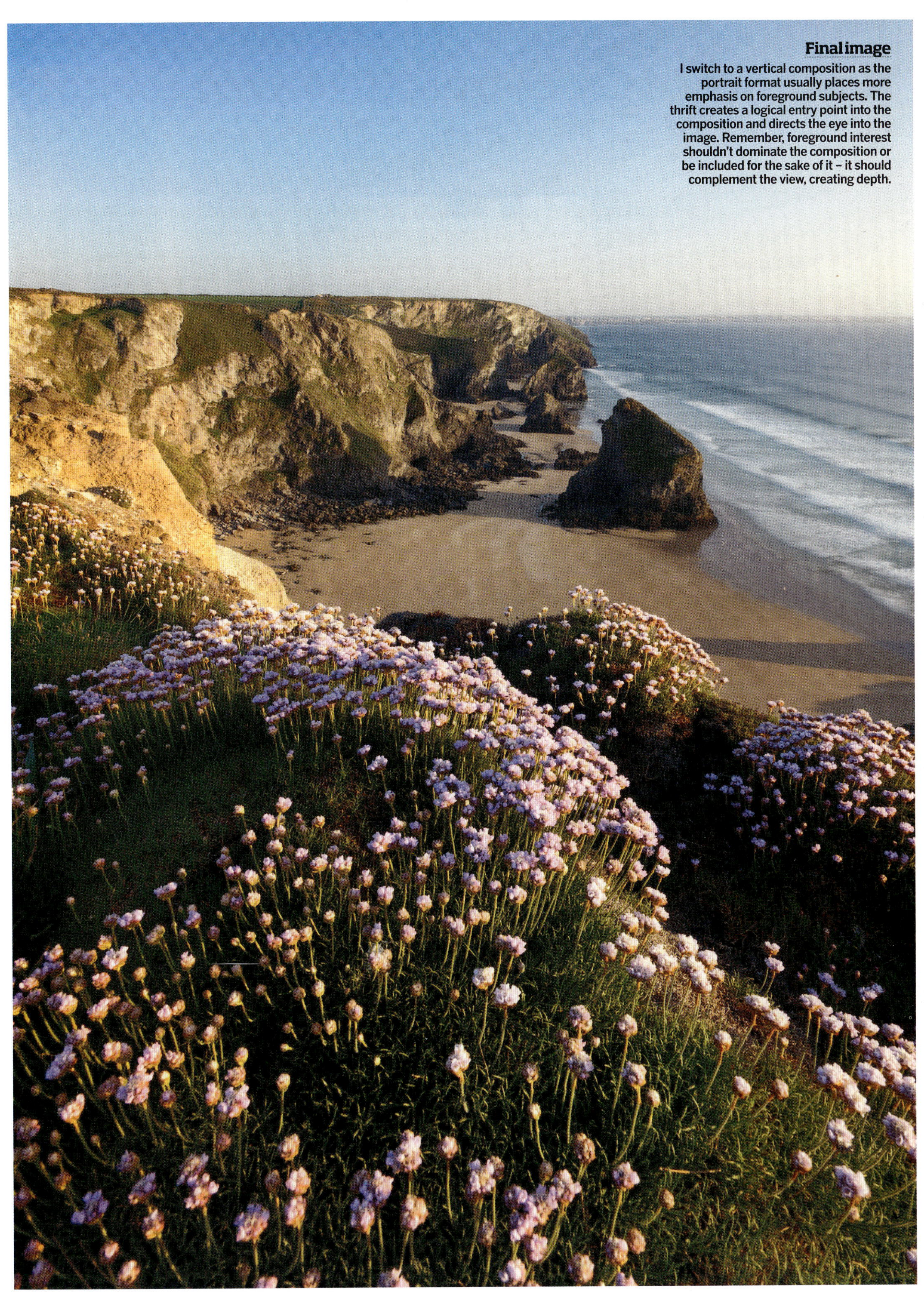

Final image

I switch to a vertical composition as the portrait format usually places more emphasis on foreground subjects. The thrift creates a logical entry point into the composition and directs the eye into the image. Remember, foreground interest shouldn't dominate the composition or be included for the sake of it – it should complement the view, creating depth.

Landscape lighting

Daylight is the most accessible and versatile light source available to photographers. We explore its many forms, look at the factors that change it and tell you how to make the most of it for landscapes

LIGHT IS THE SINGLE essential ingredient that allows us to create a photographic image. But light can take on many forms – it can be hard or soft, strong or weak, warm or cold – and each variation has a profound effect, not only on the mood and character of the landscape, but the success of every photograph we take. Time of day and weather conditions are the two main factors that affect the quality of daylight. Throw in seasonal variations and you have seemingly endless permutations that change from one minute to the next. This can be both a blessing and a curse. When things are going to plan, daylight is the most amazing light source there is. But when you crawl out of bed in the middle of the night, drive three hours in darkness to reach a location for sunrise, only to be greeted by thick cloud and drizzle when you finally get there, it can also be the most frustrating.

Essential filters

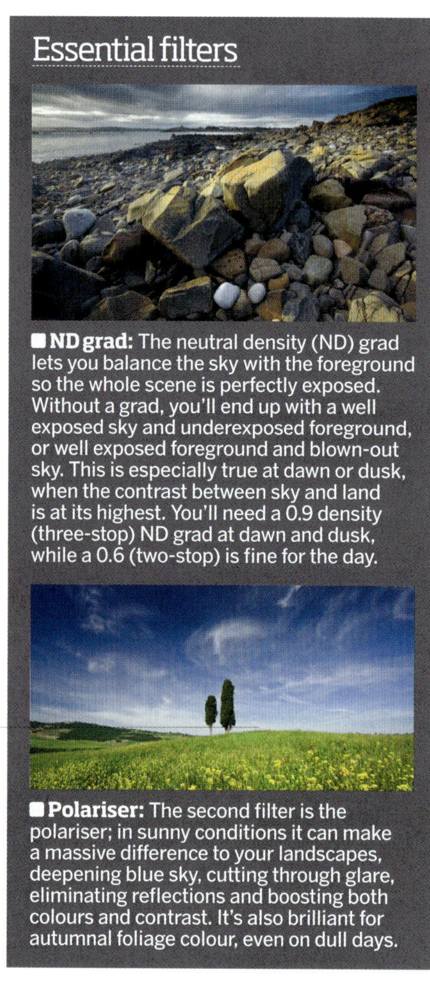

ND grad: The neutral density (ND) grad lets you balance the sky with the foreground so the whole scene is perfectly exposed. Without a grad, you'll end up with a well exposed sky and underexposed foreground, or well exposed foreground and blown-out sky. This is especially true at dawn or dusk, when the contrast between sky and land is at its highest. You'll need a 0.9 density (three-stop) ND grad at dawn and dusk, while a 0.6 (two-stop) is fine for the day.

Polariser: The second filter is the polariser; in sunny conditions it can make a massive difference to your landscapes, deepening blue sky, cutting through glare, eliminating reflections and boosting both colours and contrast. It's also brilliant for autumnal foliage colour, even on dull days.

Be prepared

Planning puts the odds of success in your favour and is easier than ever, thanks to the internet. You can check the weather forecast for the next few days, establish sunrise and sunset times for any day or location in the world, or check tide times if you're heading to the coast. The more information you gather, the more likely you are to be in the right place at the right time to take advantage of fantastic light. And if things don't go according to plan, you may end up taking photos that are better than you had hoped for, because unexpected changes in the weather often produce spectacular conditions that can't be planned for, but by being on location, you can take advantage of them. It's not down to luck that top landscape photographers produce amazing images on a regular basis – it's down to being out in the field, chasing the light.

The ability and willingness to adapt to unforeseen conditions will also help you to make the most of light because different forms of natural light suit different subjects. The flat light of an overcast day may not suit grand wide-angle views, for example, but it's ideal for shooting details in the landscape. Another option is to shoot with the intention of converting images to black & white: in which case, the quality of light isn't so important. You can also employ photographic techniques. No matter how drab the weather is, if you're on the coast you can produce amazing images using a ten-stop ND filter to record motion in the sea and contrast it with static elements, such as rocks, groynes and jetties.

The right direction

The direction from which light strikes your subject can make a big difference to the mood and impact of your images. Frontal light, where the sun is to your back, makes the world look lovely but, photographically, it's not very effective because shadows fall away from the camera, making the landscape look rather flat. Just after sunrise, or just before sunset, when the sun is low in the sky and bathes the landscape in golden light, that lack of depth can be forgiven because the light is fantastic, though you may find that you struggle to keep your own shadow out of the composition!

Side-lighting, with the sun at roughly 90° to the camera, works better because you can incorporate the shadows to make them an integral part of the composition and use them to reveal texture and detail, and add a sense of depth. Again, this is most pronounced when the sun is low in the sky, as shadows are very long and weak. Another option is to shoot into the light, a technique known as 'contre-jour'. Sunrise and sunset shots are taken in this way because the most colourful area of the sky is generally where the sun's about to rise or the moments after. You can also produce stunning images when the sun is higher in the sky, but you need to choose the right kind of scene. Coastal views or any scene containing water suit 'contre-jour' photography. Winter scenes are also ideal as sunlight reflects off the snow, ice and frost. Mist and fog work well, too, as the light burning through can create images that are incredibly atmospheric.

Ultimately, natural daylight is a law unto itself and no matter how hard you try, you'll never be able to control it. You can master it, though, through planning, patience, practice and perseverance, and once you master light, you master photography.

ALL IMAGES: LEE FROST

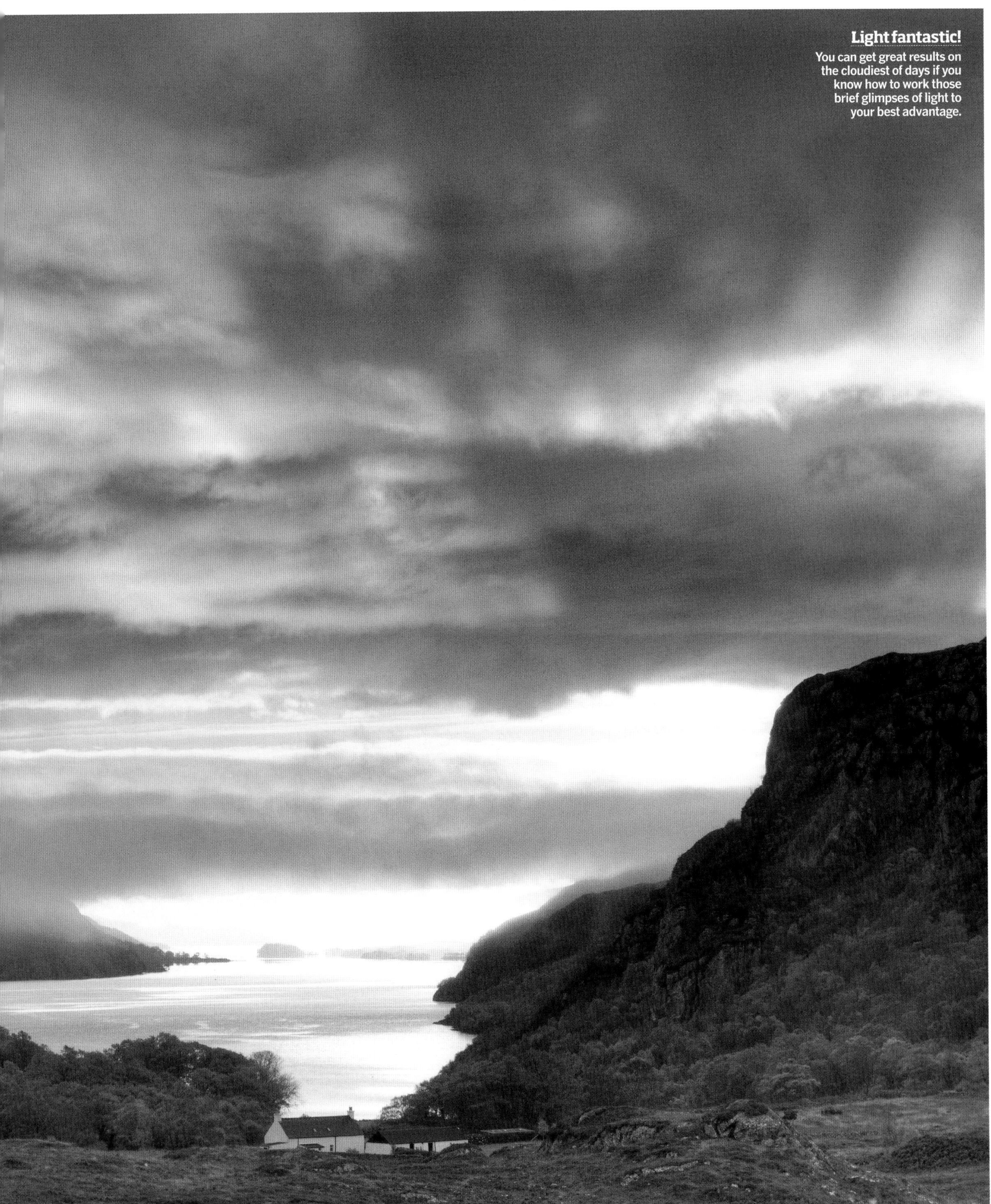

Light fantastic!
You can get great results on the cloudiest of days if you know how to work those brief glimpses of light to your best advantage.

The time of day

From the moment first light appears to the time when darkness takes over, the quality of light undergoes a myriad of amazing changes and makes a huge difference to your photographs...

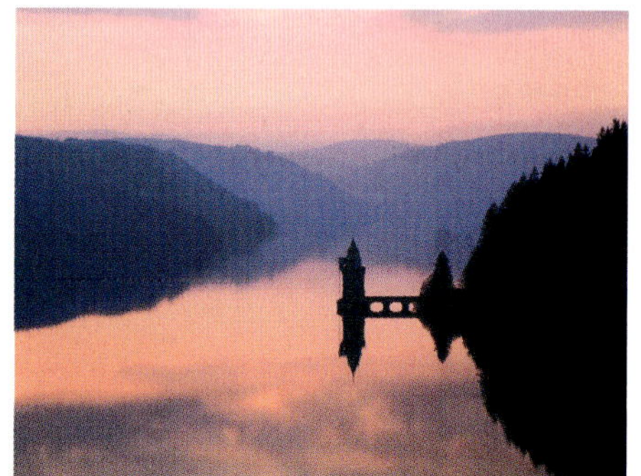

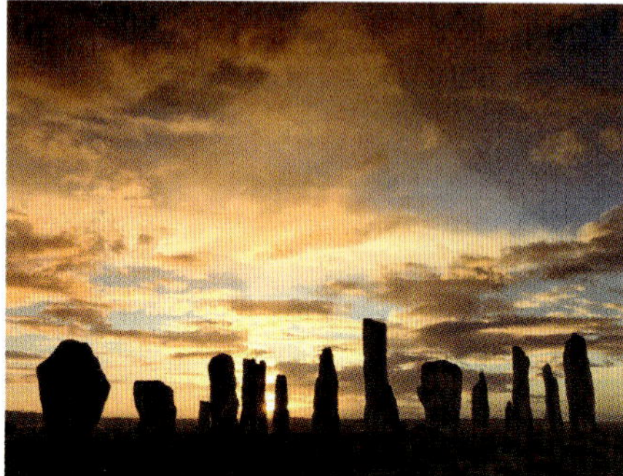

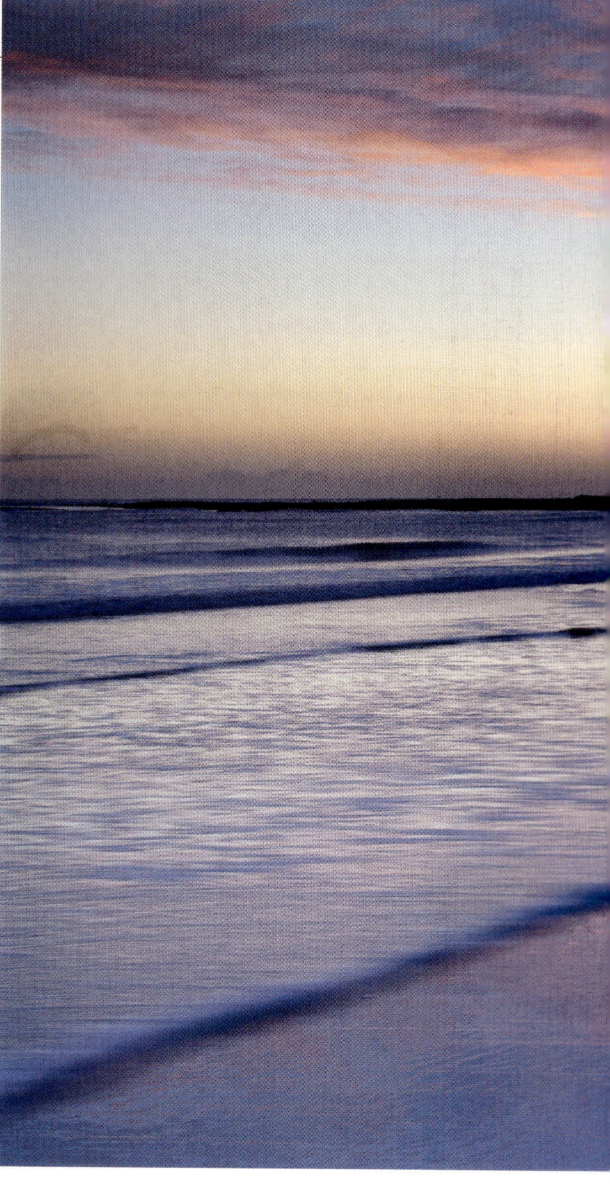

Predawn First light usually appears 30-40 minutes before sunrise. Ideally, arrive an hour before sun-up to find a viewpoint, set up your gear and start shooting as soon as colour appears. Any light on the landscape is reflected from the sky, so it's soft and shadowless, and tends to have a strong, cool cast. This contrasts well with the warm glow over the eastern horizon.

Water, wet sand and wet rocks pick up the colour in the sky, so predawn is great to shoot coastal or lake views. Ideally, there will be some broken cloud adding colour to the sky, but clear mornings can also be highly productive. Light levels are low, so expect long exposures. The contrast between the sky and land is high due to the lack of direct light, so use a 0.9ND graduate to retain detail and colour in the sky.

Sunrise By the time the sun peeps over the horizon, any colour in the sky may have gone. On clear mornings, the sun will be dazzling once it rises, but you'll be able to shoot into it for a few minutes as the sea and wet sand reflects the light to keep contrast manageable. Features such as piers, castles and lighthouses can also be captured in silhouette. Inland, contrast will be too high once the sun rises into a clear sky. At this point, turn and capture the golden light on the landscape. Ideally, let the sun side-light the scene so you can include long, raking shadows to add depth and reveal texture.

The light is warm at sunrise because the rays pass through the atmosphere at a shallow angle and the light is scattered, with many of the wavelengths at the blue end of the spectrum filtered out.

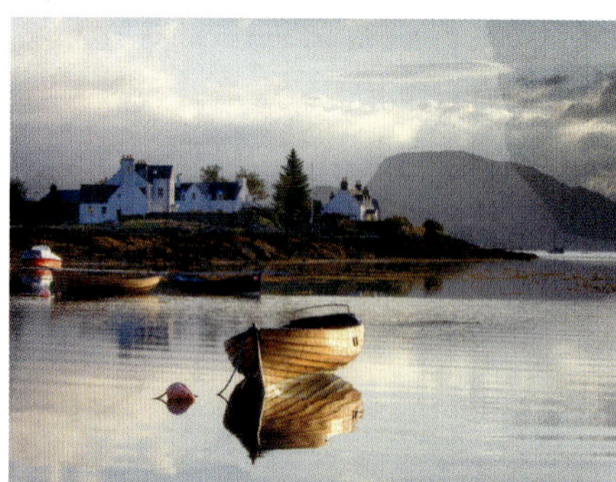

Early morning Once the sun is up, you have minutes to capture the light at its peak quality before it loses warmth. During the summer, daylight is neutral in colour two hours after sunrise and its colour temperature remains constant for about 12 hours. During spring and autumn, any warmth in the light will have gone by 8am and the colour temperature remains steady until 4pm. In winter, however, the colour temperature hardly ever reaches 5500K, even at midday, because the angle between the sun and earth is shallow all day.

The first two hours after sunrise are the best for landscape photography as the intensity of the light is reasonably low, and long shadows add depth and modelling. A polariser is also effective when the sun is low in the sky and at 90° to the camera.

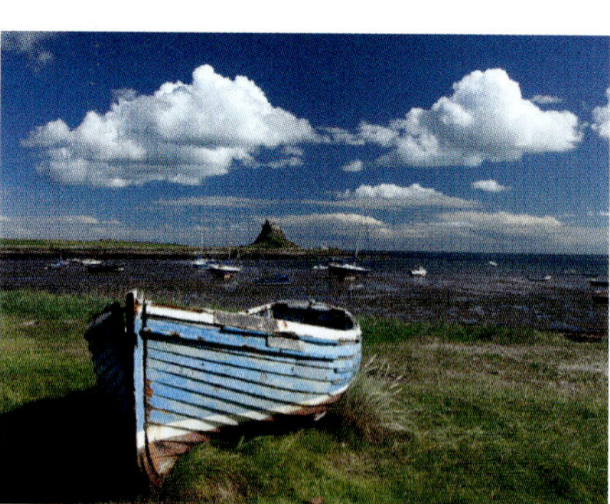

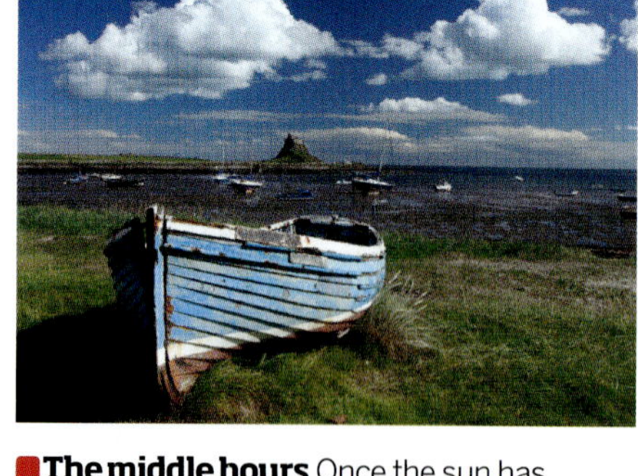

The middle hours Once the sun has been up for two hours, the quality of the light in clear, sunny weather begins to tail off. The higher the sun climbs, the more harsh and intense the light and the shorter and denser the shadows. By 9am in summer, the sun is at its 'zenith' – its highest point – and stays there until at least 4pm. The landscape looks flat, contrast is high and the light isn't attractive. The urban landscape is better suited to strong light: shoot modern architecture, using a polariser to deepen the sky, and look for abstracts and colourful details. In the countryside, capture trees against the sky from a low angle and look for reflections in water. Infrared photography works in harsh light, especially in spring and summer when there's lush foliage around.

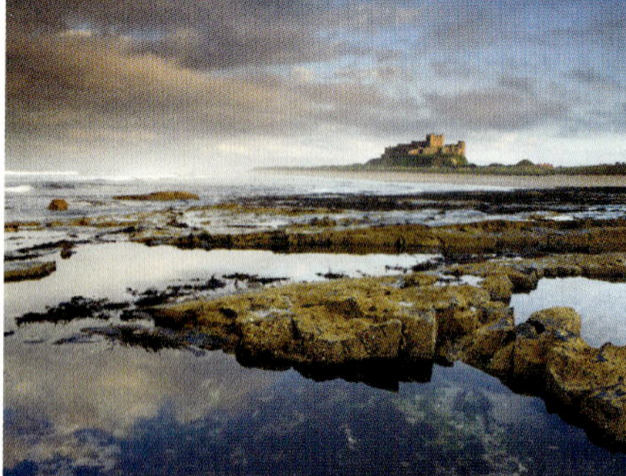

Late afternoon Once the sun begins its slow descent and the light begins to warm up, its intensity is reduced, and shadows become longer and weaker. Shape and character return to the landscape, and the longer you wait, the better it gets. In the morning, the light falls on a cold earth, but in the afternoon, the earth is warm so shadows appear neutral, not cool. The atmosphere is also denser in the afternoon, so light can appear redder than it did at the start of the day. The hour before sunset is often referred to as 'the golden hour' due to the richness of the light. Long shadows reveal texture and modelling to give your pictures depth, and because the sun is sinking and not rising, it's easier to predict how the light is going so you can choose a suitable location.

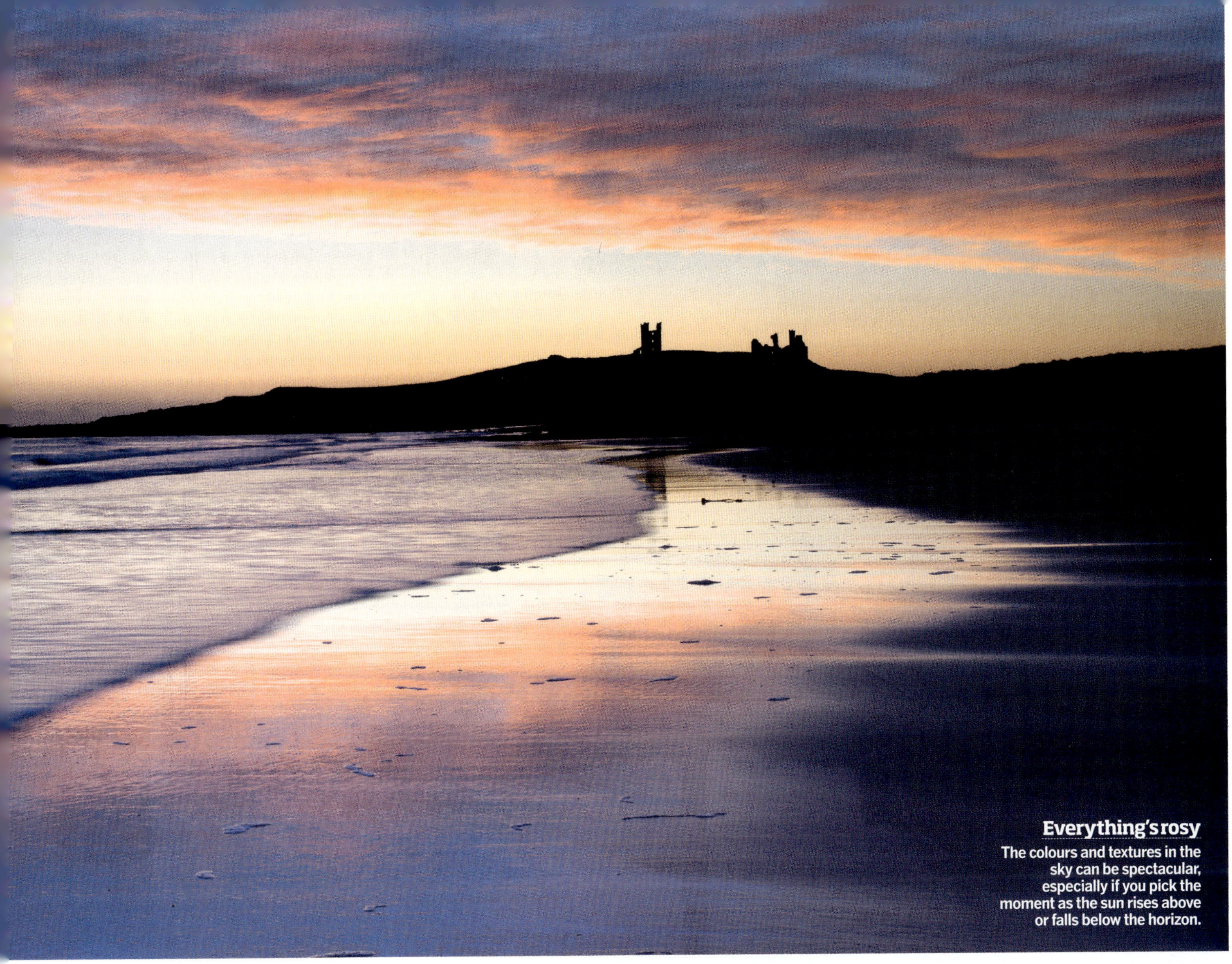

Everything's rosy
The colours and textures in the sky can be spectacular, especially if you pick the moment as the sun rises above or falls below the horizon.

ALL IMAGES: LEE FROST

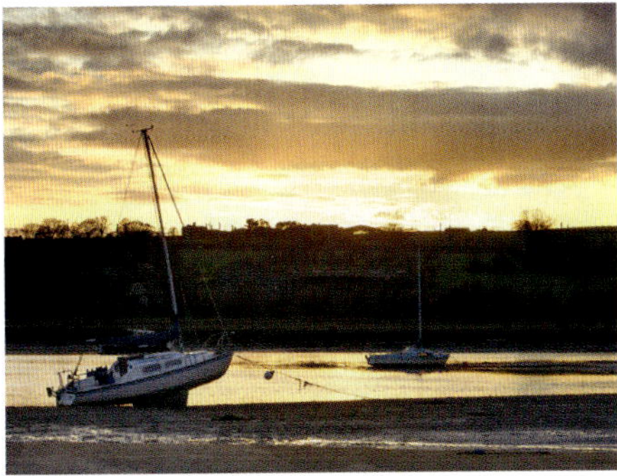

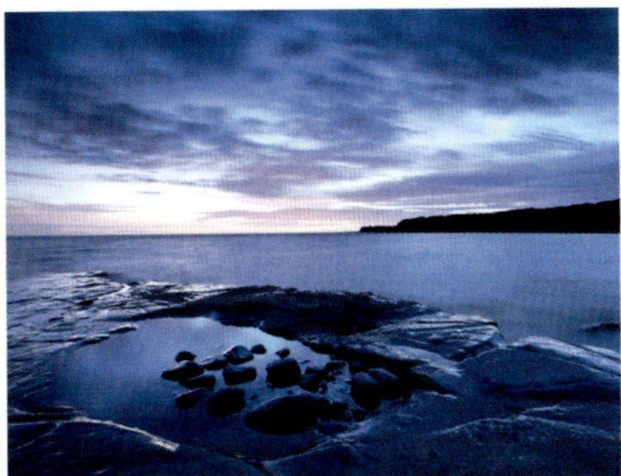

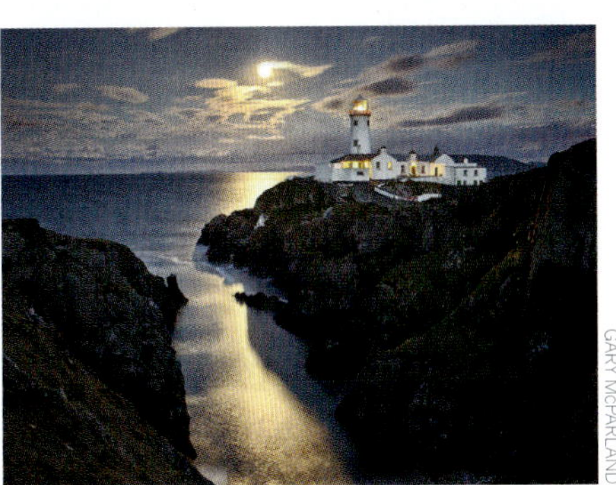

GARY McPARLAND

Sunset When a sunset seems likely, get to your location 45 minutes before so you can choose the best viewpoint, get set up and take a variety of pictures as the sun dips. Capture the landscape bathed in golden light. If the scenery is relatively flat, the light will perform its magic literally until the moment the sun sets, whereas in hilly regions, you may lose the sun half an hour before. Shooting into the sun will record anything between the sun and the camera in silhouette: a good technique when shooting water because the sun's glow and colour in the sky will be reflected, creating a backdrop to silhouettes of boats, islands, piers and so on. If flare is a problem, hide the sun behind something in the scene or wait for it to set. If you want to record detail in the foreground, use a 0.9ND grad.

Twilight Once the sun finally disappears below the horizon, light levels quickly fade and the light on the landscape is again reflected from the sky. If you're lucky, there will be a vivid afterglow in the sky created by the sun as it under-lights the clouds above the horizon, but even this will fade quickly. You'll find that colours are muted, the light is soft, shadows fade and light levels fall away. Head to the water's edge where the pastel colours left in the sky look stunning reflected in lakes and rivers. Or use those colours as a background to silhouettes. Long exposures record movement: the swaying of trees in the breeze; the movement of clouds across the sky; the motion of the sea or water flowing in rivers and streams. Keep shooting until those colours fade.

Moonlight The moon can be a lovely natural source of light. Winter scenes work well because snow and frost reflect the moonlight. Coastal views also work if you capture the shimmering silver ribbon of light from the moon on the sea. By increasing exposure, you can create surreal shots that look like they've been taken in daylight. They'll look normal, but the light will have a strange quality. You can even try recording star trails in the sky created by the rotation of the earth while the camera's shutter is open. Obviously, exposures will be long in low light, so use a tripod, and keep the ISO low – 400 or less – for high image quality. Whatever you shoot, unless the moon is obscured by cloud, you should keep it out of frame to avoid it recording as an overexposed white smudge!

Shoot a scene at dawn

Ross Hoddinott says you can't beat a sunrise for adding extraordinary colour to your landscapes…

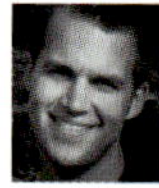

Ross Hoddinott AS A TEENAGER, I never thought I would utter these words, but… dawn is the best time of the day. The light is pure, skies are beautiful and you often have the world all to yourself. Don't get me wrong: I love my bed. But once you're up, the excitement and anticipation of what you might photograph is unrivalled.

The best dawn shots are rarely the result of chance, so plan ahead. Calculate the time and direction of sunrise for the time of year, and select your location accordingly. The weather forecast is also important: if you're hoping for light and colour, but blanket cloud is forecast, you'll be disappointed. And we've said it already, but we'll say it again: colour can begin forming in the sky up to an hour before sunrise, so arrive in plenty of time. Check your kit bag the night before, ensuring filters are clean, everything is in the right place and that batteries are fully charged. Pack a torch, too. Finally, start shooting straight away, even in extremely low light; the light recording properties of an image sensor are amazing. Exposure times will be long, but this can generate interesting cloud or water movement. The results might just surprise you.

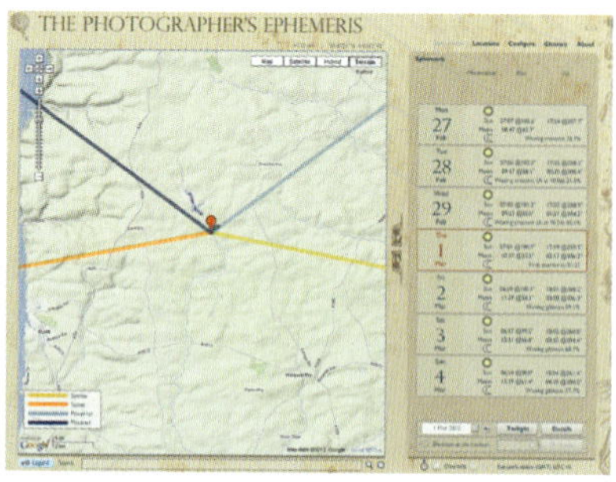

1 Be prepared Plan your shoot carefully to maximise your chances of success. Study the sun's position as this will dictate suitable dawn viewpoints. You should also know the time of sunrise and tide times if you're heading to the coast. Check the weather forecast, too. A number of good websites and phone apps can help (one of the best is www.photoephemeris.com). See page 94 for more useful websites that will help you to plan ahead.

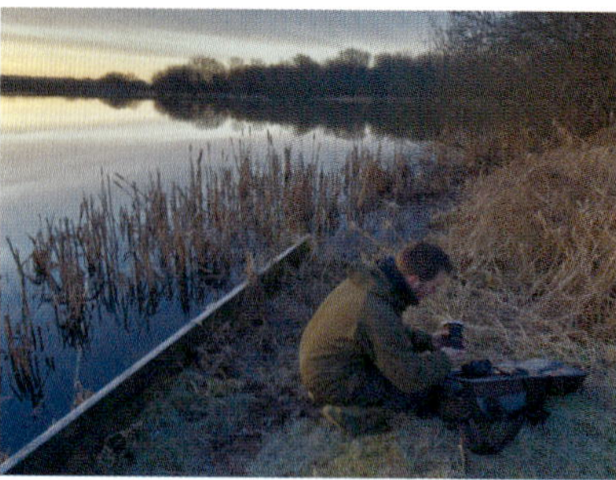

2 Travel Having chosen a location, plan to be there, ready to shoot, at least 30 minutes before sunrise. Allow sufficient time for driving, walking to your viewpoint and setting up. The best dawn colours and morning glow often appear long in advance of sunrise itself. Give yourself too much time, rather than too little; you don't want to be stuck in the car driving to your location as colour begins appearing in the sky as you've probably missed half your shoot.

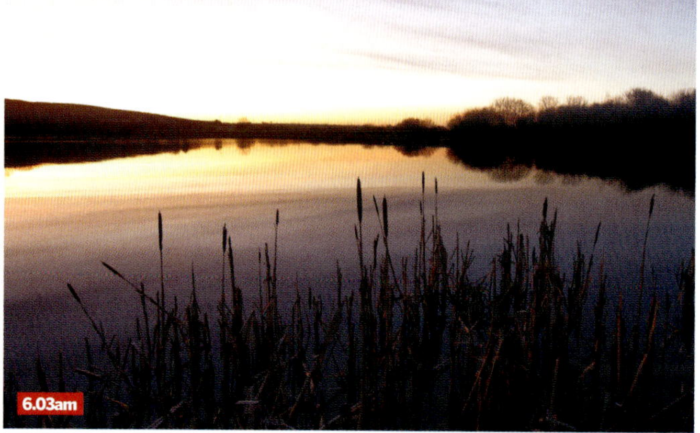

3 Overexposed sky With colour already beginning to form in the sky, I composed my shot. To guarantee front-to-back sharpness, I selected a small aperture of f/16 and focused on the hyperfocal distance. In the low light of dawn, a tripod is essential to ensure sharp results. Using multi-zone metering, I took my first frame. The foreground is correctly exposed, but the brighter sky is washed out and devoid of detail.

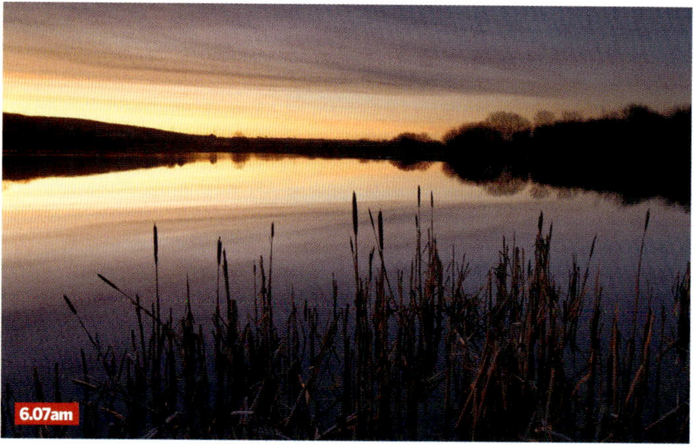

4 Graduated ND At dawn, there is usually a large contrast in light between the sky and land. To produce correctly exposed results in-camera, you could take two frames – one exposed for the land and one for the sky – and blend them during post-processing, or attach an ND grad filter. I aligned the filter, using a grad with a three-stop density (0.9ND) to lower contrast to within the camera's dynamic range.

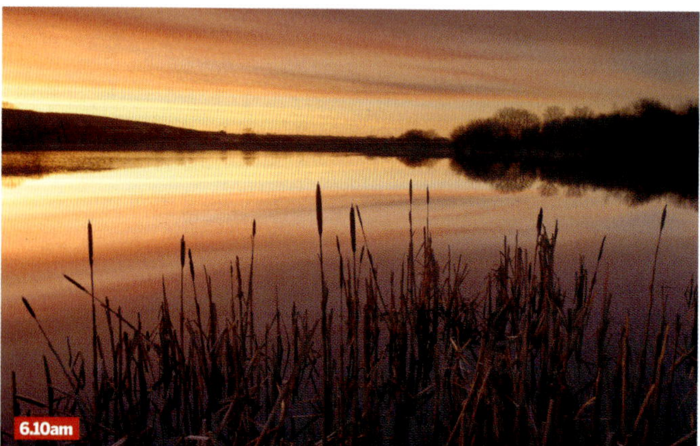

5 Pre-dawn glow Pre-dawn light is soft, cool and shadowless, which contrasts well with a warm, colourful sky. For the best colours, opt for a viewpoint facing east. With around 20 minutes until sunrise, the colours are near their best. Water scenes work well at dawn, reflecting the sky's colour and light. With the intensity of the sky changing quickly, the look and feel of your images can change from one frame to the next.

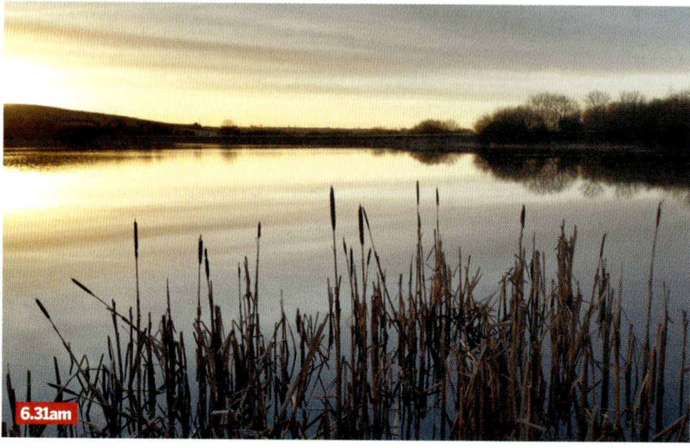

6 Sunrise Just minutes later, the sky's intensity grows too strong to control as the sun appears above the horizon. The best of the colour has gone and the highlights are bright and burnt out. However, due to the sun's low position in the sky, the light is warm and good, so don't pack up and go home just yet; instead find a different viewpoint – pointing farther away from the sun's position – and keep shooting.

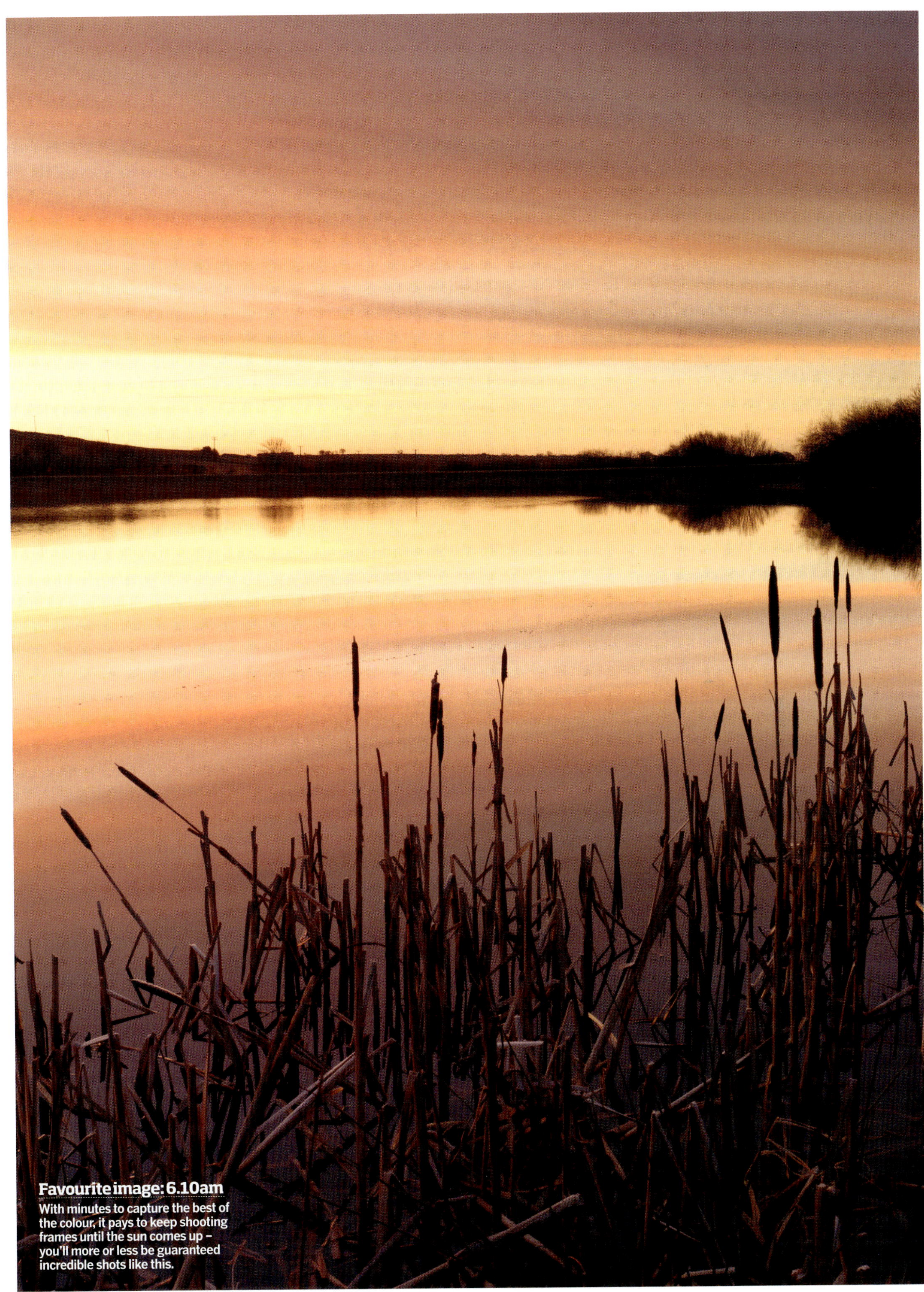

Favourite image: 6.10am
With minutes to capture the best of the colour, it pays to keep shooting frames until the sun comes up – you'll more or less be guaranteed incredible shots like this.

Watch the weather

Changes in weather have an even greater influence on the quality of light than the time of day, so if you want to take stunning shots every time, you need to be prepared to take on the elements

"THERE'S NO SUCH THING as bad weather, only inappropriate clothing," so said comedian Billy Connolly, and he was right. If the sun isn't shining and the sky isn't blue, we tend to refer to the weather as 'bad', but photographically, 'bad' can be good because it gives us variations in the quality of light to work with, adds drama and creates atmosphere. So-called 'good' weather is actually not so good for photography because the light is bland and the landscape looks picture-postcard perfect, which gets boring after a while.

Clouds have a dramatic effect on the quality of daylight because they soften and spread it so intensity is reduced, contrast falls and shadows become weaker. Clouds also add interest to the sky, and the sky can make or break a great landscape.

Days when the sky is a blanket of monotonous grey cloud are probably the least exciting for landscape photography as colours appear dull and muted, and a lack of shadows means scenery tends to look flat and uninviting. However, overcast light is ideal for capturing details in the landscape: the patterns and textures in rocks; the smooth shapes and soft colours in sea-worn boulders and pebbles; the rich colours of autumnal foliage or banks of spring flowers. Strong colours look intense in diffuse light because there's no glare to dilute saturation. Dull days are also ideal for slow shutter speed shots of waterfalls – just keep the boring sky out of the shot and you'll get some great results.

White clouds in their many shapes and forms are highly photogenic against blue sky, and you can make them stand out even more by using a polariser to deepen the blue. Keep the sun to your side for the strongest effect. Watch out for cloud patterns on the landscape, too – they can add an extra element that makes a good scene great, and are easiest to spot if you're shooting from an elevated viewpoint.

Stormy weather creates the most dramatic conditions for landscape photography – angry, dark clouds rushing across the sky, strong winds blowing and momentary breaks that allow rays of sunlight to flood through and illuminate the scene below. You can't plan for such conditions, but if you venture outdoors in stormy weather, there's always the chance that you'll be in the right place to capture them. And it will be a blessing if you do.

If the sun does break through during a storm, the landscape ends up brighter than the sky, which is a reversal of the norm. What this means in practice is that you can get away without using an ND grad as the sky won't overexpose. However, it's still worth using a 0.6ND grad to make the sky look even more dramatic than it really is.

Something else to watch out for in stormy weather is a rainbow arching across the sky. Rainbows are created when the sun shines through falling rain, so if that happens while you're out, turn your back to the sun and check the sky ahead. To reveal the colours of the bow at their best, try to catch it against dark clouds and use a telezoom to home in on part of the bow. Alternatively, use a wide-angle zoom and include the whole bow.

Mist and fog reduce the landscape to soft shapes and hazy outlines. Three dimensions become two and aerial perspective means that tones become brighter with distance. The light is diffuse, shadows don't exist and fine detail is lost. Scenes are simplified and your images should reflect that.

Telephoto lenses emphasise the effects of mist and fog by magnifying the scene and compressing perspective, so they're great for shooting the overlapping forms of hills and mountains, or picking out elements like a single tree or church spire fading into the gloom. If you want to relegate mist or fog to the distance, then use a wide-angle lens – visibility close to the camera will be much better than farther away, so you can capture plenty of foreground detail and let the rest of the scene fade away. Dense fog is heavy and damp. It snuffs out colour and turns the world to grey, so you may decide to convert your foggy landscapes to black & white. Mist is more delicate, so instead of destroying colour, it tends to merge all colours together to create very soft hues. Mist is also fine enough to let the light through, so shoot contre-jour at sunrise, when you're more likely to find mist in woodland or over water, and capture golden rays of lights bleeding through. Such conditions aren't common, but the quality of light when you get mist and sunrise coinciding is hard to beat.

Check the web

If you're planning a landscape shoot, whether it's to head out early in the morning for sunrise or to go off into the wilds for a week, use the internet to gather information that will help you make the most of the light. Here are some websites worth bookmarking:

Weather forecast

www.metoffice.gov.uk
www.bbc.co.uk/weather
www.xcweather.co.uk
www.metcheck.com

Sunrise & sunset times

www.canterburyweather.co.uk/sun/ukmap.php

Tide times

www.tidetimes.org.uk/
http://easytide.ukho.gov.uk

Planning your shoot

A more sophisticated tool is the Photographer's Ephemeris (www.photoephemeris.com). This is available as a free download for both Mac and PC (plus as a paid-for app for the iPhone) and allows you to determine not only sunrise and sunset times for anywhere in the world, any day of the year, but also the angle of the sunrise/ sunset so you can check if the sun's orb will be blocked by a range of hills, say. Moonrise and set times are also provided.

Below left: Far from ruining the image, clouds can add all-important interest to coastal views.

Below right: Simple scenes suit a misty outlook and are given an ethereal twist.

Right: Rays of light shining through storm clouds can have a really dramatic effect.

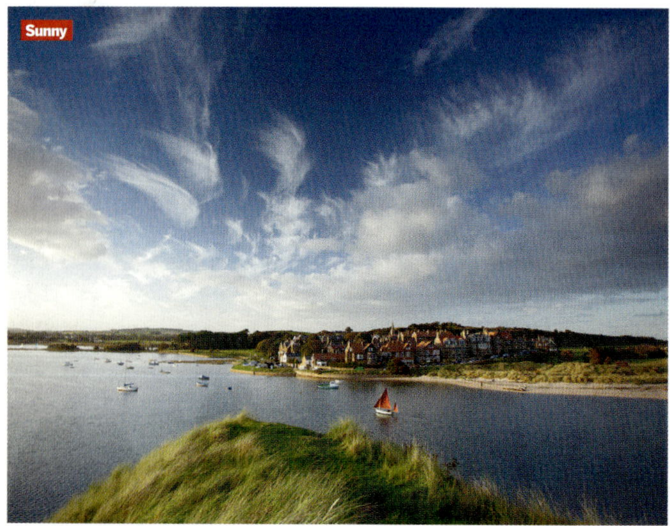
Sunny

LEE FROST

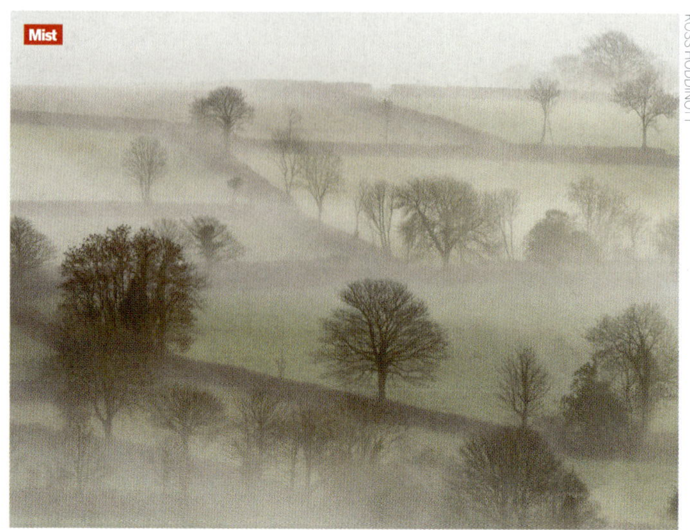
Mist

ROSS HODDINOTT

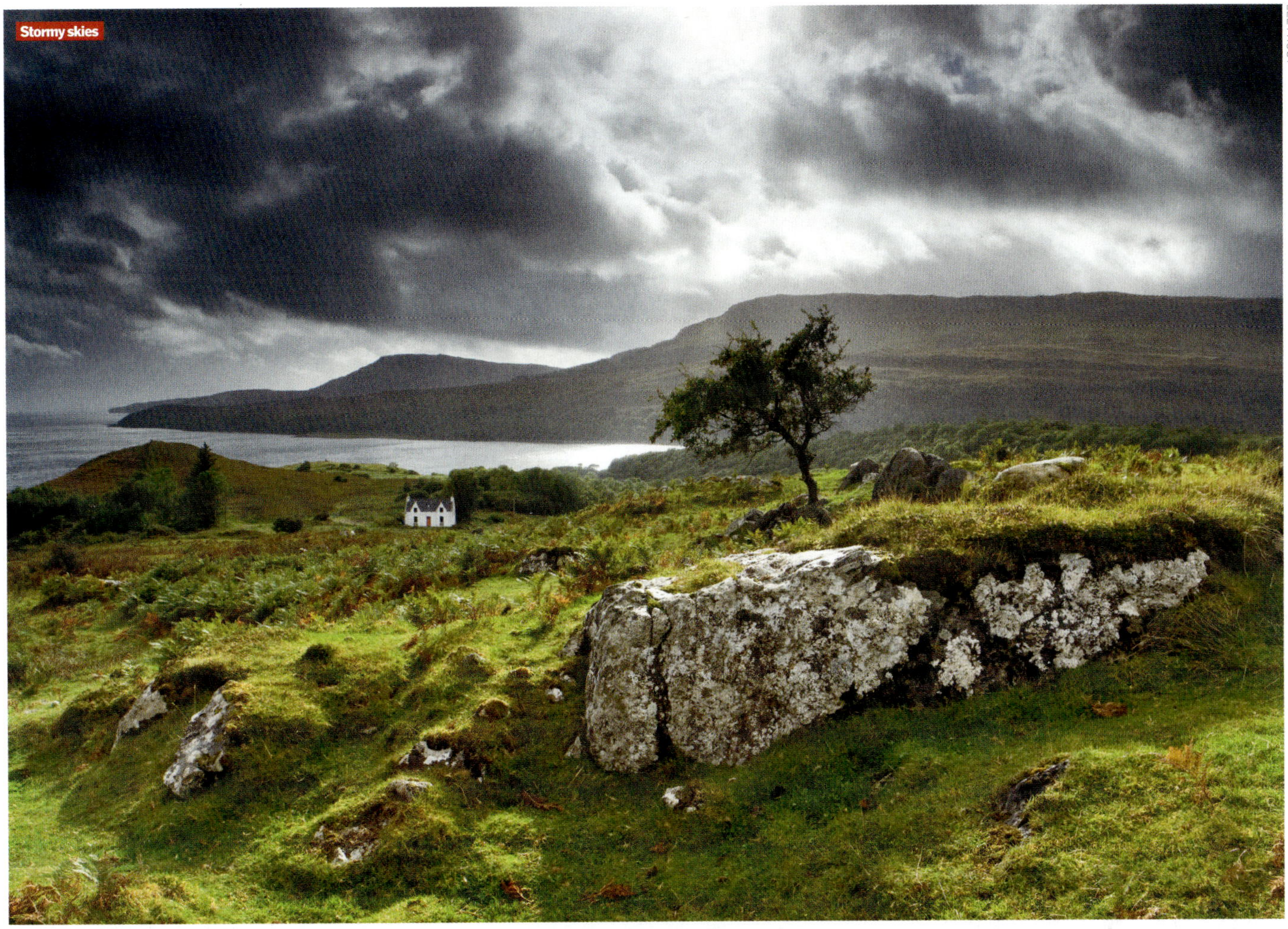

Stormy skies

LEE FROST

Colour temperature and White Balance

The colour of light is referred to as 'colour temperature', which is measured in Kelvin (K). The warmer the light is, the lower its colour temperature, and the cooler the light is, the higher its temperature.

Our eyes adapt to changes in the colour temperature automatically, so natural light always looks more or less white – this is known as chromatic adaptation. The photographic equivalent is your camera's Auto White Balance (AWB) setting. If you use AWB, you will find that it produces pleasing results in most daylight situations, but the White Balance does fluctuate so you may not record the 'colour' of the light as it really is. If you want to do that, you should set White Balance to the Daylight preset, which is 5500K. This is the colour temperature of 'mean noon daylight', so in normal daylight situations, your images will come out looking neutral. However, at sunrise and sunset the light is much warmer (lower colour temperature), so by using the Daylight White Balance preset, your camera will record that warmth. Similarly, if the light is cool, as is often the case during predawn or in bad weather, using the Daylight preset will record that coolness.

Remember, also, that if you shoot in Raw, you can adjust the colour temperature of the image later. So if you don't like the cool cast, you simply get rid of it, or if a warm image isn't warm enough, you can adjust the colour temperature to make it warmer.

Conditions	Colour temp (K)	Colour cast (Daylight WB)
Open shade under blue sky	10000K	Very blue
Shade under part cloudy sky	**7500K**	**Blue**
Overcast weather	6000K	Slightly cool
Average noon daylight	**5500K**	**None**
Morning/evening sunlight	3500K	Warm
Sunrise/sunset	**2000K**	**Very warm**

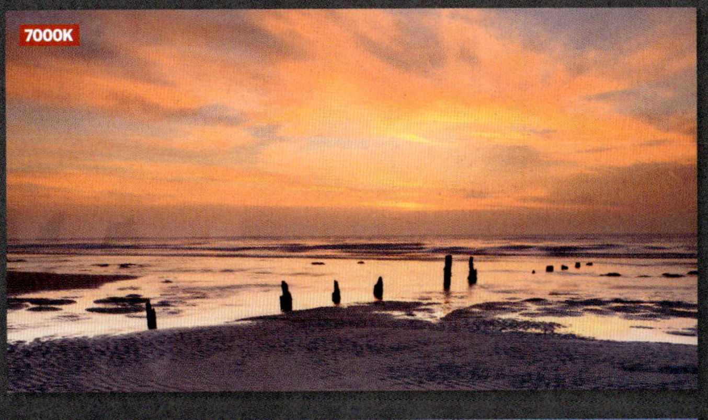
7000K

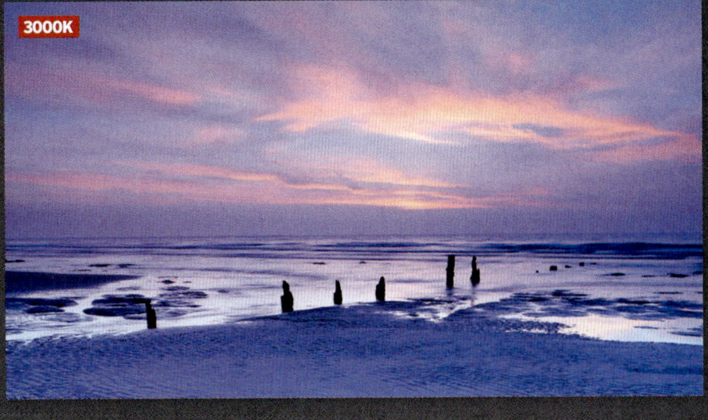
3000K

Seasonal landscape light

Although seasonal changes have more of a physical effect on the landscape, the quality of daylight also varies throughout the year. Here's our guide on how to handle landscapes in different seasons…

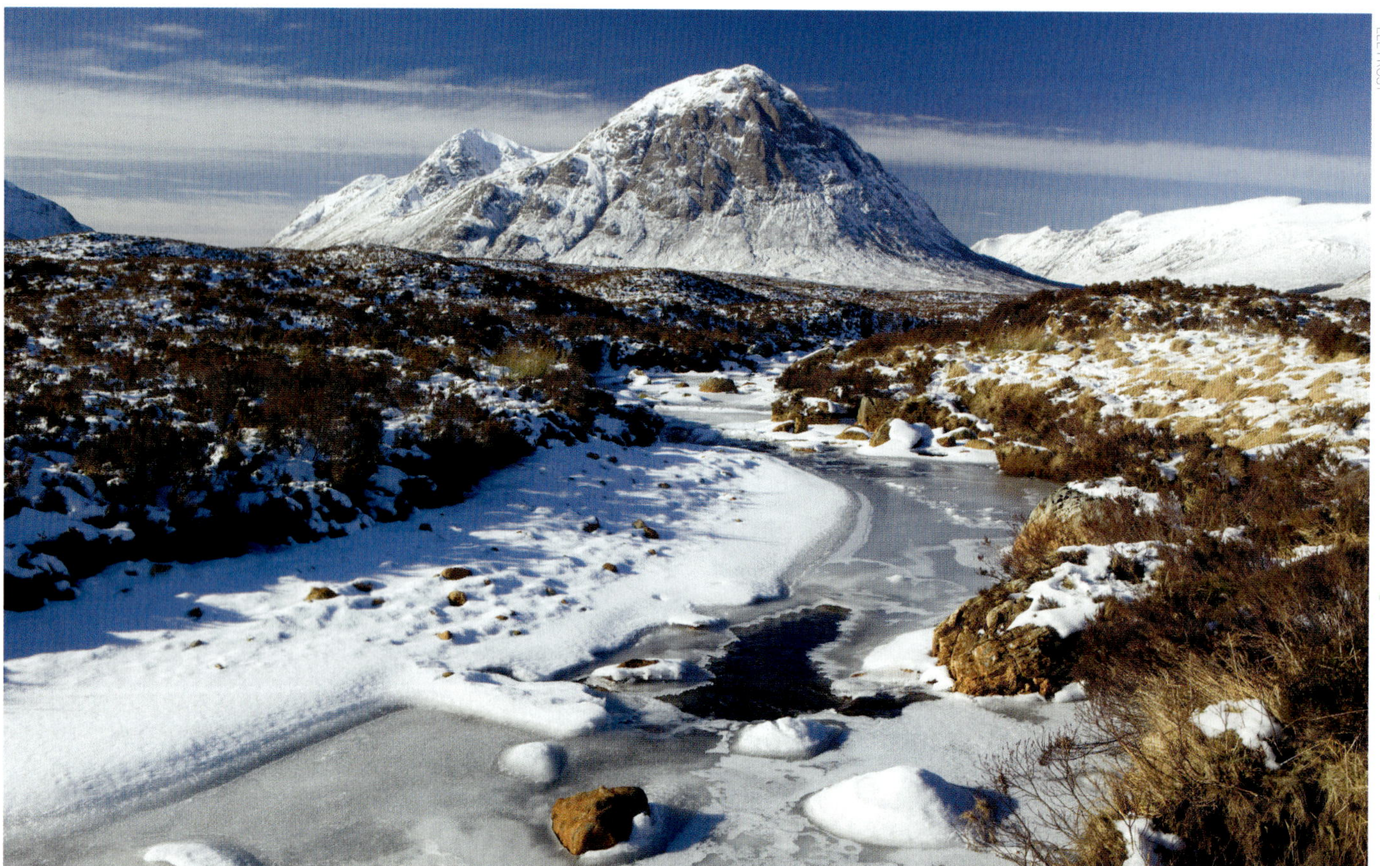

LEE FROST

1) Winter

The landscape lies dormant and bare during winter. Trees stand skeletal against the sky, while fields are brown and barren. Days are also painfully short, with the sun rising well after 8am and setting before 4pm in January.

Photographically, however, winter is a fantastic season. There are few sights more magnificent than a landscape covered in freshly fallen snow and bathed in crisp morning sunlight. But even if you're not lucky enough to get that, ice and frost are a certainty at some point as temperatures drop well below freezing.

The short days are a benefit, too, because you can shoot sunrise and sunset at civilised times. Plus the sun never climbs more than about 20° above the horizon, so the quality of light remains high from dawn to dusk, with long, weak shadows adding depth – on a clear winter's day you can get eight hours of good light.

Keep a close watch on the weather and if a clear night is forecast, prepare for an early start because that usually means ice and frost come the morning – and, if you're lucky, freezing mist for the sun to slowly burn away. Incredible pictures are guaranteed. Woodland and water locations are your best bet. As well as shooting wide-angle views, look for winter details: cobwebs covered in icy beads; the patterns in ice over ponds and puddles; frosty leaves on the ground; and so on.

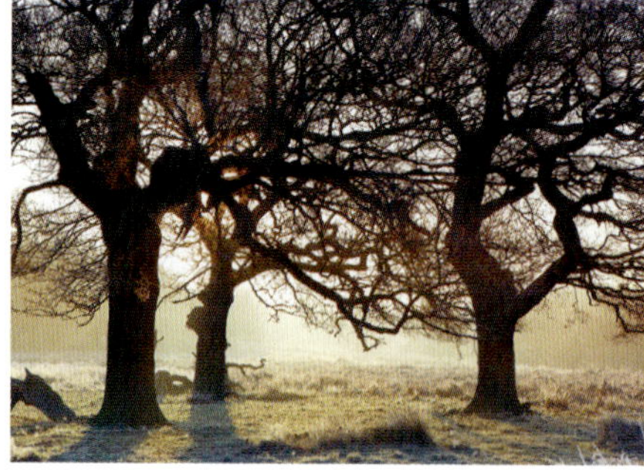

HELEN DIXON

Dawn on a freezing morning can be magical, with the sky full of pastel colours and the sun rising like a giant orange ball. Its intensity is often reduced by mist or haze, so you can include it in your shots without any risk of flare. Use your longest lens to make it nice and big.

Snow is best photographed when it has just fallen so it's pristine and fresh, and ideally in sunny weather – a glistening snowy landscape under a blue sky is hard to beat. And you needn't head to magnificent countryside to take great snow shots – a visit to your local park can be just as productive if you concentrate on simple scenes, like a single tree standing in the middle of a snow-filled field.

Winter Q&A

What should I consider when shooting snow scenes?
Exposure! All that whiteness in the scene is likely to fool your camera's metering system into underexposure, so take a shot then check the preview image and the histogram. You will almost certainly need to dial in extra exposure using the exposure compensation facility – do that in ⅓-stop increments until the highlight warnings on your preview image start to flash to indicate overexposure. Delete that shot – the one before it should be perfect.

Is it okay to use a polarising filter during winter?
Definitely, but carefully. Blue sky is bluer in winter and because more of it is polarised, the effect of a polarising filter is more obvious than at any other time of the year. In extreme cases, the sky can go almost black if you fully polarise, so you may need to wind back the effect a little.

Will my camera work okay in freezing winter weather?
Yes, but batteries drain faster so make sure yours is fully charged and ideally carry a spare. Also, avoid breathing on your lens or any filters you're using as they will mist up and take ages to clear.

HELEN DIXON

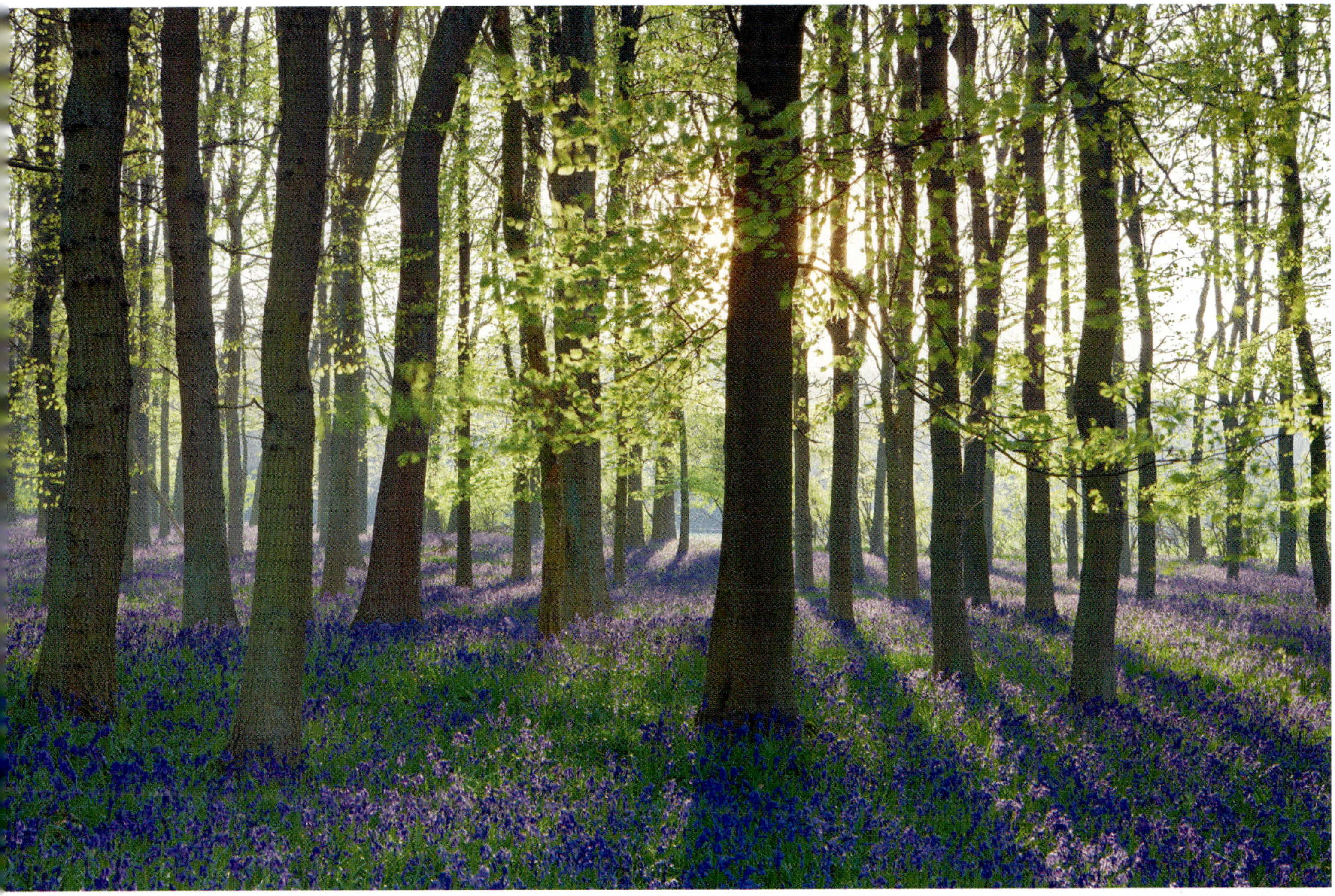

2) Spring

This season marks the dawn of new life as the landscape awakens from the dormant months of winter. Barren trees burst with buds and blossom, woodland floors, hedgerows and riverbanks are carpeted with colourful wild flowers, while desolate fields turn into beautiful patchwork quilts of green.

Scenes that looked grey and drab during winter are transformed within a few short weeks – especially if the weather turns and is mild towards the end of winter. Spring is also time for tulips, daffodils, buttercups and bluebells, turning gardens and meadows into dazzling displays of colour.

The weather during spring is changeable and unpredictable – but this has its advantages for the photographer. Brief showers cleanse the atmosphere and create rainbows arching across the countryside, shafts of sunlight burst through stormy skies to illuminate the landscape below, and light mists hang over rivers and lakes or in valley bottoms at dawn.

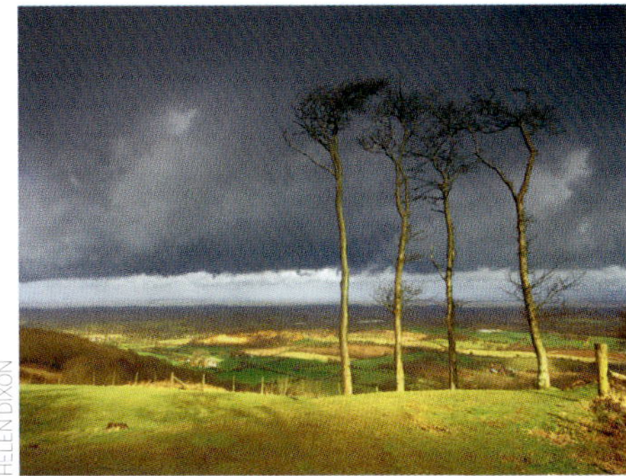

HELEN DIXON

As the weeks pass, the days also grow longer. The sun rises at around 6am during the early days of spring and sets at 8pm, but by mid-June, sunrise can be as early as 4.15am and sunset after 10.30pm in the north of Scotland. To make the most of spring conditions, rise early and stay out late. Dawn on a perfect spring morning is hard to beat, with a chorus of birdsong permeating the cool air and the first rays of sunlight slowly burning away the mist. The opportunity for amazing images is one that shouldn't be missed, and nothing quite beats that feeling of getting in touch with nature.

The intensity of colour in the spring landscape can be improved by using a polarising filter to cut through atmospheric haze and glare on the foliage. If you want to capture carpets of spring flowers, ideally wait for a bright but overcast day when contrast is low and shadows weak. This makes it easier to record the delicate colours and fine details of the blooms, especially when taking pictures in woodland where the light is patchy during sunny spells.

Spring Q&A

How do I shoot spring mist?
Mist often occurs when a mild day with rain is followed by a clear night and cold temperatures. If that's predicted in the weather forecast, set your alarm early and head out before sunrise. Mist is common near water and wetlands, and in woodland. Get to a decent location ready for sunrise: if you're lucky, the light from the rising sun will burst through the mist, creating warm rays of light that radiate from behind trees and buildings. A straight exposure should capture this effect perfectly, but, if necessary, increase the exposure by 2/3-1 stop.

What's the best shutter speed to use when shooting waterfalls?
A shutter speed around one second is usually slow enough to blur the water, but also record some texture – though you can experiment with slower speeds. What you don't want to do is overexpose the water so it comes out white.

How do I get backlit shots of flowers?
You need to shoot when the sun is low in the sky, so during early morning or late afternoon: morning is often more atmospheric. Get down low, use a telezoom to isolate a group of flowers and try to capture them against a dark background so the colours glow.

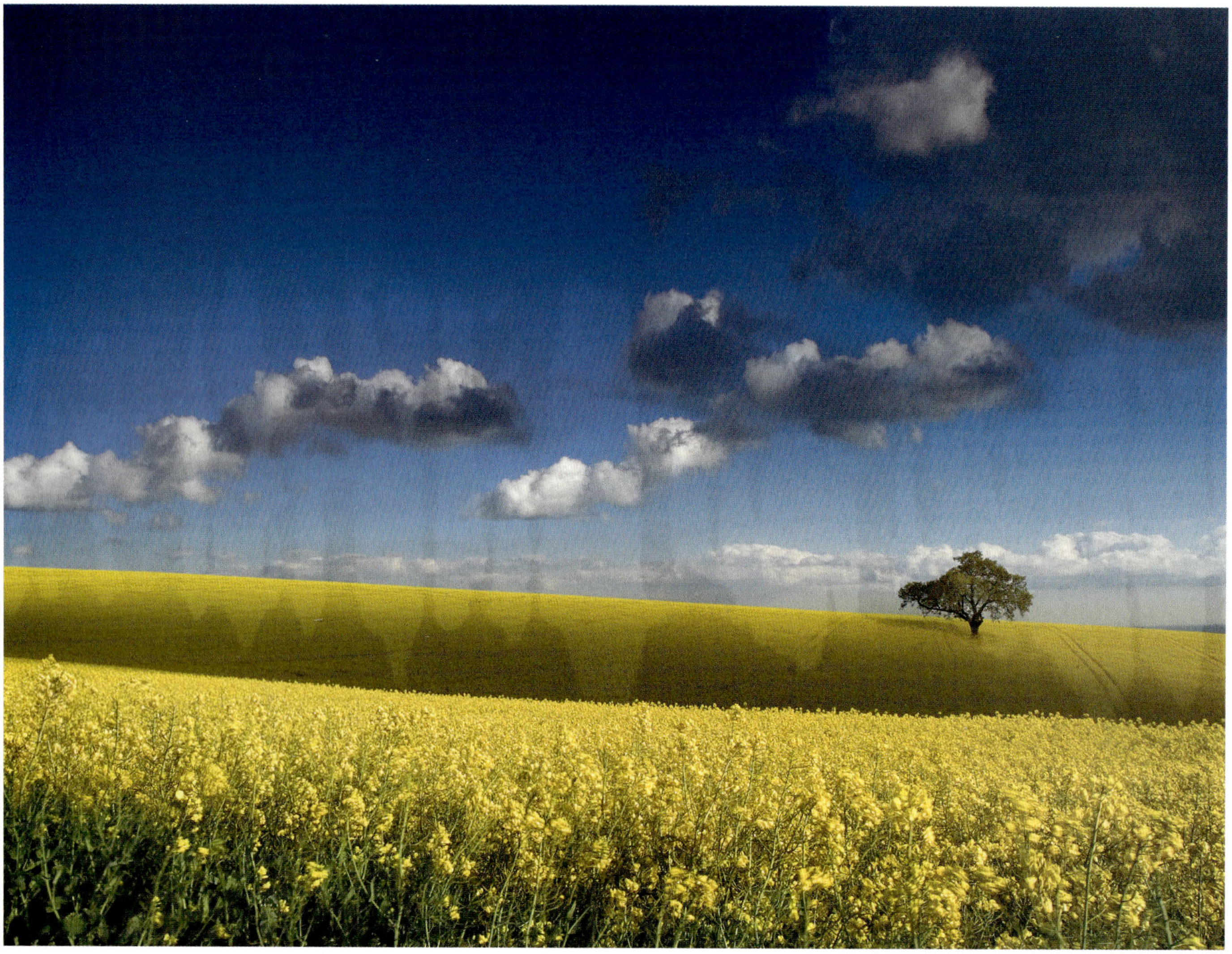

HELEN DIXON

3) Summer

Summer is the least favourite season for landscape photographers, as the light tends to be harsh and bland. Yes, the countryside does look resplendent in its lush coat of foliage, gardens and meadows are alive with colour and the days last much longer. But when the sun does shine, it can be very intense and unflattering, with a high colour temperature that makes images look cool, while heat haze tends to turn blue sky into an ugly washed-out tone. Consequently, the number of effective hours available for landscape photography are no more than on a clear winter's day.

Between 10am and 4pm in summer, the sun is overhead and the light harsh and characterless, while shadows are short and dense. For conventional landscape photography, this isn't great, but if you find scenes containing lots of colour – oilseed rape, poppy fields, sunflowers – on a sunny, blue-sky day, it's still possible to produce striking images. Use a polariser to boost contrast and clarity, and keep your composition simple.

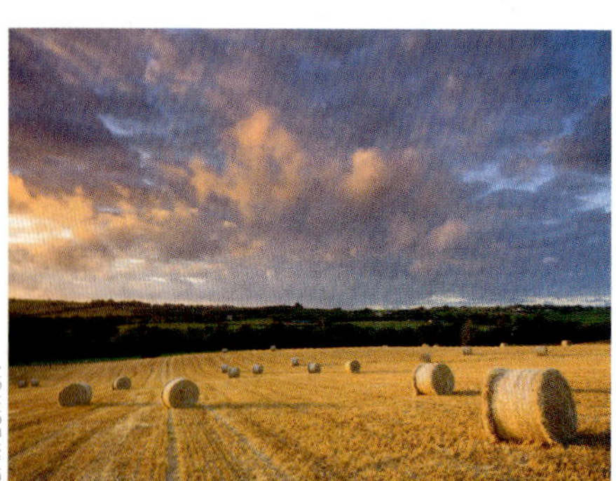

ADAM BURTON

Summer storms are also quite common, with high temperatures leading to thunder and heavy rain. This can produce amazing landscape light, but you risk a soaking to catch it! Once the rain subsides, crisp, clean light will often bathe the landscape and rainbows can appear.

The light is at its best at the extreme of the day, so get to your location very early or be prepared to stay out late. The days do get shorter as summer progresses, but 3am starts and 11pm finishes are not uncommon. You can always grab a sleep in the afternoon when the light's no good!

Wild landscapes can still look dramatic during the summer, and by early September start to turn quite autumnal, so scout out the locations nearest you that will be full of colour. Rocky, barren coastline also changes little during the summer and can be the source of great shots – especially at dawn and dusk when the light is warm.

Summer Q&A

Can I do anything about hazy skies?
Not really. Hazy skies and overcast grey skies lack texture or drama – they're just a blanket, boring tone. Using an ND grad merely darkens that tone, but rarely makes it more interesting. Exclude the sky from your compositions; maybe use a telezoom to shoot selective landscapes or concentrate on smaller details.

Is the summer a good time to use my infrared modified camera?
Definitely. There's plenty of foliage to show the ghostly infrared effect, and it doesn't matter how harsh the light is because infrared photography suits it. Use your IR camera in parks, gardens and woodland, as well as the countryside. For those without an IR modified camera, try using an infrared filter like the Hoya R72.

My summer landscapes often have an unsightly blue cast. What causes it?
High colour temperature – on a sunny blue-sky day, the colour temperature can hit 10000K. If you use Daylight White Balance, set for 5500K, your camera will record the coolness in the light. Setting White Balance to Shade will get rid of the cast – even Auto White Balance (AWB) may work. Or, if you shoot in Raw, you can correct the cast during image processing.

LEE FROST

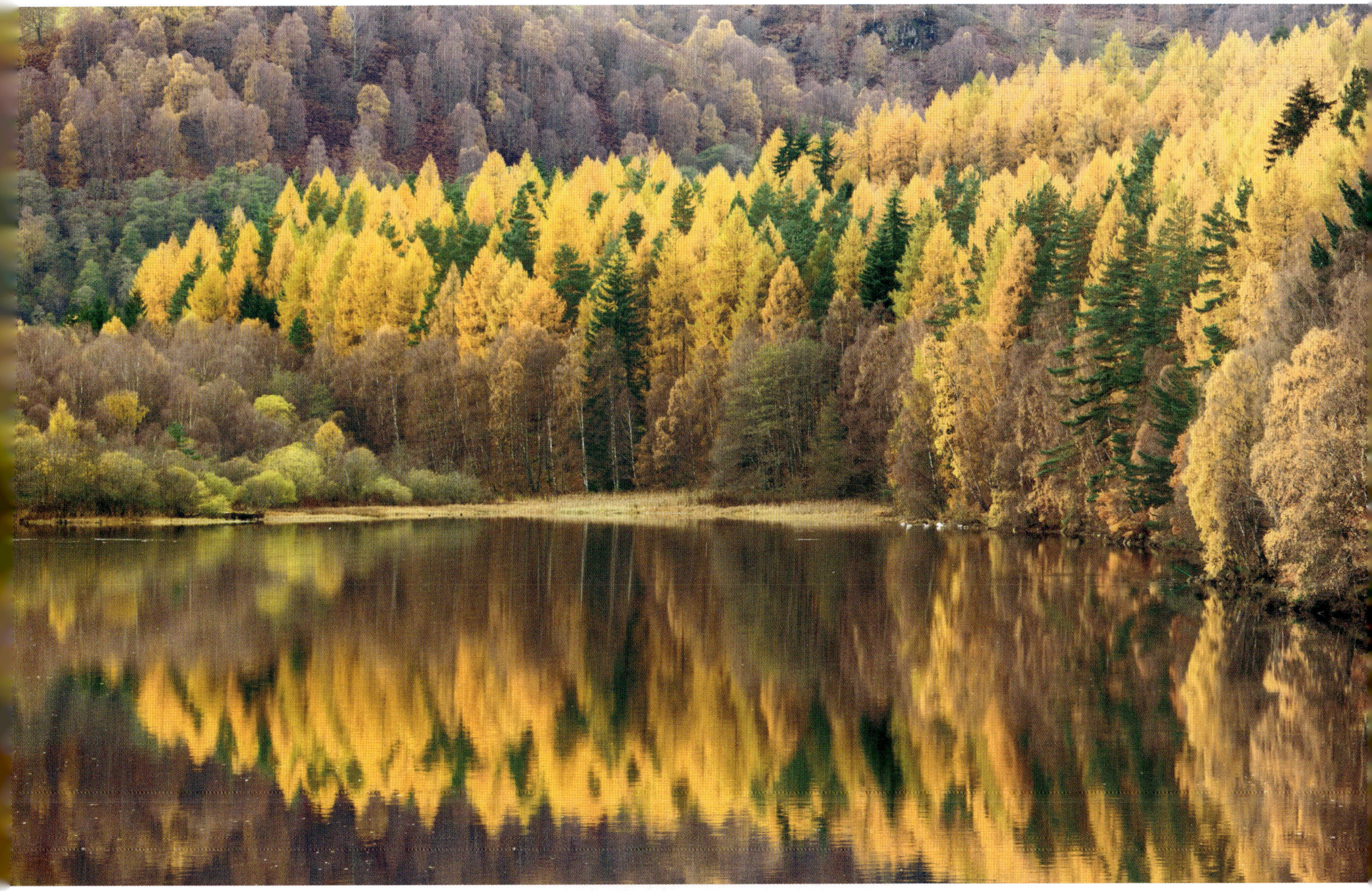

4) Autumn

Colour – that's what autumn is all about. As days shorten and temperatures fall, deciduous foliage turns a myriad of wonderful rustic colours. Hillsides covered in heather and bracken turn to gold and the landscape battens down the hatches ready for winter. Whether autumn is a hit or a flop colourwise depends on temperatures and rainfall during spring and summer: the first week in November is traditionally a time when colours peak, but the prime period can occur earlier or later.

Clear, sunny days provide the best conditions to capture autumn's beauty, especially during early morning and late afternoon when the sunlight is naturally warm and the sky a deep, velvety blue. Wild landscape looks amazing in autumn – head to regions like Rannoch Moor in Scotland or the Lake District and you can't go wrong.

If you intend to shoot deep inside woodland, ideally choose an overcast day when the light is soft and shadows weak, otherwise high contrast will be a problem. Such conditions reveal the woodland colours at their most intense, especially when enhanced by a polarising filter, which cuts through haze on the damp foliage.

Head for rivers and lakes where you can capture the autumnal colours reflecting in calm water, and as well as shooting wide-angle views, also look for details like the vibrant patterns of fallen autumnal leaves.

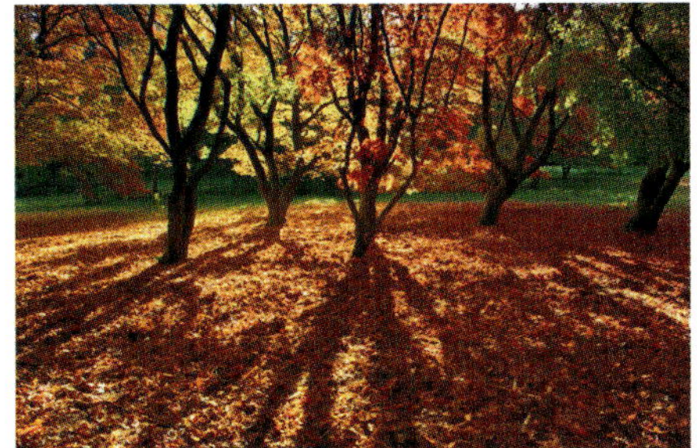

HELEN DIXON

Autumn is also good to capture the landscape being brought to life by dramatic, stormy light, with patches of sunlight breaking through the dark, brooding sky. Or why not rise early and make the most of early-morning mist around water or in woodland and valleys? If you're lucky, you may capture the first golden rays of sunlight burning though to create stunning images.

At the start of autumn, on 21 September, the sun rises around 7am and sets at 7pm, so the days are fairly long, but the quality of light remains high throughout. By day one of winter, on 1 December, the sun doesn't rise until after 8am and it sets before 4pm.

Autumn Q&A

What causes foliage to change colour in autumn?

Deciduous trees drop their leaves in readiness for winter when there's too little light for photosynthesis to occur, and they live off sugar reserves stored through the summer. Chlorophyll, which gives leaves their green colour, is necessary for photosynthesis to take place, but as the days grow shorter and the hours of darkness increase, the production of chlorophyll slows down and that's when the colour changes start to occur.

Autumnal colours reach their peak when all the chlorophyll has been destroyed and other chemicals in the leaves are revealed, such as carotenoids and anthocyanins.

Can you recommend some top autumn locations in the UK?

If the colours are good, you can take great autumn shots literally anywhere you find deciduous foliage, but check out Westonbirt Arboretum in Gloucestershire, Glen Affric in Scotland, Stourhead Gardens in Wiltshire, The New Forest in Hampshire, Grasmere and Rydal Water in the Lake District, Gwydyr Forest in North Wales and Kielder Forest, Northumberland.

Shoot a misty morning scene

Ross Hoddinott reveals how early-morning mist provides a wonderful opportunity for you to shoot ethereal, magical scenes...

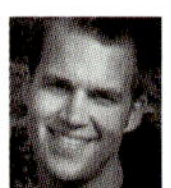

Ross Hoddinott MISTY MORNINGS ARE one of the key traits of spring. Mist can look magical, filling valleys and hanging atmospherically above fields. By reducing colour and contrast, mist simplifies the look of objects, placing more emphasis on shape instead. There are different types of mist and fog, but the most photogenic is 'radiation fog', which forms during clear, still nights when the ground loses heat by radiation and cools.

The ground chills nearby air to saturation point and mist forms. It often stays confined to low ground, forming a thin white layer at the bottom of valleys. When looking at the local weather forecast, watch for clear skies and cool, still nights – perfect conditions for mist. Also, look at the forecast for clarity. If clarity is predicted to drop to average or poor during the night, then there is a good chance you will be greeted with mist in the morning. Set your alarm early. Allow enough time to get to your intended viewpoint before sunrise, so that you can get set up and ready in advance of the best conditions. If you are driving, remember your journey will be slower due to the conditions.

A high viewpoint, from the top of a hill or valley, is often best; allowing you to get above the mist to shoot atmospheric vistas.

Often, objects are reduced to nothing more than a simple silhouette in misty weather. Therefore, look for strong, bold objects to photograph within the landscape – a church steeple, castle ruin or tree, for example. Longer focal lengths suit misty scenes the most, foreshortening perspective and allowing photographers to isolate points of interest. Light scatters and is more diffused in mist, adding to its mystical effect – often the most dramatic results come from shooting into the light. A medium telephoto lens, in the region of 100mm, is often ideal. Mist – like snow – has a habit of fooling a camera's metering system. This is because it is designed to assume that the subject is mid-tone (18% grey). Subjects that are significantly lighter or darker than mid-tone, like a misty landscape, can be exposed incorrectly. TTL metering has a tendency to underexpose mist, rendering it too dark. Consult the camera's histogram screen regularly when shooting mist. If the graph is biased to the left, this is an indication of underexposure. Apply positive (+) exposure compensation to make the image brighter, and then reshoot. You may only need to apply a third, or half a stop of compensation, but in extreme instances, you might have to dial in a stop or more of compensation. Again, use the histogram as your guide.

Having dragged yourself out of bed early to shoot the morning mist, don't overlook the picture potential of smaller, less obvious subjects – for example, dew-laden cobwebs glistening in the morning light.

Weather websites & apps

Outdoor photographers rely heavily on local weather forecasts, especially when waiting for ideal conditions leading to mist. While long-term forecasts aren't always reliable, 24- and 48-hour forecasts are often accurate. Therefore, keep a regular eye on the forecast. Mobile phone apps are an ideal source of information but you should also use websites such as www.metoffice.gov.uk

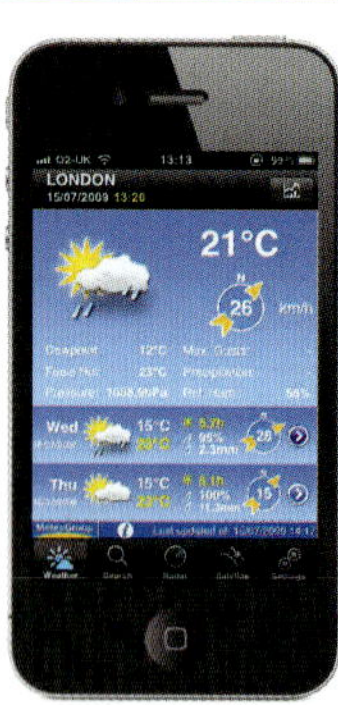

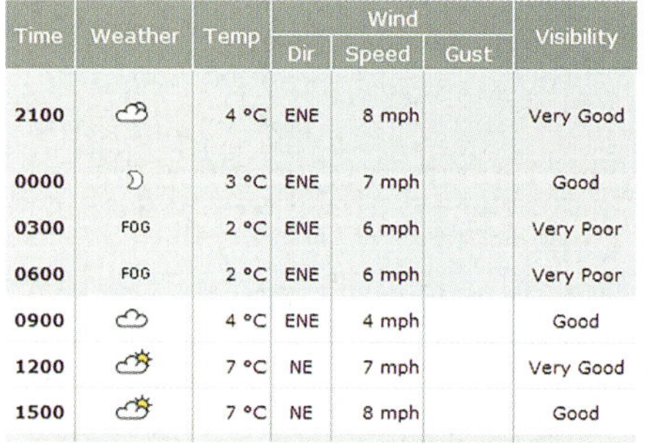

Time	Weather	Temp	Wind			Visibility
			Dir	Speed	Gust	
2100		4 °C	ENE	8 mph		Very Good
0000		3 °C	ENE	7 mph		Good
0300	FOG	2 °C	ENE	6 mph		Very Poor
0600	FOG	2 °C	ENE	6 mph		Very Poor
0900		4 °C	ENE	4 mph		Good
1200		7 °C	NE	7 mph		Very Good
1500		7 °C	NE	8 mph		Good

1 Planning I check the local weather forecast daily and notice that a clear, still night is predicted. Clarity also dropped during the night, so I am optimistic that it will be misty in the morning. I prepare my camera outfit, then set my alarm for just before sunrise.

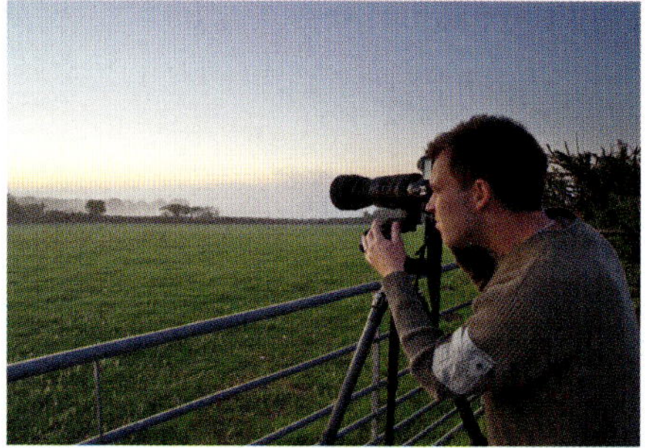

2 Viewpoint Sure enough, the landscape is shrouded in morning mist. I drive to a high viewpoint, which offers good views over the misty landscape and set up my kit. A telephoto is a good lens choice for mist as it compresses perspective, exaggerating the effect.

3 Metering Mist helps to simplify the look of the landscape, giving it a 'layered' effect. I compose my shot, and release the shutter, but the result is too dark. By looking at the histogram, I can tell the exposure is biased to the left, confirming the image is underexposed.

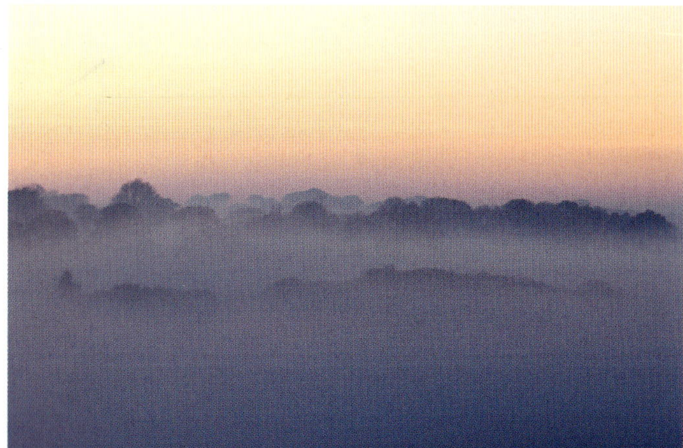

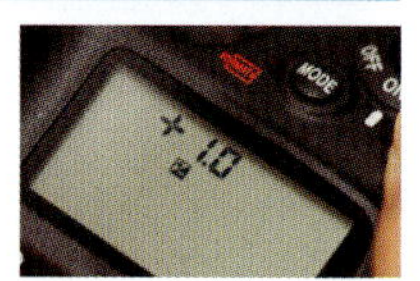

4 Exposure override The brightness of mist can fool metering systems designed to assume scenes are mid-tone. Using the camera's exposure compensation button, I dial in one stop of positive (+) compensation to lengthen the exposure time. The result is far better, but the scene lacks a focal point.

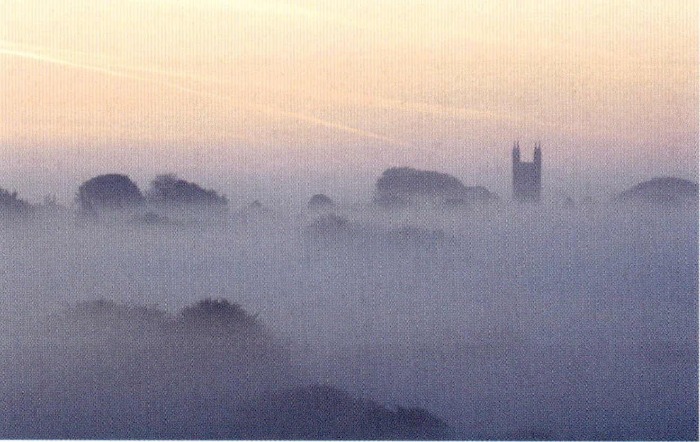

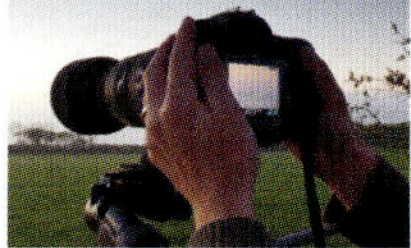

5 Composition I scan the landscape for a key point of interest to give my shot more purpose and notice a church tower sticking out above the mist. I recompose the picture to make this my main point of interest and also try a vertical composition. The result is a great springtime misty image.

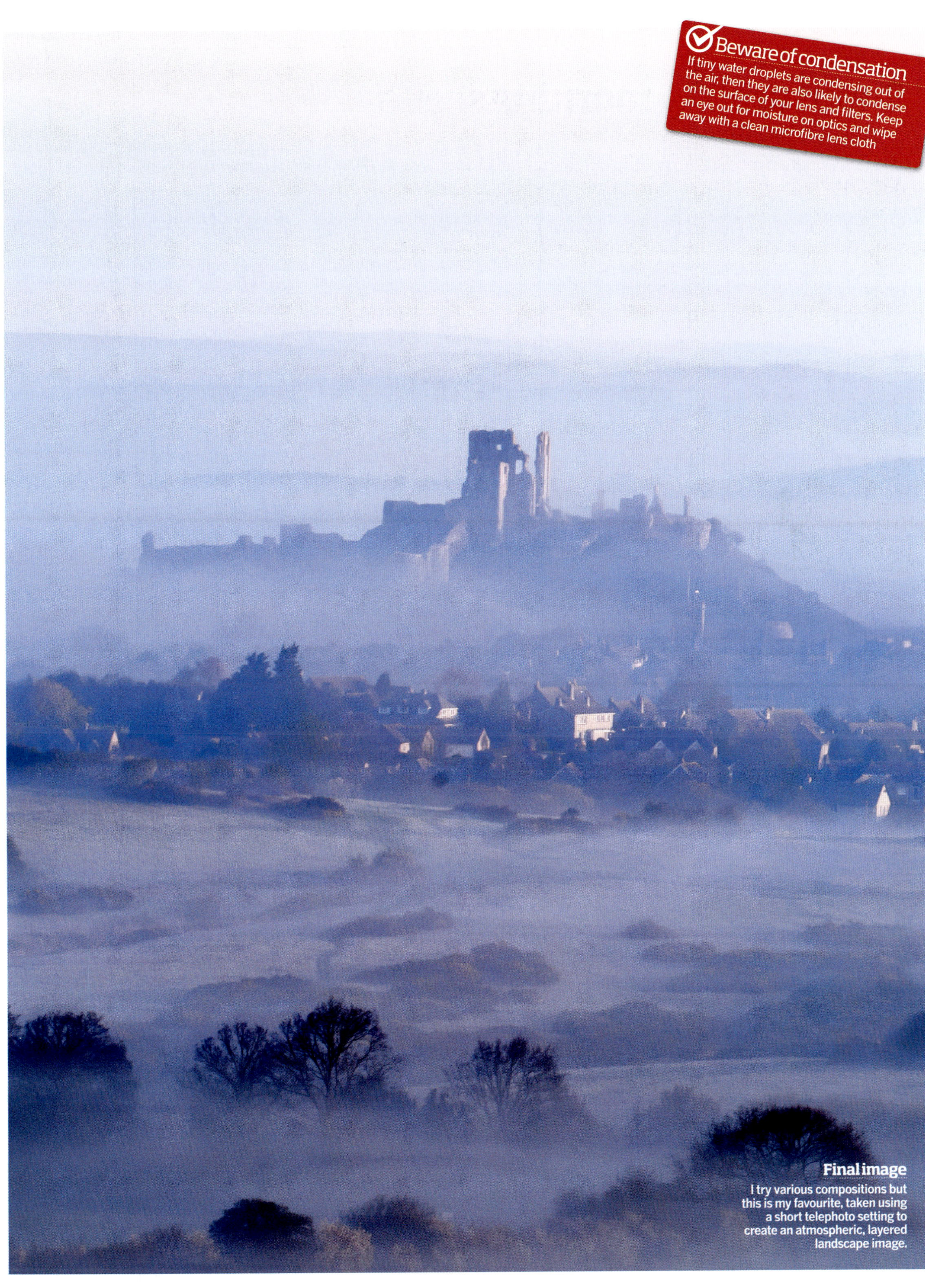

Beware of condensation

If tiny water droplets are condensing out of the air, then they are also likely to condense on the surface of your lens and filters. Keep an eye out for moisture on optics and wipe away with a clean microfibre lens cloth

Final image

I try various compositions but this is my favourite, taken using a short telephoto setting to create an atmospheric, layered landscape image.

Exposure

Digital SLRs have extremely accurate, multi-zone metering systems with a histogram function to help us check accurate exposure, so getting it right has never been easier. However, to take more creative control, you need to take things into your own hands. Here are a few techniques for perfect exposures

Mid-tone metering

Metering systems in digital cameras are calibrated to an 18% grey mid-tone. Basing exposure readings on a mid-tone such as grass is a good starting point for accurate exposures

MARK BAUER WAS LOOKING for a 'different' view of Corfe Castle in Dorset, so he sauntered along to the graveyard in the village. Having found a composition based around one of the crosses, the next problem was sorting out the exposure. Mark explains, step by step, how he tackled the challenge:

1) This is what the camera's multi-zone meter came up with, without the aid of any filtration. The scene is high in contrast, and the camera has struggled to capture all the tonal information.

2) Spot meter readings from the base of the cross and the sky revealed a difference in brightness of about 4½ stops. Setting an exposure for the land, I fitted a 0.9ND grad filter (three stops) and pulled it down below the horizon, to the edge of the darkest shadow area. I used a soft grad so that it wouldn't cut a line into the cross. As there is some loss of detail in the brighter parts of the sky, I reduced the exposure by two-thirds of a stop and re-shot.

3) The result is that the image has now been 'exposed to the right' (see over the page for details), without 'clipping' the highlights. The histogram shows that there are still dark tones, but also plenty of information in the top section, and no clipped shadows.

4) A straight conversion of the Raw file looks dull, the picture lacks contrast. For the final version, I've brought the exposure down slightly and added more contrast, especially in the shadows, to recreate the drama of the original scene. I've also tweaked the White Balance to add warmth and increased the saturation too.

5) For comparison purposes, I also took a shot that was underexposed by one stop. As you can see, it's left the shadows muddy and lacking in detail.

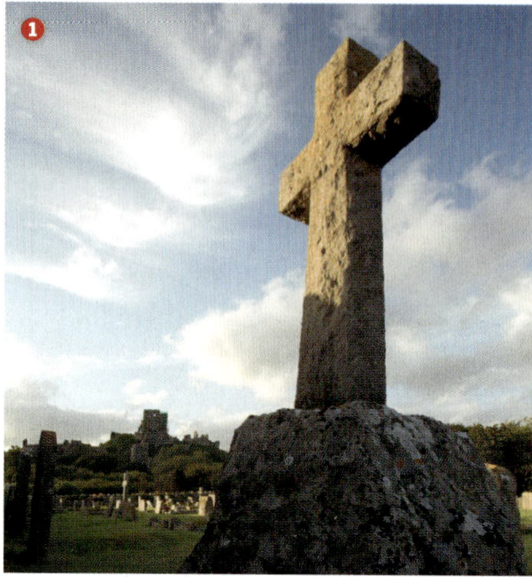

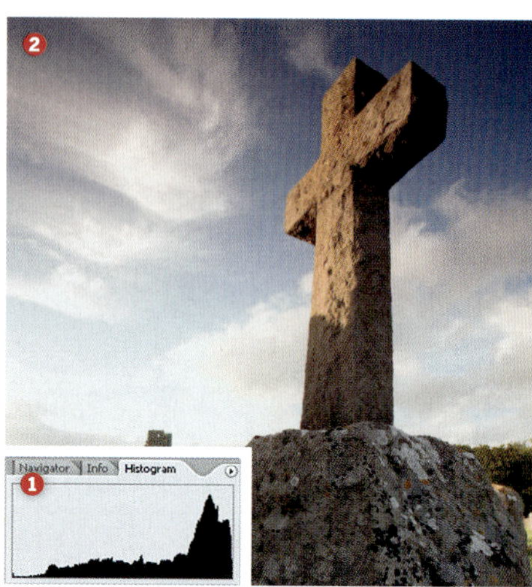

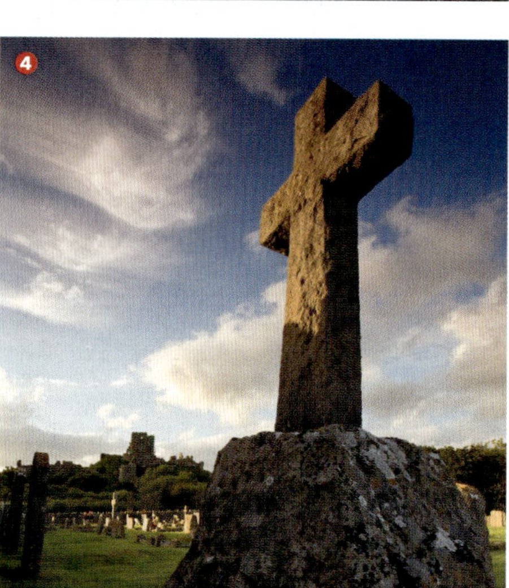

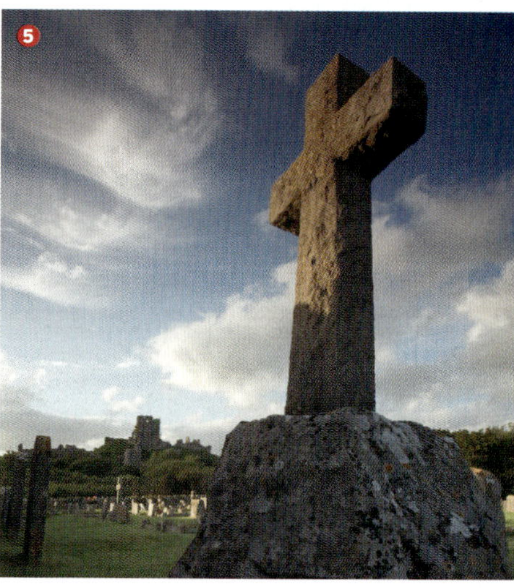

Exposure

Shadows
These two examples on the right show why it's not a good idea to underexpose and then try to open up the shadows during processing. The nearest image is around one-stop underexposed (to maintain highlight detail) and the shadow curve has been pulled up to match the exposure in the correctly exposed version on the right. As you can see, not only is there 'posterisation' in the shadows, rather than smooth tonal transitions, and tons of noise, but also the sensor has recorded significantly less detail.

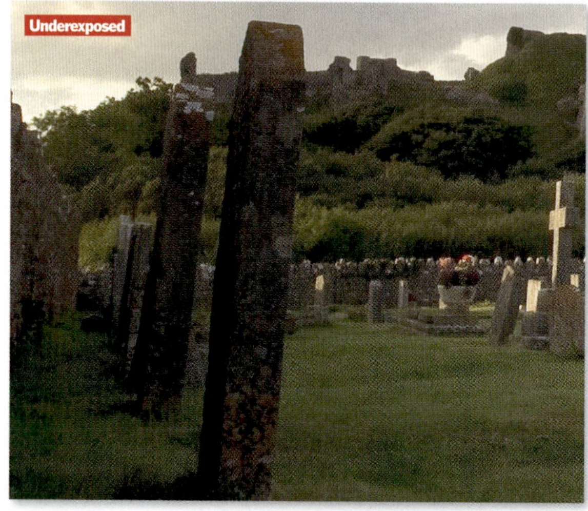
Underexposed

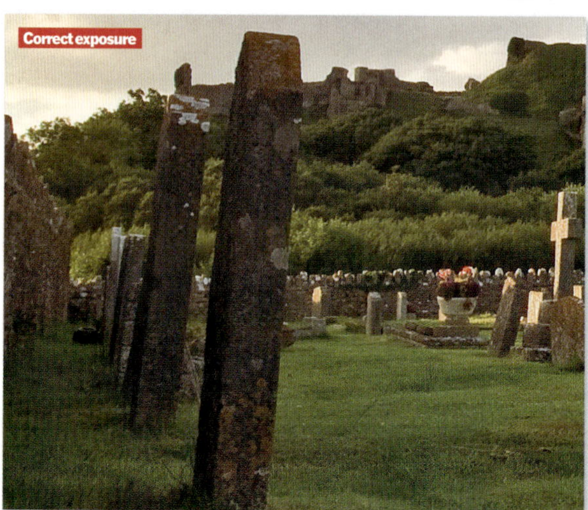
Correct exposure

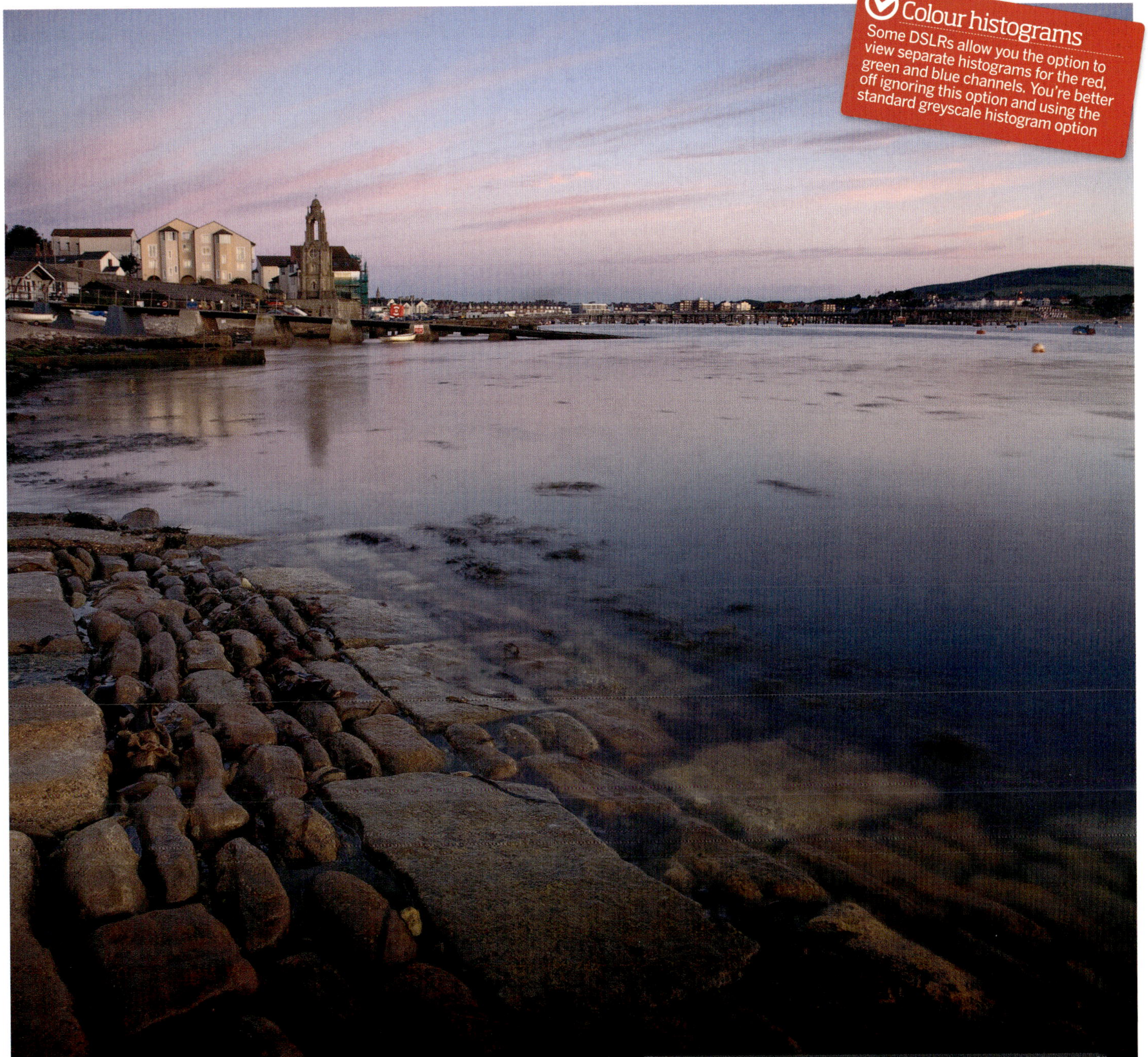

Colour histograms

Some DSLRs allow you the option to view separate histograms for the red, green and blue channels. You're better off ignoring this option and using the standard greyscale histogram option

Expose to the right

'Exposing to the right' is fast becoming a widely accepted approach to help maximise image quality – although it only applies if you shoot in Raw. With this technique you effectively push exposure settings as close to overexposure as possible without actually clipping the highlights. The result is a histogram with the majority of pixels grouped to the right of mid point – hence the name 'expose to the right'. So, when you're confident you understand exposures well enough, give this technique a try and push the exposure as far to the right of the histogram as you can, without clipping the highlights. The image will probably look a little light once in the Raw converter, but this is easily corrected with the brightness and contrast controls, and will give much better results than trying to lighten a darker image.

CCD and CMOS sensors count light in a linear fashion. Most digital SLRs record a 12-bit image capable of recording 4,096 tonal values over six stops. But the tonal values are not spread evenly across the six stops; each stop records half the light of the previous one. So, half of the levels are devoted to the brightest stop (2,048), half of the remainder (1,024 levels) are devoted to the next stop and so on. As a result, the last and darkest of the six stops only boasts 64 levels. This might seem confusing but, simply, if you do not properly use the right side of the histogram, which represents the majority of tonal values, you are wasting up to half of the available encoding levels. So if you deliberately underexpose to ensure detail is retained in the highlights – a common practice among many digital photographers – you are potentially losing a large percentage of the data that can be captured.

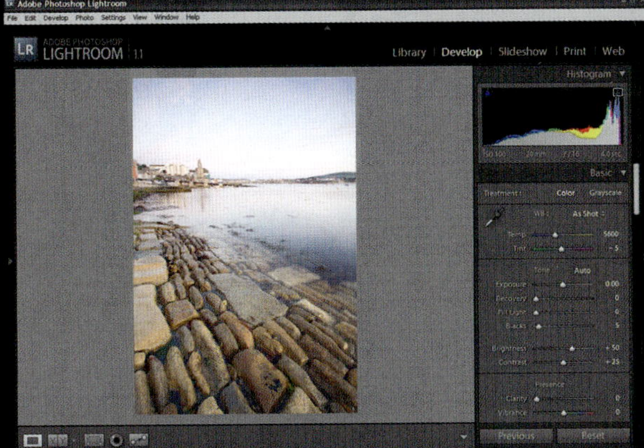

MAIN IMAGE & INSET: Exposure to the right of the histogram will capture maximum detail and minimum noise. Once in the Raw converter, the image will look too light and washed out, so use the brightness and contrast controls to adjust the image's appearance.

MARK BAUER

The basics skills for shooting water in landscapes

It's all about technique and the right gear when shooting stunning water scenics: be prepared before you head into the great outdoors

WE'RE NOT SURE if you've ever noticed, but the majority of stunning landscape images usually have some form of water in the scene. Whether it's as subtle as a small river trickling through, or as obvious as a dominating sea in a coastal seascape, water represents a key element in many landscape images.

One of the main reasons for this is because water is such a photographically pliable element. By using filters and/or manipulating the shutter speed, it's possible to record water in all manner of ways, from freezing its movement so droplets are suspended in mid-air, to using a long exposure to transform it into an ethereal mist. While potentially causing problems with our exposure, the reflective nature of water also plays its part in improving images too. On days where there is little or no wind, by heading to a lake, reservoir or any other large body of water, it's possible to produce a striking result by capturing a clean reflection of the scene on its surface. The possibilities don't stop there – rivers can be used as strong lead-in lines through the scene or, along with the likes of secluded rockpools and meandering streams littered with rocks, can form highly effective foreground interest.

The list is endless, but in this section of our guide, we provide the essentials you need to start going out to shoot water in landscapes and returning with brilliant results. What are you waiting for? Get exploring!

Choosing shutter speeds

The shutter speed you use to capture water will depend on a number of factors: if it's moving; how quickly it's moving; how much of it there is; and whether you want to stop it dead to freeze its movement or let it blur.

For big waterfalls and breaking waves, a shutter speed of 1/1000-1/2000sec will guarantee you freeze every droplet. For fast-flowing rivers and smaller waterfalls like this one pictured here, try 1/200–1/500sec, while for slower rivers and streams, 1/125–1/250sec should do the trick.

When it comes to blurring, one second will have a good effect on big waterfalls or try two seconds for smaller waterfalls. Rivers and streams need a slower speed of two to four seconds, though you can go much slower – 10-20 seconds – if you like.

Overexposure can be a problem when large volumes of water are concentrated in certain areas, so keep an eye on the histogram and use a slower speed if you start to clip the highlights. For coastal scenes, one to two seconds will blur waves, while 20-30 seconds will produce a 'milky' effect.

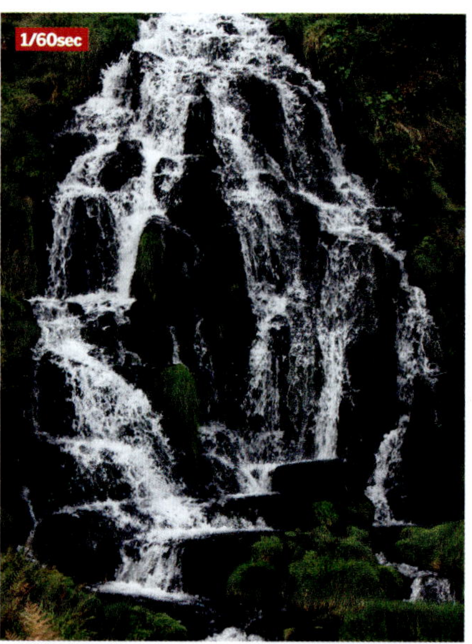
1/60sec

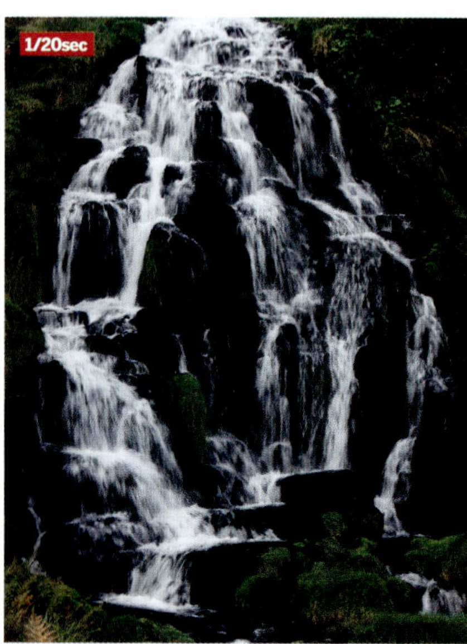
1/20sec

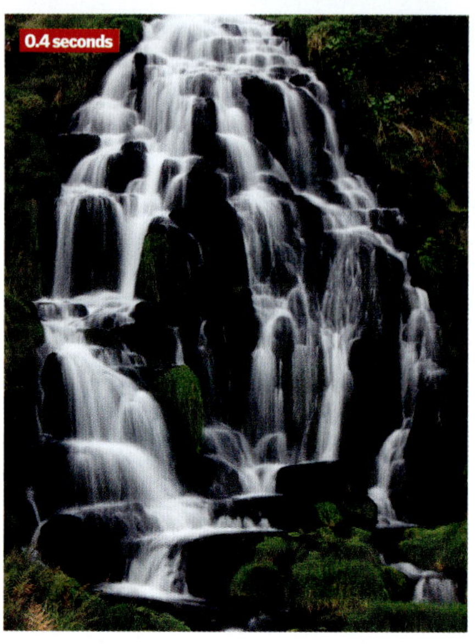
0.4 seconds

Essential gear

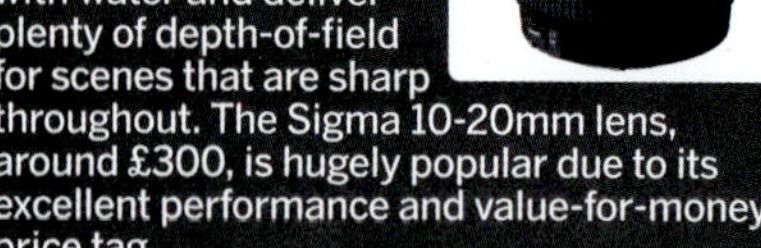

Wide-angle zoom: An ultra wide zoom like a 12-24mm or similar is ideal as it will allow you to fill the foreground with water and deliver plenty of depth-of-field for scenes that are sharp throughout. The Sigma 10-20mm lens, around £300, is hugely popular due to its excellent performance and value-for-money price tag.

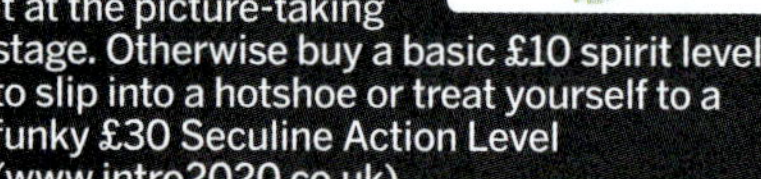

Spirit level: If your tripod kit has a spirit level, use it to ensure horizons are even – you don't want to spend ages in Photoshop levelling them if you can avoid it at the picture-taking stage. Otherwise buy a basic £10 spirit level to slip into a hotshoe or treat yourself to a funky £30 Seculine Action Level (www.intro2020.co.uk).

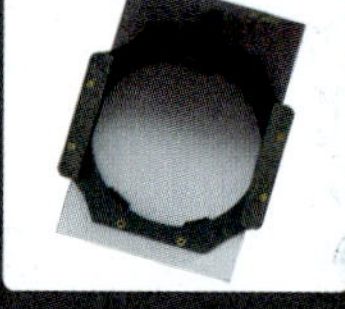

Filters: If you're serious about landscape photography, it'll pay to invest in a slot-in filter system. Cokin's P-system (www.intro2020.co.uk) represents great value for money, while if quality is paramount, look to Lee Filters' superb 100mm system – the choice of the professionals (www.leefilters.com). A polariser helps boost blue skies and deliver clear reflections off the water's surface. A 0.6 or 0.9ND filter (not ND grad!) is also worth considering, as it will allow you to use long shutter speeds in daylight to blur moving water.

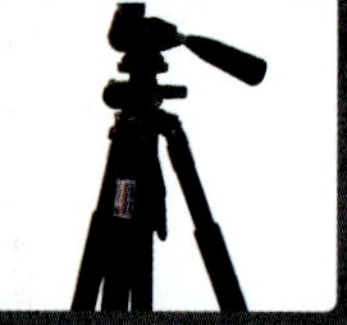

Tripod: When shooting water, you'll be looking to use small apertures to maximise depth-of-field and the slow shutter speeds require you to keep the camera stable to avoid shake. Check out the essential kit section later in this guide for advice on the best tripods to buy for outdoor photography, whatever your budget.

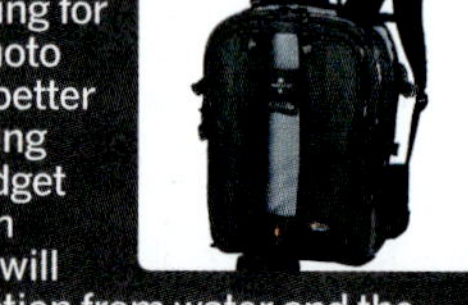

Photo backpack: When you're walking for miles on end, a photo backpack is a far better option for protecting your kit than a gadget bag. Those with an all-weather cover will offer better protection from water and the elements. Take a look at our website for reviews of some of the best: www.digitalslrphoto.com.

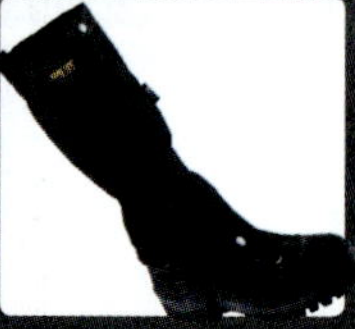

Clothing: There's nothing worse than slipping into a river and having to spend the day in wet clothes. Wear decent footwear from reputable brands such as Berghaus and consider waterproof trousers or gaiters from brands such as Paramo, as they allow you to step into rivers and stay dry.

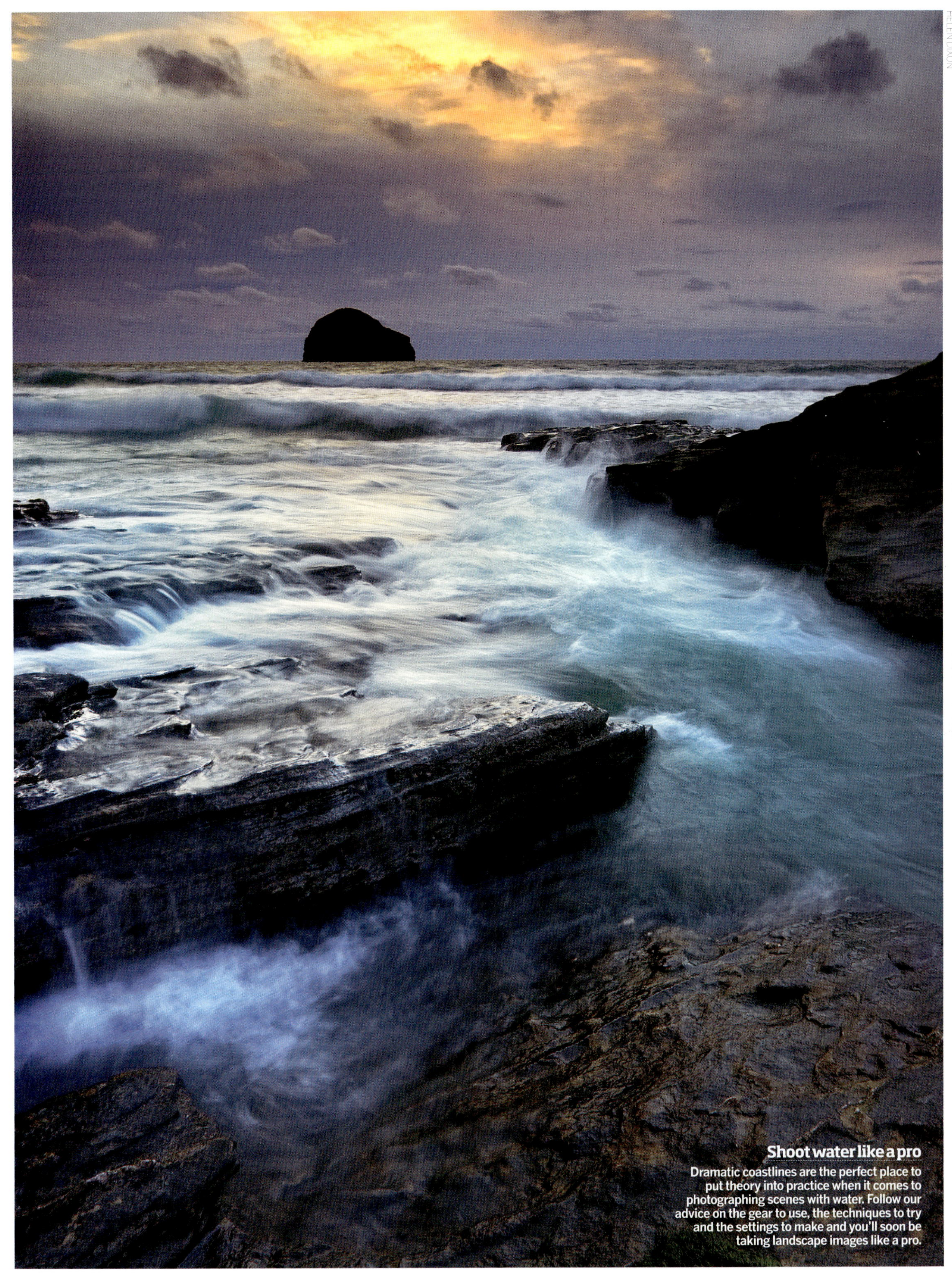

Shoot water like a pro

Dramatic coastlines are the perfect place to put theory into practice when it comes to photographing scenes with water. Follow our advice on the gear to use, the techniques to try and the settings to make and you'll soon be taking landscape images like a pro.

Capturing 'natural-looking' waves

Professional photographer Mark Bauer explains the best technique for capturing the movement of breaking waves as they hit the shore

Mark Bauer THERE'S A LOT OF debate about how best to photograph wave movement. Long exposures result in a 'misty' look that is popular with many photographers (see over the page) but is certainly not to everyone's taste as it's not authentic. When we watch waves rolling on to the shore, we see the whole movement – we don't see a moment frozen in time or mist drifting over rocks. One way to truly appreciate wave motion as the eye sees it is to use video rather than a stills camera, but by paying careful attention to shutter speeds, it *is* possible to record natural-looking waves on your DSLR.

The trick is to record the right amount of movement; if the shutter is open too long there will be too much motion blur, not long enough and the wave will appear too static. You need to find a middle ground where there's misty blur but the waves still keep their shape.

There is no simple recipe for this; the best shutter speed depends on the size and speed of the waves, how they're falling onto the shore, and also personal taste. Experimentation is the key – be prepared to shoot a lot of frames and spend a lot of time looking at the LCD monitor reviewing your images and tweaking the camera controls.

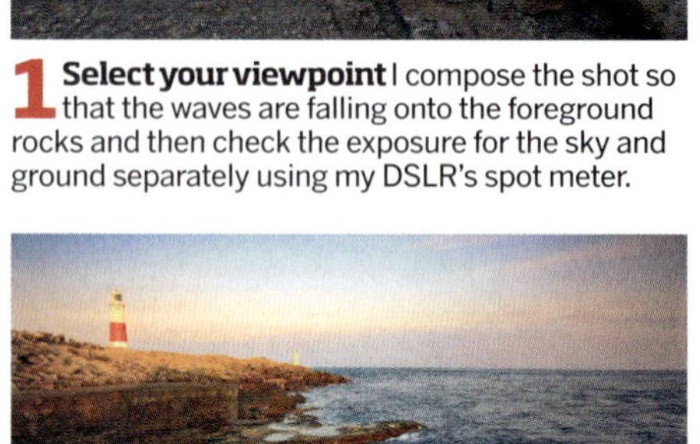

1 Select your viewpoint I compose the shot so that the waves are falling onto the foreground rocks and then check the exposure for the sky and ground separately using my DSLR's spot meter.

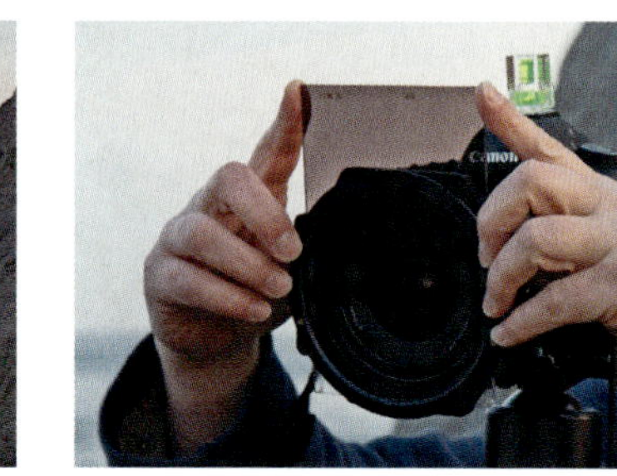

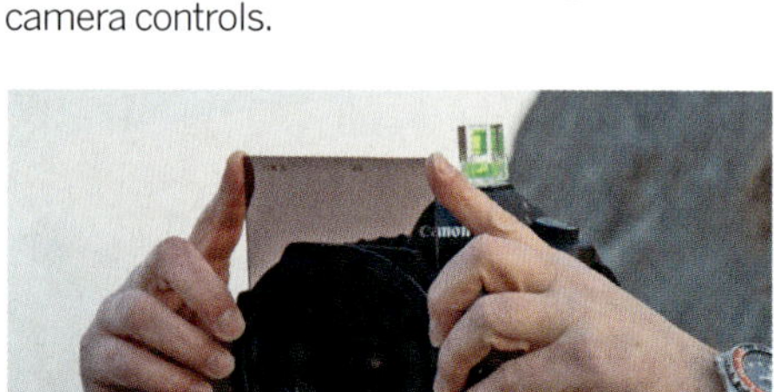

2 Use an ND grad As the sky is much brighter than the ground, I added a three-stop ND soft grad filter to balance the contrast. A soft grad means the transition line won't be too obvious.

Controlling shutter speeds

Although there's no 'ideal' shutter speed for capturing a breaking wave, as it depends on the conditions at the time, a shutter speed of between ¼ second and a couple of seconds usually provides the result you'll want.

Unfortunately, though, it's not just a matter of putting the camera into shutter-priority mode and setting the shutter speed. You will also need to make sure you're using the right aperture in order to achieve the appropriate depth-of-field and an accurate exposure. For landscapes, this is usually between f/8 and f/22 for maximum depth-of-field.

There are other ways you can control the shutter speed too. Apart from waiting for the light to change, for a faster shutter speed, you should increase the camera's ISO rating. Normally this will raise the level of noise, so you do not want to go much above ISO 800 unless you're using a professional DSLR that handles noise well.

For shutter speeds of more than 30 seconds, you will need to set your camera to Bulb mode and time the exposure manually. However, this can often result in overexposed shots, so you may need to add a 'solid' neutral density filter to reduce the amount of light falling onto the sensor. ND filters come in various strengths; the most common being one, two and three stops, and you can use several together, along with a polarising filter too, for times when you want to set extremely long exposures.

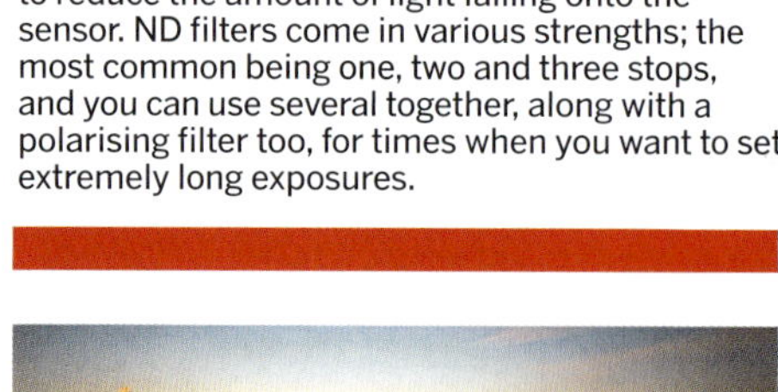

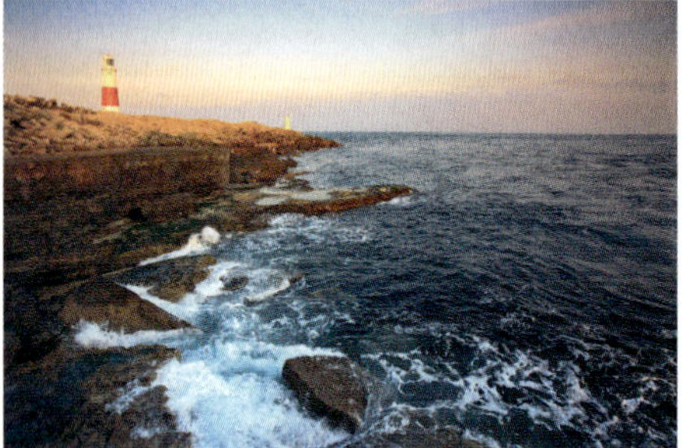

3 Take a test shot Set to shutter-priority mode, I try 1/100sec but it freezes the movement. For large waves this might convey drama, but with small waves like this it completely fails.

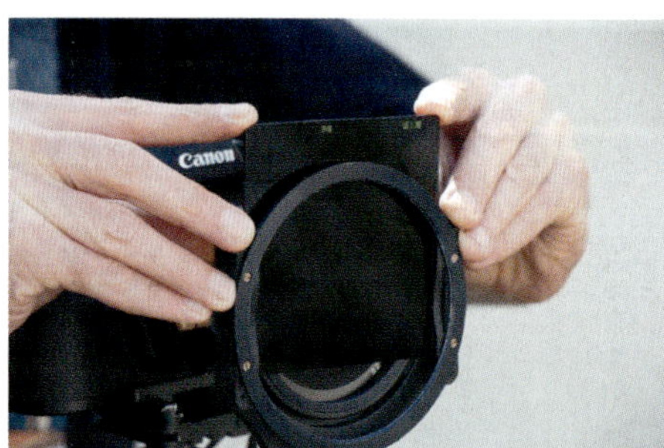

4 Replace filter In the hope of lengthening the exposure, I wait for the light levels to drop and replace the three-stop ND filter with a four-stop ND filter, giving me a ten-second exposure at f/22.

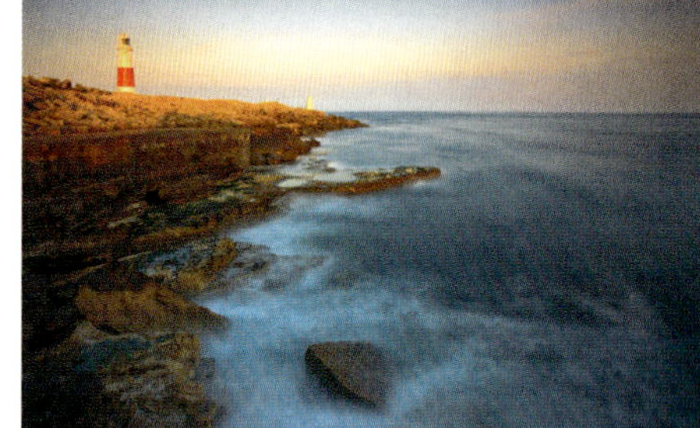

5 Not quite... This time the exposure is still not long enough to give an ethereal misty look to the water, but it doesn't capture the drama of the scene by freezing the water either.

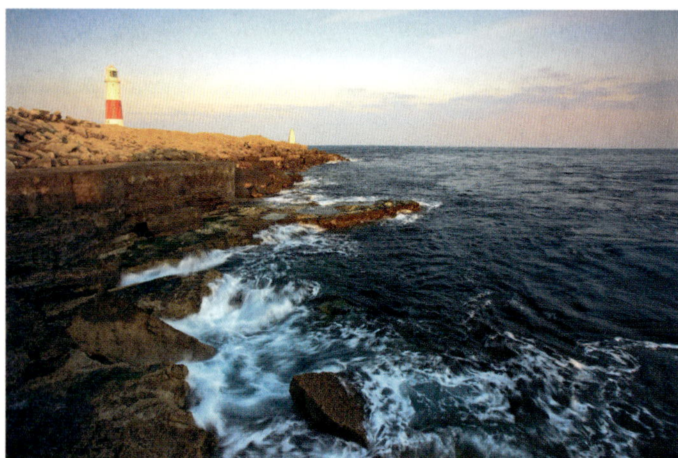

6 Shorten exposure Opening up the aperture to f/11 and swapping the four-stop ND for a two-stop enables me to shorten the exposure time to 0.3 seconds. The result is almost there, but the wave is frozen just a little too much.

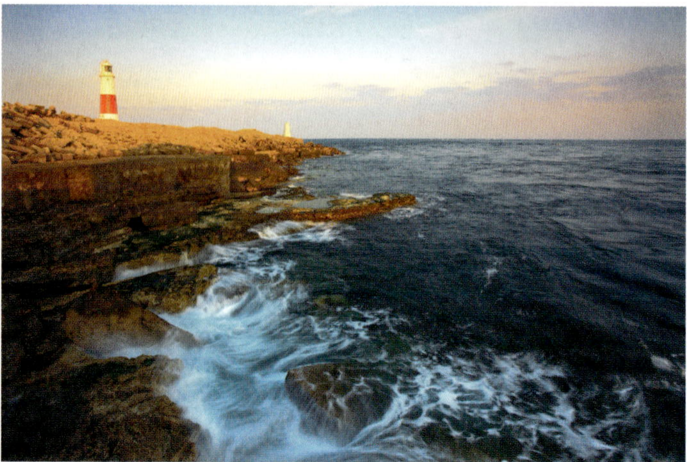

7 Lengthen exposure slightly One more attempt, with the light levels a bit lower, I get the shot I want at around 0.6 of a second. There's enough movement to create a sense of drama but the waves still keep their shape.

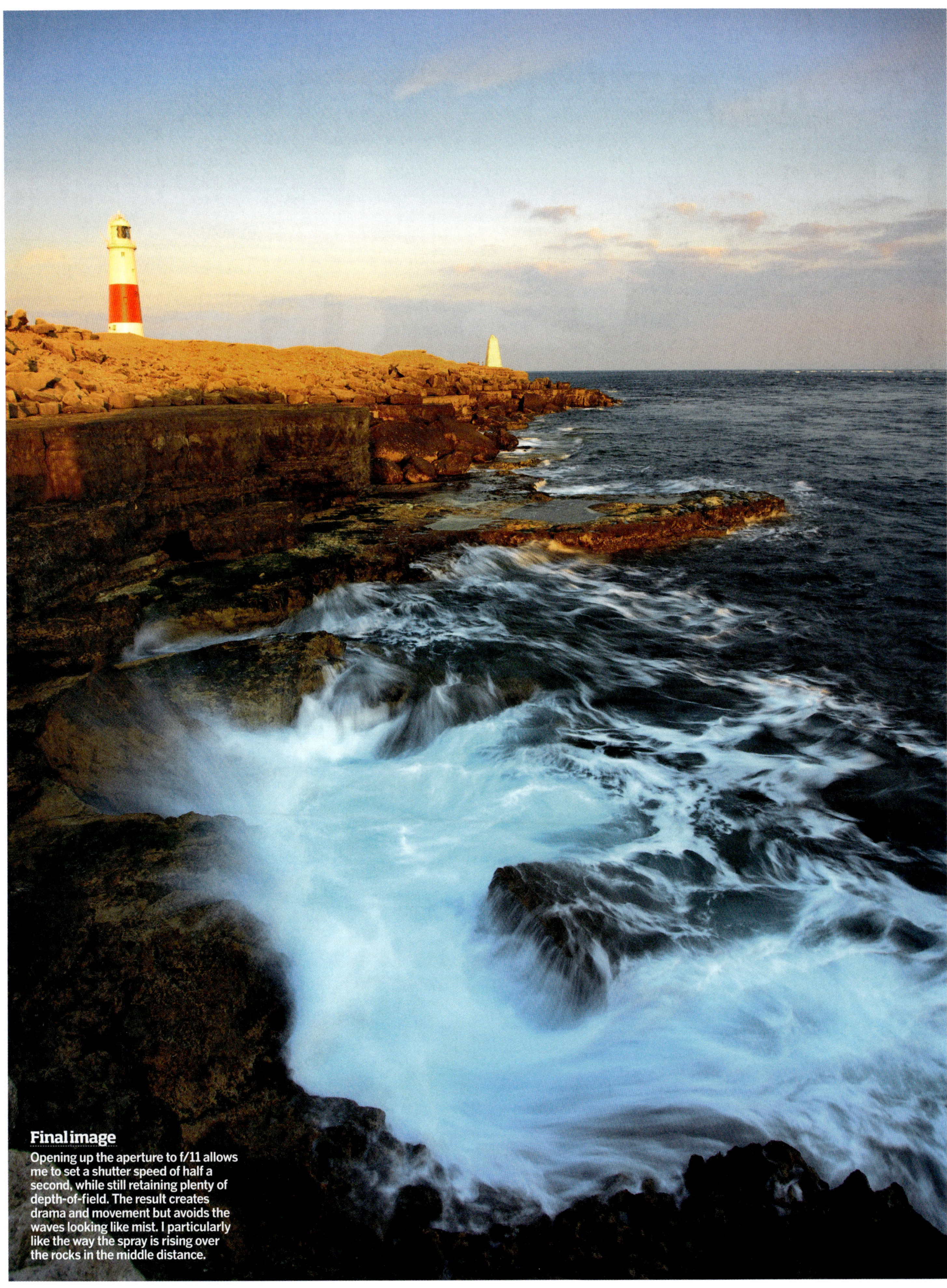

Final image

Opening up the aperture to f/11 allows me to set a shutter speed of half a second, while still retaining plenty of depth-of-field. The result creates drama and movement but avoids the waves looking like mist. I particularly like the way the spray is rising over the rocks in the middle distance.

Create misty-looking waterscapes

Outdoor photographer Ross Hoddinott leads the way to capturing ethereal images of moving water

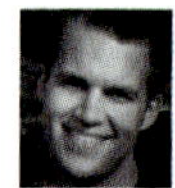

Ross Hoddinott WHEN YOU LIVE on an island the size of the UK, the coast is never far away, which is handy considering few subjects are as popular as seascapes for shooting. How you capture the water's motion, however, can make or break your photographs. While some loathe the blurry water effect, most love it. The most striking results are when you can get close to the action and where the water 'shapes' your foreground rocks as it washes over them, but getting this depends on the tide. Opt for a receding tide as it's safer to photograph, but always be mindful of large waves and put your safety above 'getting the shot'. A winter's evening is perfect for capturing long-exposure landscapes as the light is naturally soft and low. With this in mind, I visited Trebarwith Strand in North Cornwall with the sole intention of shooting moving water. I arrived an hour before sunset armed with a range of filters to help me achieve the dreamy, angel-mist water I desired.

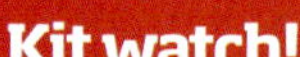

Kit watch!

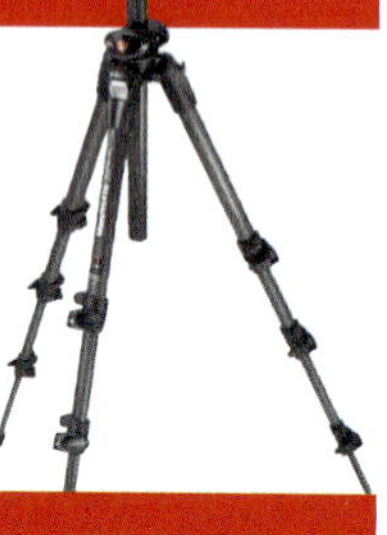

Tripod
To photograph moving water, a good, sturdy tripod is essential. A camera support will ensure that everything other than the water remains pin-sharp. Also, if you want to avoid wet feet, a decent pair of wellies are a good idea.

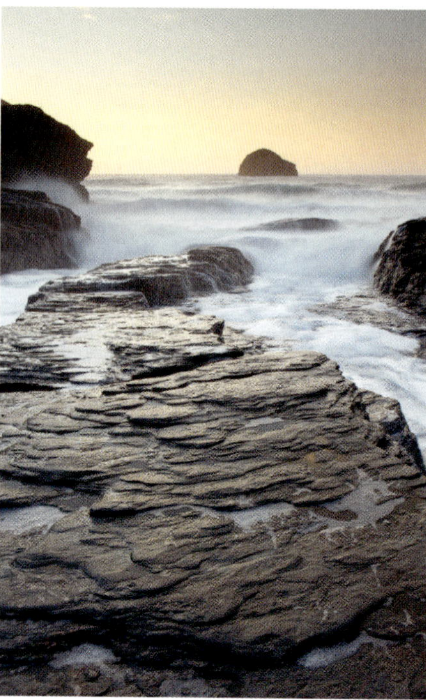

1 Choose your viewpoint There is no point going to great lengths to attractively blur the water if your composition is poor. In this instance, I looked for a rocky outcrop that would form a strong foreground and lead the eye into the image. Try to imagine how the water's motion will shape the foreground when it is blurred. A vertical composition will often help create depth in a shot.

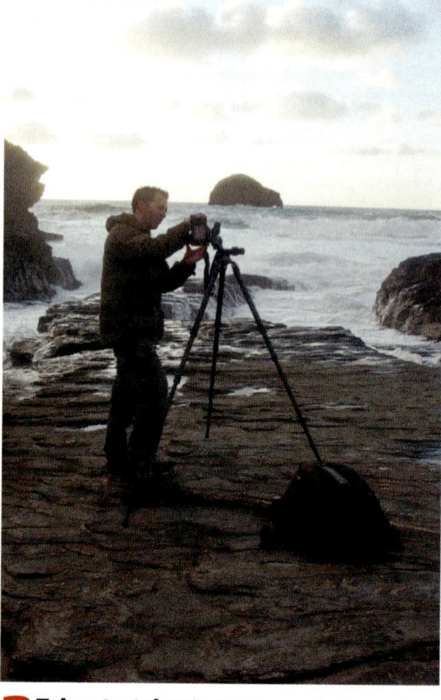

2 Take a test shot In aperture-priority mode, select f/16 for sufficient depth-of-field and ISO 100 to generate a long exposure. Avoid stopping down as far as f/22, as diffraction (softening of the image) can affect results. For me, this resulted in a shutter speed of ¼sec, which created a degree of subject motion but not as much as I wanted. It's time to artificially lengthen the exposure.

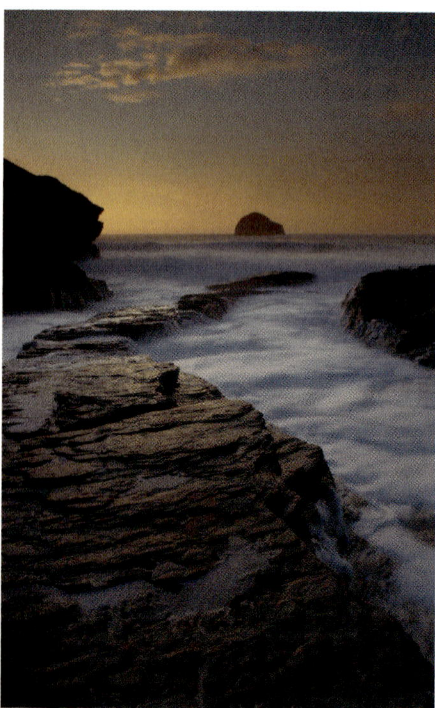

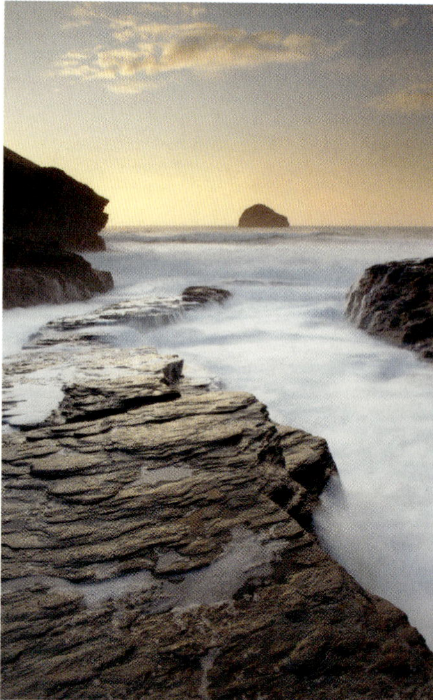

3 Add filters A stop is a doubling or halving of the exposure value. Therefore, an ND filter with a three-stop density (0.9ND) lengthens an unfiltered value of ¼sec to two seconds – a significant shift. In low light, and when using high density ND filters, TTL metering is more prone to error – particularly underexposure. Remember to regularly review images and histograms.

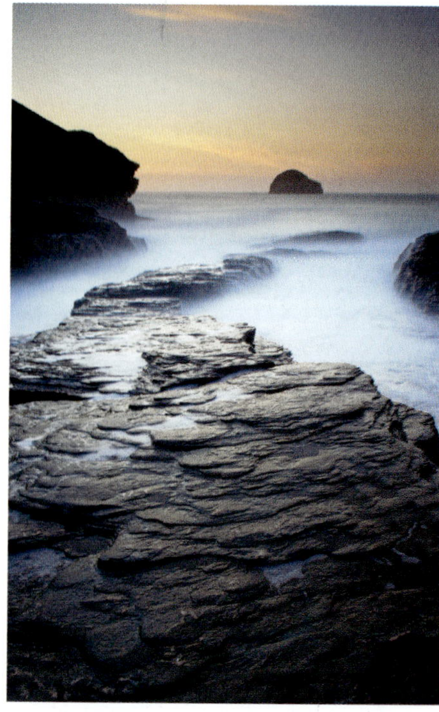

4 And wait... With the ND filter, the motion looked far more attractive, but for a real ethereal-looking result, I simply waited for the sun to lower, lengthening the shutter speed.

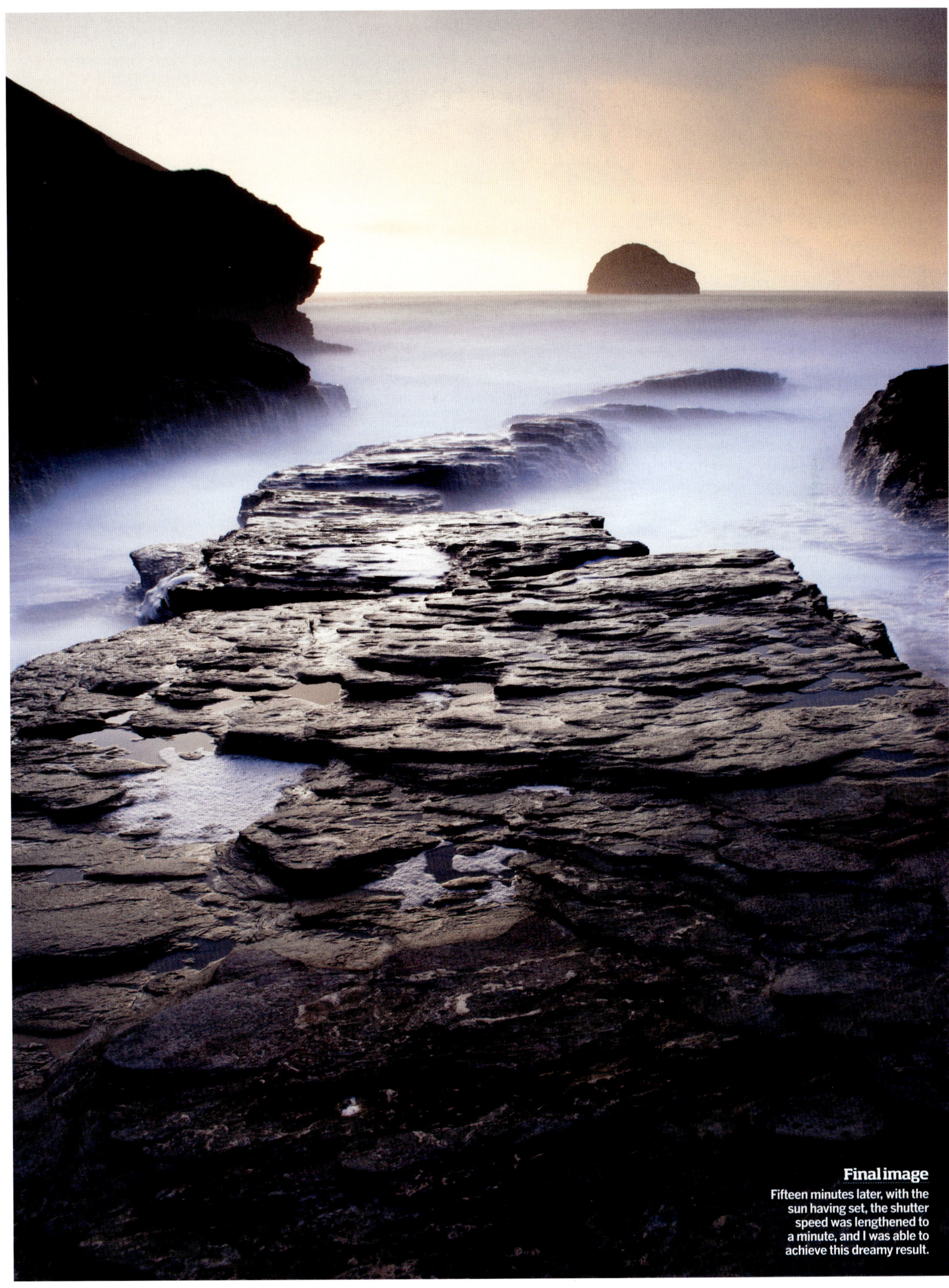

Final image

Fifteen minutes later, with the sun having set, the shutter speed was lengthened to a minute, and I was able to achieve this dreamy result.

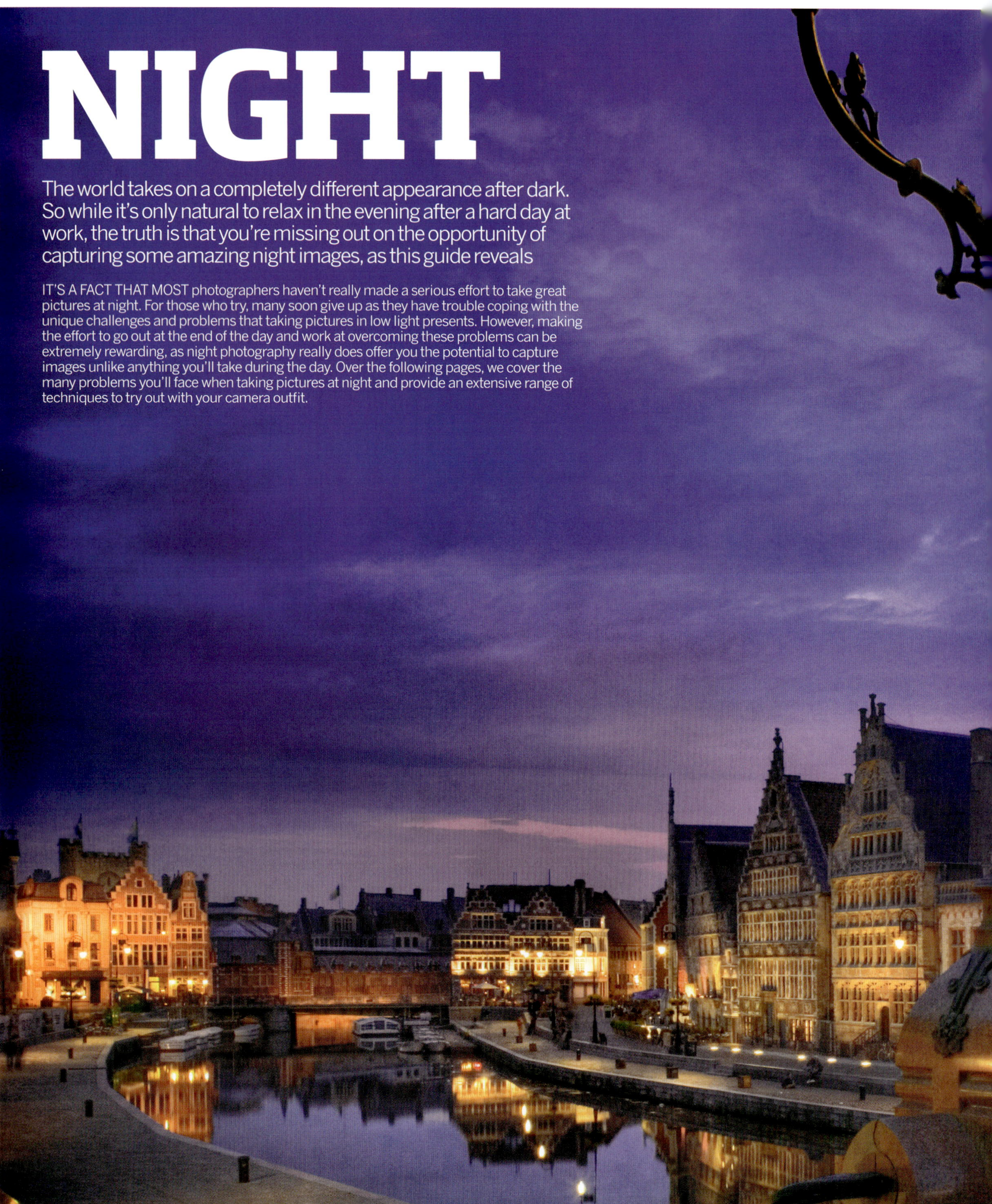

NIGHT

The world takes on a completely different appearance after dark. So while it's only natural to relax in the evening after a hard day at work, the truth is that you're missing out on the opportunity of capturing some amazing night images, as this guide reveals

IT'S A FACT THAT MOST photographers haven't really made a serious effort to take great pictures at night. For those who try, many soon give up as they have trouble coping with the unique challenges and problems that taking pictures in low light presents. However, making the effort to go out at the end of the day and work at overcoming these problems can be extremely rewarding, as night photography really does offer you the potential to capture images unlike anything you'll take during the day. Over the following pages, we cover the many problems you'll face when taking pictures at night and provide an extensive range of techniques to try out with your camera outfit.

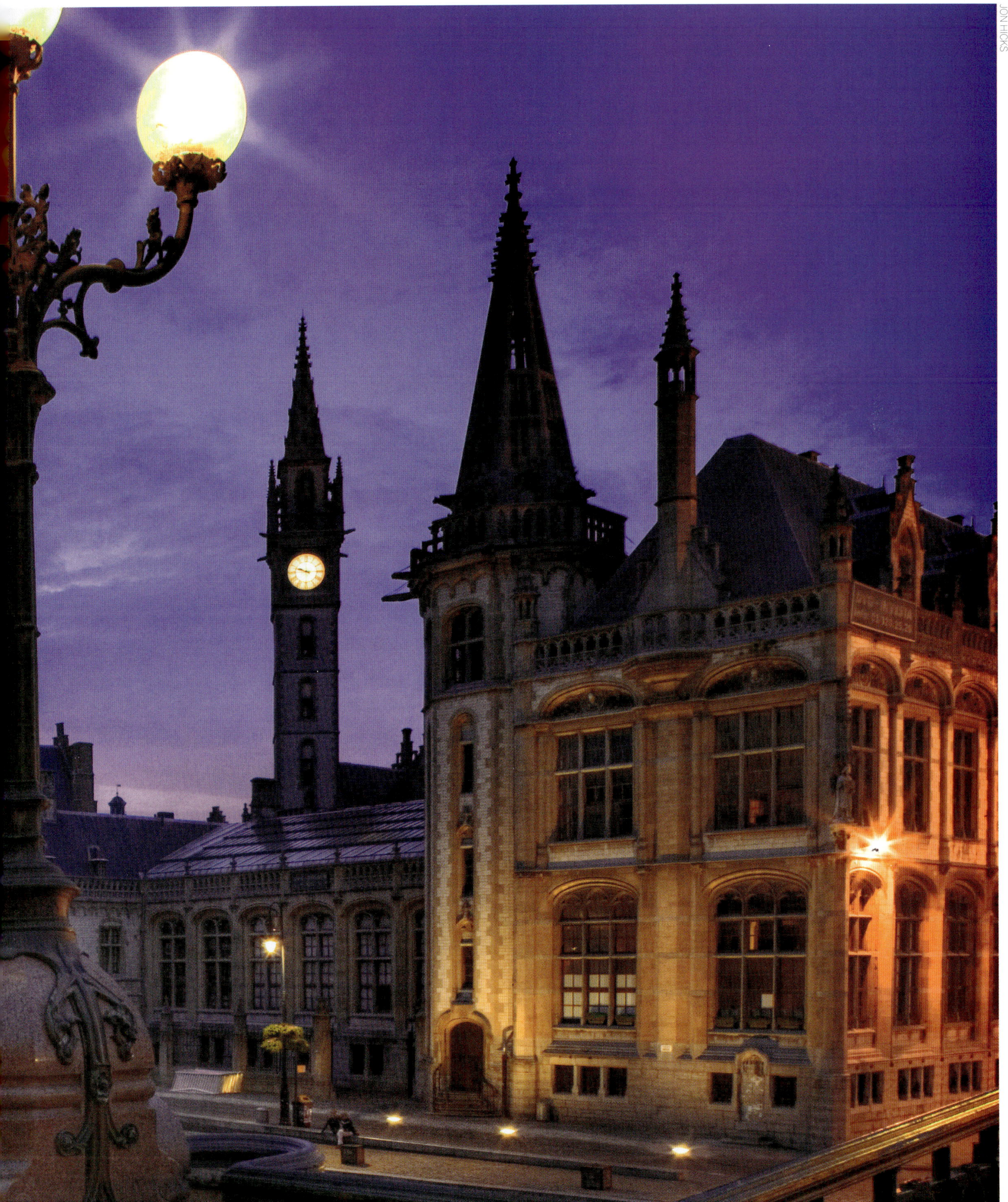

JON HICKS

Shooting outdoors in low light

There's an art to low-light photography. Our pro advice, essential techniques and key kit to use will help you take brilliant night shots

THE SAYING 'LESS IS MORE' could be applied to many things in photography. Equipment is one – you don't need loads of it to take great photographs. Composition is another – the more you cram into an image, the less appealing it's likely to be. Well, it's also the same with light. You might assume that lots of it is required to produce successful shots, but in reality, the less there is the better. Just look at these shots here if you need any convincing.

Sunrise and sunset are universally regarded as the most photogenic times of day, yet light levels are significantly lower than at midday. The urban landscape also looks far more photogenic in the evening, as daylight dies and the colourful glow of man-made illumination takes over. And if you look to the heavens on a starry night, you can't fail to be impressed by the sight of millions of tiny pinpricks of light flickering in the sea of darkness above.

But low light isn't just about the great outdoors – the same rules apply inside as well. Think about it: Does your front room look more inviting with all the lights turned on, or do you prefer the cosy glows of an open fire? Half a dozen halogen spots may stop you tripping over things, but if you want to shoot romantic portraits, a dim room will be far more effective. To show you just how amazing low light can be, we've dedicated a section of this guide to harnessing and mastering it, with a little help from some of our regular contributors. Let's see just how low they can go!

ISTOCK PHOTO

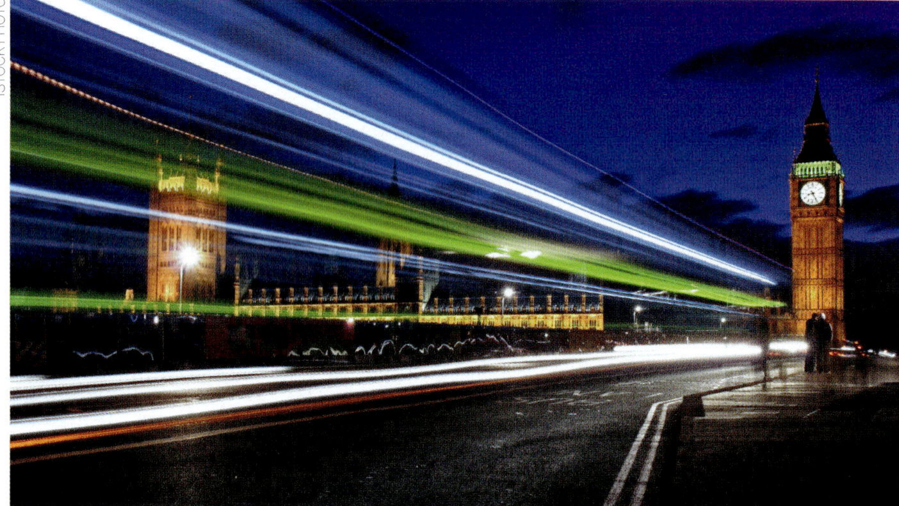

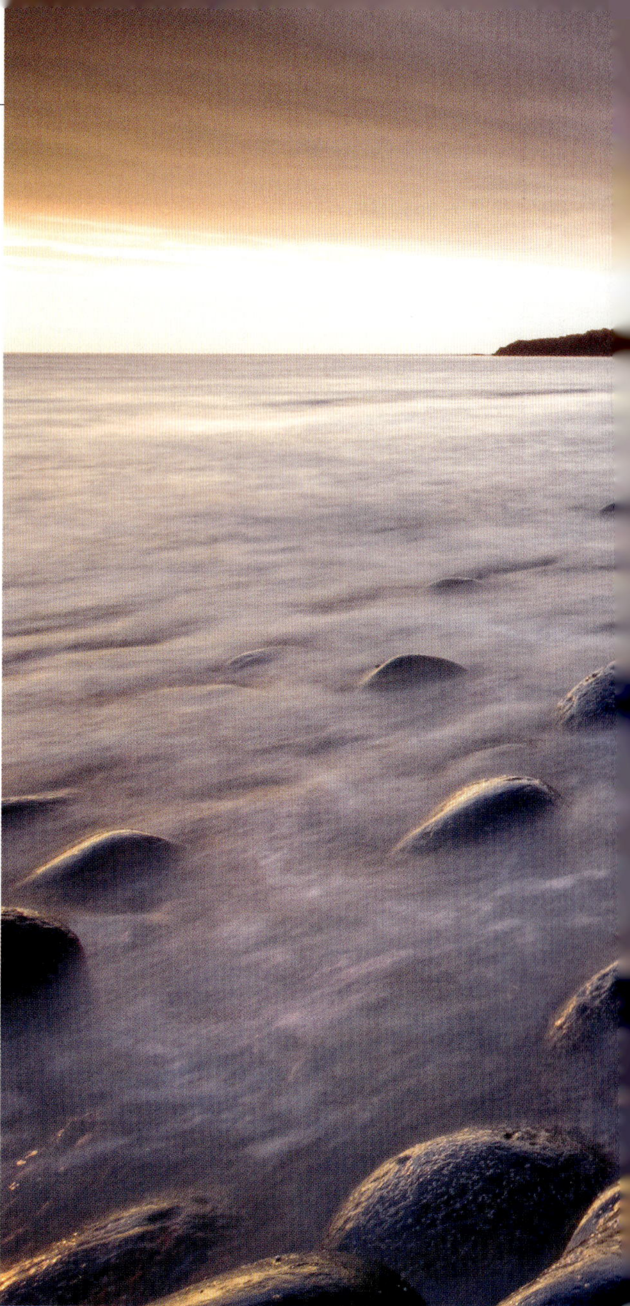

When it comes to light, quality is always more important than quantity. A little special light beats loads of mediocre light any day – or night, come to think of it. That's why low-light photography is so rewarding – whatever the subject or the situation, the light's always good, and when the light's good, the battle to create a great shot is pretty much won.

Outdoors, low-light shooting begins as the day ends and ends as the next day begins – dusk to dawn if you're confused. Sunset kicks things off. As soon as the sun dips below the horizon, day starts its slow transformation into night. Direct light on the landscape disappears and the sky overhead turns into a huge softbox that floods the earth with diffuse illumination, while the sky above the western horizon burns like fire (with any luck). Slot a hard ND grad filter into your filter holder and you can capture the lot in a single exposure – a foreground full of detail and a sky full of colour.

Twilight sees the warmth in the sky dissolve seamlessly into colder purples and blues, while daylight levels fade and scenes visibly darken. This is an ideal time to get out and shoot modern architecture as the colours in the sky are mirrored by its glass and steel surfaces. If you prefer to go wild in the country, head for water so its calm surface can do the same thing. Twilight on a lake's shore or by the sea is hard to beat in the mood stakes and low light levels mean long exposures, which gives blurry water.

The urban landscape comes to life at twilight when daylight fades enough for man-made illumination to cast its technicolour spell, but there's still enough of the natural stuff around to stop those shady spots turning black. The sky – by now a deep blue – acts like a reflector, bouncing what little light is left into the bits not hit by streetlamps or floodlights, neon signs and shop displays. This crossover period is the prime time to shoot floodlit buildings, street scenes, traffic trails – any low-light urban scene or subject where sky is included in the frame. Once the sky looks black, it's almost time to stop, although image sensors have a surprising ability to keep pulling colour from the sky long after your eyes have stopped seeing it, so don't be in too much of a hurry to head home.

Actually, you don't need to bother heading home at all, because once night arrives, you can turn your attention to the heavens. How about shooting landscapes in moonlight? Again, put water in the foreground so it picks up the shimmering silver ribbon of moonlight dancing on the inky-black surface. That contrast alone can make great shots.

Or keep the camera's shutter open for ten minutes or longer and turn night into day. This produces surreal effects because scenes look like they've been shot in broad daylight, but instead of being lit by the sun, they're lit by the moon. Whatever takes your fancy, low light offers you lots of photo opportunities.

Essential accessories

Tripod The easiest way to avoid camera shake in low light is to attach your camera to a sturdy tripod. If you haven't got one, then buy one! Look to spend around £100 for a decent model.

Remote release A very useful aid to help avoid camera shake. As well as own-brand remotes, you'll also find compatible remotes from the likes of Hähnel and Hama. Ask your photo dealer for details on what's available for your model of camera.

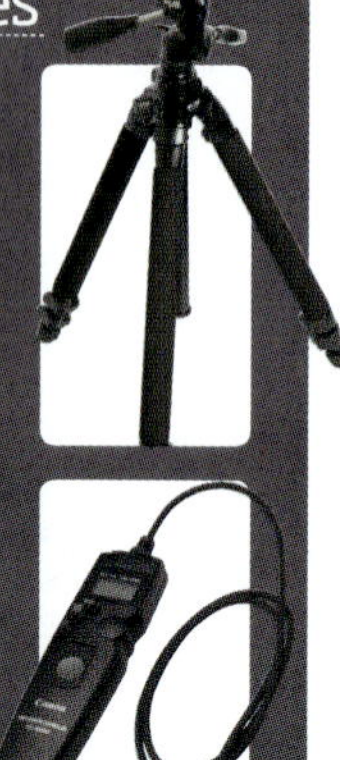

Torch It's worth keeping a small torch handy if you're setting up in very low light. Any torch is suitable, but you may want to check out the Gorillatorch, from the makers of the Gorillapod, which can be wrapped around objects to free up both your hands.

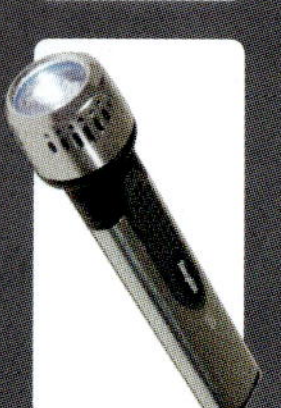

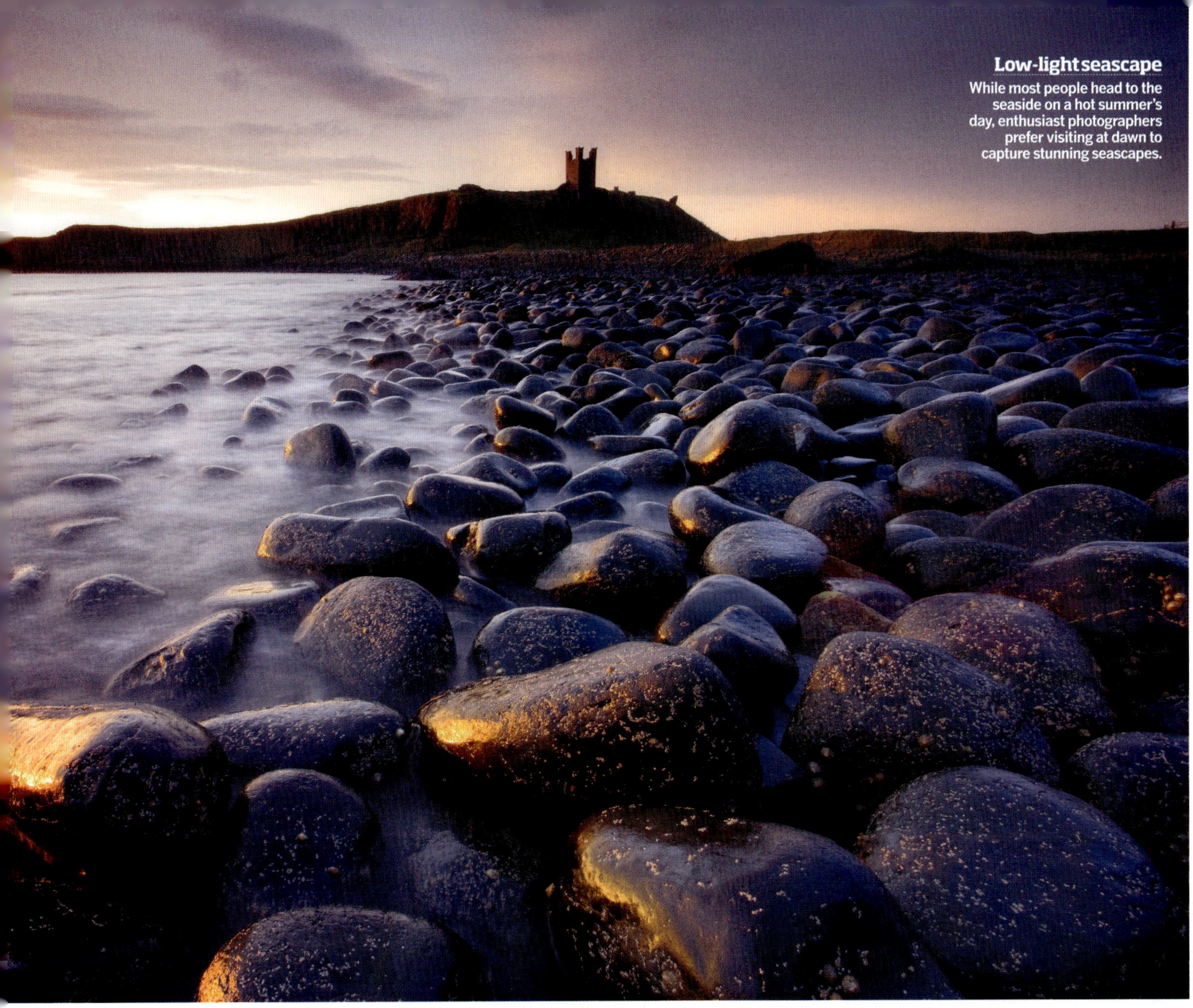

Low-light seascape

While most people head to the seaside on a hot summer's day, enthusiast photographers prefer visiting at dawn to capture stunning seascapes.

LEE FROST

Five outdoor techniques to try...

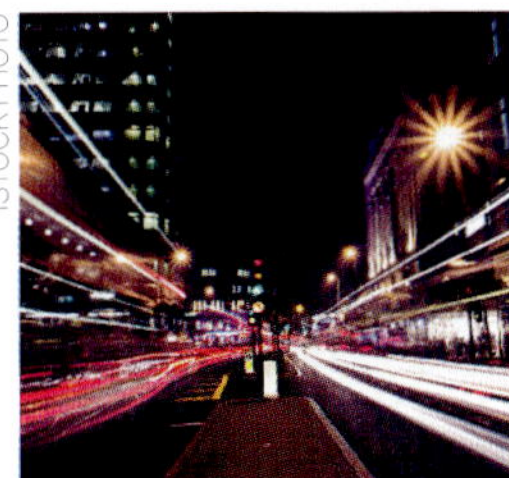

ISTOCK PHOTO

1) Traffic trails

Find an elevated viewpoint overlooking a busy road or roundabout, mount your camera on a tripod and use an exposure of 30-60 seconds to record moving traffic as colourful light trails. Include floodlit buildings or the dusk sky for added interest. This is the ideal time of year as dusk and rush hour coincide. Just take care with the traffic!

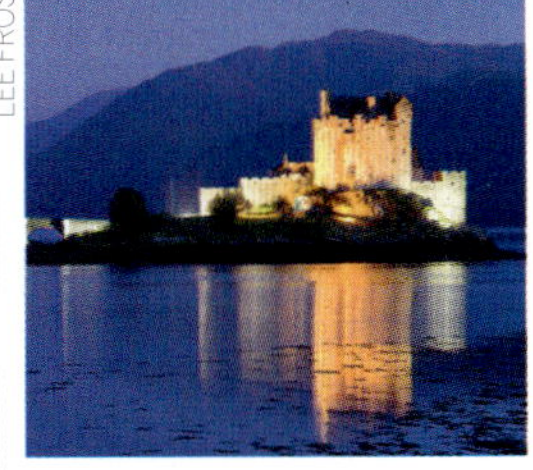

LEE FROST

2) Floodlit buildings

Another classic low-light subject that's accessible to all. Churches, castles, cathedrals, monuments; every town and city has its fair share of floodlit buildings. For best results, shoot at twilight while there's still colour in the sky and enough daylight so shadows aren't yet dark and colourful floodlighting stands out.

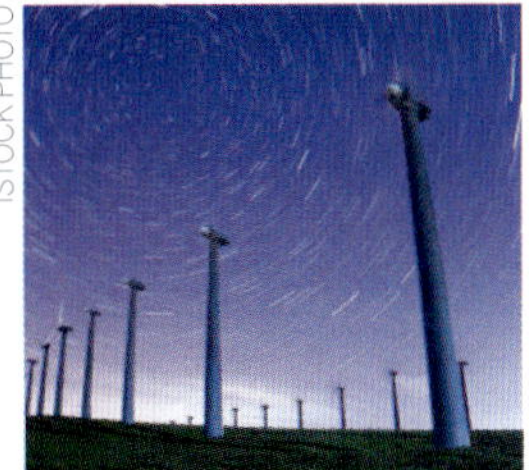

ISTOCK PHOTO

3) Star trails

Get as far away from civilisation as you can on a clear night and use a long exposure to record stars in the sky as trails of light. Point your widest lens towards the northern sky so you include the Pole Star (Polaris), lock your camera's shutter open on Bulb for two hours at f/4 on ISO 200 and see what happens. You'll be amazed by the results.

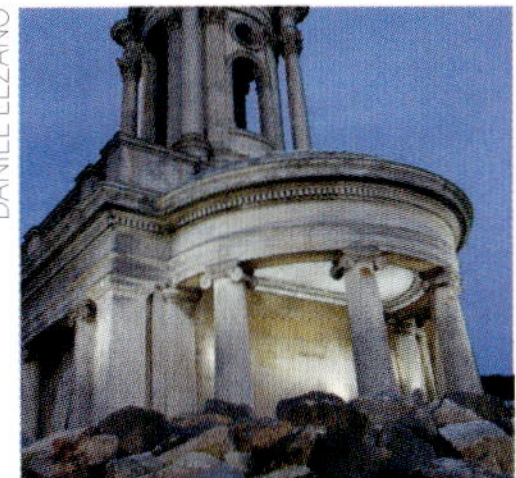

DANIEL LEZANO

4) Painting with light

Find an old building that's unlit, then as it begins to get dark, use repeated bursts from a handheld flashgun set to manual to illuminate the exterior, while your camera's shutter is locked open on Bulb. Use filters to colour the light if you like. Instead of using a flashgun, you could use a powerful torch and see what results you can produce.

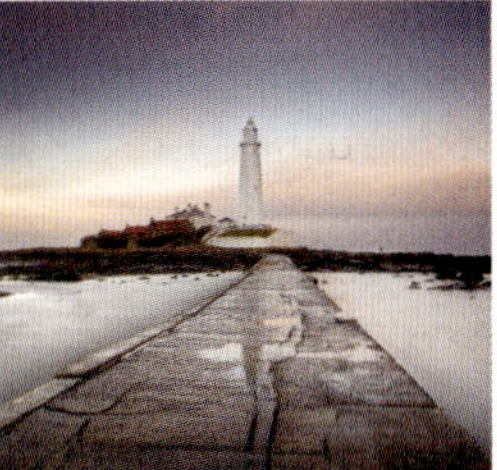

LEE FROST

5) Coastal landscapes

Head to the coast either before sunrise or just before sunset and capture stunning sea views at the fringes of the day. Light levels are low so use long exposures to record motion in the sea, while wet sand and rocks reflect the rich colours in the sky. Remember to be careful with the tides, pack a mobile and let someone know where you are.

Get prepared for the night ahead

Taking pictures at night presents a number of challenges. However, your DSLR is equipped to be able to cope with them all. We provide the best settings and techniques for ensuring you're ready to cope, too

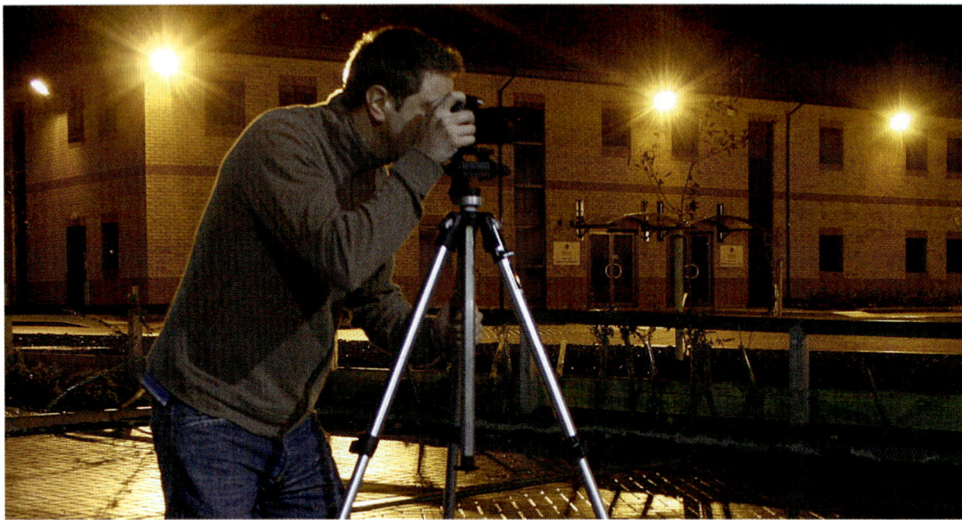

How to reduce the risk of shake without a tripod

1) Increase the ISO rating By setting a faster ISO rating, you can increase the top shutter speed available to you. The main drawback with this method is that an increase in the ISO rating also sees a gradual degradation in the image, with higher levels of noise and less realistic colours being recorded. That said, the current generation of DSLRs produce excellent images up to ISO 400 (and in some cases ISO 800), so it's only beyond these speeds that you'll notice a major drop in quality. We'd only recommend increasing the ISO rating if you're shooting handheld or have placed the camera on an unstable support. If you have your camera on a stable surface, like a tripod, then we'd use a low ISO (100-200) to ensure the best possible quality.

The following set of images shows how noise becomes progressively more evident as you increase the ISO rating. The amount of noise will vary from camera to camera – try shooting the same scene at different ISO ratings to check the noise of your camera.

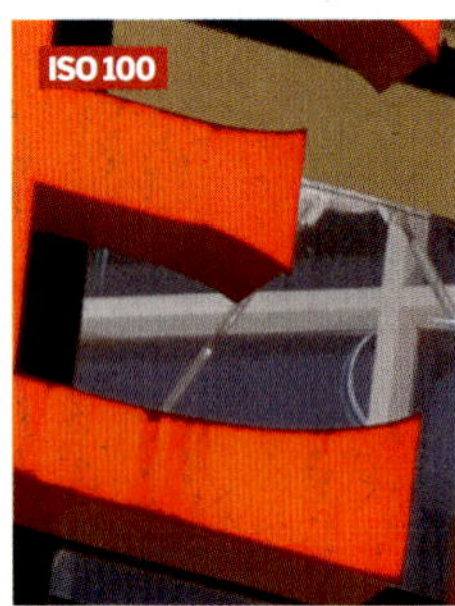
ISO 100

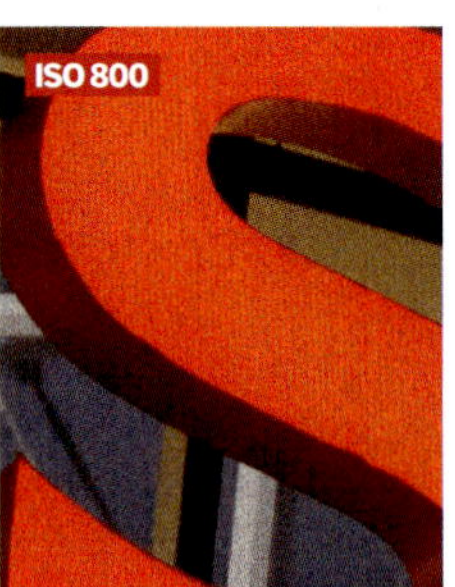
ISO 800

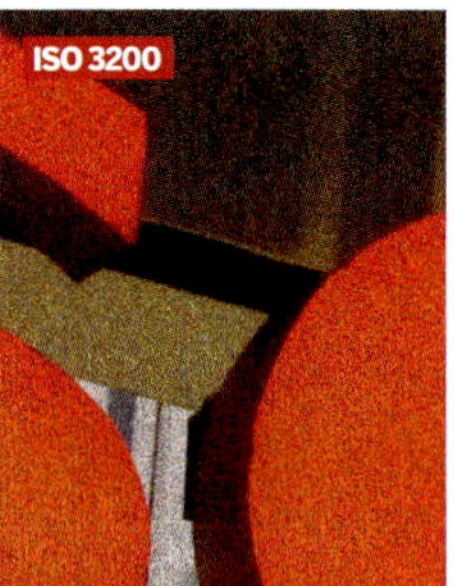
ISO 3200

2) Image stabilisation Depending on which camera you use, you'll find that either your camera body or certain lenses in the range offer image stabilisation (also referred to as shake reduction or similar). If you haven't placed your camera on a stable tripod, it's well worth activating this feature, as it can allow you to use a shutter speed three to four stops faster than without stabilisation.

3) Rest the camera You'll find that leaning against a tree or resting your camera on a wall offers better stability than handholding it, so look for objects that you can rest your DSLR on.

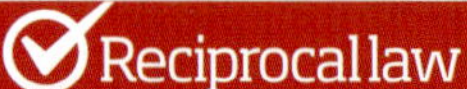

Reciprocal law

Unsure what shutter speed you can get away with when handholding? The easiest way to remember is to ensure that the shutter speed you use is a reciprocal of the focal length you use. So, if you're shooting at 100mm, ensure your shutter speed is at least 1/100sec etc

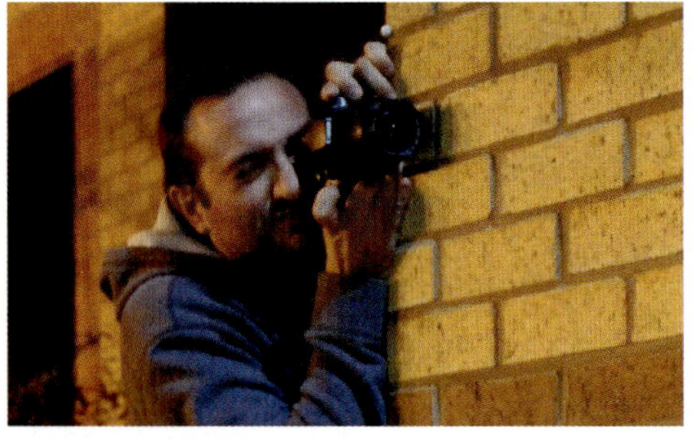

Gear up for night!

It's essential that you use some form of support for your camera and a decent tripod should be top of your list. Models like the Slik Pro 400DX or Manfrotto 190X Pro B are worth considering – check out the gear section in this guide (page 158) for further options.

If, for whatever reason, you can't use a tripod, there are other supports available, including beanpods, mini tripods and suction cups. Another accessory we'd recommend is a remote release for firing the shutter without having to touch the camera. Also, depending on what you're shooting, you could find a flashgun or a torch useful. Finally, make sure you're wrapped up nice and warm – being cold and uncomfortable won't inspire your picture taking.

Camera shake

The most obvious problem that you'll have to overcome with night/low-light photography is that of long exposure times, which create the very real risk of camera shake ruining your images. You'll most likely be looking at shutter speeds running into seconds, so your biggest challenge will be to ensure that your pictures are shake-free. The ideal scenario is to support your camera on a stable platform, such as a tripod, as this will keep your camera steady and give you complete freedom with exposures. It's vital that your camera is totally still during the exposure, so ensure you set up your tripod to be as stable as possible.

Avoid shake at the start!

What many newcomers to DSLRs do not realise is that camera shake is often caused by two actions at the start of the exposure. One is from movement caused when you press the shutter button, the other is caused by the action of the mirror inside the camera body flipping up at the start of the exposure. The following are easy ways to eliminate these problems.

✔ **Use a remote release** Almost every DSLR allows a remote release of one type or another to be used. These useful accessories allow you to take a picture without having to press the shutter button, so reducing any risk of camera shake caused by when you push down on the button. Some remotes work via infrared, while others connect into a socket on the camera body.

✔ **Self-timer** An alternative to using a remote is to fire the shutter using the self-timer. The interval between pressing the button and the shutter firing (two or ten seconds, depending on your DSLR) is enough time for any vibration to stop.

✔ **Mirror lock-up** This facility isn't one that's often spoken about, but it's well worth using if your camera has it. It works by raising the mirror prior to the exposure being taken, to avoid any risk of shake from its action.

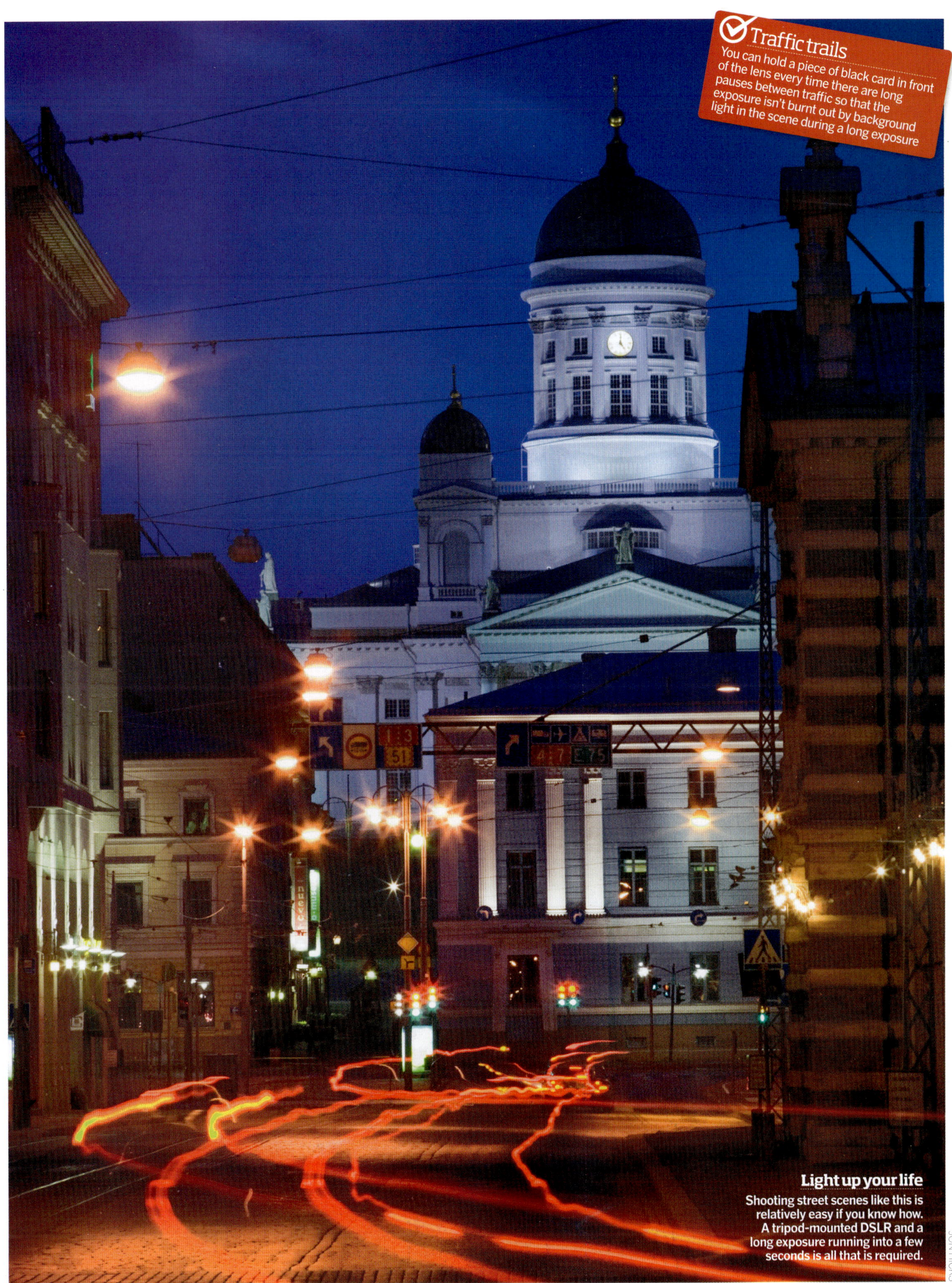

Traffic trails

You can hold a piece of black card in front of the lens every time there are long pauses between traffic so that the exposure isn't burnt out by background light in the scene during a long exposure

Light up your life

Shooting street scenes like this is relatively easy if you know how. A tripod-mounted DSLR and a long exposure running into a few seconds is all that is required.

JON HICKS

What mode should you use?

This will depend what you're trying to shoot and the technique you're using. For outdoor scenes, traffic trails or painting-with-light techniques, most people begin by using aperture-priority or shutter-priority, and setting an aperture of f/8 or a shutter speed between one and eight seconds. However, neither of these two modes is ideal – you'd be far better off setting your camera to manual (M), setting a mid-aperture like f/8 for optimum quality, then experimenting with shutter speeds and checking results on the LCD monitor. You'll get a better idea of how to do this by following our guides and trying the techniques out for yourself.

Bulb mode: Run through the shutter speeds: beyond the slowest setting (usually 30 seconds) you'll come across Bulb mode. This mode allows you to shoot images where you determine the length of the exposure, so for instance, you can shoot at 23 seconds, three minutes etc. With some DSLRs, you press the shutter button once to activate the Bulb exposure and again to end it. With others, you need to keep your finger depressed on the button during the whole exposure – this latter method runs the risk of shake, so use a remote.

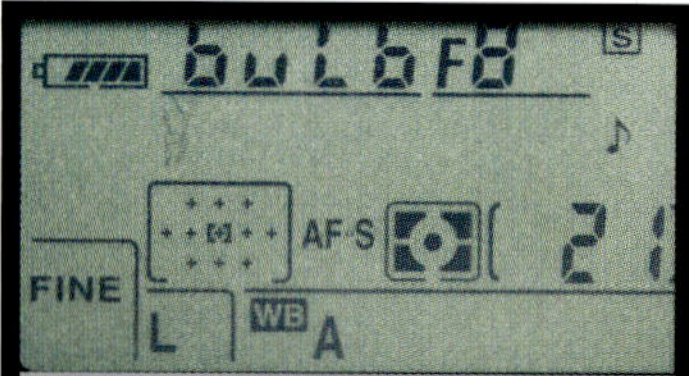

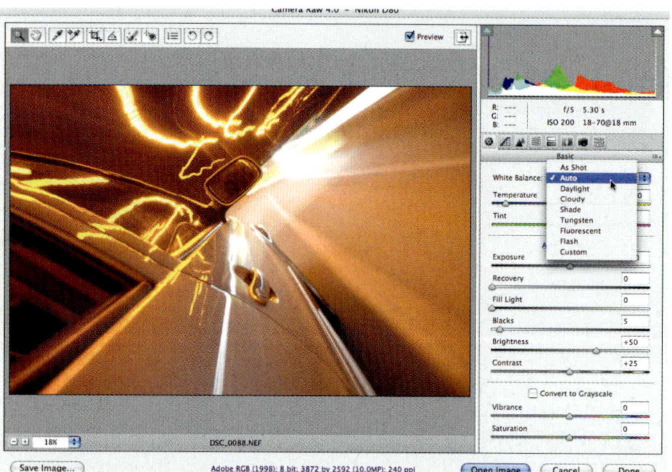

White Balance: When shooting at night, you need to be prepared for images exhibiting very unusual colours due to the use of artificial lighting. You'll find most street lighting will produce an orange cast, while floodlit buildings like cathedrals or churches often record with a bluish-white cast. We'd recommend that you shoot in Raw and try out different White Balance settings on your computer to see which works best. If you're shooting in JPEG, take a sequence of exposures set to different White Balance presets and compare the results.

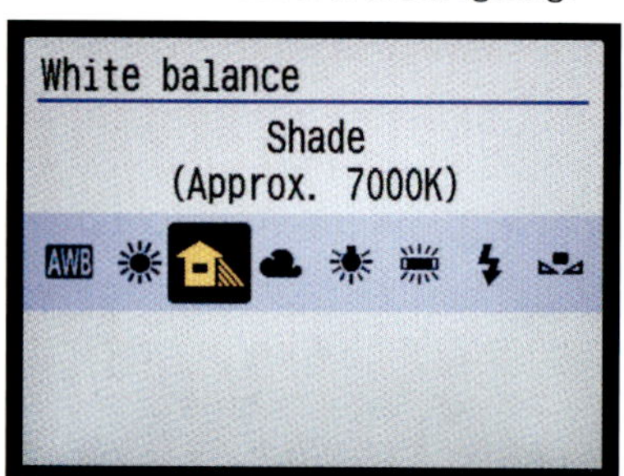

Night photography: Ideal settings

If you can set up your camera as below, then you'll be fully prepared for taking great night images

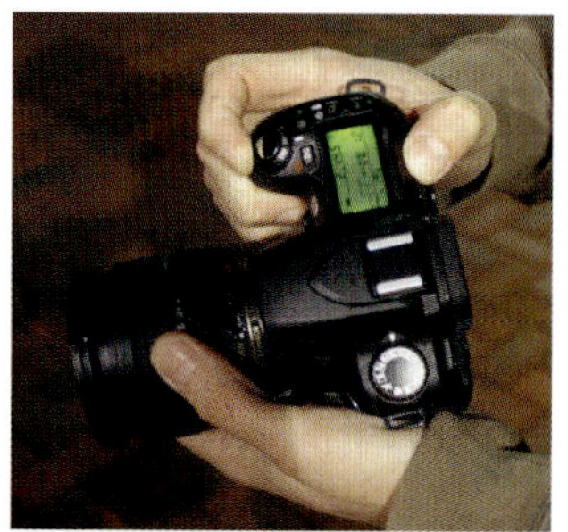

- ✔ Digital camera on a sturdy tripod
- ✔ Set to Raw (+ JPEG if available) so that colour casts can be easily managed
- ✔ ISO rating at 100 or 200 for optimum quality
- ✔ Set to manual, a mid-aperture (f/8 or f/11) and Bulb
- ✔ Mirror lock-up activated and shutter fired by self-timer or remote control

Prepare your DSLR for night shooting

If you're unsure of how to set your camera so that it's optimised for night shooting, follow our quick help operation guide

CANON EOS SERIES

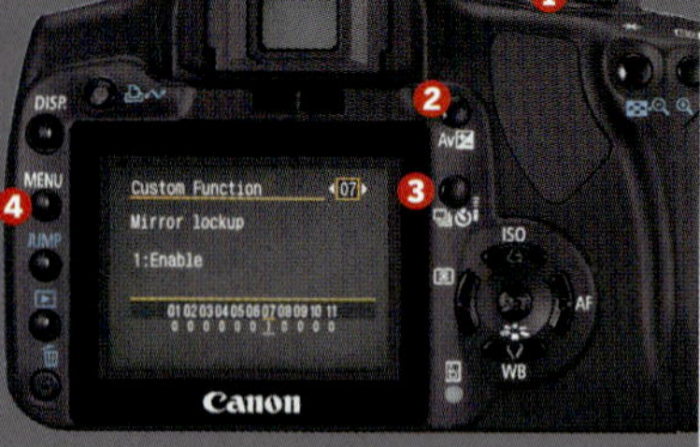

(1) Turn the mode dial to M (manual mode). To set a shutter speed, turn the dial behind the shutter button. **(2)** To set an aperture, press and hold the +/- button, then turn the dial. **(3)** To use the self-timer or remote control, press the drive button and choose the appropriate icon. **(4)** To use mirror lock-up with suitable cameras, press MENU, go to Custom Functions and choose the appropriate number. Press Set, select 1: Enable. When you want to take a picture, press the shutter button once to raise the mirror and again to take the picture.

NIKON DSLRS

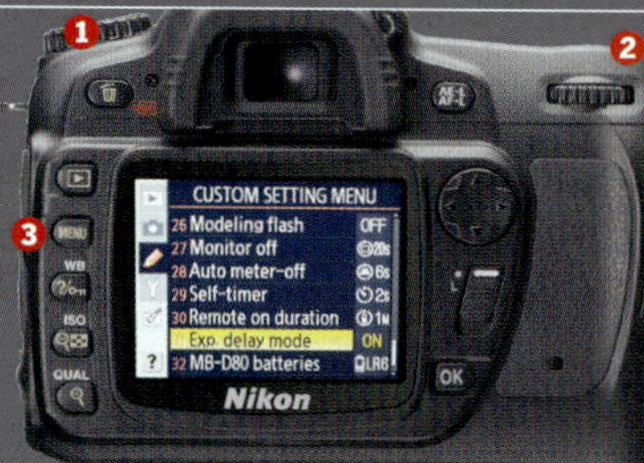

(1) Turn the mode dial to M (manual mode). To set a shutter speed, turn the rear dial. To set an aperture, turn the dial at the top of the handgrip. **(2)** To use the self-timer or remote control, press the drive button and choose the appropriate icon. **(3)** To use mirror lock-up with suitable models, press MENU, go to Custom Setting and choose the appropriate number.

OLYMPUS E-SERIES

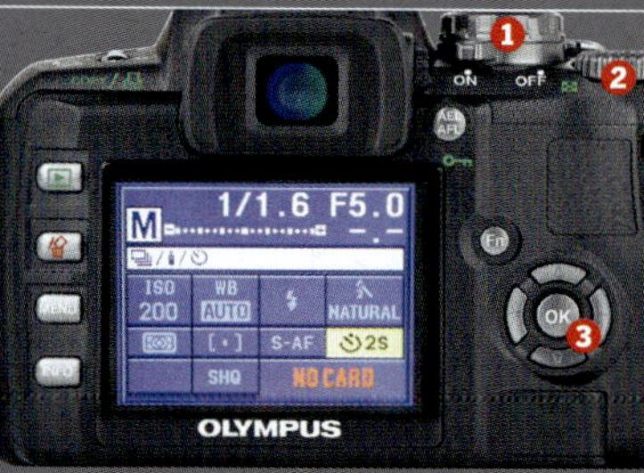

(1) Turn the mode dial to M (manual mode). To set a shutter speed, turn the dial on the top-plate. **(2)**To set an aperture, press and hold the +/- button on the top-plate, then turn the dial. **(3)**To use the self timer or remote control, press OK, move to the drive icon on the LCD, press OK and select the appropriate icon.

PENTAX K-SERIES

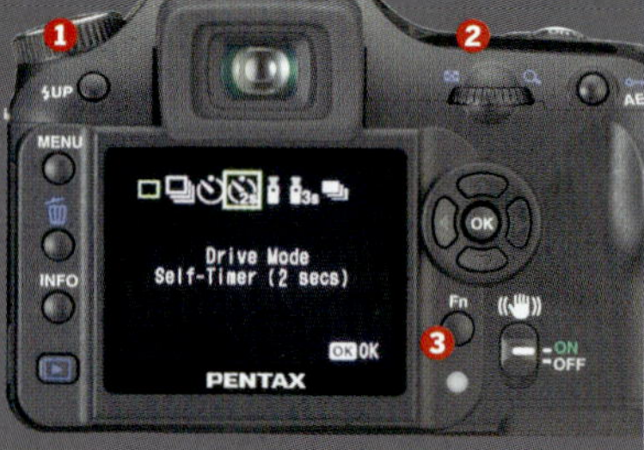

(1) Turn the mode dial to M (manual mode). To set a shutter speed, turn the rear dial. **(2)** To set an aperture, press and hold the +/- button, then turn the dial. **(3)** To use the self-timer or remote control, press the Fn button, press the up button on the four-way control and select the appropriate icon, then press OK to set. You'll find that selecting the two-second self-timer also engages a mirror lock-up facility.

SONY ALPHA SERIES

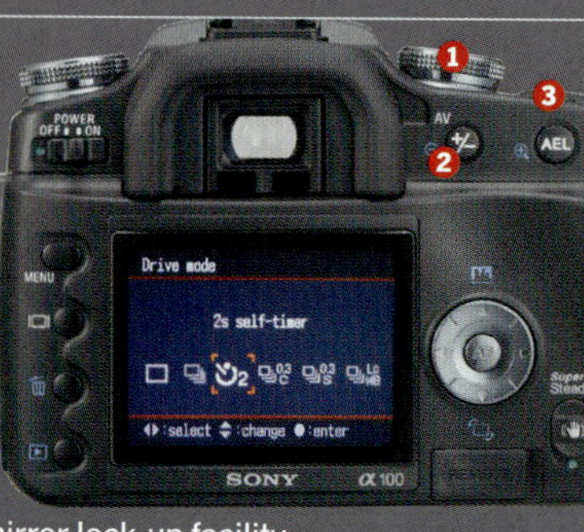

(1) Turn the mode dial to M (manual mode). To set a shutter speed, turn the dial in front of the shutter button. **(2)** To set an aperture, press and hold the +/- button, then turn the dial. **(3)** To use the self-timer, press the drive button and choose the appropriate icon. You'll find that selecting the two-second self-timer also engages a mirror lock-up facility.

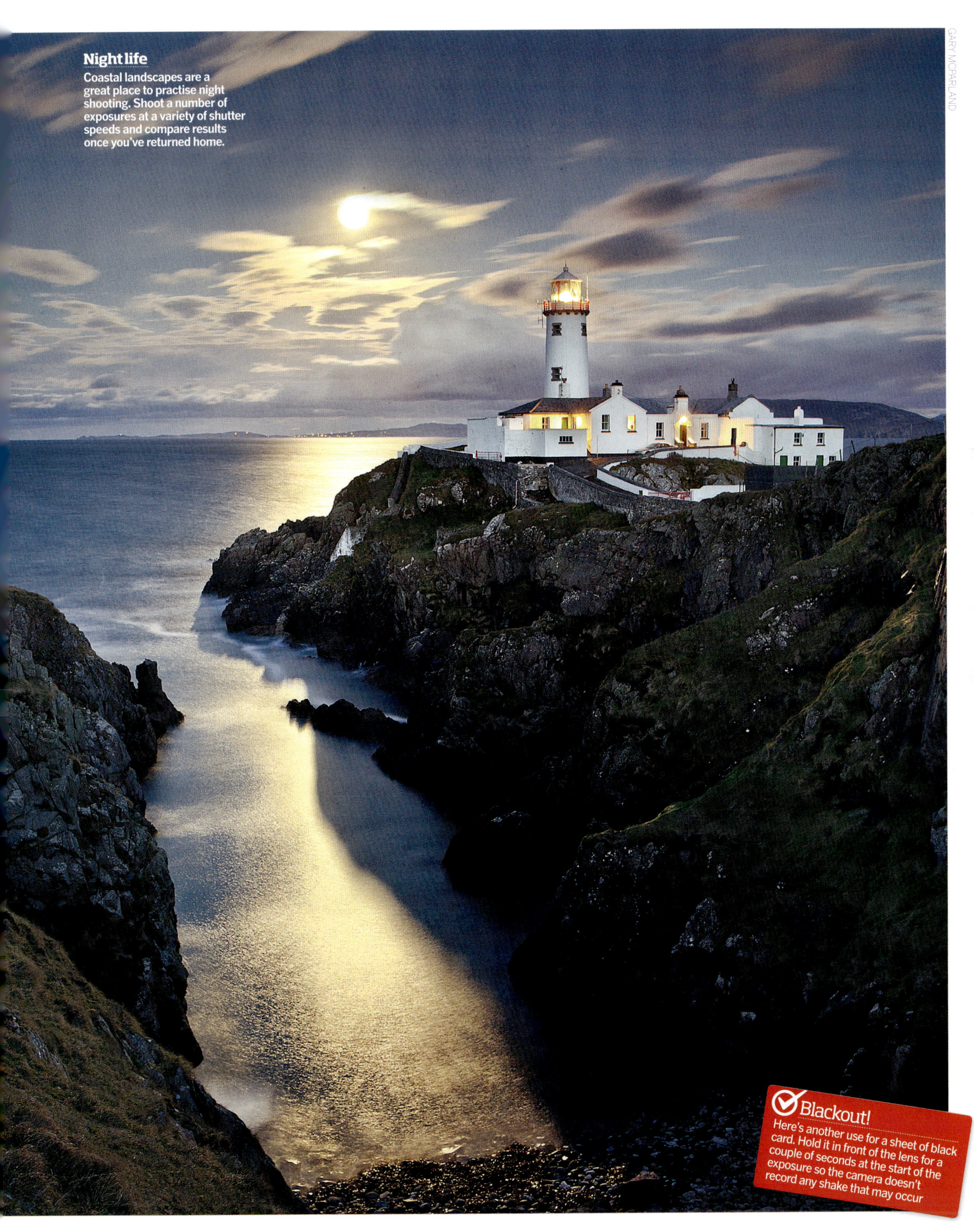

Night life

Coastal landscapes are a great place to practise night shooting. Shoot a number of exposures at a variety of shutter speeds and compare results once you've returned home.

GARY MCPARLAND

Blackout!

Here's another use for a sheet of black card. Hold it in front of the lens for a couple of seconds at the start of the exposure so the camera doesn't record any shake that may occur

Urban landscapes

Master the main techniques for shooting cityscapes at night

FROM TUDOR BUILDINGS to modern glass skyscrapers and derelict warehouses, there are plenty of photo opportunities in an urban environment and they all look fabulous when lit up at night.

Before embarking on your night of photography, spend time planning your shoot – it's vital to successful night shots, particularly if you're visiting a location for the first time. Train times, the location of the nearest station, earmarking landmarks and viewpoints, where to park, printing off a street map and knowing what time sunset occurs are all great timesavers, allowing you to concentrate on getting great shots when you arrive. Take inspiration from other people's images, too, to give you a starting point. Arrive at your location several hours before dusk so you can wander around and familiarise yourself with the scene, and test out various focal lengths and compositions before the sun starts to set. Look out for trees, tunnels or bridges to frame a picture. Statues can make good foreground interest, making shots feel three-dimensional by adding scale. Don't just look for wide cityscapes, zoom in and concentrate on high-rises or deserted streets. Adding movement to night shots can also improve the composition and dynamism, so keep a lookout for traffic and people. Try placing water in the foreground, too, to pick up the reflections from the buildings' lights, giving your image stunning symmetry and contrast. Suitable subjects include a river, lake or wet pavement after a rainy period.

The best light for urban nightscapes is the 'crossover period', when the ambient daylight balances with the artificial lights of the buildings. At this point, the blue or orange sunset sky has darkened and you can clearly see the streetlights, but there is still enough daylight to reveal shadow detail. This moment after sunset varies depending on season, weather conditions and how bright the buildings are. You're best to shoot about 15 minutes after sunset, or when the city lights are switched on, and continue until the sky loses all colour and turns black. Shoot a bracketed sequence of images (in one-stop increments above and below the camera's metered exposure) every few minutes, over a 20-minute period, so that you can choose the most balanced shot later and also see how the balance of ambient/artificial light subtly changes. Once the sky turns black, you could continue shooting with the view of converting the shots to black & white.

When you've found a location and decided on a suitable composition, your next job is to concentrate on focus and exposure. Even the best autofocus systems can struggle in low-light conditions, so do a test shot and zoom in to check sharpness. If the focus is out, alter the focus point manually to find a bright area with strong contrasting lines and refocus – then switch to manual focus to stop the system from hunting again. If your camera has LiveView, set it to Tripod Mode via the menu and use this to help manually focus. A remote release can also make a huge difference to sharpness, so ensure you use one.

Your camera's metering system is usually very accurate – but there are instances where they can struggle, like in dim light. As urban night scenes usually consist of large areas of darkness broken up by small areas of light from street lamps, glowing windows and signs, the extreme dynamic range makes giving a correct exposure quite a challenge. Too much and highlight detail is lost, too short an exposure and there's very little detail in the shadow areas as they merge together.

For bright cityscapes, use the camera's multi-zone metering pattern, which takes an average reading of the whole scene. Use centre-weighted or spot metering for individual buildings, otherwise you risk underexposing them.

The best way to judge the accuracy of the exposure is to use the camera's histogram: be watchful of the right-hand side to make sure no highlights are clipped. Bracketing exposures (see your camera's manual for details on how to do this) can improve your chances of getting an accurate exposure, but in some cases you may need to blend parts of the exposures together in Photoshop to create one image with high dynamic range. You can do this by dragging the three exposures on top of one another and then using Layer Masks to reveal lost shadows or highlights from the various exposures.

When composing your pictures, keep an eye out for lights just out of frame in case they cause flare. Use your hand to test for flare by placing it around the edge of your lens. It can be obvious, but sometimes there can be a very subtle loss of contrast: use a lens hood or hold a piece of black card between the light and lens, being careful not to get it in frame.

Diffraction is also something to watch out for as it affects image quality due to optical aberrations. To minimise diffraction, avoid using the smallest apertures and instead stick to using anywhere between f/11 and f/16 – go beyond this and diffraction is a real risk.

One interesting and pretty aspect of diffraction is the star effect that appears around hot spots of light, such as street lamps. These look best with lenses that have an odd number of diaphragm blades (ideally seven or nine) as it doubles the number of 'diffraction spikes': seven blades create a 14-pointed star. The smaller the aperture, the more refined and elegant the effect is, but use f/22 or smaller with caution.

Know your rights

One problem when shooting buildings at night is police or security guards sniffing around using the infamous anti-terrorist laws. In cities like London the latter can get quite aggressive, so know your rights. They cannot touch you, your memory card or your camera: it would be breaking the law. Always be polite, but firm. If you're on private land (which is often not signposted) and you are asked to leave, agree and quickly move on.

Right: This image was taken in manual mode, using centre-weighted metering and an exposure of eight seconds at f/11.
Below: This series of pictures shows the 'crossover period' and how quickly the ambient light drops and balances with the city lights.

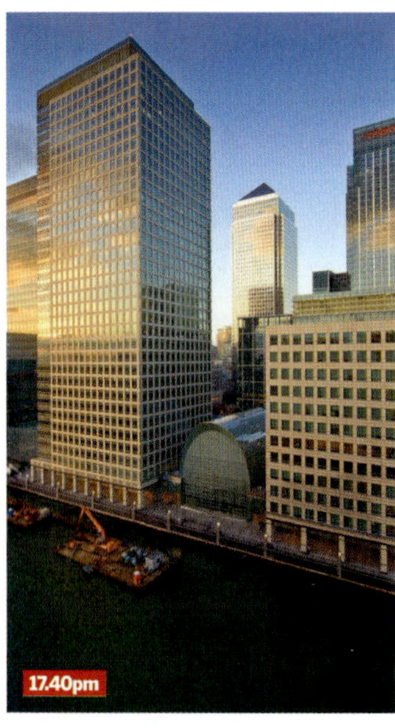
17.40pm

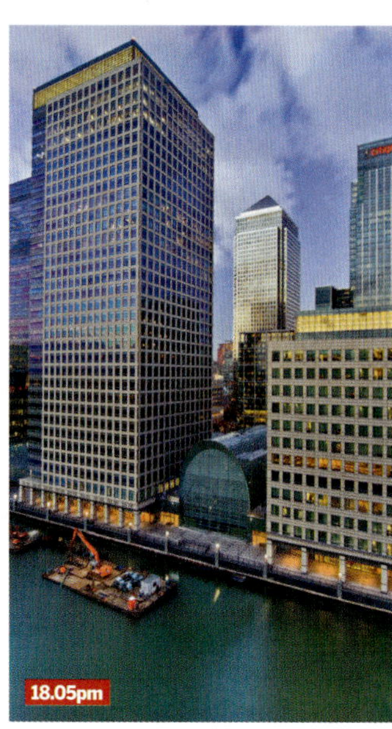
18.05pm

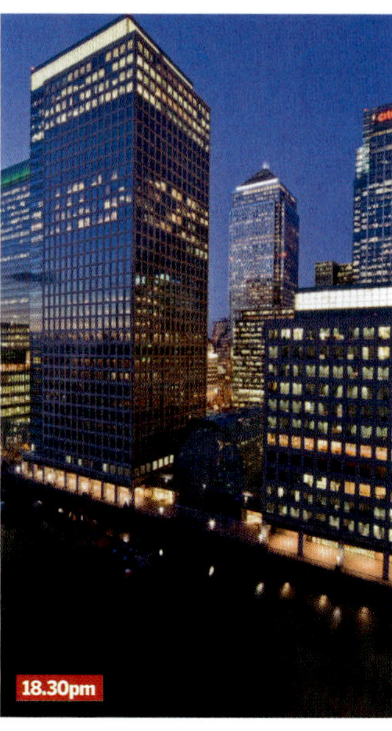
18.30pm

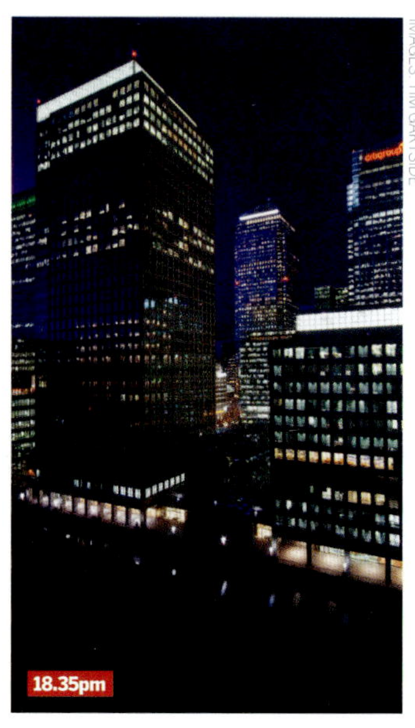
18.35pm

IMAGES: TIM GARTSIDE

TIM GARTSIDE

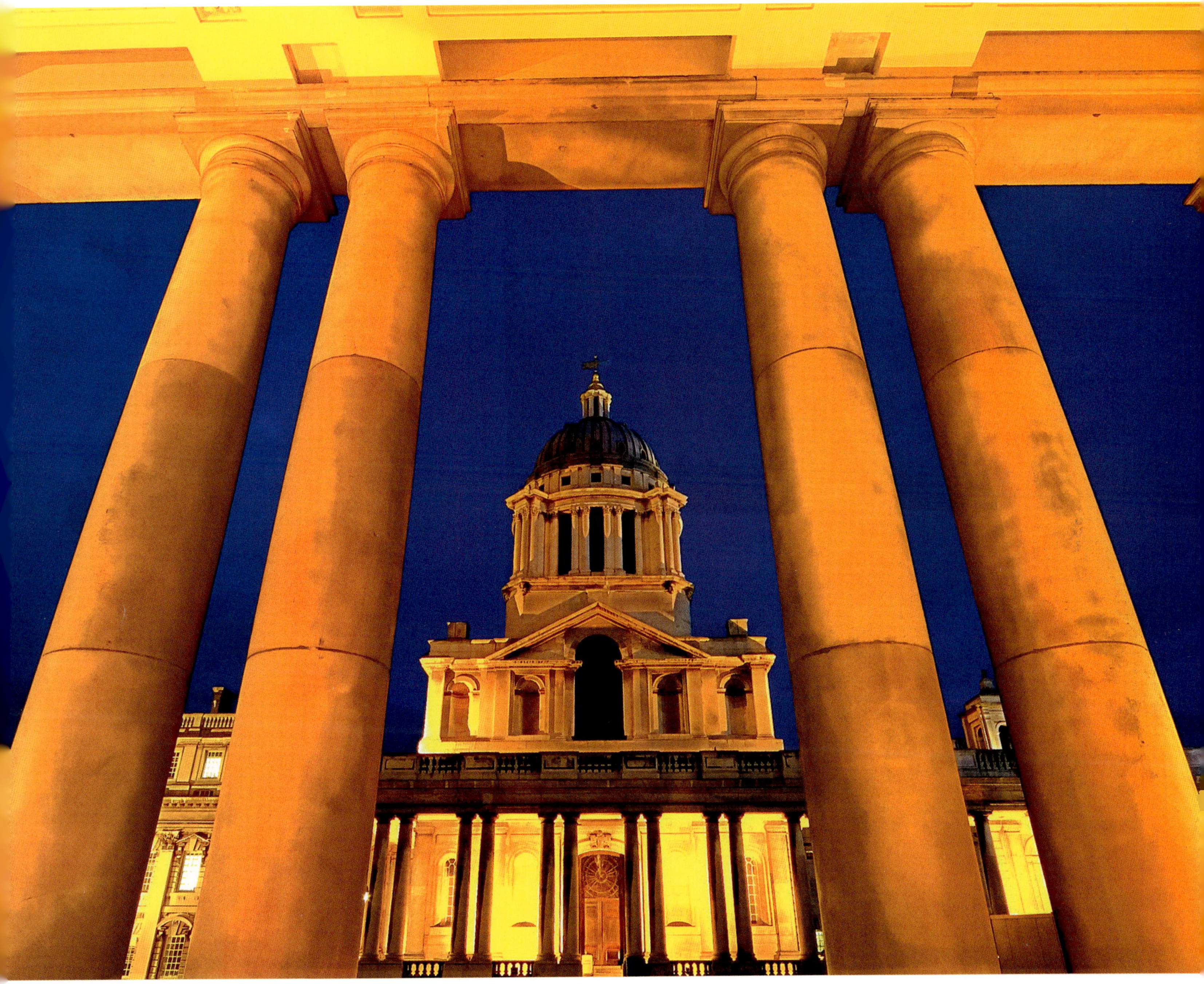

How to shoot floodlit buildings

As night falls, many historical and modern buildings become floodlit, creating some beautiful architectural shots. In order to capture the ambience, you need to master the exposure as, quite often, the building will be several stops brighter than its surroundings. For the best results, photograph early in the 'crossover' period, before the sky gets too dark, and use spot metering to take a reading from a mid-tone area, then take a test shot. Check the histogram for shadow/highlight clipping and adjust the exposure accordingly.

Often the camera's metering system is fooled into underexposing a scene if there's a large bright area, like a floodlit building. Get around it by adding 1 or 1.5 stops of positive exposure to compensate; adjust the shutter speed or dial in the equivalent stops of positive exposure compensation. In some instances, features – like the new and much brighter lights in Big Ben's clock face – overexpose and are difficult to control as they exceed the camera's dynamic range, which is when bracketing exposures and restoring lost shadows and highlights in post-production become a normal part of digital workflow.

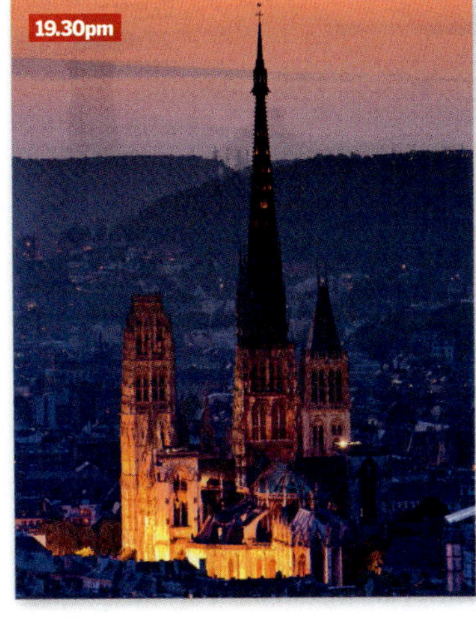

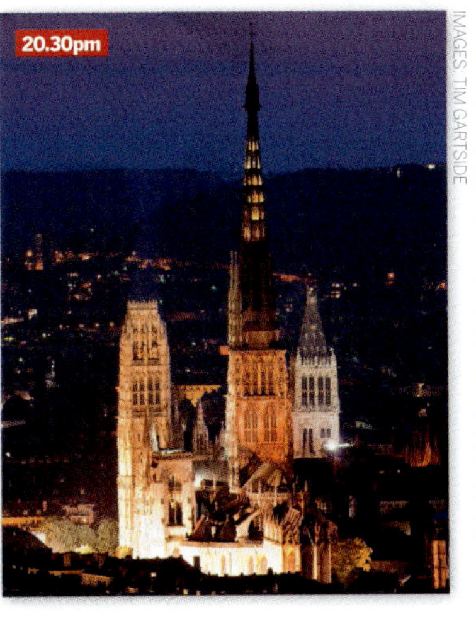

IMAGES: TIM GARTSIDE

Get creative: Traffic trails

New to night photography and want to practise your techniques? Then head to a main road near you with your camera and a tripod

FOR ANYONE LOOKING TO DEVELOP their skills at night photography, there are few subjects as accessible and relatively straightforward to photograph as traffic trails. The technique behind it is simple: you set up your camera so that it's aimed at a road and you fire a long exposure while the traffic zooms by. The aim is to capture the lights from the passing traffic as streaks of white (headlights) and red (tail lights). It's one of the easiest night techniques that you can try, so you should really give it a go.

Set your camera on a tripod and compose the scene so that the road is prominent in the frame. You then have a choice of which exposure mode to use. We'd recommend you select manual (M), rate the ISO at 100-200 and set a mid-aperture like f/8 or f/11 to give the optimum quality. Then it's simply a case of deciding how long you'd like the exposure to be. You can set particular shutter speeds, or you can set Bulb and use whatever length of exposure you like. We'd suggest you shoot in sequences that increase/decrease in one-stop intervals – eg two secs, four secs, eight secs, 15 secs etc – as you can compare the results on the monitor and determine which works best. Bear in mind that the speed of the traffic will greatly influence this – slow-moving vehicles will produce shorter trails than traffic moving at speed. You should also consider different viewpoints to shoot traffic trails from. While setting up the camera at normal working heights is an obvious start, you should also try shooting from a higher vantage point (eg the upper floor of a building or a footbridge), as well as getting down low to make it appear as if trails are streaking through the air. Our step-by-step below provides a beginner-style approach to trying out traffic trails.

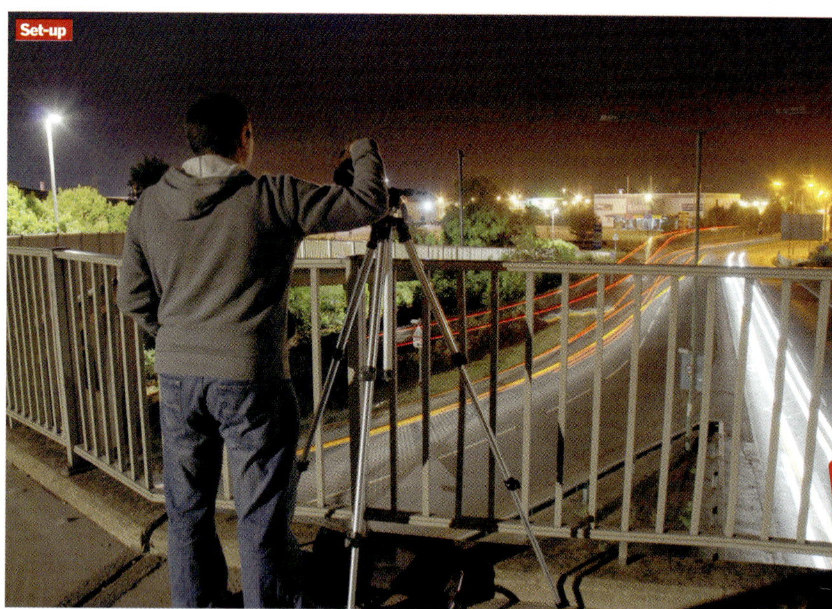

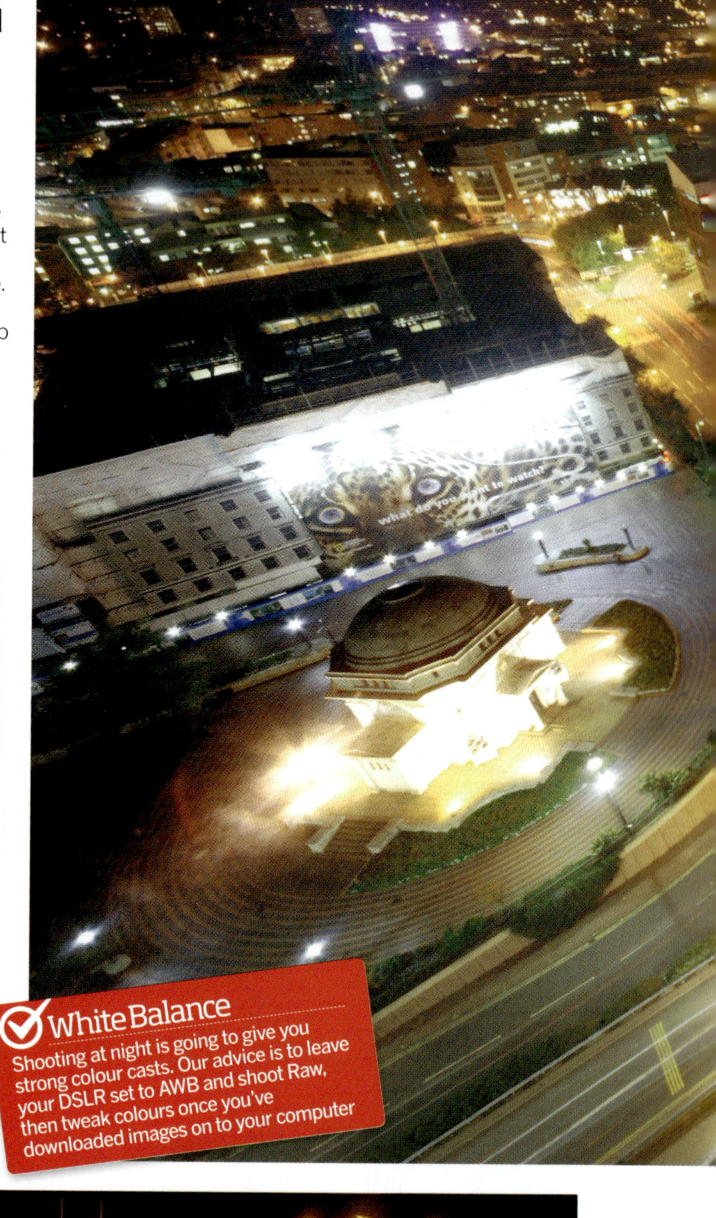

White Balance
Shooting at night is going to give you strong colour casts. Our advice is to leave your DSLR set to AWB and shoot Raw, then tweak colours once you've downloaded images on to your computer

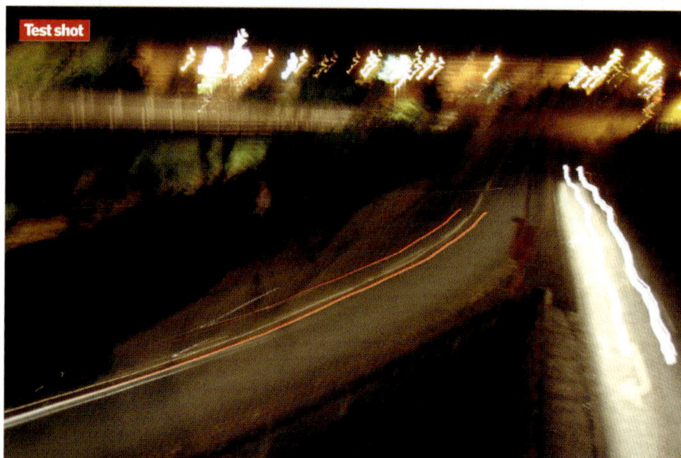

1 Beanbag test This test shot was taken with the camera resting on a beanbag on the railings. As you can see, the vibration of the traffic has travelled through the railings and beanbag, and caused serious camera shake. There is no doubt that you can't beat the trusty tripod.

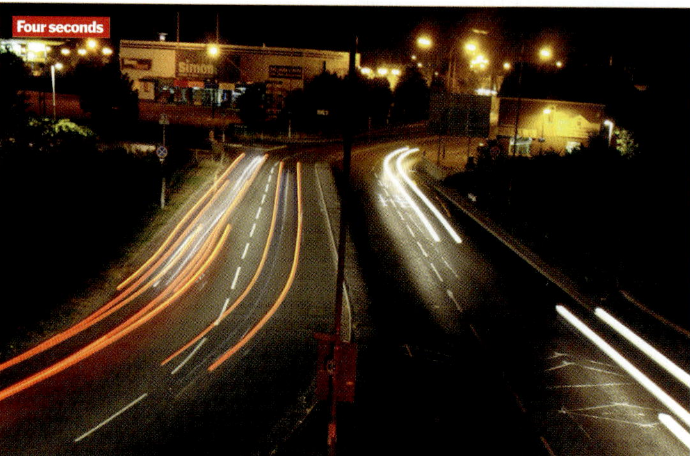

2 Four-second exposure The first of our shutter speed sequence is a four-second exposure. A quick review of the LCD monitor shows that when shooting cars within a 40mph speed limit, we're going to need much longer exposure times to capture traffic trails that extend through the entire frame.

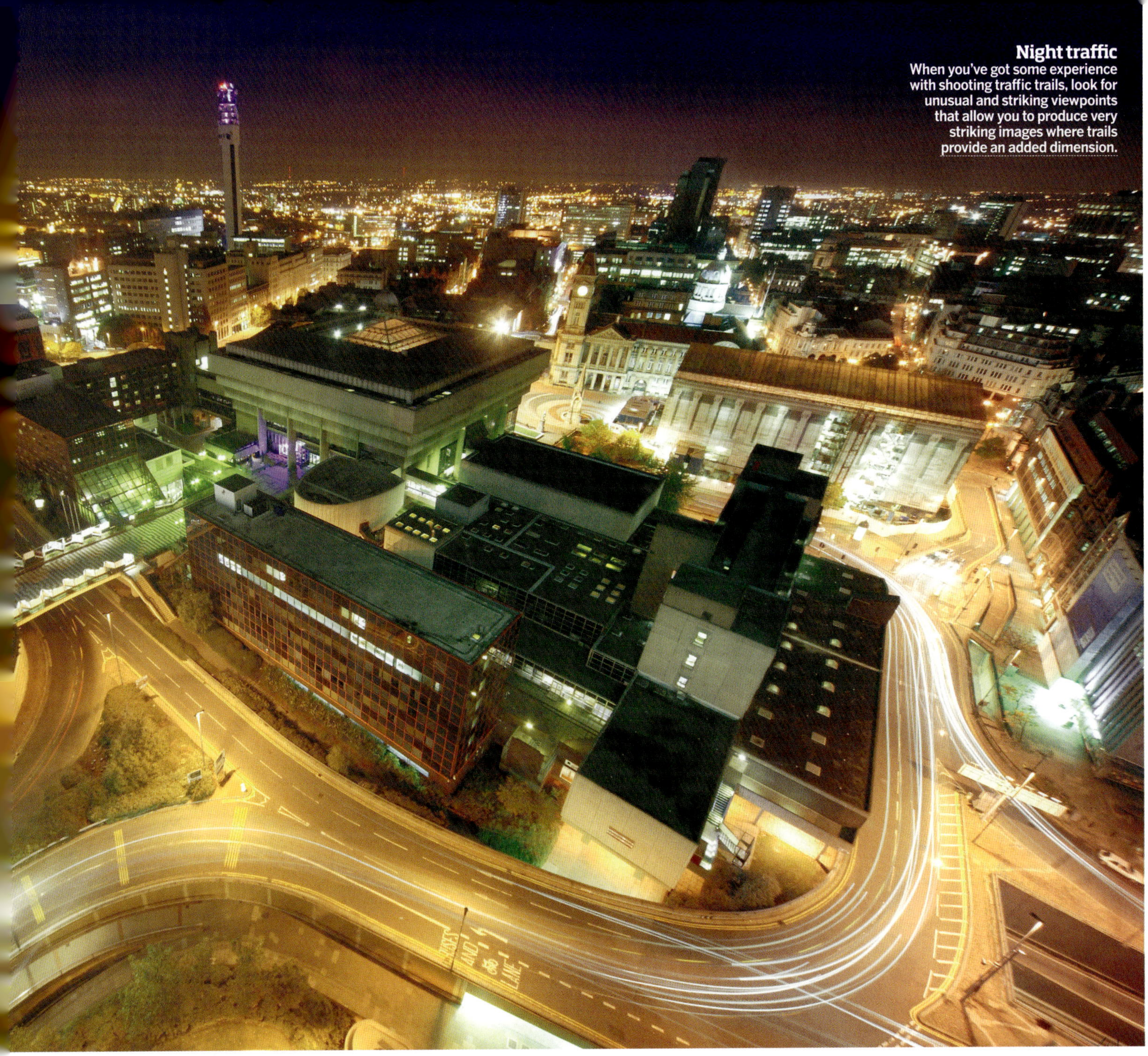

Night traffic

When you've got some experience with shooting traffic trails, look for unusual and striking viewpoints that allow you to produce very striking images where trails provide an added dimension.

PAUL WARD

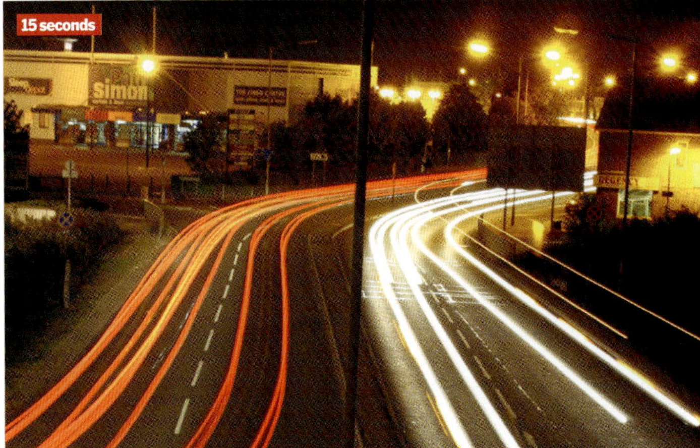

3 15-second exposure A much longer exposure time has allowed the traffic trails to extend through the entire frame and the colours of the trails are nice and punchy. The ambient light levels are well controlled too, so there are no burnt-out areas of the frame.

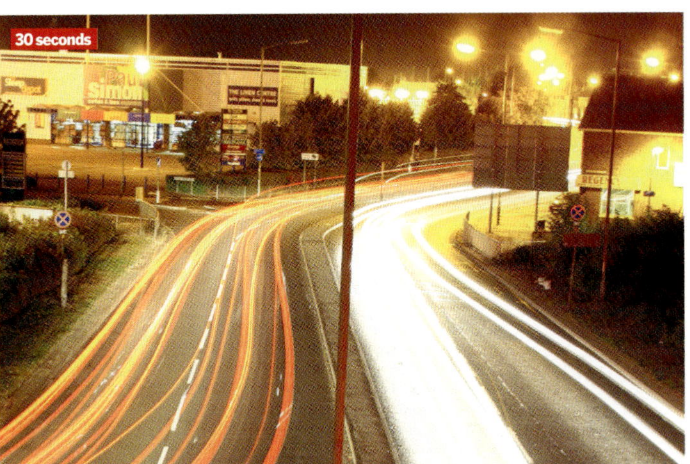

4 30-second exposure While the extra time allows more light trails to be recorded, there is a point where too much light starts to burn out the traffic trails. If this happens, either select a smaller aperture, shorten the exposure time or lower the ISO rating (or combine two or more of these methods).

Painting with flash

Ross Hoddinott shows how any external flashgun can be used to paint subjects with bursts of light

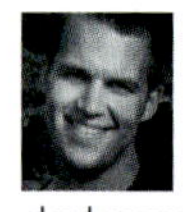

Ross Hoddinott THE WORD PHOTOGRAPHY quite literally means 'painting with light', so it is an apt title for this unusual night technique. Painting with light is a method that involves using a long exposure, up to a minute or more, in near or total darkness. Then, whilst the shutter is open, the photographer manually illuminates the subject using an artificial light source – like a flashgun or torchlight. The resulting images have a surreal, atmospheric feel to them, created by the uneven illumination of the artificial light source combined with any ambient light.

At first, the concept of painting with light might sound bizarre, but it is great fun to try and the results can be striking. Also, whilst this technique might rely heavily on trial and error, it is not difficult to attempt. First, you need to identify a suitable subject. Practically anything can work, big or small. However, larger subjects, like trees and buildings, often create the most eye-catching results. Old ruins, dilapidated buildings and – if you're not easily spooked – gravestones work especially well.

The technique relies on it being dark. However, arrive at your location while it is still light so you can easily compose your shot. This will also help you familiarise yourself with your surroundings; you will be wandering around in the dark and don't want to be tripping over. Whilst it can be tempting to begin shooting immediately after sundown, don't – if there is too much ambient light, the effect of your torch or flashgun will be diluted and ineffective. Wait patiently until it is sufficiently dark, remembering to wrap up warm, and keep a torch with you at all times for safety.

Generally speaking, it is best to shoot around an hour after sundown when there is still some colour in the sky. There is no set rule regarding the length of exposure required; it is a hit-or-miss affair. Begin by using a 30-second exposure, combined with a small aperture of f/16 or f/22. However, you may find that the best results are achieved at a minute or longer. To shoot exposure times this long, it will be necessary to employ your camera's Bulb setting. Be prepared to experiment and review images after every frame; you can then adjust settings accordingly. With your camera set up on a sturdy tripod and exposure set, release the shutter using either a remote release or the self-timer. By doing so, you can be in position ready to begin painting. A flashgun is ideal for illuminating larger, outdoor subjects. You will need to fire the flash on full power several times to create a decent exposure. Walk around the subject, directing the flash burst towards the areas you want lit. You can emphasise certain regions by giving them repeated flashes. To minimise being recorded in the shot, make sure you wear dark clothing and keep moving as you paint!

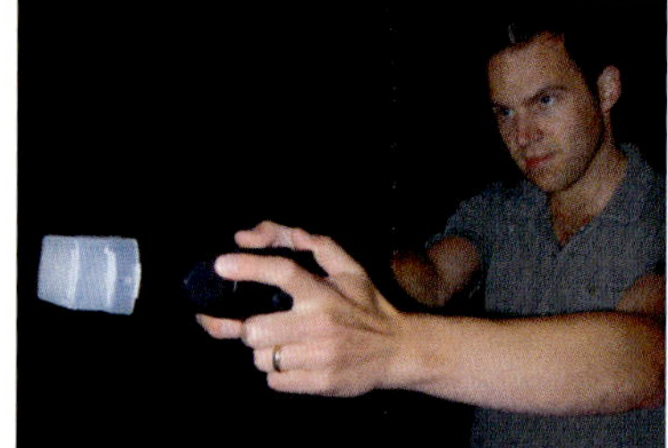

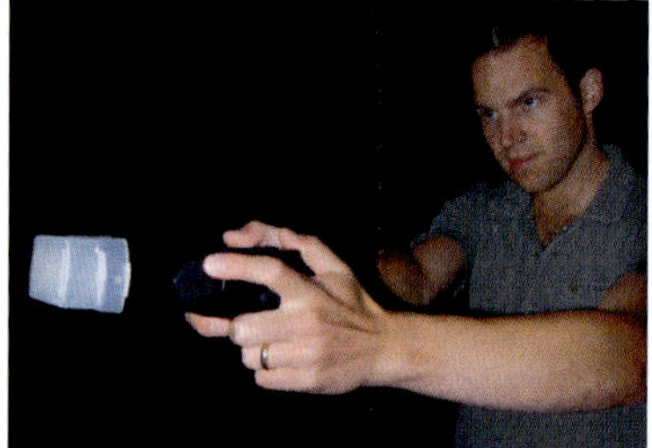

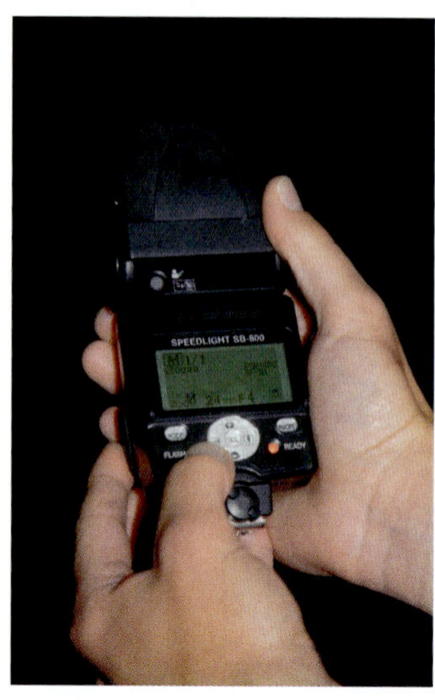

Bulb setting

Most digital cameras usually have a maximum automatic exposure of 30 seconds. For exposures longer than this, the camera needs to be set to Bulb or 'B'. Using this setting, the shutter will remain open for as long as the shutter release button is depressed – either manually or via a remote. The term 'Bulb' refers to old-style pneumatically-actuated shutters – squeezing an air bulb would open the shutter and releasing the bulb would close it again. When using the Bulb setting, exposure has to be timed manually, meaning a degree of trial and error is usually required.

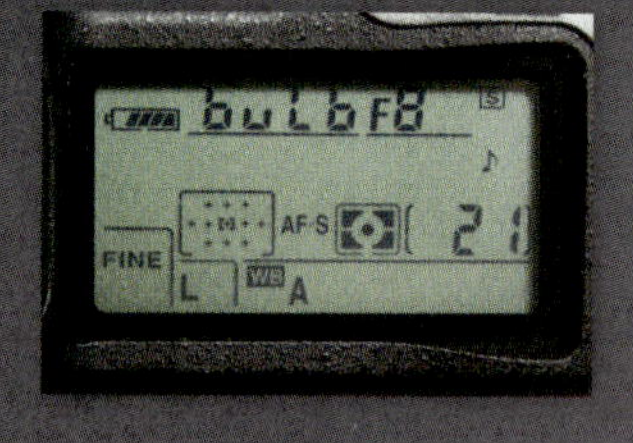

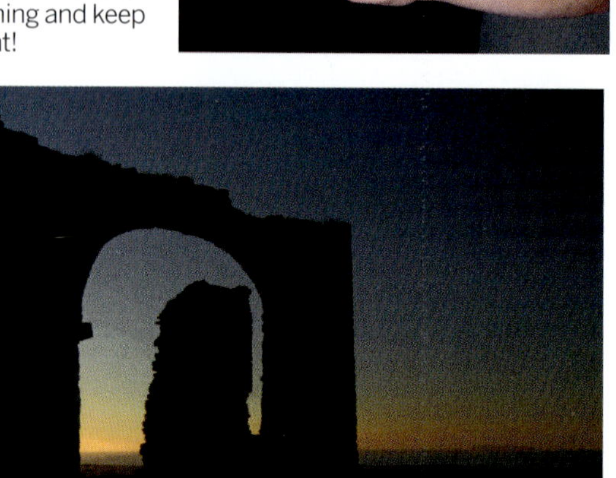

1 Set up The sun might have set, but there is too much ambient light to begin 'painting'. However, it gives me time to set up the camera on a sturdy tripod, arrange composition and take a test shot while it's still light.

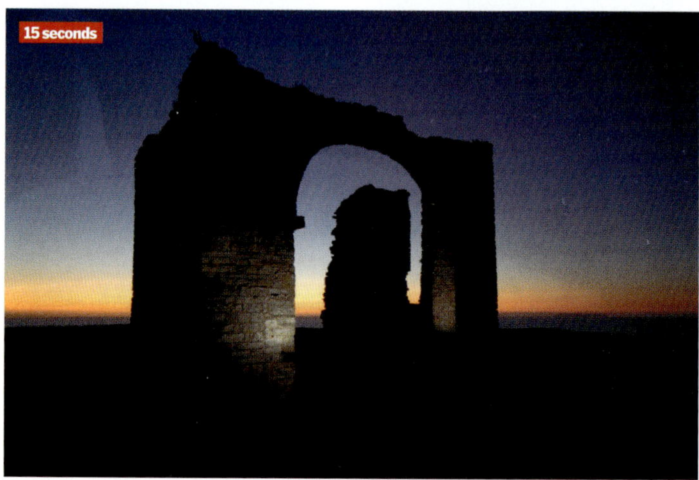

2 Test shot The first attempt was taken using an exposure of 15 seconds. However, this didn't allow sufficient time for me to illuminate the ruins of this folly properly and the effect of the flash isn't obvious enough.

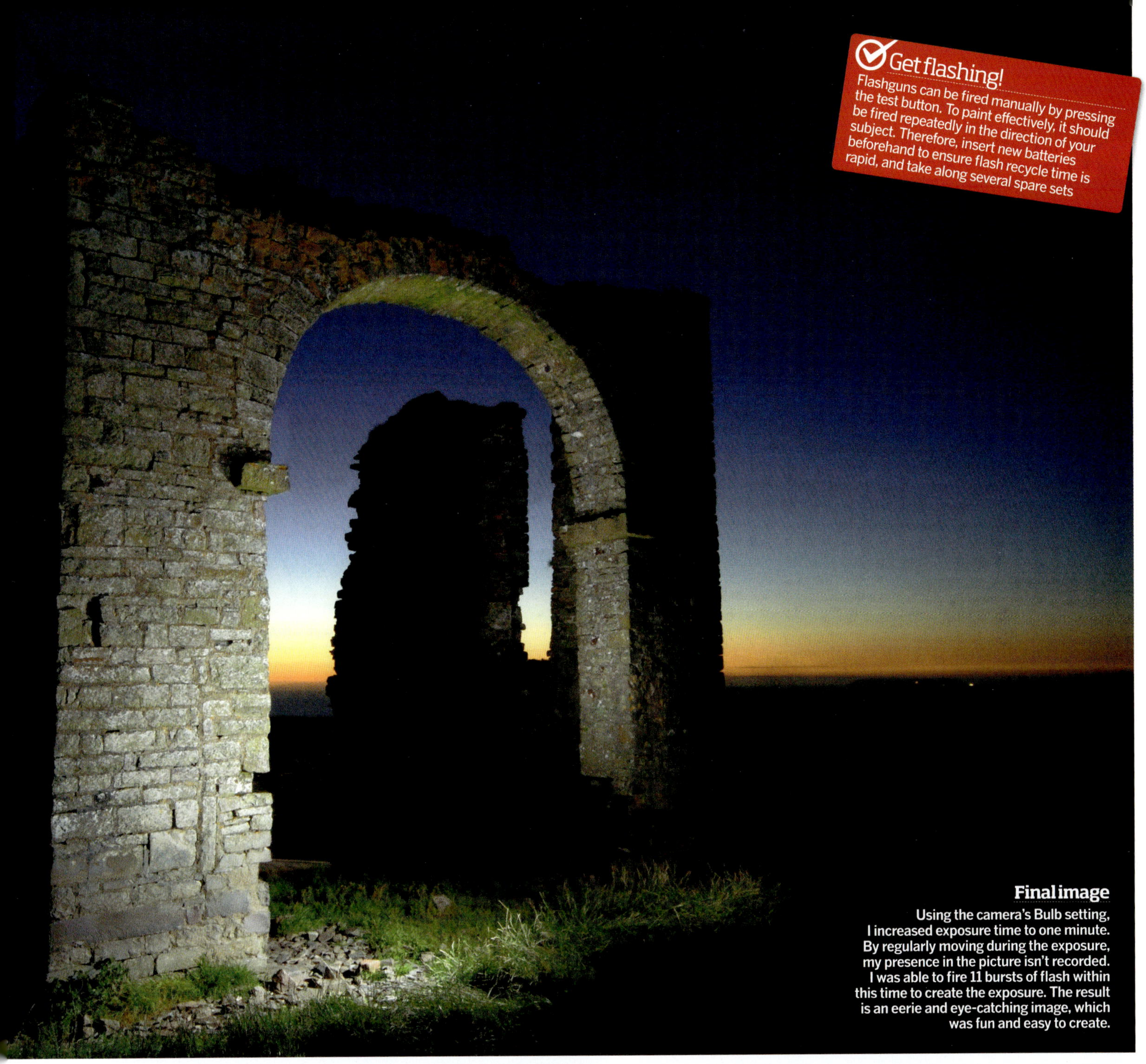

Get flashing!

Flashguns can be fired manually by pressing the test button. To paint effectively, it should be fired repeatedly in the direction of your subject. Therefore, insert new batteries beforehand to ensure flash recycle time is rapid, and take along several spare sets

Final image

Using the camera's Bulb setting, I increased exposure time to one minute. By regularly moving during the exposure, my presence in the picture isn't recorded. I was able to fire 11 bursts of flash within this time to create the exposure. The result is an eerie and eye-catching image, which was fun and easy to create.

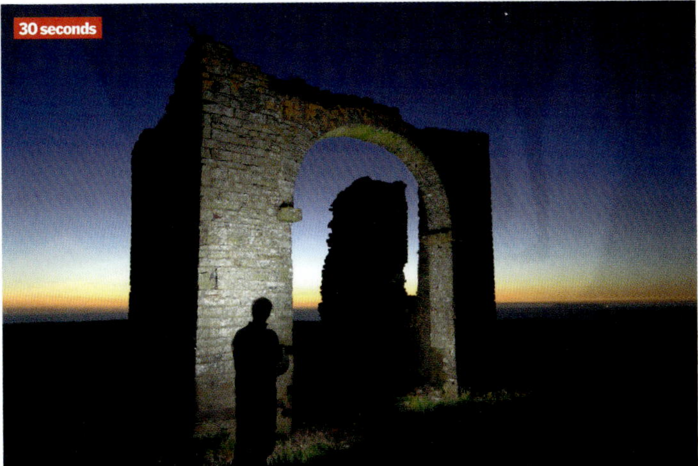

30 seconds

3 Try a longer exposure An exposure of 30 seconds allowed time for twice as many flash bursts as step 2. The folly is far better illuminated, but by remaining still in one position, my outline has accidentally been recorded.

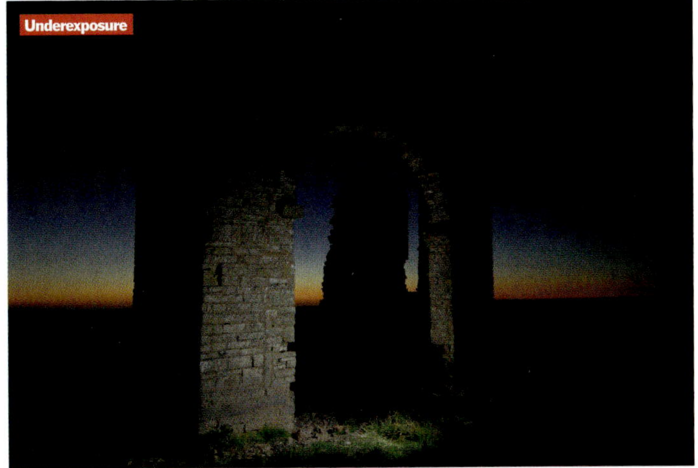

Underexposure

4 Adjust exposure Achieving the correct exposure is hit and miss. Although an hour after sundown, the light is still growing steadily darker; without adjusting exposure time, images may underexpose, as it has here.

Put your subject in the spotlight

The humble torch can be a fantastic tool to produce amazing pictures. Here's how...

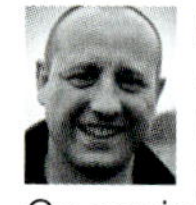

Mark Bauer DULL WEATHER AND a lack of light are no excuse to pack up your camera gear and leave a perfectly good landscape behind. Go equipped with your own light source and you won't miss a shot. A powerful torch, for instance, can shed some light during a long exposure on subjects that would otherwise be too dark for a camera to record well, thus making them stand out from a night scene. It's a brilliant technique that can produce some eye-catching results. The colour contrast between the cool ambient light and the torch's warm light can add a huge shot of impact. So, with this in mind, on a dull evening, I took a trip to Poole Harbour in Dorset to try out this technique on the boats on the sand at low tide. Why don't you try, too?

Shed some light on the matter!

It's surprising how many different types of torches there are, and some are better suited to this technique than others. The brightness of torches is often expressed in 'candelas' or 'candle power'. If you're painting a large object, such as a building, you might want to use a more powerful torch, perhaps one that's ten-million candle power. The type of bulb is important, too, as they have different colour temperatures altering your White Balance – another reason why it's best to shoot in Raw.

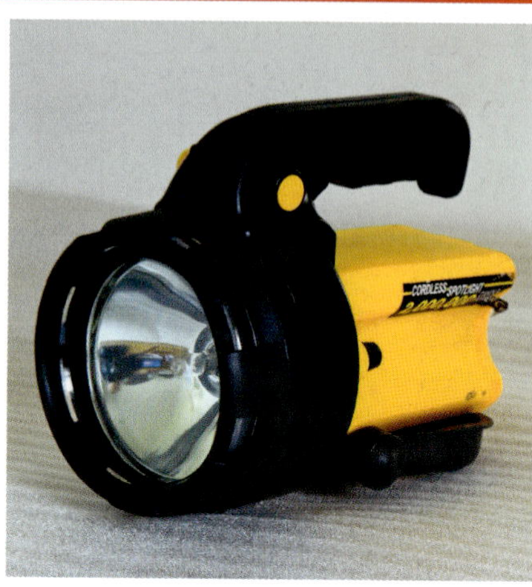

1 Select your subject First, I tried to find the right boat. After a couple of test shots, I realised I needed a boat that wasn't too tatty and that leaned towards the camera. While this boat had the streetlights of Sandbanks twinkling in the background, the boat wasn't particularly photogenic. It was a little too early in the evening, too, as everything was grey – I waited until it got darker.

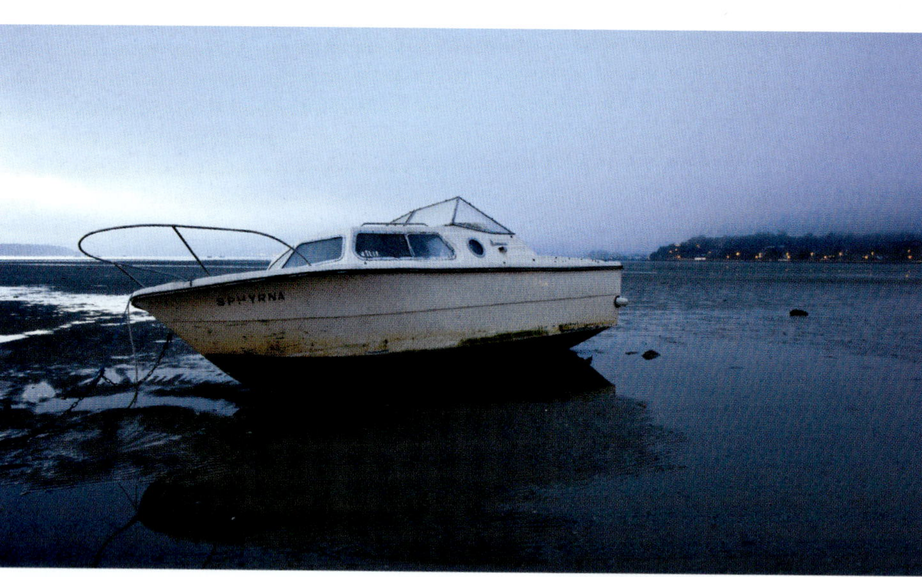

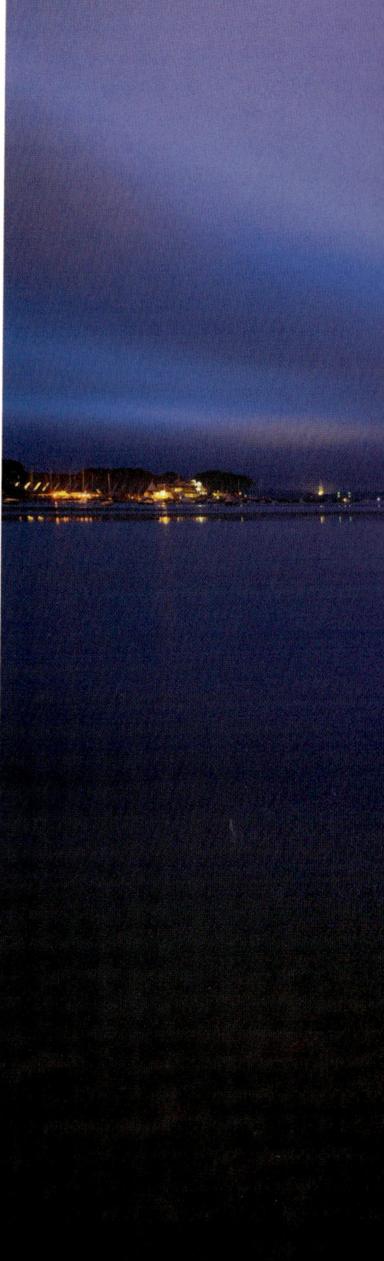

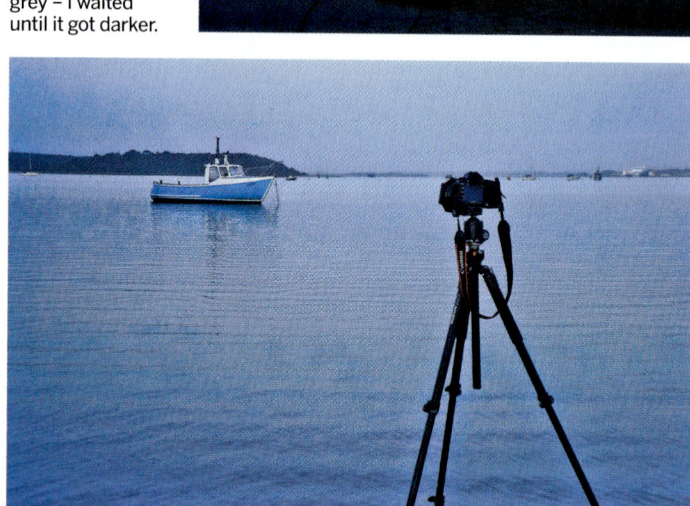

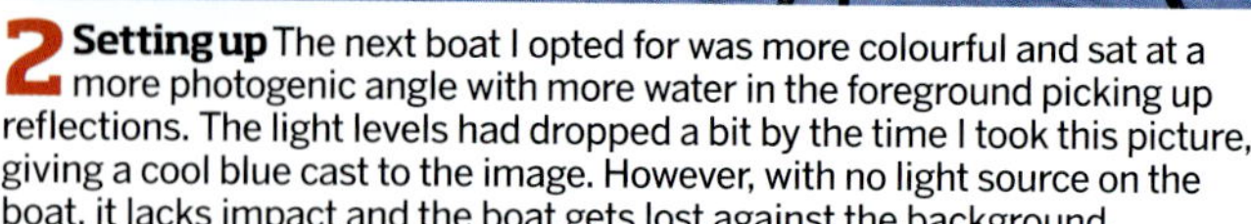

2 Setting up The next boat I opted for was more colourful and sat at a more photogenic angle with more water in the foreground picking up reflections. The light levels had dropped a bit by the time I took this picture, giving a cool blue cast to the image. However, with no light source on the boat, it lacks impact and the boat gets lost against the background.

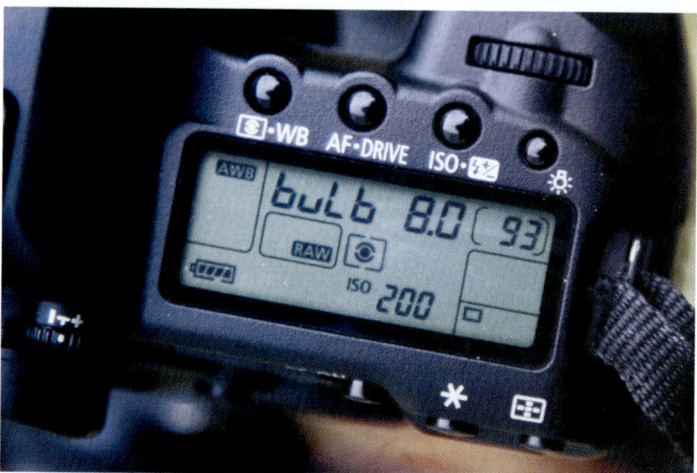

3 Set exposure I took a spot meter reading from the sky so it would record as a mid-tone. My initial settings were ISO 100 and f/16, which resulted in an exposure of 24 minutes! This was way too long and increased the risk of the tripod sinking into the wet sand and ruining the shot. So I increased ISO to 200 and set f/8, then, using the Bulb setting, set an exposure of three minutes.

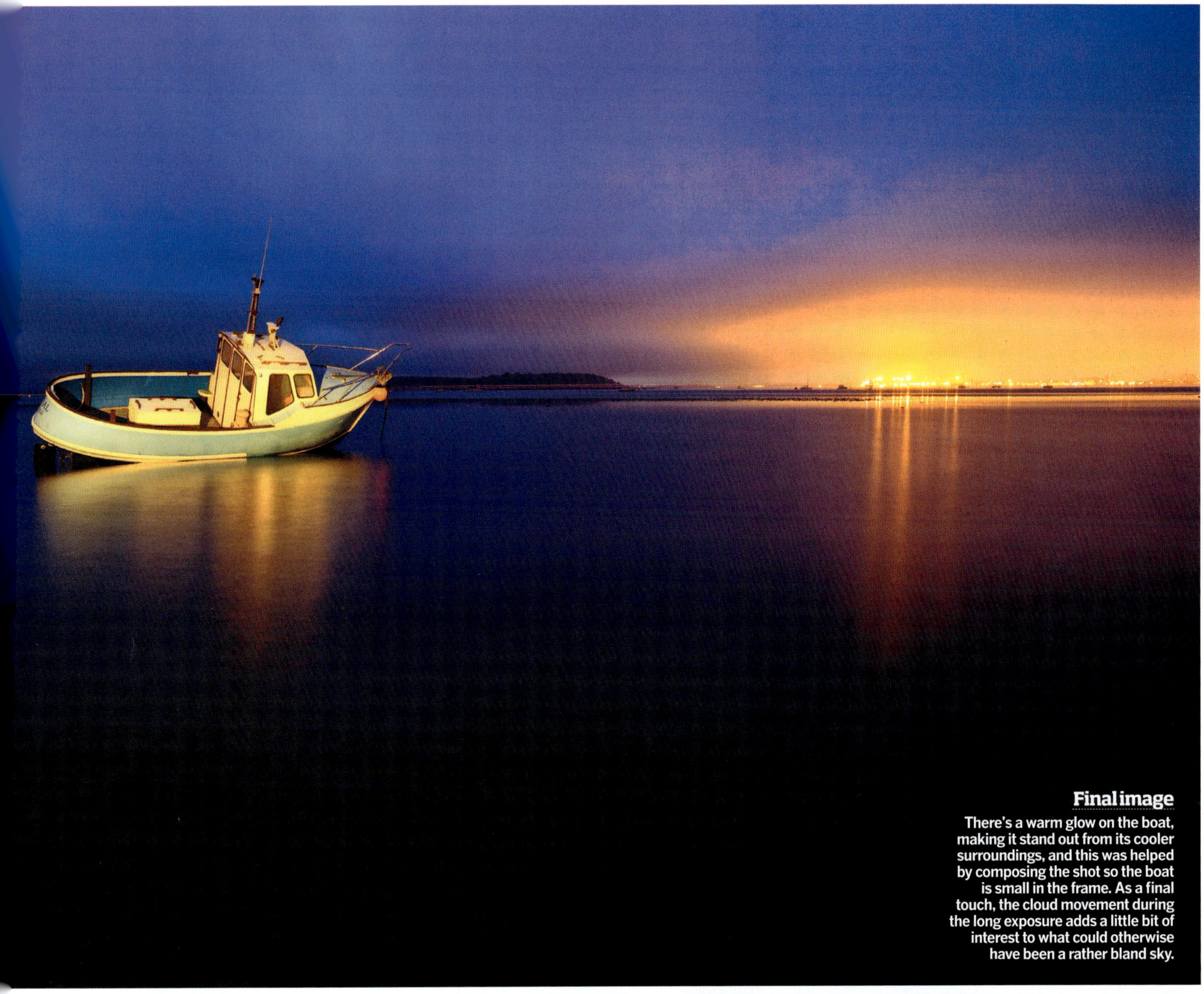

Final image

There's a warm glow on the boat, making it stand out from its cooler surroundings, and this was helped by composing the shot so the boat is small in the frame. As a final touch, the cloud movement during the long exposure adds a little bit of interest to what could otherwise have been a rather bland sky.

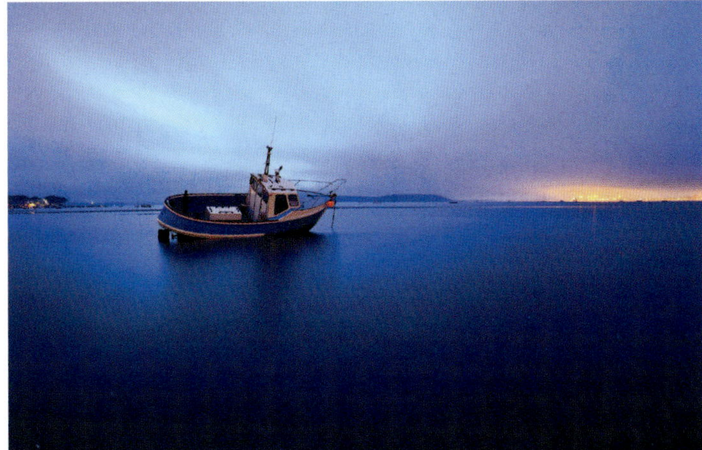

4 Paint light with a torch I then started painting the boat with light. How long you need to do this for depends on several factors: how powerful your torch is; how close you are to the subject you're illuminating; and how reflective the subject is. I kept the beam of the torch moving during the exposure, while I stood out of frame, making sure that I lit the boat evenly.

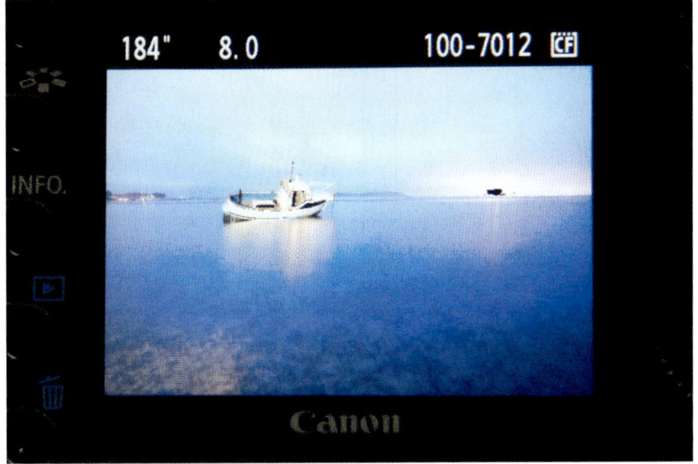

5 Adjust the light Getting the right amount of light on the boat was a matter of trial and error. As you can see from the review image on the LCD monitor, I overcooked this one by shining the torch on the boat for around two minutes during a three-minute exposure. I reshot, this time 'painting' the boat for 90 seconds – probably a good starting point for most images of this type.

Moonlit landscapes

The brightness of the moon can create other-worldly landscape scenes. Here's how to use the moon to your best advantage

JUST BECAUSE THE SUN has gone down doesn't mean you can't capture beautiful landscapes. Using moonlight is in fact simpler than photographing at dusk as the light is less variable. Shooting moonlit landscapes is not that different from shooting in daylight, but a lot easier than shooting at sunset, because moonlight is a lot stronger than the last light of the day. That said, you need to pay similar attention to the angle and position of the moon, as you would the sun. A high moon casts strong downward shadows, while a low moon creates long shadows and much softer lighting. It's the optimum light for landscapes and occurs shortly after sunset, just as the moon begins to rise.

Exposure is the main challenge when it comes to moonlight, as it's several thousand times weaker than sunlight. A further complication is the fact that the moon moves fairly quickly, so exposures more than a couple of minutes long can render it a streak in the sky. One solution is to keep the moon out of frame and simply shoot a landscape exposed by its light. Landscapes illuminated exclusively by a full moving moon that softens shadows can make eerie, ethereal pictures. Use too long of an exposure, though, and the light becomes flat. If you want the moon in the picture, but the exposure is too long, take the correct exposure for the foreground, immediately followed by a shorter exposure for the sky, and then merge the two in post-production.

The length of an exposure depends on the intensity of the moon: a full moon on a clear night is great for illuminating landscapes where you want extensive depth-of-field. But if the moon isn't as strong or prominent, you'll find you may need to compromise on depth-of-field by using a wide aperture to reduce exposure times. Remember, though: if you use a wide aperture, focusing is critical. The best times to shoot are when there's a full moon or during the two days before and after the full moon, when it wanes into and wanes out of its full phase. Note also that layers of cloud affect the exposure, just like it does during the day.

For extra visual interest, try shooting with a river, lake or sea in the foreground, so you can capture the light beams glistening off the surface – you'll find that the reflected light also brightens the whole scene. You could also introduce flash or a torch into your shoot, using it to paint the foreground.

When setting up your camera, apply the same techniques already explained in this guide: use Bulb or manual mode, work out the exposure, focus manually if possible and fire the shutter using a remote release. When working out the exposure for a moonlit scene, multi-zone metering works well. Then follow this technique: take a test shot in aperture-priority mode at your highest ISO rating and widest aperture to give yourself a base shutter speed, then use reciprocity failure to work out the exposure for a decent aperture and low ISO rating. Alternatively, switch to spot metering and meter off the brightest part in the scene, then add two stops of extra exposure because the metering system will otherwise render your highlights as a mid-tone.

Once you've mastered star trails and moonlit landscapes, try shooting auroras, meteor showers or even have a go at deep-space photography!

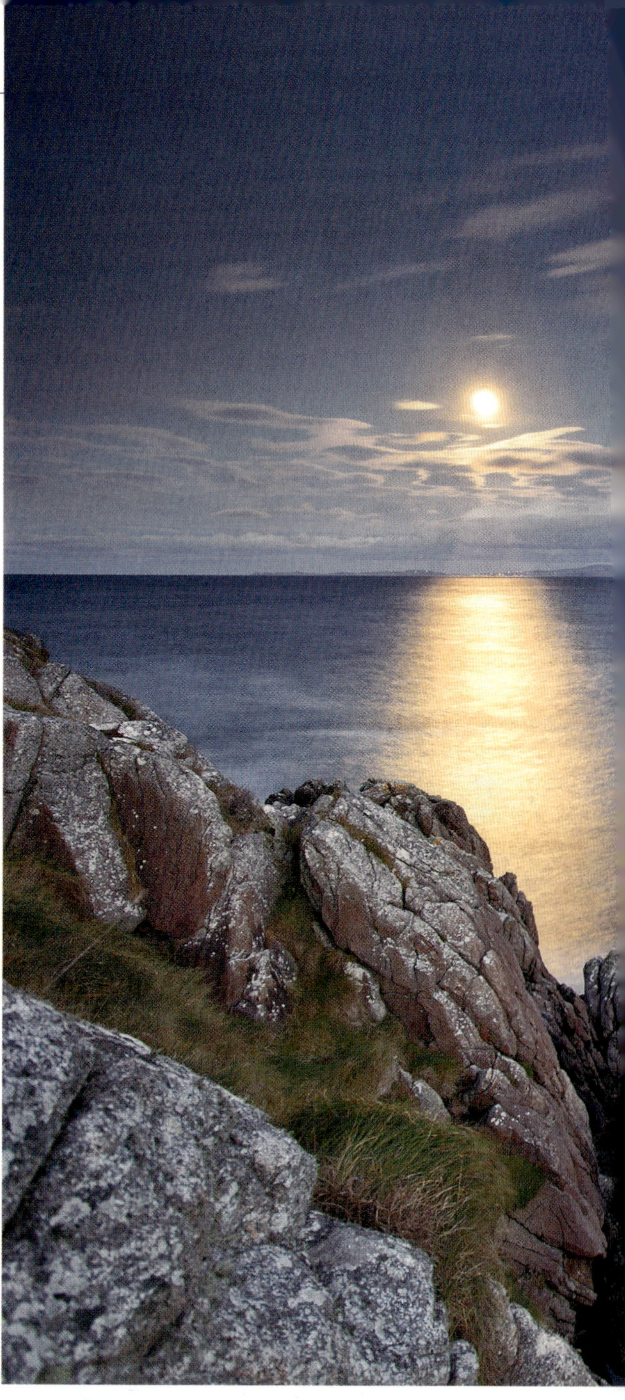

Right: Moonlighting: For every exposure of this scene, the f/stop and ISO had to be adjusted to keep the shutter speed between 15 and 30 seconds in order to freeze the moon's motion.

Below: This shot of Swaledale comprises a four-minute exposure for the foreground and a 30-second exposure for the sky.

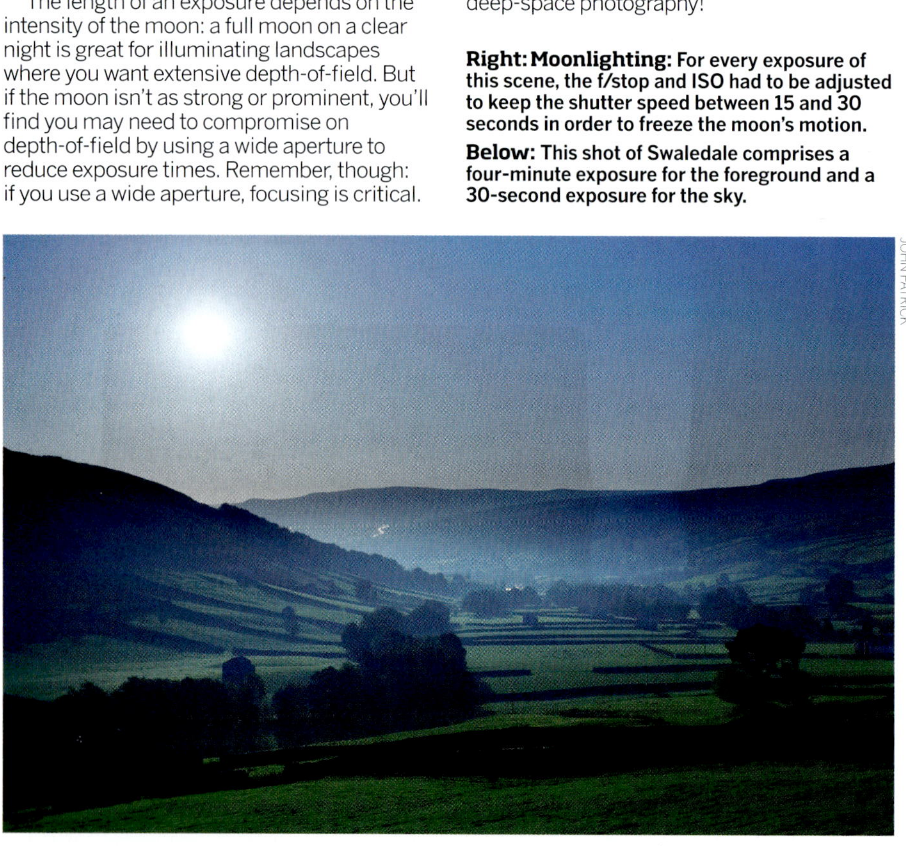

JOHN PATRICK

Reciprocity law

With low-light photography, it's important to remind yourself about the interchangeable relationship between shutter speeds and apertures so that you can work out the required exposure.

It takes a bit of brainpower, but you can now download apps to your smartphone that can help you calculate equivalent exposures. Basically, every time you stop down your aperture, you need to increase your shutter speed to double the exposure time, so if you go from f/4 to f/5.6, the shutter speed needs to double from, say, two seconds to four seconds.

Reciprocity law failure is when the camera fails to accurately meter a scene in low light and fails to meter a sufficient exposure time for the length of shutter speed. It's much less common with digital cameras than film, but you may find you need to add an extra stop or two of exposure to ward off underexposure when shooting moonlit shots like the ones on these pages.

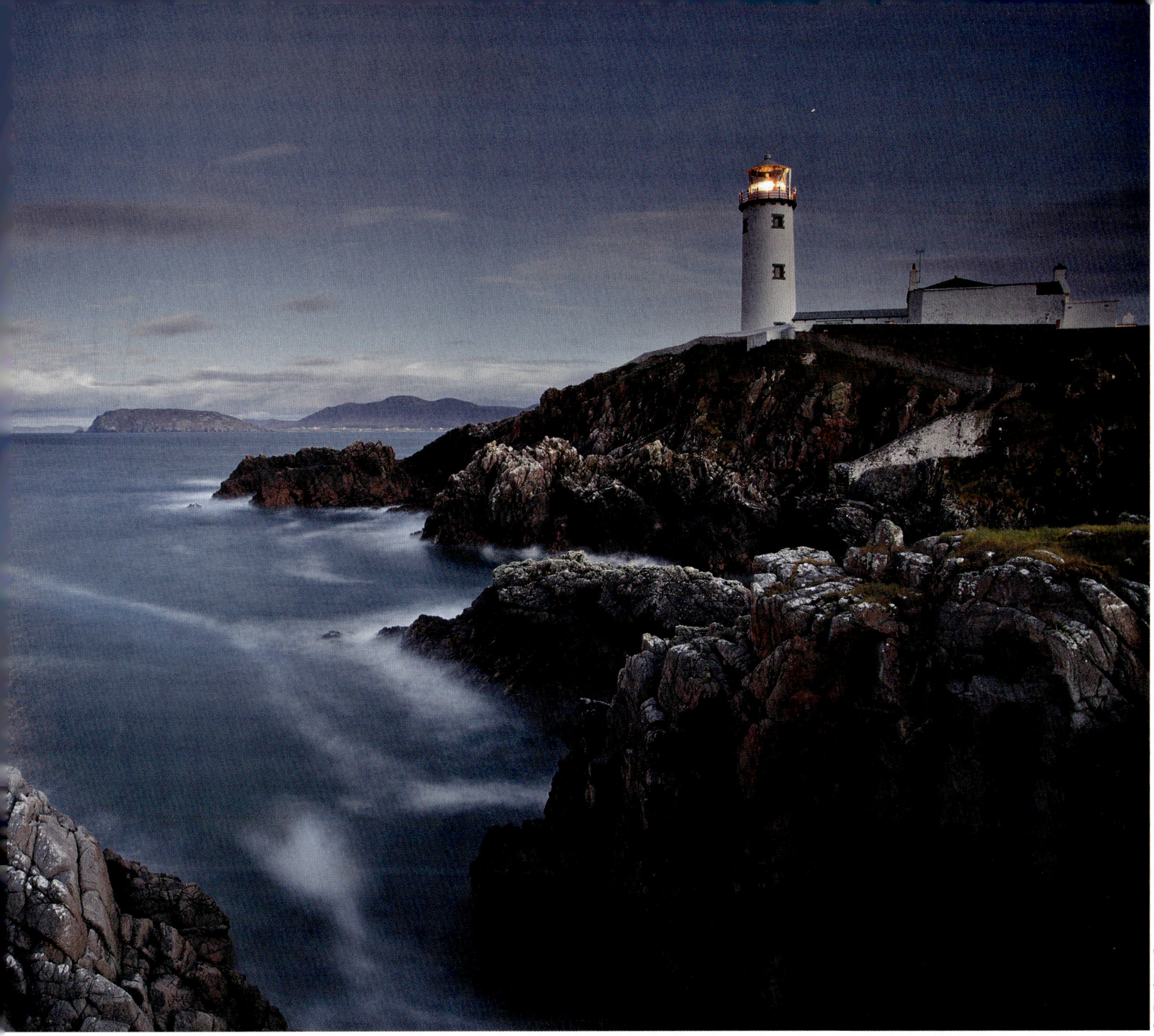

GARY McPARLAND

How to shoot the moon

For those of us who don't have the resources for deep-space photography of the Milky Way galaxy, the nearest thing we have to the mysticism of space is the moon. You don't need any special equipment to photograph the moon, only what you'd normally use for most night photography, but a decent telephoto zoom would be an asset – in particular, those extending to at least 300mm. If you don't have a suitable lens, you could invest in a teleconverter to extend the reach. Remember that an APS-C camera has a crop factor of x1.5, so the equivalent focal length of a 200mm lens is 300mm.

It's easy to underestimate the moon's brightness, which is why getting the exposure correct can be quite tricky. Most first attempts at lunar photographs result in an overexposed circle where the moon should be. The first step to avoiding this is to pick a spot where there is no ambient light from traffic or streetlights, on a clear night, with no cloud. There is a little trial and error needed to get the perfect exposure as it changes depending on the shooting conditions, but set your camera to manual mode and use 1/250sec at f/8 (ISO 100) as a starting point. Take a series of bracketed exposures (in one-stop increments) around this setting and review them on the LCD monitor.

We'd recommend you change the shutter speed rather than the aperture. Depending on the phase of the moon, its brightness, your location and the atmospheric conditions, you may find you need to lengthen or shorten the exposure to capture enough tonal detail on the lunar surface.

Position your focus point over the moon, lock on to it using autofocus and then switch to manual focus to stop it hunting. Use a remote release or the self-timer to minimise the risk of shake blurring the result.

You're likely to have to crop the image in Photoshop and do a little work on the tonality by adjusting the Levels to draw out more detail on the moon's surface.

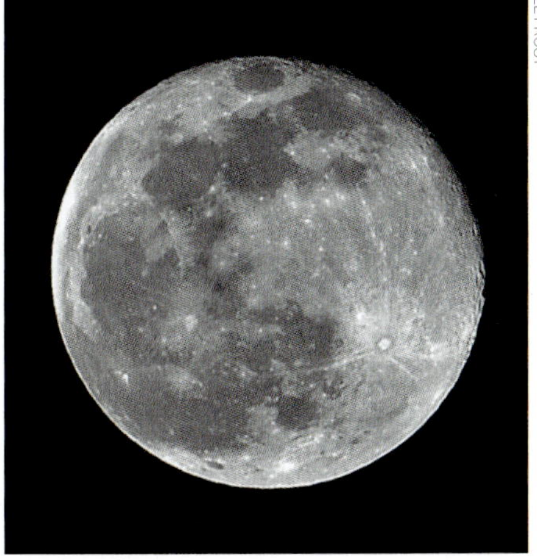

LEE FROST

FILTERS

Lee Frost reveals the importance of filters for landscape photographers

IMAGINE YOU'RE ABOUT TO BE SHIPWRECKED on a desert island and the captain of the vessel has given strict instructions that you can only take three filters overboard with you. Okay, so it's a rather extreme scenario, but – hey – worse things have happened at sea! The question is, which three would you take?

As a child of the Cokin era, I managed to amass more filters than your average camera shop. I had bits of plastic (okay, okay, C39 resin) that could add fake rainbows to my images, ruin a perfectly nice sky by turning it tobacco, reduce attractive scenes to impressionistic smudges, turn bright points of light into brilliant explosions of colour, and perform all sorts of other weird and wonderful tricks. I never used the things, of course, because most of the effects were horrible. But you weren't a proper photographer unless you carried at least a dozen of them everywhere, and if the worst came to the worst, they were ideal for making a sow's ear from a silk purse. I've got hundred of examples to prove it.

Fortunately, after numerous failed attempts I managed to kick my Cokin addiction, so out went all the filters that weren't essential – which actually left very few. Later still, I jumped on the digital bandwagon, which meant I could jettison even more (mainly the colour correction and conversion filters that have been replaced by White Balance and colour temperature adjustments).

Today, I'm left with only three filter types: Neutral Density (ND) grads, a polariser and solid Neutral Density (ND) filters. For landscape and general photography, they're all you need, and all three can be used individually or in combination to help you get the most from a scene.

Some of you may be thinking, 'Why bother with filters at all when the effects can be added in Photoshop?' Well, if you're thinking that, chances are you've never used them, because while the effects some filters have can be replicated in Photoshop, others can't. And anyway, even if they could all be, surely it's better to get your photographs as close to completion in-camera as possible, rather than spending ages at your computer trying to sort them out in post-production?

For information on filter systems, take a look at the panel below, then read on to see the difference my three favourite filters could make to your landscape images.

Which filter system?

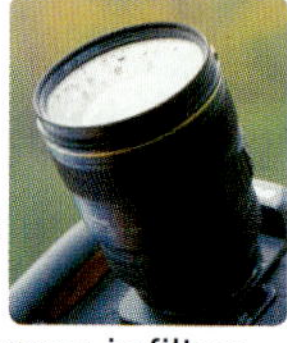

Screw-in: These high-quality glass filters screw directly onto the filter thread of your lens, making them fast and easy to use. You'll find numerous polarisers and ND screw-in filters (including B+W's ten-stop ND) but virtually no ND grads. While offering excellent optical quality, screw-in filters have one big disadvantage: if you have numerous lenses, you'll most likely need to buy several sizes of screw-in filters. Brands to consider include B+W, Hoya, Jessops and Tiffen.

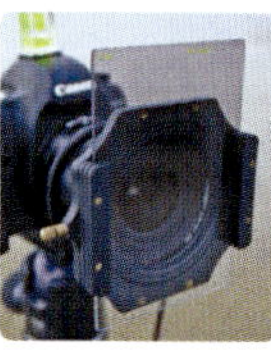

Slot-in: Your best choice when investing in a filter system is the slot-in variety. You buy rings that screw on to your lenses and a single holder that slips on to these rings – this way you only need one filter. Polarisers, NDs and ND grads are all available as slot-in filters. Cokin (P or X-Pro) and Formatt (Hitech) are good first systems, while Lee Filters is the professionals' choice.

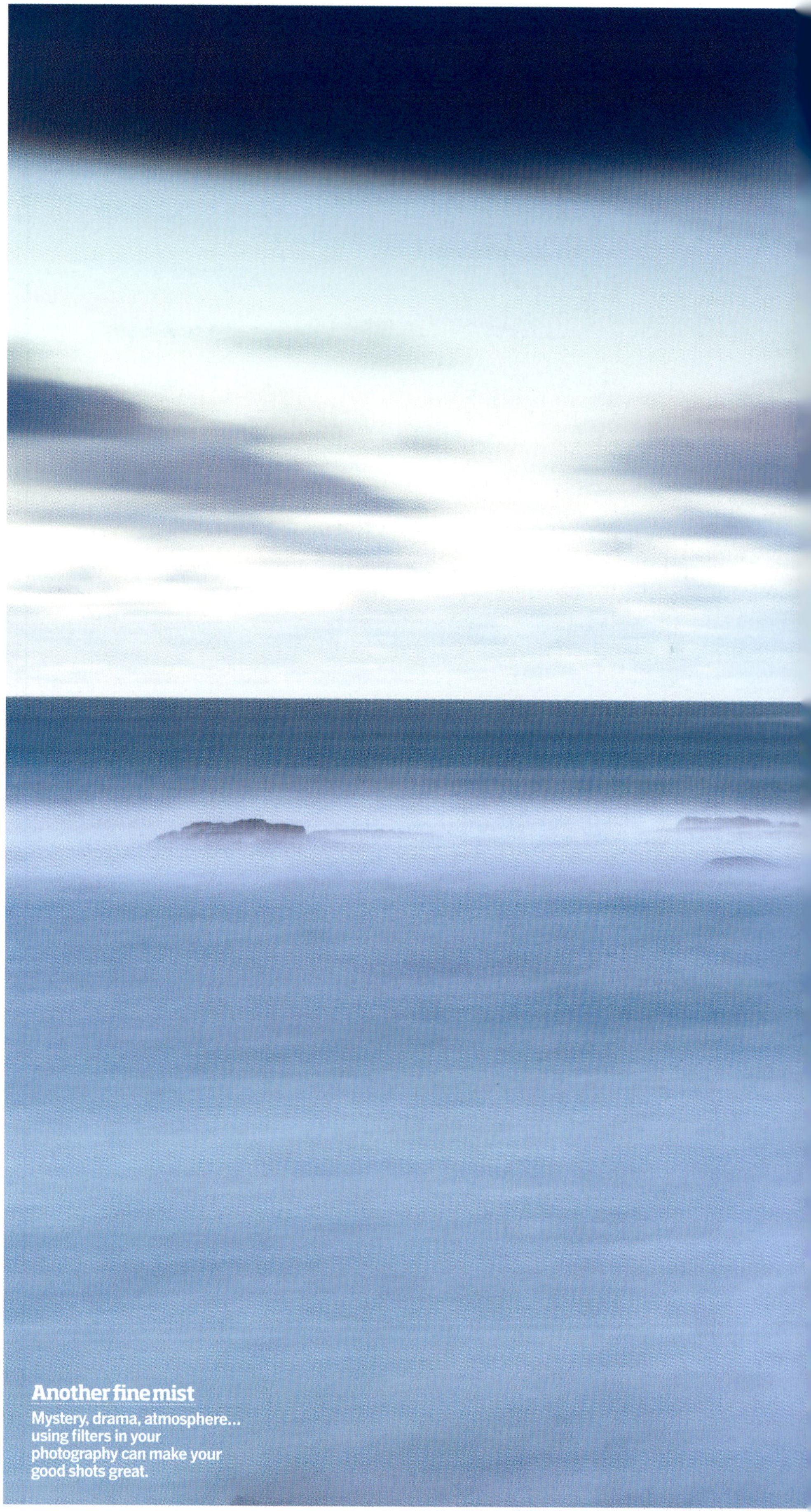

Another fine mist
Mystery, drama, atmosphere... using filters in your photography can make your good shots great.

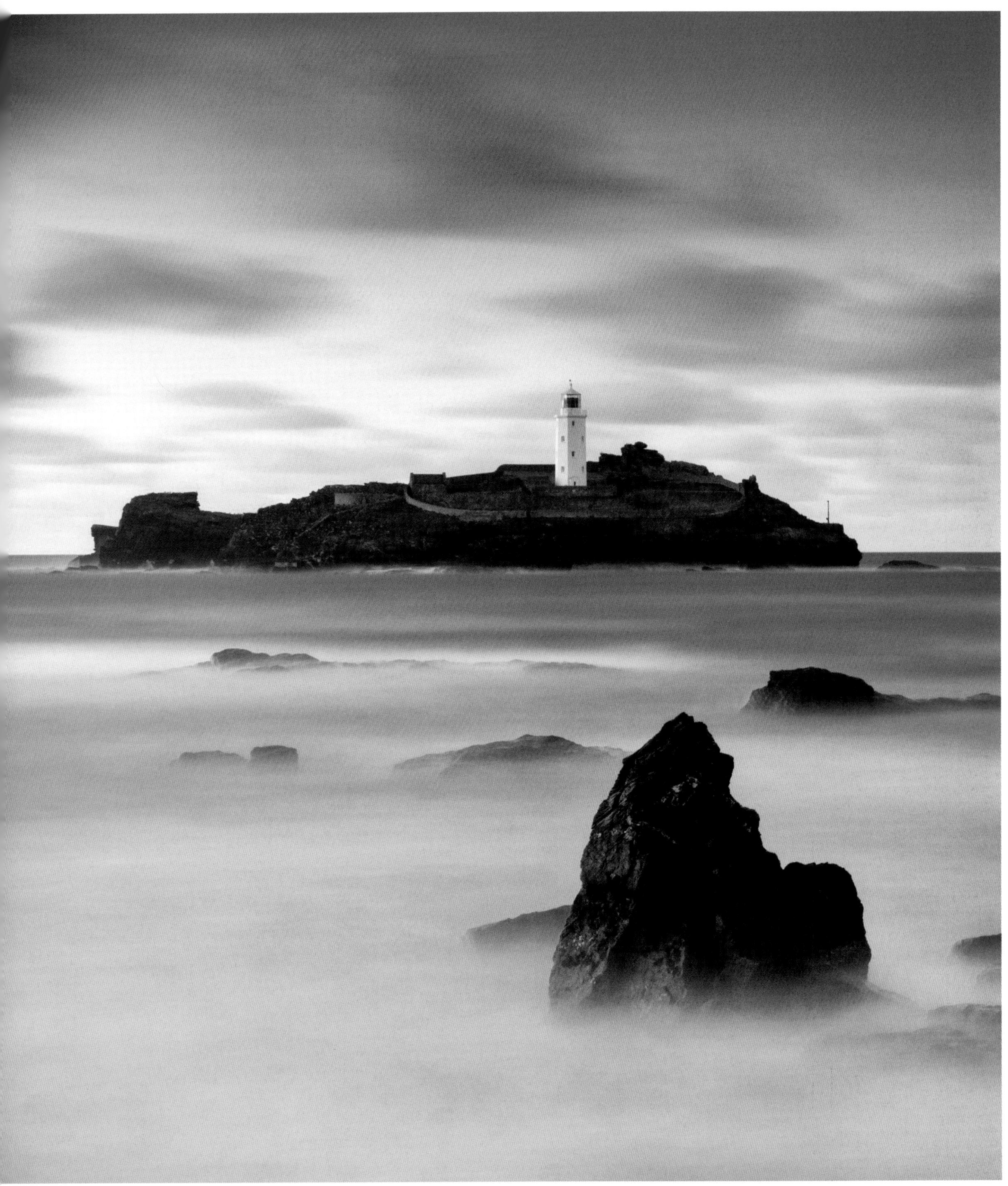

ND graduates

Make bland skies a thing of the past by using a Neutral Density graduate filter

HOW MANY TIMES have you composed a great shot with a dramatic sky only to discover that when you check the picture you've taken the landscape looks fine, but the sky is overexposed and washed out?

Naïve photographers shrug their shoulders and think, 'Oh, I'll rescue that later', which is fine if there's something to rescue. But if the sky's so overexposed that no detail has been recorded, there won't be. More experienced shooters take two photographs of the scene – one exposing for the sky, the other for the landscape – then combine them in Photoshop. This method works well, but does mean more time in front of a computer than a camera. The quickest and easiest solution is to use an ND grad filter.

ND grads are grey on the top half – that's the Neutral Density part – and clear on the bottom half. The idea is that the grey part of the grad tones down the brightness of the sky so that when you expose for the landscape, the sky is also correctly exposed, instead of being completely blown out.

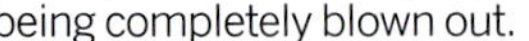

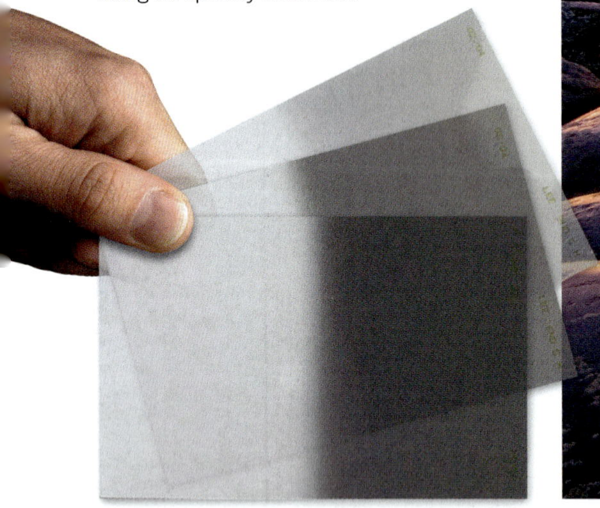

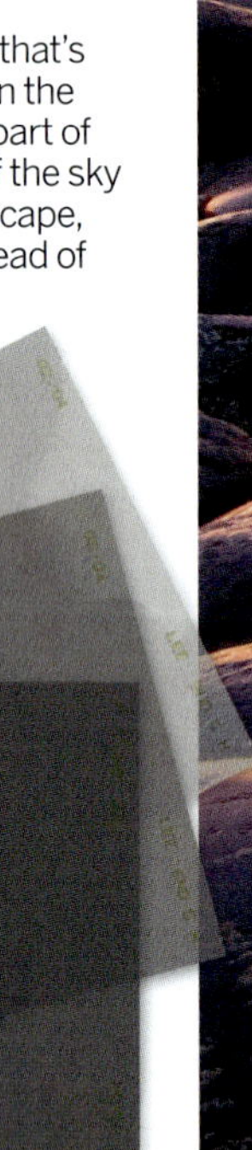

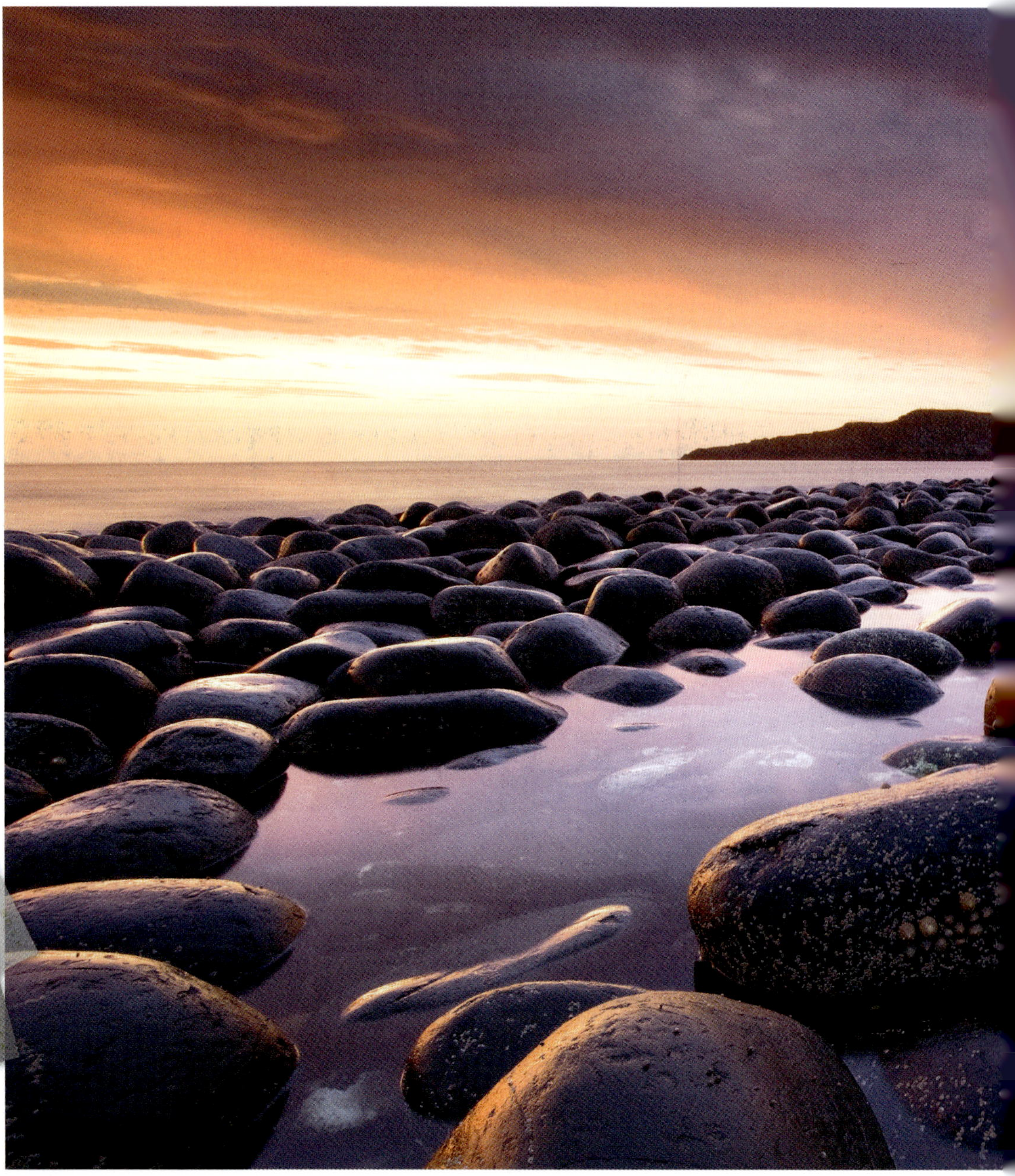

ND grads & exposure

Before multi-zone metering was introduced, exposure readings had to be taken with a light meter and set manually on the camera before attaching an ND grad to the lens in order to avoid getting an overexposed image. Metering systems these days are much more intelligent; now you can compose your shot, align the grad ready for use and meter with it on the lens. The reason for this is that a multi-zone metering pattern takes a number of exposure readings from different parts of the image area, therefore the darkness of the filter doesn't influence the final exposure in a negative way. In fact, it helps your camera obtain an accurate reading, as when an ND grad is fitted, the Neutral Density part of the filter darkens the sky area so that the contrast between the sky and foreground is reduced. Hey presto: a perfectly exposed landscape.

Technique watch!

Choose the right density

To produce a convincing result you need to choose the right density of ND grad. Fortunately, making the right choice isn't difficult as there are only three main densities to choose from: 0.3, 0.6 and 0.9, which reduce the brightness of the sky by one, two and three stops respectively. Some manufacturers also produce a 1.2ND grad, which tones down the sky by four stops. The weakest, 0.3ND, is only of use when you need a very subtle effect, while the stronger 0.9ND is mainly used at dawn and dusk when the sky's really bright but there's no direct light on the landscape. That just leaves the 0.6ND grad, which is the best choice for general use. If in doubt, take a test shot with a 0.6ND grad, check the image on your camera's preview screen, then switch to either a 0.3ND or, more likely, a 0.9ND, if the effect isn't right.

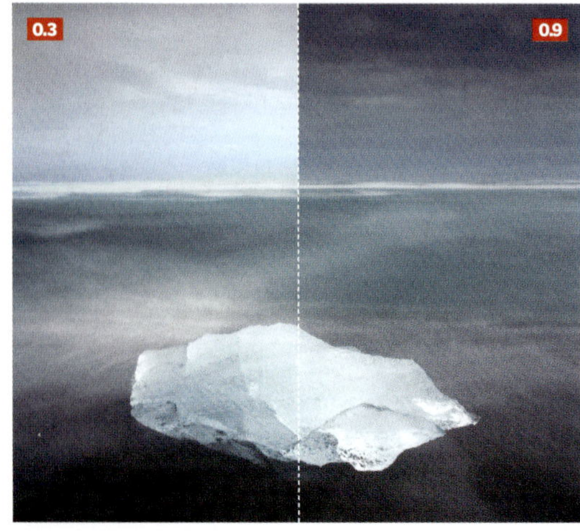

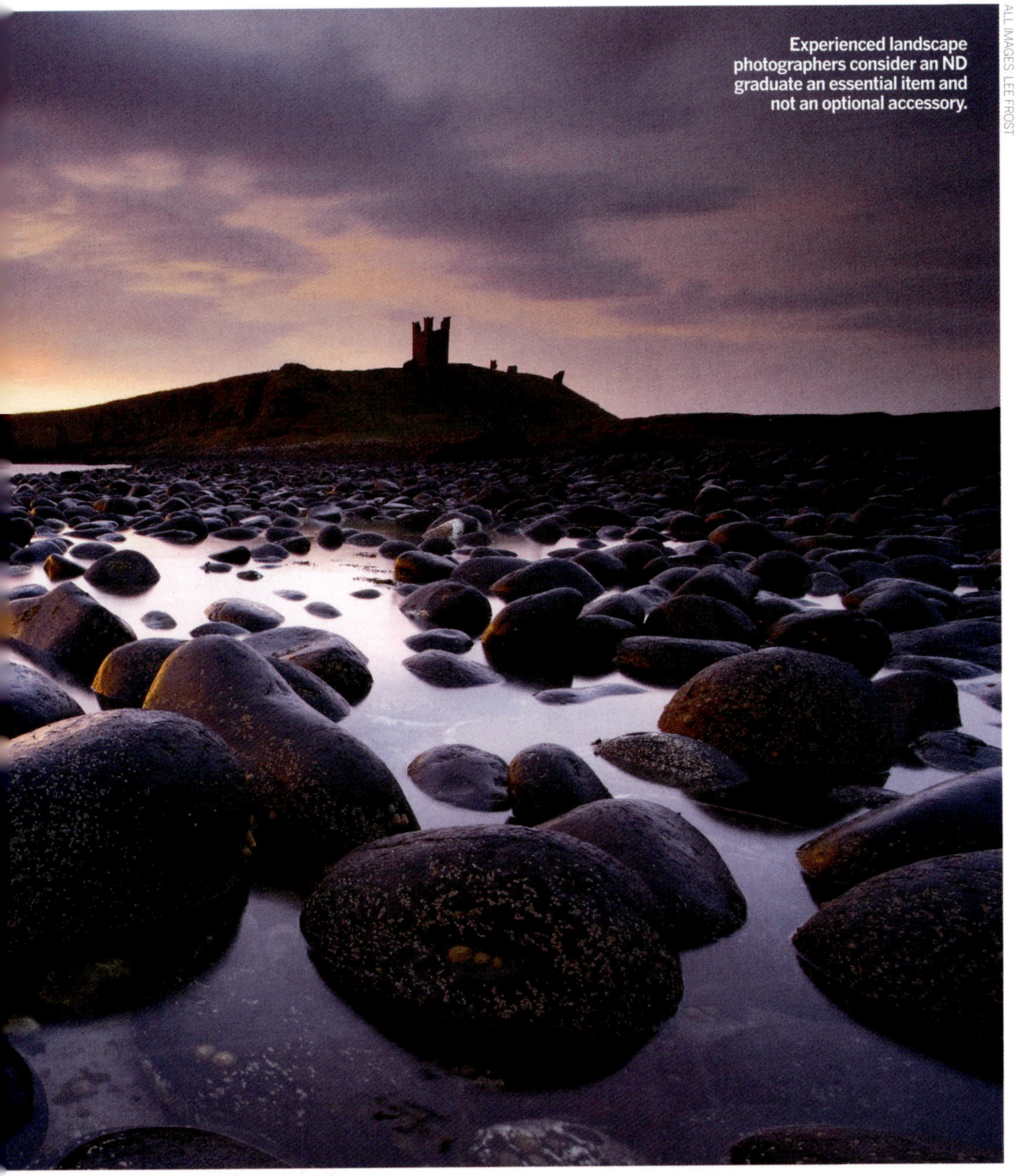

Experienced landscape photographers consider an ND graduate an essential item and not an optional accessory.

ALL IMAGES: LEE FROST

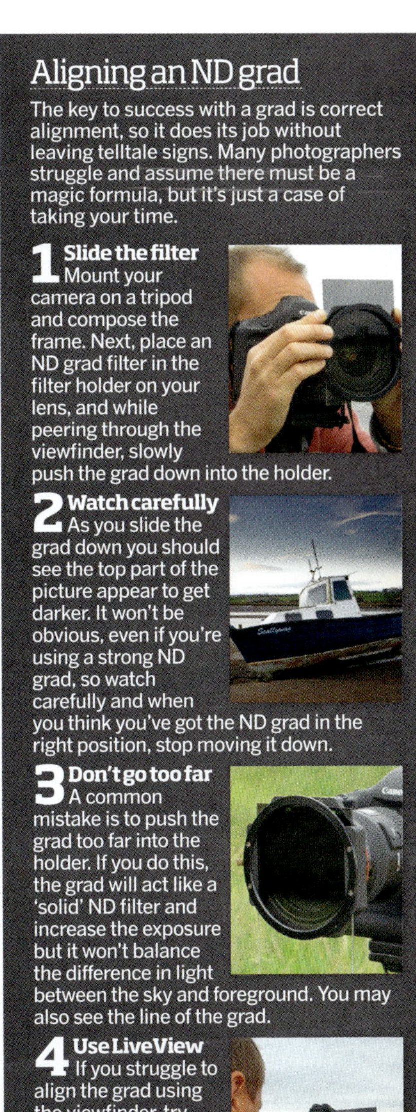

Aligning an ND grad

The key to success with a grad is correct alignment, so it does its job without leaving telltale signs. Many photographers struggle and assume there must be a magic formula, but it's just a case of taking your time.

1 Slide the filter Mount your camera on a tripod and compose the frame. Next, place an ND grad filter in the filter holder on your lens, and while peering through the viewfinder, slowly push the grad down into the holder.

2 Watch carefully As you slide the grad down you should see the top part of the picture appear to get darker. It won't be obvious, even if you're using a strong ND grad, so watch carefully and when you think you've got the ND grad in the right position, stop moving it down.

3 Don't go too far A common mistake is to push the grad too far into the holder. If you do this, the grad will act like a 'solid' ND filter and increase the exposure but it won't balance the difference in light between the sky and foreground. You may also see the line of the grad.

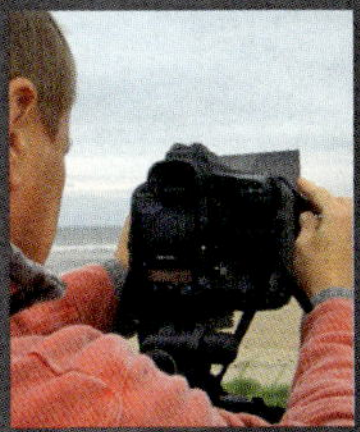

4 Use LiveView If you struggle to align the grad using the viewfinder, try using LiveView. You may find it simpler to do this as you're seeing the exact effect the filter is having on the image, making it easier to accurately align it.

Technique watch!

Hard or soft grads?

There are two types of ND grad: Hard and Soft. This refers to the way in which the Neutral Density (grey) part of the filter graduates down to clear: with hard grads the change is quite sudden; whereas with soft grads it's gentle. Newcomers to ND grads assume that soft grads are easier to use because if you align them incorrectly it's less likely that you'll see the line of the grad in your picture. However, hard grads are also quite forgiving and give a more defined effect, making them the best choice.

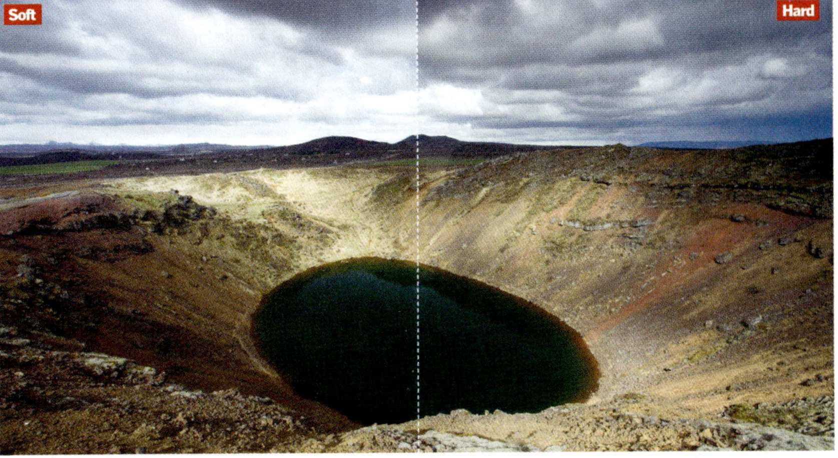

Polariser

A circular polariser will be your best friend, boosting colour impact and reducing reflections

WHEN LIGHT STRIKES a surface, some of the rays scatter in all directions thus becoming polarised, causing reflections and glare that reduces colour saturation – particularly on shiny surfaces such as paintwork and foliage. Polarising filters prevent this from happening by only allowing light rays to enter your lens that are travelling from one direction – effectively blocking out polarised light. Doing this offers three distinct advantages for landscape photography.

The most obvious benefit is that blue sky is deepened, because it contains a lot of polarised light. Using a polariser allows you to add visual impact to images by providing a strong, punchy blue backdrop. Another benefit is that glare on non-metallic surfaces is reduced, so the colours in a scene appear richer and more saturated. The third advantage to using polarisers is that reflections are eliminated, so you can see through windows and into rivers.

Using a polariser is easy because you can see the effect it has simply by rotating it slowly in its mount on your lens while looking through the camera's viewfinder. Blue sky goes darker and white clouds stand out, reflections come and go, glare disappears. When you're happy with what you see, simply stop rotating and fire. To get the best possible results, however, you should also bear in mind certain factors.

Although polarisers generally work best in bright, sunny weather when there's more polarised light around, they can be used in dull, overcast conditions, too, in order to remove glare and reflections. Autumnal woodland scenes usually look much better if you shoot them through a polariser, as glare is reduced, so the rich colours of the foliage really come through.

When using a polariser to deepen blue sky, keep the sun at a right angle to the camera so you're aiming towards the area of sky where maximum polarisation occurs. That way, you'll get the strongest effect. If the sun is behind you, or you're shooting into the sun, a polariser won't make much difference. Polarisation in the sky also tends to be better when the sun is low in the sky – so early morning and evening give better results than in the middle of the day.

Polarisation is uneven across the sky, so take care when using ultra wide-angle lenses or zooms with a focal length wider than 24mm (16mm on APS-C sensors) as the sky in your images may record darker on one side than the other: the effect can look very odd. This can be corrected in Photoshop later, but it's tricky. You should also note that glare will only be removed from non-metallic surfaces such as paintwork, foliage and plastic. To remove reflections from surfaces such as water and glass, the angle between the reflective surface and the lens axis must be around 30°. You can find this by making slight adjustments to your position then rotating the polariser to see what happens.

Finally, polarising filters can give your pictures a slight blue colour cast when used in bright, sunny weather. To remove this, either adjust your camera's White Balance setting or correct the cast when you process the Raw file on your computer.

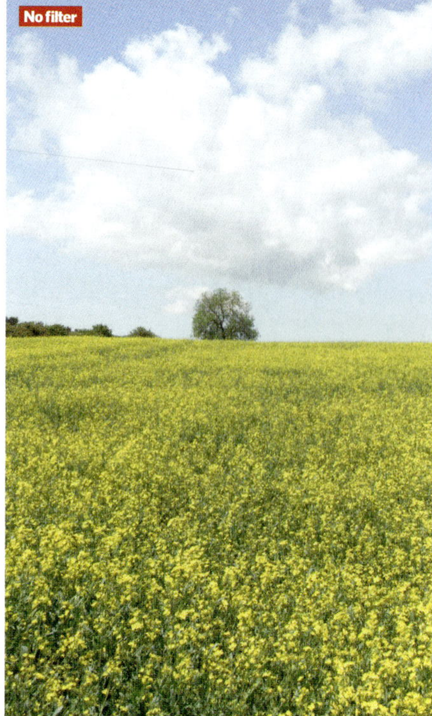

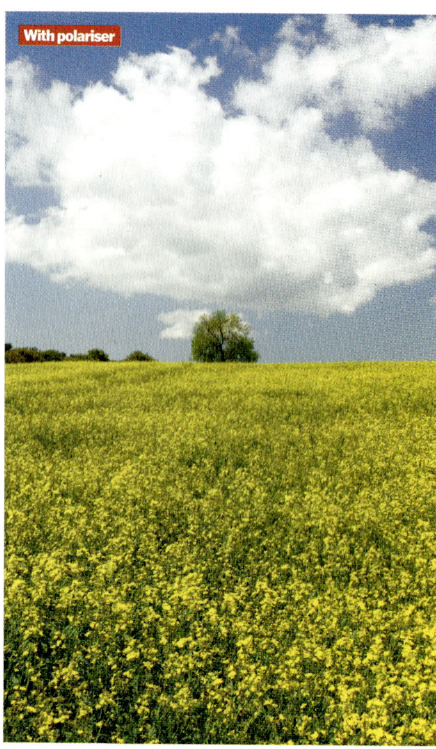

Technique watch!

Circular or linear?
There are two types of polarising filters available: linear and circular. Avoid linear. You need to use a circular polariser with your digital camera as linear polarisers are used on certain older non-autofocus film SLRs. Both types do exactly the same job, but a circular polariser is manufactured differently to ensure correct exposure when used with autofocus DSLRs and CSCs.

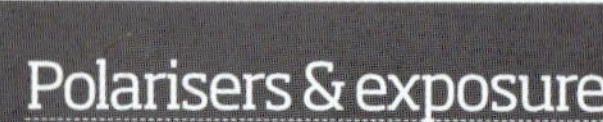

Polarisers & exposure

When you use a polariser, it reduces the light entering your lens by two stops. This means if you have an exposure of 1/125sec at f/11 without a polarising filter in place, the exposure would drop to 1/30sec at f/11 once you fitted it. Your camera accounts for this light loss automatically, so you don't need to compensate, but you need to be aware of it because the shutter speed can easily become very slow when using a polariser – even in bright sunlight – so the risk of camera shake is increased. That said, this light loss can be a benefit when you want to use a slower shutter speed, as the polariser acts like a 0.6-density ND filter (covered overleaf). When shooting waterfalls, for example, the polariser not only gives you a slower shutter speed to blur the water, but also removes reflections from water and glare from wet rocks and foliage, giving a better result.

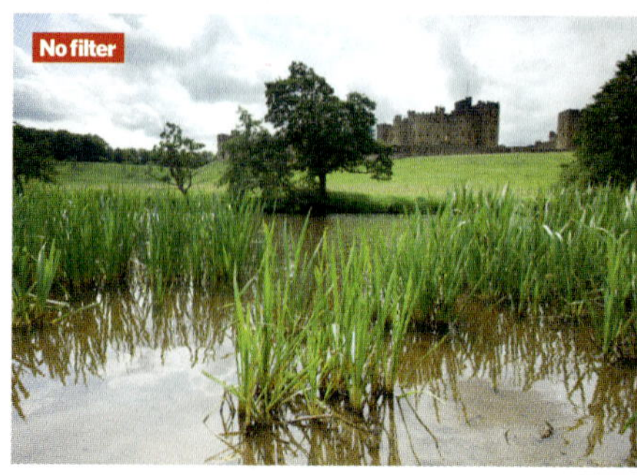

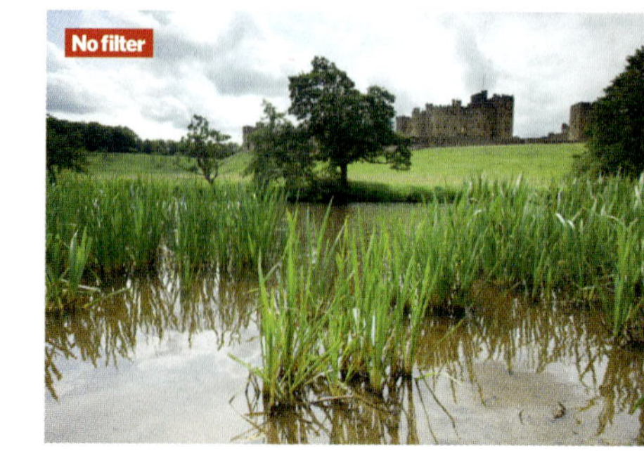

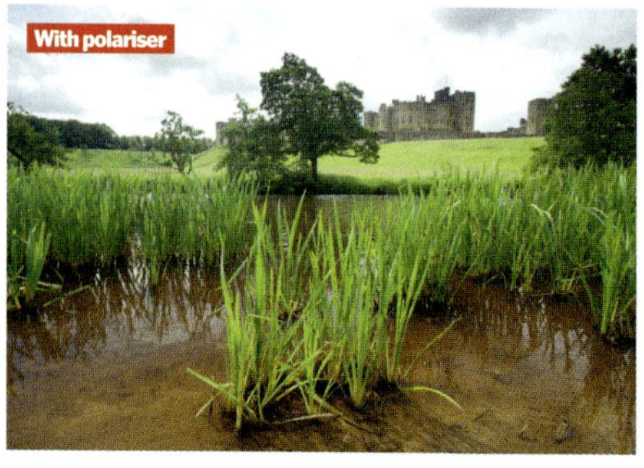

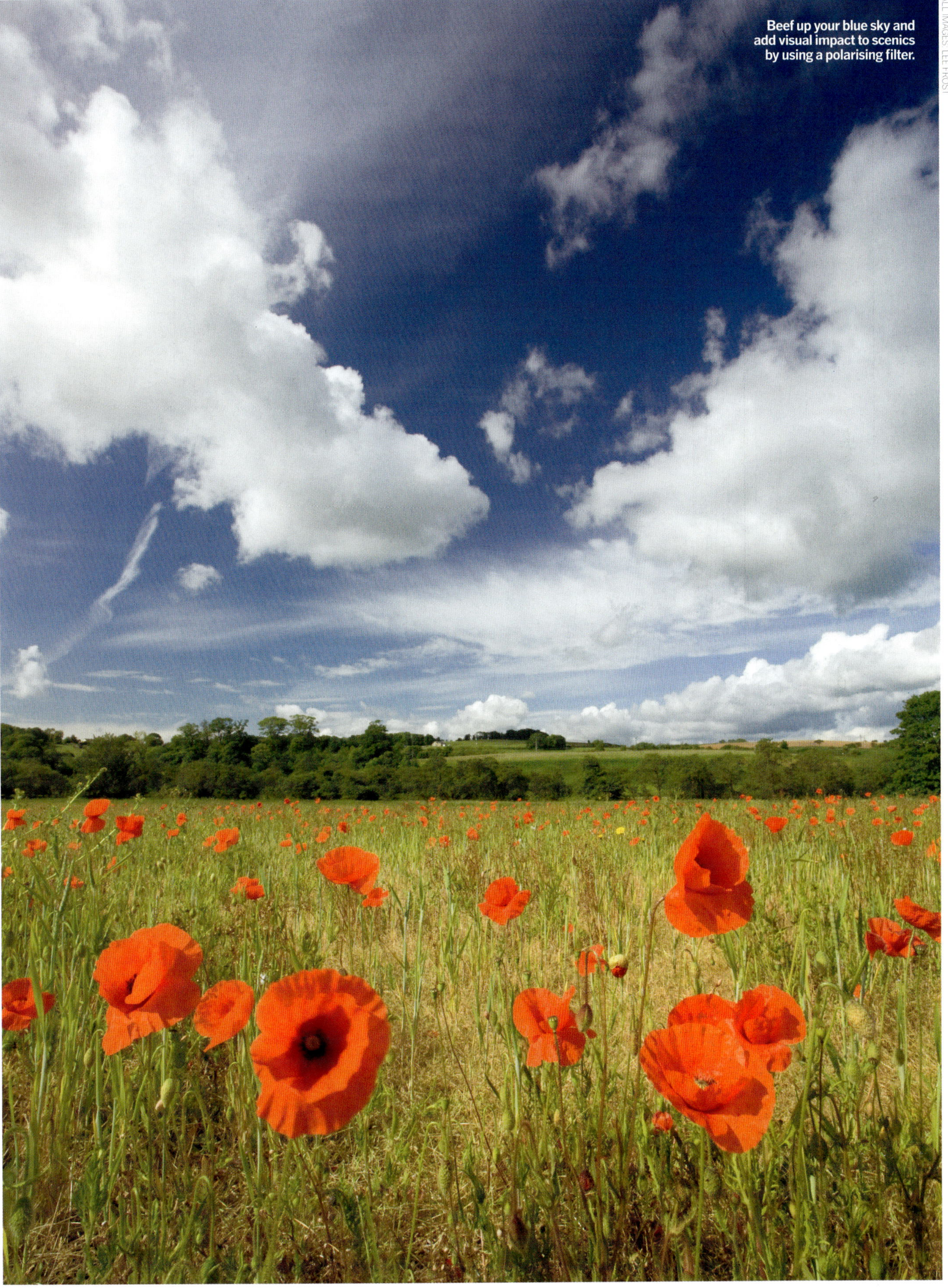

Beef up your blue sky and add visual impact to scenics by using a polarising filter.

Neutral Density (ND) filters

Lengthen exposure times for creative effects using a Neutral Density filter

ND FILTERS ARE SPECIALLY made to reduce the amount of light entering your lens without changing the colour balance – hence the name Neutral Density. They do a similar job to ND grad filters, but instead of affecting just part of the image (usually the sky with ND grads), they have a uniform effect on the whole image.

ND filters are mainly used to increase the exposure required for an image, so you can use a slower shutter speed to record motion. The classic subject that they're used for is waterfalls, recording the moving water as a graceful blur. But they can be used to introduce or increase motion in all kinds of subjects – crowds of commuters pouring off a train, traffic moving along busy roads, trees blowing in the wind, waves washing over rocks and so on. They're ideal for use in bright conditions when the lowest ISO rating and smallest aperture aren't enough to give you the slow shutter speed that you desire.

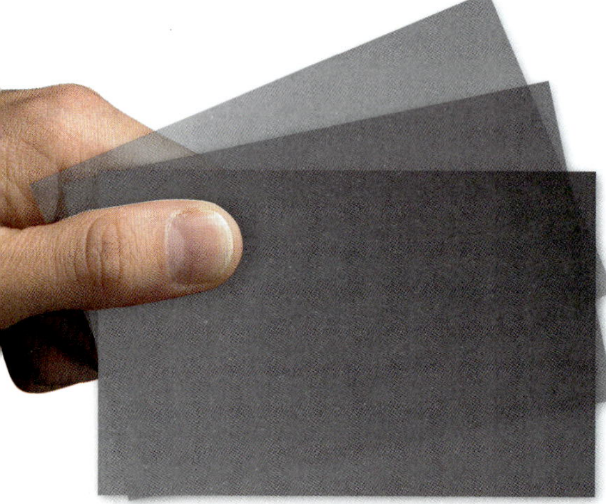

Exposure chart

If you're using weaker ND filters, up to a 1.2 density, your camera's TTL metering will be able to give accurate exposure readings with the filter on the lens. Once density goes beyond 1.2, however, you may find that underexposure occurs because the filter density fools the camera's metering.

To avoid exposure error, take a meter reading without the ND filter on the lens, then calculate the required exposure with it in place and set the exposure on your camera manually. If you have an iPhone there's a useful app called ND Calc that will do this for you. Alternatively, refer to the table below. Once the required exposure goes beyond 30 seconds you will have to set your camera to its Bulb (B) mode and time the exposure using the timer on the camera or smartphone, a remote release, your wristwatch or by counting elephants – you decide! We'd recommend that you photocopy and cut out the exposure chart below and keep it along with your ND filter for easy reference.

No filter	With 0.6ND	With 0.9ND	With 1.2ND
1/500sec	1/125sec	1/60sec	1/30sec
1/250sec	**1/60sec**	**1/30sec**	**1/15sec**
1/125sec	1/30sec	1/15sec	1/8sec
1/60sec	**1/15sec**	**1/8sec**	**1/4sec**
1/30sec	1/8sec	1/4sec	1/2sec
1/15sec	**1/4sec**	**1/2sec**	**One second**
1/8sec	1/2sec	One second	Two seconds
1/4sec	**One second**	**Two seconds**	**Four seconds**
1/2sec	Two seconds	Four seconds	Eight seconds
One second	**Four seconds**	**Eight seconds**	**16 seconds**
Two seconds	Eight seconds	16 seconds	32 seconds
Three seconds	**16 seconds**	**32 seconds**	**One minute**
Four seconds	32 seconds	One minute	Two minutes

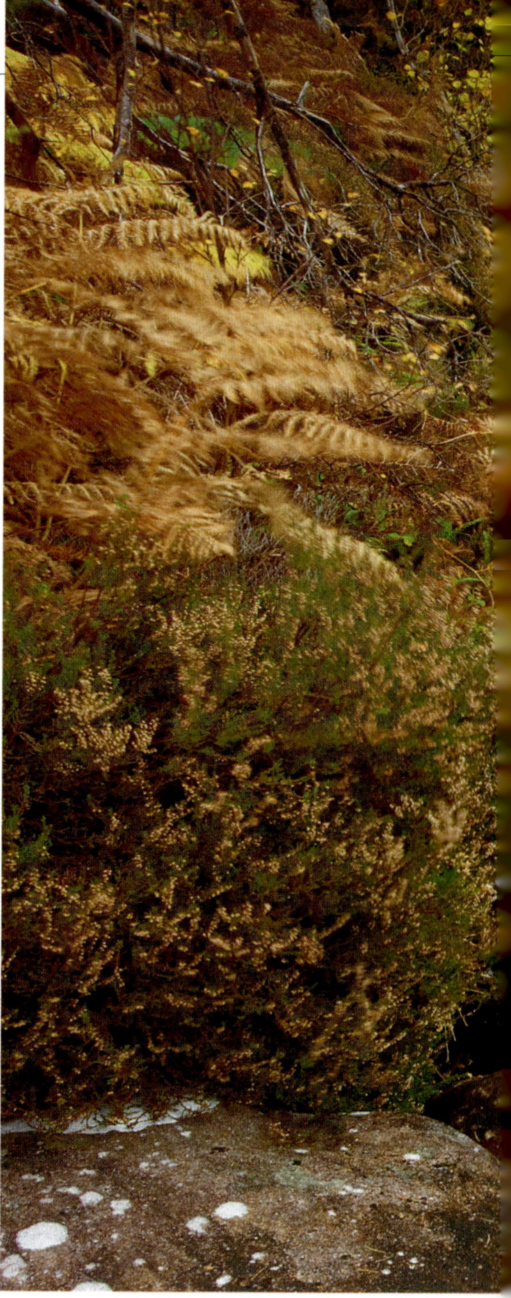

Technique watch!

Different densities

The amount of exposure increase an ND filter requires depends on its density. The weakest ND worth bothering with is a 0.6ND (4x), which requires a two-stop exposure increase. A polariser also requires an exposure increase of two stops and so can be used like a 0.6ND filter. Next up is a 0.9ND (8x), which requires a three-stop exposure increase, followed by a 1.2ND (16x) that requires a four-stop increase. This is where the density of conventional ND filters end, though you can combine two or more for a cumulative effect – a 0.6ND and a 0.9ND together will require a five-stop exposure increase, for example.

The alternative is to use a more extreme ND filter, with a density of 1.8 (six stops) or more. These filters were originally designed for photographing industrial processes that involved extreme brightness but are now popular with photographers as they allow exposures in daylight of several minutes. Turn over for our favourite: the 3.0ND, which requires an exposure increase of ten stops – that's 1,000x more than the unfiltered exposure!

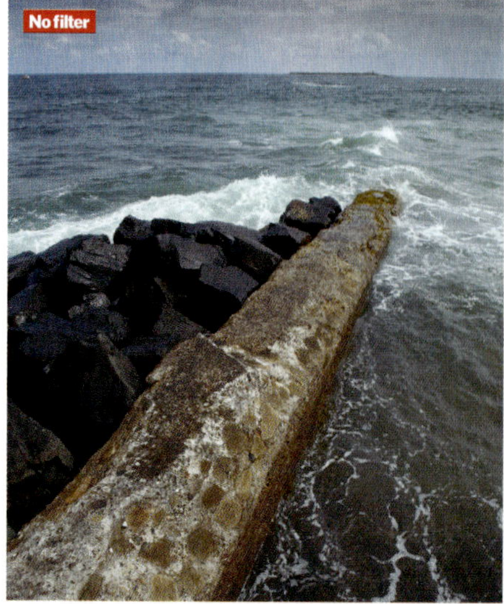
No filter

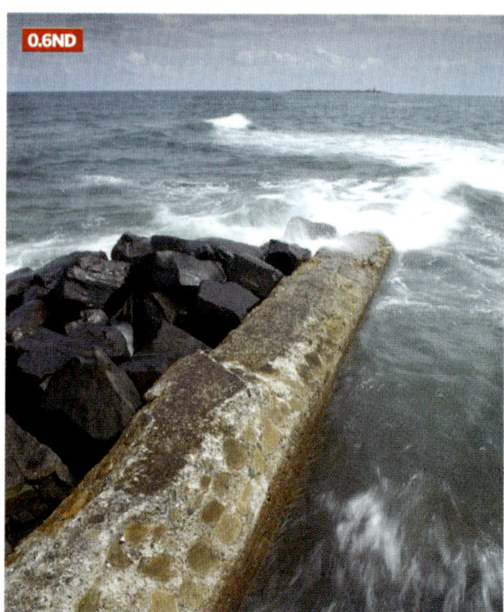
0.6ND

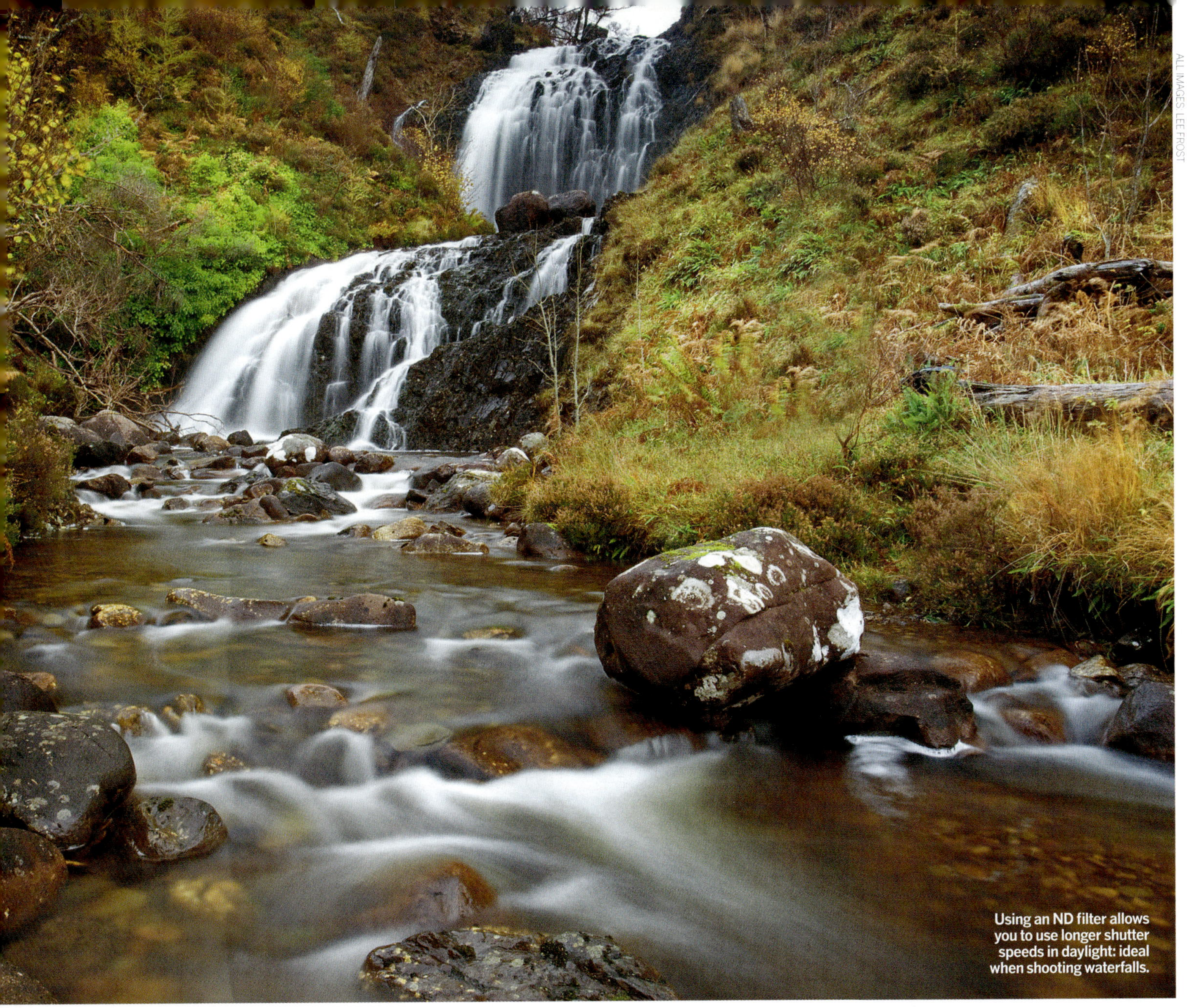

ALL IMAGES: LEE FROST

Using an ND filter allows you to use longer shutter speeds in daylight: ideal when shooting waterfalls.

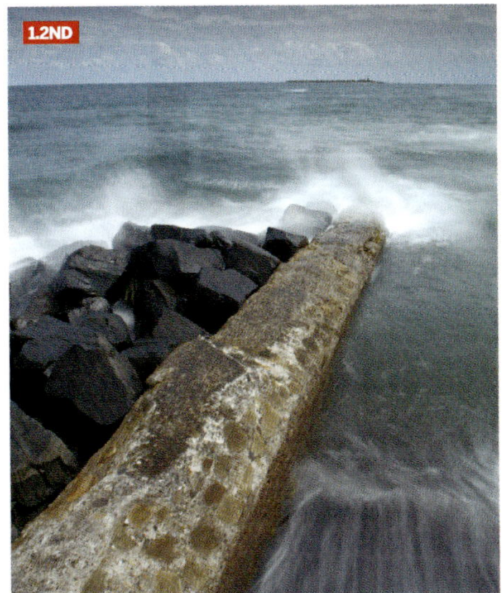

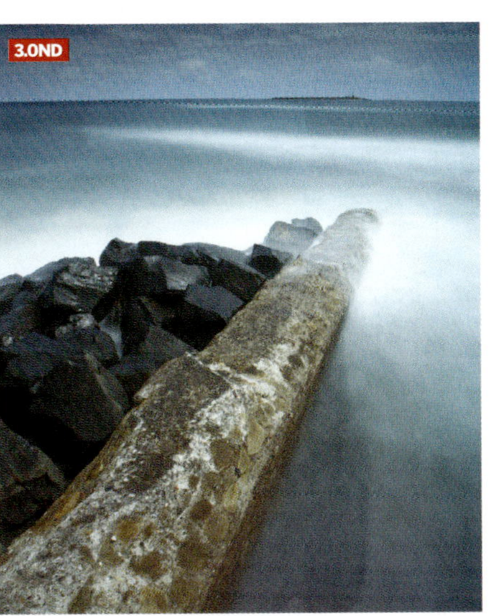

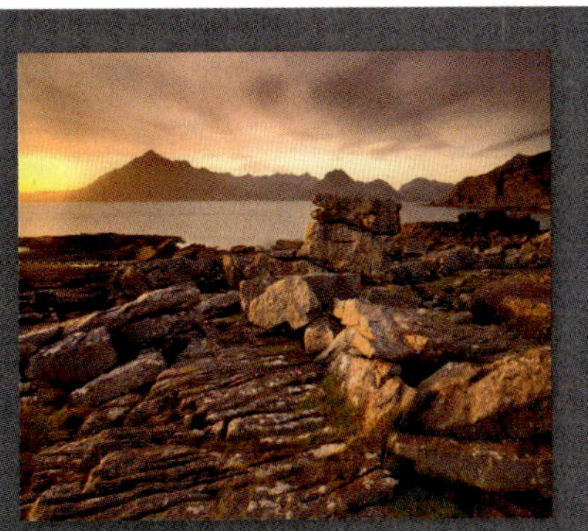

Colour casts

While ND filters should be neutral, once you combine them for higher density (and a longer exposure), you'll see that colour casts appear. This is most noticeable with ten-stop ND filters – the B+W 3.0 adds a very warm colour cast while the Lee Big Stopper adds a cool blue cast. These can enhance the look of the image, but if you prefer, you can adjust the colour temperature when you process the Raw file.

Ten-stop ND filters

Use a ten-stop ND filter and you'll find you can create colour and black & white fine-art landscapes with ease

THE FIRST THING YOU'LL NOTICE when using a ten-stop ND filter is that it's so dense, you can't see through it. In bright sunlight you might just make out a faint image through the viewfinder, but its brightness is 1,000x less than if you didn't have the ten-stop ND in place. To take a photograph you must therefore mount your camera on a tripod, compose the scene, set focus to manual (as AF won't work through it), align your ND grad in its holder if you're using one, then finally position the ten-stop ND. Some of the latest cameras have LiveView that's sensitive enough to see through a ten-stop ND, so if you need to adjust the composition or move the camera and shoot from a different spot, you may be able to do so without taking the ten-stop ND filter off. For most of us, though, removing the filter to see through the viewfinder is unavoidable. That's why a slot-in filter like Lee Filter's Big Stopper or HiTech's Pro Stop is more versatile than the B+W screw-in filter – you can simply remove it from its holder and leave everything else in place, whereas the B+W has to be unscrewed from the lens.

The longest exposure you can achieve using your camera's programmed shutter speed range is 30 seconds. More often than not, you'll be using exposures much longer than that with the ten-stopper, so you'll need to set your camera to Bulb (B) mode in order to keep the shutter open. Trying to keep exposures under 30 seconds for convenience, by opening up the aperture or increasing the ISO rating, is completely defeating the object because you'll get the best effects by using exposures of several minutes.

In terms of subject matter, any scene containing moving elements is ideal. The sky is an obvious candidate: on a windy day, clouds are transformed into ghostly streaks as they drift overhead, and you won't know quite how they're going to record until the exposure ends and you can review the shot. Trees and grass swaying in the breeze also take on a totally different appearance when exposed for several minutes, adding a strong sense of motion to an image.

Coastal scenes are perhaps the most effective subjects for the ten-stop ND. The sea is constantly moving, so over the course of a few minutes any texture in its surface is lost and it takes on a smooth, milky appearance that contrasts well with static elements such as piers, lighthouses, headlands, jetties and rocks. Clouds work well, too, rendering as streaks in the sky. Or for something completely different, try shooting urban scenes with a ten-stop ND. Anything moving through the scene while the shutter is open – people and traffic mostly – won't record. This means you can capture something that we never see with the naked eye – busy streets completely deserted!

Wide-angle lenses are more effective than telephotos when using a ten-stop ND because you can emphasise the sky and the foreground, which is where most of the motion is recorded. Move in close to a static feature in the foreground and contrast it with moving water, or get down low with a wide lens so you're looking up at the sky.

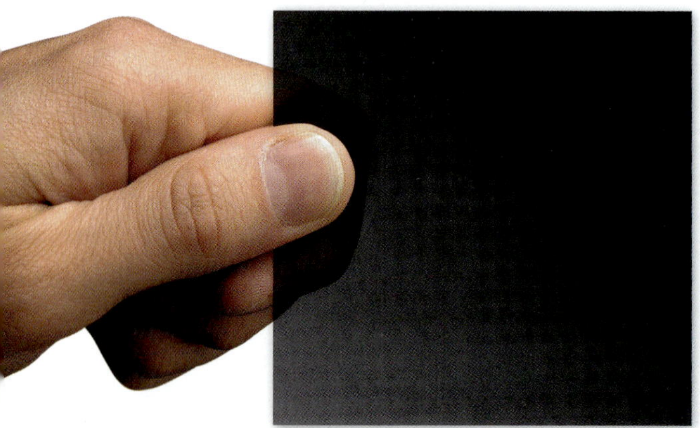

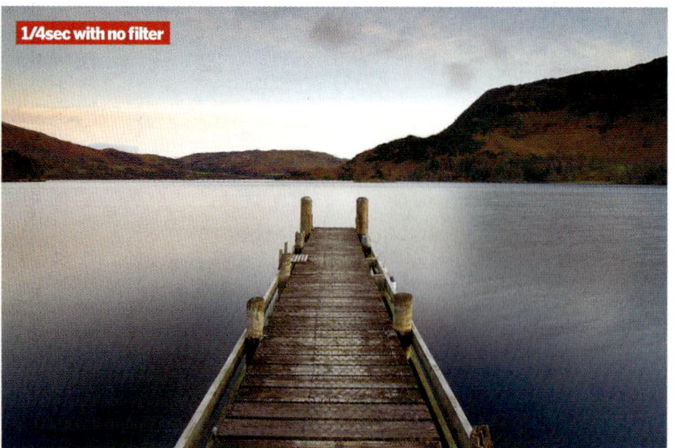
1/4sec with no filter

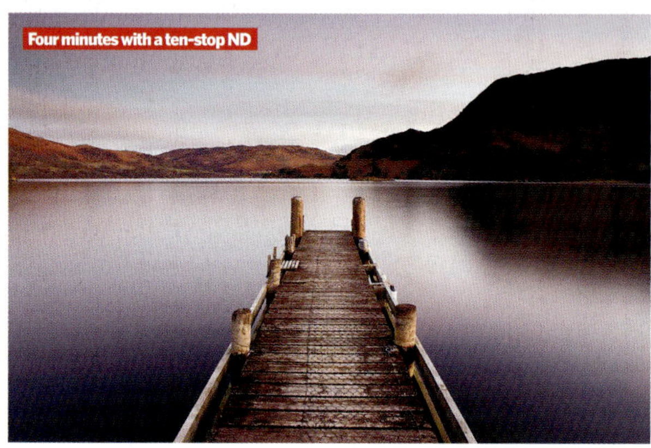
Four minutes with a ten-stop ND

Bright sunshine gives the least effective light for ten-stop shots as it's harsh and flat, plus the higher light levels mean you won't be able to achieve really long exposures – even with your lens stopped right down and the ISO rating at its minimum setting. Dawn and dusk, on the other hand, are perfect for creating atmospheric images, along with early morning and evening when the sun's low in the sky and the light is warm. The B+W 3.0 ten-stop ND has a warm colour cast, which is ideal for enhancing shots taken at either end of the day. Stormy weather can produce dramatic results, too, as there's more movement in the sky and sea, while on overcast days the soft light and gentle tones result in simple, graphic images.

Although you'll be shooting in colour, ten-stop shots look amazing in black & white – especially if you're not keen on the filter's inherent colour cast. To maximise the impact and drama, when converting your picture to monochrome, treat the sky and the rest of the scene as separate elements by adjusting their tonality separately, using tools such as Levels and Curves. The end result may look nothing like the original scene, but that doesn't matter because as soon as you put a ten-stop ND filter on your lens, you're taking a step back from reality anyway.

Exposure chart

The chart on the right reveals the increase of exposure times when using a ten-stop ND filter. It's a key reason why you're recommended not to use the Long Exposure Noise Reduction system on your camera, as this function takes the same amount of time as the exposure. For instance, when you shoot a two-minute exposure, you'll need to wait another couple more minutes for the image to write and be viewable on the LCD monitor. We'd suggest you switch Noise Reduction off and control noise in post-production.

Unfiltered	3.0ND (Ten-stop)
1/500sec	Two seconds
1/250sec	**Four seconds**
1/125sec	Eight seconds
1/60sec	**16 seconds**
1/30sec	32 seconds
1/15sec	**One minute**
1/8sec	Two minutes
1/4sec	**Four minutes**
1/2sec	Eight minutes
One second	**16 minutes**
Two seconds	32 minutes
Three seconds	**48 minutes**
Four seconds	One hour

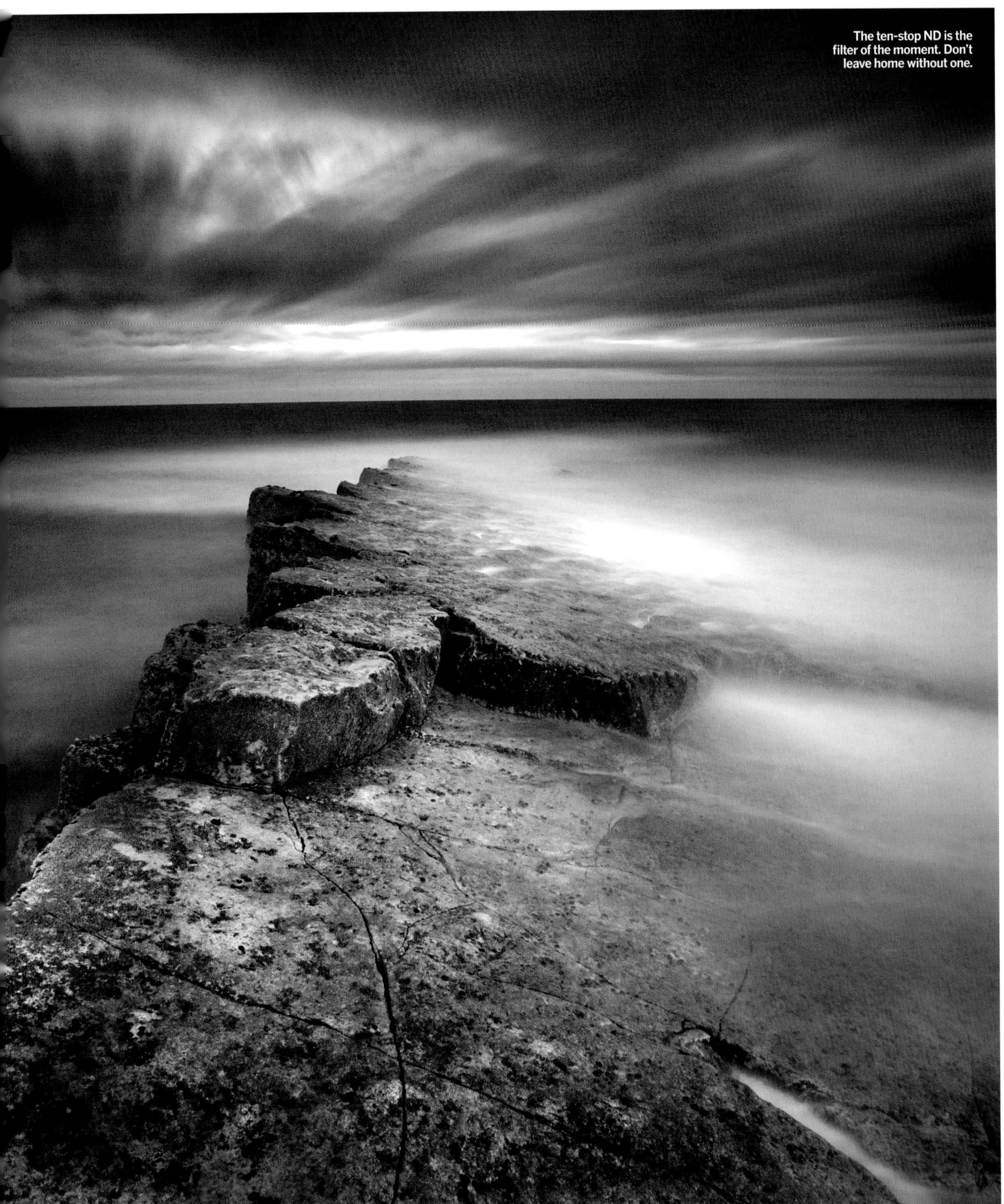

The ten-stop ND is the filter of the moment. Don't leave home without one.

Filter brands

There aren't too many brands of filter but the choice they offer can be confusing. We've highlighted the tried-and-tested filter brands that offer great value as well as high-quality products

B+W

www.daymen.co.uk

This prestigious German brand is renowned for producing screw-in filters with optimum quality, both in terms of the metal filter ring and the manufacturing process behind its premium, optical glass. It's a very popular brand with pros but it does cost around twice as much as other brands. If you need the ultimate in quality from a screw-in filter, then B+W is the option for you, otherwise, Hoya is a great choice. One string in its bow is the ten-stop ND filter, which has proven incredibly popular for daytime long-exposure photography.

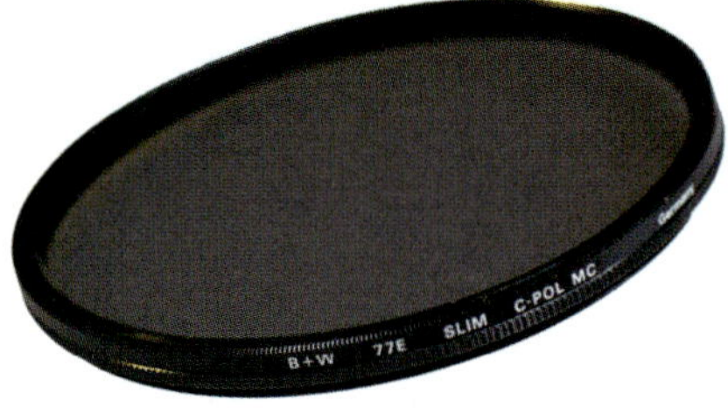

Hoya

www.intro2020.co.uk

Hoya produces around 60% of the world's optical glass, so you can be assured it offers excellent quality and value. Hoya offers the most extensive range of any screw-in filter system, with literally every type of filter you can imagine. What's more, for popular types of filter such as polariser or UV, it has a number of options to suit all levels of photographer, from amateur through to pro. Its filters boast several cutting-edge technologies, for instance, the HD series boasts hardened glass and several layers of multi-coating to improve contrast and reduce flare, while the Pro 1 Digital series has been exclusively designed for use with digital cameras. The extensive Super HMC series covers the majority of filter types and provides fantastic quality at a great price. It's worth downloading Hoya's filter brochure to get a better idea of the full range of filters on offer.

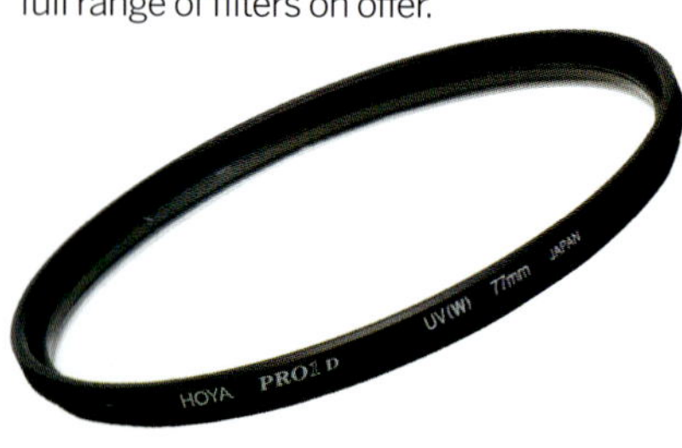

Cokin

www.intro2020.co.uk

For many photographers over the decades, the search for high-quality and affordable slot-in filters started and ended with Cokin. This isn't a surprise as this manufacturer was the innovator of creative filters for amateur photographers and has led the way ever since.

Cokin offers four filter sizes: 67mm (A-series); 84mm (P-series); 100mm (Z-Pro); and 130mm (X-Pro) . The A-series is aimed more for use with compacts or camcorders, so the P-series is the best introductory option. If you use wide-angle lenses with a focal length wider than 28mm, you should consider the Z-Pro range, while the X-Pro is more for medium-format photographers. All the ranges offer plenty of options but the P-series has everything the DSLR photographer may ever need, with over 140 filters to choose from, including polarisers and a variety of ND grads. Filter rings are available for threads up to 82mm and the P-holder accepts up to three filters at a time. The Z-Pro series is a better choice for landscape photographers – in particular those with ultra-wide zooms. Adaptor rings are available from 49mm to 96mm and filters are 100mm square, except for the grads which are 100x150mm.

All the filters are made from CR39 optical resin and deliver high-quality results, and because it's such a popular range, filters are very well priced. The ND Grad Kit for the P-series is affordable at £50 and consists of a Cokin P filter holder, one P121L ND2 Light Grad, one P121M ND4 Grad and one P121S ND8 Soft Grad filter. The Cokin P164 circular polariser is around £50, while for the Z-Pro, you're looking at around £225 for the Z164! Adaptor rings cost in the region of: A-series: £8; P-series: £11; X-Pro: £50; and Z-Pro: £22.

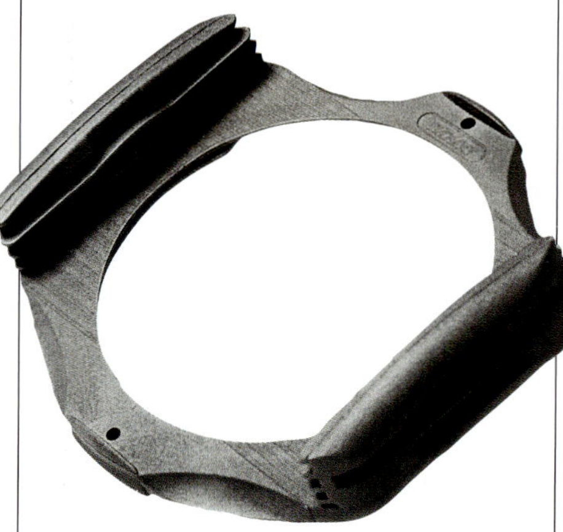

Jessops

www.jessops.com

Its range of screw-in filters may be limited to 20 or so protection and polarising filters, but with prices starting at £20 for a 52mm Skylight or UV, it's a good place to start your filter collection. They're well made too, so you won't have to worry about quality. Most filters are kept in stock in-store as well as being available for home delivery.

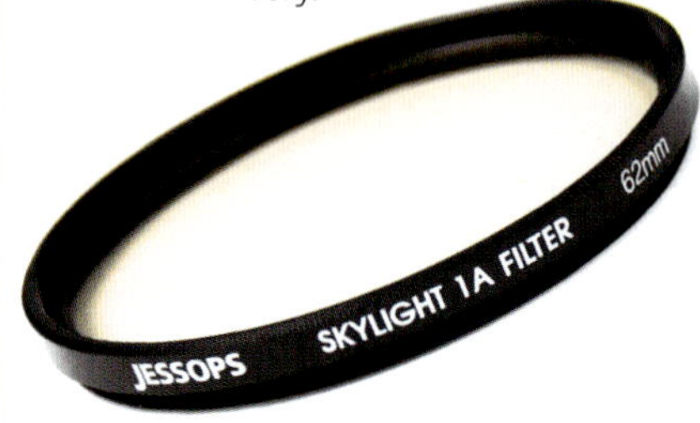

Lee Filters

www.leefilters.com

Lee Filters is the ultimate choice for the discerning photographer. Loved by pros and relished by enthusiasts, Lee Filters are as good as it gets in terms of optical quality, but due to the stringent manufacturing processes involved, expect it to command high prices. Its brilliant 100mm system is the cornerstone of its success, with a high-quality and versatile holder that can be made to your own specification to hold varying numbers of filters. The filters themselves are brilliant quality and are manufactured from a number of materials, including glass, resin and polyester. Various kits are available and we'd recommend the £200 Digital Starter Kit, which comprises an assembled holder, 0.6ND ProGlass ND hard grad, 0.6ND and cleaning cloth, all packed neatly into a pouch. The other kit is the £150 Starter Kit, which includes an assembled filter holder, 0.6ND grad, cleaning cloth, Coral 3 grad and pouch. Its ten-stop 'Big Stopper' ND (around £130) is the best on the market. Adaptor rings from 49mm to 77mm cost £19, 82mm and 86mm are £41, while 93mm, 95mm and 105mm rings are £55. The filter holder (the Foundation Kit) is £55. If you intend making a living from photography and investing in expensive lenses, then these are the filters you should aspire to own.

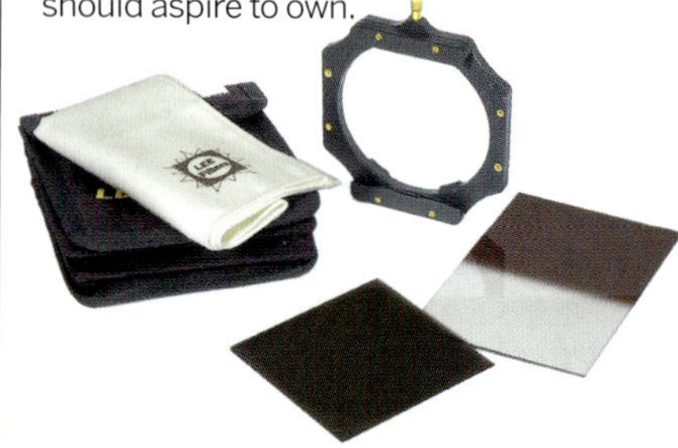

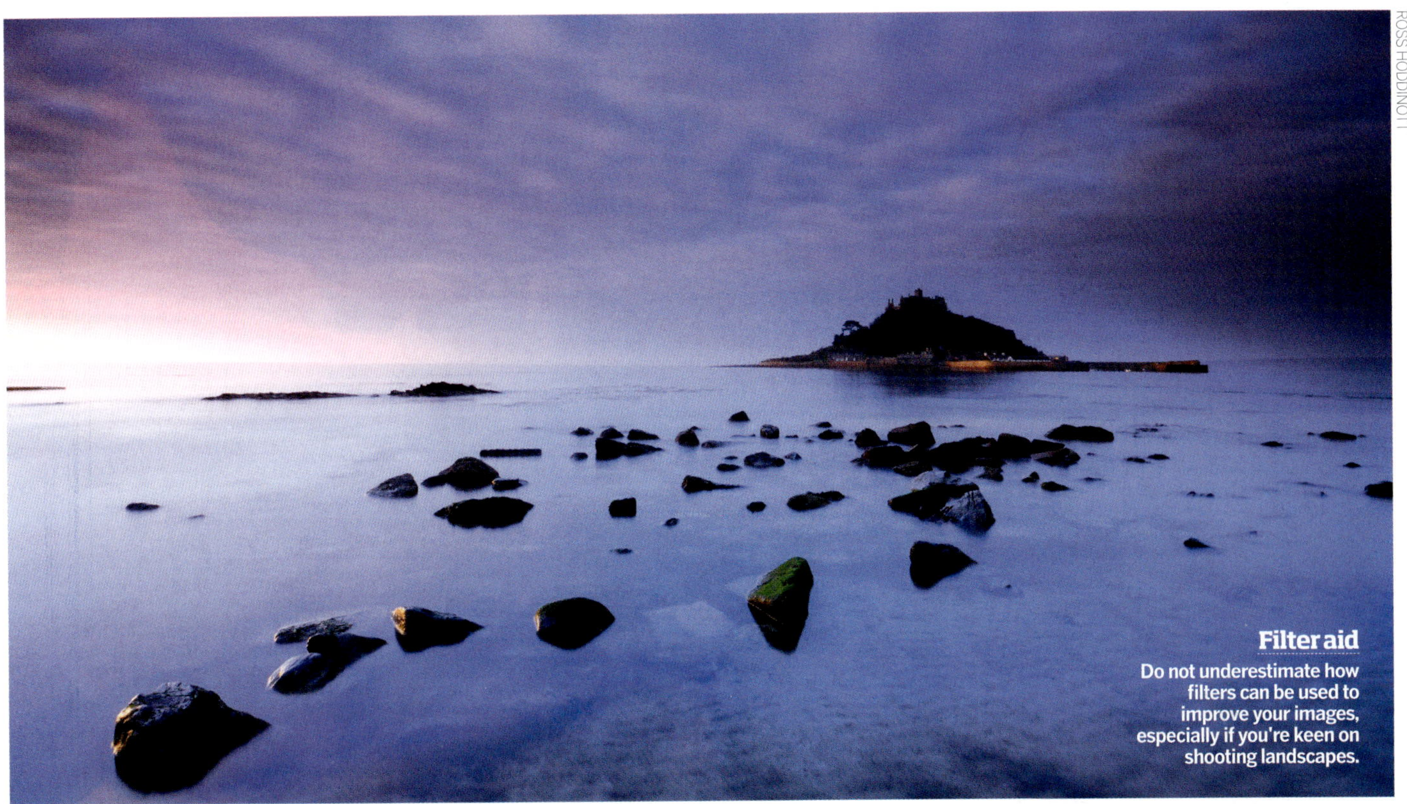
ROSS HODDINOTT

Filter aid
Do not underestimate how filters can be used to improve your images, especially if you're keen on shooting landscapes.

Formatt (Hitech)

www.formatt.co.uk

Formatt makes a range of filters for movies and stills photography. Its Hitech filters are aimed specifically at digital SLR photographers, made from optical resin and are manufactured in the UK to extremely high standards to provide excellent optical quality. The 67mm, 85mm and 100mm filter systems are compatible with other slot-in brands and include an extensive range of graduates. As well as hard- and soft-edged ND grads (from 0.3-1.2), it offers a huge choice of colour grads, as well as the Blender, which graduates the effect through the entire length of the filter. Hitech also boasts the Pro Stop, a ten-stop ND filter that costs only £50 for the 85mm version, or £75 for the 100mm. An ND grad kit with 0.3, 0.6 and 0.9ND grads costs £38 (85mm); £85(100mm) and £111 (100x150mm). The circular polariser costs £133 (85mm) or £139 (100mm). A plastic holder costs under £10 and plastic adaptor rings costs around £5 from 49mm to 77mm.

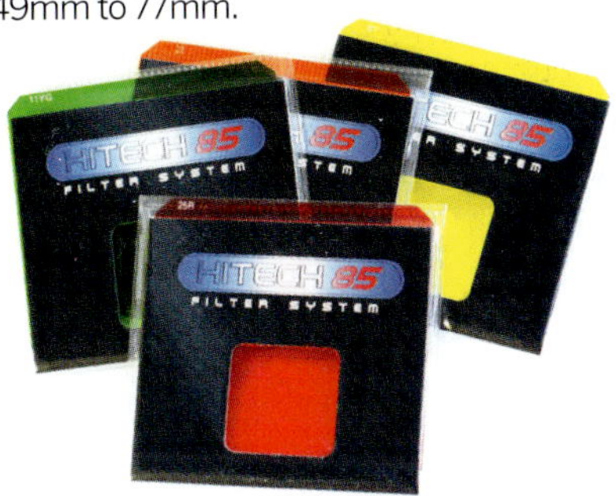

Kood

www.kood-international.com

Kood has its own range, with screw-in filters imported from Japan and slot-in filters manufactured in the UK. The range of screw-in filters isn't large but includes polarisers, protection and close-up filters, as well as various special-effect items such as starburst and colour correction filters. Kood also has a good range of stepping rings, too. Kood offers four sizes of slot-in filters – 67mm, 84mm, 100mm and 130mm – so its filters are compatible with all the major slot-in brands. Made from CR39 optical resin, they offer decent quality and are a good budget buy. Kood isn't available from all high-street outlets, so visit its website for your nearest stockist. Kood's Circular Polariser and ND grads in sizes 84mm to 130mm cost between £25 and £35, and can be purchased from Kood direct as well as a number of camera dealers.

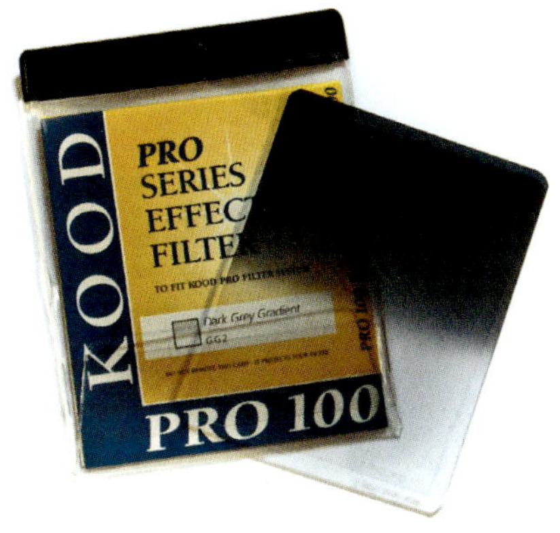

Unknown brands

Search the web and you'll find filters from little-known brands like Helios. Most stem from China and as there are no official UK importers, it's hard to judge optical quality so the safest bet is to stick with recognised filter brands

Tiffen

www.tiffen.com

Tiffen is an American brand that has been around for decades and is particularly popular in the movie industry. Its range of screw-in filters isn't as comprehensive as Hoya's, but it does cover all the key types including protection filters, polarisers and Neutral Density filters. It also has a number of special-effect filters, in particular lots of diffusion filters including soft-focus, mist and fog, but these aren't filters you'd use on a regular basis. While the range is relatively small, quality is very high and Tiffen filters come with a ten-year guarantee. You'll also find that prices are competitive, too, making them a decent alternative to brands like Hoya, although the latter is more likely to be stocked by your local photo dealer.

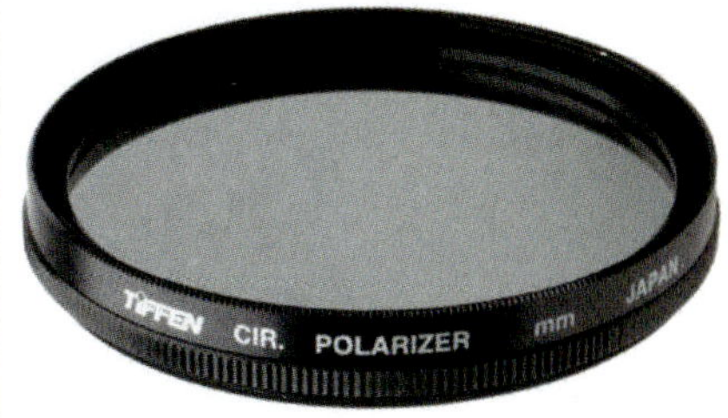

Close-up filters

These useful accessories offer an affordable way to shoot great close-ups

CLOSE-UP FILTERS offer a great introduction to the world of macro photography, without the need to spend hundreds on a dedicated macro lens. Technically speaking, they're not actually a filter, but a dioptre. However, they are commonly regarded as one and produced by the majority of the major filter brands. They are a screw-in type filter, attaching to the front of the lens and acting like a magnifier. By doing so, they reduce the lens's minimum focusing distance.

Typically, they are of a single-element construction and manufactured in a range of four strengths: +1, +2, +3 and +4. The higher the number, the nearer it is possible to focus and therefore the greater the magnification. Some brands also offer a powerful +10 dioptre, which is normally a two-element construction to help optimise image quality.

It is possible to couple close-up filters together to create a greater level of magnification. If you decide to do this, attach the most powerful one on your lens first and the weakest last. However, combining three or more filters will degrade image quality and exaggerate any optical flaws, which is why it is recommended that you attach a maximum of two at any one time. They can be purchased in a set or individually. Expect to pay around £20 for a single filter. Naturally, at this price, it is unrealistic to expect them to match the optical quality of a macro lens, or extension tube, and they are prone to spherical aberration (softening of the image). However, this can be kept to a minimum by selecting a mid-range aperture of f/8 or f/11 and, considering their price tag, they are capable of excellent results. They are best combined with a prime focal length lens, as opposed to a zoom. A standard 50mm lens is an ideal focal length, but short telephoto lenses, up to 135mm, are also well suited. That said, it's possible to get decent results when used with standard zooms, so if you like close-ups, give them a try.

"Close-up filters offer a great introduction to the world of macro photography"

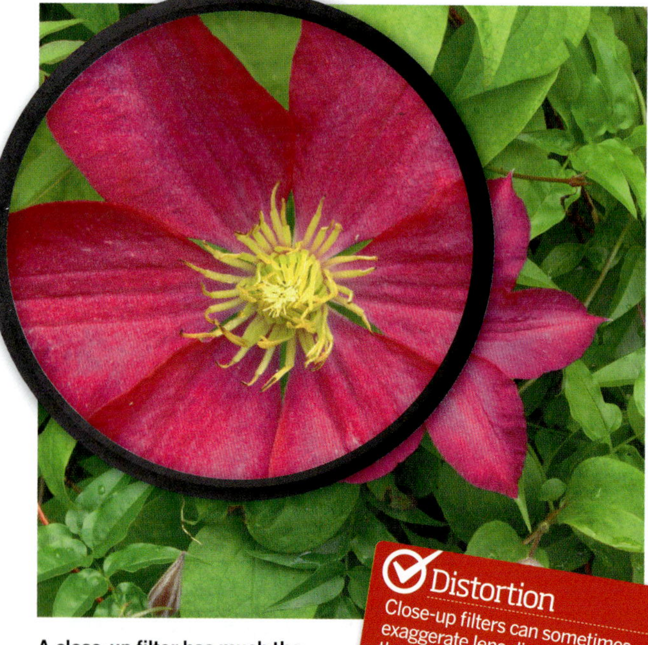

A close-up filter has much the same effect as a magnifying glass and is ideal when you want to increase the size of a small object, like a flower, in the frame.

Distortion

Close-up filters can sometimes exaggerate lens distortion at the edges of the frame, so avoid using them with wide-angle lenses whenever possible

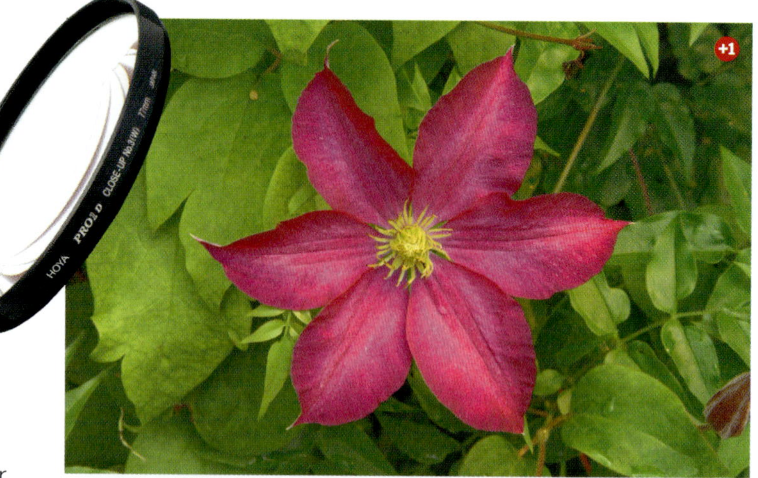

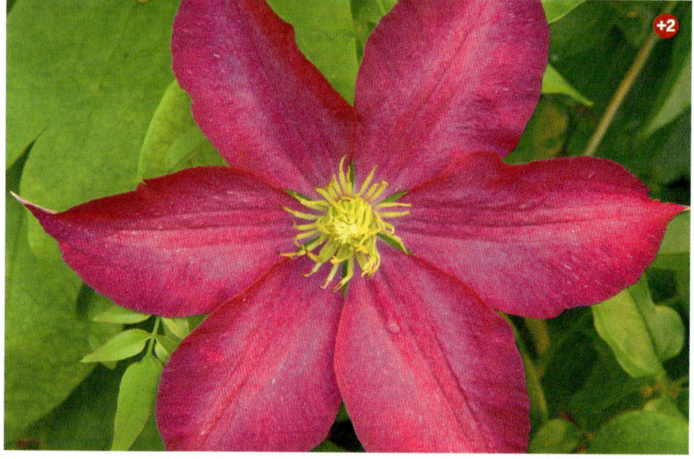

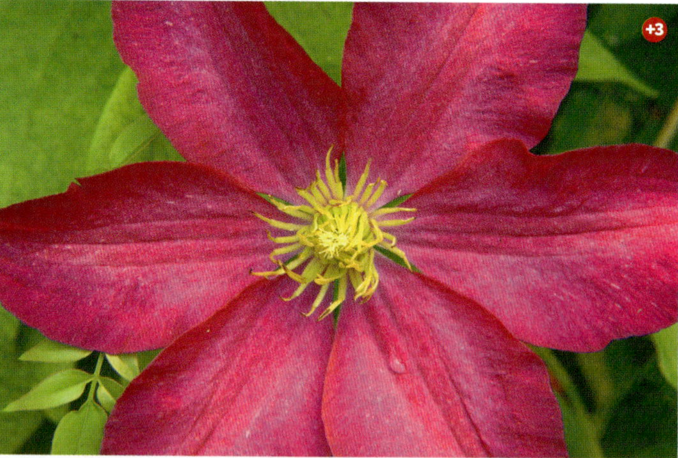

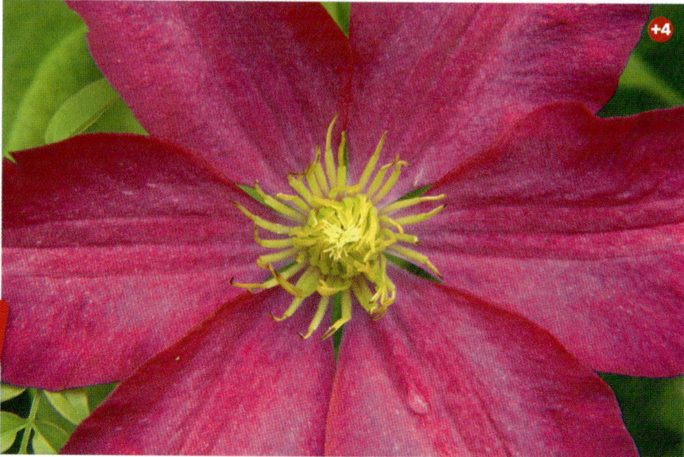

In-camera filtration

Try using your camera's White Balance settings for creative filtration

THE COLOUR TEMPERATURE of light is measured in degrees of Kelvin (K) and is handled by your camera's White Balance system. Light is considered neutral at around 5500K, with lower temperatures appearing warmer and higher temperatures getting cooler. By intentionally mismatching the WB setting with the available light, it's possible to creatively play with how colours are recorded. For example, shooting a sunlit landscape with the WB to Cloudy produces a warm hue. In contrast, select a lower setting, for example 3000K – or the Tungsten WB preset – and the photo will look cooler. Once you understand the creative potential of WB, you can begin using it as a form of convenient in-camera filtration – available at all times at the simple flick of a switch. Most DSLRs allow you to set the WB value manually for added control, so don't feel you have to rely on the camera's preset values. Whilst often the best effect will be subtle, don't be afraid to experiment – sometimes the most pleasing result will be one boasting a strong, artificial tint. Some images benefit from a little extra warmth – especially portrait and scenics. However, a blue cast can convey a sense of coolness and mystery and, while fewer subjects suit a colder colour temperature, it's an effect not to be overlooked.

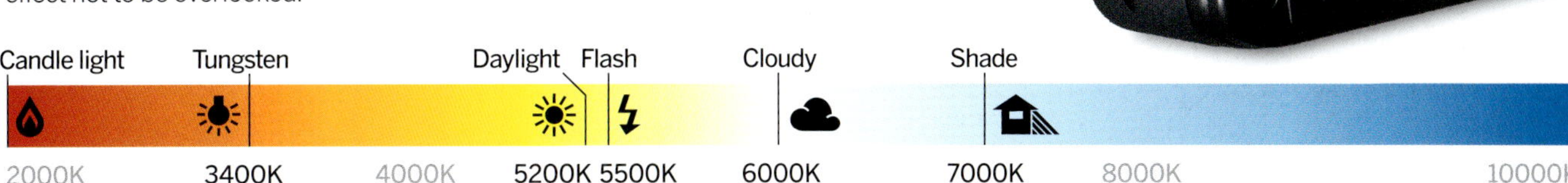

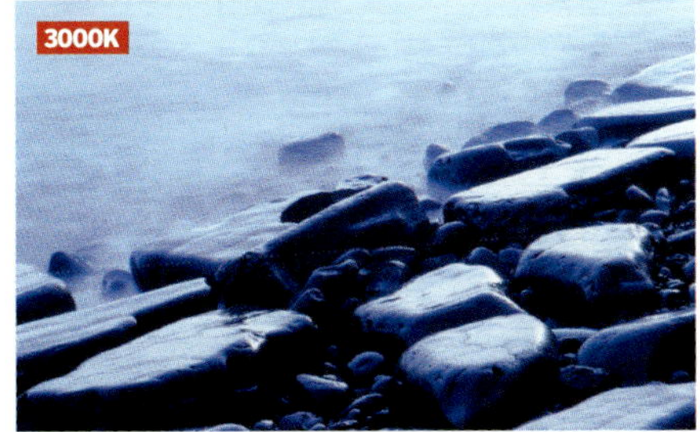

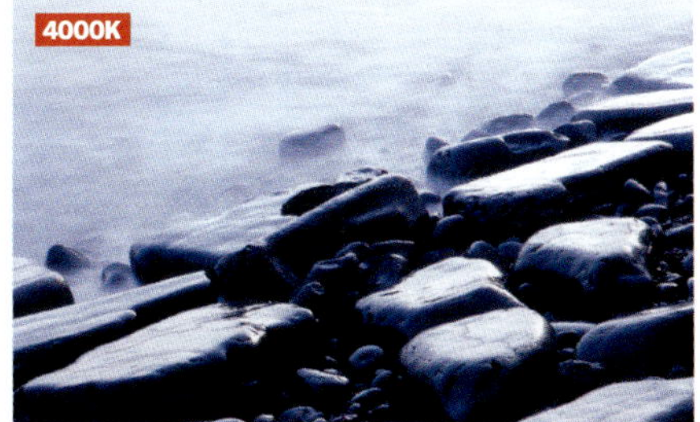

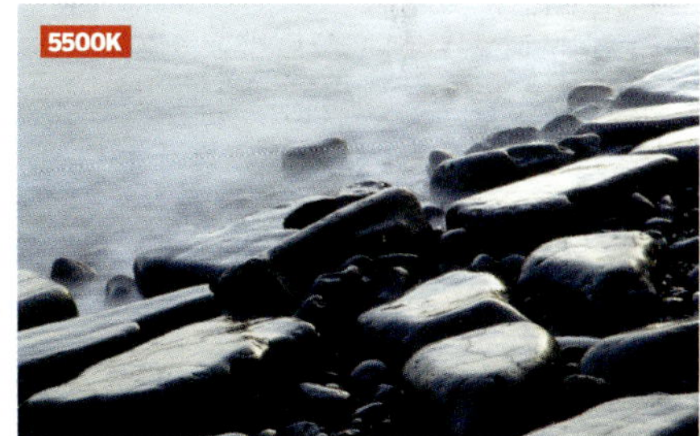

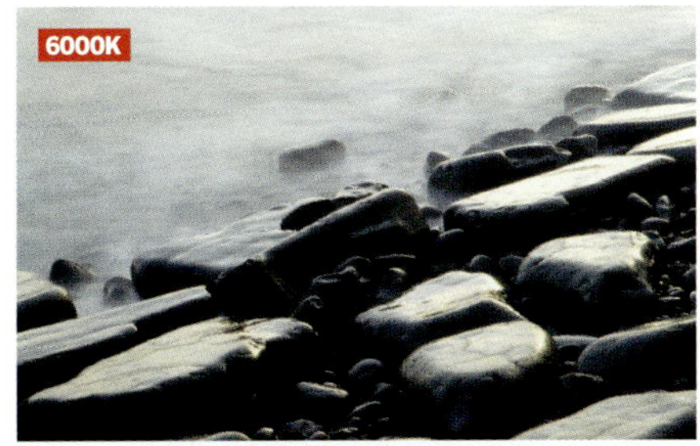

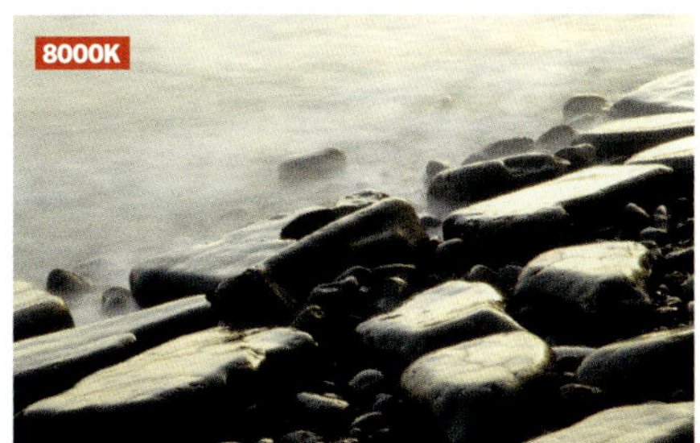

"Once you understand the creative potential of White Balance, you can begin using it as a form of convenient in-camera filtration"

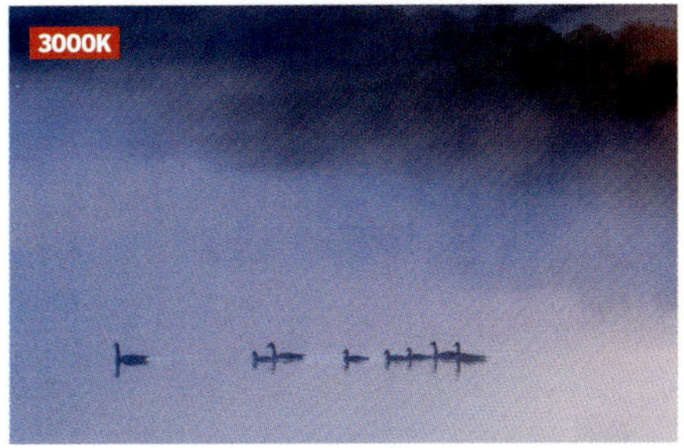

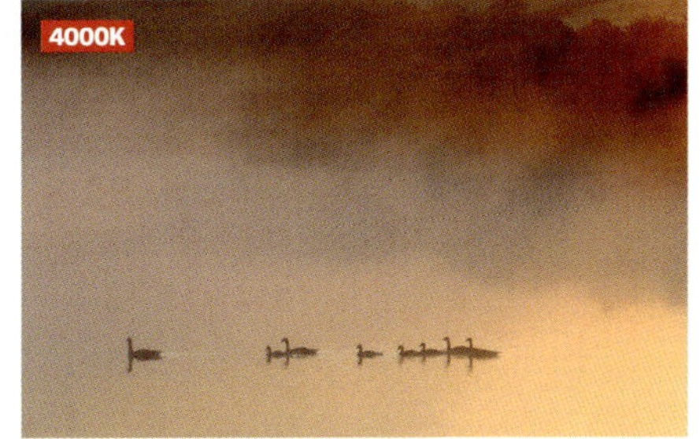

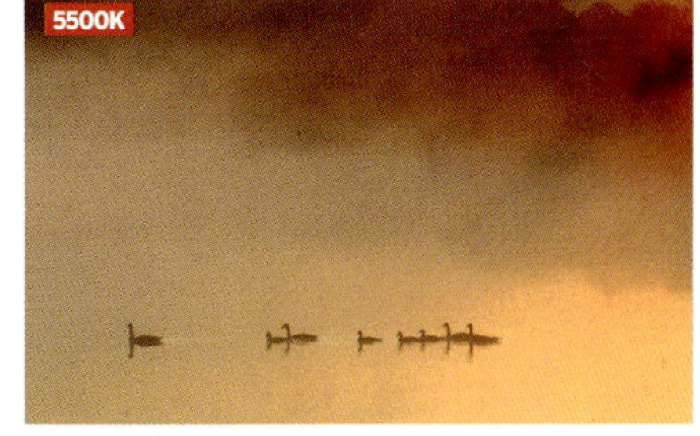

White Balance comparison
A colour cast will greatly alter the feel, mood and look of a scene or subject. Digital SLR photographers can 'filter' their images quickly and easily by simply mismatching the White Balance setting with the ambient light. Different scenes will suit different colour shifts. For example, in the first sequence (water and rocks) a cool blue hue works best; whilst in the second (geese at sunrise) a warmer hue is better suited. In both instances, a technically inaccurate White Balance preset suits the image far better than the correct White Balance setting.

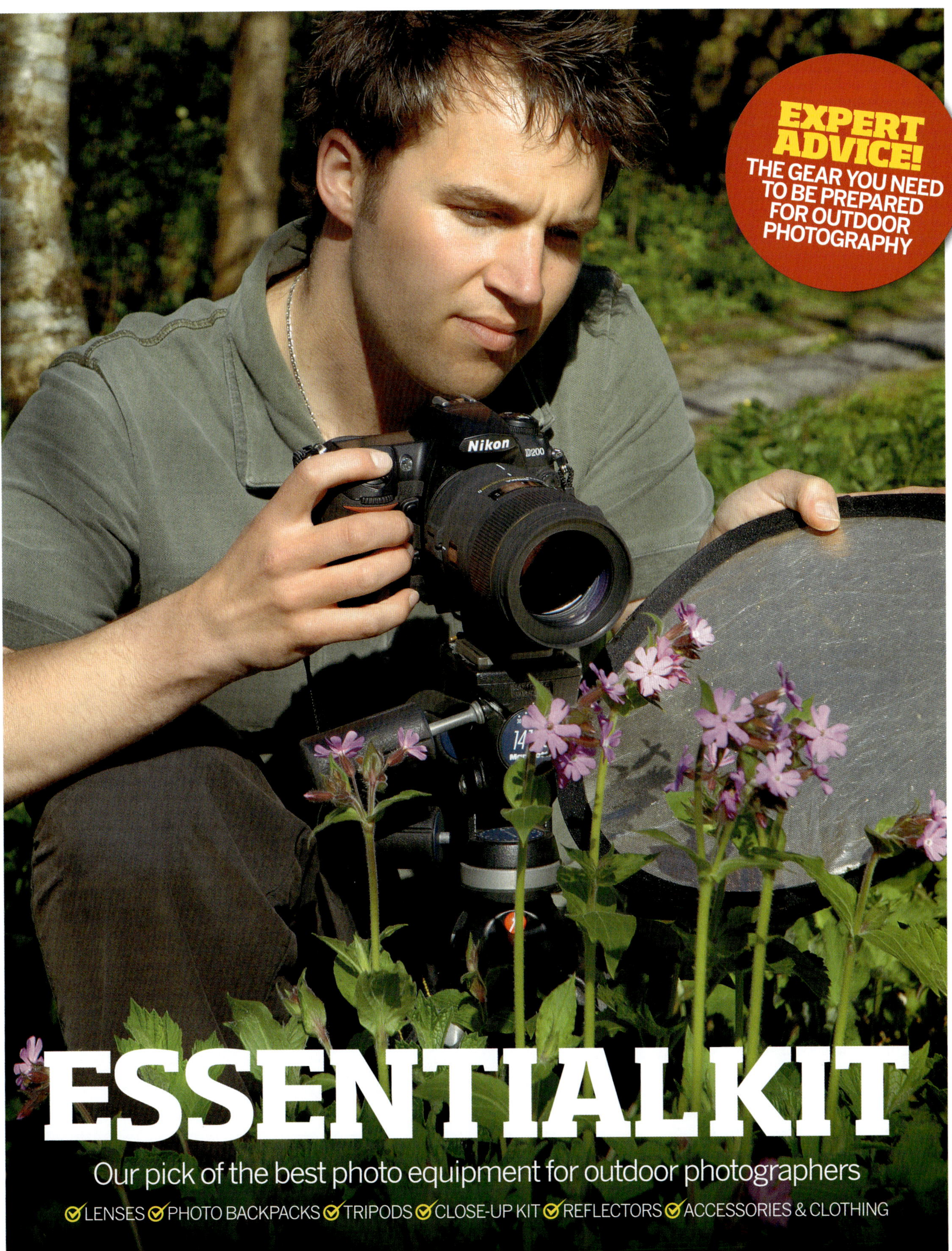

ESSENTIAL KIT

Our pick of the best photo equipment for outdoor photographers

✓LENSES ✓PHOTO BACKPACKS ✓TRIPODS ✓CLOSE-UP KIT ✓REFLECTORS ✓ACCESSORIES & CLOTHING

Fundamentals of lenses

Follow our essential advice to choosing the right lens for your needs

THE KEY WITH CHOOSING LENSES is to put together a system that serves all your needs. What those needs are will depend on the subjects you tend to shoot – specialist subjects such as sport, nature and close-ups have more specific optical requirements. However, most of us like to try a bit of everything, so a more general selection will be required. In terms of focal lengths, if you have lenses covering 15mm to 300mm on a full-frame DSLR (12mm to 200mm for APS-C sensors) you'll be equipped for just about any situation. The wider focal lengths are ideal for scenic photography – landscapes, architecture, street scenes, travel – the mid-range focal lengths are great for portraiture, details and general use, while telephotos suit sport, candids and nature. Saying that, you can take brilliant landscapes with a telephoto and amazing nature shots with an ultra-wide, so use your imagination and make the most of all your lenses.

In this digital age, lens quality is more important than ever. High-resolution sensors are so good that they can easily out-resolve inferior lenses, so any flaws in optical design will be highlighted. These problems are at their worst in ultra wide-angle zooms, where chromatic aberration, diffraction, vignetting, distortion and loss of sharpness at the image corners are all common problems – and the less you pay for the lens, the more it's likely to suffer; though not in all cases. Telezooms tend to suffer less from all of the above because their optical design isn't as extreme, but they don't escape completely and the more pixels your camera has, the, more your images will highlight any problems.

Optical flaws can be corrected, to an extent, during post-production, but it's preferable if they don't exist in the first place, or are at least minimised. The best way to ensure that is by buying the best lenses you can afford. Don't necessarily take the price of a lens as the only indicator of quality, as certain lenses from certain manufacturers have reputations, both good and bad. Instead, read reviews and ask the opinion of other photographers. Whether you buy prime (fixed focal length) or zoom lenses is down to you and your budget.

Lens choice: Prime v zoom

A prime lens has a fixed focal length while a zoom's is variable. Both have advantages and disadvantages. In general, primes offer higher image quality, faster maximum apertures and are more compact and lightweight, but buying several proves costly. A zoom is more versatile and saves money as it covers a range of focal lengths. Quality isn't as high (but comes close) and the maximum aperture is slower, but its convenience makes it more popular.

Primes tend to have the edge in terms of image quality, but zooms are more versatile and you'd be hard-pressed to tell the difference between a shot taken using a £500 zoom and another shot with a £1,000 prime lens. Lenses from independent manufacturers such as Sigma and Tamron should be considered alongside the likes of Canon and Nikon – optically they're often as good but at more attractive prices. Whichever lenses you buy, to get the best optical performance from them, always use a mid-range aperture of f/8 or f/11 whenever you can. Image quality is at its lowest at the widest and smallest apertures, especially with wide-angle zooms, and at its sharpest at mid-apertures.

Main types of lenses for digital photography

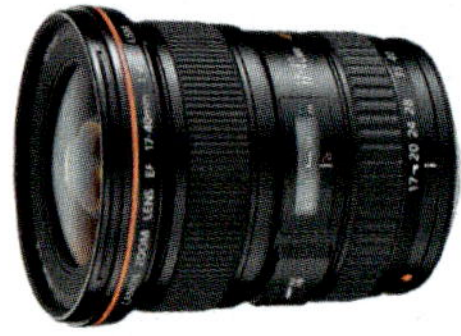

1) Wide-angle

With a wider field-of-view than the human eye can see, wide-angle lenses allow you to include more of the scene in the image frame, making it the ideal choice when shooting scenics or taking pictures indoors or when space is tight. There's an extensive choice of primes and zooms available, so you're not short of options. Wide-angles allow you to exaggerate perspective, excentuating depth, which can lead to creative results. But you do need to be aware of its tendency to distort, especially subjects that are towards the edges of the frame. While this can be used to your advantage, it can also ruin your images. See page 146 for details on wide-angles.

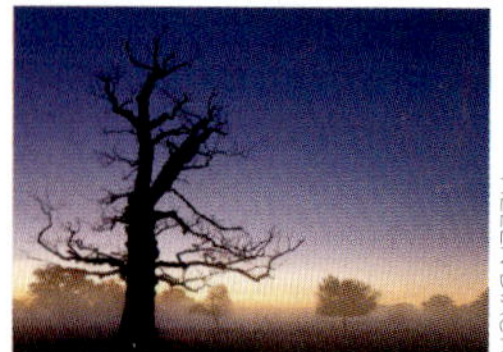

HELEN DIXON

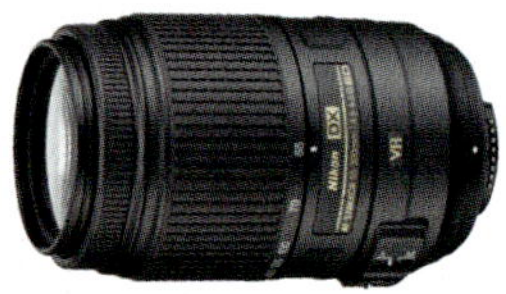

2) Telephoto

A telephoto zoom is often the first lens a DSLR or CSC photographer will add to their outfit. The extra pulling power a telephoto gives is ideal for filling the frame with relatively small or distant subjects. It's also ideal when you're trying to take pictures of a subject without it being aware, such as wildlife or when shooting candids. As it's a lens that compresses perspective, it's perfect for producing flattering portraits. The 50-200mm and 70-300mm telezooms are popular but need to be used with care to avoid the problem of camera shake. If you can afford to, invest in a telephoto with a maximum aperture of f/2.8. See page 148 for more details on telephotos.

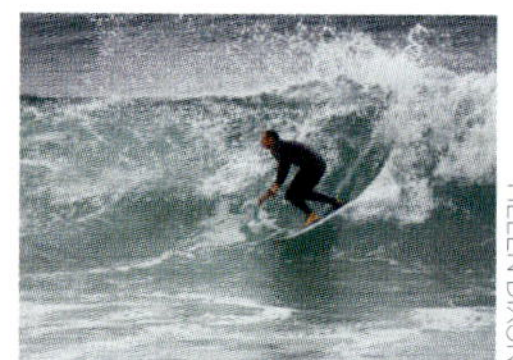

HELEN DIXON

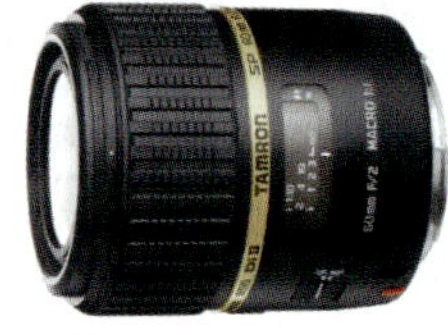

3) Macro

Physically, macro lenses look just like a regular lens, but the major difference is they can focus much closer, allowing you to fill the frame with tiny subjects such as insects and butterflies. They're also specially designed for use at close focusing distances, so optical quality is superb. The focal length tends to be either 50/55mm or 90/105mm. Both are useful and the vast majority offer 1:1 (life-size) reproduction, but the longer focal lengths are more suited to photographing nature because they have a longer working distance, which means that you don't have to get particularly close and risk frightening your subjects away.

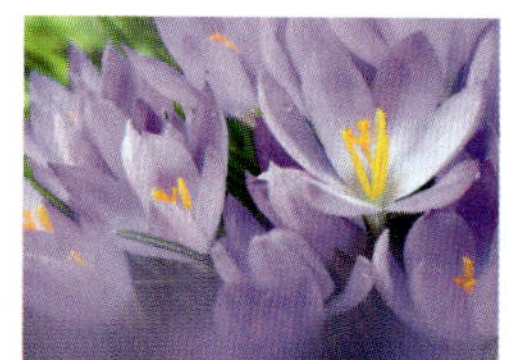

HELEN DIXON

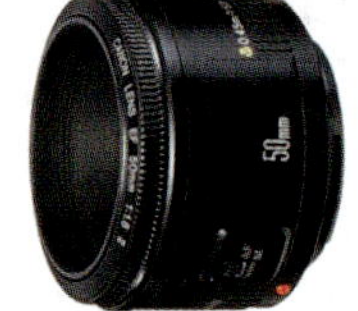

4) Standard

Once upon a time, SLRs were sold with a 50mm 'standard' lens so every keen photographer had one. Today you get a standard zoom instead like the 18-55mm or 18-105mm. However, it's worth investing in a 50mm prime because for little outlay you get a compact and lightweight lens that's pin-sharp, focuses down to just a few inches, has a super-fast maximum aperture of at least f/1.8, if not f/1.4 or f/1.2, and is perfect for handheld, low-light photography. Use with an APS-C sensor and you have a brilliant 75-80mm portrait lens which, used at its widest aperture, will give minimal depth-of-field and produce superb images.

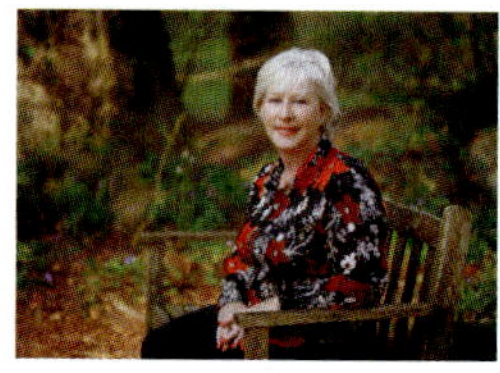

BJORN THOMASSEN

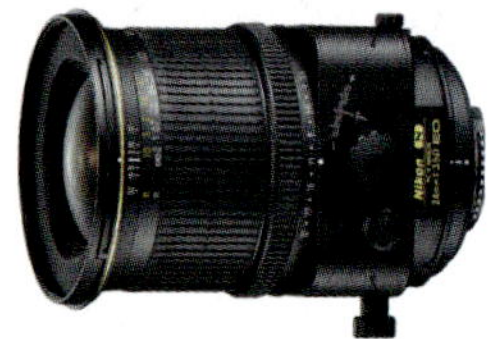

5) Tilt and shift

These expensive lenses serve two purposes. First, they prevent converging verticals when shooting architecture. Instead of leaning back to include the top of a building, you can shift the front of the lens up but keep the camera back parallel to the subject building. Second, the 'tilt' facility lets you angle the front section of the lens down so the plane of focus is parallel with the plane of the camera's sensor, thus increasing depth-of-field without having to set a smaller aperture. By tilting the other way depth-of-field is reduced to almost nothing producing unusual effects – similar effects can also be achieved using a Lensbaby for a fraction of the cost.

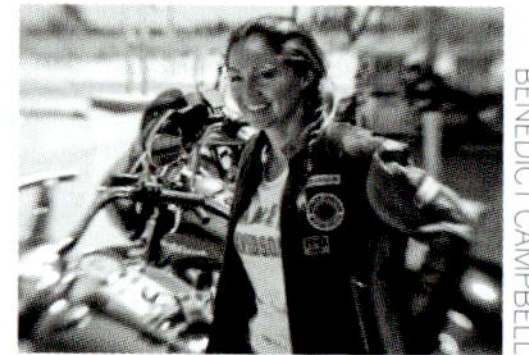

BENEDICT CAMPBELL

Understanding effective focal length

Most lenses available for use on your digital camera were designed for 35mm film SLRs or full-frame digital SLRs that have a sensor the same size as a 35mm film frame (24x36mm). However, only a handful of digital SLRs at present actually have a full-frame sensor, while the vast majority use an APS-C sized sensor that's smaller than full-frame 35mm. This means that the focal length of 'normal' lenses is increased, to what is usually termed the effective focal length. The amount of increase can be calculated using a magnification factor (MF) and this is governed by the size of the sensor in the camera. Most cameras have an MF of 1.5x, although for Canon it is 1.6x and for Four Thirds cameras 2x.

For landscape and other subjects where wide-angle lenses are mainly used, this focal length increase is a disadvantage. For example, an ultra-wide 17-40mm zoom will effectively work like a 25-60mm standard zoom on a digital camera with a MF of 1.5x. To get the same effect as a 17-40mm zoom you would therefore need something like a 10-20mm or 12-24mm zoom. For sport, nature and other subjects requiring telephoto lenses, the focal length increase is more beneficial because it makes modest lenses more powerful. A 70-300mm zoom effectively becomes a 105-450mm zoom on a camera with a MF of 1.5x, for example, so you can fill the frame with more distant or smaller subjects.

Another factor to consider is that lenses are at their sharpest in the centre and at their softest towards the edges. Cameras with an APS-C sensor therefore get the best from full-frame lenses as they use the sharper central area of the lens's image circle and exclude the outer limits of the image circle where image quality is lower. Understanding focal length can be confusing, but our tables below should help you understand it better.

Camera brand/models	Multiplication factor
Canon	
All EOS models (except below)	**1.6x**
EOS-1D series	**1.3x**
EOS 5D & EOS-1DS series	**1x**
Fujifilm	
All S-series models	**1.5x**
Nikon	
All D-series (except below)	**1.5x**
D700 and D3 series	**1x**
Olympus & Panasonic	
All digital SLRs and CSCs	**2x**
Pentax	
All *ist and K-series models	**1.5x**
Samsung	
All GX and NX series models	**1.5x**
Sigma	
All SD models	**1.7x**
Sony	
All Alpha & NEX (except below)	**1.5x**
Alpha 850 and 900	**1x**

Effective focal length The table above shows the effective focal length increase on the majority of popular brands of DSLR and CSC cameras. Use this magnification factor with the table on the right to work out the effective focal length of popular prime an zoom lenses.

Sensor sizes These images were all taken with a 35mm lens from the same spot and show the effect of the magnification factor.

Focal length on lens	Sensor size: Full-frame	APS-H	APS-C	APS-C (Canon)	Four Thirds & Micro Four Thirds
	1x	**1.3x**	**1.5x**	**1.6x**	**2x**
14mm	14mm	18mm	21mm	22mm	28mm
15mm	**15mm**	**19mm**	**22mm**	**23mm**	**30mm**
20mm	20mm	26mm	30mm	32mm	40mm
24mm	**24mm**	**31mm**	**36mm**	**38mm**	**48mm**
28mm	28mm	36mm	42mm	45mm	56mm
50mm	**50mm**	**65mm**	**75mm**	**80mm**	**100mm**
85mm	85mm	110mm	127mm	136mm	170mm
100mm	**100mm**	**135mm**	**150mm**	**160mm**	**200mm**
10-17mm	10-17mm	13-22mm	15-25mm	16-27mm	20-34mm
10-20mm	**10-20mm**	**13-26mm**	**15-30mm**	**16-32mm**	**20-40mm**
10-22mm	10-22mm	13-29mm	15-33mm	16-35mm	20-44mm
11-18mm	**11-18mm**	**14-23mm**	**16-27mm**	**18-29mm**	**22-36mm**
12-24mm	12-24mm	16-31mm	18-36mm	19-38mm	24-48mm
16-35mm	**16-35mm**	**21-45mm**	**24-53mm**	**26-56mm**	**32-70mm**
17-35mm	17-35mm	22-45mm	25-53mm	27-56mm	34-70mm
17-40mm	**17-40mm**	**22-52mm**	**25-60mm**	**27-56mm**	**34-80mm**
18-55mm	18-55mm	23-71mm	27-82mm	29-88mm	36-110mm
18-200mm	**18-200mm**	**23-260mm**	**27-300mm**	**29-320mm**	**36-400mm**
18-270mm	18-270mm	23-351mm	27-405mm	29-432mm	36-540mm
24-105mm	**24-105mm**	**31-136mm**	**36-157mm**	**38-168mm**	**48-210mm**
28-70mm	28-70mm	36-91mm	42-105mm	45-112mm	56-140mm
28-300mm	**28-300mm**	**36-390mm**	**42-450mm**	**45-480mm**	**56-600mm**
55-200mm	55-200mm	71-260mm	82-300mm	88-320mm	110-400mm
70-300mm	**70-300mm**	**91-390mm**	**105-450mm**	**112-480mm**	**140-600mm**
100-400mm	100-400mm	130-520mm	150-600mm	160-600mm	200-800mm

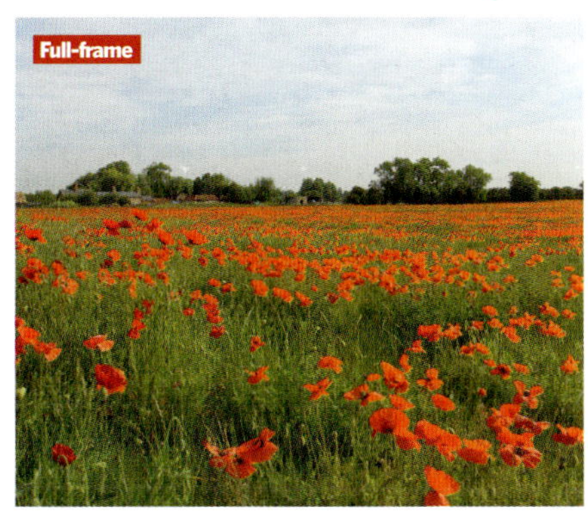

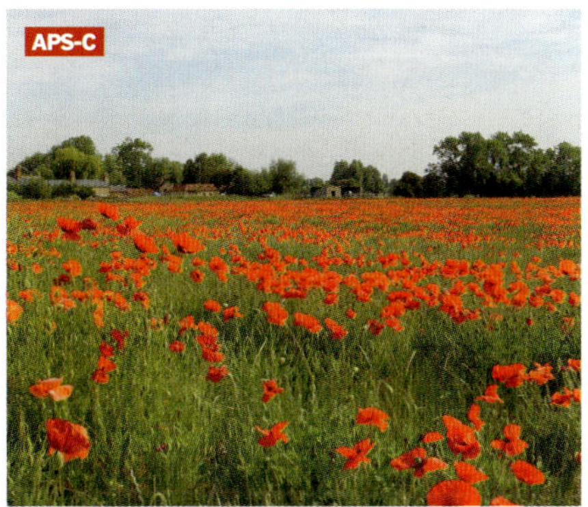

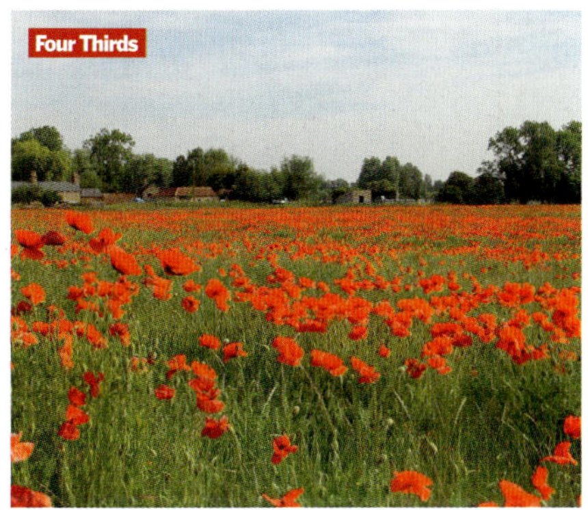

Wide-angle lenses

With an extensive field-of-view, wide-angles are ideal for filling the frame with stunning scenes or shooting in cramped conditions

PEERING THROUGH your camera's viewfinder for the first time with a wide-angle lens fitted is like looking out on another world. Suddenly you can see considerably more than is possible with the naked eye, and the initial reaction is one of amazement and excitement. Nearby features loom large in the frame, while everything else seems to rush off into the distance with dramatic effect. Lines and shapes are distorted, perspective is exaggerated so that the elements in a scene seem to be spaced out much more than they are in reality and even the most ordinary subjects and scenes can be turned into dynamic compositions.

Any lens with a focal length less than the standard is considered a wide-angle. In full-frame format, that's anything less than 50mm, and anything less than 32mm in APS-C format, though 35mm is the first proper wide-angle focal length (or 22mm for APS-C). Generally, 24mm and 28mm are considered to be 'normal' wide-angle focal lengths, and are the best choice for general use when shooting landscapes, architecture and other scenic subjects. They have a broad angle-of-view and strong wide-angle characteristics, but are still relatively easy to use, so producing a tight composition rather than one full of empty space isn't that difficult.

Once focal length drops to 21mm (14mm in APS-C format) or less, you're into ultra wide territory. These lenses can produce fantastic results as their effects are extreme: depth-of-field extends from just a few inches to infinity at small apertures such as f/11 or f/16, so you can really exploit foreground interest knowing that everything will be sharply focused from front-to-back. Small changes in camera position will also dramatically change the juxtaposition of elements in the frame and the way they relate to each other, so you can literally create images from nothing – try shooting from a really low viewpoint and you'll see what we mean. You do need to use ultra wides with care, though. Perspective is exaggerated so much and the angle-of-view is so wide that you can easily end up with empty, boring compositions. It's absolutely vital to get close to an important feature in the scene and use it to dominate the composition. Ultra wides are also ideal for exploiting lines in a scene or making the most of frames to direct attention towards the main subject.

Though mainly used for scenic photography, wide-angle lenses do have other uses. The minimum focusing distance is usually just a few inches, so you can produce stunning nature shots by moving in close to your subject and capturing it in its natural habitat. The same applies with people – instead of using a telezoom to shoot head-and-shoulders portraits, switch to a wide and go for a more environmental approach. Wide-angles are also perfect for close-range candids or reportage photography.

Don't fancy sticking your camera in someone's face? Then shoot from the hip with the lens set to f/8, and the focus at around two metres; this way you can fire away without anyone realising that you're taking their photo.

Beyond ultra wide, you enter the wacky world of the fisheye lens, so-named because its bulging front element looks like a fish's eye. These have an amazing 180° angle-of-view that swallows up everything in front of you and distorts anything near the edge of the frame considerably. There are two types of fisheye lens: circular and full-frame. The former produces a circular image in the middle of the frame and tends to have a focal length around 8mm on full-frame (Sigma makes a 4.5mm for APS-C sensors), whereas the latter fills the whole picture area and has a focal length of 15mm or 16mm. If you're thinking of buying a fisheye, choose the full-frame type as the effect isn't so extreme, so they're more useful on a day-to-day basis. That said, obvious distortion is unavoidable, so any fisheye lens has limited use compared to ultra wides.

Although we've stated specific wide-angle focal lengths, most photographers invest in wide-angle zooms rather than prime lenses as they're more versatile. The 24-70mm 'standard' zoom (16-35mm/17-40mm for APS-C sensors) makes a good starting point, but if you like the idea of wide-angle photography, it won't be long before you're keen for something wider. For full-frame users, the 16-35mm/17-40mm range is ideal, while for APS-C sensors, 10-20mm/12-24mm is very popular. You should rarely need anything wider, but if you do, Canon makes an 8-15mm for full-frame and APS-C sensors, while Sigma offers an 8-16mm for APS-C. Now that's what we call wide!

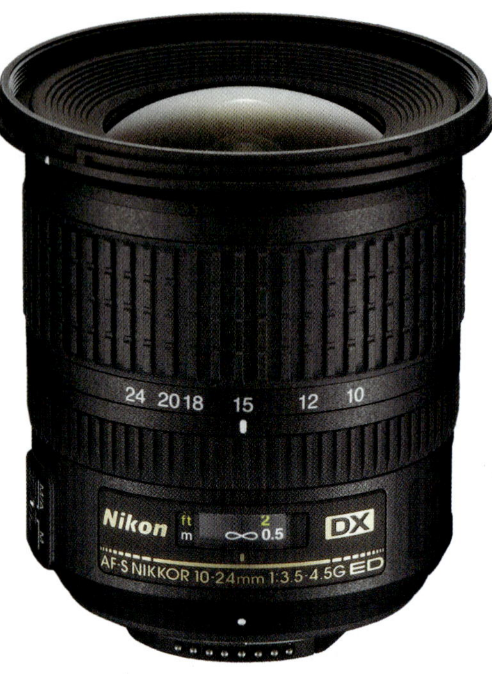

Ultra wide zooms: The versatility of ultra wide-angle zooms and their impressive image quality makes them the best all-round choice.

Wide-angle lenses: Common problems

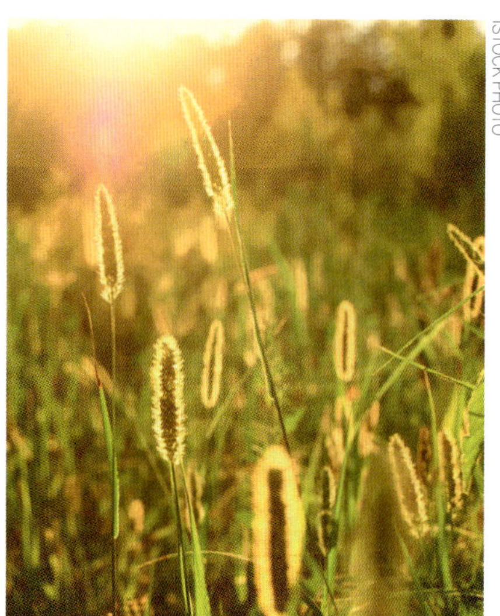

ISTOCK PHOTO

1) Flare: Flare is more likely with wide-angle lenses due to their broad angle-of-view. To prevent it, keep the front element and any filters placed over it clean, and use your hand, a sheet of card or your jacket to shade if there are bright light sources (in particular, the sun) just out of frame.

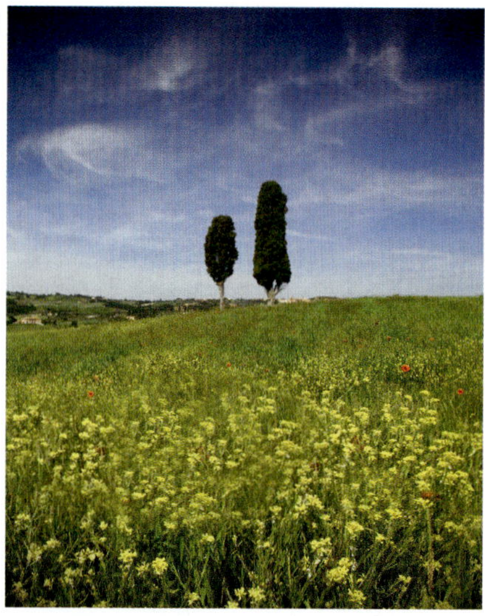

LEE FROST

2) Light fall-off: Wide-angle zooms tend to suffer from natural light fall-off (darkening of the image corners) due to their design. This can work well on some images as it helps to keep the viewer's attention on the main subject, but if you don't like it, it's easy to remove it during Raw file processing.

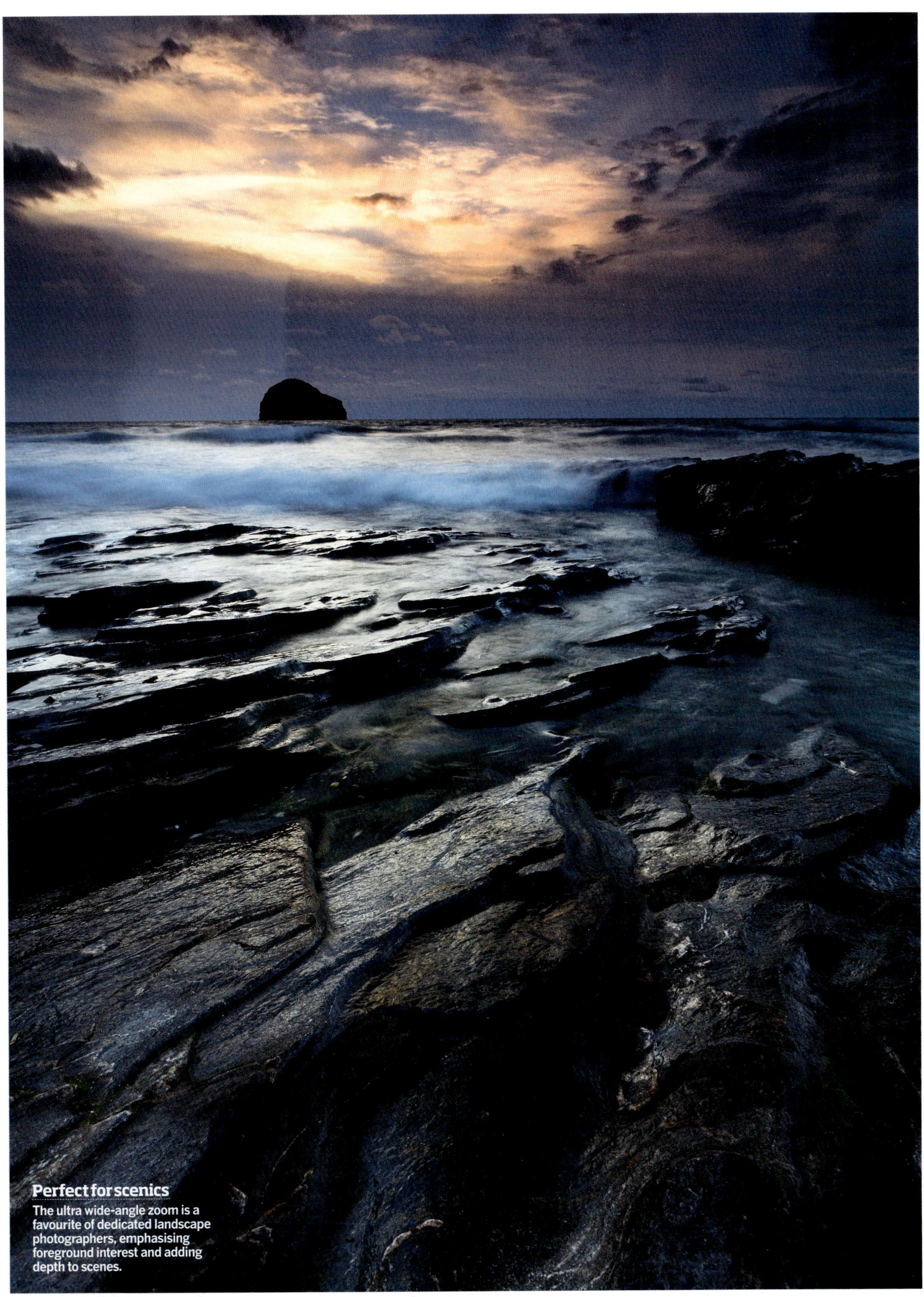

Perfect for scenics

The ultra wide-angle zoom is a favourite of dedicated landscape photographers, emphasising foreground interest and adding depth to scenes.

Telephoto lenses

If you're unable to get physically closer to your subject, the solution is to use a lens with pulling power to bring your subject closer to you

ANY LENS WITH A FOCAL LENGTH greater than 50mm (32mm in APS-C format) is considered a telephoto, and as you'd probably imagine, they do exactly the opposite job to wide-angle lenses.

• The angle-of-view is smaller than a standard or wide-angle lens, so they 'see' less than the naked eye and magnify your subject to make it appear bigger in the viewfinder.

• Depth-of-field is reduced, so at wide apertures such as f/2.8 or f/4, only a small area of the scene will record in sharp focus. Depth-of-field increases at smaller apertures such as f/16 or f/22, but never to the same extent as with wide-angle lenses.

• Perspective is compressed so the elements in a scene appear closer together than they really are. This effect is known as 'foreshortening'.

The longer the focal length of the lens, the more pronounced these characteristics are – for instance, a 300mm focal length will magnify your subject more, give less depth-of-field at any aperture, and greater foreshortening than a 100mm lens, but less than a 500mm.

The moderate focal lengths from 80-200mm are invaluable for general use, which is why zoom lenses covering this focal length range are purchased in such large numbers. The lower end (80-100mm) is ideal for portraiture, as a short telephoto gives slight compression of perspective, which flatters facial features. Prime lenses with a focal length of 100mm or 105mm are often referred to as portrait lenses. Depth-of-field is also shallow at wide apertures, so you can throw the background out of focus to concentrate attention on your focal point. The top end (100-200mm) is ideal for candids, close-range action, isolating interesting details in the landscape or on buildings and so on.

A 300mm or 400mm focal length is the next step up for most photographers, especially those interested in sport or nature photography, as it allows you to fill the frame with your subject from further away. Such focal lengths are ideal for sunrise and sunset shots, as they exaggerate the size of the sun's orb to make it much bigger. Foreshortening (also known as perspective compression) is also much more obvious so you can really crowd the features in a scene together – great for cityscapes, avenues of trees, misty mountains and other scenes or subjects that contain repeated features.

Beyond 400mm, you're really into long telephoto territory where the lenses are big, heavy and expensive. There are a few zooms that go all the way to 400mm or 500mm but prime lenses are more common once you get to this range. Serious nature photographers use a 500mm or 600mm as standard, while few dedicated sports snappers are without at least a 500mm.

Once you get into these focal lengths, the effects are amazing. Subjects that appear distant to the naked eye suddenly fill your camera's viewfinder. Depth-of-field is also severely limited so only one element is sharply focused, and perspective is compressed to the extent that distant features appear crowded together. And remember that if you use an APS-C camera, as most of you will, telephoto power is increased further, so a 70-300mm zoom is effectively a 105-450mm lens.

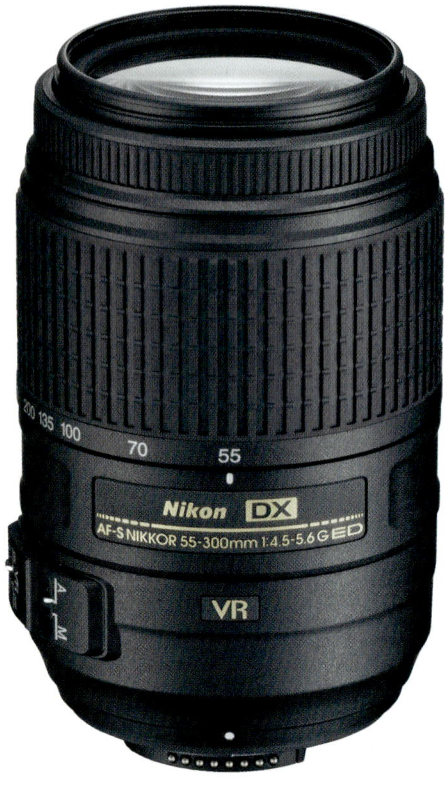

Pulling power: The latest telephoto zooms are extremely compact and lightweight considering the enormous pulling power they offer.

Add pulling power with a teleconverter

Teleconverters fit between your camera body and lens to increase the focal length of that lens. The minimum focusing distance of the original lens also remains the same, so you can get really close to your subject.

The most common teleconverter is a 2x, which doubles the focal length – turning a 70-200mm zoom into a 140-400mm on a full-frame DSLR and a whopping 220-600mm on a DSLR with an APS-C sensor! You can also get 1.4x converters that increase focal length by a more modest 40%.

There are drawbacks to using teleconverters. With a 2x version you lose two stops of light, so an f/4 lens effectively becomes an f/8 lens. This darkens the viewfinder image and means that you have to use slower shutter speeds or a higher ISO to keep the shutter speed reasonable to freeze subjects or avoid camera shake. On slow telezooms with a maximum aperture of f/4-5.6, you may find that the autofocusing doesn't work at the longer end due to the loss of light. A 1.4x converter only loses one stop so is a better option in that respect.

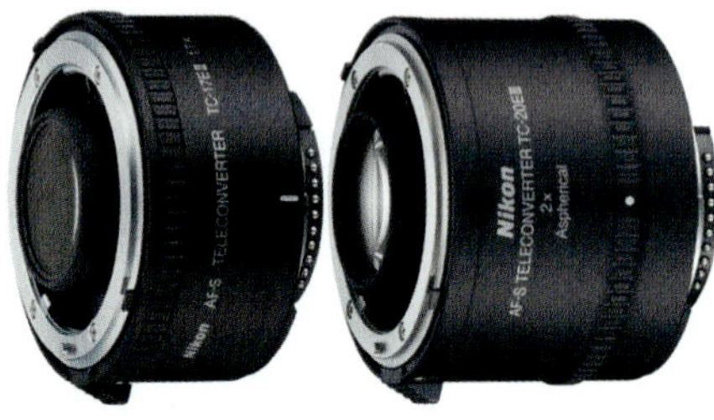

The optical quality of the lens is also reduced when you attach a teleconverter, so your images won't be as sharp. To minimise this, we suggest buying the best teleconverter that you can afford – ideally with seven elements – and stop your lens down to a mid-range aperture, such as f/8 or f/11.

Despite their flaws, if you want to take long telephoto shots occasionally and can't justify buying the real thing, teleconverters are an ideal solution. They also save carrying lots of lenses around, which can be a real advantage when you need to travel light.

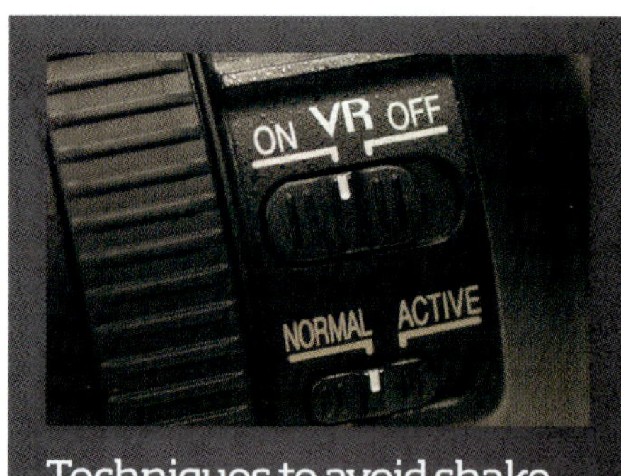

Techniques to avoid shake

The risk of camera shake proportionally rises with the size and weight of the lens, so when using telezooms and telephotos, you need to take extra care if you want to end up with pin-sharp shots. Image stabilisation offers a major benefit as it allows you to hand-hold at slower shutter speeds than normal – so if you're going to be using telephoto lenses, stabilisation is important. Other ways to reduce the risk of shake while hand-holding are to adopt a stable stance – feet slightly apart, back straight, left hand supporting the lens – and fire the shutter after exhaling so your body's more relaxed. It's important to gently squeeze rather than jab the shutter. If necessary, look for some kind of support – a wall, post, tree stump; anything that you can rest the lens on. Or use a monopod to support the lens, but still retain your freedom of movement – sports photographers favour monopods.

A tripod provides ultimate support, though it's a good idea to use the camera's mirror lock-up facility to reduce mirror 'slap', which can cause vibrations, and to fire the shutter with a remote release so you don't have to touch the camera.

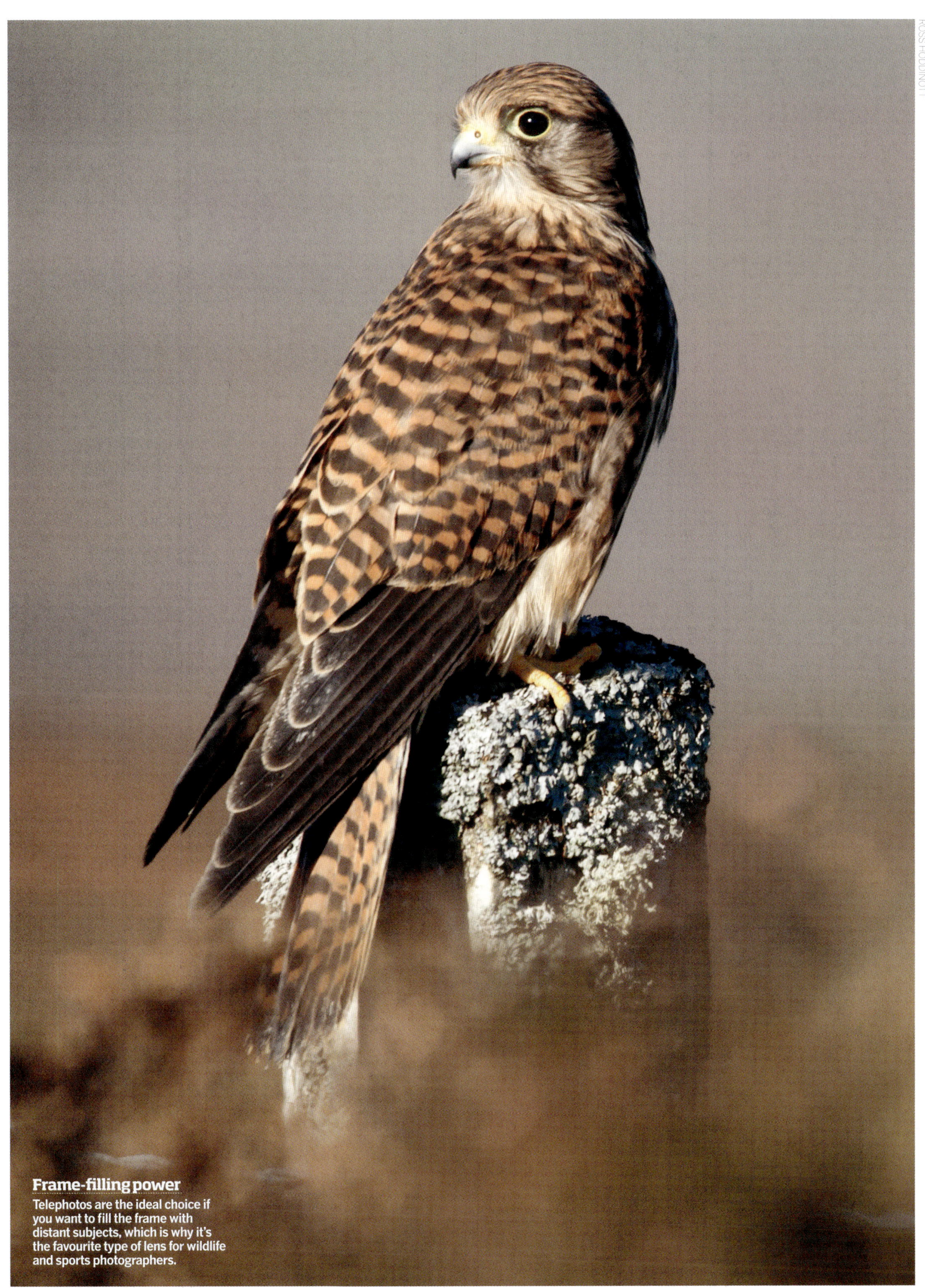

ROSS HODDINOTT

Frame-filling power

Telephotos are the ideal choice if you want to fill the frame with distant subjects, which is why it's the favourite type of lens for wildlife and sports photographers.

Our shortlist of the best value lenses

These lenses have been highlighted as they offer great value and excellent performance

Tamron 10-24mm f/3.5-4.5 Di II LD

www.intro2020.co.uk

MAIN SPECIFICATIONS

Guide price: £500
Street price: £350
Lens construction: 12 elements in nine groups
Aperture range: f/3.5-4.5 to f/22
Filter thread: 77mm
Dimensions: 83.2x86.5mm
Weight: 406g
Fittings: Canon, Nikon, Pentax and Sony

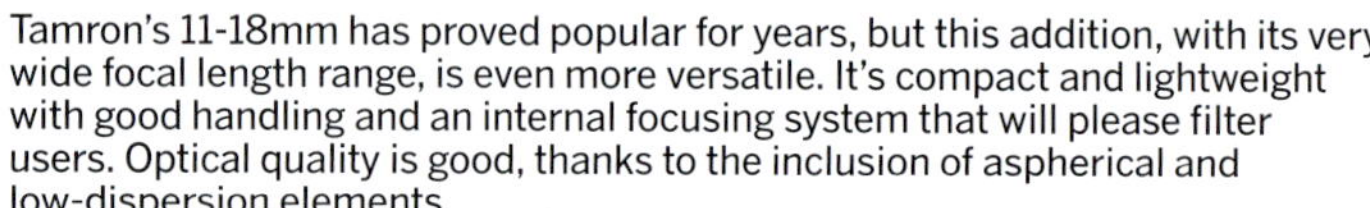

Tamron's 11-18mm has proved popular for years, but this addition, with its very wide focal length range, is even more versatile. It's compact and lightweight with good handling and an internal focusing system that will please filter users. Optical quality is good, thanks to the inclusion of aspherical and low-dispersion elements.

Tamron AF 55-200mm f/4-5.6 LD Di II Macro

www.intro2020.co.uk

MAIN SPECIFICATIONS

Guide price: £180
Street price: £100
Lens construction: 13 elements in nine groups
Aperture range: f/4-5.6 to f/32
Filter thread: 52mm
Dimensions: 71.6x83mm
Weight: 300g
Fittings: Canon and Nikon

Normally sharpness falls off as you zoom through the focal lengths, but this lens retains good sharpness throughout. Its wide zoom ring is very easy to use. The autofocus turns in a good performance – it's not the quickest or quietest, but is accurate and performs well in low light. It's light and compact, and is a great budget telezoom.

Tamron AF 18-270mm f/3.5-6.3 Di II VC Macro

www.intro2020.co.uk

MAIN SPECIFICATIONS

Guide price: £500
Street price: £400
Lens construction: 18 elements in 13 groups
Aperture range: f/3.5-6.3 to f/22
Filter thread: 72mm
Dimensions: 79.6x101mm
Weight: 560g
Fittings: Canon and Nikon

The Tamron 18-270mm boasts an incredible 15x zoom range, giving an effective focal length of 28-419mm, making this suitable for almost every type of subject. The addition of image stabilisation gives it a four-stop benefit, so it can be used hand-held in low-light conditions or at longer focal lengths, with a reduced risk of shake.

Tamron SP AF 60mm f/2 Di II L Macro

www.intro2020.co.uk

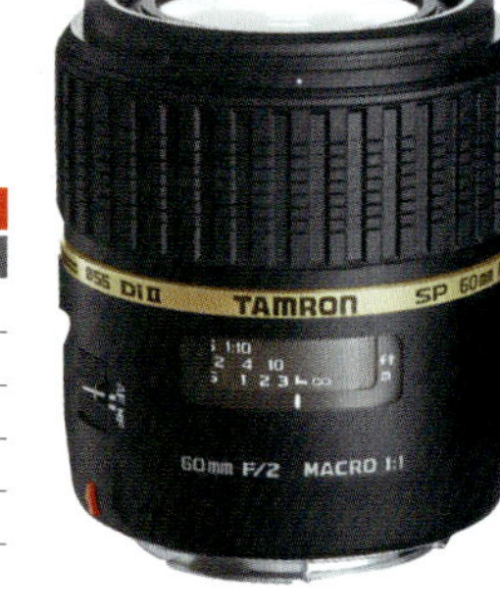

MAIN SPECIFICATIONS

Guide price: £550
Street price: £400
Lens construction: 14 elements in ten groups
Aperture range: f/2 to f/22
Filter thread: 55mm
Dimensions: 73x80mm
Weight: 400g
Fittings: Canon, Nikon and Sony

Designed for exclusive use with DSLRs with APS-C sensors, this lightweight lens holds an ace card in the form of its maximum aperture of f/2, which gives a couple of big advantages over its rivals. As well as a brighter viewfinder image, it creates a very shallow depth-of-field – highly desired by macro photographers. Image quality is superb.

Voigtlander 20mm f/3.5 Color Skopar SL II

www.robertwhite.co.uk

MAIN SPECIFICATIONS

Guide price: £475
Street price: £475
Lens construction: Nine elements in six groups
Aperture range: f/3.5 to f/22
Filter thread: 52mm
Dimensions: 63x28.8mm
Weight: 205g
Fittings: Nikon and Pentax

This manual-focus lens is one of the most affordable prime lenses on the market and one of the smallest and lightest. The manual-focus action is smooth and the barrel boasts a clear hyperfocal scale. Optically, this lens is a very good performer with excellent sharpness once stopped down. A great budget prime lens.

Sigma 120-400mm f/4.5-5.6 DG OS HSM

www.sigma-imaging-uk.com

MAIN SPECIFICATIONS

Guide price: £749
Street price: £600
Lens construction: 21 elements in 15 groups
Aperture range: f/4.5-5.6 to f/32
Filter thread: 77mm
Dimensions: 92x203mm / **Weight:** 1,640g
Fittings: Canon, Nikon, Pentax, Sigma and Sony

Despite its focal length, this high-ratio zoom is relatively compact and includes an Optical Stabiliser (OS), a rear focusing system and HyperSonic Motor (HSM) for quiet, high-speed focusing. Its minimum focusing distance is 150cm with a magnification of 1:4.2 – something that is sure to appeal to enthusiastic nature photographers.

Equipment for close-ups

Many standard zooms boast a useful reproduction ratio of around 1:4 – quarter life-size. This is ideal to get you started, but if you want to get even nearer to your subjects, you may need to invest in a close-up attachment or dedicated macro lens. Here, we look at the most popular and widely used options and cover the merits of each type

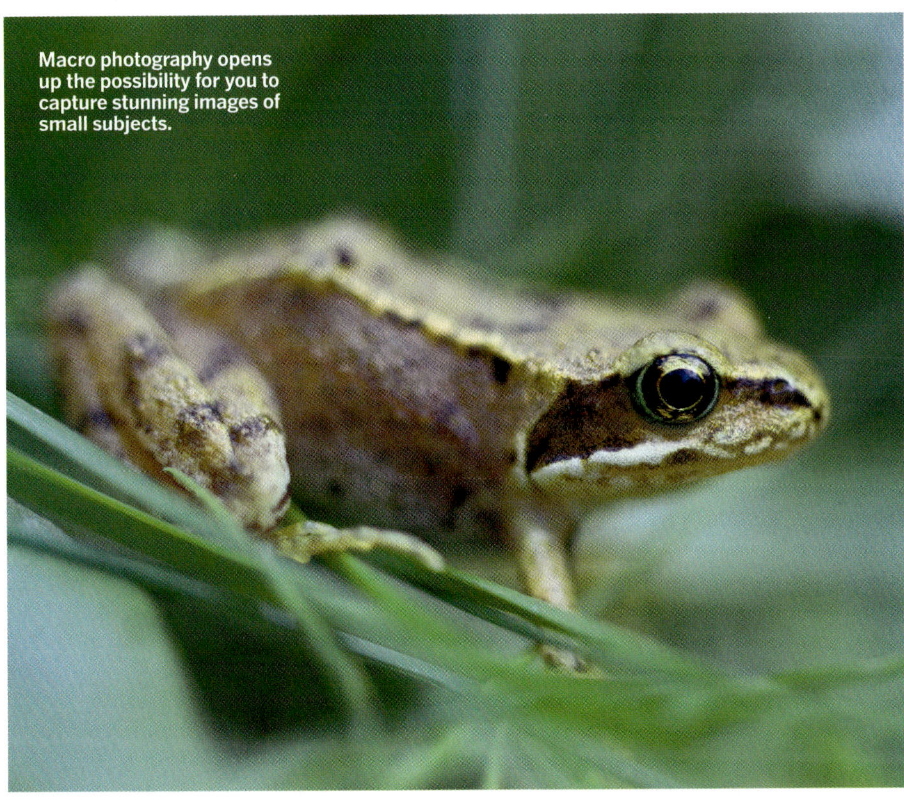

Macro photography opens up the possibility for you to capture stunning images of small subjects.

Useful close-up accessories

Tripod: At high magnification, the effect of camera movement is exaggerated. A tripod is the best form of support. A flexible design is best suited to shooting close-ups as it lets you get low.

Reflector: Small, collapsible reflectors can be angled to bounce light accurately onto your subject. The intensity of the light can be adjusted by moving the reflector closer or further away.

Wimberley Plamp: This is an articulated arm with a clamp fixed at either end. One end can be attached to a tripod leg, while the other can be used to hold a reflector.

Ringflash: A ringflash is designed specifically for close-up work. It attaches directly to the front of the lens, so the burst can illuminate close-up subjects. Twin flash units work in a similar way.

Remote release: Depressing the shutter release button while using a high magnification, and a slow shutter speed, can cause slight camera vibration. A remote release allows you to trigger the shutter without any fear of camera shake.

Close-up filters

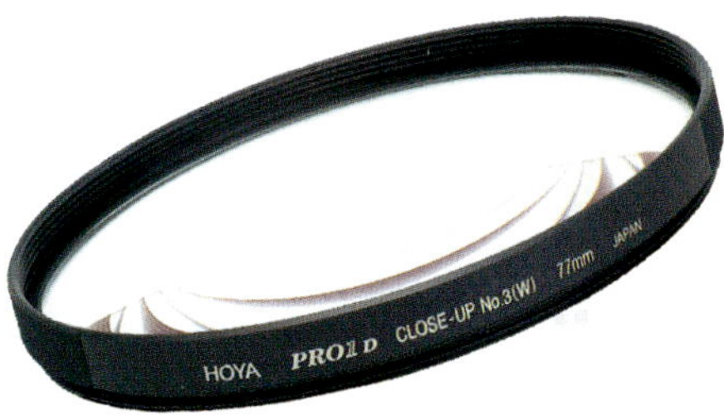

Close-up filters screw to the filter thread of your lens and work like a magnifying glass. Depending on the brand and size, they can cost as little as £10. They are normally of a single element construction and available in progressive strengths, stated in dioptres. +1, +2, +3 and +4 are the most popular, although a two-element +10 dioptre is also available. The higher the number, the nearer the lens can focus and the higher the magnification. Although they can be used in combination, image quality will degrade if you attach more than two at one time. Close-up filters do not affect normal camera functions, so are easy to use and well suited to giving beginners a taste of close-up photography. Despite their modest price, they can produce excellent results and, being so small and lightweight, can easily be used hand-held without affecting stability.

Auto extension tubes

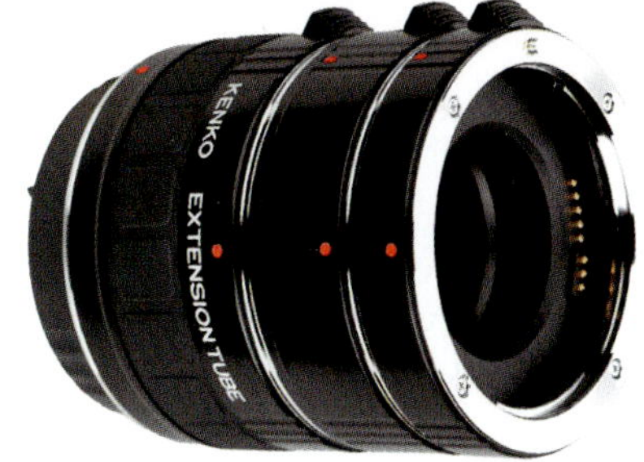

Extension tubes are hollow rings that fit between the camera and lens. They work by increasing the distance between the sensor and lens, allowing the camera to focus closer than normal and increase magnification. They lack any optics and so do not affect the image quality of the lens they're coupled with, making the image quality superior to close-up filters. They can be purchased individually or in a set of three lengths: 12mm, 25mm and 36mm. Their level of magnification is calculated by dividing the amount of extension by the focal length of the lens being used. For example, 25mm of extension used with a 50mm standard lens results in a 1:2 reproduction – or half life-size. To achieve 1:1 life-size, the extension would need to equal the focal length of the lens attached. Therefore, they are most effective when combined with relatively short focal lengths.

Macro lens

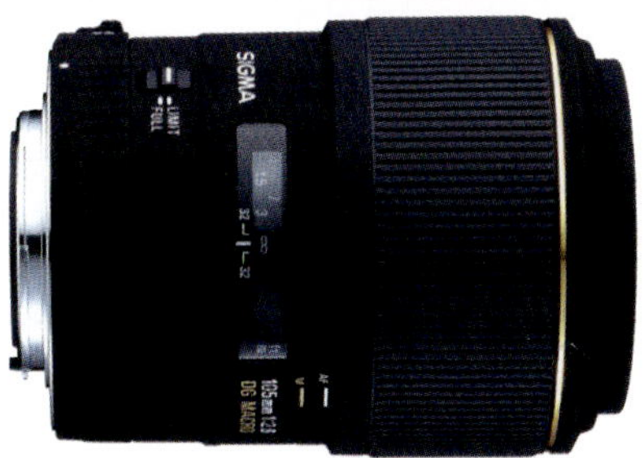

A macro lens is optimised for close focusing. While they are highly corrected to give their best results at close range, they can also be for general use and are popular among portrait photographers. At its minimum focusing distance, a dedicated macro lens will normally produce 1:1 reproduction. They are available in a range of focal lengths: short macro lenses, in the region of 50mm to 70mm, are lightweight and compact, making them easy to use hand-held. However, at their maximum magnification, they don't have a generous working distance. Therefore, this focal length is not the best if you wish to photograph subjects that are easily disturbed, such as insects like butterflies. Generally speaking, focal lengths upwards of 90mm are a better choice. They provide a greater subject-to-camera distance and make it easier to isolate your subject.

Buyers' Guide: Lighting aids

When working with ambient light, reflectors and diffusers are an inexpensive and versatile aid to help you manipulate light to provide the best possible results. We cover the best options from the most popular brands

California Sunbounce

www.theflashcentre.com

The stability, build and light weight of California Sunbounce has made it a favourite with professionals. The reflector panels are fitted to aluminium frames that come in various sizes and are quick and easy to assemble, disassemble and pack up for storage and transportation. There is a good choice of reflective panels available, although not every colour is suitable for every frame (the downloadable PDF catalogue has a useful easy-reference table).

While you can buy extra panels to use with a frame, the difference in price for complete kits and individual panels isn't that wide, so it's often worth buying the complete outfit to save you having to swap panels while on location. As with other brands, there are silver/white and gold/white reflector options, but you'll find that there are other reflective finishes eg zebra/white (zebra is a mix of gold and silver), as well as a number of translucent diffuser options too.

Made for pro use, they're expensive but will last for years of heavy use and are produced from the best possible materials.

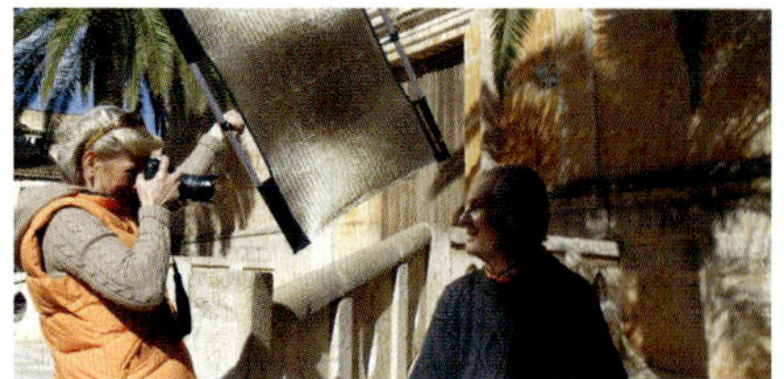

The range is extensive, so contact importers The Flash Centre for details, or download the catalogue at: www.sunbounce.com.

Because the number of options is huge, we've listed the different reflector ranges below and stated the price of the two most popular colours. While a number of sizes are available, we'd recommend the Mini or Pro as your first choice, and the Mega (stated as Big in the catalogue) if you're a very keen enthusiast. Here are the main options:

Micro-mini: (60x90cm)
Silver/white: £101; Zebra/white: £125
Mini: (90x125cm)
Silver/white: £156; Zebra/white: £190
Pro: (130x190cm)
Silver/white: £235; Zebra/white: £275
Big: (180x245cm)
Silver/white: £370; Zebra/white: £430

While translucent panels are available for the Pro and Mega panels, for diffusing purposes we'd recommend the Sun Swatter. This large diffuser is ideal for outdoors as it can be held by a boon over the subject and outside the image area. It's easy to build and designed to be used in windy conditions. There are two sizes and several options for the light-reducing value of the translucent material (1/3, 2/3 or one-stop diffusion). We'd recommend a smaller Sun Swatter with a 1/3 or 2/3-stop diffuser as a good first option. Other reflectors in the range include the Sun-Mover, which allows additional control of the spread of light and the Sun Cage – a purpose-made mobile studio.

Sun Swatter (130x190cm)
1/3 stop complete £230
Sun Swatter (130x190cm)
2/3 Stop complete £240
Sun Swatter Giant (180x245cm)
1/3 Stop complete £385
Sun Swatter Giant (180x245cm)
2/3 Stop Complete £400

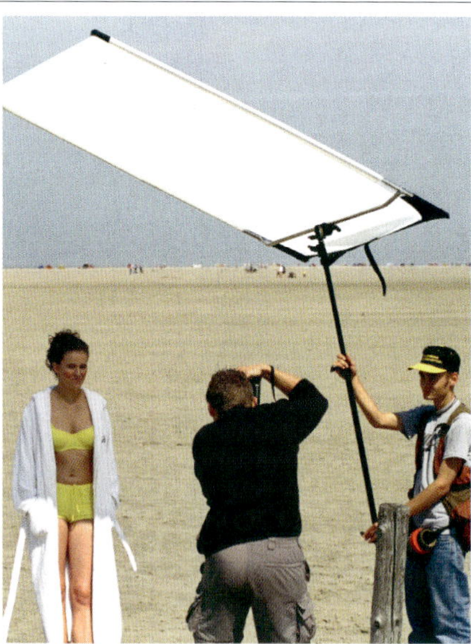

Kenro

www.kenro.co.uk

Kenro produces a circular and a rectangular 5-in-1 kit. The circular reflectors measure 12in, 22in, 32in and 42in, and cost £16, £30, £55 and £68 respectively. The rectangular kits measure 28x44in, 36x48in and 40x66in, and cost £56, £75 and £99 respectively. All the kits are supplied in a bag with a translucent panel and a reversible gold, silver, white and black cover.

Kenro also offers a range of reflectors and diffusers with handles called Easy Grips. It has three 60x90cm (24x36in) models in the range: the £41 translucent and the £45 silver/white and sunlight/white variants. Each 5-in-1 reflector kit features a translucent panel over which a reversible gold, silver, white or black cover can be attached. It folds down into a handy round zip bag when not in use.

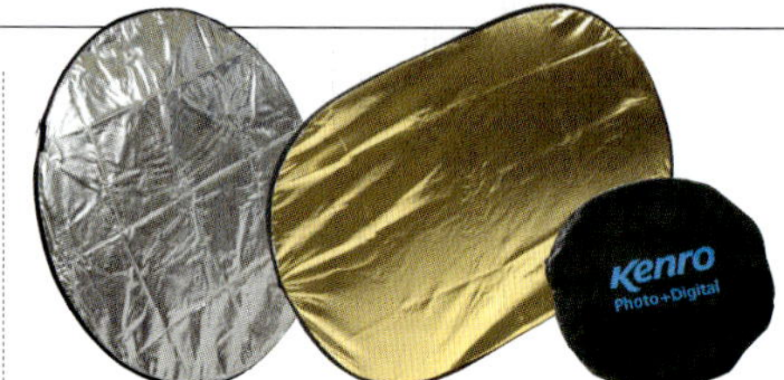

Calumet

www.calumetphoto.co.uk

Calumet is a major photo retailer and has an extensive number of own-brand photo accessories, including its ZipDisc range of collapsible reflectors. These include two colour reflectors, translucent panels and four-colour sleeves (gold/silver/white/black). The ZipDisc kits are as follows:

■ Translucent white ZipDisc panel
The circular diffuser at the heart of its 5-in-1 kit is available on its own, too.
56cm £15; 81cm £26; 107cm £37; 130cm £46

■ Zigzag gold-silver/White ZipDisc
The gold-silver side combines gold and silver for added warmth to the subject.
56cm £15; 81cm £26; 107cm £37

■ Silver/white ZipDisc
The classic hand-held reflector. Supplied with a zip case.
56cm £15; 81cm £26; 107cm £37

■ ZipDisc Four-colour cover
This four-colour (gold, white, silver and black) sleeve cover can be used on any round or oval reflector.
56cm (22in) ZipDisc reversible: £13
81cm (32in) ZipDisc reversible: £15
107cm (42in) ZipDisc reversible: £16

■ 5-in-1 kit
This is a combination of the ZipDisc translucent panel and the four-colour sleeve. We've tested the 81cm 5-in-1 in our comparison test.
56cm £21; 81cm £34; 107cm £41

Please note that if you visit Calumet's website, you may get a little confused about the product descriptions, so if you've any queries, phone the customer service line on 08706 030303.

Elemental

www.studio-flash.com

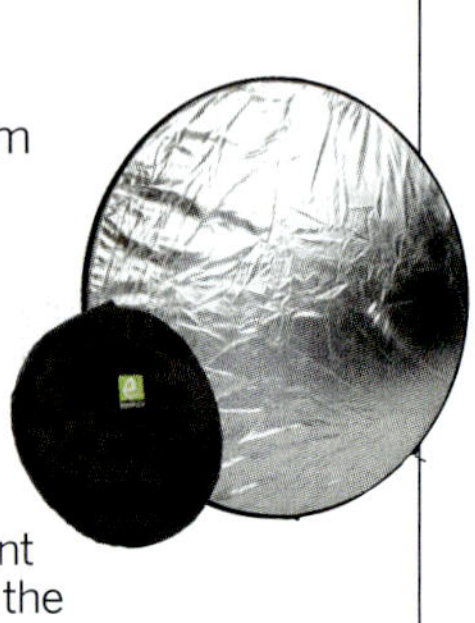

Budget studioflash specialists Elemental currently only has two collapsible reflectors in its range, but we've included them in this guide as they represent excellent value for money. Both the 80cm and 107cm 5-in-1 kits comprise a white diffuser with an interchangeable gold, silver and white reflector cover, all supplied in a black bag. The 80cm costs £25, while the 107cm is £35. Elemental also has a reflector arm available for £25.

Interfit

www.interfitphotographic.com

Interfit is one of the UK's leading brands of studio equipment and has an extensive range of reflectors, from hand-helds to larger stand-supported types, so you've plenty of choice!

Soft sun/white; silver/white and silver/gold
Round, collapsible reflectors available in three finishes and four sizes.
30cm £10.50; **56cm** £16.50; **82cm** £27.60; **107cm** £39

5-in-1 kits
These feature a translucent reflector, with a four-colour overlay sleeve (gold, silver, black and white), supplied in a zip-up bag. They are available in three sizes, as follows.
56cm £26.50: **82cm** £37; **107cm** £44

Easy Grip
Interfit's Easy Grip reflector has a thick handle for one-handed use and measures 90x60cm (36x24in). It is available in the following colours: sunlight/white; gold/silver; silver/white and ½-stop translucent and costs £40.

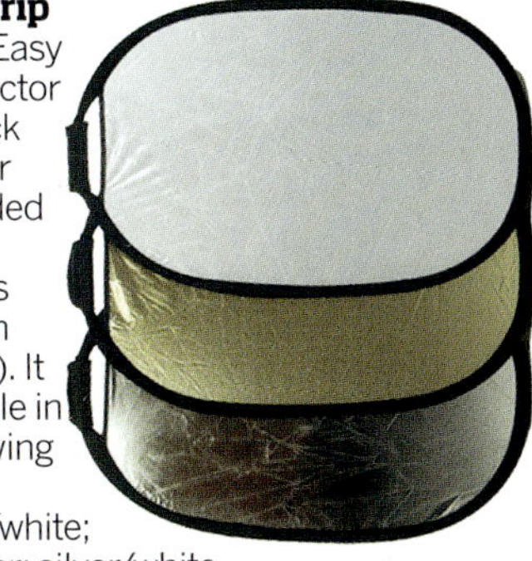

Portrait Reflector Kit
Interfit's Portrait Reflector Kit is essentially three reflector panels attached to a frame that fits easily on a lighting stand. Each 90x60cm (36x24in) panel can be individually positioned for improved lighting control. The kit is supplied with one silver/gold panel and two sunlight/silver panels, and costs £100.

The Large Flat Panel Reflector
Studio-based photographers may be interested in these large reflector panels, made for full-length portraits and fashion shoots. The Large Flat Panel Reflector measures 89x178cm (35x70in) and is supplied complete with a stand and a rotating/tilting bracket for using the panel vertically or horizontally. Silver/gold and white/black versions are available for £82.

Flexi-lite 5-in-1
This stand-mounted panel reflector is aimed at pros and can be used hand-held or on location. The aluminium frame has a boon arm that can be positioned at any angle. Various kits are available in medium (100x150cm) or large (150x200cm). The INT303 has a gold/silver/black/white cover and costs £306.

Lastolite

www.lastolite.com

Lastolite is one of the world's leading studio accessory brands and is particularly renowned for its lighting aids, so it's no surprise to discover it has an extensive range of products. Many are designed for specific pro uses, so due to space constraints, we've selected the products most suitable for general portrait photography. A comprehensive brochure PDF can be downloaded from Lastolite's website if you'd like to check out the entire range.

Collapsible reflectors: When it comes to collapsible reflectors, no brand has as many options as Lastolite. Its round reflectors are available in 30cm, 50cm, 76cm, 95cm and 120cm diameters and there is a huge 1.8x1.2m rectangular option, too. All of these are available in the following finishes: silver/white; Sunfire/white, silver/gold, Sunfire/silver; gold/white and Sunlite/soft silver. A two-stop diffuser is also available in all sizes from 50cm upwards. Guide prices for silver/white are as follows.
30cm £13; **50cm** £24; **75cm** £35; **95cm** £58; **120cm** £75; **1.8x1.2m** £91

Bottletops 5-in-1 kit: This includes a diffuser panel with elasticated covers. The kit comprises the diffuser panel and a gold/white and Sunfire/silver cover and comes in four sizes: 50cm (£41), 75cm (£47), 95cm (£57) and 120cm (£85).

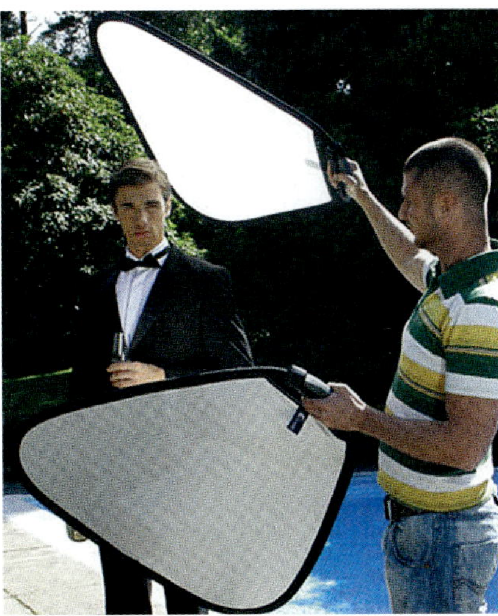

TriGrip: The original TriGrip was the first collapsible reflector to feature a handle and proved extremely popular. The design has been updated, with a new moulded handle improving handling and there are now three sizes in the range: the £47 Mini TriGrip (45cm); £62 TriGrip (75cm) and £77 Large TriGrip (1.2m). For each size, you can choose reflectors in silver/white, gold/white, Sunfire/silver and Sunlite/Softsilver finishes, as well as a one-stop or two-stop diffuser. Accessories for the TriGrip include a support bracket and the TriFlip, a set of seven reflector covers that can be placed over a TriGrip to offer the ultimate in versatility. You can also buy a £185 TriFlip 8:1 kit that supplies a two-stop diffuser (Mini TriGrip or TriGrip) with seven colour sleeves.

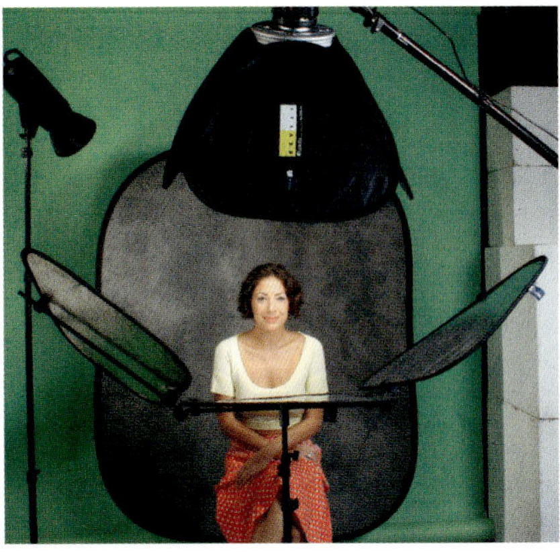

Triflector: The MkII kit consists of a support frame with three collapsible panels, all easily packed away in a case weighing a total of only 1.2kg. The panels are available in the following reflective finishes: Sunfire/silver, silver/white, gold/white and a 1.2-stop diffuser. A kit is £123; extra sets of panels range from £33-£45.

UpLite 4:1: A set of self-supporting 120x90cm reflector panels for use by photographers working on their own, who need to bounce light at an angle from the floor. The angle can be adjusted from 30-80° and the two panels can also be separated for hand-held use. The UpLite comes in two versions: the Cool Tone has sunlite/softsilver and silver/white reflective surfaces; while the Warm Tone has gold/white and Sunfire/silver reflective surfaces. It comes supplied with a waterproof shower cap and a carry case, and costs £120.

Skylite: Best suited for serious photographers looking for a lightweight, durable and large diffuser that can also double up as a reflector. The rigid, hollow aluminium frame supports a diffuser (0.75 or 1.25 stop) or reflector (gold/silver, silver/white, black/white or Sunfire/white) via secure Velcro fastenings. The Skylite can be bought in a number of kit forms and three sizes are available as follows: small 1.1x1.1m (1.3kg); medium 1x2m (2kg) and large 2x2m (2.3kg). The standard kit includes the frame, silver/white and translucent fabrics and carry bag, and are priced at around £138, £180 and £260 for the small, medium and large respectively.

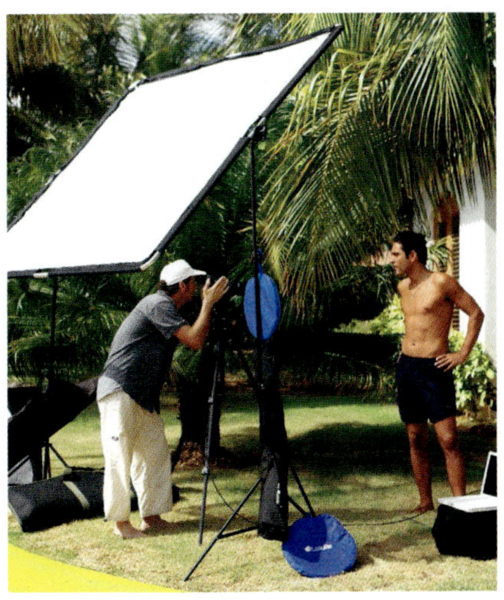

5-in-1 reflector kits

If you're looking to buy your first lighting aid, make it one of these 5-in-1 kits. They offer silver, white, gold and (rarely used) black finishes to suit a variety of shooting situations. The translucent panel, which these reflective sleeves wrap around, can be used as a soft white reflector, although its efficiency is poor. You can also use it to shade your subject, but we'd recommend purchasing a purpose-built diffuser, too, as it works far better. As we discovered when conducting this test, in all areas including build quality, the kits are very similar, so for most photographers, the cheapest option may well be the best one. We've highlighted the major differences below, but in truth, they're all very similar products.

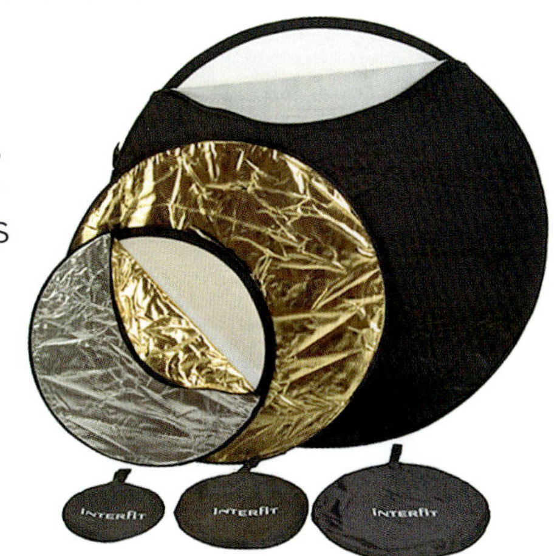

Elemental 5-in-1 (107cm)

www.studio-flash.com

Guide Price: £35
Street Price: £35

Better known for their excellent range of budget studioflash equipment, Elemental also offers a couple of 5-in-1 reflector kits that represent excellent value. This 107cm kit comes in its own black zip-up bag and, once removed, the 5-in-1 reflector looks and handles much like the similarly priced Interfit. The translucent panel is nicely manufactured and the coloured sleeve has a slot for the panel's tab to slip through when zipped up. The sleeve can be used to give a silver/black or gold/white effect, and is thick and well put together. This is a great budget option and excellent value for money.

Verdict

An excellent budget buy.

Build quality (panel)	★★★★★
Build quality (sleeve)	★★★★½
Versatility	★★★★
Performance	★★★★★
Value for money	★★★★★
OVERALL	★★★★★

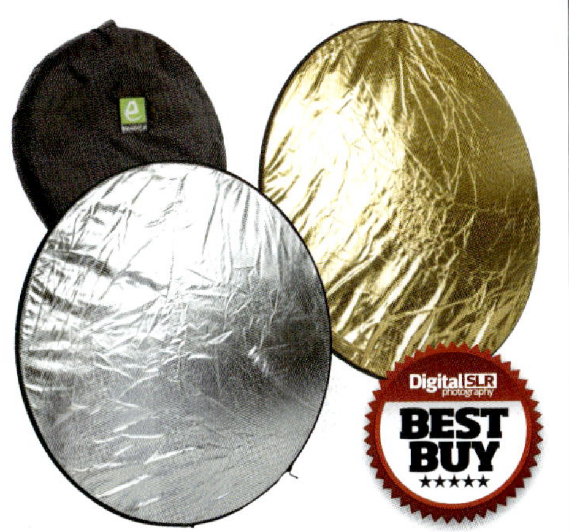

Interfit 265 (107cm)

www.interfitphotographic.com

Guide Price: £44
Street Price: £38

The white surface of the well-made translucent panel offers a ½-stop efficiency and has a thick black edge and small cloth tab for hanging off a hook. The sleeve is made from thick material and can be wrapped around to give silver/black or gold/white options. The zip has a smooth action and at its end, the sleeve has a gap for the tab to stick through. Interfit makes a large number of reflector kits, so you should have no trouble finding the most suitable size for you. Better still, they're available at an excellent price. A high-quality piece of equipment, supplied in a well-constructed zip-up black bag.

Verdict

An excellent, affordable kit.

Build quality (panel)	★★★★★
Build quality (sleeve)	★★★★½
Versatility	★★★★
Performance	★★★★★
Value for money	★★★★★
OVERALL	★★★★★

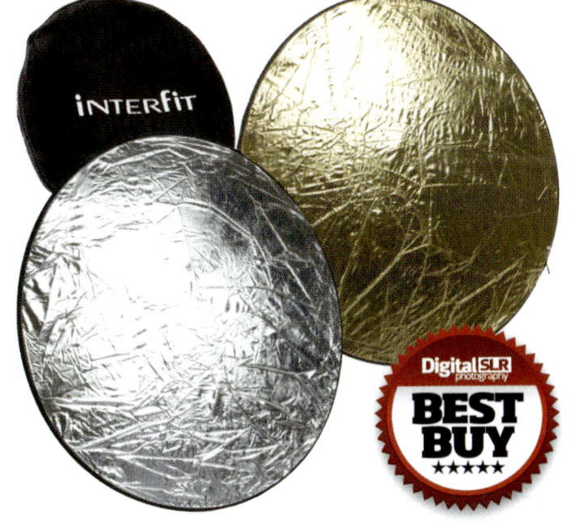

Lastolite Bottletop 4896 (120cm)

www.lastolite.com

Guide Price: £85
Street Price: £80

This 120cm kit is the largest in the range, and also the biggest and most expensive 5-in-1 in our test. It's also different in a number of ways. First, the 5-in-1 kit is made up of a panel and two reversible elasticated sleeves: a gold/white and a silver/sunfire. This has a number of benefits: it's quicker to change from one to another as there is no zip, and you can fit one over each side of the panel, allowing you to have different combinations to suit your liking. The build quality is first-rate, and spare panels are available so you can place a sleeve on each and have two reflectors at the ready.

Verdict

Versatile and made to last.

Build quality (panel)	★★★★★
Build quality (sleeve)	★★★★★
Versatility	★★★★★
Performance	★★★★★
Value for money	★★★★
OVERALL	★★★★★

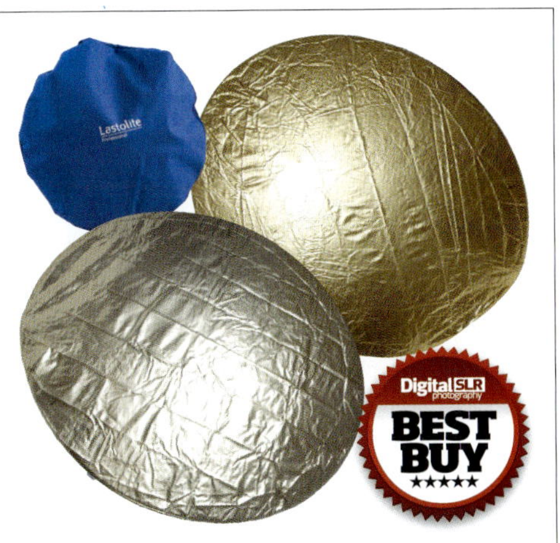

Bags and backpacks

Expert advice on storage to protect your camera gear

MOST OUTDOOR PHOTOGRAPHERS prefer backpacks as they distribute weight over your shoulders and back, making it far easier to carry gear over long distances. The daypack holds photo gear in the bottom section and general items in the top compartment, while dedicated photo backpacks are designed with larger kits in mind. Consider the following:

Comfort: As you carry more kit, the weight increases, so shoulder straps are important. The wider and more padded they are, the less they dig into your shoulders. Waist straps are useful, as they relieve tension from the lumbar region and help keep your back straight. Another important factor is the bag's frame. Some are sturdier than others which may seem uncomfortable at first, but it helps keep your back straight on long treks.

Capacity: Think about how much kit you plan to carry. All the bags here have adjustable compartments, so are quite versatile.

Build quality: How well the backpack is put together, including the stitching, zippers and weatherproofing, determines how long it ought to last, how strong it is and how well it protects your equipment.

Features (see panel below): Some photographers just want a bag with lots of space, others are more demanding over specific features. Most have front pockets, designed to help you organise your memory cards and batteries into used and unused.

Price: We have stated the average street price from a number of popular retailers and not the manufacturer's guide price.

Features

1) Straps Check to see if the straps are adjustable, padded and wide, to stop them from cutting into your shoulders on long journeys. Also look for waist straps.

2) Padding Some bags have pressure pads on the back, which will take a lot of the strain out of long journeys and spread the weight of the gear over a larger area.

3) Storage/capacity Does the bag hold all the equipment you will need for your photography? If there is too much empty space, the bag will be unbalanced, which can be bad for your back. All the bags in this test feature adjustable dividers and offer quite a bit of versatility.

4) Weatherproofing/ rain cover Most bags are weather resistant. Some are weatherproof, and others have all-weather covers that can be pulled out from a hidden compartment, usually on the base.

5) Laptop compartment Make sure that the laptop compartment is big enough for your computer, as they vary in size. The padding is also important here.

6) Accessory clips Some bags allow you to attach further bags, tripods and monopods, but some are only compatible with the manufacturer's own clip systems.

7) Zips If you go out a lot in bad weather or near water, make sure that the zips are up to it. Wildlife photographers should also consider the noise made by the zips as animals can be easily frightened off.

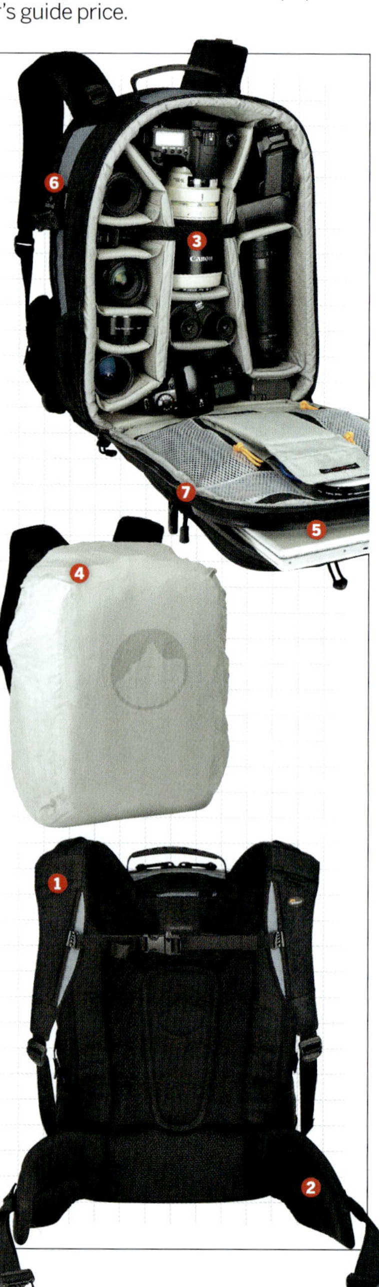

Kit watch!

Fitting and wearing a bag properly
If you're carrying a lot of heavy kit, it's important that your bag sits correctly on your back or at your side. This advice can prevent all kinds of back and posture problems. With a backpack, ensure that both straps are over your shoulders and tightened so that the bag sits in the centre of your back. If it has waist and chest straps, make sure you use them to distribute the weight evenly across your back, rather than just your shoulders. For shoulder bags, pull the strap over your head to the opposite shoulder. This will distribute the weight better than if it were on the closest shoulder and stop it from slipping off your shoulder or being easily snatched.

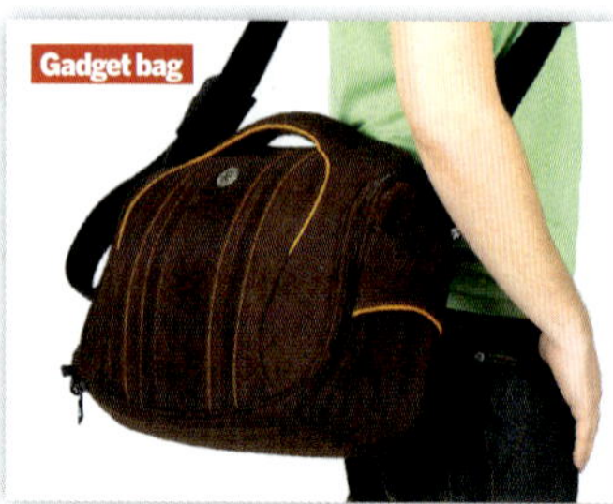

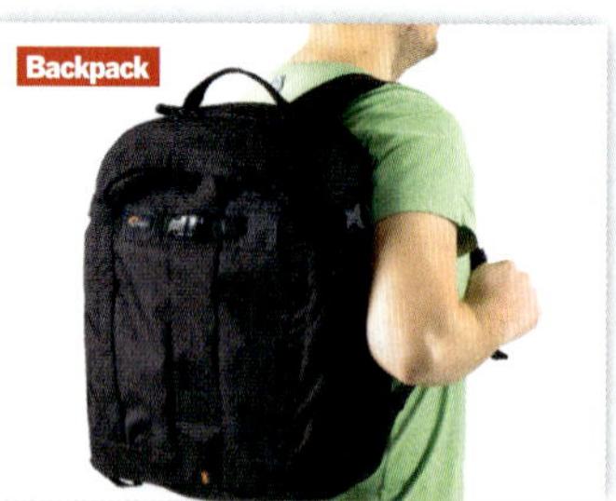

Lowepro CompuDay Photo 250

Dimensions: 40x32x18cm
Weight: 900g
Warranty: Lifetime
Contact: 01902 864646
Website: www.lowepro.com

This laptop bag has plenty of room for everyday items and a padded side compartment big enough for a DSLR with standard zoom. While the camera aspect is not exactly an afterthought, the large and deep main compartment is better suited to a flask and sarnies than anything specifically photographic. There are no dividers, but there's room for a spare lens or flashgun if protected in a soft wrap. The top zip also has a rain flap. It's a great concept for carrying a camera alongside your general workday kit. There are pockets for documents and a separate interior bag for a laptop charger and leads. The harness is simple, just shoulder straps, though the contoured shape makes it easy to carry the bag over one shoulder with quick access to the camera.

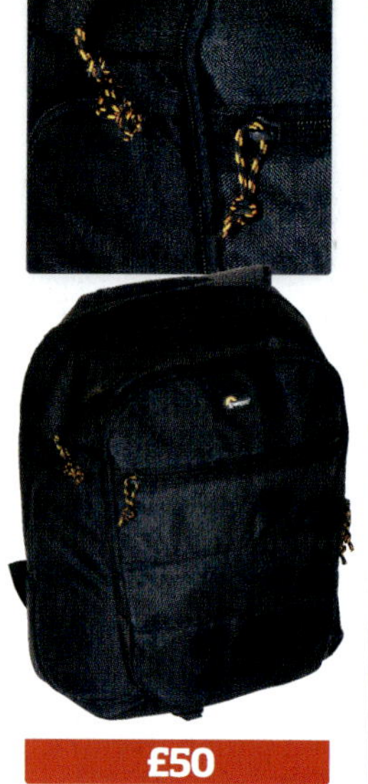

£50

Vanguard UP-Rise 45

Dimensions (outer): 43x32x22cm
Weight: 1,600g
Warranty: Limited lifetime
Contact: 01782 753304
Website: www.vanguardworld.co.uk

The UP-Rise tag refers to Vanguard's expansion system, supposedly unzipping extra space when needed, but in practice with the UP-Rise 45 it makes barely any difference. Not that it is short on space, or features. The main compartment is large enough for a DSLR with up to 70-200mm zoom attached, plus two or three extra lenses and a flashgun. Grabbing the camera through the side flap is easy, with lesser-used items accessed by unzipping the back. The padded top compartment is large, and the bottom can be detached to swing down and form one very large holdall. There are a number of thoughtful touches, like the camera compartment secured with fast-pull twin zips, plus Velcro and a clip. There are dual grab handles, a rain cover and a good tripod slot with adjustable straps.

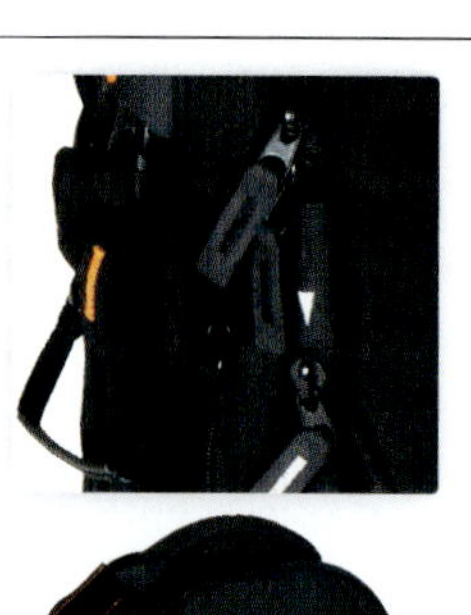

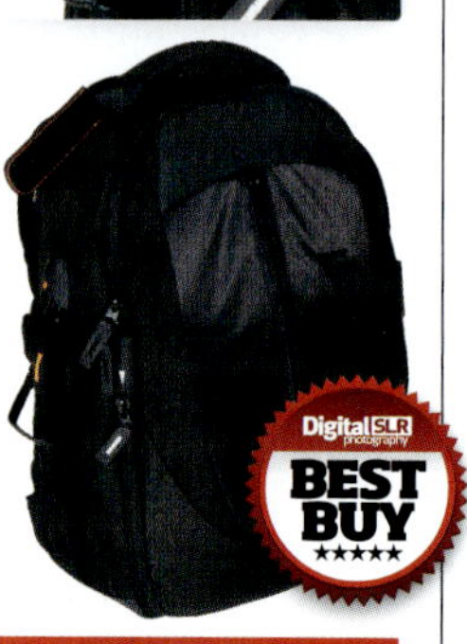

£55

Tamrac Evolution 6

Dimensions: 42x26x19cm
Weight: 1,510g
Warranty: Five years
Contact: 01628 674411
Website: www.intro2020.co.uk

This is one of Tamrac's clever Evolution series, which includes two larger versions in the range. There are three ways of carrying it, as a backpack, or as either left- or right-handed sling. There are three entry points to the main camera compartment, from both sides and the front. It works well as a sling for fast access, with the other shoulder strap and waistband tucked away behind the rear padding. Camera access is through the side, where there's room for a DSLR and medium-sized zoom. There's also enough space for another lens or maybe two, plus flash, and you can get at those either through the front flap, or from the opposite side. The top compartment has useful extra capacity, wide enough for a 70-200mm zoom. The outer is well padded, but any equipment in there would need its own protection.

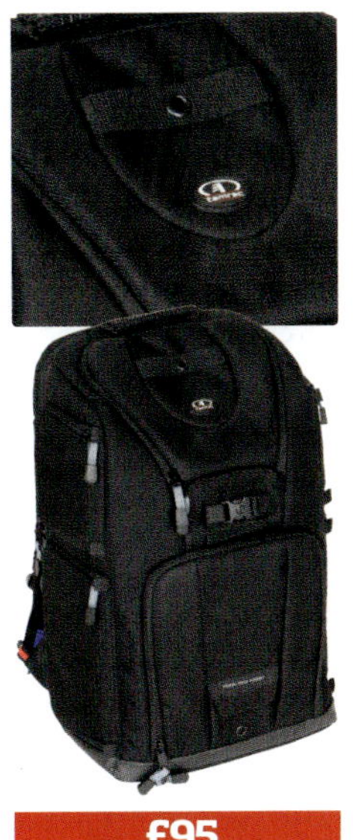

£95

Tamrac Aero Speed Pack 85

Dimensions: 36x23x50cm
Weight: 1,600g
Warranty: Five years
Contact: 01628 674411
Website: www.intro2020.co.uk

With space to hold personal and camera gear, the Aero Speed Pack 85 is well designed, with an alternate layout that allows you to carry more gear. It can hold a large DSLR, at least three lenses and it's also compatible with Tamrac's Strap Accessory System to slip on extra pouches. There's both side and front entry access, which makes getting gear out a little quicker, although you still need to take this backpack off first. The top of the bag has room for a light coat, lunch and a few other essentials, but there's no laptop compartment. Other pockets are limited, too; there are a couple of side mesh pockets, and Velcro and zipped pouches for storing memory cards and batteries. Padding on the rear and non-slip straps is thin and there's no sternum strap, waist belt or rain cover either.

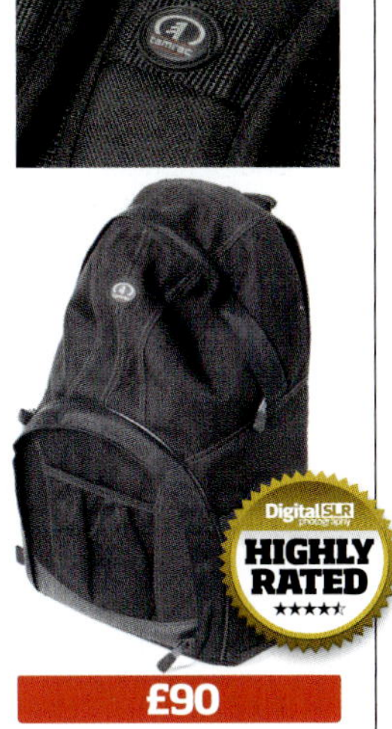

Digital SLR Photography HIGHLY RATED ★★★★½

£90

Hama Defender 170 Backpack

Dimensions: 40x26x45cm
Weight: 2,800g
Warranty: 30 years
Contact: 0845 2304262
Website: www.hama.co.uk

This large backpack has two compartments, both of which feature generous space. The lower compartment fits a large DSLR with 24-70mm f/2.8 attached, a long zoom, flashgun, two small primes and even a second body. The flexible dividers make it versatile, too, as the whole padded section can also be removed, and there's a large 17in laptop compartment. The construction is robust with Ultra Dobby Nylon, protected zips, tough belts, strong metal hooks and a rubber base that covers the bottom, so no problems leaving it on wet ground. The shoulder straps are adjustable, but not very well padded, and there's a waist belt, lumbar support and padding on the rear for improved comfort. Features are good, too, with a detachable microfibre cloth, memory card wallet, rain cover and several pockets.

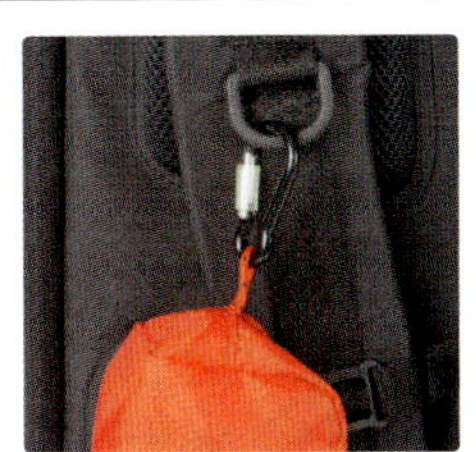

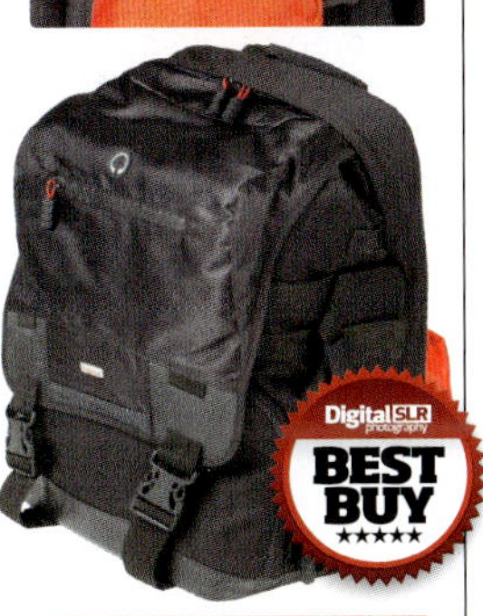

Digital SLR Photography BEST BUY ★★★★★

£110

Lowepro Flipside 400 AW

Dimensions: 45x30x24cm
Weight: 1,540g
Warranty: Lifetime
Contact: 01902 864646
Website: www.lowepro.com

This is a serious backpack, designed for carrying lots of camera gear with comfort and security. The whole of the back unzips to open a storage area the full size of the bag, large enough for a couple of cameras, four or five lenses up to almost any length, flash and accessories. When you're carrying it, there's no access to the main compartment – for you or anyone else. Comfort is assured by shoulder straps and chest strap, the waist band is deep and heavily padded, and includes accessory loops. Lowepro claims you can rotate the bag around to your front and access gear while it's attached to your waist, but that's asking a lot when it's full. The front compartment is quite shallow and thinly padded, but deep and large enough for small personal items and an iPad, but not a laptop.

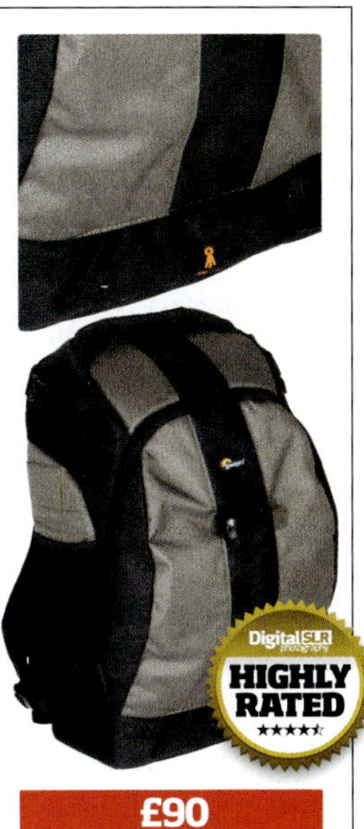

Digital SLR Photography HIGHLY RATED ★★★★½

£90

Lowepro Pro Runner 450 AW

Dimensions: 34x29x50.5cm
Weight: 2,700g
Warranty: Lifetime
Contact: 01902 864646
Website: www.lowepro.com

The Pro Runner 450 AW holds a lot of gear, with room for two large DSLRs with zooms attached, and space for several extra lenses, flashguns, a third body and a 17in laptop, too. The shoulder straps are thickly padded and adjustable, and the waist belt and carry handle will be appreciated when carting about all that weight. The compression straps help reduce the bulk on the 450 AW for easier transportation, there's a built-in all-weather cover and loops are handy for carrying a tripod. The front pocket will hold a few personal items, the three internal pockets feature windowpane panels to help keep things like filters on display, and there are two dedicated memory card pouches, too. This bag is a great option for carrying a large outfit as well as personal gear.

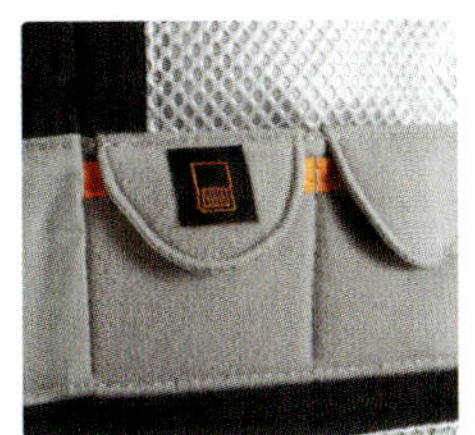

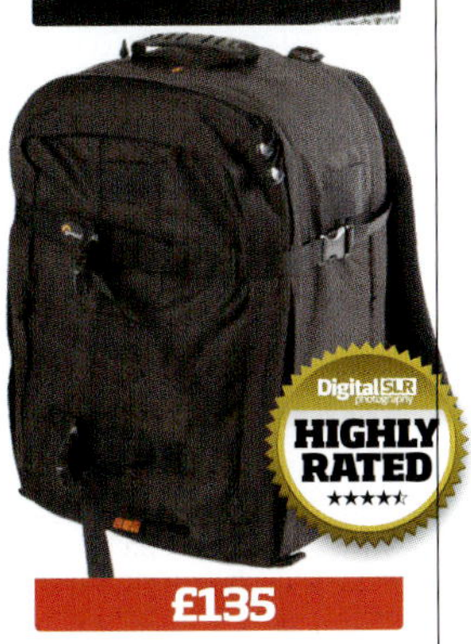

Digital SLR Photography HIGHLY RATED ★★★★½

£135

Tamrac Expedition 7x

Dimensions: 33x34x50cm
Weight: 2,900g
Warranty: Five years (limited)
Contact: 01628 674411
Website: www.intro2020.co.uk

The Expedition 7x boasts lots of room and a comfortable harness system. There's loads of padding on the shoulder straps, lumbar support and waist belt, together with airflow channels to keep you cool. There's no rain cover, but water-resistant zips and a lock-down rain flap help protect your gear. The dual-hinge divider system helps you carry one or two DSLRs with zooms attached, with room to spare for other lenses, and you can boost capacity with Tamrac's Modular Accessory System and Strap Accessory System. There's a 15in laptop compartment and two 'wing' accessory pockets with Tamrac's Memory and Battery Management System for organising essentials. There's also a plastic reinforced pocket which provides protection for fragile accessories and acts as a tripod footrest.

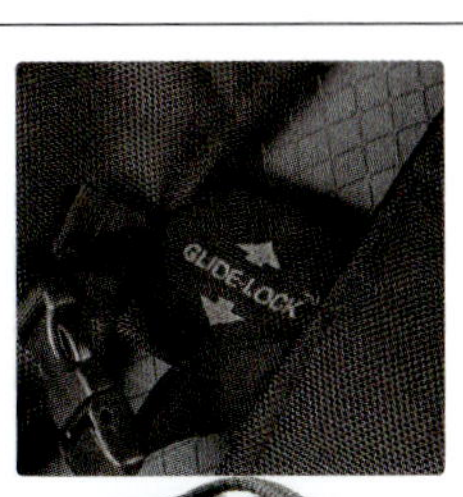

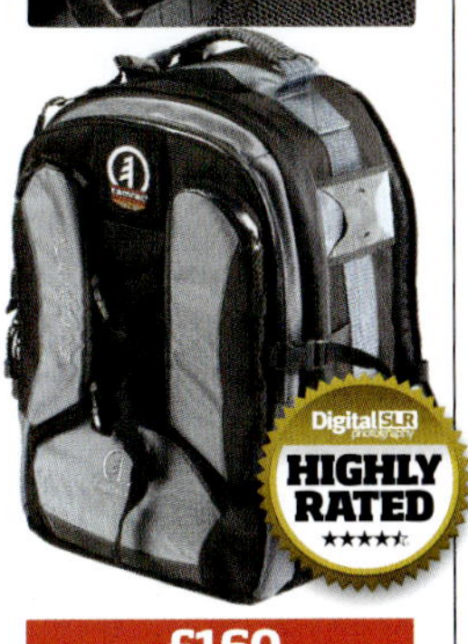

Digital SLR Photography HIGHLY RATED ★★★★½

£160

Tripods for outdoor use

Don't leave home without a three-legged friend

A TRIPOD SHOULD BE VIEWED as an essential part of your outfit. You'll usually be using a small aperture setting to maximise depth-of-field, along with a low ISO rating to give the highest quality results, which will result in long shutter speeds. Handholding might be feasible with some shots, but with a tripod you never need to worry about the shakes. You'll also find that, by using a tripod, you can spend more time and attention on fine-tuning the framing of the scene to get the best possible composition. You'll discover a huge variety of tripods on offer, so choosing one isn't straightforward, but there are two key factors to consider. The first is stability – while cheaper models may be tempting, they may not provide a stable platform, so ensure you pick a model that is sturdy enough to keep your kit totally still when shooting. The second factor to think about is how much a tripod weighs, which is important as you'll be carrying it, along with the rest of your gear, for considerable distances. Most tripods are made from aluminium, which is sturdy and fairly lightweight, although decent models weigh around 2kg or more. If you want a tripod that's as sturdy but far lighter, you'll want a carbon-fibre model, although you'll have to be prepared to pay a premium for one. Our selection of tripods have all received the highest ratings in *Digital SLR Photography* magazine. We've chosen examples that cover various price ranges to ensure you find one that suits your budget. Bear in mind that with the more expensive models, you buy the tripod and the head separately.

Features

1) Head There are various tripod heads available, from ball-and-socket to three-way pan-and-tilt. Some have interchangeable heads. . When choosing a tripod, attach your DSLR securely and ensure the head is free from movement.

2) Quick-release plate These allow you to quickly attach and detach your DSLR to/from the tripod. All of the tripods in this review have one.

3) Leg locks Most of the tripods here feature 'clip' locks, which are easy to use and provide a firm lock.

4) Leg sections Tripods with three leg sections or fewer tend to be the most sturdy, as the more sections you have, the less stable they can become.

5) Spirit levels Useful for landscape photography, many tripods feature built-in spirit levels to make sure your images are straight. If not, your local photo store should sell one that slots straight on to your hotshoe.

6) Bag hook Some tripods have hooks on the central column, from which a bag can be hung, using its weight to add stability to the tripod in windy conditions.

7) Tripod feet Spikes are good for grip outdoors but will scratch flooring. Rubber feet offer good grip indoors and outside and are the best choice for general use.

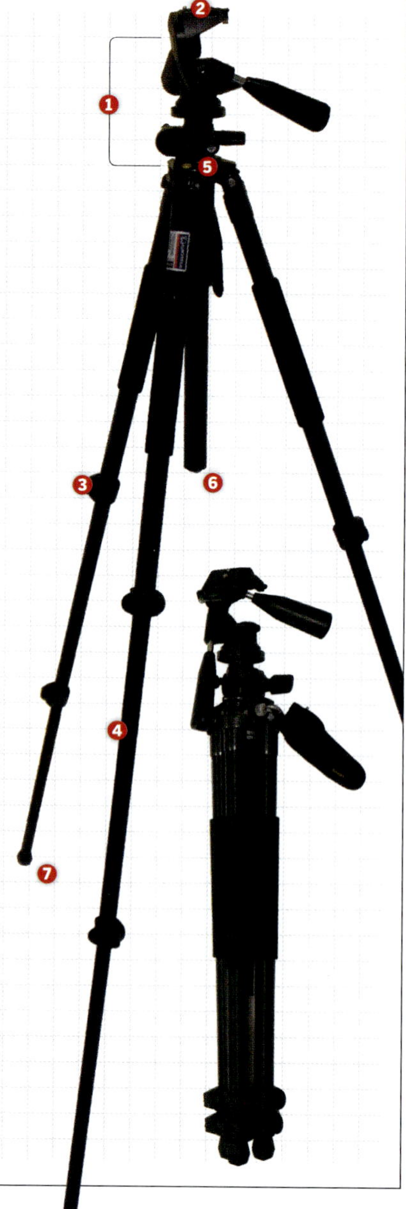

Kit watch!

Interchangeable tripod heads

Most high-end tripods aren't supplied with a head. This allows users to choose their preferred legs and a specialist or general-purpose head. The two most common types of heads are as follows:

Ball-and-socket: These range from very simple heads with one control to complex units with panoramic locks and gauges, grip-locks and hydraulic ball-locking systems. Usually stronger and quicker to adjust than pan-and-tilt heads, they allow free movement in all directions. 'Slipping' used to be a problem; not so much now, though.

Three-way heads: Commonly known as pan-and-tilt heads, these are great for all types of photography. Panning gauges, showing the shooting angle, are useful for panoramic shots, although there are specialised heads made for this, too. Fluid heads have the smoothest panning motion, making them ideal for sports photographers.

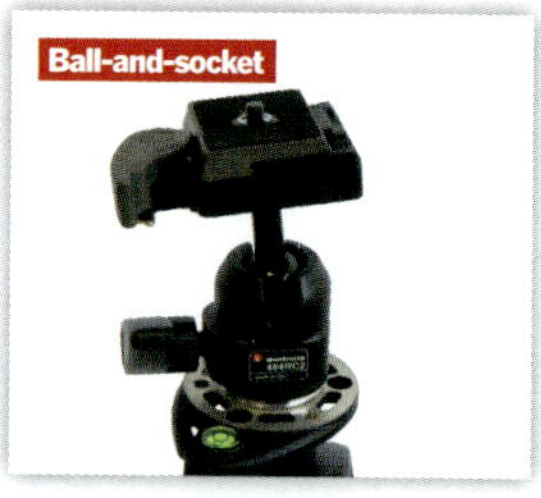
Ball-and-socket

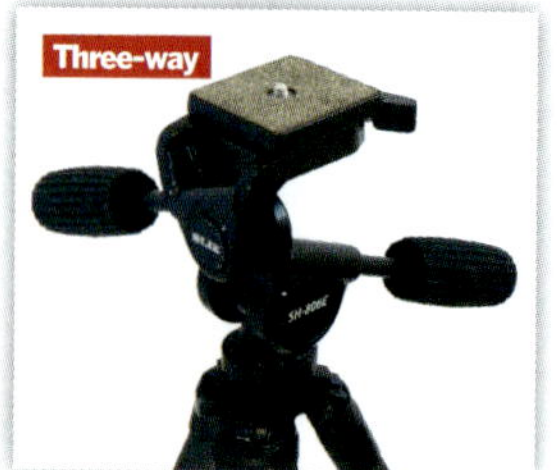
Three-way

Giottos MTL9351B + MH5011 head

Length (closed): 64cm
Number of leg sections: 3
Height (legs extended): 159cm
Maximum load: 5kg
Weight: 2.1kg
Website: www.giottos-tripods.com

Solid aluminium legs with foam insulators keep hands from freezing to them on cold days. The nuts and locks are a combination of plastic and die-cast aluminium, and are as solid as could be hoped for at this price. The three-way head is easily controllable and features three spirit levels in addition to the one on the legs, so there's no excuse for wonky horizons! It has a lockable rotational central column, which can be removed and reinserted horizontally or inverted for macro or copy work. The tripod is very sturdy for the price, and comes with its own tool kit in case you need to make any adjustments. There is also a hidden bag hook underneath the central column. The MTL9351B had no problems coping with our mid-range Nikon DSLR and would provide a very suitable platform on which the amateur landscaper could mount his DSLR.

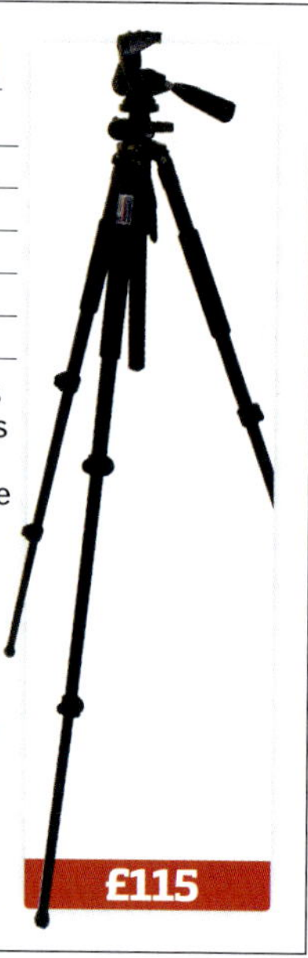

£115

Giottos Vitruvian VGR8255 kit

Length (closed): 40cm
Height (legs extended): 136cm
Number of leg sections: 5
Maximum load: 4kg
Weight: 1.28kg
Website: www.giottos-tripods.com

Boasting the 'reverse technology' design, the legs of the Vitruvian fold 180° to surround the centre column, reducing the length to only 40cm. Open the legs and it extends to an impressive 1.36m (1.57m with centre column raised, too). Made from six-layer carbon-fibre, it's lightweight and stable with aluminium alloy in the main casting adding to its robustness, while a hook on the centre column can hold ballast. Twist locks are fast and easy to use and the centre column can be removed to transform it into a monopod. The supplied ball-and-socket head provides a smooth action and has a friction lock, spirit level and quick-release plate with safety lock. The maximum load of 4kg makes this a suitable choice for most. An aluminium version (VGR9255) has a virtually identical spec, weighs 1.5kg and costs around £180.

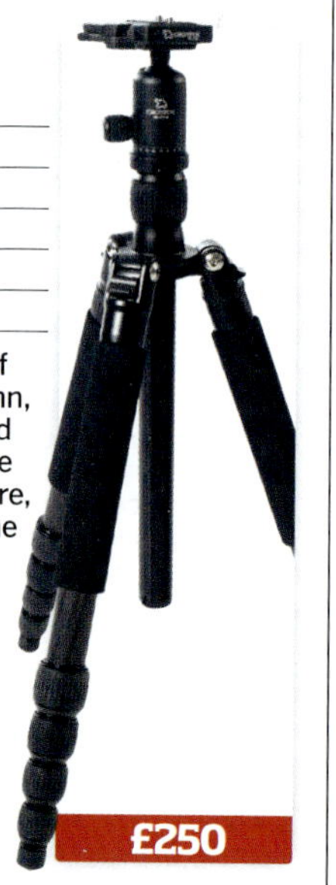

£250

Giottos MTL8240B + MH1302-652 head

Length (closed): 51cm
Height (legs extended): 148cm
Number of leg sections: 4
Maximum load: 3kg
Weight: 1.375kg
Website: www.giottos-tripods.com

This tripod is exceptionally light, yet sturdy, although the maximum load may prove restrictive for some. The rubberised twist locks are secure and easy to use and foam leg grips give a comfortable grip in cold weather. The three-position angle locks ensure the legs don't slip, which is reassuring to those using expensive kit. The central column is reversible for low-level and macro shots, and has a bag hook. The ball-and-socket head is also very secure, and it is easy to manoeuvre the head into just about any position. It has a variable friction control, allowing the user a great deal of control, which means precision adjustments are quick and easy to implement. The three spirit levels help to ensure that horizontals and verticals are perfectly aligned, making this a great all-round tripod for almost any type of photography.

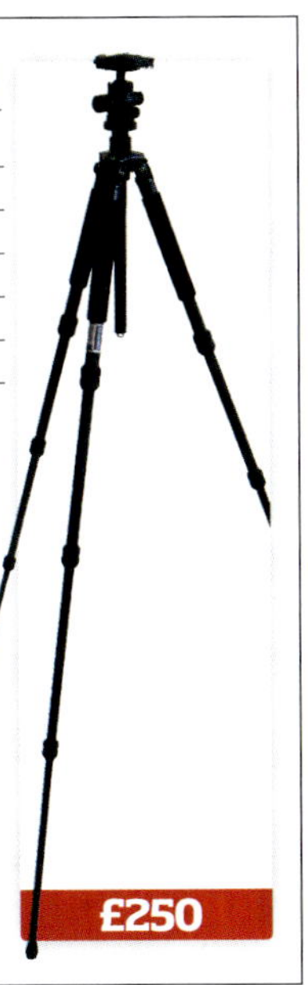
£250

Manfrotto 190CXPRO3 + 494RC2 head

Length (closed): 58cm
Height (legs extended): 146cm
Number of leg sections: 3
Maximum load: 5kg
Weight: 1.62kg
Website: www.manfrotto.co.uk

This Manfrotto is exceptionally light and its sleek design looks fantastic. Despite its thin legs, it was sturdy and supported our test camera with ease. The twist locks are strong and quick to use. The central column can be raised and moved into horizontal position without removing it from the legs, making the tripod perfect for macro and low-level shots. The multi-position leg locks have a depressable button, making them easier and nicer to use than those that have clips that must be lifted. The ball-and-socket head is smooth and easy to use, as one switch controls everything. This is ideal for quick positioning, but not as precise as some of the other heads on test. There is a spirit level to ensure your tripod is level, and the centre column boasts a bag hook, allowing extra weight to be attached for stability in high winds.

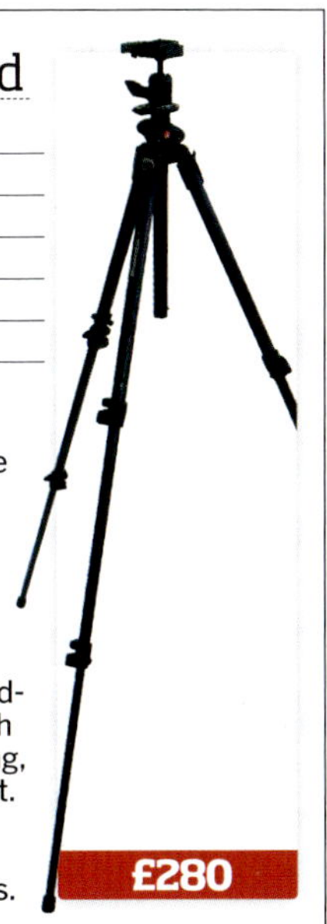
£280

Manfrotto 190X PROB + 460MG head

Length (closed): 57cm
Height (legs extended): 146cm
Number of leg sections: 3
Maximum load: 5kg
Weight: 2.25kg
Website: www.manfrotto.co.uk

This aluminium tripod from Manfrotto is one of the lightest in this price category. The legs are sturdy and support the camera well in all positions. The flip locks are easy to use and very secure, and there are vari-position locks to keep the legs secure at different settings. Perhaps the most interesting feature of the legs is that the central column can be switched to horizontal position for macro shots without removing it from the legs; an excellent feature as it makes the process easy and fast to carry out. The head is versatile, as it can pan, tilt and swivel in just about any direction, and is easy to operate. The lack of panning handles may be a dealbreaker, but the head is so versatile that it more than makes up for it. Spirit levels are on the head and central column brace, and a bag hook can be found on the legs.

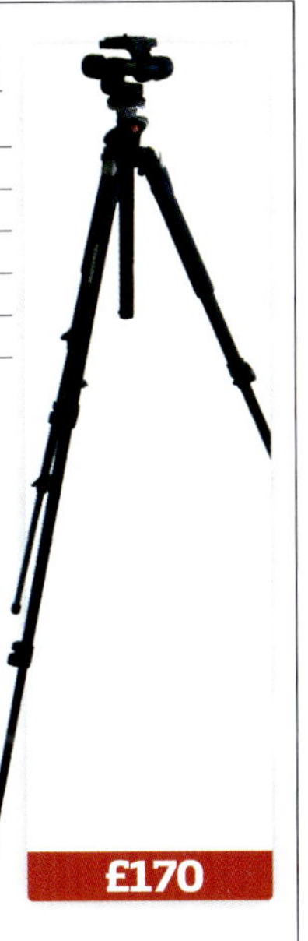
£170

Velbon Sherpa 435 + PHD-41Q head

Length (closed): 53cm
Height (legs extended): 161cm
Number of leg sections: 3
Maximum load: 3kg
Weight: 1.92kg
Website: www.intro2020.co.uk

At the more affordable end of the market is this combined head-and-legs set from Velbon. The tripod's aluminium legs have three sections, locked in place with easy-to-open, clip-style locks. The centre column is adjustable and reversible for low-angle shooting. For an entry-level model, the PHD-41Q head is a good buy, too. It's bigger and more sturdy than others in this bracket and will take loads of up to 3kg, no problem. We like the relative simplicity; using it quickly becomes second nature. Two padded handles control movement, and one unscrews and fits inside the other when the tripod is stored. A well-designed quick-release plate completes the package. A cracking buy for the beginner or intermediate photographer who wants a general-purpose tripod.

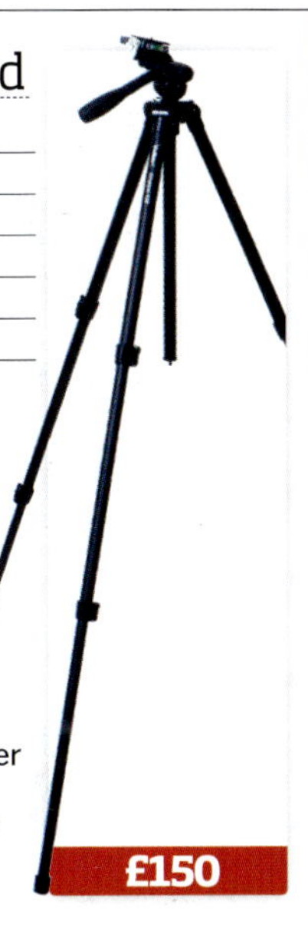
£150

Manfrotto 055XPROB + 322RC2 head

Length (closed): 65.5cm
Height (legs extended): 178.5cm
Number of leg sections: 3
Maximum load: 7kg
Weight: 3.15kg
Website: www.manfrotto.co.uk

The build quality of this die-cast aluminium tripod is excellent. The sturdy 055XPROB features the same dual-positioning central column as the 190XPROB, as well as a spirit level, bag hook and foam leg grips, which protect the user's hands in cold weather. The legs each have a four-position lock, which makes it versatile and secure. You'll either love or hate the trigger-style grip head, but we found it incredibly quick and easy to adjust, getting your camera into just the right position with the minimum of fuss. Not having to tighten levers saves time and reduces the risk of knocking the head out of place. The head has its own spirit level, allowing you to make sure your camera is level. This head is particularly useful when combined with the versatility of the central column of the tripod and when shooting macro.

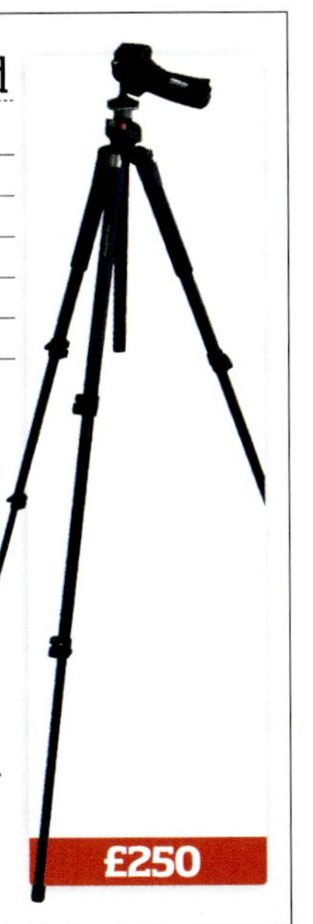
£250

Slik Pro 700DX + 700DX pan-&-tilt head

Length (closed): 76cm
Height (legs extended): 190cm
Number of leg sections: 3
Maximum load: 6.8kg
Weight: 3.2kg
Website: www.intro2020.co.uk

The largest tripod in this category feels as though it could withstand any treatment. It's sturdy, simple and stylish, and it certainly looks like a tripod for serious use. Although it is quite heavy, it is still very portable. The locks are strong and secure, yet easy to open, while the reversible central column allows users to take low-level and macro shots with ease. This is particularly effective when used with the legs open wide, which can be done easily using the three-position locks to hold them firmly in position. The pan-and-tilt head features a panning lock and has a very smooth panning motion. The quick-release plate is circular, making it easy to attach and detach the camera. There are two spirit levels which help to keep horizontals and verticals straight. Although there is no bag hook, the tripod is so sturdy you are unlikely to miss it.

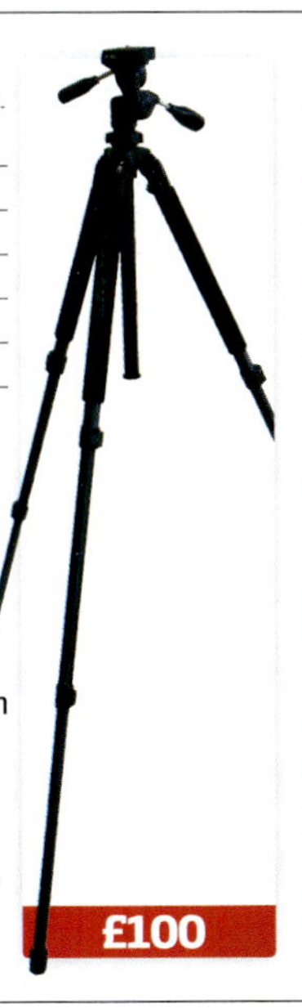
£100

Clothing accessories

Be prepared to brave all weather conditions

Dedicated outdoor photographers are often shooting from before dawn until after dusk, so have to dress appropriately if they're to stay the distance. As well as thick clothing for cold temperatures and high winds, you should also consider breathable garments to allow perspiration to evaporate and comfortable footwear that can handle hours of trudging along countryside, rocky mountains and wet bogs. Be protected from the elements by following our guide…

1) Keep your head warm with a beanie hat! You lose close to a third of your body heat through your head, so it's important to wear a hat or cap in cold conditions. While baseball caps are okay, they don't cover your ears, aren't made of insulating material and the peak will get in the way when holding the camera to your eye. Beanies are also available in a range of styes to suit your fashion sense (or lack of it!).

2) Keep your fingers nimble! Cold winds can freeze your fingers, making it more difficult to press buttons and tweak controls on your DSLR. The easiest solution is to wear gloves, although standard types are thick and still make it difficult to operate your camera. Our favourites are made by Outdoor Designs (www.outdoordesigns.co.uk) and are well worth trying out. The Takustretch has a grip palm and is made from wind-resistant materials to keep your hands warm. Better still is the Konagrip convertible, a windproof fleece glove with leather grip palm and flip-over finger mitt.

3) Wear good footwear! You're more than likely going to cover miles in pursuit of stunning landscapes, so your average trainers aren't the best choice. Depending on how far you plan to walk, the type of terrain and time of year, you should look to wear shoes that are comfortable, hard-wearing and practical. Walking boots are best for serious treks and the likes of the £90 Berghaus Explorer Trek (www.berghaus.com) are ideal, offering comfort, durability and support. You'll find them available for men and women in various colours. Another great option is Patagonia's Snoutler hiking shoes (www.patagonia.com), which are extremely comfortable and lightweight and incredibly durable. They're fashionable, too, and very well priced at around £90.

4) Don't forget your socks! Cold or wet feet make walking around a real misery, as can wearing too thick a sock in warmer conditions. It's worth buying a couple of pairs of decent socks to suit the season and type of shoe you wear. Bridgedale (www.bridgedale.com) are leaders in this department, offering socks to suit cold weather, light treks or longer walks where comfort is essential. They've a bewildering choice on offer, but we'd recommend the Endurance Trekker and Comfort Trekker for longer walks, and the lightweight Bamboo Crew in warmer weather.

5) Keep your body warm and dry! The humble fleece is an unsung hero in outdoor clothing, proving relatively lightweight, incredibly warm and very hard-wearing. They're also available in various designs and colours, too, so are as fashionable as they are practical. You'll find all high-street fashion stores stock their own brands, but we'd really recommend that you check out those from outdoor specialists like Patagonia, Paramo and Berghaus as they're generally made from better quality materials. In cold weather, the general rule is to wear one or two thin layers as opposed to one thick layer as the air between each layer is warmed up. So a fleece top with an outer fleece is a good option to consider. If it's especially cold or windy, a windproof jacket adds an extra layer of protection. For this guide, we tried out a number of fleeces and found the Patagonia R1 Pullover and Berghaus Arana to be excellent choices as a fleece top. The Berghaus Aura is a decent choice as an outer layer, while we found that Paramo's Pajaro and Cascada (www.paramo.co.uk) offered superb protection from the wind and sea spray when shooting by the coast. Incidentally, when choosing colours, bear in mind bright reds are great for visibility, so perfect when heading to remote locations, but not such a good choice if you ever plan on stalking wildlife!

6) Protect your legs! In truth, few amateur photographers head outdoors in anything other than a pair of jeans and while they're comfortable, they're not ideal when the going gets wet. If the weather is unpredictable or you know you'll be shooting near the coast, consider a pair of waterproof trousers. Again, outdoor specialists are best, with Paramo's Cascada trousers generally considered to be one of the best.

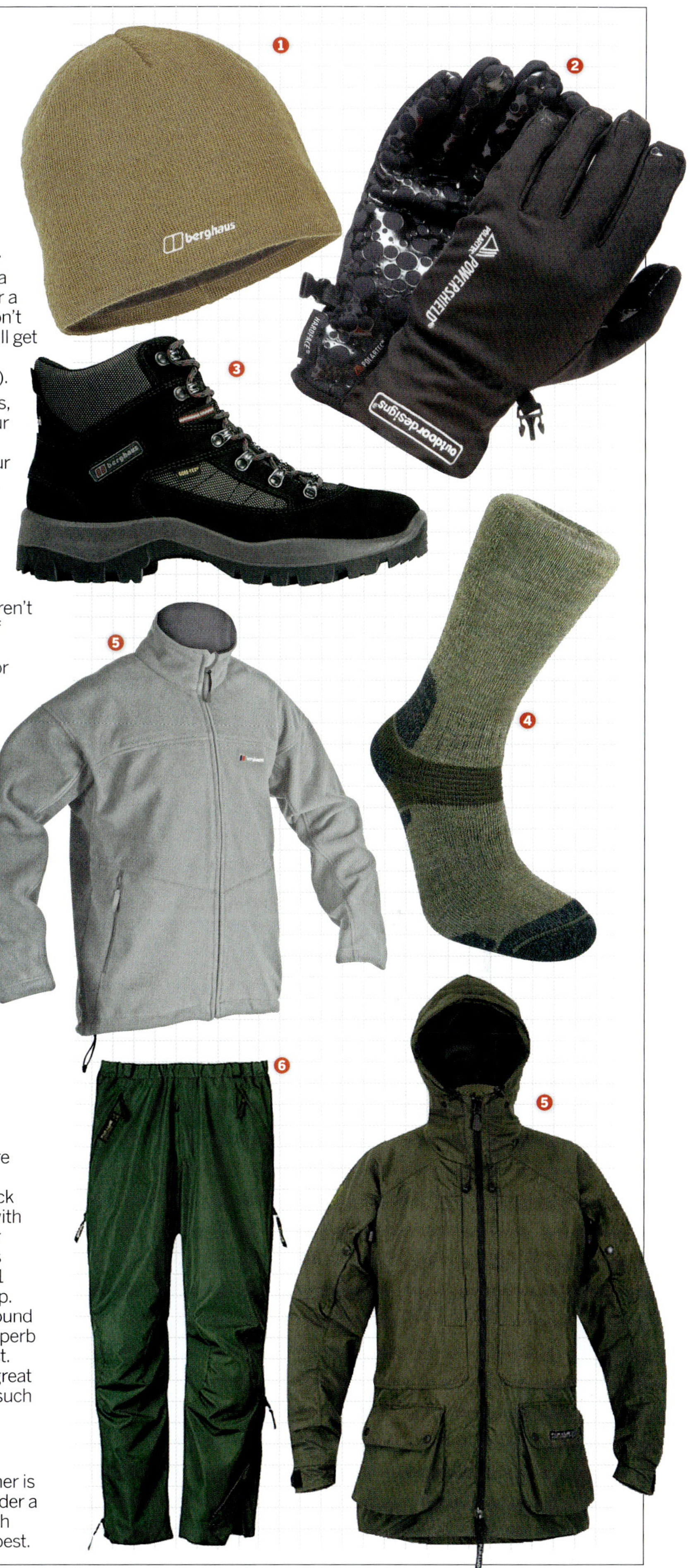

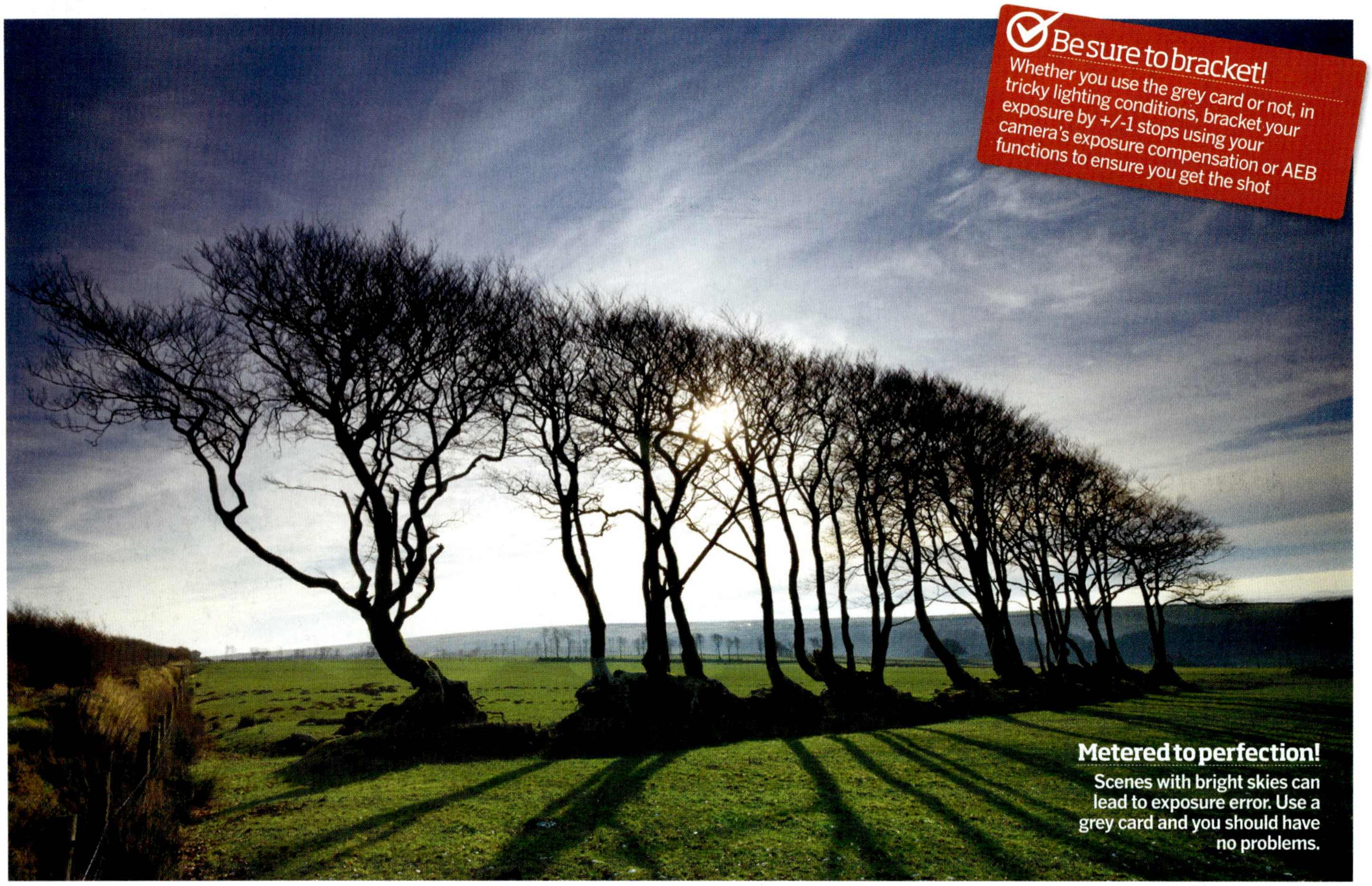

ADAM BURTON

Be sure to bracket!
Whether you use the grey card or not, in tricky lighting conditions, bracket your exposure by +/-1 stops using your camera's exposure compensation or AEB functions to ensure you get the shot

Metered to perfection!
Scenes with bright skies can lead to exposure error. Use a grey card and you should have no problems.

How to use your metering & White Balance cards

The 18% grey card can be used to ensure perfect exposures when shooting in tricky lighting conditions. Both reference cards can also be used to set a custom White Balance. Depending on the camera you use, you need to take a White Balance reading off the grey or the white card (your camera's instructions will show you how)

DIGITAL SLRS USE SOPHISTICATED exposure systems and all work using the same assumption that the average of the scene that is being metered from is a mid-tone, or 18% grey to be exact; ie the average of all dark, light and mid-tones mixed together is 18% grey. It's the basis of all metering patterns and works surprisingly well, but while it's fine for the majority of shooting situations, it can lead to incorrect exposures when the scene or subject is considerably lighter or darker in tone than 18% grey. For example, very dark areas can fool the metering system into overexposure. Similarly, very light subjects, such as a snow scene, can fool the camera into underexposing them – making them appear darker than they are – as the light meter will take a reading designed to render them as a mid-tone. As a camera is trying to render an image 'grey', it's your job to ensure you compensate to keep the tones true to life. You can do this by using one of your DSLR's exposure override facilities, such as exposure compensation or the AE-Lock button, or by metering from an area of the scene that has a mid-tone. And that's where our grey card comes in. Using it is very simple as our step-by-step guide below illustrates. Remember that you need to place the grey card in similar lighting to your scene: for instance, don't place it in a shaded area if your scene is bathed in sunlight. Also make sure that the card fills the metering area – we recommend you use spot or partial metering as the card won't need to fill the entire image area, but any is suitable. You can either lock the exposure using your camera's AE-Lock facility or note the aperture and shutter speed, and then switch to manual mode and set these (although this method isn't suitable to days where lighting is variable). The card has AF reference lines to help your camera's autofocus lock on to it. However, you don't necessarily need it to be in focus to work correctly. The grey card (as well as the white card) can also be used to take a custom White Balance reading from, too.

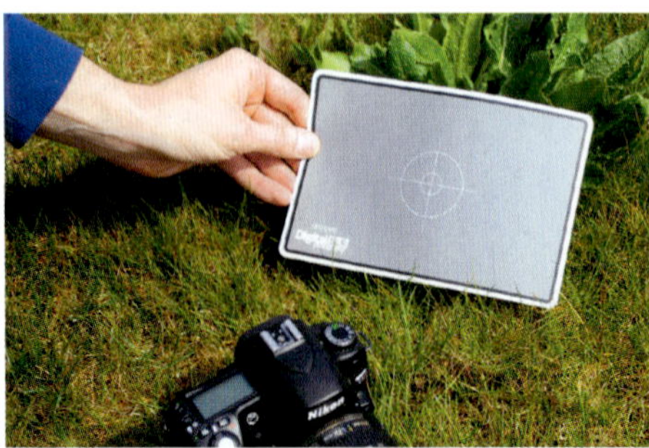

1 Getting started Place your grey card on the ground angled towards you and ensure it's located in a spot that is bathed in the same light as the majority of the scene you plan to shoot.

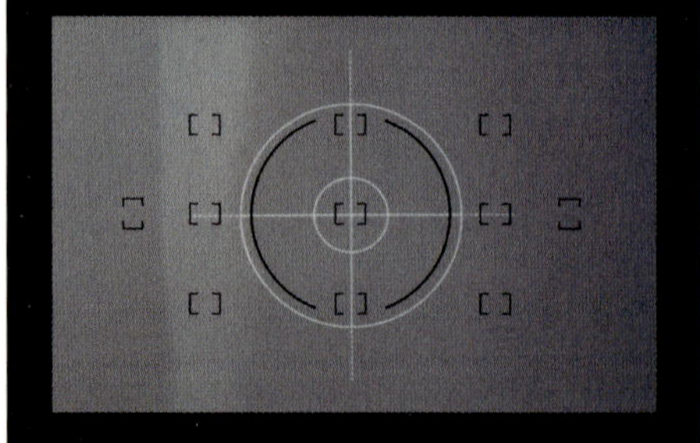

2 Take a meter reading Ensure that the entire metering area is filled by the grey card (in this instance we're using multi-zone metering) and lock the exposure with the AE-Lock button.

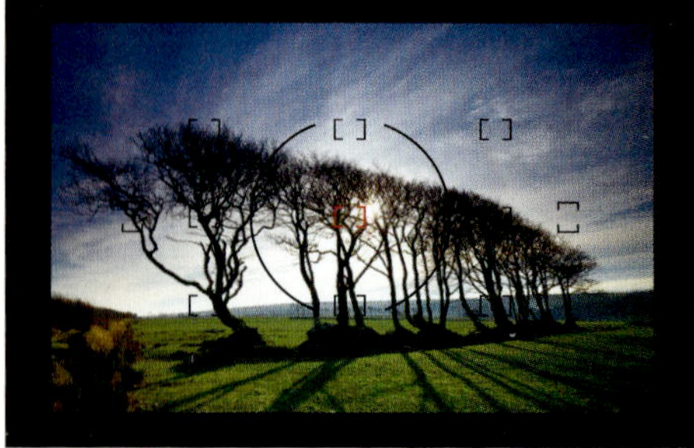

3 Compose & shoot With this exposure locked, you can compose your scene and take your shots. When you check it on your LCD monitor, the exposure should be perfect.